Cassell's Dictionary of English Idioms

CASSELL'S DICTIONARY OF
English Idioms

Rosalind Fergusson

CASSELL

Cassell
Wellington House
125 Strand
London
WC2R 0BB

First published 1999
by Cassell & Co.

This edition 2002

© Cassell & Co. 1999

Distributed in the United States by Sterling Publishing Co. Inc.
387 Park Avenue South, New York, NY 10016–8810

British Library Cataloguing in Publication Data
A catalogue entry for this book is available from the British Library

ISBN 0–304–36384–7

Printed and bound in Great Britain by
Bookmarque Ltd, Croydon, Surrey

Contents

Acknowledgements

Editor	Rosalind Fergusson
Publisher	Richard Milbank
Database Editor	Rebecca Skipwith
Proof-readers	Jessica Feinstein
	Alice Grandison
	Michael Janes
Database Technology	Gentian I.T. Consultants
Typesetting	Gem Graphics

How to use *The Cassell Dictionary of English Idioms*

About this book

An idiom can be defined as a phrase whose meaning cannot be readily understood from its component parts. The level of idiomaticity within these phrases can vary greatly, from the proverbial type of idiom, e.g. **too many cooks spoil the broth**, whose application is entirely metaphorical and whose practical meaning has nothing to do with cooking soup, through those which contain idiomatic and unidiomatic elements, e.g. **dead duck**, which certainly refers to something defunct, though not necessarily to a duck, to phrasal verbs, e.g. **to pick up**, whose idiomaticity consists in the combination of the two elements.

The Cassell Dictionary of English Idioms is devoted to these untranslatable and often highly colourful phrases, whose use and misuse forms a daily part of the English language. It provides a useful reference for native speakers and foreign learners and includes expressions in current use from North America, Australia, New Zealand and the whole of the British Isles as well as a smattering of archaic and dated phrases.

Definitions are given in plain English often supported by examples to illustrate usage and notes on the origin and history of the idioms.

A note on the positioning of entries

Every effort has been made to devise an objective and consistent system for the placement and cross-referencing of idioms in this volume.

To enable the user to track down what are often complex, multi-word phrases with a confusing number of potential points of definition, idioms are listed under keywords both at their point of definition and at points of cross reference. The point of definition is generally the first 'significant' and non-variable word in the phrase in question: a noun, verb or adjective, though practical considerations dictate a number of exceptions to this general rule (see below). Cross-references are given at all nouns contained in an idiom following the element at which it is defined. For example, **to bell the cat** is defined at 'bell' and has a cross-reference at 'cat'; **all work and no play makes Jack a dull boy** is defined at 'work', with cross-references at 'play', 'jack' and 'boy'.

Certain nouns, verbs and adjectives are not considered 'significant', usually because they are in such frequent use that the idioms they would otherwise have to house would be too numerous. The words in question are:

> **all, any, bad, be, bear, beat, best, better, bring, call, carry, come, cut, draw, enough, every, fall, find, get, give, go, good, have, hold, keep, know, lay, leave, let, look, make, many, more, much, one, pass, pay, play, pull, put, run, say, see, send, set, show, side, some, stand, take, throw, turn, way, worse, worst**.

It should be noted that in the absence of any more significant elements these words have been used as points of definition and occasionally, where they have been considered semantically strong enough, they have been used as keywords even when there is a 'significant' alternative, e.g. **good egg** is defined at 'good'. Where no significant element is present in a particular idiom, its placement has been a matter of editorial judgement based on reasonable expectations of where the user might look for it, e.g. **after all** is defined at 'all', where the emphasis suggests that it should go.

A note on the form of idioms presented

Where possible the idioms have been presented in their 'core form', i.e. in such a form as to account for as many collocations or variations in usage as the user is likely to come across in Standard English.

Sometimes a word or group of words within an idiom can be replaced by another word or group of words. These possible variants are indicated in the form in which the idiom is presented, and combined by means of an oblique, as in **with a pinch/ grain of salt**. The alternative forms range from straightforward synonymic variants – as in the foregoing example – to structural variants reflecting two-way shifts in the semantic and syntactic interaction of the component parts of the idiom as shown. Thus the idiom presented in the form **to give someone/ get the push** reflects usages that denote (a) the *active* role of terminating someone's contract (*His employer gave him the push*) or (b) the *passive* role of being on the receiving end of that action (*He got the push*). In cases of simple synonymic alternatives (**with a pinch/ grain of salt**), the order of the alternative elements reflects their perceived frequency of use.

Sometimes an idiom contains elements which can be considered optional, i.e. which can be used as part of the idiom but which can also equally well be omitted. These elements are indicated in the form of the idiom by round brackets, e.g. **to scrape (the bottom of) the barrel**.

Variant and optional elements are never used as points of definition or cross-reference, thus **with a pinch/ grain of salt** is defined at 'salt', rather than at 'pinch' or 'grain', while **to scrape (the bottom of) the barrel** is defined at 'scrape', with a cross-reference at 'barrel', but not at 'bottom'.

To aid the user, variable pronouns such as 'someone' and 'something' have often been inserted to indicate the appropriate position of subject or object.

Definitions and examples

Definitions have been phrased to mirror as closely as possible the form of the idiom given. Where an idiom includes syntactic variants (as in **to give someone/ get the push**) the equivalent meanings are represented in the same way in the definition by the use of an oblique (i.e. 'to dismiss someone/ be dismissed from employment'). Variable pronouns used in the idiom are also included in the same form in the definition. Optional elements used in the idiom are represented in the definition by round brackets where their addition alters the meaning of the idiom. Every effort has been made to ensure that idioms are not defined with other idioms or by the use of any opaque idiomatic expressions. The one exception to this rule relates to where there is a direct North American English equivalent for a British English idiom, as with the North American idiom **to be rained out**, which is a direct equivalent of the British idiom **to be rained off**. In such cases the British expression is given as the definition of the North American, to help the user appreciate the equivalence.

Examples have been included in many entries in the dictionary to assist the user. These serve two purposes: either to exemplify the most recognizable usage of the idiom, or to reflect a usage which cannot be directly inferred from the form of the idiom given, as in the example *a behind-the-scenes investigation* which demonstrates the attributive use of the idiom **behind the scenes**.

Labels

Descriptive labels in brackets have been added where appropriate. They fall into three main categories – stylistic labels, e.g. (coll.), (poet.), (dated); geographical labels, e.g. (N Am.), (Sc.); and field labels, e.g. (Law), (Mil.). A list of abbreviations appears on p. xi.

Cross-references

The word cross-referred to appears as small capitals for usual lower case, e.g. **to wet one's whistle** WET.

Symbols

Obsolete and archaic phrases and meanings are preceded by a dagger sign †

Chief Abbreviations

All are given here in roman, though some may also appear in italics as labels.

attrib.	attributive, attribute
Austral.	Australia, Australian
b.	born
c.	circa
cent.	century
coll.	colloquial
*Cor.	Epistle to the Corinthians
constr.	construction, constructed; construed
*Dan.	Daniel
derog.	derogatory
*Deut.	Deuteronomy
dial.	dialect, dialectal
*Eccles.	Ecclesiastes
esp.	especially
euphem.	euphemism
*Exod.	Exodus
*Ezek.	Ezekiel
facet.	facetious
fig.	figurative, figuratively
*Gen.	Genesis
Her.	Heraldry
Hist.	History
*Hos.	Hosea
*Isa.	Isiah
imper.	imperative
impers.	impersonal
Ir.	Irish
iron.	ironical, ironically
lit.	literal, literally
*Jer.	Jeremiah
*John	Gospel according to St John
*Josh.	Joshua
*Judg.	Judges

*Kgs.	Book of Kings
*Lam.	Lamentations
*Luke	Gospel according to St Luke
†Macc.	Book of Maccabees
*Mal.	Malachi
*Matt.	Gospel according to St Matthew
Math.	Mathematics
Mil.	Military
Mus.	Music
N Am.	North America, North American
Naut.	Nautical
neg.	negative, negatively
New Zeal.	New Zealand
*Pet.	Epistle of Peter
Philos.	Philosophy
pl.	plural
poet.	poetical, poetry
p.p.	past participle
Print.	Printing
*Prov.	Proverbs
*Ps.	Psalms
*Rev.	Revelation
*Rom.	Epistle to the Romans
*Sam.	Book of Samuel
Sc.	Scottish
sl.	slang
*Tim.	Epistle to Timothy
Theol.	Theology
US	United States of America
usu.	usually

*indicates a book of the Bible
†indicates a book of the Apocrypha

THE DICTIONARY OF
ENGLISH IDIOMS

A

from A to B from one point or position to another (*a car that will get me from A to B*).

from A to Z from beginning to end.

abeyance

in abeyance 1 suspended, temporarily out of use. **2** (*Law*) waiting for an occupant or owner.

abide

to abide by 1 to comply with, to act upon (terms, a decision). **2** to stay faithful to (a promise).

ability

to the best of one's ability as well as one can.

aboard

all aboard! a call to warn passengers to board a ship, train etc. that is about to depart.

abode

of no fixed abode FIX.

†to make abode to dwell, to reside.

about

all about it the whole of the matter.

to be about to to be on the point of (doing something).

to be (all) about to be essentially, to have as its main point (*It's all about creating the right image*).

above

above all principally, before everything else.

above and beyond in addition to, in excess of (*above and beyond what was required*).

above oneself arrogant; conceited.

abroad

†all abroad at a loss, astray.

from abroad from a foreign country.

absence

absence makes the heart grow fonder a period of separation can make people like each other better. [From *The Isle of Beauty* (1850) by T. Haynes Bayley.]

conspicuous by one's absence CONSPICUOUS.

abstract

in the abstract without reference to individual cases, abstractly, ideally, theoretically.

access

easy of access EASY.

accident

by accident 1 unintentionally. **2** by chance, fortuitously.

chapter of accidents CHAPTER.

acclamation

by acclamation by a large majority or unanimously, without a ballot.

accord

according as in proportion to.

according to 1 in proportion or relation to (*according to age and experience*). **2** as stated or reported by. **3** depending on. **4** in conformity with (*went according to plan*).

of one's own accord voluntarily.

with one accord with the assent of all.

accordance

in accordance with in conformity with, in such a way as to correspond to (*carried out in accordance with your instructions*).

account

by all accounts according to what most people say, in most people's opinion.

for account of to be sold on behalf of, to be accounted for to.

in account with having business relations with.

of no account valueless, negligible.

on account 1 on credit. **2** as an interim payment.

on account of for the sake of, because of (*Don't worry on my account*).

on no account under no circumstances.

on one's own account 1 for one's own purpose or benefit. **2** at one's own risk; on one's own responsibility.

to account for 1 to give, or to serve as, an explanation of. **2** to render an account for (expenditure, payments made etc.). **3** to give a formal explanation or justification of (*Can you account for your movements on the night of the murder?*). **4** to kill or defeat (an enemy, opponent). **5** to constitute, to make up.

to call/ bring to account 1 to require an explanation from. **2** to reprimand.

to give a good account of oneself to be successful, to do oneself credit.

to hold to account to hold responsible.

to keep account of to keep a record of.

to leave out of account to disregard.

to make account of 1 to set a value upon. **2** to consider.

to settle/ square accounts with to have one's revenge on.

to take account of 1 to pay attention to, to consider. **2** to make allowance for (*take account of someone's age*).

to take into account to take account of.

to turn to (good) account to derive advantage from.

ace

ace in the hole (*N Am.*) ace/ card up one's sleeve.

black as the ace of spades BLACK.

to hold all the aces to be in a position of supreme advantage or control.

to play one's ace to make use of the most effective thing one has available.

within an ace of very close to, within a hair's breadth of (*He came within an ace of colliding with a lorry*).

Achilles

Achilles heel a person's vulnerable point or fatal weakness. [The mother of the Greek hero Achilles held him by the heel when she dipped him in the river Styx to make him invulnerable. He was subsequently killed by an arrow wound to his unprotected heel.]

acid

acid test 1 an absolute and definite test. **2** a critical ordeal. [From the use of nitric acid to test gold.]

to put on the acid (*Austral.*) to scrounge, to cadge.

acquaintance

nodding acquaintance NODDING.

to make one's acquaintance with to meet or encounter (someone or something) for the first time.

to make the acquaintance of to get to know.

to scrape acquaintance with SCRAPE.

acquire

acquired taste something which one learns to like.

act

in the (very) act in the actual commission of some deed (*caught in the act*).

old pals act OLD.

to act counter to to disobey (orders etc.).

to act for to be the (esp. legal) representative of.

to act one's age to behave in a manner befitting a person of one's age or maturity (*Stop fooling around and act your age!*).

to act on/ upon 1 to follow, to carry out (advice, recommendation). **2** to have an effect on, to influence.

to act out to represent (a scene, one's desires) in physical action or by performance.

to act up 1 (*coll.*) to behave badly. **2** (*coll.*) to function badly, to give trouble.

to do a disappearing act DISAPPEAR.

to get in on the act (*coll.*) to become involved in an undertaking, esp. so as to benefit.

to get one's act together 1 (*coll.*) to organize or prepare oneself properly. **2** (*coll.*) to start to behave in a more responsible or more appropriate way.

to put on an act (*coll.*) to pretend.

to read the riot act READ.

action

actions speak louder than words what one actually does is more important than what one merely says one will do.

action stations! 1 a command to military personnel to take up positions for battle. **2** a signal to get ready for immediate action or an imminent event (esp. when this is planned or arranged).

in action 1 a working, operating. **b** (of artillery) firing. **2** in combat, fighting (*killed in action*).

out of action not working, unable to operate.

piece of the action PIECE.

to go into action 1 to begin to take action, esp. energetically. **2** to go into battle.

to suit the action to the word SUIT.

to take action to do something, esp. something energetic or decisive or something intended as a protest.

actress

as the actress said to the bishop (*coll.*) used to draw attention to a suggestive double meaning in the preceding remark (*I'm sure you'll rise to the occasion, as the actress said to the bishop*).

Adam

†**Adam's ale** water.

not to know someone from Adam to have no idea at all who someone is.

add

to add fuel to the fire to exacerbate a difficult situation.

to add in to include.

to add insult to injury to cause further offence to someone one has already offended.

to add on to attach as a supplement or extension.

to add to to increase.

to add up 1 to perform the operation of addition. **2** to produce a correct total when added. **3** to make sense (*It doesn't add up*).

to add up to 1 to amount to. **2** to mean, to have as an effect.

addition

in addition as well, also.

address

to address oneself to 1 to speak to. **2** to apply oneself to, to deal with.

to pay one's addresses to to court.

admit

to **admit of** to allow of, to be capable of.

to **admit to** to acknowledge one's guilt or responsibility in respect of.

ado

without further/ more ado straight away, without delay.

advance

in advance 1 beforehand (*pay in advance*). **2** in front.

to **advance on** to move towards menacingly.

to **make advances to** to try to establish a sexual or business relationship with.

advantage

to **advantage** so as to display the best points (*The evening light set the garden off to advantage*).

to **have the advantage of 1** to be in a better position than. **2** to recognize (someone) who does not recognize you (*I'm afraid you have the advantage of me – have we met before?*).

to **take advantage of 1** to make good use of, to profit by. **2** to exploit or abuse unscrupulously or unfairly. **3** (*euphem.*) to seduce.

to **turn to advantage** to derive benefit from (a thing originally seen as a handicap).

advice

to **take advice 1** to seek advice, esp. from an expert. **2** to act on advice given.

advocate

devil's advocate DEVIL.

aegis

under the aegis of under the leadership, encouragement or patronage of.

afar

from afar from a great distance away.

affirmative

in the affirmative so as to indicate agreement, approval, consent; yes (*answer in the affirmative*).

afflicted

to **be afflicted with** to suffer from.

afoul

to **fall/ run afoul of** (*N Am.*) to fall/ run foul of.

after

after you a polite formula inviting someone to go ahead.

again

again and again with frequent repetition, repeatedly.

age

of a certain age CERTAIN.

of age (*Law*) having reached the full legal age (18).

over-age over a certain age limit.

this day and age DAY.

to **act one's age** ACT.

to **come of age 1** to reach the age of 18, to become an adult. **2** to reach maturity or full development (*Rock music has finally come of age*).

under age not old enough to do an activity legally.

agenda

on the agenda requiring attention, needing to be done.

aggregate

in the aggregate collectively.

agony

to **pile on the agony** (*coll.*) PILE.

agree

to **agree to differ** to give up trying to convince each other.

to **be agreed** to have reached agreement.

ahead

ahead of 1 in front of, in the line of progress of. **2** further on than, making better progress than. **3** in advance of (*ahead of his time*). **4** awaiting (someone) in the future (*Who knows what lies ahead of us?*).

to be ahead to be in the lead, to be winning.

aid

in aid of 1 in support of, so as to help. **2** (*coll.*) intended for (*What's all this in aid of?*).

aim

to be aimed at 1 to have as its target. **2** to have as its object.

to take aim to direct a gun, missile etc. (at).

air

airs and graces would-be elegant or genteel mannerisms intended to impress.

breath of fresh air BREATH.

by air in an aircraft.

change of air CHANGE.

hot air HOT.

in the air 1 (of an opinion, feeling) perceptible; current or becoming current. **2** (of a project, plan) as yet unsettled, in the process of being decided.

off the air not broadcasting, not being broadcast.

on the air broadcasting, being broadcast.

thin air THIN.

to air a grievance to state a cause of complaint.

to clear the air CLEAR.

to give oneself/ put on airs to behave in an affected or haughty manner.

to go up in the air (*coll.*) to become very angry.

to take air to become public.

to take the air to go for a walk or ride in the open air.

to walk/ tread on air to feel elated (*I was walking on air for days afterwards*).

up in the air as yet unsettled, in the process of being decided.

with one's nose in the air NOSE.

alarm

false alarm FALSE.

alarum

alarums and excursions confused noise or activity. [From a stage direction used in Shakespeare's plays to indicate the noise and confusion of battle.]

Albion

perfidious Albion PERFIDIOUS.

ale

Adam's ale ADAM.

cakes and ale CAKE.

alec

smart alec SMART.

alert

on alert (of troops etc.) in a state of enhanced readiness to respond to an attack, a crisis etc.

on the alert 1 on the watch. **2** on one's guard. **3** ready, prepared.

alive

alive and kicking 1 (*coll.*) still living and active. **2** (*coll.*) in a very lively state.

alive and well still alive or in existence (esp. despite contrary assumptions).

look alive! get busy, make haste.

all

after all 1 when everything has been taken into account. **2** in spite of everything that was done, said etc. **3** against expectation or probability.

all and sundry everyone, anyone who cares to do something.

all but almost.

all for (*coll.*) very much in favour of.

all in 1 including everything. **2** (*coll.*) exhausted.

all in all all things considered.

all of as much, far etc. as, no less than (*all of thirty miles to Bath*).

all out 1 with maximum effort (*go all out to win*). **2** at full speed.

all over 1 completely; everywhere. **2** finished (*it's all over*). **3** (*coll.*) typical of (*That's him all over*). **4** (*coll.*) excessively attentive to (*He was all over her*).

all the to an even greater degree (*That makes it all the easier*).

all together in a body, altogether.

all very well used to express rejection of or scepticism about a positive statement (*That's all very well, but who's going to pay for it?*).

and all (*coll.*) too, as well.

and all that with all the rest of it.

at all 1 in any respect, to any extent, in any degree. **2** of any kind, whatever.

in all in total, altogether.

alley

blind alley BLIND.

allow

to allow for to make allowance or deduction for.

to allow of to accept, to admit.

allowance

to make allowance(s) for 1 to take (mitigating circumstances) into account. **2** to consider, when making a decision.

alone

let alone 1 not to mention. **2** much less.

to go it alone to carry on single-handedly.

to leave alone 1 not to interfere with. **2** to have no dealings with (*You should leave drugs well alone*).

to let alone 1 not to interfere with. **2** not to do or deal with. **3** not to mention.

to stand alone to be unique or unrivalled.

along

all along throughout, all the time (*She had known all along*).

along with in company or together with.

aloof

to stand/ keep aloof 1 to take no part in, to keep away; to remain by oneself. **2** to remain unsympathetic.

alpha

alpha and omega the beginning and the end; the essential or most important part, point etc. [From the first and last letters of the Greek alphabet, and from the Bible: "I am Alpha and Omega, the beginning and the ending" (Rev. i.8).]

altar

to lead to the altar LEAD[1].

altogether

in the altogether (*coll.*) in the nude.

amen

amen to that! used to express agreement or the hope that the previous speaker's wish will be fulfilled.

to say amen to to express agreement with or approval of.

amends

to make amends to compensate or make up (for).

analysis

in the final/ last/ ultimate analysis in the end, when everything has been taken into consideration.

anchor

at anchor 1 held by an anchor. **2** at rest.

sheet anchor SHEET[2].

to cast anchor CAST.

to drop anchor DROP.

to weigh anchor WEIGH.

ancient

ancient history 1 history of ancient times, esp. to the end of the Western Roman Empire, AD 476. **2** (*coll.*) information, gossip etc. that is widely known.

and

and/ or indicating that either or both of two possibilities may occur, be chosen etc.

angel

fools rush in where angels fear to tread FOOL.
on the side of the angels SIDE.

anger

more in sorrow than in anger SORROW.

angle

at right angles RIGHT ANGLE.

another

ask me another ASK.
you're another (*dated, sl.*) you are a liar, fool or rascal (a retort to abuse etc.).

answer

not to take no for an answer NO².
to answer back to reply rudely or cheekily.
to answer for 1 to be responsible or answerable for. **2** to speak as a representative of. **3** to express one's confidence in; to vouch for.
to answer to 1 to correspond, to suit. **2** to be responsible or answerable to.
to know all the answers to be very knowledgeable or well-informed, esp. when this is a cause for conceit (*You think you know all the answers*).

ant

to have ants in one's pants (*coll.*) to be extremely fidgety and restless.

ante

to up the ante UP.

anvil

on the anvil in preparation.

any

any longer for any further length of time; now, from this point on.
any old (*coll.*) any, no matter which or what.
any old how (*coll.*) haphazardly, in a disorderly fashion.
not having any (*coll.*) unwilling to tolerate or put up with something; unwilling to participate in something (*I asked him to help, but he wasn't having any*).

anybody

anybody's guess something that is difficult to determine or predict (*Whether it will work or not is anybody's guess*).
to be anybody's 1 (of a game, contest) to be evenly balanced. **2** (*coll.*) (of a person) to be easily seduced, bribed etc. by anybody.

anything

anything but not at all (*It's anything but easy*).
anything doing anything going on.
if anything possibly even (*If anything, it's too short*).
like anything (*coll.*) very fast, vigorously, intensely etc.

apart

apart from 1 with the exception of, leaving out. **2** in addition to.

ape

the naked ape NAKED.
to go ape (*N Am.*) to go berserk, to go crazy.

appear

to appear in print to have one's work published.

appearance

to all appearances so far as could be ascertained, apparently.

to enter an appearance ENTER.

to keep up/ save appearances 1 to keep up an outward show of affluence, respectability etc. **2** to conceal the absence of something desirable.

to put in/ make an appearance to attend a function or to visit a person, usu. briefly.

appetite

to whet someone's appetite WHET.

apple

apple of Sodom 1 a mythical fruit, said to resemble an apple, but turning to ashes. **2** †anything disappointing.

apple of someone's eye a person or thing that is very dear or precious to someone. [The phrase originally referred to the pupil of the eye, formerly supposed to be a solid body.]

rotten apple ROTTEN.

she's apples (*Austral., coll.*) everything is fine.

the Big Apple BIG.

apple-cart

to upset the apple-cart UPSET.

apple pie

apple-pie bed a bed prepared as a practical joke, with sheets folded short or tucked in hard so as to prevent one stretching one's full length.

apple-pie order perfect order.

apply

to apply oneself to work, study etc. in a concentrated and diligent fashion.

appro

on appro on approval.

approval

on approval 1 on trial to ascertain if suitable. **2** (of goods) to be returned if not suitable.

apron

tied to someone's apron strings TIE.

apropos

apropos of 1 with regard to, concerning. **2** as suggested by.

area

grey area GREY.

argue

to argue the toss to continue to dispute about a matter that has already been decided. [Alluding to the toss of a coin.]

ark

out of the ark (*coll.*) extremely old or old-fashioned. [A reference to Noah's ark, described in the Bible (Gen. vi–ix).]

arm[1]

an arm and a leg (*coll.*) a great amount of money (*cost an arm and a leg*).

arm in arm with the arms interlinked.

at arm's length 1 at a distance. **2** at a sufficient distance to avoid undue familiarity (*kept us at arm's length*). **3** (of negotiations) such that each party preserves its freedom of action.

babe in arms BABE.

in arms (of a baby) needing to be carried, too young to walk.

in someone's arms being embraced by someone.

in the arms of Morpheus asleep. [Morpheus was the Greek god of sleep and dreams.]

long as your arm LONG.

on someone's arm (of a person) walking

arm in arm with someone or
supported by someone's arm.
shot in the arm SHOT.
the long arm of the law LONG.
to chance one's arm CHANCE.
to give one's right arm RIGHT.
to twist someone's arm TWIST.
under one's arm held between the arm
and the body.
within arm's reach that can be reached
without moving from one's position.
with open arms OPEN.

arm²

to arms! 1 take your weapons. **2** prepare
for battle.
to bear arms 1 to be a soldier. **2** (*Her.*) to
be entitled to a coat of arms.
to lay down one's arms 1 to cease fighting.
2 to surrender.
to order arms ORDER.
to present arms PRESENT².
to reverse arms REVERSE.
to secure arms SECURE.
to shoulder arms SHOULDER.
to slope arms SLOPE.
to take (up) arms to prepare or begin to
fight.
to trail arms TRAIL.
under arms 1 bearing arms. **2** ready for
service. **3** in battle array.
up in arms 1 (*coll.*) angry, indignant,
protesting. **2** in revolt.

armed

armed to the teeth armed with every
possible weapon.

armour

a chink in someone's armour CHINK.
knight in shining armour KNIGHT.

around

all around (*N Am.*) all round.
to have been around 1 (*coll.*) to have
acquired a wide experience. **2** (*coll.*) to
be worldly-wise and shrewd.

arrears

in arrears 1 behindhand, esp. in
payment. **2** unpaid; undone,
uncompleted.

arrest

under arrest in legal custody.

arrive

to arrive at 1 to reach, to get to. **2** to
agree upon (a decision); to attain to
(a conclusion).

arrow

straight as an arrow STRAIGHT.

arse

not to know one's arse from one's elbow
(*taboo sl.*) to be utterly ignorant or
incompetent.
to arse about/ around (*taboo sl.*) to act
in a stupid or irritating manner.
to kiss someone's arse KISS.

art

state-of-the-art STATE.
the healing art HEALING.
to get something down to a fine art FINE¹.

as

as and when to the degree and at the
time that.
as for regarding, concerning.
as from from (the specified time or
date).
as if/ though as it would be if (*You look
as if you'd seen a ghost!*).
as it is in the present state, actually.
as it were in a certain way, to some
extent, so to speak (*You are their
leader, as it were*).
as of as from.
as per according to (*as per your
instructions*).
as to respecting, concerning.
as was (*coll.*) in a previous state.

ascend
to ascend the throne to become king or queen.

ascendant
in the ascendant 1 dominant, predominant, supreme. **2** rising or increasing in influence.

ash
in sackcloth and ashes SACKCLOTH.
to be/ lie in ashes to be utterly destroyed (*His hopes lay in ashes*).
to turn to dust and ashes DUST.

aside
aside from 1 with the exception of, leaving out. **2** in addition to.

ask
ask me another (*coll.*) I don't know.
I ask you! 1 used to express disapproval or dismay. **2** used rhetorically to solicit the agreement of the person one is speaking to.
if you ask me in my opinion.
to ask a blessing to say grace before a meal.
to ask after to request information about, esp. about (the health of) another person.
to ask for to behave in such a way as to invite (trouble etc.).
to ask for it (*coll.*) to act in such a way as to make trouble, unpleasant consequences etc. inevitable.
to ask for trouble (*coll.*) to lack caution (*Leaving your car unlocked is asking for trouble*).
to ask the hand of to ask permission to marry (a woman).

asking
for the asking (obtainable) for nothing or for very little effort.

aspersion
to cast aspersions on CAST.

ass[1]
to make an ass of to treat as a fool, to make ridiculous.
to make an ass of oneself to make oneself appear foolish, to play the fool.

ass[2]
to kick (some) ass KICK.

at
at it 1 at work, engaged, busy. **2** (*coll.*) engaged in a habitual (usu. disapproved of) activity. **3** (*coll.*) having sexual intercourse.
at that moreover.
where it's at 1 (*sl.*) where the really important or fashionable activity is taking place. **2** (*sl.*) where the real significance lies.

attempt
†**to attempt the life of** to try to kill.

attendance
in attendance waiting, attendant (on).
to dance attendance on DANCE.

attitude
to strike an attitude STRIKE.

attrition
war of attrition WAR.

aunt
Aunt Sally 1 a game in which a figure, often with a pipe in its mouth, is set up, and the players endeavour to knock the figure down or break the pipe by throwing sticks or balls at it. **2** an object of ridicule.
my giddy/ sainted aunt (*coll.*) used to express surprise, disbelief etc.

auspice
under the auspices of under the leadership, encouragement or patronage of.

avail

of no avail in vain.

to avail oneself of to take advantage of, to make use of.

to little/ no avail ineffectually, with little/ no useful result (*We tried to persuade him, but to little avail*).

without avail in vain.

average

on (an) average 1 usually, typically.
2 taking the mean calculated from a number of examples.

to average out to attain an acceptable level in the long run.

to average out at to come to (a certain figure) when the average is calculated.

avoid

to avoid like the plague to make every effort to avoid (someone or something).

awake

awake to aware of.

awakening

to have/ get a rude awakening RUDE.

awash

awash with full of, having an abundance of; having too much or too many of.

away

away back long ago.

away from it all in or to a place without the stresses of everyday life (*get away from it all for a few days*).

away with take away, get rid of.

far/ out and away beyond comparison, by a large margin (*far and away the best*).

awe

to keep in awe to restrain by fear.

axe

to give someone/ get the axe to dismiss someone/ be dismissed from employment.

to have an axe to grind to have an ulterior motive, or a personal interest or grievance, that causes one to act in a particular way. [From a story told by Benjamin Franklin (1706–90): when he was a boy, a man had shown interest in his father's grindstone and asked to see it in action. Once it was turning, the man produced an axe of his own that needed sharpening.]

†**to put the axe on the helve** to remove a doubt or solve a puzzle. [The helve is the handle of an axe.]

aye[1]

aye aye, sir (*Naut., also facet.*) yes, sir; very well, sir.

the ayes have it the motion is passed.

aye[2]

for (ever and) aye for ever, to all eternity.

B

B
from A to B A.

not to know B from a bull's foot to be grossly ignorant or illiterate.

babe

babe in arms 1 a child who is too young to walk. **2** a naive or gullible person.

baby

to be left holding/ carrying the baby 1 (*coll.*) to be left to bear the brunt of something. **2** (*coll.*) to be landed with something.

to throw the baby out with the bathwater to reject the essential along with the inessential.

to wet the baby's head WET.

back

at someone's back 1 pursuing someone. **2** giving support to someone.

at the back of one's mind not consciously thought of.

back and belly all over, completely.

back and forth 1 forwards and backwards. **2** repeatedly from one place to another and back again.

back number 1 a past issue of a newspaper or magazine. **2** (*sl.*) an out-of-date person or thing.

back of (*N Am.*) behind.

back of beyond an extremely remote place (*live in the back of beyond*).

behind someone's back secretly, surreptitiously; without someone's knowledge.

clap on the back CLAP.

eyes in the back of one's head EYE.

like the back of a bus (*coll.*) very ugly (*a face like the back of a bus*).

like water off a duck's back WATER.

mind your back(s) MIND.

on one's back 1 floored. **2** at the end of one's tether. **3** laid up.

on the back of 1 weighing as a heavy burden on. **2** in addition to.

pat on the back PAT.

slap on the back SLAP.

stab in the back STAB.

the shirt off one's back SHIRT.

the straw that broke the camel's back STRAW.

to back away to withdraw.

to back down/ out 1 to move backwards. **2** to retreat from a difficult situation.

to back into 1 to knock into (someone or something) with a backward motion. **2** (of a train, car etc.) to move backwards into.

to back off 1 to withdraw, to retreat. **2** to stop pursuing a course.

to back on to to have its back next to (*a house backing on to the recreation ground*).

to back out of to decide not to do something that one had promised to do.

to back the field to bet against all the horses except one.

to back the wrong horse to make a bad choice.

to back up 1 to support. **2** to confirm. **3** to render support to (a team-mate) in cricket and other games. **4** (*Comput.*) to duplicate (a computer data file) as

security against damage to the original.
5 (of water) to build up behind
something. **6** to reverse (a vehicle) to
an intended position. **7** to build up
into a queue (of traffic etc.).

to back water to reverse the motion of
the oars when rowing.

to break the back of BREAK.

to fall off the back of a lorry to be stolen
or acquired by dubious means.

to get off someone's back to stop
harassing someone.

to have a monkey on one's back MONKEY.

to have one's back to the wall to be in a
desperate position.

to know like the back of one's hand to
know thoroughly or intimately.

to make a rod for one's own back ROD.

to pat on the back PAT.

to put/ get someone's back up to cause
resentment or annoyance to someone.
[From the way a cat arches its back in
anger.]

to put one's back into to make a strenuous
effort to perform (a task).

to see the back of to get rid of (*glad to see
the back of them*).

to slap on the back SLAP.

to stab in the back STAB.

to turn one's back to turn away, to flee.

to turn one's back on/ upon 1 to abandon,
to forsake. **2** to ignore.

with one hand/ arm tied behind one's back
TIE.

with one's back to/ up against the wall in
a critical position.

you scratch my back and I'll scratch yours
SCRATCH.

backbone
to the backbone thoroughly.

back door
by/ through the back door secretly or
unofficially.

backroom
backroom boys (*coll.*) scientists and

others who work in the background
unrecognized.

back seat
back-seat driver 1 a passenger in a car
who offers unwanted advice. **2** a
person who offers advice on matters
which do not concern them.

to take a back seat 1 to accept an
inferior role. **2** to withdraw from the
forefront.

backward
backwards and forwards 1 to and fro. **2** in
an uncertain or vacillating manner.

not backward in coming forward (*coll.*)
not shy or reticent.

to bend/ fall/ lean over backwards to go to
great pains, esp. to help.

backyard
in one's own backyard near one's own
home, close by, locally.

bacon
to bring home the bacon 1 (*coll.*) to
succeed. **2** (*coll.*) to provide a living.
[Possibly from a whole pig or a side of
bacon awarded as a prize.]

to save someone's bacon SAVE.

bad
bad blood mutual hostility or ill feeling.

bad egg (*coll.*) a useless or lazy person, a
ne'er-do-well.

bad form 1 bad manners (*It's bad form to
talk with your mouth full*). **2** lack of
breeding.

bad lot 1 (*coll.*) a useless or lazy person.
2 a poor speculation or unfavourable
situation (*make the best of a bad
lot*).

bad show (something) badly done.

from bad to worse to a worse state from
an already bad one.

not (so) bad quite good.

to go bad to decay.

to go to the bad to go to ruin.

too bad (of circumstances etc.) beyond
rectification, esp. in a dismissive
sense (*It's too bad we didn't win the
lottery*).

to the bad **1** to ruin. **2** to the wrong side
of an account.

badly

badly off not wealthy or fortunate.

bag

bag and baggage with all one's
belongings.

bag of bones a living skeleton, someone
very thin.

in the bag (*coll.*) secured or as good as
secured. [Possibly from a hunter's bag
of game.]

someone could not punch their way out of
a paper bag PUNCH.

the whole bag of tricks WHOLE.

to give someone the bag to hold to slip off,
to leave someone in the lurch.

to let the cat out of the bag CAT.

to pack one's bags PACK.

baggage

bag and baggage BAG.

bail

to bail out **1** (*Law*) to procure release on
bail from prison. **2** to rescue from
difficulty.

to give leg bail LEG.

to jump bail JUMP.

to stand/ go bail (*Law*) to secure freedom
until trial for an accused person on
payment of surety.

to surrender to bail SURRENDER.

bait

to rise to the bait RISE.

baker

baker's dozen thirteen. [From the former
practice of giving an extra loaf of bread
free with every dozen sold, esp. to
avoid accusations of short weight.]

the butcher, the baker, the candlestick
maker BUTCHER.

balance

in the balance in an uncertain state.

off balance at a disadvantage (*caught off
balance*).

on balance taking all factors into
consideration.

to hang in the balance HANG.

to hold the balance to have the power of
deciding.

to keep one's balance **1** not to tumble, to
avoid falling. **2** to remain sane and
sensible.

to lose one's balance LOSE.

to redress the balance REDRESS.

to strike a balance STRIKE.

to tip the balance TIP².

bald

bald as a coot completely bald. [Alluding
to the broad white base of the bill
across the coot's forehead.]

to go at it bald-headed to attack or
undertake something boldly, regardless
of consequences. [A reference to the
Marquis of Granby, commander-in-
chief at the Battle of Warburg in 1760,
whose hat and wig fell off as he led a
cavalry charge.]

bale

to bale out to escape from or help out of
a difficulty.

ball¹

cold enough to freeze the balls off a brass
monkey COLD.

on the ball **1** alert. **2** in control.

the ball is in someone's court it is
someone's move, it is someone's turn
to act. [Referring to the game of
tennis.]

to balls up/ make a balls of (*sl.*) to make a
mess of; to botch, to do badly.

to have the ball at one's feet to have a
chance or opportunity. [Referring to
the game of football.]

to keep the ball rolling to keep the conversation, debate, activity or game from flagging.

to play ball (*coll.*) to cooperate.

to start/ set the ball rolling to start a conversation, debate, activity or game.

ball[2]

to have a ball (*coll.*) to have a good time.

to open the ball OPEN.

ballgame

a different/ whole new ballgame (*coll.*) something quite different.

ballistic

to go ballistic (*sl.*) to become explosively angry, to lose one's temper.

balloon

to go down like a lead balloon LEAD[2].

when the balloon goes up when the action begins, when the troubles start. [Referring to a military observation balloon or a barrage balloon.]

ballpark

ballpark figure (*coll.*) an approximate amount.

in the right ballpark RIGHT.

banana

to be/ go bananas (*sl.*) to be or go mad.

band[1]

†**in bands** in prison.

band[2]

to beat the band very loudly, vigorously or well (*The kids were screaming to beat the band*).

when the band begins to play 1 when things get lively. **2** when trouble begins.

bandbox

like something out of a bandbox immaculately smart.

bandwagon

to climb/ jump on the bandwagon to try to be on the winning side, to join something that seems certain of success. [A bandwagon was a horse-drawn vehicle carrying a group of musicians at the head of a procession, esp. in a US electoral campaign. People would show their support for the politician or party by climbing aboard.]

bandy

to bandy words to wrangle (with).

bang

bang goes something said when something suddenly comes to an end or the prospect of something suddenly vanishes (*Bang goes my pay rise!*).

bang off (*sl.*) immediately.

bang on (*coll.*) exactly right.

bang to rights (*sl.*) caught in the act.

to bang away at to do something violently or noisily.

to bang on (*coll.*) to talk loudly or at great length.

to bang up (*sl.*) to imprison or lock up.

to go (off) with a bang to go very well, to succeed.

bank

to bank on to rely on (*Don't bank on it*).

to break the bank BREAK.

banner

to carry the banner for to support.

to follow the banner of FOLLOW.

baptism

baptism of fire 1 the baptism of the Holy Ghost, martyrdom. **2** a soldier's first experience of actual war. **3** a difficult or frightening introduction to something.

bar[1]

behind bars in jail.

to be called to the bar (*Law*) to be admitted as a barrister.

to be called within the bar (*Law*) to be made a Queen's (or King's) Counsel.

to prop up the bar PROP.

bar²

bar none without exception.

bare

the bare bones the essentials.

to bare one's soul to reveal one's inner feelings, personal details etc.

to lay bare 1 to reveal. **2** to strip.

with one's bare hands without using tools or weapons.

bargain

into/ in the bargain over and above what is stipulated.

off one's bargain released from a purchase or engagement.

to bargain away to exchange for something of less value.

to bargain on/ for to count on, to expect (*got more than we bargained for*).

to drive a good bargain DRIVE.

to drive a hard bargain DRIVE.

to make the best of a bad bargain to do the best one can in adverse circumstances.

to strike/ make a bargain to come to terms.

bargepole

would not touch with a bargepole TOUCH.

bark

someone's bark is worse than their bite said of someone who seems angry or threatening but won't actually do anything to hurt you.

to bark up the wrong tree 1 to be on a false scent. **2** to accuse the wrong person.

barleycorn

John Barleycorn JOHN.

barrack

barrack-room lawyer 1 a soldier who argues with those in authority. **2** a person who gives advice in a pompous or insistent way, esp. when not qualified to do so.

barrel

lock, stock and barrel LOCK.

to have someone over a barrel 1 to have power over someone. **2** to have someone at a disadvantage. [From a former method of resuscitating a drowned person by placing them over a barrel and rolling it backwards and forwards to empty water from their lungs.]

to scrape (the bottom of) the barrel SCRAPE.

barren

barren of devoid of.

barter

to barter away 1 to dispose of by barter. **2** to part with for a consideration (usu. an inadequate one).

base

to make/ get to first base FIRST.

to make/ get to first base with FIRST.

to touch base TOUCH.

bash

to have a bash at to attempt.

basket

to put all one's eggs in one basket EGG.

bat¹

off one's own bat on one's own initiative, by one's own exertions. [From the game of cricket.]

right off the bat (*N Am.*, *coll.*) straight away.

to bat around 1 (*sl.*) to potter. **2** to discuss (an idea).

to carry one's bat in cricket, to be not out at the end of an innings.

bat²

blind as a bat BLIND.

like a bat out of hell (*coll.*) extremely quickly.

to have bats in the belfry (*coll.*) to be crazy, to suffer from delusions.

bat³

not to bat an eyelid/ eyelash/ eye 1 not to blink. **2** to show no surprise or emotion.

bate

with bated breath 1 with breath held in check. **2** in suspense, anxiously (*waited with bated breath*).

bathwater

to throw the baby out with the bathwater BABY.

batten

to batten down the hatches 1 (*Naut.*) to secure the hatches of a ship, esp. before a storm. **2** to prepare for action, trouble, danger etc.

battery

to turn someone's battery against themselves to use someone's own arguments to prove them wrong.

battle

battle royal 1 a general engagement. **2** a free fight, a general row. **3** a cock-fight in which more than two game cocks are engaged.

half the battle HALF.

pitched battle PITCH.

running battle RUNNING.

to battle one's way to make one's way fighting.

to do battle to take part in a battle, contest or struggle.

to fight a losing battle FIGHT.

to have the battle to be victorious.

to join battle JOIN.

bawl

to bawl out (*coll.*) to reprove fiercely.

bay

at bay in a position of defence, cornered by pursuers or enemies. [From hunting, referring to the baying of a pack of hounds that have cornered their prey.]

to bring/ drive to bay 1 to come to close quarters with (the animal hunted). **2** to reduce to extremities.

to hold/ keep at bay 1 to keep back (assailing hounds or other pursuers) from attacking. **2** to keep (something undesirable) at a distance.

to stand at bay to turn to face assailing hounds or one's pursuers.

be

been (and gone) and (*sl.*) used to express surprise or annoyance at what someone has done (*He's been and gone and sold it!*).

be that as it may even if that is true.

the be-all and end-all the sole object or idea in view. [From Shakespeare's *Macbeth*: "that but this blow / Might be the be-all and the end-all here", referring to the assassination of Duncan.]

to be at to occupy oneself with.

to be off to leave.

to be oneself to act in one's normal manner.

beach

not the only pebble on the beach ONLY.

bead

to draw a bead on to aim at. [A bead is the front sight of a gun.]

to tell/ say one's beads to recite the rosary, to say one's prayers.

beam

broad across/ in the beam BROAD.

off (the) beam 1 off the course indicated by a radio beam. **2** off the mark.

on the beam 1 on the course indicated by a radio beam. **2** on the mark. **3** (*Naut.*) at right-angles to the keel.

beam-ends

on one's beam-ends 1 (*Naut.*) (of a ship) thrown so much to one side that the beams are in the water. **2** (*coll.*) penniless, quite destitute. [The beam of a ship or boat is the transverse timber that supports the deck. If its ends are in the water, the vessel is likely to capsize or sink.]

bean

full of beans FULL.

not a bean (*sl.*) no money.

to spill the beans SPILL.

bear[1]

like a bear with a sore head in a very bad mood, irritable.

bear[2]

to bear against 1 to rest upon. **2** to be in contact with.

to bear away 1 to carry off. **2** to win. **3** (*Naut.*) to change the course of a ship or boat away from the wind.

to bear down 1 to overwhelm, to crush, to subdue. **2** to use the abdominal muscles to assist in giving birth.

to bear down on 1 to sail in the direction of. **2** to approach purposefully. **3** to make (someone) worried or depressed.

to bear hard 1 to press, to urge. **2** to have a grudge against. **3** †to resent.

to bear hard/ heavily on to oppress.

to bear off 1 to carry off. **2** to win.

to bear on 1 to press against. **2** to be relevant to.

to bear out to confirm, to justify.

to bear up 1 to endure problems cheerfully (*bearing up under the strain*). **2** (*Naut.*) to change the course of a ship or boat towards the wind.

to bear upon to be relevant to.

to bear with to put up with, to endure, wait for (*Bear with me a minute*).

to bring to bear to apply, to bring into operation.

beard

to beard the lion in his den to confront a fearsome or powerful person on their own territory.

bearing

to get/ find one's bearings to establish or re-establish one's position.

to lose one's bearings LOSE.

beat

to beat about (*Naut.*) to tack.

to beat back to compel to retire in a confrontation.

to beat down 1 to throw or cast down. **2** to force down (a price) by haggling. **3** to force (a seller) to lower a price by haggling. **4** to come down from the sky strongly (*The sun beat down*).

to beat into 1 to knock into by striking. **2** to instil.

to beat it (*sl.*) to go away.

to beat off to drive away by blows.

to beat out 1 to extend by beating, to hammer out. **2** to extinguish by beating.

to beat someone to it to reach somewhere or achieve something before another person (*I was going to say that, but you beat me to it*).

to beat up 1 to injure seriously by beating. **2** to bring (cream, eggs etc.) to a fluid or semi-fluid mass by beating. **3** (*Naut.*) to make way against wind or tide.

to beat up and down to run first one way, then another, as a hunted animal.

to beat up for to make great endeavours to procure (*beat up for recruits*).

beaten

off the beaten track 1 away from the places people usually go. **2** unusual.

beating

to take a beating to suffer verbal or physical punishment.

to take some/ a lot of beating to be difficult to improve upon.

beauty

beauty is in the eye of the beholder some people find attractive what others find unattractive.

beauty is only skin deep physical attractiveness is superficial and may hide less desirable features.

beaver

eager beaver EAGER.

to beaver away at to work hard at. [The beaver is thought to be an industrious animal.]

beck

at someone's beck and call 1 ready to obey someone's orders instantly. **2** subject to someone's every whim.

become

to become of to happen to, to befall (*I wonder what became of her*).

bed

apple-pie bed APPLE PIE.

bed of nails/ thorns an unpleasant or difficult situation.

bed of roses a comfortable place or situation (*Don't expect marriage to be a bed of roses*).

†to be brought to bed to be delivered of a child.

to bed out to plant out in beds.

to get out of bed on the wrong side to begin the day in a bad mood. [From a superstition that it is unlucky to get out of bed on the left side, or to put one's left foot to the floor first.]

to go to bed 1 to retire at the end of the day. **2** to have sexual intercourse (with).

to have made one's bed and have to lie in it to suffer for one's own misdeeds or mistakes (*You've made your bed, now you must lie in it: don't expect any help from us*).

to make a bed to put a bed in order after it has been used.

to make up a bed to prepare sleeping accommodation at short notice.

to put to bed 1 to settle (a child etc.) in bed for the night. **2** to complete work on (a newspaper) so that it can go to press.

to take/ keep to one's bed to be confined to/ remain in bed (from sickness etc.).

bee

busy as a bee BUSY.

busy bee BUSY.

the bee's knees (*coll.*) (someone or something) wonderful, admirable (*She thinks she's the bee's knees*). [Possibly referring to the part of a bee's legs where pollen is carried.]

the birds and the bees BIRD.

to have a bee in one's bonnet to have a crazy fancy or obsession.

beef

to beef up (*coll.*) to strengthen, to reinforce.

beeline

to make a beeline for to make straight for. [From the idea that bees fly along a direct route back to the hive.]

beer

beer and skittles enjoyment or pleasure (*It's not all beer and skittles*).

to be small beer SMALL BEER.

beetle

to beetle along/ off to hurry, scuttle along.

beetroot

red as a beetroot RED.

beforehand

to be beforehand with to forestall or anticipate.

beg

to beg off to seek to be released from some obligation (*He begged off helping with the washing-up*).

to beg one's bread to live by begging.

to beg someone's pardon to apologize.

to beg the question 1 to assume the thing to be proved. **2** to raise the question. **3** (*coll.*) to avoid facing the difficulty.

to beg to differ to disagree.

to go begging 1 to be acceptable to nobody. **2** to be left after everyone has eaten etc. (*Is this piece of toast going begging?*).

beggar

beggars can't be choosers those who need something must take what is available, however undesirable.

to beggar description to go beyond one's power of expression. [From Shakespeare's *Antony and Cleopatra*: "For her own person, / It beggar'd all description", referring to the beauty of Cleopatra.]

begin

to begin at to start from.

to begin on/ upon to start work on.

to begin with 1 to take first. **2** firstly.

beginning

the beginning of the end the point at which the outcome becomes clear.

behalf

in behalf of (*N Am.*) on behalf of.

on behalf of 1 on account of, for the sake of. **2** representing. **3** (*coll.*) on the part of.

behaviour

on one's best behaviour behaving well when particularly required to do so.

beholder

beauty is in the eye of the beholder BEAUTY.

being

in being existing.

to call into being to give existence to, to create.

belfry

to have bats in the belfry BAT².

belief

beyond belief incredible.

to the best of my belief as far as I know.

believe

believe it or not (*coll.*) although it may seem incredible (the statement is true).

to believe in 1 to trust in the effectiveness of validity of (*believe in corporal punishment*). **2** to accept as true the existence of (*believe in ghosts*).

to believe one's eyes/ ears (*usu. with neg.*) to accept that what one is seeing/ hearing is true (*I could hardly believe my eyes*).

to make believe to pretend.

would you believe it? (*coll.*) does this not seem incredible?

bell

clear as a bell CLEAR.

saved by the bell SAVE.

sound as a bell SOUND².

to bear away the bell to carry off the prize.

to bear the bell to be first.

to bell the cat 1 to be a ringleader in a hazardous movement. **2** to grapple with a dangerous opponent. [From a story about a group of mice who decided to tie a bell round the neck of the cat so that they would hear it coming. However, none of their number was willing to perform this dangerous task.]

to curse by bell, book and candle CURSE.

to give someone a bell (*coll.*) to telephone someone.

to ring a bell RING².

belly

back and belly BACK.

to go belly up 1 (*esp. N Am., coll.*) to go bankrupt. 2 (*esp. N Am., coll.*) to die.

belt

belt and braces offering double security.

to belt out to sing or emit (a sound) loudly or with enthusiasm.

to belt up 1 (*often imper., sl.*) to stop talking. 2 to fasten with a belt. 3 to put a seat belt on.

to hit below the belt HIT.

to tighten one's belt TIGHTEN.

under one's belt secured in one's possession (*You need to get some qualifications under your belt.*). [Possibly alluding to food that has been eaten and digested.]

bench

on the bench serving as a judge or magistrate.

to be raised to the bench RAISE.

bend

around the bend (*N Am., coll.*) round the bend.

bent double stooping.

on bended knee(s) 1 with the knees bent. 2 in submission or supplication (*She begged me on bended knee to let her stay*).

round the bend (*coll.*) crazy, insane (*You're driving me round the bend*).

to bend someone's ear (*coll.*) to talk to someone, esp. boringly or at length (*He's been bending my ear about his new car all morning*).

to bend the brows to frown.

to bend the elbow (*coll.*) to be fond of drinking alcohol.

to bend the knee 1 to kneel in submission. 2 to submit.

to bend the rules to ignore or overlook a rule, esp. on a particular occasion or for a good reason (*I think we can bend the rules and let the children in, just this once*).

benefit

to give someone the benefit of the doubt to assume that someone is innocent, or that they are telling the truth, in the absence of any evidence to the contrary. [Of legal origin.]

bent

to the top of one's bent TOP¹.

berserk

to go berserk to lose control of one's actions in violent rage.

berth

to give a wide berth to WIDE.

beside

beside oneself out of one's wits (with worry etc.)

best

all the best used to express goodwill on taking leave.

as best one can/ may as successfully as one can under the circumstances.

at best as far as can be expected.

at one's best in prime condition, in one's prime.

past one's best no longer in one's prime.

Sunday best SUNDAY.

to be (all) for the best to have a happy or successful outcome, though immediately unpleasant.

to do one's best to do one's utmost.

to get the best of to get the advantage or victory over.

to give best to to concede defeat to, to give way to.

to give it best (*Austral.*) to give in without trying further.

to have the best of to have the advantage or victory over.

to make the best of 1 to make the most of. 2 to be content with.

to the best of to the utmost extent of.

with the best of them without having to be ashamed of one's ability etc. (*I can talk computers with the best of them*).

bet

to bet one's boots to be absolutely certain (*You can bet your boots he'll forget*).

to bet one's bottom dollar to predict with the utmost confidence.

to hedge one's bets HEDGE.

you bet (*sl.*) certainly, of course, depend upon it.

better

better half one's wife.

better off 1 in better circumstances. **2** wealthier.

for better (or) for worse whatever the circumstances. [From the marriage ceremony, in which husband and wife vow to take each other "for better for worse, for richer for poorer" etc.]

for the better tending towards improvement.

had better would be wiser to (do), would be advised to (do) (*You'd better lock the door*).

no better than one should be having dubious morals.

to better oneself to get on, to get a better job.

to get the better of to defeat, to outwit.

betting

what's the betting? I think it very likely (that).

between

between ourselves in confidence.

between you and me (and the gatepost) in confidence.

in between intermediate(ly).

betwixt

betwixt and between 1 (*coll.*) neither one thing nor the other. **2** (*coll.*) half and half. **3** (*coll.*) middling.

bias

on the bias (of material) cut diagonally, slanting obliquely.

bib

best bib and tucker one's best clothing, one's smartest outfit. [A bib was a fancy or formal shirt front worn by men, and a tucker a piece of ornamental lace worn by women around the neck and shoulders.]

to poke/ stick one's bib in (*Austral., sl.*) to interfere.

bid

to bid fair to seem likely, to promise well.

to bid farewell/ welcome to salute at parting or greet on arrival.

to bid up to raise the price of a commodity at auction by a succession of overbids.

to make a bid for to make an attempt to gain (*made a bid for freedom*).

bidding

to force the bidding FORCE.

bide

to bide one's time 1 to await an opportunity patiently. **2** †to abide, to stay. **3** †to continue, to remain.

big

Big Brother a sinister and ruthless person or organization that exercises totalitarian control. [From George Orwell's novel *1984* (1949), in which Big Brother is the head of the Party, which controls the state. Every movement of the citizens is monitored and the slogan "Big Brother is watching you" appears in every public place.]

big cheese/ noise/ shot (*sl.*) an important person.

big deal (*sl., iron.*) a derisory exclamation or response.

big fish in a little pond a person who is important or influential, but only within a limited area or among a small group.

big talk boasting, bragging.

big time (*coll.*) the highest rank in a profession, esp. in entertainment (*He's hit the big time*).

in a big way 1 (*coll.*) to a considerable degree. **2** (*coll.*) very enthusiastically.

the Big Apple (*N Am., sl.*) New York City.

to be big of someone (*coll., usu. iron.*) someone is very generous or magnanimous (*That's big of you!*).

to come/ go over big to impress.

to give a big hand to to clap, to applaud.

too big for one's boots/ breeches unduly self-important.

what's the big idea? (*coll.*) what is the purpose of this?

bike

on your bike! (*sl.*) go away!

to get off one's bike (*esp. Austral.*) to become angry.

bill¹

to fill/ fit the bill to prove satisfactory, to be what is required.

to foot the bill FOOT.

to head/ top the bill 1 to have one's name at the top of a playbill. **2** to be the star attraction.

bill²

to bill and coo 1 (*dated*) to kiss and fondle. **2** (*dated*) to make love.

bill of goods

to sell someone a bill of goods SELL.

bill of health

clean bill of health CLEAN.

billy-o

like billy-o (*sl.*) vigorously, strongly. [Possibly from a personal name, or from the steam engine Puffing Billy.]

bind

to bind down to restrain by formal stipulations.

to bind over (*Law*) to place under legal obligation.

to bind up to bandage.

bird

a bird in the hand (is worth two in the bush) something in one's possession (is of greater value than what one might obtain).

a little bird told me LITTLE.

bird of passage 1 a migratory bird. **2** a person who travels frequently and rarely stays long in one place.

birds of a feather (flock together) people of similar character or interests (are attracted to one another).

early bird EARLY.

fine feathers make fine birds FINE.

free as a bird FREE.

like a bird without difficulty or resistance.

rare bird RARE.

(strictly) for the birds worthless, not serious.

the bird is/ has flown the person concerned has escaped.

the birds and the bees (*euphem.*) reproduction; the facts of life.

the early bird catches the worm EARLY.

to give someone/ get the bird 1 to hiss or boo someone/ be hissed or booed. **2** to dismiss someone/ be dismissed. [From the hissing sound made by geese.]

to kill two birds with one stone KILL.

bird's-eye

bird's-eye view a view from high above.

birth

of gentle birth GENTLE.

to give birth (to) to have a baby, to bring forth young etc.

birthday

in one's birthday suit naked, in the nude. [From the nakedness of a newborn baby.]

biscuit

to take the biscuit 1 (*coll.*) to be the best of the lot. **2** (*coll.*) to be incredible. **3** (*iron.*) to be the most foolish, unacceptable etc. (*I've heard some crazy suggestions, but that takes the biscuit!*).

bishop

as the actress said to the bishop ACTRESS.

bit¹

a bit 1 a little. **2** rather, somewhat.
bit by bit gradually, piecemeal.
bit of all right/ crumpet/ skirt/ stuff (*sl., offensive*) a sexually attractive woman.
bit of rough (*sl.*) a man who is sexually attractive because of his lack of sophistication.
bit of the other (*sl.*) sexual intercourse.
bit on the side 1 (*sl.*) a sexual relationship outside one's marriage. **2** (*sl.*) the person with whom one is having an affair.
devil a bit DEVIL.
every bit as just as (*This book is every bit as good as her last one*).
not a bit not at all.
not a blind bit of BLIND.
to bits 1 into pieces, completely apart (*took the radio to bits*). **2** (*coll.*) very much (*thrilled to bits*).
to do one's bit to do one's share.

bit²

a bit and a sup something to eat and drink.
to champ at the bit CHAMP.
to draw bit 1 to stop a horse by pulling the reins. **2** (*fig.*) to stop; to slacken speed.
to take the bit between one's teeth 1 to become unmanageable. **2** to act decisively. [When a horse takes the bit between its teeth, it is no longer under the rider's control.]

bitch

son of a bitch SON.

bite

someone's bark is worse than their bite BARK.
to bite back to avoid saying (e.g. something hurtful).
to bite off to seize with the teeth and detach.
to bite off more than one can chew to undertake more than one can manage (*I think I've bitten off more than I can chew with this project*).
to bite one's lip 1 to express vexation. **2** to repress anger, laughter or other emotion.
to bite (on) the bullet to submit to an unpleasant situation, to face up to something. [Injured soldiers were given a bullet to bite on while being treated without anaesthetic.]
to bite someone's head off (*coll.*) to snap at someone, to be irritable.
to bite the dust 1 to fail. **2** to die. **3** to be humiliated. [Alluding to a person falling face down when killed.]
to bite the hand that feeds one to be ungrateful to a benefactor.
to put the bite on (*Austral., N Am., sl.*) to borrow or extort money from.
two bites at the cherry TWO.

biter

the biter bit the cheater cheated; the wrongdoer paid back.

bitten

bitten with infected by (a passion etc.).
once bitten twice shy after an unpleasant experience, one is more cautious.

bitter

bitter pill something which is unwelcome or difficult to accept (*It's a bitter pill to swallow*).
to the bitter end until the very end, esp. of something difficult or unpleasant. [Of nautical origin: the bitter end is the loose end of any rope or the end of an anchor

rope attached to a fixture on the deck.]

black

black and blue 1 discoloured by bruising. **2** livid.

black as the ace of spades 1 completely black. **2** very dirty.

black in the face livid with annoyance, exertion etc.

black sheep a bad member of a group or family (*Uncle Tom is the black sheep of the family*).

black spot 1 an area of a road where accidents are common. **2** any dangerous area.

in black and white in writing or print.

in the black in credit, not overdrawn. [From the use of black ink on the credit side of an account.]

like the Black Hole of Calcutta dark, airless, hot and overcrowded. [Alluding to an incident in 1756, when 146 British prisoners were confined in a small prison in Calcutta; all but 23 died of suffocation overnight.]

not as black as one is painted better than one's reputation.

blame

blame it! used as a mild oath.

to be to blame to be culpable.

to have only oneself to blame to be solely responsible for one's own problems.

blanch

to blanch over to try to conceal or misrepresent (e.g. a fault).

blank

blank cheque 1 a cheque with the amount left for the payee to insert. **2** complete freedom of action.

to draw a blank not to succeed in finding what one is looking for. [From a kind of lottery in which winning tickets are numbered and losing tickets are blank.]

blanket

born on the wrong side of the blanket BORN.

wet blanket WET.

blast

at full blast FULL.

to blast off 1 (of a missile or space vehicle) to be launched. **2** (*coll.*) to start.

blaze¹

like blazes (*sl.*) furiously.

to blaze away 1 (of a fire) to burn brightly and strongly. **2** to fire continuously (with guns). **3** to work continuously and enthusiastically.

to blaze out 1 to cause to flare away. **2** to subside with a flare.

to blaze up 1 (of a fire) suddenly to burst into flames. **2** to burst into anger.

what the blazes! (*sl.*) what the hell!

blaze²

to blaze a trail 1 to mark out a route. **2** to pioneer something. [From a white mark (blaze) made on a tree by chipping off bark, used to indicate the path of an explorer.]

blaze³

to blaze abroad to spread (news).

bleed

to bleed like a (stuck) pig to lose a large amount of blood.

to bleed white to drain of money, resources etc.

bless

(God) bless me! an expression of surprise etc.

(God) bless you! 1 used to express endearment, gratitude etc. **2** said to someone who has just sneezed.

to bless oneself to make the sign of the cross (as a defence against evil spirits).

to bless one's stars to be very thankful.

blessing

blessing in disguise something that turns out to be unexpectedly advantageous. [Perhaps from the poem 'Reflections on a Flower Garden' (1746) by James Harvey: "E'en crosses from his sovereign hand / Are blessings in disguise."]

mixed blessing MIXED.

to ask a blessing ASK.

to count one's blessings COUNT.

to give one's blessing to to state one's approval of.

blind

blind alley 1 a street, road or alley walled up at the end. **2** a situation leading nowhere.

blind as a bat having very poor eyesight.

blind spot 1 (*Anat.*) a part of the retina insensitive to light, owing to the passage through it of the optic nerve. **2** a point within the service area of a radio station where signals are received very faintly. **3** a tendency to overlook faults etc. **4** a failure of understanding or judgement. **5** a weakness.

blind to incapable of appreciating.

not a blind bit of (*sl.*) not any, not the slightest (amount of).

the blind leading the blind those with little or no knowledge or experience trying to guide or teach others. [From the Bible: "And if the blind lead the blind, both shall fall into the ditch" (Matt. xv.14).]

there's none so blind as those who will not see said when someone refuses to be persuaded or convinced.

to blind someone with science to overawe someone with esp. spurious knowledge.

to go it blind to act recklessly.

to turn a blind eye to to pretend not to see, to overlook.

blink

on the blink (*coll.*) (of a machine) not functioning properly.

blinker

to wear blinkers WEAR.

block

chip off the old block CHIP.

on the block (*N Am.*) being auctioned.

to block in to sketch roughly the broad masses of (a picture or drawing).

to block out 1 to mark out (work) roughly. **2** to exclude (something painful) from memory.

to block up 1 to confine. **2** to fill in (a window or doorway) with bricks.

to do one's block (*Austral., New Zeal., coll.*) to be very angry.

to put one's head on the block HEAD[1].

to put the blocks on to prevent from going ahead.

blockade

to run a blockade to pass through a blockading force.

blood

bad blood BAD.

blood and thunder melodramatic or sensational (literature etc.).

blood is thicker than water relatives are more important than friends.

flesh and blood FLESH.

in cold blood COLD.

in one's blood inborn; in one's character.

more than flesh and blood can stand FLESH.

new blood NEW.

out for someone's blood 1 wanting revenge on someone. **2** wanting to kill someone.

someone's blood is up someone is angry or ready to fight.

to chill someone's blood CHILL.

to get blood from a stone to obtain the unobtainable (*Getting information from the local council is like getting blood from a stone*).

to **make someone's blood boil** to make someone furious.

to **make someone's blood curdle** to terrify someone, as with a ghost story.

to **make someone's blood run cold** to horrify someone.

to **spill someone's blood** SPILL.

to **stir the blood** STIR.

to **sweat blood** SWEAT.

to **taste blood** TASTE.

young blood YOUNG.

bloody

to **bloody someone's nose** to hurt someone's pride.

bloody murder

to **cry/ scream bloody murder** MURDER.

bloom

in bloom flowering, blossoming.

to **take the bloom off** to make stale.

blot

blot on the escutcheon a stain on the reputation of a person, family etc.

blot on the landscape an unsightly building, an eyesore.

to **blot one's copybook 1** (*coll.*) to commit an indiscretion. **2** (*coll.*) to spoil one's good record. [A copybook is a book in which specimens of good handwriting are written clearly to be copied esp. by children learning to write.]

to **blot out** to obliterate, to efface.

blow¹

blow it! damn, confound it.

I'll be blowed! (*coll.*) used to express astonishment etc.

to **blow a coal 1** to fan a quarrel. **2** to stir up strife.

to **blow a fuse/ gasket** to lose one's temper.

to **blow a kiss** to kiss one's hand and blow the air towards someone.

to **blow away 1** (*sl.*) to kill or destroy. **2** (*sl.*) to defeat. **3** (*sl.*) to amaze.

to **blow away the cobwebs** to refresh oneself in the open air.

to **blow great guns** (of wind) to blow tempestuously. [Of naval origin, alluding to the sound or effect of cannon fire.]

to **blow hot and cold 1** to vacillate. **2** to do one thing at one time, and its opposite at another. [From Aesop's fable about a satyr who watched a man blow on his hands to warm them and on his food to cool it, and thought he was blowing hot and cold with the same breath.]

to **blow in 1** to break inwards. **2** to make an unexpected visit.

to **blow it/ something** (*coll.*) to lose a chance or advantage by committing a blunder.

to **blow off 1** to escape with a blowing noise, as steam. **2** to discharge (steam, energy, anger etc.). **3** to break wind.

to **blow one's own trumpet** to boast, to sing one's own praises.

to **blow one's stack** (*N Am., coll.*) to blow one's top.

to **blow one's top/ lid** (*coll.*) to lose one's temper.

to **blow out 1** to extinguish by blowing. **2** to clear by means of blowing. **3** (of a tyre) to burst. **4** (of a fuse) to melt. **5** (*N Am., sl.*) to defeat soundly. **6** (*N Am., sl.*) to break.

to **blow over** to pass away, to subside.

to **blow sky-high** to blow up, to destroy completely.

to **blow someone's mind** (*sl.*) to give someone drug-induced hallucinations or a similar experience.

to **blow the gaff** to let out the secret, to give information.

to **blow the socks off** (*coll.*) to astonish.

to **blow the whistle on** (*coll.*) to inform on (someone) or bring (something) to an end (*She blew the whistle on the corrupt practices of her employers*). [Alluding to the whistle blown by a referee or umpire in certain games.]

to blow up 1 to inflate. **2** to scold, to
censure severely. **3** to ruin. **4** to
explode. **5** to destroy by explosion.
6 (*coll.*) to enlarge (a photograph).
7 (*coll.*) to exaggerate. **8** (*coll.*) to arise.
9 (*coll.*) to lose one's temper.

blow²

at one blow in one action.
to come to blows to begin fighting.
to exchange blows EXCHANGE.
to strike a blow for STRIKE.

blue

blue-eyed boy/ girl (*coll., usu. derog.*)
someone especially favoured by a
person or group.
bolt from the blue BOLT¹.
boys in blue BOY.
out of the blue unexpectedly. [Referring
to the sky.]
to look blue to look frightened or
depressed.
until one is blue in the face forever and
without success.

blue moon

once in a blue moon 1 very rarely, seldom.
2 never. [From the rare phenomenon of
atmospheric conditions causing the
moon to appear blue in colour.]

blue murder

to cry/ scream blue murder MURDER.

bluey

to hump one's bluey HUMP.

bluff

to call someone's bluff to challenge
someone who is bluffing. [From the
game of poker.]

blunder

to blunder upon to find or discover by
chance.

blush

at (the) first blush FIRST.

to put to the blush 1 to cause to blush.
2 to make ashamed.
to spare someone's blushes SPARE.

board

above board (done) openly, without
dishonesty or trickery. [From card-
games, in which anything a player
does below the board (or table) is
likely to be dishonest or illegal.]
across the board affecting or applying in
all cases (*a 5% pay increase across the
board*). [Originally a betting term in
US horse racing.]
back to the drawing board DRAWING
BOARD.
board and lodging meals and sleeping
quarters.
on board in or into a ship, train, bus or
aeroplane.
stiff as a board STIFF.
to board out 1 to accommodate or be
accommodated away from home.
2 to take one's meals out.
to go by the board 1 to fall overboard.
2 to be ignored, rejected or unused (*All
our plans went by the board*).
to sweep the board SWEEP.
to take on board to consider (an idea etc.)
(*They took our suggestions on board*).
to walk the boards WALK.

boat

in the same boat SAME.
to push the boat out PUSH.
to rock the boat ROCK².

bob

to bob up to emerge suddenly.

Bob

Bob's your uncle everything is all right or
easily accomplished (*You just press
this switch, and Bob's your uncle*). [A
reference to Robert Cecil, Lord
Salisbury (1830–1903), and his nephew
Arthur James Balfour (1848–1930),
who was given important posts in

government while his uncle was prime minister.]

bobtail
ragtag and bobtail RAGTAG

bodikin
od's bodikins OD.

body
body and soul/ bones altogether.

body blow 1 in boxing, a punch landing between the breastbone and navel. **2** a harsh disappointment or setback, a severe shock.

in a body all together.

over my dead body DEAD.

to body forth 1 to give mental shape to. **2** to exhibit, to typify.

to have more ... in one's little finger than someone has in their whole body LITTLE FINGER.

to keep body and soul together to survive, to maintain life (*hardly enough to keep body and soul together*).

bog
to bog down 1 to overwhelm, as with work. **2** to hinder (*Don't get bogged down in the details*).

to bog off (*sl.*) to go away.

boil
to boil away to evaporate in boiling.

to boil down 1 to lessen the bulk of by boiling. **2** to condense.

to boil down to to amount to; to mean (*What it boils down to is this: we can't afford it*).

to boil over 1 to bubble up, so as to run over the sides of the vessel. **2** to be effusive. **3** to lose one's temper.

to come to the boil 1 to reach boiling point. **2** to reach an important or critical stage (*The match really came to the boil after half-time*).

to go off the boil 1 to fall below boiling point. **2** to become less active or enthusiastic.

bold
bold as brass utterly impudent or audacious.

to make/ be so bold to venture, to presume (*if I may make so bold*).

bolster
to bolster up to support, aid or abet.

bolt¹
bolt from the blue 1 lightning from a cloudless sky. **2** an unexpected sudden event (*His resignation was a bolt from the blue*).

bolt upright straight upright.

nuts and bolts NUT.

to bolt in to shut in.

to bolt on 1 to fasten by bolts. **2** to add on.

to bolt out to exclude.

to have shot one's bolt SHOOT.

to shoot one's bolt SHOOT.

bolt²
to bolt out to separate by sifting.

bomb
to go down a bomb (*coll.*) to be very successful or well received.

to go like a bomb 1 (*coll.*) to go very fast (*Our new car goes like a bomb*). **2** (*coll.*) to sell very well.

to make/ earn a bomb (*coll.*) to make or earn a lot of money.

to put a bomb under someone (*coll.*) to urge someone to do something.

bond
in bond in a bonded warehouse and liable to customs duty.

bone
a bone to pick with someone a cause of quarrel with or complaint against someone (*I've got a bone to pick with you*). [Probably an allusion to the inevitable dispute or fight when two animals pick at the same bone.]

bag of bones BAG.

bone of contention a subject of dispute. [Alluding to dogs fighting over a bone.]

bred in the bone BREED.

close to/ near the bone 1 tactless. **2** indecent. **3** destitute, hard up.

dry as a bone DRY.

the bare bones BARE.

to be (all) skin and bone SKIN.

to bone up (on) (*sl.*) to study hard, to swot.

to feel something in one's bones FEEL.

to make no bones about 1 to do or speak about without hesitation or scruple. **2** to present no opposition to. [Possibly from someone looking for bones in their soup or stew, or a reference to throwing dice (which were originally made from bones).]

to make old bones OLD.

to point a/ the bone POINT.

to the bone 1 to the inmost part (*chilled to the bone*). **2** to the minimum (*The budget has been cut to the bone*).

to work one's fingers to the bone WORK.

bonnet

to have a bee in one's bonnet BEE.

boo

would not say boo to a goose would never venture to say anything, is very timid.

book

by the book 1 with exact information. **2** according to the rules.

closed book CLOSED.

in my book according to my view of things.

in someone's bad/ black books regarded with disfavour by someone.

in someone's good books regarded with favour by someone.

like a book formally, pedantically, as if one were reciting from a book.

not in the book not allowed.

one for the book worth recording.

on the books on the official list of names.

open book OPEN.

to book in to register one's arrival.

to book up to buy tickets in advance.

to bring to book to convict, to call to account.

to cook the books COOK.

to curse by bell, book and candle CURSE.

to go by the book to proceed according to the rules.

to kiss the book KISS.

to read someone like a book READ.

to suit someone's book SUIT.

to take a leaf out of someone's book LEAF.

to throw the book at 1 (*coll.*) to charge with every offence possible. **2** (*coll.*) to punish severely.

turn-up for the book(s) TURN-UP.

without book 1 from memory. **2** without authority.

boot[1]

boot and saddle used as a command to mount.

the boot is on the other foot/ leg the situation is reversed.

to bet one's boots BET.

to boot out (*sl.*) to dismiss, to sack.

to die with one's boots on DIE[1].

to give someone/ get the (order of the) boot to dismiss or sack someone/ be dismissed or sacked.

to hang up one's boots HANG.

to have one's heart in one's boots HEART.

to put/ stick the boot in 1 to kick brutally. **2** (*sl.*) to cause further upset or harm to someone already in distress.

tough as old boots TOUGH.

boot[2]

to boot into the bargain, besides, in addition.

bootstrap

to pull oneself up by the bootstraps to achieve or improve one's situation by one's own efforts.

booty

to play booty 1 to join with confederates so as to victimize another player. **2** to play to lose.

bore

to bore the pants off someone (*coll.*) to bore someone greatly.

to bore to tears to bore utterly, to weary greatly.

born

born again 1 regenerated. **2** renewed. **3** reformed, converted.

born and bred by birth and upbringing (*a Northerner born and bred*).

born in/ out of wedlock legitimate/ illegitimate.

born in the purple of high and wealthy, esp. royal or imperial, family. [From the purple robes worn by emperors, kings etc.]

born on the wrong side of the blanket (*coll.*) illegitimate.

born to destined to.

born with a silver spoon in one's mouth fortunate in being born into a family with wealth and social class. [Perhaps an allusion to the type of silver spoon normally given as a christening present.]

in all one's born days (*coll.*) in all one's life so far (*Never in all my born days have I heard such nonsense!*).

not born yesterday (*coll.*) not inexperienced, not gullible.

not to know one is born not to realize how lucky or cosseted one is (*You don't know you're born: I used to start work at six o'clock in the morning*).

there's one born every minute there are plenty of foolish or gullible people around. [From a remark attributed to the US showman Phineas T. Barnum (1810–91): "There's a sucker born every minute."]

borne

borne in upon one 1 having become one's firm conviction. **2** realized by one.

borrowed

borrowed plumes decorations or honours to which one is not entitled.

borrowed time time that one did not expect to have, esp. additional days to live.

bosom

bosom friend a dearest and most intimate friend.

in one's bosom 1 clasped in one's embrace. **2** in one's inmost feelings.

the bosom of one's family the midst of one's family.

viper in one's bosom VIPER.

both

to cut both ways to have both good and bad consequences (*It cuts both ways: you'll have more time to spare, but less money*).

to have it both ways to have or alternate between two incompatible things.

bother

cannot be bothered will not make an effort.

bottle

on the bottle drinking (alcohol) heavily.

to bottle out (*sl.*) to fail to do something because of fear.

to bottle up 1 to conceal. **2** to restrain or repress (one's emotions).

to crack a bottle CRACK.

to hit the bottle HIT.

to lose one's bottle LOSE.

bottom

at bottom 1 in reality. **2** at heart.

bottom drawer a drawer in which a woman keeps her new clothes etc. before marriage.

bottoms up! (*coll.*) a drinking toast.

on one's own bottom independently.
the bottom has fallen out of the market
demand has dropped suddenly.
to be at the bottom of to be the cause of.
to bottom out (of prices etc.) to drop to,
and level out at, the lowest point.
to get to the bottom of to investigate and
discover the real truth about.
to knock the bottom out of KNOCK.
to touch bottom TOUCH.

bottom dollar
to bet one's bottom dollar BET.

bounce
to bounce back to recover quickly or
easily.

bound¹
by leaps and bounds LEAP.

bound²
out of bounds (of an area etc.) forbidden,
prohibited.
to beat the bounds to mark the boundary
of a parish by striking it with light
rods.

bound³
bound up in busy or occupied with.
bound up with 1 intimately associated
with. **2** having identical aims or
interests with.

bow¹
more than one string to one's bow STRING.
to draw the long bow LONG.

bow²
to bow and scrape to be obsequious.
to bow down 1 to bend or kneel in
submission or reverence. **2** to crush, to
make stoop.
to bow out 1 to make one's exit. **2** to
retire, to retreat (*time to bow out and
let a younger person take over*).
to make one's bow to exit or enter
formally.
to take a bow to acknowledge applause.

bow³
shot across the bows SHOT.

bowl
to bowl along to move rapidly and
smoothly.
to bowl out 1 to dismiss (a batsman or
side) in cricket. **2** (*sl.*) to find out.
3 to convict.
to bowl over 1 to knock over. **2** to throw
into a helpless condition. **3** (*coll.*) to
impress (*bowled over by her
performance*).

box¹
in the box seat in the most advantageous
position, best placed.
in the wrong box WRONG.
to box in to surround, to enclose.
to box off 1 (*Naut.*) to veer (a ship) in a
particular manner when near the
shore. **2** to partition off.
to box the compass 1 to name the points
of the compass in proper order. **2** to go
right round (in direction, political
views etc.) and end at the starting
point.
to box up 1 to shut in. **2** to squeeze
together.

box²
to box clever (*coll.*) to act in a clever or
cunning way.

boy
all work and no play makes Jack a dull boy
WORK.
backroom boys BACKROOM.
boys in blue policemen; the police.
boys will be boys 1 used to defend the
boisterous behaviour of boys. **2** said
jocularly when men behave
childishly.
broth of a boy BROTH.
jobs for the boys JOB.
man and boy MAN.
oh boy! used to express surprise,
appreciation, delight or derision.

old boy network OLD.

to separate/ sort out the men from the boys MAN.

whipping boy WHIPPING.

brace

belt and braces BELT.

brain

brain drain (*coll.*) the emigration of academics or scientists looking for better pay or conditions.

to beat one's brains to puzzle, to ponder laboriously.

to cudgel one's brains CUDGEL.

to have something on the brain to be obsessed with something, to be unable to get something out of one's mind (*I've had that tune on the brain all day*).

to pick someone's brains PICK.

to rack one's brains RACK[1].

branch

olive branch OLIVE.

root and branch ROOT.

to branch out to broaden one's activities.

brass

bold as brass BOLD.

brassed off (*sl.*) fed up.

brass hat (*coll.*) a staff officer.

brass neck (*coll.*) impudence, audacity (*He had the brass neck to ask for his money back*).

brass tacks 1 (*coll.*) details. 2 (*coll.*) the essential facts of the matter. [Possibly from rhyming slang for 'facts'.]

not a brass razoo (*Austral., New Zeal., coll.*) no money at all.

top brass TOP[1].

brass farthing

not a brass farthing (*coll.*) no money at all.

not to give a brass farthing (*coll.*) to be totally unconcerned.

brass monkey

cold enough to freeze the balls off a brass monkey COLD.

brave

to brave it out to bear oneself defiantly in the face of blame or suspicion.

breach

†to stand in the breach to bear the brunt of an attack.

to step into the breach STEP.

bread

bread and butter 1 a slice of buttered bread. 2 basic means of subsistence, livelihood (*bread-and-butter earnings*). 3 plain and practical, routine and basic (*bread-and-butter issues*).

bread-and-butter letter a letter of thanks for hospitality.

bread and circuses free food and entertainment, esp. to placate the population. [From Juvenal's *Satires* (2nd century AD), originally referring to ways of preventing unrest among the populace of ancient Rome.]

bread buttered on both sides 1 fortunate circumstances. 2 ease and prosperity.

daily bread DAILY.

half a loaf is better than no bread HALF.

the best thing since sliced bread THING.

to beg one's bread BEG.

to break bread BREAK.

to cast one's bread upon the waters CAST.

to know which side one's bread is buttered (on) SIDE.

to take the bread out of someone's mouth to take away someone's means of living.

breadth

a hair's breadth HAIR.

break

break a leg! (*sl.*) used to wish someone good luck, esp. in the theatre. [According to theatrical superstition, it is unlucky to say 'Good luck!' to someone before a performance. The phrase may be of German origin, and is probably unconnected with the fact that the US actor John Wilkes Booth broke his leg after assassinating President Abraham Lincoln in 1865.]

break of day dawn.

to break a head to injure someone.

to break a way to make a way by forcing obstacles apart.

to break away 1 to remove by breaking. **2** to start away. **3** to revolt, to rebel (from).

to break bread 1 to take a meal (with). **2** to take Communion (with).

to break bulk to begin to unload or unpack.

to break camp to take down one's tent in preparation for leaving.

to break cover to dart out from a hiding place.

to break down 1 to destroy, to overcome. **2** (of a machine) to stop working. **3** to collapse, to fail. **4** to lose control of oneself. **5** to analyse (costs etc.) into component parts.

to break even to emerge without gaining or losing (*We won't make a profit, but we should break even*).

to break free/ loose 1 to escape from captivity. **2** to shake off restraint.

to break ground 1 to plough, to dig (esp. uncultivated or fallow ground). **2** to open trenches. **3** to commence operations. **4** (*Naut.*) to begin to weigh anchor.

to break in 1 to tame. **2** to make (shoes etc.) more comfortable by wearing them. **3** to enter a building by using force. **4** (*Austral., New Zeal.*) to bring (land) into cultivation.

to break in on to disturb or interrupt.

to break into 1 to enter by force. **2** to interrupt. **3** to suddenly burst out with. **4** to suddenly change to (a faster pace).

to break new/ fresh ground 1 to do something not previously done. **2** to make a start. **3** to cut the first sod.

to break off 1 to detach from. **2** to cease, to desist.

to break one's duck to score one's first run in a game of cricket. [A duck in cricket is a score of zero, from the round shape of a duck's egg.]

to break one's word to break one's promise, to fail to fulfil an undertaking.

to break on the wheel to torture or execute by stretching on a wheel, and breaking the limbs with an iron bar.

to break open 1 to force a door or cover. **2** to penetrate by violence.

to break out 1 to burst loose, to escape. **2** to begin suddenly, to burst forth (*War broke out*). **3** to appear (as an eruption on the skin). **4** to exclaim. **5** to release (a flag). **6** to open (a container) and remove the contents.

to break rank(s) 1 (of soldiers) to fall out of line. **2** to lose solidarity.

to break service/ someone's serve to win a game of tennis in which the opposing player served.

to break someone's heart to cause someone overwhelming grief.

to break step to cease marching in unison.

to break the back of 1 to overburden. **2** to perform the greater part of (a piece of work).

to break the bank 1 to win the limit set by the management of a gambling house for a particular period. **2** to leave someone penniless (*Five pounds won't break the bank*).

to break the ice 1 to prepare the way. **2** to take the first steps, esp. towards overcoming formality or shyness between two or more people (*a few party games to break the ice*).

to break the mould 1 to make unique. **2** to effect a fundamental change.

to break the news to tell something that has just happened.

to break through 1 to force a way through. **2** to achieve success.

to **break to pieces** to break into separate fragments.

to **break up 1** to disintegrate. **2** to lay open (ground etc.). **3** to dissolve into laughter. **4** to separate. **5** to cause to separate. **6** to come to an end. **7** to bring to an end, to destroy. **8** to start school holidays. **9** (*esp. N Am.*) to be upset or excited.

to **break wind** to discharge wind from the anus.

to **break with 1** to cease to be friends with. **2** to quarrel with.

to **make a break for it** to attempt to escape.

breakfast

to **have someone for breakfast** to crush or destroy someone.

breast

to **beat one's breast** to show grief or sorrow.

to **breast the tape** in a race on foot, to touch or break the tape across the course to win.

to **make a clean breast of** CLEAN.

breath

breath of fresh air 1 a small amount of fresh air. **2** a refreshing change.

in the same breath SAME.

out of breath gasping for air after exercise.

short of breath SHORT.

to **catch one's breath** CATCH.

to **draw breath 1** to pause, to have a break. **2** to live, to breathe.

to **gather (one's) breath** GATHER.

to **hold one's breath 1** to stop breathing for a short time. **2** to wait in anxious or eager expectation.

to **save one's breath (to cool one's porridge)** SAVE.

to **take breath** to pause.

to **take one's breath away** to astonish, to delight (*The view took my breath away*).

to **waste one's breath** WASTE.

under/ below one's breath in a low voice, in a whisper.

with bated breath BATE.

breathe

not to breathe a word to keep silent, to keep a secret.

to **breathe again/ freely/ easily** to be relieved from fear or anxiety.

to **breathe down someone's neck** to cause someone discomfort with one's close supervision or constant attention.

to **breathe in/ out** to inhale/ exhale.

to **breathe one's last** to die.

to **breathe upon** to tarnish.

breed

bred in the bone 1 hereditary. **2** firmly established.

to **breed in and in** to breed always with or from near relatives.

to **breed like rabbits** (*derog.*) to have many children.

to **breed true** always to produce young in harmony with the parental type.

breeze

to **breeze in** to enter in a carefree or casual manner.

to **breeze up 1** to begin to blow freshly. **2** to sound louder on the breeze. **3** to approach in a carefree or lively manner.

brew

to **brew up** (*coll.*) to make tea.

brick

like a ton of bricks TON.

to **bang/ knock/ run one's head against a brick wall** HEAD[1].

to **brick up** to block up with brickwork.

to **drop a brick** DROP.

to **make bricks without straw** to perform the impossible. [From the Bible: "Ye shall no more give the people straw to make brick" (Exod. v.7).]

to **see through a brick wall** to be

unusually discerning; to have extraordinary insight.

bridge

to cross a bridge when one comes to it CROSS.

water under the bridge WATER.

brief

in brief briefly.

to be brief to use few words.

to hold a brief for 1 to argue in support of. **2** (*Law*) to be retained as counsel for.

bright

bright and breezy carefree, cheerful or lively.

bright and early very early in the morning.

bright as a button very clever or alert.

bright-eyed and bushy-tailed (*coll.*) radiant with health and vigour.

bright lights 1 the area of a city where places of entertainment are concentrated. **2** the city.

bright spark (*coll., also iron.*) a clever, witty or lively person.

to look on the bright side to be optimistic.

brim

to brim over to overflow.

bring

to bring about 1 to cause to happen. **2** (*Naut.*) to change the course of (a ship).

to bring around (*N Am.*) to bring round.

to bring back to recall to memory (*It brought back the time we got lost in the forest*).

to bring down 1 to humble, to abase. **2** to shoot, to kill. **3** to lower (a price). **4** to carry on (a history) to a certain date. **5** to depose, to overthrow (*a scandal that brought down the government*). **6** (*sl.*) to make unhappy. **7** (*coll.*) to demean.

to bring forth 1 to bear, to produce, to give birth to. **2** to cause.

to bring forward 1 to produce, to adduce. **2** to carry on (a sum) from the bottom of one page to the top of the next (in bookkeeping). **3** to move to an earlier date or time.

to bring home to 1 to cause to realize. **2** to prove conclusively to, to convince.

to bring in 1 to produce, to yield. **2** to introduce (an action or bill). **3** to return (a verdict).

to bring low 1 to overcome. **2** to humiliate. **3** to depress. **4** to reduce in wealth, position, health etc.

to bring off 1 to bring away (from a ship, the shore etc.). **2** to procure the acquittal of. **3** to accomplish.

to bring on 1 to cause to begin. **2** to introduce for discussion. **3** to cause to develop (more quickly).

to bring out 1 to express, to exhibit, to illustrate. **2** to introduce to society. **3** to launch (as a company). **4** to produce upon the stage. **5** to publish. **6** to expose or reveal (*brings out the worst in me*).

to bring over 1 to convert. **2** to cause to change sides.

to bring round 1 to revive. **2** to convert (*At first she was against the idea, but I managed to bring her round*).

to bring through to help (someone) through a crisis, illness etc.

to bring to 1 to restore to health or consciousness. **2** (*Naut.*) to check the course of (a ship).

to bring to pass to cause to happen.

to bring under to subdue.

to bring up 1 to educate, to rear. **2** to raise (a subject) for discussion. **3** to vomit. **4** to come to a stop. **5** to continue a further stage. **6** (*Naut.*) to cast anchor.

to bring upon oneself to be responsible for (one's own problems).

brink

on the brink of on the point of.

bristling

bristling with full of, with many of.

Bristol

(all shipshape and) Bristol fashion in good order. [Dating from the time when Bristol was a major port, renowned for its efficiency.]

broad

broad across/ in the beam 1 (of a ship) wide. **2** (of a person) having wide hips, having large buttocks.

in broad daylight in the clear light of day (*They were robbed in the street in broad daylight*).

to be as broad as it is long 1 to be equal on the whole. **2** to be the same either way.

to have broad shoulders to be willing or able to take on a great deal of responsibility etc.

broke

to go for broke (*sl.*) to risk everything in a venture.

broken

broken home the home of children with separated or divorced parents.

broken reed an unreliable or weak person.

broom

a new broom sweeps clean NEW.

new broom NEW.

broth

broth of a boy a high-spirited fellow.

too many cooks spoil the broth COOK.

brother

am I my brother's keeper? I am not responsible for the actions or affairs of others. [From the Bible (Gen. iv.9), said by Cain when asked by God where his murdered brother Abel was.]

Big Brother BIG.

brow

by the sweat of one's brow SWEAT.

to bend the brows BEND.

to knit one's brows KNIT.

brown

browned off 1 (*sl.*) disappointed. **2** (*sl.*) bored, fed up.

in a brown study in a daydream, deep in thought.

to do brown (*sl.*) to take in, to deceive.

brunt

to bear the brunt to take the main force (e.g. of an attack).

brush

daft as a brush DAFT.

tarred with the same brush TAR.

to brush aside to ignore or dismiss curtly (*They brushed aside our objections*).

to brush off to dismiss or rebuff curtly.

to brush over to paint lightly.

to brush up 1 to clean by brushing. **2** to revive, to tidy one's appearance. **3** to refresh one's memory or knowledge (*I'd better brush up my Spanish before I go on holiday*).

brute

brute force (and ignorance) sheer strength or violence, rather than skill or subtlety, used to achieve something (*We'll have to use brute force*).

bubble

to bubble over to overflow with laughter, anger etc.

buck

the buck stops here this person or organization must take responsibility. [From a sign that the US president Harry S. Truman (1884–1972) placed on his desk.]

to buck up 1 to hurry. **2** to improve. **3** to become cheerful or lively.

to pass the buck (*sl.*) to shift responsibility to someone else. [The buck is an object (originally a buckhorn knife, a piece of buckshot or a silver dollar) passed to a player with a particular responsibility, such as dealing the cards or declaring the first stake, in certain card games.]

bucket
to cry buckets CRY.
to kick the bucket KICK.

buckle
to buckle down to make a determined effort.
to buckle to to set to work, to set about energetically.
to buckle under to give way under stress.

bud
in bud about to flower or grow leaves.
to nip in the bud NIP.

buddy
to buddy up to become friendly.

budge
to budge over/ up to move along to make room for someone.

budget
on a budget with a restricted amount of money to spend.

buff
in the buff (*coll.*) naked. [From the colour of the skin.]

bug
snug as a bug in a rug SNUG.
to bug off (*esp. N Am., sl.*) to go away.
to bug out 1 (*esp. N Am., sl.*) (of eyes) to protrude. 2 (*esp. N Am., sl.*) to depart hurriedly.

bugger
bugger all (*sl.*) nothing (*I've done bugger all this afternoon*).
to bugger about/ around (*sl.*) to mess about and waste time.
to bugger off (*sl.*) to leave.

build
to build in to incorporate (into a structure etc.).
to build on 1 to found or rely on (as a basis). 2 to add to (a building).

to build something on sand to establish something on an insecure basis. [From the Bible: "every one that heareth these sayings of mine, and doeth them not, shall be likened unto a foolish man, which built his house upon the sand" (Matt. vii.26)]
to build up 1 to establish or strengthen by degrees. 2 to increase. 3 to block up. 4 to erect many buildings in (an area). 5 to praise.
to build upon to found or rely on.

bulge
to get/ have the bulge on (*sl.*) to get/ have an advantage over (someone).

bulk
in bulk 1 (of cargo) loose in the hold. 2 in large quantities.
to break bulk BREAK.

bull
bull in a china shop a tactless or clumsy person, a blunderer.
cock and bull story COCK¹.
John Bull JOHN.
like a bull at a gate forcefully or vigorously, without tact or finesse (*He went at it like a bull at a gate*).
like a red rag to a bull RED RAG.
not to know B from a bull's foot B.
to take the bull by the horns to grapple with a difficulty boldly.

bulldoze
to bulldoze one's way (*coll.*) to make one's way by force.

bullet
to bite (on) the bullet BITE.
to give someone/ get the bullet (*sl.*) to dismiss someone/ be dismissed.
to sweat bullets SWEAT.

bully
bully for you! (*sometimes iron.*) well done!, bravo!

bum

bum steer misleading information.

on the bum scrounging, begging.

the bum's rush 1 (*N Am., sl.*) forcible ejection, as from a gathering. **2** (*N Am., sl.*) dismissal (of an idea or person).

bump

to bump into 1 to collide with, to hit. **2** to meet unexpectedly (*I bumped into Mary at the airport*).

to bump off (*coll.*) to murder.

to bump up to increase (prices).

bun

to have a bun in the oven (*sl.*) to be pregnant.

to take the bun 1 (*coll.*) to be the best of the lot. **2** (*coll.*) to be incredible.

bunch

bunch of fives a fist.

bundle

bundle of nerves (*coll.*) a very timid, anxious person.

to bundle off 1 to send away hurriedly or unceremoniously. **2** to dismiss.

to bundle up 1 to gather into a bundle. **2** to clothe warmly.

to go a bundle on 1 (*sl.*) to like enormously (*I don't go a bundle on their choice of wallpaper*). **2** (*sl.*) to be enthusiastic for.

bung

to go bung 1 (*Austral., coll.*) to die. **2** (*Austral., coll.*) to go bankrupt.

bunk

to bunk off to play truant.

to do a bunk to run away.

buoy

to buoy up 1 to keep afloat. **2** to hearten or encourage (*buoyed up by the news*). **3** to bring to the surface.

burn

burnt offering 1 an offering or sacrifice made to a deity by fire. **2** (*facet.*) food ruined by burning.

to burn a hole in someone's pocket (of money) to cause someone to want to spend it immediately (*His winnings were burning a hole in his pocket*).

to burn away to consume entirely by fire.

to burn down to reduce or be reduced to ashes.

to burn in to render indelible by or as by burning.

to burn low (of fire) to be nearly out.

to burn off to remove (paint) by means of softening with a blowlamp or hot iron.

to burn one's boats/ bridges to commit oneself to something without possibility of retreat. [From a military practice of destroying the boats or bridges used by an army to cross a river.]

to burn one's fingers/ get one's fingers burnt to hurt or bring trouble on oneself by meddling.

to burn out 1 to consume the inside or contents of. **2** (*coll.*) to exhaust or render inoperative through overwork or overheating (*You'll be burnt out by the time you're thirty*). **3** to eradicate or expel by burning.

to burn the candle at both ends to expend one's energies or exhaust oneself, esp. by staying up late and getting up early.

to burn the midnight oil to study or work far into the night.

to burn to a cinder to burn thoroughly; to render useless, inedible etc. by burning.

to burn to a crisp to overcook something to the point where it is burnt and uneatable.

to burn up 1 to destroy or get rid of, by fire. **2** to blaze, to flash into a blaze. **3** (*coll.*) to drive fast. **4** (*N Am., sl.*) to be furious or make furious.

to go for the burn (*coll.*) to try to achieve the burning sensation in the muscles

produced by strenuous exercise, to
exercise hard.

burner

on the back/ front burner (*coll.*) having
low/ high priority (*put the project on
the back burner*).

burst

bursting at the seams too full for comfort.
to burst in 1 to enter suddenly. **2** to
interrupt.
to burst out 1 to break out. **2** to begin
suddenly to laugh, cry etc. **3** to
exclaim.
to burst up 1 (*coll.*) to go bankrupt. **2** to
collapse.

Burton

gone for a burton 1 (*sl.*) dead. **2** (*sl.*)
absent, missing. **3** (*sl.*) ruined,
destroyed. [Probably a reference to
beer brewed in Burton-upon-Trent in
Staffordshire. The phrase originated
in the RAF in World War II and was
applied to airmen who failed to return
from a mission, especially those shot
down over water. There may be a
connection between a drink of beer
and 'the drink' meaning 'the sea'.]

bury

to bury one's head in the sand to ignore
the facts. [An allusion to ostriches,
which were once thought to bury
their heads in the sand when danger
approached, believing that they
could not be seen if they could not
see.]
to bury the hatchet to forgive and forget,
to effect a reconciliation. [From the
North American Indian custom of
burying a tomahawk on the conclusion
of peace.]

bus

like the back of a bus BACK.

bush

bush telegraph the rapid dissemination
of rumours, information etc.
to beat about the bush 1 to approach a
matter in a roundabout way. **2** to be
hesitant or irresolute.
to beat around the bush (*N Am.*) to beat
about the bush.
to go bush (*Austral.*) to go into the bush;
to leave civilization.
to take to the bush 1 to take refuge in the
backwoods. **2** (*Austral., Hist.*) to make
one's home in the bush and live by
robbing travellers etc.

bushel

to hide one's light under a bushel HIDE[1].

business

business end (*coll.*) the point (of a tool or
weapon).
funny business FUNNY.
like nobody's business NOBODY.
monkey business MONKEY.
on business with a particular (esp.
work-related) purpose.
to have no business to to have no right
to.
to make it one's business to undertake (to
do something) (*I made it my business
to put the matter right*).
to mean business MEAN[1].
to mind one's own business MIND.
to send someone about their business
to send someone off brusquely or
summarily.

busman

busman's holiday (*coll.*) a holiday spent
doing one's everyday work. [From the
days of horse-drawn buses, when a
driver would sometimes take a holiday
on his own bus in order to keep an eye
on his horses.]

bust

to bust a gut (*coll.*) to make a great effort
(*I bust a gut to get it finished in time*).

to **bust up 1** to quarrel and separate. **2** to bring or come to collapse.

to **go bust** to go bankrupt.

busy

busy as a bee very busy, continuously occupied.

busy bee a busy worker.

but

but for were it not for (*We'd have been here ages ago but for the traffic*).

but me no buts bring forward no objections.

but that were it not that.

but yet however, on the other hand.

no buts about it undoubtedly, indisputably.

butcher

the butcher, the baker, the candlestick maker all and sundry. [From the nursery rhyme beginning "Rub-a-dub-dub, three men in a tub".]

butt

to **butt in** to interfere, to interrupt.

to **butt out 1** (*esp. N Am., sl.*) to stop interfering. **2** (*N Am., sl.*) to stop doing something.

butter

bread and butter BREAD.

bread-and-butter letter BREAD.

to **butter up** (*coll.*) to flatter.

to **look as if butter wouldn't melt in one's mouth** to look innocent.

butterfly

butterflies in the stomach (*coll.*) nervous tremors in the stomach.

button

bright as a button BRIGHT.

buttoned up 1 (*coll.*) formal and inhibited. **2** (*coll.*) silent.

on the button (*esp. N Am., sl.*) precisely.

to **button one's lip** (*sl.*) to stay silent.

to **press the button** PRESS.

to **press the panic button** PRESS.

buy

to **buy in 1** to buy back for the owner (at an auction). **2** to obtain a stock of (anything) by purchase. **3** to purchase (stock) and charge the extra cost to the person who had undertaken to deliver it.

to **buy into** to purchase a share of or interest in (e.g. a company).

to **buy it** (*sl.*) to be killed.

to **buy off 1** to pay a price to, for release or non-opposition. **2** to get rid of by a payment.

to **buy out 1** to purchase the release of (a member of the forces) from service. **2** to buy a majority share in or complete control over (e.g. a property, a company), thereby dispossessing the original owner(s). **3** to buy off. **4** †to redeem.

to **buy over** to bribe.

to **buy time** to delay something.

to **buy up** to purchase all the available stock of.

buzz

to **buzz about** to hover or bustle about in an annoying manner.

by

by and by 1 soon, presently. **2** later on. **3** (*N Am.*) the future, time to come.

by and large on the whole. [Originally a nautical term, referring to a course or passage that uses a variable wind to the best advantage.]

by oneself 1 alone, without help. **2** on one's own initiative.

by the way/ by(e) casually, incidentally, apart from the main subject (*We've run out of coffee, by the way*).

bygone

let bygones be bygones let us think no more of past injuries.

C

cabbage
not as green as one is cabbage-looking
GREEN.

caboodle
the whole (kit and) caboodle WHOLE.

cackle
to cut the cackle to get down to business.

Cain
to raise Cain RAISE.

cake
cakes and ale a good time. [From
    Shakespeare's *Twelfth Night*: "Dost
    thou think, because thou art virtuous,
    there shall be no more cakes and ale?"]
icing on the cake ICING.
piece of cake PIECE.
slice of the cake SLICE.
to go/ sell like hot cakes HOT.
to have one's cake and eat it to take
    advantage of two alternatives, one of
    which excludes the other (*You can't
    have your cake and eat it*).
to take the cake 1 (*sl.*) to come first.
    2 (*iron., sl.*) to be the most foolish,
    unacceptable etc. [From the prize of a
    cake awarded to the best performers of
    the cakewalk, a dance with high
    marching steps.]

Calcutta
like the Black Hole of Calcutta BLACK.

calends
at the Greek calends GREEK.

calf
calf love romantic attachment between a
    boy and a girl.
golden calf GOLDEN.
in/ with calf (of a cow, elephant,
    rhinoceros etc.) pregnant.
to kill the fatted calf KILL.

call
at someone's beck and call BECK.
call of nature a need to urinate or
    defecate.
close call CLOSE¹.
on call 1 (of a doctor etc.) available to be
    summoned if required. 2 (of a loan
    etc.) to be repaid on demand.
to call away to summon away, to divert.
to call back 1 to revoke, to withdraw.
    2 to visit again. 3 to call later by
    telephone.
to call down to invoke.
to call for 1 to desire the attendance of.
    2 to appeal for, to demand. 3 to require,
    to necessitate (*Urgent action is called
    for*). 4 to visit a place to bring (a
    person or thing) away. 5 to signal for
    (trumps).
to call forth 1 to elicit. 2 to summon to
    action.
to call in 1 to summon to one's aid (*We
    called in a consultant*). 2 to withdraw
    (money) from circulation. 3 to order
    the return of. 4 to pay a short visit (on,
    at etc.).
to call off 1 to summon away, to order
    (an animal or person) to stop attacking
    etc. 2 to cancel (*The meeting was
    called off*).

to call on 1 to invoke, to appeal to. 2 to pay a short visit to.

to call out 1 to say loudly, to shout. 2 to summon (troops etc.) to service. 3 to order (workers) to strike. 4 to elicit. 5 to challenge to a duel or fight.

to call over to read aloud.

to call up 1 (*Mil.*) to mobilize. 2 to make a telephone call to. 3 to rouse from sleep. 4 to cause to remember or imagine. 5 to summon to appear. 6 to require payment of.

to pay a call (*coll.*) to urinate or defecate.

within call within hearing.

calm

calm before the storm a relatively quiet and peaceful period before a crisis or commotion.

to calm down to make or become calm.

camel

the straw that broke the camel's back STRAW.

to strain at a gnat and swallow a camel STRAIN.

camera

in camera 1 in private. 2 (*Law*) in a judge's chamber, or with the public excluded from the court (*a trial held in camera*).

off camera not being filmed.

on camera being recorded on film.

camp¹

camp follower 1 a civilian who follows an army in the field. 2 a hanger-on.

foot in both camps FOOT.

to break camp BREAK.

to camp out 1 to lodge in a tent etc. in the open. 2 to sleep outdoors. 3 to place (troops) in camp.

camp²

to camp it up to act in an exaggeratedly camp manner, to overact.

can

can it! (*sl.*) stop doing that!

can of worms (*coll.*) a complicated and potentially problematic issue or situation.

in the can 1 filmed or recorded, processed and ready for release. 2 (*fig.*) arranged. [Referring to a shallow metal container for film.]

to carry the can (*coll.*) to take responsibility, to accept blame. [Of military origin, referring to a can containing the beer supply for a group of soldiers. Carrying the can was regarded as a menial task.]

cancel

to cancel out to neutralize, counterbalance or compensate for (one another).

candle

not (fit/ able) to hold a candle to not to be comparable with, to be greatly inferior to. [In the days before electric lighting, apprentices would hold a candle to assist their masters at work.]

(the game is) not worth the candle WORTH.

to burn the candle at both ends BURN.

to curse by bell, book and candle CURSE.

candlestick

the butcher, the baker, the candlestick maker BUTCHER.

cannon

cannon fodder (*facet.*) soldiers, esp. infantrymen, regarded as expendable.

canoe

in the same canoe SAME.

to paddle one's own canoe PADDLE.

canter

in/ at a canter easily.

canvas

to win by a canvas WIN.

under canvas 1 in a tent or tents. 2 with sails set.

cap

cap in hand in a humble or servile
manner (*The management was forced
to go cap in hand to the union*).
[Removing one's cap or hat in the
presence of others is a sign of respect.]

feather in one's cap FEATHER.

if the cap fits (wear it) if the general
remark applies to you, take it to
yourself. [Originally referring to a
jester's cap as appropriate headgear for
a foolish person.]

to cap it all (*coll.*) as a finishing touch.

†**to cap verses** to reply to a verse quoted
by quoting another that rhymes or is
otherwise appropriate.

to pass/ send round the cap to make a
collection of money.

to put on one's thinking cap THINKING.

to set one's cap at (*dated*) to try to attract
or win (a particular person, esp. a
man) for love or marriage. [Perhaps an
allusion to the ornate headgear
formerly worn by young women on
social occasions.]

†**to throw one's cap over the windmill** to
behave in a reckless or unconventional
manner.

capacity

to capacity fully, to the limit.

caper

to cut a caper/ capers 1 to skip about
playfully. **2** to act in an ostentatious
manner.

capful

capful of wind (*Naut.*) a light gust.

capital

to make capital out of to make profit
from, to turn to one's advantage (*The
opposition made capital out of the
government's U-turn*).

with a capital A etc. used for emphasis
(*This is sexism with a capital S!*).

capitalize

to capitalize on to use to one's advantage.

captain

captain of industry a powerful or
influential person in industry; the
head of a large industry.

carbon

carbon copy 1 a duplicate of something
typed, written or drawn, made by
placing carbon paper between two or
more sheets of paper before typing etc.
2 a person, thing or event etc. that is
identical or very similar to something
else.

card

house of cards HOUSE.

in the cards (*N Am.*) on the cards.

on the cards possible; not improbable.
[From the use of cards in fortune-
telling.]

to get one's cards to be dismissed or made
redundant. [Referring originally to an
employee's National Insurance card
and other documents held by an
employer during a period of
employment.]

to hold all the cards to be in a position of
control.

to play one's cards close to one's chest to
be secretive about one's intentions,
resources etc.

to play one's cards well/ right to be a good
strategist, to take the appropriate
action to gain an advantage.

to put/ lay one's cards on the table to
disclose one's situation, plans etc.

to shuffle the cards SHUFFLE.

to speak by the card SPEAK.

to stack the cards STACK.

to throw up the cards to give up.

trump card TRUMP.

care

care killed the cat don't worry. [An
allusion to the proverbial nine lives of

a cat, implying that even the most
resilient can be killed by worry.]
care of at or to the address of.
for all someone cares (*coll.*) referring to
someone's lack of concern or interest
(*For all you care she could be dead*).
in care (of a child) in the guardianship of
the local authority.
not to care a curse to regard something as
worthless or as too contemptible to
trouble about.
**not to care two hoots/ a fig/ a pin/ a
button** not to care at all.
(someone) couldn't care less (*coll.*) used to
express (someone's) complete
indifference.
to care for 1 to provide for; to look after.
2 to like, to be fond of.
to take care of 1 to look after (*He takes
care of his elderly mother*). **2** to
provide or pay for (*I put money aside
in order to take care of the bills*). **3** to
deal with.
to take/ have a care 1 to be careful,
cautious or vigilant. **2** (*coll.*) to look
after oneself.
who cares? (*coll.*) I don't care.

carpet
on the carpet 1 under consideration.
2 (*coll.*) being reprimanded. [Referring
originally to the carpet in a room
where the master or mistress of the
house reprimanded a servant.]
to put out the red carpet RED CARPET.
to sweep/ brush under the carpet to
conceal or ignore deliberately (a
problem etc.).

carrot
carrot and stick reward and punishment,
esp. as alternative means of
persuasion. [Alluding to means of
persuading a donkey to move on or to
go faster.]

carry
to carry all before one 1 to bear off all the

honours. **2** to win or gain complete
success, unanimous support etc.
to carry away 1 to remove. **2** (*usu. pass.*)
to excite, to inspire, to deprive of
self-control (*Don't get carried away!*).
3 (*Naut.*) to break or lose (a rope, mast
etc.).
to carry back 1 to take back. **2** in
accounting, to apply (a loss etc.) to the
income of the previous year for tax
purposes.
to carry forward to transfer to another
page or column.
to carry it off to succeed, esp. under
difficult circumstances.
to carry off 1 to remove. **2** to win. **3** to do
or handle successfully. **4** to cause to
die.
to carry on 1 to conduct or engage in (a
business, a conversation etc.). **2** to
continue. **3** to behave in a particular
way, esp. to flirt outrageously or have
an affair (*carrying on with the man
next door*). **4** to make a fuss.
to carry oneself to behave (in a particular
way).
to carry out 1 to perform. **2** to
accomplish.
to carry over 1 to carry forward. **2** to
postpone to a future occasion.
to carry through 1 to accomplish. **2** to
bring to a conclusion in spite of
obstacles.
to carry with one 1 to bear in mind.
2 to convince.

cart
in the cart (*sl.*) in a predicament, in
trouble.
to cart off (*coll.*) to remove by force.
to put the cart before the horse to reverse
the natural or proper order.
to upset the apple-cart UPSET.

carve
to carve out 1 to take (a piece) from
something larger. **2** to create or
establish by one's own effort (*to carve*

out a career). **3** (*Law*) to create a small estate out of a larger one.

to carve up 1 to divide into pieces or portions, to subdivide (esp. land). **2** to drive into the path of (another vehicle), esp. in an aggressive or dangerous manner after overtaking.

case

as the case may be according to the circumstances, depending on the situation.

case in point an apt or relevant instance.

hard case HARD.

in any case in any event, whatever may happen.

in case 1 if, supposing that. **2** lest (*Take a map in case you get lost*).

in case of in the event of.

†in good case in good condition.

in no case under no circumstances.

in that case if that should happen, if that is true.

in the case of regarding.

it's a case with (*sl.*) it's all up with.

just in case as a precaution (*I'll bring my umbrella just in case*).

to be the case to be so (*If that's the case, there's nothing more we can do*).

to rest one's case REST¹.

cash

cash down with money paid on the spot.

in cash 1 having money. **2** with cash as opposed to cheques or credit.

out of cash having no money.

to cash in to exchange for money.

to cash in on (*coll.*) to profit from (*They tried to cash in on our good fortune*).

to cash in one's chips (*sl.*) to die. [Chips are counters used as tokens in gambling games.]

to cash up to add up the money taken (in a shop etc.) at the end of the day.

cast

cast in the same mould very alike.

ne'er cast a clout till May is out do not stop wearing warm winter clothes until the end of May (or until the may blossom appears).

to cast about/ around to make an extensive mental, visual or physical search (*to cast about for inspiration*).

to cast adrift to cause or leave to drift.

†to cast a glamour over to bewitch, to enchant.

to cast anchor 1 to drop the anchor into the sea. **2** (of a person) to settle down.

to cast an eye over to look at in a cursory manner (*I cast an eye over the figures*).

to cast a shadow over to have a dispiriting effect on (*The bad news cast a shadow over the proceedings*).

to cast ashore (of the sea, waves etc.) to throw or deposit on the shore.

to cast aside 1 to reject. **2** to give up.

to cast aspersions on to make disparaging or slanderous remarks about.

to cast away 1 to reject. **2** to shipwreck.

to cast back to turn (one's mind) back to the past.

to cast down 1 to throw down. **2** to deject.

to cast forth 1 to throw away. **2** to emit.

to cast light on to elucidate, to explain.

to cast loose to set loose, to detach.

to cast lots to determine by the throw of a dice or other contrivance.

to cast off 1 to discard. **2** to untie (a rope), to unmoor (a boat). **3** in knitting, to finish by looping together the last row of stitches. **4** (*Print.*) to estimate the amount of space a piece of copy will occupy.

to cast on in knitting, to make the first row of loops or stitches.

to cast one's bread upon the waters to be generous without expecting any reward. [From the Bible: "Cast thy bread upon the waters: for thou shalt find it after many days" (Eccles. xi.1).]

to cast oneself on to take refuge with.

to cast out to expel.

to cast pearls before swine to offer something valuable or beautiful to someone who does not appreciate it. [From the Bible: "neither cast ye your pearls before swine, lest they trample them under their feet" (Matt. vii.6).]

to cast something in someone's teeth to upbraid someone with something.

to cast the first stone to be the first to accuse or criticize, though not oneself blameless. [From a judgement made by Jesus in the Bible: "He that is without sin among you, let him first cast a stone at her" (John viii.7), referring to a woman who was to be stoned for adultery.]

to cast up 1 to reckon, to add. **2** to vomit. **3** to cast ashore.

caste

to lose caste LOSE.

castle

an Englishman's home is his castle ENGLISHMAN.

castles in the air/ in Spain visionary or unrealizable projects, daydreams.

cat

a cat may look at a king all people are equal, regardless of class, and even the lowliest have their rights.

care killed the cat CARE.

cat's paw 1 a light wind which just ripples the surface of the water. **2** (*Naut.*) a turn in the bight of a rope to hook a tackle on. **3** a dupe used as a tool. [From a fable by La Fontaine (1621–95) in which a monkey used a cat's paw to pick roasted chestnuts from the fire.]

curiosity killed the cat CURIOSITY.

fat cat FAT.

like a cat on a hot tin roof/ on hot bricks in a state of agitation.

like a scalded cat SCALD.

like something the cat brought/ dragged in (*coll.*) very bedraggled or dishevelled.

no room to swing a cat ROOM.

not to have a cat in hell's chance (*sl.*) to have no chance at all.

the cat has (got) someone's tongue (*coll.*) someone is silent (*Has the cat got your tongue?*).

the cat's whiskers/ pyjamas (*sl.*) the best or greatest person or thing (*He thinks he's the cat's whiskers*).

to bell the cat BELL.

to fight like cat and dog FIGHT.

to fight like Kilkenny cats FIGHT.

to grin like a Cheshire cat GRIN.

to let the cat out of the bag to give away a secret, esp. unintentionally. [Possibly referring to a trick in which gullible customers were sold a cat in a bag, having been told that the bag contained a piglet.]

to play cat and mouse with to tease or toy with an opponent or victim, esp. before defeating or destroying them.

to put/ set the cat among the pigeons to stir up trouble.

to rain cats and dogs RAIN.

to see which way the cat jumps 1 to wait until others have made up their mind. **2** to remain uncommitted.

to whip the cat WHIP.

when the cat's away the mice will play said when people take advantage of the absence of someone in authority.

catch

to catch a cold 1 to contract a cold. **2** (*coll.*) to run into difficulties.

to catch a crab in rowing, to sink an oar too deep and be pushed backwards by the resistance of the water, or to miss a stroke and fall backwards.

to catch at to attempt to seize.

to catch a Tartar to find an opponent stronger than was expected.

to catch fire 1 to ignite. **2** to become excited.

to catch it (*sl.*) to get a scolding (*You'll catch it if your mother finds out*).

to catch on 1 (*coll.*) to become popular (*It'll never catch on*). **2** to understand.

to catch one's breath 1 to stop breathing momentarily. **2** to regain even breathing after exertion or a shock.

to catch one's death of cold to catch a very bad cold or chill.

to catch out 1 to discover (someone) in error or wrongdoing. **2** in cricket, to dismiss (a batsman) by catching the ball.

to catch sight of to begin to see, to glimpse or notice.

to catch someone napping 1 to find someone asleep. **2** to take someone unawares, to catch someone unprepared or at a disadvantage.

to catch someone on the hop to catch someone by surprise.

to catch someone on the wrong foot to take someone unprepared or at a disadvantage.

to catch someone red-handed to catch someone in the very act of committing a crime or doing something wrong. [From the blood-covered hands of a murderer.]

to catch someone's eye to attract someone's attention.

to catch someone with their trousers/ pants down (*coll.*) to catch someone in an embarrassing or ill-prepared position.

to catch the sun 1 to be in a sunny place. **2** to become sunburnt.

to catch up 1 to reach (a person, vehicle etc. that is ahead). **2** to make up arrears. **3** (*often pass.*) to involve (*He was caught up in a plot to assassinate the president*). **4** to raise and hold.

you wouldn't catch me (*coll.*) I would never do the thing mentioned (*You wouldn't catch me wearing a hat like that!*).

cause

in the cause of in order to defend or support.

lost cause LOST.

to make common cause COMMON.

to show cause (*Law*) to allege with justification.

caution

to throw caution to the winds to behave in an utterly reckless manner.

cave

to cave in 1 to fall in, to collapse. **2** to give in, to yield.

caviar

caviar to the general something too refined to be generally appreciated. [From Shakespeare's *Hamlet*: "The play, I remember, pleased not the million; 'twas caviar to the general." In this context the word 'general' refers to the general public.]

cease

without cease without pausing or stopping.

ceiling

glass ceiling GLASS.

to hit the ceiling HIT.

cent

not to have a red cent RED CENT.

centre

right, left and centre RIGHT.

centuplicate

in centuplicate a hundredfold.

Cerberus

sop to Cerberus SOP.

ceremony

to stand on ceremony to be rigidly punctilious, to insist on observing formalities (*There's no need to stand on ceremony – call me Bill*).

without ceremony informally.

certain

for certain definitely.

of a certain age (*euphem.*) middle-aged, no longer young.

to make certain to ensure, to secure.

certainty

for a certainty without doubt.

cess

bad cess to you (*Ir., sl.*) may ill luck befall you.

chaff

to separate the wheat from the chaff SEPARATE[1].

chair

to take a chair to sit down.

to take the chair to preside at a meeting.

chalk

by a long chalk LONG.

(different as) chalk and cheese completely or fundamentally different.

to chalk out to sketch out, to plan.

to chalk up 1 to record or register (*We had chalked up a high score*). **2** to charge to an account, to give or take credit for (*Chalk it up!*).

to walk one's chalks WALK.

to walk the chalk WALK.

champ

to champ at the bit to be impatient. [Referring to the part of the horse's bridle that passes through its mouth.]

chance

by any chance 1 as it happens. **2** perhaps.

by chance accidentally, undesignedly.

chance in a million a very remote possibility.

even chance EVEN[1].

fat chance FAT.

fighting chance FIGHTING.

ghost of a chance GHOST.

half a chance HALF.

†how chance ...? how was it that ...?

main chance MAIN.

not a dog's chance DOG.

not to have a cat in hell's chance CAT.

not to have a snowball's chance in hell SNOWBALL.

on the chance 1 on the possibility. **2** in case.

on the off chance OFF CHANCE.

sporting chance SPORTING.

to chance it to take the risk.

to chance one's arm to make a speculative attempt, to try something not very likely to succeed.

to chance on/ upon to come upon accidentally.

to fancy one's chances FANCY.

to stand a chance to have a prospect of success (*She stands a good chance of promotion*).

to take a chance to take a risk, to risk failure.

to take chances to behave in a risky manner.

to take one's chances to trust to luck.

chancery

in chancery 1 in a hopeless predicament. **2** in boxing, having one's head under an opponent's arm. **3** (*Law*) in litigation.

change

change of air 1 a different climate. **2** variety in experience, activity etc. (*We moved to France as we fancied a change of air*).

change of heart a change of attitude, opinion etc., which often results in the reversal of a decision (*I had a change of heart and let them stay*).

to change colour 1 to turn pale. **2** to blush.

to change countenance to change the expression on one's face because of emotion.

to change down in driving etc., to engage a lower gear.

to change gear 1 to engage a different gear in a motor vehicle. **2** to change pace.

to change hands to pass from one person's ownership to another's (*The house has changed hands four times since then*).

to change one's mind to form a new plan or opinion.

to change one's spots/ skin to undergo an unlikely change of character. [From the Bible: "Can the Ethiopian change his skin, or the leopard his spots?" (Jer. xiii.23).]

to change one's tune to alter one's attitude or tone.

to change over to change from one state, position, situation, system etc. to another (*change over to the metric system*).

to change sides to alter one's allegiance, to change one's party.

to change step in marching, to adjust one's step so as to make one's other leg mark the main beat.

to change the subject 1 to abandon the topic under discussion and introduce another. **2** the formula one uses when doing this.

to change up in driving etc., to engage a higher gear.

to get no change out of 1 (*coll.*) to fail to gain information from (*You'll get no change out of him*). **2** (*coll.*) not to be able to take any advantage of.

to ring the changes RING[2].

to take one's change 1 to exact revenge. **2** to get even with someone.

chapter

chapter and verse a full and precise reference in order to verify a fact or quotation (*I can't give you chapter and verse*). [From the chapters and verses into which the books of the Bible are divided.]

chapter of accidents 1 a series of accidents. **2** an unfortunate coincidence.

to the end of the chapter END.

character

in character typical of a person, consistent with a person's character.

out of character not in character (*Her behaviour was quite out of character*).

charge

free of charge FREE.

in charge 1 on duty. **2** in command.

in charge of responsible for.

on a charge having been charged with a crime.

to give in charge 1 to commit to the care of another. **2** to hand over to the custody of a police officer.

to lay a charge to make an accusation.

to lay something to the charge of someone to accuse someone of something.

to return to the charge RETURN.

to reverse the charges REVERSE.

to take charge to assume control, command, responsibility etc. (*I took charge of the situation*).

to take in charge to arrest, to take into custody.

charity

charity begins at home one should take care of the people closest to one before offering help or financial support to others (*The government is spending too much on foreign aid: charity begins at home*).

cold as charity COLD.

charm

like a charm perfectly (*It worked like a charm*).

Charybdis

between Scylla and Charybdis SCYLLA.

chase

go and chase yourself (*coll.*) go away!

to chase rainbows to pursue an illusory aim.

to chase the dragon (*sl.*) to smoke heroin.

to chase up (*coll.*) to pursue or

investigate in order to obtain
information etc.

to give chase to to pursue.

wild-goose chase WILD.

chat

to chat up (*sl.*) to chat to in order to
establish a (sexual) relationship.

chatter

the chattering classes (*derog. or facet.*)
intellectuals etc. considered as a social
group enjoying political, social or
cultural discussion.

chaw

to chaw up (*N Am., sl.*) to defeat or
destroy completely.

cheap

cheap as dirt very cheap.

on the cheap 1 cheaply (*how to
redecorate your house on the cheap*).
2 in a miserly way.

to feel cheap FEEL.

to hold cheap not to value highly (*They
held our friendship cheap*).

to make oneself cheap to behave with
undignified familiarity.

cheat

to cheat on (*coll.*) to be unfaithful to
(one's wife, husband, lover etc.).

check

in check 1 under control or restraint (*Try
to keep your temper in check*). **2** (of a
king in chess) exposed to direct attack.

to check in to register on arrival at a
hotel, at work etc.

to check off to mark or tick (an item on a
list etc.).

to check on 1 to keep watch on. **2** to
check up on.

to check out 1 to complete the formalities
for leaving a hotel, place of work etc.
(*We have to check out of the hotel
before 10 o'clock*). **2 a** to test for

accuracy, quality etc.; to prove to be
accurate or of requisite quality etc.
(*check out a witness's statement*).
b (*coll.*) to investigate, look at or visit
(*You must check out the museums
while you're in London*). **3** (*N Am., sl.*)
to die.

to check over to examine for faults, errors
etc.

to check through to examine carefully (a
series of items) (*to check through the
records*).

to check up 1 to investigate. **2** to make
sure.

to check up on to investigate.

to hand/ pass in one's checks (*N Am.*) to
die. [Checks are counters used as
tokens in gambling games.]

to take a rain check RAIN CHECK.

cheek

cheek by jowl 1 side by side. **2** in the
closest proximity.

tongue-in-cheek TONGUE.

to turn the other cheek OTHER.

with one's tongue in one's cheek TONGUE.

cheer

to cheer up 1 to make more cheerful. **2** to
become more cheerful.

cheese

cheesed off (*coll.*) bored, annoyed.

(different as) chalk and cheese CHALK.

hard cheese HARD.

say cheese! used by photographers to
encourage people to smile.

to cheese it 1 (*N Am., sl.*) to run away.
2 (*dated, sl.*) to desist.

cheque

blank cheque BLANK.

cherry

two bites at the cherry TWO.

Cheshire

to grin like a Cheshire cat GRIN.

chest

to get off one's chest 1 (*coll.*) to unburden oneself of (a secret etc.) (*It might help to get the whole thing off your chest*). **2** (*coll.*) to admit, to declare.

to play one's cards close to one's chest CARD.

to put hairs on someone's chest HAIR.

chestnut

old chestnut OLD.

to pull the chestnuts out of the fire (*dated*) to help someone out of a difficult situation, esp. by taking risks oneself. [From a fable by La Fontaine (1621–95), in which a monkey used a cat's paw to pick roasted chestnuts from the fire.]

chew

to chew on 1 to grind continuously with the teeth. **2** to ruminate on.

to chew out (*N Am., coll.*) to reprimand.

to chew over 1 to discuss. **2** to think about (*I've been chewing over your suggestion*).

to chew the cud 1 to ruminate. **2** to reflect.

to chew the fat/ rag 1 (*sl.*) to chat. **2** (*sl.*) to grumble, to complain.

to chew up 1 to damage or destroy by chewing or by a similar grinding action. **2** (*usu. pass., coll.*) to make nervous or worried.

chicken

chicken-and-egg of or denoting a situation in which it is impossible to distinguish between cause and effect. [From the riddle 'Which came first, the chicken or the egg?']

chicken feed 1 food for poultry. **2** (*coll.*) an insignificant sum of money. **3** (*coll.*) a trifling amount or matter.

no chicken no longer young; older than he or she appears.

spring chicken SPRING.

to chicken out (*coll.*) to lose one's nerve.

to count one's chickens (before they are hatched) COUNT.

chief

too many chiefs and not enough Indians too many people in charge and not enough people to do the work.

child

child's play easy work.

from a child since childhood.

quick with child QUICK.

spare the rod and spoil the child SPARE.

the child is father of the man a child's character shows what kind of an adult they will become. [From the poem 'My Heart Leaps Up' (1802) by William Wordsworth.]

to get with child (*dated*) to make pregnant.

with child (*dated*) pregnant.

childhood

second childhood SECOND.

chill

to chill out (*esp. N Am., coll.*) to relax.

to chill someone's blood to terrify someone.

to take the chill off to warm slightly.

chime

to chime in 1 to join in. **2** to express agreement.

chimney

to smoke like a chimney SMOKE.

chin

chin up! (*coll.*) cheer up!

to keep one's chin up (*coll.*) to remain cheerful in adversity.

to stick one's chin out STICK².

to take it on the chin to face up to (misfortune, defeat etc.) courageously.

China

for all the tea in China TEA.

china
bull in a china shop BULL.

chink
a chink in someone's armour a weak or
vulnerable point in someone's
character etc.

chip
chip off the old block a person resembling
one of their parents, esp. in character
or in behaviour.
chip on one's shoulder a grievance, a
disposition to feel badly treated.
[Of N Am. origin, referring to a way of
giving vent to one's feelings by putting
a chip of wood on one's shoulder and
fighting anyone who dared to knock it
off.]
to cash in one's chips CASH.
to chip at (*Austral.*) to jeer at, to nag.
to chip in 1 (*coll.*) to cut into a
conversation. 2 (*coll.*) to contribute
(money).
to have had one's chips 1 (*coll.*) to be
defeated. 2 (*coll.*) to be unable to avoid
death.
to spit chips SPIT.
when the chips are down (*coll.*) at a
moment of crisis; when it comes to the
point. [Alluding to the moment in a
gambling game when the bets have
been placed but the outcome is still
unknown.]

chirpy
chirpy as a cricket very lively and
cheerful.

choice
for/ from choice by preference.
Hobson's choice HOBSON.
spoilt for choice SPOIL.
you pays your money and you takes your
choice MONEY.

choke
to choke back to suppress (*He choked
back his anger*).

to choke down 1 to swallow with
difficulty. 2 to choke back.
to choke off to discourage, to suppress.
to choke up to fill up until blocked.

choose
†cannot choose but have no alternative
but.
there's nothing/ little to choose between
them they are almost equal, esp.
equally good or bad.
to choose sides (of team leaders) to select
team members from the group
available.

chooser
beggars can't be choosers BEGGAR.

chop¹
to chop in to intervene suddenly in a
conversation.
to chop up to cut into small pieces, to
mince.
to get the chop 1 (*sl.*) to be dismissed
(from a job etc.) (*The managing
director got the chop*). 2 (*sl.*) to be
killed. 3 (*sl.*) (of a project etc.) to be
cancelled.

chop²
to chop and change 1 to vary
continuously, to fluctuate. 2 to
vacillate.
to chop logic to wrangle pedantically.

chop³
not much chop (*Austral., New Zeal.*) not
very good.

chord
to strike a chord STRIKE.
to touch the right chord TOUCH.

chorus
in chorus in unison, together.

Christ
for Christ's sake used as a solemn

adjuration or an expression of
exasperation etc.

chuck

to chuck away 1 (*coll.*) to discard.
2 (*coll.*) to waste.
to chuck in (*coll.*) to abandon, to give up
(*She chucked in her job*).
to chuck it (*sl.*) to stop, to desist.
to chuck out 1 (*coll.*) to eject forcibly
from a meeting, building etc. (*We got
chucked out of the disco*). **2** (*coll.*) to
throw away.
to chuck up 1 (*coll.*) to chuck in. **2** (*esp.
N Am., sl.*) to vomit.
to get the chuck (*sl.*) to be dismissed
(from a job etc.).

chum

to chum up to become friendly (with).

chump

off one's chump (*sl.*) crazy.

church

poor as a church mouse POOR.
to go into the Church 1 to take holy
orders. **2** to become a minister of
religion.

churn

to churn out to produce rapidly and
prolifically, usu. without concern for
quality (*churning out romantic
novels*).

cinder

to burn to a cinder BURN.

circle

to circle back to go back to the starting
point following a circular or indirect
route.
to circle in to confine.
to come full circle FULL.
to go round in circles to make no progress
in spite of one's efforts.
to run round in circles (*coll.*) to be very
active without achieving much.

to square the circle SQUARE.
vicious circle VICIOUS.

circulation

in circulation 1 (of money) serving as
currency. **2** in general use.
3 participating in social or business
activities.
out of circulation not in circulation.

circumstance

force of circumstances FORCE.
in reduced circumstances REDUCE.
in/ under no circumstances not at all,
never, in no case.
in/ under the circumstances in the
particular situation for which
allowance should be made (*He did
very well under the circumstances*).

circus

bread and circuses BREAD.
three-ring circus THREE.

civil

to keep a civil tongue in one's head to
remain polite.

civvy

in civvy street (*sl.*) in civilian life as
opposed to the armed forces.

claim

to jump a claim JUMP.
to lay claim to to assert that one owns or
has a right to.
to stake one's claim STAKE[1].

clam

to clam up to become silent. [Alluding to
the tightly closed shell of a clam.]

clamp

to clamp down (on) to impose (heavier)
restrictions (on); to attempt to suppress
(*They announced their intention to
clamp down on pornography*).

clanger
to **drop a clanger** DROP.

clap
clap on the back congratulations (*She deserves a clap on the back*).
to **clap on** to add hastily.
to **clap up 1** to make hastily. **2** †to conclude (a bargain etc.) hastily. **3** †to imprison hastily.

clapper
like the clappers (*sl.*) extremely fast (*going like the clappers*). [Perhaps alluding to the clapper in a rattle or bell, which moves back and forth very quickly.]

claret
to **tap the claret** TAP.

clasp
to **clasp hands** to hold or shake hands firmly or fervently.
to **clasp one's hands** to put one's hands together with the fingers interlaced.

class
in a class of one's/ its own of matchless excellence.
the chattering classes CHATTER.

claw
to **claw back 1** to get back by clawing or with difficulty. **2** to take back (part of a benefit or allowance etc.) by extra taxation etc.
to **claw up** (*dial., sl.*) to beat soundly.
to **get one's claws into 1** to display extreme jealousy or disapproval of. **2** to entrap (a potential marriage partner).

clay
feet of clay FOOT.

clean
clean as a whistle very clean.

clean bill of health 1 a document certifying the health of a ship's company. **2** a statement that a person is in good health or a thing in good condition.
clean sheet/ slate a new start, all debts etc. written off.
to **clean down** to brush or wipe down.
to **clean one's plate** to eat all the food on one's plate.
to **clean out 1** to clean thoroughly. **2** to strip. **3** (*sl.*) to deprive of all money.
to **clean up 1** to clear away a mess. **2** to put tidy. **3** to make oneself clean. **4** to collect all the money, profits etc. (*hoping to clean up if their rival goes bankrupt*).
to **come clean** (*coll.*) to confess.
to **make a clean breast of** to confess all that one knows about.
to **make a clean sweep of 1** to get rid of entirely. **2** to win all the prizes in (a competition etc.).
to **show a clean pair of heels** to run away.
with clean hands without blame or guilt, without being implicated.

cleaner
to **take someone to the cleaners 1** (*sl.*) to deprive someone of all their money, goods etc. **2** (*sl.*) to criticize someone severely.

clear
clear as a bell perfectly clear, esp. in sound quality.
clear as crystal perfectly clear or plain.
clear as mud (*coll., iron.*) not clear at all.
in clear not in code.
in the clear free from suspicion.
out of a clear sky as a complete surprise.
to **clear away 1** to remove. **2** to remove plates etc. after a meal. **3** to disappear. **4** to melt away.
to **clear off 1** to remove. **2** (*coll.*) to depart (*Clear off and don't come back!*).
to **clear one's throat** to make one's voice clear with a slight cough.

to **clear out 1** to empty. **2** to eject. **3** (*coll.*) to depart.

to **clear someone's name** to prove someone's innocence and restore their reputation.

to **clear the air 1** to make the air cooler, fresher etc. **2** to remove misunderstandings or suspicion.

to **clear the decks** to prepare for action.

to **clear the way 1** to remove obstacles (*to clear the way for negotiations*). **2** to stand aside, to get out of the way.

to **clear up 1** to become bright and clear. **2** to elucidate. **3** to tidy up. **4** to disappear.

to **get clear 1** to disengage oneself. **2** to be released.

cleft stick

in a cleft stick in a difficult situation, esp. one where going forward or back is impossible.

clever

clever clogs/ Dick (*coll.*) a person who shows off their own cleverness.

click

to **click on** to select (an item on a computer screen) by pressing one of the buttons of a computer mouse.

climb

to **climb down 1** to descend, esp. using hands and feet. **2** to abandon one's claims, to withdraw from a position, opinion etc.

to **climb into 1** to enter, esp. with effort or by climbing (*They climbed into the truck*). **2** to put on (clothes).

cling

clinging vine a person who is excessively dependent on, or monopolizes the attention of, another.

to **cling together 1** to form one mass. **2** to resist separation.

clip

to **clip the wings of** to put a check on the ambitions of.

cloak

cloak-and-dagger involving mystery and intrigue (*cloak-and-dagger tales*). [Originally from a Spanish phrase meaning 'cloak and sword', applied to a type of 17th-century play in which the main characters wore cloaks and carried swords. It was subsequently used of French and English melodramas involving intrigue and adventure.]

under the cloak of hidden by, using as a disguise or pretext (*under the cloak of darkness*).

clock

against the clock 1 (of a task etc.) to be finished by a certain time. **2** (of a race etc.) timed by a stopwatch or similar device.

round the clock continuously, for 24 hours a day (*work round the clock*).

to **beat the clock** to complete a task within the allotted time.

to **clock in/ on** to register on a specially constructed clock the time of arrival at work.

to **clock out/ off** to register on a specially constructed clock the time of departure from work.

to **clock up** to register (a specified time, speed etc.).

to **hold the clock on** to be responsible for timing (a race etc.).

to **put/ turn the clock back** to go back to an earlier state.

to **watch the clock** WATCH.

clockwork

like clockwork with unfailing regularity; mechanically, automatically; very smoothly (*It all went like clockwork*).

regular as clockwork REGULAR.

close¹

close by within a short distance; very near.

close call (*esp. N Am.*) a close shave.

close on nearly (*We lived there close on twenty years*).

close shave a situation in which danger or trouble is only just avoided.

close to near.

close to home uncomfortably close to the truth.

to go close (of a racehorse) to (almost) win.

too close for comfort uncomfortably close.

close²

to close down 1 (of a factory, shop etc.) to cease work or business, esp. permanently. **2** (of a radio or television station) to go off the air.

to close in 1 to shut in, to enclose. **2** to come nearer. **3** to get shorter (*The days are closing in*).

to close on 1 to shut over. **2** to grasp. **3** to catch up with (*They're closing on us*).

to close one's eyes (*euphem.*) to die.

to close one's mind to refuse to consider something, often unreasonably.

to close out to terminate (a business, an account etc.).

to close ranks to maintain solidarity.

to close the door to to exclude the possibility of.

to close up 1 to block up, to fill in. **2** to come together.

to close with 1 to agree or consent to. **2** to unite with. **3** to grapple with (*to close with the enemy*).

closed

behind closed doors in private.

closed book 1 a subject or person one knows nothing about. **2** a matter that has been concluded.

close quarters

at close quarters 1 in direct contact, esp. with an enemy. **2** very near.

to come to close quarters to come into direct contact, esp. with an enemy.

closet

to be closeted with to hold a confidential conversation with.

to come out of the closet to declare or make public one's inclinations, intentions etc., esp. to declare one's homosexuality.

cloth

to cut one's coat according to one's cloth COAT.

clothing

wolf in sheep's clothing WOLF.

cloud

cloud-cuckoo-land 1 a utopia. **2** a fantastic and impractical scheme for social, political or economic reform. [From the name of an imaginary city built in the air by the birds in Aristophanes' play *The Birds* (414 BC).]

every cloud has a silver lining something good will always come of misfortune (*Unemployment gave me more time to spend with my family: every cloud has a silver lining*).

in the clouds 1 mystical, unreal. **2** absent-minded.

on cloud nine (*coll.*) very happy, elated. [Originally 'on cloud seven', seven being a mystic or sacred number; nine is also considered lucky, being a multiple of three (representing the Trinity and other examples of triadic unity).]

under a cloud in temporary disgrace or misfortune; under suspicion (*Your predecessor left under a cloud*).

with one's head in the clouds HEAD¹.

clout

ne'er cast a clout till May is out CAST.

clover

(like pigs) **in clover 1** in enjoyable circumstances. **2** in luxury. [Clover is a rich and nutritious food for farm animals.]

club

in the (pudding) club (*sl.*) pregnant.
join the club! JOIN.
to club together to join together for a common object (*We clubbed together to buy him a present*).

clue

not to have a clue 1 (*coll.*) to have no idea whatever. **2** (*coll.*) to be utterly incompetent.
to clue up (*sl.*) to inform (*clued up on the latest computer trends*).

clutch

to clutch at to try to seize or grasp.

clutter

to clutter up to fill untidily.

coach

to drive a coach and horses through DRIVE.

coal

to blow a coal BLOW[1].
to carry coals to put up with insults.
to carry coals to Newcastle to bring things to a place where they abound; to do anything superfluous or unnecessary. [Referring to Newcastle-upon-Tyne as a former centre of the British coal-mining industry.]
to haul over the coals HAUL.
to heap coals of fire on someone's head HEAP.

coast

the coast is clear 1 the road is free. **2** the danger is over. [The phrase originally referred to smuggling.]

coat

to cut one's coat according to one's cloth to adapt to one's personal (esp. financial) circumstances.
to turn one's coat to change sides, to be a turncoat. [Soldiers of fortune would line their uniform with the colours of the opposing side; if they felt they were losing the battle they could turn their coat inside out and join the enemy.]

coat-tail

on someone's coat-tails gaining an undeserved benefit from the success of another.

cobweb

to blow away the cobwebs BLOW[1].

cock[1]

cock and bull story a silly, exaggerated story. [Perhaps from the many fables that feature birds and animals, or from tales told at coaching inns called the Cock and the Bull.]
cock-of-the-walk 1 a masterful person. **2** a leader, a chief.
to live like fighting cocks LIVE[1].

cock[2]

to cock a snook 1 to make a gesture of derision (at) with the thumb to the nose and the fingers spread. **2** to express defiance or laugh (at someone's authority etc.).
to cock up (*sl.*) to ruin by incompetence; to bungle.
to go off at half-cock/ half-cocked HALF-COCK.

cocked hat

to knock into a cocked hat KNOCK.

Cocker

†**according to Cocker** properly, correctly. [Referring to the English mathematician Edward Cocker (1631–75).]

cockle
to warm the cockles of the heart WARM.

coffin
nail in the coffin of NAIL.

cog
cog in the machine a person playing a
small and unimportant part in any
enterprise.

cognizance
to have cognizance of to know.
to take cognizance of to take into
consideration.

coil[1]
to coil up 1 to twist into rings or a spiral
shape. 2 to be twisted into such a
shape.

coil[2]
this mortal coil MORTAL.

coin
the other side of the coin OTHER.
to coin a phrase (*iron.*) said before or
after using a cliché.
to coin it (in) (*sl.*) to make money rapidly.
to coin money (*sl.*) to make money
rapidly.
to pay someone back in their own coin to
give someone the same treatment that
they have given others, to give tit for
tat.

cold
cold as charity cold-hearted,
unsympathetic.
cold comfort poor consolation,
depressing reassurance.
cold enough to freeze the balls off a brass
monkey (*coll.*) (of the weather)
extremely cold. [A monkey was a
metal rack on which cannonballs were
stacked on warships. If the rack was
made of brass, in very cold weather it
would contract more rapidly than the

iron cannonballs, causing the pile to
collapse.]
cold feet (*coll.*) loss of courage or
confidence (*to get cold feet*).
cold steel cutting weapons, such as sword
and bayonet, as opposed to firearms.
cold storage 1 the preservation of
perishable foodstuffs by refrigeration.
2 abeyance (*to put a project into cold
storage*).
cold sweat sweating accompanied by
chill, caused esp. by fear (*wake up in a
cold sweat*).
in cold blood 1 without feeling, callously
or ruthlessly (*murdered in cold blood*).
2 without passion or excitement,
deliberately.
in the cold light of day after calm and
reasoned consideration.
out in the cold ignored or neglected (*I
was left out in the cold*).
to catch a cold CATCH.
to catch one's death of cold CATCH.
to give someone the cold shoulder (*coll.*)
to shun or snub someone. [Possibly
from the cold leftovers served to
unwelcome guests.]
to leave cold (*coll.*) to fail to excite or
interest (*My wife is fond of jazz, but it
leaves me cold*).
to pour/ throw cold water on to be
discouraging about or critical of (*pour
cold water on an idea*).

collar
hot under the collar HOT.
to feel someone's collar FEEL.
to slip the collar SLIP[1].

collect
to collect on (*coll.*) to make money out of.
to collect oneself to recover one's self-
possession.

colour
horse of another/ a different colour
HORSE.
to change colour CHANGE.

to join the colours JOIN.

to nail one's colours to the mast NAIL.

to sail under false colours SAIL.

to see the colour of someone's money (*coll.*) to receive payment, or proof that money will be paid, before supplying goods or services (*Make sure you see the colour of their money before you start work*).

to show one's true colours TRUE.

under false colours FALSE COLOURS.

with flying colours FLYING.

column

to dodge the column DODGE.

comb

to comb out 1 to tidy or arrange with a comb. 2 to remove with a comb. 3 to find and remove. 4 to search thoroughly.

to go over with a fine-tooth comb FINE-TOOTH COMB.

come

as... as they come being the most typical or supreme example (*She's as lazy as they come*).

as it comes without additions or alterations.

come again? say that again.

come along make haste.

come off it (*coll.*) stop behaving or talking so stupidly or pretentiously.

come on 1 hurry up. 2 proceed. 3 used to express encouragement.

come to that (*coll.*) in fact.

come what may whatever happens.

how come? (*coll.*) how did that happen?

if it comes to that in that case.

to come in the future (*in days to come*).

to come about 1 to result, to come to pass. 2 (*Naut.*) to change direction, esp. by tacking.

to come across 1 to meet with accidentally. 2 (*coll.*) to be perceived (as) (*He came across as a nice enough chap*).

to come across with (*sl.*) to provide or hand over.

to come along to make progress.

to come and go 1 to appear and disappear. 2 to pass to and fro. 3 to pay a short call.

to come apart to separate or break into parts or pieces (*It came apart in my hands*).

to come around (*N Am.*) to come round.

to come at 1 to reach, to attain, to gain access to. 2 to attack.

to come away 1 to move away, to leave. 2 to become parted or separated.

to come back 1 to return. 2 to recur to memory. 3 to retort. 4 to become popular or fashionable again.

to come before to be dealt with by (*to come before an industrial tribunal*).

to come between 1 to damage a relationship between (two people) (*Don't let this come between us*). 2 to separate.

to come by 1 to pass near. 2 to call, to visit. 3 to obtain, to gain.

to come down 1 to descend, to fall. 2 to be humbled. 3 to decide. 4 to be handed down.

to come down on 1 to reprimand. 2 to chastise. 3 to pay out.

to come down to 1 to amount to. 2 to have as result.

to come down with 1 to contract (an ailment). 2 to hand over (money).

to come for 1 to come to fetch or receive (*I've come for my money*). 2 to attack.

to come forward 1 to make oneself known, to identify oneself (*No witnesses to the crime have come forward*). 2 to offer oneself. 3 to move forwards.

to come from behind to make a late spurt to win after lagging behind.

to come home 1 to return home. 2 to affect closely. 3 to be fully comprehended.

to come in 1 to enter. 2 to advance or approach, to arrive at a destination.

3 to become fashionable. **4** to be received. **5** to prove to be (*to come in useful*). **6** to play a role, to have a function (*This is where the torch comes in*). **7** to accrue. **8** to assume power. **9** (*coll.*) to secure an advantage or chance of benefit.

to come in for 1 to arrive in time for. **2** to obtain, to receive (*The design came in for a lot of criticism*).

to come into 1 to join with. **2** to comply with. **3** to acquire, to inherit.

to come it over someone (*coll.*) to act in a superior manner towards someone.

to come near 1 to approach. **2** nearly to succeed.

to come of 1 to be descended from. **2** to proceed or result from (*Nothing came of the scheme*).

to come off 1 to part from. **2** to be detachable. **3** to fall off. **4** to take place. **5** (*coll.*) to be accomplished. **6** to fare (*to come off best*). **7** (*sl.*) to experience orgasm. **8** to appear. **9** to escape.

to come on 1 to advance. **2** to prosper (*coming on well*). **3** to appear. **4** to begin to perform, speak, play, be broadcast etc. **5** to happen, to arise. **6** to begin (*It came on to rain*). **7** to come upon.

to come out 1 to emerge. **2** to be revealed, to become public. **3** to be introduced into society. **4** to be published. **5** to declare something openly, esp. one's homosexuality. **6** to go on strike. **7** to turn out. **8** to be covered (in) (*She came out in a rash*). **9** (*N Am.*) to make profession of religion. **10** to be removed or solved.

to come out of to issue forth, to proceed from.

to come out with to utter, to disclose (*He comes out with the craziest things!*).

to come over 1 to cross over. **2** to change sides. **3** to affect. **4** (*coll.*) to become (*I came over dizzy*). **5** to make a casual visit. **6** to be perceived (as).

to come round 1 to change one's opinion.

2 to recover consciousness. **3** to make a casual visit. **4** to recur. **5** to cheat.

to come through 1 to survive. **2** to be successful. **3** to be received.

to come to 1 to amount to. **2** to recover consciousness (*I came to in the back of a van*). **3** (*Naut.*) to cease moving. **4** to reach. **5** to consent. **6** (*Naut.*) to sail close to the wind.

to come to oneself to recover consciousness.

to come to pass to happen.

to come under 1 to be classed as. **2** to be subject to (authority, influence etc.).

to come up 1 to ascend. **2** to arise. **3** to be introduced as a topic. **4** to happen. **5** to become public or fashionable. **6** (*Naut.*) (of a rope) to slacken.

to come up against to encounter or confront (a difficulty etc.).

to come upon 1 to attack. **2** to befall. **3** to find, to discover. **4** to meet with unexpectedly.

to come up to 1 to approach. **2** to be equal to. **3** to amount to.

to come up with 1 to produce (*Is that the best you can come up with?*). **2** to overtake.

where one came in back at the beginning.

comer

all comers anyone who accepts a challenge.

comfort

cold comfort COLD.
creature comforts CREATURE.
too close for comfort CLOSE[1].

comforter

Job's comforter JOB.

coming

not to know whether one is coming or going to be totally confused, esp. because very busy.

to have it coming (*coll.*) to deserve what (unpleasant thing) is about to happen (*She had it coming to her*).

command

at command 1 ready for orders. **2** at one's disposal.

at someone's command in accordance with someone's instructions.

in command of having control over.

under command of commanded by.

commend

†**commend me to 1** remember me to.

highly commended almost as good as the top prizewinner(s).

comment

no comment (*coll.*) I refuse to answer or comment.

commentary

running commentary RUNNING.

commission

in commission 1 (of a naval ship) prepared for active service. **2** entrusted with authority. **3** in operation, in working order. **4** entrusted to a commission instead of the constitutional officer.

on commission a percentage of the proceeds of goods sold being paid to the agent or retailer.

out of commission (of a ship, machine etc.) not in service or operation, not in working order.

commit

to commit oneself 1 to pledge or bind oneself. **2** to involve or compromise oneself (*reluctant to commit herself*).

to commit to memory to learn by heart.

to commit to paper to write down, to record.

common

above the common superior to most.

common as muck very vulgar or ill-bred.

common ground matter in a discussion accepted by both sides (*Is there any common ground between the parties?*).

common knowledge something widely known.

common or garden (*coll.*) ordinary (*It's just a common or garden cold, nothing serious*).

common touch an ability to interact with ordinary people (*a prince with the common touch*). [From Rudyard Kipling's poem 'If' (1910): "If you can talk with crowds and keep your virtue, / Or walk with Kings – nor lose the common touch".]

in common shared with another or others (*They have nothing in common*).

in common with the same way as, like.

out of the common extraordinary, unusual.

to make common cause to unite for a specific purpose.

commons

short commons SHORT.

company

in company with others, not alone.

in company with together with.

present company excepted PRESENT[1].

to be in good company to discover that the experience of others is similar to one's own (*Don't worry, you're in good company: none of us has ever ridden a horse before!*).

to keep company (with) 1 to associate (with). **2** to court.

to keep someone company to go or be with someone (*He stayed at home to keep me company*).

to part company PART.

two's company, three's a crowd TWO.

compare

beyond compare peerless, unequalled.

to compare notes to exchange information or opinions.

comparison

beyond comparison 1 totally different. **2** beyond compare.

in/ by comparison with compared with.
to bear/ stand comparison (with) to be as
  good (as) or better (than).

compass
to box the compass BOX[1].

complete
complete with having (an important or
  desirable accessory) (*The computer
  comes complete with a range of
  software*).

compliance
in compliance with in accordance with.

compliment
compliments of the season greetings
  appropriate to the season, esp.
  Christmas.
to fish for compliments FISH.
to pay a compliment to utter or perform a
  compliment.
to return the compliment RETURN.

comport
to comport with to suit, to agree with.

composed
composed of made up of, comprising.

compound
to compound the felony to make a bad
  situation worse. [Of legal origin,
  referring to the acceptance of money
  in exchange for overlooking a crime.]

con
pros and cons PRO.

conceit
out of conceit with no longer fond of or
  inclined to.

conception
to have no conception of to be unable to
  imagine (*They have no conception of
  the amount of work involved*).

concern
to have a concern in to have an interest
  in.
to have no concern with to have nothing
  to do with.
to whom it may concern to whomever has
  an interest in this matter (used to
  address the reader of a letter of
  reference etc.).

concerned
as far as I am concerned in my opinion,
  as regards my interests.

concert
in concert 1 acting together. 2 (of
  musicians) performing live on stage.

conclude
to conclude in short, finally.

conclusion
foregone conclusion FOREGONE.
in conclusion to conclude.
to come to a conclusion to make a
  decision or judgement after
  considering the evidence (*I came to
  the conclusion that he didn't really
  want the job*).
to jump to conclusions JUMP.
to try conclusions TRY.

concrete
concrete jungle a modern city or town
  considered as an unattractive or
  dangerous place.
in the concrete in the sphere of reality,
  not of abstractions or generalities.

condition
conditioned by 1 depending on. 2 limited
  by.
†in a delicate/ interesting condition
  pregnant.
in condition in good condition, in a good
  state of health or fitness.
in no condition to not fit to.
on condition that provided that, with the
  stipulation that.

out of condition in bad condition, in a
bad state of health or fitness.

conference
in conference at a meeting, engaged in
consultation or discussion.

confidence
in confidence as a secret.
in someone's confidence entrusted with
someone's secrets.
to take into one's confidence to reveal
one's secrets to, to talk confidentially
to (*He took me into his confidence*).

confine
to be confined 1 to be in labour or
childbirth. **2** to give birth to a child.

conflict
in conflict in opposition.

conjunction
in conjunction with together with.

conjure
to conjure up 1 to cause to appear by or
as if by magic. **2** to bring to the mind,
to evoke (*to conjure up an image*).

conk
to conk out 1 (*coll.*) to break down, to fail
(*The car conked out halfway up the
hill*). **2** (*coll.*) to die. **3** (*coll.*) to
collapse from exhaustion.

connection
in connection with connected with.
in this/ that connection in relation to
this/ that matter.

connive
to connive at to disregard or tacitly
encourage (a wrong or fault).

conquest
to make a conquest of to win the love or
admiration of.

conscience
for conscience's sake 1 for the sake of
one's conscientious scruples. **2** for the
sake of one's religion.
in all conscience (*coll.*) in all reason or
fairness (*I can't in all conscience
charge them the full amount*).
in conscience 1 in truth. **2** assuredly.
on my conscience most assuredly (a
strong asseveration).
on someone's conscience causing
someone to feel guilt or remorse (*He
had her death on his conscience*).
to have the conscience to to have the
assurance or impudence to.

consent
with one consent unanimously.

consequence
in consequence as a result.
of no consequence of no importance or
relevance.
to take the consequences to accept the
(usu. unpleasant) results.

consider
all things considered THING.

consideration
in consideration of 1 as a payment for, in
return for. **2** because of.
to take into consideration to bear in
mind, to take into account (*You must
take his lack of experience into
consideration*).
under consideration being considered;
under discussion.

conspicuous
conspicuous by one's absence noticeably
or significantly absent (*The father of
the bride was conspicuous by his
absence*).

conspiracy
conspiracy of silence an agreement not to
talk about a particular subject.

constable

to outrun the constable OUTRUN.

contact

to be in contact with **1** to be touching. **2** to be in communication with. **3** to be in close proximity or association with.

to come into contact with to meet, to come across.

to make contact **1** to complete an electric circuit. **2** to touch. **3** to establish communication.

contempt

beneath contempt utterly contemptible.

familiarity breeds contempt FAMILIARITY.

to hold in contempt to scorn, to despise.

content

to one's heart's content HEART.

contention

bone of contention BONE.

in contention competing.

context

in context with the connected words, circumstances etc.

out of context without the connected words, circumstances etc. (*Her remarks were quoted out of context*).

contract

to contract in to agree to participate in some scheme, esp. a pension scheme.

to contract out **1** to agree not to participate in a scheme (*contract out of the state pension scheme*). **2** to offer (work) to outside contractors (*All the school's catering is now contracted out*).

contradiction

contradiction in terms a statement that is obviously self-contradictory or inconsistent.

contrary

on the contrary **1** on the other hand. **2** quite the reverse.

to the contrary to the opposite effect.

contravention

in contravention of violating, infringing.

control

in control controlling.

out of control not or no longer controlled.

under control being controlled.

convenience

at one's convenience at a time that is suitable to one.

at one's earliest convenience EARLY.

to make a convenience of to take advantage of or impose on (a person).

converge

to converge on to approach and meet at (a place) from different directions (*The police and emergency services converged on the scene*).

conversation

conversation piece **1** a representation of figures in familiar groupings. **2** something that provides a topic of conversation.

conversation stopper (*coll.*) a remark to which there is no ready reply.

to make conversation to engage in polite talk.

convert

to convert to one's own use to appropriate or make use of (another's property) wrongfully.

conviction

the courage of one's convictions COURAGE.

to carry conviction to be convincing.

convoy

in convoy travelling together, with or without an escort.

cooee

within (a) cooee (*Austral., New Zeal., coll.*) within calling distance (of).

cook

to be cooking (*coll.*) to be happening (*What's cooking?*).

to cook someone's goose 1 (*coll.*) to ruin someone's chances. **2** (*coll.*) to spoil someone's plans.

to cook the books (*coll.*) to falsify the accounts.

to cook up (*coll.*) to concoct (an excuse, a story etc.).

too many cooks spoil the broth something will not be done properly if too many people are involved.

cookie

the way the cookie crumbles WAY.

cool

cool as a cucumber very unemotional, imperturbable (*Despite the emergency, she remained cool as a cucumber*).

cool, calm and collected in control of one's emotions.

to cool it (*sl.*) to calm down.

to cool one's heels (*coll.*) to be kept waiting.

to keep one's cool (*coll.*) to remain calm.

to lose one's cool LOSE.

to play it cool (*coll.*) not to show emotion, to keep calm.

coop

to fly the coop FLY².

coot

bald as a coot BALD.

cop

fair cop FAIR.

not much/ no cop (*sl.*) worthless.

to cop a plea (*N Am., sl.*) to arrange more lenient treatment by the court in return for an admission of guilt by the accused.

to cop it 1 (*sl.*) to be caught or punished (*You'll cop it!*). **2** (*sl.*) to be killed.

to cop out 1 (*sl.*) to refuse or avoid responsibility or a task. **2** (*sl.*) to give up, to stop. **3** (*sl.*) to break a promise.

copy

carbon copy CARBON.

copybook

to blot one's copybook BLOT.

core

to the core thoroughly (*rotten to the core*).

corn

to tread on someone's corns TREAD.

corner

all/ the four corners of the earth FOUR.

hole-and-corner HOLE.

in a (tight) corner in a position of difficulty or embarrassment (*Thanks for getting me out of a tight corner!*).

just around the corner 1 (*coll.*) very close. **2** (*coll.*) imminent (*Better times are just around the corner*).

out of the corner of one's eye indirectly or surreptitiously.

to cut corners 1 to take short cuts. **2** to sacrifice quality in favour of speed (*We must increase our productivity without cutting corners*).

to drive into a corner DRIVE.

to turn the corner 1 to go round a corner into the next street. **2** to pass the crisis of an illness. **3** to get past a difficulty.

correct

to stand corrected to acknowledge a mistake (*I stand corrected*).

cost

at all costs regardless of the cost (*to be avoided at all costs*).

at any cost regardless of the cost.

at cost at cost price.

at the cost of involving or resulting in the loss or sacrifice of.

to cost a bomb/ a packet/ the earth (*coll.*) to be very expensive.

to cost someone dear to cause someone great expenditure, severe loss etc. (*His mistake cost him dear*).

to count the cost COUNT.

to quit cost QUIT.

to someone's cost with consequent loss, expense or disadvantage to someone (*I found to my cost that it was not as easy as it looked*).

cosy

to cosy up 1 (*coll.*, *esp. N Am.*) to try to ingratiate oneself (with). 2 (*coll.*, *esp. N Am.*) to snuggle up (to).

cottage

love in a cottage LOVE.

cotton

to cotton on 1 (*coll.*) to be attracted (to). 2 (*coll.*) to begin to understand. 3 (*coll.*) to make use of.

to cotton to (*N Am.*, *coll.*) to take a liking to.

cotton wool

wrapped (up) in cotton wool WRAPPED.

couch

couch potato (*sl.*) an inactive person who watches an excessive amount of television instead of taking part in other forms of entertainment or exercise.

cough

to cough down to silence (a speaker) by a noise of or like coughing.

to cough out to say with a cough.

to cough up 1 to eject by coughing. 2 (*sl.*) to produce (money or information), esp. under duress (*Come on, cough up!*).

counsel

to keep one's own counsel to keep a matter secret.

to take counsel (with) to seek advice (from).

count

not counting excluding.

out for the count 1 unconscious. 2 fast asleep. 3 thoroughly dispirited or dejected. 4 in boxing, having been counted out.

to count against to be a factor against (*Your age may count against you*).

to count down to count in reverse order, towards zero, in preparing for a particular event.

to count for to be a factor in favour of.

to count heads to count the number of people present.

to count in to include.

to count noses 1 to count the number of people present. 2 to count votes, supporters etc. [Perhaps from a horse-dealer's method of counting stock.]

to count on 1 to rely on (*I'm counting on you*). 2 to consider as certain (*Don't count on it*).

to count one's blessings to be thankful for the good things one has.

to count one's chickens (before they are hatched) to make plans that depend on something uncertain (*Don't count your chickens: you haven't got the job yet*).

to count out 1 to reckon one by one from a number of units by counting aloud. 2 to count aloud (the number one is taking from a larger amount). 3 (*coll.*) to exclude, not to count in (*If it involves getting up early, you can count me out!*). 4 in children's games, to select or reject by means of a counting rhyme etc. 5 to declare (a boxer) defeated upon their failure to stand up within 10 seconds of the referee beginning to count. 6 to adjourn a meeting, esp. of Parliament, after counting those present and finding they are not sufficient to form a quorum.

to count sheep to count to oneself as a remedy for insomnia.

to count the cost 1 to calculate the damage or loss that has resulted or would result from some action. **2** to consider the risks entailed in some action.

to count the days/ hours to wait impatiently for something.

to count up to calculate the sum of.

to keep count to keep an accurate record of a numerical series.

to lose count LOSE.

to stand up and be counted to make one's opinions, feelings etc. publicly known (*It's time for those who oppose this plan to stand up and be counted*).

to take the count in boxing, to be counted out.

countenance

in countenance 1 in favour. **2** confident, assured.

out of countenance 1 out of favour. **2** abashed. **3** dismayed.

to change countenance CHANGE.

to keep in countenance to support.

to keep one's countenance to continue to look composed, to refrain from laughter.

to lose countenance LOSE.

to put out of countenance to abash, to cause to feel ashamed.

counter[1]

over the counter 1 (of medicines) sold without prescription. **2** (of the buying and selling of shares) through a broker, because the shares are not on the official list of a stock exchange.

to nail to the counter NAIL.

under the counter 1 referring to trade in black market goods. **2** secret(ly). **3** surreptitious(ly).

counter[2]

to run/ go counter in hunting, to go in the opposite direction to that of the quarry.

to run/ go counter to 1 to disobey (orders etc.). **2** to happen, behave etc. in a way other than (what is expected) (*The results ran counter to our previous findings*).

country

across country not using roads etc.

country cousin (*often derog.*) a relation of countrified ways or appearance.

line of country LINE[1].

to go/ appeal to the country to hold a general election, to appeal to the electors.

up country away from the coast or from the capital city.

courage

Dutch courage DUTCH.

the courage of one's convictions the courage to act in accordance with one's beliefs (*You must have the courage of your convictions and tell them what you think*).

to lose courage LOSE.

to pluck up/ screw up courage to summon up boldness or bravery (*He finally plucked up courage to ask her out*).

to take courage 1 to pluck up courage. **2** to derive courage (from a thought, piece of news etc.).

to take one's courage in both hands to summon up the courage necessary to do something.

course

horses for courses HORSE.

in due course DUE.

in (the) course of 1 in the process of. **2** during.

in the course of time 1 as time passes. **2** eventually.

matter of course MATTER.

of course 1 naturally. **2** admittedly (*I may be wrong, of course*). **3** certainly (*Of course you may go*).

off course not on course.

on course following the correct course, on target, on schedule (*on course for completion in June*).

par for the course PAR.

to run/ take its course to develop naturally and come to a natural end (*Let the disease run its course*).

to stay the course STAY.

court

friend at court FRIEND.

in court attending legal proceedings as one of the parties to a case or as counsel.

out of court 1 without the case being heard in a civil court (*The dispute was settled out of court*). **2** not entitled to be heard in court. **3** not worth considering (*Our complaints were ruled out of court*).

the ball is in someone's court BALL[1].

to go to court to begin legal proceedings.

to hold court to preside over one's admirers.

to laugh out of court LAUGH.

to pay court to to behave flatteringly or amorously (towards someone).

to take to court to begin legal proceedings against (*threatened to take us to court if we refused*).

courtesy

by courtesy as a matter of courtesy, not of right.

by courtesy of with the permission or agreement of.

cousin

country cousin COUNTRY.

†to call cousins to profess kinship with.

Coventry

to send to Coventry to ostracize, to refuse to have communication or dealings with. [The phrase may have originated in the English Civil War, when ostracized Royalists were sent to the Parliamentarian stronghold of Coventry. An alternative explanation is that the people of Coventry reputedly refused to have dealings with soldiers stationed there.]

cover

from cover to cover from beginning to end (of a book).

to break cover BREAK.

to cover a multitude of sins to include a wide range of different things. [From the Bible: "charity shall cover the multitude of sins" (I Pet. iv.8).]

to cover for to substitute for or replace (an absent fellow worker).

to cover in 1 to fill in. **2** to finish covering, e.g. with a roof.

to cover one's tracks 1 to remove all signs of one's passing. **2** to remove all evidence of what one has done.

to cover up 1 to cover completely. **2** to conceal (esp. something illegal).

to take cover to go into shelter in a place of protection.

under cover 1 concealed; acting under an assumed identity (*a spy working under cover at the Foreign Office*). **2** protected; sheltered by a roof etc. (*They left under cover of darkness*). **3** enclosed in an envelope addressed to another person.

under separate cover SEPARATE[2].

cow

milch cow MILCH.

sacred cow SACRED.

till the cows come home (*coll.*) forever (*wait till the cows come home*).

crab

to catch a crab CATCH.

crack

crack of dawn the first light of dawn (*We had to be up at the crack of dawn to catch the plane*).

crack of doom the end of the world at

Judgement Day, or the noise of thunder supposed to accompany this.

(fair) crack of the whip a (fair) opportunity or chance (*He was never given a fair crack of the whip*).

not all it's cracked up to be not as good as people say.

to crack a bottle to open and drink the contents of a bottle, e.g. of wine.

to crack a crib (*sl.*) to break into a house.

to crack down (on) (*coll.*) to take very strict measures (against) (*cracking down on shoplifters*).

to crack it (*coll.*) to succeed.

to crack on (*coll.*) to boast or brag (*cracking on about her new car*).

to crack the whip to exercise discipline, authority or control in a strict or severe manner.

to crack up 1 to suffer a mental or physical breakdown. **2** (*coll.*) to begin laughing uncontrollably.

to get cracking to make a prompt and active start to something.

to have a crack at (*coll.*) to have a try, to attempt.

to paper over the cracks PAPER.

cradle

from the cradle from infancy.

from the cradle to the grave throughout one's life.

cramp

to cramp someone's style 1 to spoil the effect a person is trying to make. **2** to impede a person's actions or self-expression.

crank

to crank up 1 to start (an engine) with a crank handle. **2** (*coll.*) to increase (speed, power etc.).

cranny

every nook and cranny NOOK.

crap¹

to crap it (*sl.*) to be afraid.

to crap out (*sl.*) to opt out through fear, exhaustion etc.

crap²

to crap out 1 to make a losing throw in the game of craps. **2** to be unsuccessful.

crash

to crash out 1 (*sl.*) to fall asleep. **2** (*sl.*) to become unconscious. **3** (*sl.*) to sleep in improvised accommodation (*I crashed out on the floor of my sister's flat*).

craven

to cry craven CRY.

craw

to stick in someone's craw STICK².

crazy

like crazy (*sl.*) extremely.

cream

to cream off to remove (the best part) from something (*The grammar schools creamed off the most able pupils*).

to skim the cream off SKIM.

crease

to crease up (*coll.*) to double up with laughter.

creature

creature comforts comforts of or relating to the body, esp. food and drink.

creature of habit a person who follows the same routine every day.

credence

to give credence to to believe, to accept (*He gave no credence to their theories*).

credit

on credit with an agreement to pay at some later time.

to do someone credit to be a source or cause of honour, esteem or heightened reputation for (*Your children do you credit*).

to get (the) credit for to receive credit for something done.

to give credit to to believe.

to give someone credit for 1 to give someone praise or honour for (something done). **2** to ascribe (a good quality or ability) to someone (*Give me credit for a bit of intelligence!*). **3** to enter (an amount) in a person's account.

to one's credit as something which can be considered praiseworthy, honourable etc. (*To his credit he rejected the bribe*).

creek

up shit creek (without a paddle) SHIT.

up the creek 1 (*sl.*) in trouble or difficulty. **2** (*sl.*) mad.

creep

to creep up on 1 to approach slowly, stealthily and without being noticed. **2** to develop slowly and imperceptibly.

to give someone the creeps to make someone feel frightened, horrified or disgusted.

crest

on/ riding the crest of a wave at the peak of one's success; enjoying prolonged success.

crib

to crack a crib CRACK.

cricket[1]

not cricket unfair, not honest (*That's simply not cricket!*).

cricket[2]

chirpy as a cricket CHIRPY.

crimp

to put a crimp in (*N Am., coll.*) to obstruct, hinder or thwart.

crisp

to burn to a crisp BURN.

crock

crock of gold unattainable wealth or reward. [An allusion to the pot of gold allegedly to be found at the end of the rainbow.]

crocodile

crocodile tears hypocritical tears, a false show of grief. [From the belief that crocodiles made a show of grief to attract victims or wept while eating their prey.]

Croesus

rich as Croesus RICH.

crook

by hook or by crook HOOK.

to go crook (at/ on) (*Austral., New Zeal., coll.*) to become angry (with), to reprimand.

crop

neck and crop NECK.

to crop out 1 to come to light. **2** (*Geol.*) (of an underlying stratum) to come out at the surface by the edges.

to crop up 1 to arise unexpectedly. **2** (*Geol.*) to crop out.

cropper

to come a cropper 1 (*coll.*) to fall. **2** (*coll.*) to fail.

cross

cross as two sticks very irritable; in very bad humour. [From the superstition that crossed sticks foreshadow an impending quarrel.]

on the cross 1 diagonally. **2** (*sl.*) unfairly, fraudulently.

to cross a bridge when one comes to it to cope with a difficulty only when it occurs, not to anticipate difficulties unnecessarily (*The committee might* *object, but we'll cross that bridge when we come to it*).

to cross one's fingers 1 to put one finger across an adjacent one as a sign of wishing for good luck. **2** to hope for good luck. [From superstitious use of the sign of the cross (representing Christ's Crucifixion) to avert bad luck.]

to cross one's heart (and hope to die) to promise or aver something solemnly.

to cross someone's mind to occur to someone's memory or attention (*It never crossed my mind that she might be in danger*).

to cross someone's palm (with silver) to give money to (e.g. a fortune-teller) as payment.

to cross swords to have a fight or argument (with).

to cross the floor (of an MP etc.) to change party-political allegiance. [Referring to the central area of any parliamentary chamber where parties sit on opposite sides.]

to cross the path of 1 to meet with. **2** to thwart.

to cross the Rubicon to take an irrevocable step. [The Rubicon was a river separating Julius Caesar's territory from Italy. The irrevocable step of crossing it with his invading army in 49 BC led to war with Rome.]

to cross wires/ get one's wires crossed 1 to have a crossed line on a telephone. **2** to have a misunderstanding, to be at cross purposes.

to have a cross to bear to have a particular responsibility, affliction or misfortune (*We all have our cross to bear*).

to take up the cross to sacrifice self for some pious object.

cross purpose

at cross purposes misunderstanding or

unintentionally acting counter to each other (*talking at cross purposes*).

crossroads

at a/ the crossroads at a point at which an important decision must be made or a new direction taken (*Her career is at the crossroads*).

crow

as the crow flies in a direct line.

stone the crows! STONE.

to eat crow EAT.

to have a crow to pluck with someone (*dated*) to have some fault to find with or an explanation to demand from someone.

to pluck/ pull a crow to contend for trifles.

crowd

to crowd out 1 to force (a person or thing) out by leaving no room. **2** to fill to absolute capacity.

to follow the crowd FOLLOW.

two's company, three's a crowd TWO.

crown

to crown it all (*coll.*) as a finishing touch.

cruel

to be cruel to be kind to do or say something unpleasant to someone for their own good (*You have to be cruel to be kind*).

crunch

when it comes to the crunch (*coll.*) at the decisive or critical moment.

crush

†**to crush a cup/ pot** to open a bottle and drink the contents.

to crush out to extinguish.

to have a crush on (*coll.*) to be infatuated with (someone).

crust

upper crust UPPER.

cry

a far cry FAR.

for crying out loud (*coll.*) used to express impatience or annoyance.

great cry and little wool GREAT.

in full cry FULL.

to cry against to exclaim loudly by way of threatening or censure.

to cry buckets to weep profusely.

†to cry craven to surrender.

to cry down 1 to decry, to depreciate. **2** to shout down. **3** †to overbear.

to cry for the moon to ask for something one cannot have.

to cry halves to demand a share of something.

†to cry havoc to give the signal for violence or devastation. [From Shakespeare's *Julius Caesar*: "Caesar's spirit, ranging for revenge, ... Shall in these confines, with a monarch's voice / Cry, 'Havoc!' and let slip the dogs of war." The cry of 'Havoc!' was an old military command to massacre without mercy.]

†to cry mercy to beg pardon.

to cry off to withdraw from something promised or agreed on (*The buyers cried off at the last minute*).

to cry one's eyes/ heart out to weep abundantly and bitterly.

to cry out to shout, to clamour.

to cry out against to exclaim loudly by way of censure or reproach.

to cry out for to require or demand urgently (*The system is crying out for modernization*).

to cry over spilt milk to waste time regretting something that cannot be undone (*It's no use crying over spilt milk*).

to cry shame on to protest against.

to cry stinking fish to decry or condemn something, esp. one's own wares.

to cry up to extol, to praise highly.

to cry wolf to raise a false alarm, esp. repeatedly. [From a fable about a shepherd boy who repeatedly called for help when his sheep were not in danger, so his cries were ignored when the wolf finally arrived.]

crying

crying need an urgent need.

crying shame a great shame.

crystal

clear as crystal CLEAR.

cuckoo

cloud-cuckoo-land CLOUD.

cuckoo in the nest an unwanted and alien person, an intruder. [The cuckoo lays its eggs in other birds' nests.]

cucumber

cool as a cucumber COOL.

cud

to chew the cud CHEW.

cudgel

to cudgel one's brains to try hard to recollect or find out something.

to take up (the) cudgels (for) 1 to fight (for). **2** to defend vigorously.

cue

on cue at the right time.

to cue in 1 to give a cue to. **2** to inform.

to take one's cue from to follow the example of or take advice from.

cuff

off the cuff extempore, without preparation (*speak off the cuff; an off-the-cuff speech*). [Perhaps from notes scribbled on the cuffs of one's shirt before making a speech.]

cup

in one's cups (*dated*) intoxicated.

one's cup of tea one's preferred occupation, company etc. (*My husband loves gardening, but it's not my cup of tea*).

someone's cup is full someone feels very happy or full of emotion. [From the Bible: "thou anointest my head with oil; my cup runneth over" (Ps. xxiii.5).]

there's many a slip 'twixt cup and lip SLIP[1].

cupboard

cupboard love greedy or self-interested love.

curate

curate's egg something of which some parts are good and some parts bad (*like the curate's egg, good in parts*). [From a *Punch* cartoon (1895) that depicts a curate eating a bad egg at breakfast with his bishop. Asked by his host if the egg is to his liking, he replies, "Parts of it are excellent."]

cure

†**to do no cure** to take no care.

curiosity

curiosity killed the cat a warning against inquisitiveness. [An allusion to the proverbial nine lives of a cat, which will not protect them from the perils of curiosity.]

curl

out of curl limp, out of condition.

to curl one's lip to express scorn or contempt.

to curl up 1 to go into a curled position. **2** (*coll.*) to be embarrassed or disgusted.

current

to pass current to be generally accepted as true, genuine etc.

curry

to curry favour to ingratiate oneself with superiors by officiousness or flattery. [The phrase originated as 'to curry favel (or fauvel)', from an Old French phrase meaning 'to groom a chestnut

horse'. In a 14th-century French story, Fauvel was a horselike character known for his cunning and duplicity, who was curried (or rubbed down) by those who wanted to gain his favour.]

curse

not to care a curse CARE.

to curse by bell, book and candle to excommunicate solemnly by a ceremony in which these objects were used symbolically.

curtain

curtain lecture a reproof or lecture from a wife to a husband after they have retired to bed. [Referring to the curtains around a four-poster bed.]

Iron Curtain IRON.

to be curtains for someone (*sl.*) to be the death, ruin or end of someone. [From the closing of the curtains at the end of a theatrical performance.]

to ring down the curtain RING[2].

to ring up the curtain RING[2].

curtsy

to drop a curtsy DROP.

cuss

not to give a tinker's cuss TINKER.

custody

to give into custody to hand over or consign to the police etc.

to take into custody to arrest.

cut

a cut above (*fig.*) superior to.

cut and dried 1 pre-arranged, already decided; inflexible. **2** (of opinions) unoriginal, trite.

cut and thrust 1 in a debate etc., a lively exchange of opinions. **2** in a sword fight, cutting and thrusting. **3** a hand-to-hand struggle.

the cut of someone's jib (*orig. Naut., sl.*) someone's physical appearance (*I don't *like the cut of his jib*). [Possibly referring to the shape of a ship's jib sail, which was once an indication of her nationality. Alternatively, the phrase may be old nautical slang for the shape of someone's nose.]

to be cut out for to be naturally fitted for (*I'm not cut out for this kind of work*).

to cut across 1 to pass by a shorter course so as to cut off an angle. **2** to go contrary to (usual procedure etc.) (*Attitudes towards closer ties with Europe cut across traditional party divisions*).

to cut and come again to help oneself and return for more later if one desires (*There's plenty of food, so you can cut and come again*).

to cut and run to depart rapidly. [Of nautical origin, referring either to the cutting of an anchor rope or to the cutting of ties used to lash up the sails on a square-rigged ship.]

to cut away 1 to detach by cutting. **2** to reduce by cutting.

to cut back 1 to prune. **2** to reduce (*cutting back on expenditure*).

to cut down 1 to fell. **2** to compress, to reduce (*cut the article down by 200 words*).

to cut in 1 to interrupt, to intrude. **2** (*coll.*) to allow to have a share in. **3** to drive in front of another person's car so as to affect their driving. **4** (of an electrical device) to start working. **5** to insert something within something else. **6** to take a woman away from her dancing partner.

to cut into 1 to make a cut in (something). **2** to reduce or interfere with (*It cuts into her schedule*).

to cut it out to desist from doing something annoying (*Cut it out you two – I'm trying to read*).

to cut off 1 to remove by cutting, to eradicate. **2** to intercept. **3** to prevent from access. **4** to sever. **5** to discontinue. **6** to bring to an untimely end, to kill. **7** to disinherit (*His father threatened to cut him off without a penny*).

to cut out 1 to shape by cutting. **2** to remove or separate by cutting. **3** to supplant. **4** to cease doing, taking or indulging in something unpleasant or harmful (*trying to cut out smoking once and for all*). **5** to cease operating suddenly and unexpectedly or by the automatic intervention of a cut-out device. **6** (*Hist., Naut.*) to enter a harbour and seize and carry off (e.g. a ship) by sudden attack. **7** to relinquish a game as the result of cutting the cards.

to cut under to undersell.

to cut up 1 to cut in pieces. **2** to criticize severely. **3** to distress deeply (*She is terribly cut up about the death of her mother*). **4** in a vehicle, to drive across the line of travel of (another driver) unexpectedly and dangerously.

to cut up well (*coll.*) to leave plenty of money.

cylinder
to be firing on all cylinders FIRE.

D

dab
dab hand (*coll.*) an expert (at).

daddy
sugar daddy SUGAR.
the daddy of them all (*coll.*) the supreme
   example of something.

daft
daft about (*coll.*) very fond of.
daft as a brush (*coll.*) very silly or
   foolish.

dag
to rattle one's dags RATTLE.

dagger
at daggers drawn **1** on hostile terms.
   2 ready to fight.
cloak-and-dagger CLOAK.
to look daggers to look with fierceness.

daily
daily bread necessary food and
   sustenance, means of living. [From
   the Lord's Prayer in the Bible: "Give
   us this day our daily bread" (Matt.
   vi.11).]
daily dozen (*coll.*) daily physical
   exercises.

daisy
fresh as a daisy FRESH.
pushing up (the) daisies PUSH.

dale
up hill and down dale HILL.

damage
what's the damage? (*sl.*) what is the total
   cost?, how much do I owe you?

damn
damn all absolutely nothing.
damn well whether you like it or not,
   definitely.
not to give a damn to be totally
   unconcerned.
to damn with faint praise to praise with
   so little enthusiasm that it suggests
   dislike or disapproval. [From
   Alexander Pope's *Epistle to Dr*
   Arbuthnot (1735): "Damn with faint
   praise, assent with civil leer, / And,
   without sneering, teach the rest to
   sneer."]

damned
a damned good try (*coll.*) an exceedingly
   good try.
to be damned if **1** certainly will not
   (*I'll be damned if I offer to help her*
   again). **2** certainly do not (*I'm*
   damned if I know what's wrong with
   it).
to see someone damned first (*coll.*) to
   refuse categorically to do what
   someone wants.

damnedest
to do one's damnedest to do one's very
   best.

Damocles
sword of Damocles SWORD.

damp

damp squib a failed attempt, a disappointing event.

to damp down 1 to stifle (an emotion etc.). **2** to fill (a furnace) with coke to prevent the fire going out.

damper

to put a damper on 1 to discourage, to stifle (*The bad news put a damper on the celebrations*). **2** to reduce the chances of success of.

dance

to dance attendance on 1 to pay assiduous court to. **2** to be kept waiting by.

to dance to someone's tune to act according to someone's instructions or wishes, esp. weakly or sycophantically.

to lead someone a (merry) dance LEAD[1].

to make a song and dance SONG.

dander

to get one's dander up to become angry.

danger

in danger of liable to.

Darby

Darby and Joan an elderly married couple living in domestic bliss. [From a ballad written by Henry Woodfall and first published in 1735, supposedly based on a couple of Woodfall's acquaintance, John Darby and his wife.]

dare

I dare say I suppose (*I dare say you're right*).

dark

dark horse 1 a person who keeps their opinions and thoughts secret. **2** a person of unknown capabilities. [From horse racing, where the term refers to a horse of untested but promising potential.]

in the dark 1 without light. **2** in ignorance (about) (*Management kept us in the dark about the takeover*).

leap in the dark LEAP.

shot in the dark SHOT.

to keep something dark to keep silent about something.

to whistle in the dark WHISTLE.

darken

not to darken someone's door not to appear as a visitor (*Go away and never darken my door again!*). [Alluding to the shadow cast by a visitor.]

dash

dash it (all)! (*coll.*) used to express annoyance.

to cut a dash to make a fine impression.

to dash off/ down to write down or complete in a hurry (*He dashed off a note to his wife*).

date

out of date no longer in fashion or use.

past its/ one's sell-by date SELL-BY DATE.

to date up till now.

to make/ have a date (*coll.*) to make or have an appointment.

up to date recent, modern, abreast of the times.

daughter

†**daughter of Eve** (*often derog.*) a woman, usu. with an implication of curiosity, vanity etc.

like mother, like daughter MOTHER.

to kiss/ marry the gunner's daughter GUNNER.

Davy

Davy Jones's locker the sea as the tomb of the drowned. [The identity of Davy Jones is unknown.]

dawn

crack of dawn CRACK.

to **dawn on** to gradually become apparent
to (*It dawned on me why he had
seemed reluctant to leave*).

day

all in a/ the day's work something one has
to do regularly.

all (the) day throughout the day.

any day now in the very near future.

at the end of the day END.

a year and a day YEAR.

break of day BREAK.

day after day with monotonous
regularity, every day continuously.

day and night 1 throughout both day and
night (*work day and night*). **2** always.
3 by or in both day and night.

day by day gradually, every day (*His
health is improving day by day*).

day in, day out every day, constantly.

day of reckoning 1 the day of settling
accounts. **2** (*fig.*) the Day of Judgement.

early days EARLY.

every dog has its day DOG.

evil days EVIL.

from day one from the very start.

from day to day as the days pass; daily.

halcyon days HALCYON.

happy as the day is long HAPPY.

high days and holidays HIGH DAY.

in all one's born days BORN.

in someone's day 1 when someone was
popular, successful, prosperous etc.
2 when someone was young (*In my
day there were no computers*).

in the cold light of day COLD.

late in the day LATE.

nine days' wonder NINE.

not one's day a day on which things go
wrong for one.

not to have all day (*coll.*) to have a
limited amount of time (*Hurry up – I
haven't got all day!*).

one of these (fine) days 1 shortly; in the
near future. **2** at some unspecified time
in the future.

one of those days a day on which things
go wrong for one.

one/ some day 1 shortly; in the near
future. **2** at some unspecified time in
the future.

order of the day ORDER.

rainy day RAINY.

red-letter day RED-LETTER.

Rome was not built in a day ROME.

salad days SALAD.

someone's days are numbered someone
will not live much longer.

that'll be the day (*coll.*) that day will
never come.

the good old days GOOD.

the other day OTHER.

the present day PRESENT[1].

this day and age the present historical
period (*Nobody should be forced to
beg on the streets in this day and age*).

those were the days used to express
nostalgia for the past.

time of day TIME.

to call it a day to stop what one is doing,
esp. work (*It's getting late: let's call it a
day*).

to have a field day FIELD DAY.

to have had one's day to be no longer
popular, successful, prosperous, useful
etc.

to have one's day to experience a period
of success or good fortune.

to have seen better days to be on the
decline (*These boots have seen better
days*).

to know the time of day TIME.

to make a day of it to spend a day in
enjoyment or festivity.

to make someone's day to make someone
very happy.

tomorrow is another day TOMORROW.

to name the day NAME.

to one's dying day DYING.

to pass the time of day TIME.

to save the day SAVE.

to see the light of day LIGHT[1].

to this day even now; up till the present.

to win/ gain/ carry the day to be
victorious.

woe worth the day! WOE.

daylight

in broad daylight BROAD.

to beat/ knock the living daylights out of LIVING.

to scare/ frighten the living daylights out of LIVING.

to see daylight 1 to begin to understand. **2** to draw near to the end of a task.

dead

dead against absolutely opposed to.

dead and buried long forgotten.

dead as a dodo completely obsolete or defunct. [The dodo is an extinct flightless bird.]

dead as a doornail utterly dead.

dead duck (*coll.*) a person or idea doomed to failure.

dead from the neck up (*coll.*) completely stupid.

dead letter 1 a letter which cannot be delivered by the post office, and is opened and returned to the sender. **2** a law or anything that has become inoperative.

dead loss 1 (*coll.*) a useless person, thing or situation. **2** a loss with no compensation whatever.

dead men's shoes 1 inheritances, legacies. **2** an opportunity for promotion arising from someone's retirement or death (*waiting for dead men's shoes*).

dead of night the middle of the night.

dead on the mark absolutely straight.

dead ringer (*coll.*) a person or thing exactly resembling someone or something else (*He's a dead ringer for the president*).

dead to the world (*coll.*) fast asleep.

dead wood 1 useless people or things (*The new management are planning to cut away a lot of dead wood*). **2** (*Naut.*) the built-up timbers fore and aft above the keel.

enough to wake the dead ENOUGH.

let the dead bury their dead one should concern oneself with the present rather than dwelling on the past. [From the Bible, Matt. viii.22.]

over my dead body (*coll.*) without my agreement, against my opposition.

the quick and the dead QUICK.

to be left for dead to be assumed to be dead and consequently abandoned.

to cut dead to refuse to acknowledge the presence of (*The next time I saw her, she cut me dead*).

to make a dead set at 1 to attack with determination. **2** to try to win the affections of.

wouldn't be seen dead in/ with/ etc. would never wear/visit/be seen at or in the company of etc. (*I wouldn't be seen dead in flared trousers; He wouldn't be seen dead in a nightclub*).

deaf

deaf as a post completely deaf.

to fall on deaf ears (of a request etc.) to be ignored.

to turn a deaf ear to to refuse to listen to.

deal

a (great/ good) deal 1 a large quantity. **2** to a large extent; by much, considerably (*a great deal better*).

big deal BIG.

raw deal RAW.

square deal SQUARE.

to deal by to act towards.

to deal in to be engaged in commercially, to trade in.

to deal with 1 to take action in respect of, to handle. **2** to have to do with. **3** to behave towards. **4** to consider judicially.

dealings

to have dealings with to deal or associate with.

dear

to hold dear to regard with affection.

death

at death's door close to death.

death warrant 1 an order for the execution of a criminal. **2** an act or measure putting an end to something.

fate worse than death FATE.

in at the death present at the finish.

kiss of death KISS.

like death warmed up/ over (*coll.*) very ill or tired (*You look like death warmed up*).

like grim death GRIM.

matter of life and death MATTER.

pale as death PALE[1].

sick to death SICK.

sure as death SURE.

to be the death of 1 to cause the death of. **2** (*coll.*) to amuse (someone) greatly. **3** (*coll.*) to be a source of great worry to (*That child will be the death of me*).

to catch one's death of cold CATCH.

to death to the greatest degree, as much as possible (*bored to death*).

to dice with death DICE.

to do to death 1 to overuse (*The phrase has been done to death*). **2** to kill.

to dress to death DRESS.

to flog to death FLOG.

to put to death to execute.

to ride to death RIDE.

to the death until one of the antagonists is killed or defeated (*fight to the death*).

unto death to the last, forever.

debt

in debt under obligation to pay something due.

in someone's debt under an obligation to someone.

deceive

to be deceived to be mistaken.

to deceive oneself to ignore the truth.

decent

to be decent (*coll.*) to be sufficiently clothed to be seen in public (*Don't come in – I'm not decent!*).

deck

below deck(s) in or to the area below the main deck of a ship.

on deck 1 on an uncovered deck on a ship. **2** (*esp. N Am.*) ready for action etc.

to clear the decks CLEAR.

to deck out to adorn, to beautify.

to hit the deck HIT.

to sweep the decks SWEEP.

declare

I (do) declare! used to express surprise, disbelief etc.

to declare an/ one's interest (often of a Member of Parliament) to make known one's usu. financial interest in a company about which there is (parliamentary) discussion.

to declare for/ against to side with/ against.

to declare off to refuse to proceed with (an engagement or contract).

to declare oneself 1 to avow one's intentions. **2** to disclose one's character or attitude.

decline

to go into a decline to deteriorate gradually in health, vigour etc.

deed

in word and deed WORD.

deep

in deep water in trouble.

of the deepest dye of the most extreme or worst kind (*a villain of the deepest dye*).

deep end

to be thrown in at the deep end to be given the most difficult part to do first, to be required to start without much experience. [Alluding to the deep end of a swimming pool.]

to go (in) off the deep end to give way to one's anger.

to jump in at the deep end JUMP.

default

by default (happening) only because something else has not happened (*Since no one else applied, he got the job by default*).

in default of instead of (something wanting).

to make default to fail to appear in court, or to keep any engagement.

defensive

on the defensive 1 ready to defend oneself. **2** over-anxious to defend oneself against (expected) criticism.

defiance

in defiance of in disobedience or disregard of, in opposition to.

to set at defiance (*dated*) to defy.

degree

by degrees gradually, step by step.

one degree under (*coll.*) slightly unwell.

third degree THIRD.

to a degree (*coll.*) to a certain extent, somewhat.

to the nth degree N.

deliver

stand and deliver! (*Hist.*) the traditional utterance of a highwayman at a hold-up, ordering the victims to hand over their money and valuables.

to be delivered of to give birth to.

to deliver oneself of to communicate in a speech or recitation.

to deliver out to distribute.

to deliver over to put into someone's hands.

to deliver the goods (*coll.*) to carry out or produce something promised or expected.

to deliver up to surrender possession of.

delusion

delusions of grandeur a false belief that one is very grand or important.

demand

in demand much sought after (*Houses like this are very much in demand*).

on demand whenever requested (*Should abortion be available on demand?*).

demesne

held in demesne (*Law*) occupied by the owner, not tenants.

den

to beard the lion in his den BEARD.

Denmark

like Hamlet without the Prince of Denmark HAMLET.

denominate

denominated in expressed as a value in (a particular monetary unit).

dent

to make a dent in to lessen or diminish (*The holiday made a dent in my savings*).

deny

to deny oneself to refrain or abstain from pleasures, to practise self-denial.

depend

depending on according to.

depend upon it! you may rely upon it, you may be certain!

it all/ that depends 1 it/ that is conditional. **2** perhaps.

deposit

on deposit 1 when buying on hire purchase, payable as a first instalment. **2** in a deposit account.

depth

in depth thoroughly, in detail.

out of one's depth 1 in water deeper than one's height. **2** faced with a situation, problem etc. that is beyond one's knowledge or capability (*He's out of* *his depth in a senior management position*).

to plumb the depths (of) PLUMB[1].

deputy

by deputy by proxy.

derision

to hold in derision to hold in contempt, to make a laughing-stock of.

derry

to have a derry on (*Austral.*) to be biased against.

descend

to be descended from to be a descendant of.

to descend on to visit, esp. unexpectedly (*The whole family descended on us at the weekend*).

description

to answer/ fit the description to have the qualities or features described.

to beggar description BEGGAR.

deserts

to get one's just deserts JUST.

deserving

deserving of having deserved (*deserving of praise*).

design

by design intentionally, deliberately.

to have designs on to scheme to take possession of (*She has designs on our shop*).

desire

to leave a lot/ much to be desired to be distinctly unsatisfactory.

despite

†**despite of** in spite of.

†**to do despite to** to dishonour.

detail

beaten in detail (*Mil.*) defeated by detachments or in a series of partial engagements.

in detail minutely; item by item (*described in detail*).

to go into detail to mention all the particulars about something.

deuce

the deuce to pay serious consequences.

to play the deuce with (*dated*) to spoil completely, to ruin.

device

to leave someone to their own devices to leave someone to do as they please (*Left to his own devices, he would probably stay in bed all morning*).

devil

a devil of a (*coll.*) difficult or trying (*a devil of a problem*).

better the devil you know (than the devil you don't) it is better to remain in a situation that is undesirable but familiar than to exchange it for something unknown and possibly worse.

between the devil and the deep blue sea torn between two equally undesirable alternatives. [Of nautical origin, probably referring to the precarious position of a sailor applying pitch to a particular seam of a wooden ship.]

devil a bit not at all.

devil a one not a single one.

devil's advocate 1 a person who puts the opposing view in a discussion without necessarily holding that view. **2** (*Hist.*) an official of the Roman Catholic Church appointed to oppose a proposed canonization or beatification.

he that sups with the devil must have a long spoon SUP.

like the devil energetically or fast (*run like the devil*).

speak/ talk of the devil said when the person who is the subject of conversation arrives.

the devil finds work for idle hands people who do not keep busy may become involved in mischief or crime.

the devil has (all) the best tunes virtuous, moral or worthy pursuits are not the most enjoyable, interesting or attractive. [From a remark made by Charles Wesley (1707–88) in defence of setting the words of hymns to the tunes of popular songs.]

the devil looks after his own bad people seem to have more success than good people.

the devil's own job (*coll.*) a very difficult task (*I had the devil's own job persuading her*).

the devil take the hindmost one must look after one's own interests.

the devil to pay serious consequences. [In old nautical terminology, the devil was one of the seams between the planks of a wooden ship that had to be 'payed' (packed with pitch) regularly to prevent leakage. This may have been a difficult or dangerous task because of the length or location of the seam in question.]

the very devil (*coll.*) something very difficult.

the world, the flesh and the devil WORLD.

to give the devil his due to give a person one dislikes credit for their good qualities (*To give the devil his due, he's very good at dealing with awkward customers*).

to go to the devil 1 to be damned. **2** (*imper.*) go away!

to play the devil with to worry, to ruin.

to raise the devil RAISE.

what/ who etc. the devil an expression of surprise or annoyance (*What the devil was that?*).

you little/ young devil a playful, semi-ironical address.

devour

to devour the way (*poet.*) to move extremely quickly.

diamond

diamond cut diamond (*dated*) a meeting of two equally clever people.

rough diamond ROUGH.

dice

no dice (*sl.*) an expression of refusal or lack of success.

to dice with death to take great risks.

to load the dice against someone LOAD.

Dick

Tom, Dick and Harry TOM.

dido

†**to cut (up) didoes** to behave extravagantly or rowdily. [A dido is a prank or caper.]

die¹

never say die never give up.

to die away to become gradually less distinct.

to die back (of a plant) to die from the tip to the root.

to die down 1 (of plants) to die off above ground, with only the roots staying alive in winter. **2** to become less loud, intense etc., to subside.

to die for extremely attractive (*a figure to die for*).

to die game (*dated*) to maintain a resolute attitude to the last.

to die hard to be difficult to eradicate or suppress (*Old habits die hard*).

to die in harness to continue to the last in one's business or profession.

to die in one's shoes to meet a violent death, esp. by hanging.

to die in the last ditch to resist to the uttermost.

to die laughing (*fig.*) to laugh immoderately at something.

to die like a dog to die miserably or shamefully.

to die off 1 to die in large numbers. **2** to languish.

to die out to become extinct.

to die with one's boots on to die fighting.

to do or die to make a last desperate attempt.

die²

straight as a die STRAIGHT.

the die is cast an irrevocable decision has been taken. [A translation of the Latin phrase *alea iacta est*, allegedly used by Julius Caesar when he took the irrevocable step of crossing the Rubicon with his invading army, provoking war with Rome.]

diet

to be/ go on a diet to follow/ begin to follow a strict plan of eating so as to lose weight.

†**to take diet** to follow a strict plan of eating for medical reasons.

differ

to agree to differ AGREE.

to beg to differ BEG.

to differ in kind to differ in nature not merely in degree.

difference

to make a difference 1 to have an effect. **2** to behave differently.

to make no difference to have no effect.

to split the difference SPLIT.

with a difference 1 with something distinctive added (*a soap opera with a difference*). **2** differently. **3** (*Her.*) as a mark of distinction.

difficulty

with difficulty awkwardly, not easily.

dig

to dig a pit for to try to trap.

to dig in (*coll.*) to begin eating.

to dig oneself in 1 to take up permanent

quarters; to refuse to budge. **2** to make oneself indispensable.

to dig one's heels in to be obstinate.

to dig one's own grave to cause oneself harm or trouble (*You're digging your own grave by drinking so much*).

to dig out 1 to obtain by digging. **2** to obtain by research.

to dig through to open a passage through.

to dig up 1 to excavate. **2** to extract or raise by digging. **3** to break up (ground) by digging. **4** to obtain by research (*I managed to dig up some interesting information about his early life*).

to have a dig at to make a cutting or sarcastic remark about.

dignity

beneath someone's dignity degrading, in someone's own opinion (*She considers it beneath her dignity to make the tea*).

to stand on one's dignity to assume a manner showing one's sense of self-importance.

dilemma

on the horns of a dilemma HORN.

diligence

†**to do one's diligence** to do one's best.

dime

a dime a dozen cheap, ordinary.

on a dime 1 (*N Am., coll.*) within a very short distance. **2** (*N Am., coll.*) very quickly.

din

to din into to teach by constant repetition (*grammatical rules dinned into us at school*).

dine

to dine on to eat (something) for dinner.

to dine out to be invited out to dinner.

to dine out on to be popular socially

because of (something interesting to recount) (*I dined out on that story for months*).

to dine with Duke Humphrey (*Hist.*) to go dinnerless. [An allusion to Duke Humphrey's Walk, a part of old St Paul's where people were supposed to stroll while others were dining.]

dinkum
fair dinkum FAIR.

dinner
dressed up like a dog's dinner DRESS.
more ... than someone has had hot dinners HOT.

dint
by dint of by force of; by means of (*by dint of hard work*).

dip
to dip deep 1 to plunge far in. **2** to investigate.
to dip into 1 to draw upon (e.g. resources). **2** to read from cursorily. **3** to take a brief interest in.
to dip one's wick (*taboo sl.*) (of a man) to have sexual intercourse.
to dip out (*Austral., sl.*) to miss out (on).
to dip the flag (*Naut.*) to lower and then raise a flag as a salute.

direction
step in the right direction STEP.

dirt
cheap as dirt CHEAP.
to dish the dirt DISH.
to do someone dirt (*sl.*) to behave maliciously towards someone.
to eat dirt EAT.
to throw dirt at (*coll.*) to speak maliciously about.
to treat like dirt TREAT.

dirty
dirty dog (*coll.*) a dishonest or untrustworthy person.

dirty look (*coll.*) a glance of disapproval or dislike (*She gave me a dirty look*).
dirty money 1 money obtained by dishonest or immoral means. **2** extra pay for unpleasant or dirty work.
dirty old man 1 a man who is sexually interested in younger women. **2** a lecherous man.
dirty trick 1 a contemptible or unfair act. **2** (*pl.*) underhand politics or business methods, used to discredit rivals.
dirty weekend a weekend holiday with a sexual partner.
dirty word 1 (*coll.*) a swear word or taboo word. **2** something currently out of favour or very much disliked (*Socialism is almost a dirty word these days*).
dirty work 1 (*coll.*) dishonesty, trickery, foul play (*I won't do your dirty work for you*). **2** work that involves dirtying one's hands and clothes.
to do the dirty on (*coll.*) to play an underhand trick on (*One of our contractors did the dirty on us*).

disadvantage
at a disadvantage in an unfavourable situation or position.

disappear
disappearing act a sudden departure, esp. in order to avoid something unpleasant.

discount
at a discount 1 at a reduced price. **2** below par. **3** not held in much esteem.

discretion
at discretion according to one's own judgement.
at the discretion of according to the judgement of.
discretion is the better part of valour it is wiser to avoid danger or unpleasantness than to be recklessly

courageous. [From Shakespeare's
Henry IV, Part I: "The better part of
valour is discretion; in the which
better part I have saved my life."]
to use one's discretion USE[2].

discriminate

to discriminate against to distinguish or
deal with unfairly or unfavourably
(*The system discriminates against the
self-employed*).

disgrace

in disgrace having lost respect, out of
favour.

disguise

blessing in disguise BLESSING.
in disguise wearing a disguise.

disgust

in disgust with a feeling of disgust (*We
walked out in disgust*).

dish

to dish out (*sl.*) to distribute freely.
to dish the dirt to spread gossip (about).
to dish up 1 to serve up. **2** (*coll.*) to
present in an attractive or new way.

dispatch

hatches, matches and dispatches HATCH[2].
mentioned in dispatches MENTION.

dispense

to dispense with 1 to do without. **2** to
grant exemption from.

displease

to be displeased at/ with to be annoyed or
vexed at or with; to disapprove of.

disposal

at the disposal of 1 available for the use of
(*facilities at the disposal of our
guests*). **2** in the power of, at the
command of.

dispose

to dispose of 1 to put into the hands of
someone else. **2** to get rid of (*dispose
of nuclear waste*). **3** to sell. **4** to finish,
to settle (*We soon disposed of the
washing up*). **5** to kill. **6** to prove
wrong (*She easily disposed of his
argument*). **7** to use up. **8** to apply to
any purpose (*yours to dispose of as
you see fit*). **9** to alienate. **10** to
dismiss. **11** to put away, to stow away.

dispute

beyond/ past/ without dispute without the
possibility of being disputed (*The
excellence of her work is beyond
dispute*).

dissociate

to dissociate oneself from to deny any
connection or association with.

distance

at a distance from a long way off.
to go the distance 1 to complete
something one has started. **2** to endure
to the end of a game or bout in sport.
to keep at a distance not to become too
friendly with.
to keep one's distance 1 to behave
respectfully. **2** to behave with reserve
or coldness.
within a measurable distance of
MEASURABLE.
within spitting distance SPITTING.
within striking distance STRIKING.
within walking distance WALKING.

distraction

to drive to distraction DRIVE.

distress

in distress 1 in a state of anguish or
danger (*a damsel in distress*). **2** (of a
ship) in a disabled or perilous
condition.

disuse

to fall into disuse to stop being used.

ditch
to die in the last ditch DIE[1].

ditchwater
dull as ditchwater DULL.

dither
all of a dither (*coll.*) very agitated or indecisive.

ditto
to say ditto to repeat, to endorse.

divide
to divide against itself to split into opposing groups.

do
do as I say, not as I do follow my advice rather than my example (used esp. when someone fails to practise what they preach).

do as you would be done by treat others as you would like to be treated. [From the Bible: "And as ye would that men should do to you, do ye also to them likewise" (Luke vi.31). The saying was popularized in its current form by the name of a character in Charles Kingsley's *The Water Babies* (1863).]

dos and don'ts rules.

fair dos FAIR.

how do? hello, an informal greeting.

how do you do? used as a conventional form of greeting.

to be/ have (something) to do with to be connected with, to be about (*His work has something to do with investment banking*).

to do about to do (something) in order to deal with (*Can you do something about that smell in the bathroom?*).

to do away with 1 (*coll.*) to remove, to abolish. **2** (*coll.*) to kill.

to do by to treat, to deal with (*hard done by*).

to do down 1 (*coll.*) to get the better of, to cheat. **2** (*coll.*) to humiliate.

to do for 1 to put an end to, to ruin, to kill. **2** (*coll.*) to do domestic work for.

to do in 1 (*sl.*) to kill. **2** (*coll.*) to exhaust.

to do out (*coll.*) to decorate (a room).

to do out of (*coll.*) to deprive unfairly of (*I was done out of what I was owed*).

to do over 1 (*sl.*) to attack, to beat. **2** (*sl.*) to decorate (a room). **3** (*N Am.*) to perform a second time. **4** to cover with a coating.

to do to to treat, to deal with.

†to do unto to treat, to deal with.

to do up 1 to renovate, to decorate. **2** to dress up or make (oneself) up. **3** to fasten (*can't even do up his own shoelaces*). **4** to pack in a parcel.

to do well to prosper, to profit.

to do with 1 to need, to want (*I could do with a drink*). **2** to have business or a connection with. **3** to dispose of. **4** to handle, to treat.

to do without to dispense with.

dock[1]
to be in/ put into dock (*coll.*) to be/ send away for repairs.

dock[2]
in the dock charged with an offence.

doctor
just what the doctor ordered exactly what was needed.

to go for the doctor 1 (*Austral., sl.*) to make a supreme effort. **2** to bet all one's money.

dodge
to dodge the column (*coll.*) to avoid work, duty, responsibility etc. [Of military origin, referring to a column of men.]

dodo
dead as a dodo DEAD.

dog
dirty dog DIRTY.

dog eat dog (*also attrib.*) ruthless pursuit

of one's own interests (*It's dog eat dog out there*; *Advertising is a dog-eat-dog business*).

dog in the manger a person who prevents other people from enjoying what they cannot enjoy themselves; a churlish person. [From Aesop's fable about a dog that sat on a pile of hay in a manger and refused to let a hungry ox come near to eat its fodder.]

dog's dinner/ breakfast (*sl.*) a mess.

dressed up like a dog's dinner DRESS.

every dog has its day everyone can expect a period of success or good fortune at some time in their lives.

give a dog a bad name if a person gets a bad reputation, it is difficult to regain people's good opinion.

hair of the dog (that bit one) HAIR.

like a dog with two tails very happy.

love me, love my dog LOVE.

lucky dog LUCKY.

not a dog's chance not the slightest chance.

shaggy-dog story SHAGGY.

sick as a dog SICK.

sly dog SLY.

there's life in the old dog yet LIFE.

the tail wags the dog TAIL¹.

to die like a dog DIE¹.

to dog it (*N Am., coll.*) to be lazy, to slack.

to fight like cat and dog FIGHT.

to give to the dogs to throw away.

to go to the dogs (*sl.*) to deteriorate physically or morally, to go to ruin (*This country has gone to the dogs!*).

to help a lame dog over a stile HELP.

to keep a dog and bark oneself to do the work one employs someone else to do.

to lead a dog's life LEAD¹.

to let sleeping dogs lie SLEEP.

to let the dog see the rabbit (*coll.*) to give someone a chance to see, take part etc.

top dog TOP¹.

to put on the dog (*N Am., coll.*) to behave in a pretentious manner.

to rain cats and dogs RAIN.

to throw to the dogs to throw away.

you can't teach an old dog new tricks TEACH.

dogged

it's dogged as does it (*coll.*) it pays to be persistent.

doghouse

in the doghouse (*sl.*) in disfavour.

doldrums

in the doldrums 1 in low spirits, in the dumps. **2** (*Naut.*) becalmed.

dole

on the dole (*coll.*) receiving unemployment benefit.

to dole out to distribute in small quantities.

doll

to doll up (*coll.*) to dress up, to make (oneself) look smart.

dollar

sixty-four thousand dollar question SIXTY.

to bet one's bottom dollar BET.

to look/ feel (like) a million dollars MILLION.

dollop

all the dollop (*sl.*) the whole thing.

done

done brown (*sl.*) cheated completely.

done for (*coll.*) in serious difficulty, doomed, dead or nearly dead.

done in/ up (*coll.*) worn out, exhausted.

done to a turn cooked exactly right. [Originally referring to the turning of a spit when roasting meat.]

over and done with OVER.

the done thing socially acceptable behaviour (*not the done thing*).

to be done with to have finished with.

to get done with (*coll.*) to finish with.

to have done to have finished.

to have done with to have no further concern with.

donkey

donkey's years (*coll.*) a long time (*I haven't seen him for donkey's years*). [Possibly alluding to the longevity of a donkey or, punningly, to the length of its ears.]

donkey work drudgery, routine work.

to talk the hind legs off a donkey TALK.

doodah

all of a doodah (*coll.*) flustered, in a state of confusion.

doom

crack of doom CRACK.

prophet of doom PROPHET.

doomsday

till doomsday for ever.

door

at death's door DEATH.

behind closed doors CLOSED.

by/ through the back door BACK DOOR.

foot in the door FOOT.

next door to NEXT DOOR.

not to darken someone's door DARKEN.

open door OPEN.

out of doors outside the house; in or into the open.

to beat a path to someone's door PATH.

to close the door to CLOSE².

to keep the wolf from the door WOLF.

to lay (something) at the door of to blame for (something).

to leave the door open to ensure that an opportunity remains available to one.

to lie at the door of LIE².

to lock the stable door after the horse has bolted LOCK.

to open the door to OPEN.

to show someone the door to turn someone out; to send someone away unceremoniously.

to shut the door on SHUT.

to turn from the door 1 to refuse to admit. 2 to refuse (a beggar or petitioner).

within doors inside the house.

doornail

dead as a doornail DEAD.

doorstep

on one's doorstep very close to one's home (*with such beautiful countryside on your doorstep*).

dope

to dope out (*sl.*) to devise, to discover.

dose

like a dose of salts very quickly and thoroughly (*The burglars went through the house like a dose of salts, taking everything of value*). [Alluding to mineral salts used as a laxative.]

doss

to doss down to go to sleep in a makeshift bed.

dot

on the dot (of) (*coll.*) precisely (at) (*The coach will leave at nine o'clock on the dot*).

the year dot YEAR.

to dot and carry one (*dated*) to put down the units and transfer the tens to the next column in a sum (used by or to schoolchildren).

to dot the i's and cross the t's 1 (*coll.*) to be precisely exact. 2 (*coll.*) to put the finishing touches to an undertaking.

dote

to dote on to be foolishly fond of.

dotted line

to sign on the dotted line SIGN.

dotty

dotty about/ on (*coll.*) excessively or foolishly fond of (*dotty about horses*).

double

at the double 1 very fast. **2** at twice the normal speed.

double Dutch 1 incomprehensible talk or language, gibberish (*Computer manuals read like double Dutch to me*). **2** (*N Am.*) a skipping game in which one rope is turned clockwise and the other anticlockwise, the skipper jumping over each rope in turn.

double quick 1 very quickly. **2** very quick (*He completed the job in double quick time*).

double whammy (*coll.*) a twofold blow or misfortune. [Originally from the US comic strip *Li'l Abner.*]

on the double (*N Am.*) at the double.

to double and twist to add one thread to another and twist them together.

to double back to go back in the direction one has come from.

to double up 1 to bend one's body into a stooping or folded posture. **2** to collapse with pain or laughter (*doubled up with pain*). **3** to make (another person) double up. **4** to share a room or bed with someone (*There aren't enough beds: the children will have to double up*). **5** to use the winnings from a bet to make another bet. **6** to fold or become folded.

doubt

beyond doubt definitely true.

doubting Thomas a person who persists in doubt until they have tangible evidence. [From Thomas the apostle who would not believe in the Resurrection until he had seen Jesus (John xx.24–25).]

in doubt uncertain (*The future of the company is in doubt*).

no doubt certainly, very likely, admittedly.

to give someone the benefit of the doubt BENEFIT.

to hang in doubt HANG.

to make no doubt to be sure.

without (a) doubt definitely.

douse

to douse the glim (*dated, sl.*) to put out the light.

dovecote

to flutter the dovecotes FLUTTER.

down

down and out 1 utterly destitute and without resources. **2** in boxing, unable to continue the fight.

down under (*coll.*) (in or to) Australia or New Zealand.

down with abolish (*Down with fascism!*).

to be down on 1 to disapprove of, to be severe towards (*Why are you so down on her?*). **2** to pounce upon.

to down tools 1 to stop work. **2** to go on strike.

to have a down on (*coll.*) to have a grudge against.

to put a down on (*sl.*) to inform against.

downer

on a downer depressed, pessimistic.

downgrade

on the downgrade (*N Am.*) in decline.

doze

to doze off to fall into a light sleep.

dozen

a dime a dozen DIME.

baker's dozen BAKER.

by the dozen in large numbers (*She smokes cigarettes by the dozen*).

daily dozen DAILY.

six (of one) and half a dozen (of the other) SIX.

to talk nineteen to the dozen TALK.

drab

dribs and drabs DRIB.

drag

to drag in to introduce (a subject) gratuitously or irrelevantly.

to drag one's feet/ heels (*coll.*) to go slowly deliberately (*The government is dragging its feet on tax reform*).

to drag out to make (something) last longer than necessary.

to drag something out of someone to get information from someone with difficulty.

to drag through the mud to disgrace publicly, to denigrate.

to drag up 1 (*coll.*) to mention (an unpleasant event or story). **2** (*coll.*) to bring up or rear in a careless fashion (*Where were you dragged up?*).

to look as if one has been dragged through a hedge backwards (*coll.*) to look untidy or dishevelled.

dragon

to chase the dragon CHASE.

drain

brain drain BRAIN.

down the drain (*coll.*) wasted (*two days' work down the drain*).

to laugh like a drain LAUGH.

drake

to play ducks and drakes with DUCK.

draught

on draught (of beer) able to be obtained by drawing off from a cask.

to feel the draught FEEL.

draw

quick on the draw QUICK.

the luck of the draw LUCK.

to draw and quarter (*Hist.*) to disembowel and dismember after hanging, as a penalty (*hung, drawn and quartered*).

to draw a veil/ curtain over 1 to conceal discreetly. **2** to refrain from mentioning.

to draw away to get further in front.

to draw back 1 to move back. **2** to withdraw; to be unwilling to fulfil a promise.

to draw in 1 to involve (*If they start fighting, don't get drawn in*). **2** to entice, to inveigle. **3** (of days) to close in, to shorten. **4** (of a train) to arrive at a station.

to draw near/ nigh to approach (*Christmas is drawing near*).

to draw off 1 to withdraw, to retire, to retreat. **2** to rack (wine etc.).

to draw on 1 to lead to as a consequence. **2** to allure, to attract, to entice. **3** to approach. **4** to put on (clothes or shoes). **5** to make use of (*The book draws on her experience as a psychologist*).

to draw out 1 to lengthen, to protract (*long-drawn-out negotiations*). **2** to set in order for battle. **3** to induce to talk; to elicit. **4** to write out. **5** (of days) to become longer. **6** (of a train) to leave the station.

to draw over 1 to bring over. **2** to induce to change parties.

to draw rein/ bridle 1 to stop one's horse, to pull up. **2** to abandon an effort, enterprise etc.

to draw up 1 to compose. **2** to put into proper form. **3** to put (oneself) into a stiff erect attitude (*She drew herself up to her full height*). **4** to come to a stop. **5** to range in order, or in line of battle.

to draw up with to gain on, to overtake.

to hold to a draw to draw with (an opponent), esp. against expectation.

drawer¹

bottom drawer BOTTOM.

out of the top drawer TOP¹.

top drawer TOP¹.

drawer²

hewers of wood and drawers of water HEWER.

refer to drawer REFER.

drawing board

back to the drawing board back to start again after an unsuccessful attempt (*Our original idea was rejected and we had to go back to the drawing board*).

dream

beyond one's wildest dreams WILD.
like a dream very smoothly; very successfully (*It all went like a dream*).
pipe dream PIPE.
to dream away to spend (time) idly.
to dream up (*coll.*) to invent (an idea or excuse).

dredge

to dredge up 1 to lift with a dredge. **2** to find or reveal (something previously obscure or well hidden).

dree

to dree one's weird (*Sc.*) to abide by one's lot.

dreg

not a dreg not a drop, not the least part (left).
to drain/ drink to the dregs to enjoy to the full.

dress

dressed to kill dressed to be as attractive as possible.
dressed up like a dog's dinner dressed too flamboyantly.
dressed (up) to the nines (*coll.*) very smartly or glamorously dressed. [The phrase 'to the nines' may be a corruption of 'to then eyne', meaning 'to the eyes'.]
to dress down 1 (*coll.*) to chastise, to reprimand severely. **2** (*coll.*) to dress casually or informally.
to dress to death (*dated*) to overdress.
to dress up 1 to clothe elaborately. **2** to invest with a fictitious appearance (*old ideas dressed up as something new*). **3** to wear fancy dress. **4** to decorate, to adorn.

drib

dribs and drabs (*coll.*) small numbers at a time (*They arrived in dribs and drabs*).

drift

to catch/ get the drift of to understand (*Do you catch my drift?*).

drill

no names, no pack drill NAME.

drink

in drink (*dated*) intoxicated.
meat and drink MEAT.
the worse for drink (*coll.*) drunk.
to drink deep 1 to take a long draught. **2** to drink to excess.
to drink down 1 to destroy the memory of by drinking. **2** to beat (someone) in drinking.
to drink in 1 to absorb readily; to receive greedily, as with the senses. **2** to gaze upon, listen to etc. with delight (*drinking in her every word*).
to drink like a fish to drink to excess.
to drink off to swallow at a single draught.
to drink someone under the table to drink as much as or more than someone else but remain comparatively sober while the other person gets completely drunk.
to drink the health of to wish health to in drinking, to toast.
to drink to to salute or wish health to in drinking, to toast.
to drink up to swallow completely.

dripping

to be dripping with to have a large number or amount of.

drive

to drive a coach and horses through (*coll.*) to demolish (an argument or idea) by pointing out the obvious faults.
to drive a good bargain to make a good deal or agreement.

to drive a hard bargain to insist on advantageous terms that are hard for the other party to accept in a deal or agreement.

to drive at (*fig.*) to hint at, to mean (*What are you driving at?*).

to drive away 1 to force to a distance. **2** to scatter. **3** to go away in a car etc.

to drive home 1 to force (something) completely in (*I drove the nail home*). **2** to explain (something) emphatically and make sure it is understood (*in an attempt to drive the message home*).

to drive in 1 to hammer in. **2** (*Mil.*) to force to retreat on their supports.

to drive into a corner to force into a situation from which there is no escape.

to drive off 1 to compel to move away. **2** †to put off, to defer.

to drive out 1 to expel; to oust. **2** to take the place of. **3** (*Print.*) to space widely.

to drive to distraction to cause intense irritation to (*His ceaseless prattle drove us to distraction*).

to drive to drink (*coll.*) to annoy or frustrate intensely (*It's enough to drive you to drink!*).

to drive up the wall (*coll.*) to madden, to annoy greatly.

driver

back-seat driver BACK SEAT.
in the driver's seat in control.

driving

in the driving seat in control.
to be the driving force behind something to initiate or encourage some plan or enterprise.

drop

a drop in the ocean/bucket a very small or insignificant amount. [From the Bible: "Behold, the nations are as a drop of a bucket, and are counted as the small dust of the balance" (Isa. xl.15).]

at the drop of a hat immediately.

drop dead! (*sl.*) used to express contempt or dismissal.

drop-dead gorgeous (*sl.*) stunningly attractive.

drop it! (*sl.*) stop doing, or talking about, that!

fit/ ready to drop completely exhausted.

to drop a brick to say the wrong thing, to commit a blunder.

to drop a clanger to make a conspicuous mistake or blunder.

to drop a curtsy to curtsy.

to drop a hint to make a seemingly casual suggestion.

to drop anchor to let down the anchor.

to drop asleep to fall asleep.

to drop astern 1 to move or pass towards the stern. **2** to reduce speed so as to allow another to pass ahead.

to drop a stitch in knitting, to let a stitch fall off the end of the needle.

to drop away 1 to depart. **2** to desert a cause (*Support began to drop away*).

to drop back/ behind to fall behind, to be overtaken.

to drop back into to revert to (a former habit).

to drop down to descend a hill.

to drop in/ by 1 to make an informal visit. **2** to call unexpectedly.

to drop into 1 (*coll.*) to make an informal visit to (a place). **2** (*coll.*) to develop (a habit).

to drop into someone's lap 1 to give someone responsibility for (something, a situation etc.). **2** to be obtained or achieved without effort (*He seems to expect promotion to drop into his lap*).

to drop like a hot potato to cease to have anything to do with (a person or subject that suddenly becomes risky or controversial).

to drop off 1 to decrease, to become less. **2** (*coll.*) to fall gently asleep. **3** to set down (a passenger) from a vehicle.

to drop on (*sl.*) to scold, to punish.

to drop one's aitches/ h's not to pronounce the *h* at the beginnings of words such as 'horse' and 'have'.

to drop out (*coll.*) to refuse to follow a conventional lifestyle, esp. to leave school or college early. [Popularized in the 1960s, perhaps by the words of Timothy Leary (1920–96): "Turn on, tune in and drop out."]

to drop someone a line to write someone a short letter.

to drop to (*sl.*) to become aware of.

to drop to the rear to drop back, to fall behind.

to have had a drop too much (*coll.*) to have had slightly too much to drink.

to have the drop on (*coll.*) to have an advantage over.

to let drop to disclose, seemingly without any intention of so doing (*She let drop that she was thinking of selling the house*).

drown

a drowning man will clutch at a straw/ straws a person in a desperate situation will resort to any remedy or measure, however inadequate.

like a drowned rat soaked to the skin.

to drown one's sorrows to drink alcohol in order to forget one's problems and sorrows.

to drown out 1 to drive out by a flood. **2** to overpower by a volume of sound.

drub

to drub into to instil into.

drug

drug on the market a commodity which is so common as to be unsaleable.

drum

to beat the drum for (*coll.*) to try to raise interest in. [From the former practice of beating a drum to attract attention before a public announcement.]

to drum into to instil into.

to drum out (*Mil.*) to expel from a regiment with disgrace, to cashier.

to drum up to canvass (aid or support).

drunk

drunk as a lord very drunk.

dry

dry as a bone completely dry.

dry as dust very uninteresting.

dry run 1 shooting practice without live ammunition. **2** (*coll.*) a practice run, a rehearsal.

to dry out 1 to become dry. **2** to undergo treatment for alcohol or drug abuse.

to dry up 1 to deprive totally of moisture. **2** to dry dishes after they have been washed. **3** (of moisture) to disappear. **4** to cease to flow, to cease to yield water. **5** (of an actor) to forget one's lines. **6** (*sl.*) to stop talking or doing something. **7** to deprive of energy. **8** to lose all moisture. **9** to become withered.

duck[1]

dead duck DEAD.

lame duck LAME.

like a dying duck in a thunderstorm DYING.

like water off a duck's back WATER.

to break one's duck BREAK.

to play ducks and drakes with 1 to squander. **2** to throw into confusion. [From a game that involves skimming flat stones across the surface of a stretch of water.]

to take to (something) like a duck to water to discover a natural aptitude for (something).

duck[2]

to duck out of (*coll.*) to dodge (a responsibility etc.).

duckling

ugly duckling UGLY.

dudgeon
in high dudgeon HIGH.

due
due to because of.

in due course when the right time comes.

to fall/ become due to become payable; to mature as a bill.

to give someone their due to be fair to someone.

to give the devil his due DEVIL.

to pay one's dues 1 to fulfil one's obligations. **2** to achieve success after enduring a period of hardship.

duff¹
up the duff (*Austral., sl.*) pregnant. [A duff is a large round pudding.]

duff²
to duff up to beat up.

Duke Humphrey
to dine with Duke Humphrey DINE.

dull
dull as ditchwater very uninteresting or unentertaining.

to dull the edge of to make less intense.

dumb
to dumb down (*sl.*) to bring or come down to a lower level of understanding.

to strike dumb STRIKE.

dummy
to dummy up (*N Am., sl.*) to say nothing.

to sell a dummy SELL.

dump
to dump on (*esp. N Am.*) to treat badly.

dumps
(down) in the dumps low-spirited, depressed.

duplicate
in duplicate in the original plus a copy.

duration
for the duration (*sl.*) so long as a situation or war lasts (*evacuated to the countryside for the duration*).

dust
dry as dust DRY.

in the dust 1 humiliated. **2** dead.

like gold dust GOLD DUST.

not to see (someone) for dust to be suddenly left abandoned by (someone) (*Mention the word 'marriage' and you won't see him for dust!*).

to bite the dust BITE.

to dust down 1 to dust off. **2** (*coll.*) to scold, to reprimand.

to dust off 1 to remove dust from. **2** to reuse (an old idea or plan).

to dust someone's jacket to give someone a beating.

to kick up/ raise a dust to make a disturbance.

to kiss the dust KISS.

to lick the dust LICK.

to shake the dust off one's feet SHAKE.

to throw dust in the eyes of to mislead, to deceive, to delude.

to turn to dust and ashes to become utterly worthless or destroyed (*All our hopes turned to dust and ashes*).

when the dust settles when a situation calms down.

dusty
not so dusty (*sl.*) pretty good.

Dutch
double Dutch DOUBLE.

Dutch courage false courage, esp. inspired by alcohol. [The use of the word Dutch in a derogatory manner, often to describe something that is not what it seems, dates from the Anglo-Dutch wars of the 17th century.]

Dutch treat (*coll.*) an outing with each person paying their own share.

Dutch uncle a person who criticizes in a stern, blunt manner. [The Dutch have a reputation for strict discipline.]

to go Dutch to share the cost of a meal, etc.

Dutchman

I'm a Dutchman 1 used to express denial or disbelief (*If that is justice, then I'm a Dutchman!*). **2** used to add emphasis (*It'll rain tomorrow, or I'm a Dutchman!*).

duty

off duty not engaged in one's appointed duties.

on duty engaged in performing one's appointed duties.

to do duty for 1 to serve in lieu of someone or something else. **2** to serve as a makeshift for.

dwell

to dwell on/ upon 1 to think for a long time or continually about (something unpleasant). **2** to speak or write at length about. **3** to prolong (a sound).

dye

dyed-in-the-wool fixed in one's opinions (*a dyed-in-the-wool conservative*). [From the practice of dying wool before spinning to give a more permanent result.]

of the deepest dye DEEP.

dying

like a dying duck in a thunderstorm very weak or woebegone.

to be dying for/ to do something to be eager for/ to do something (*I'm dying for a drink*).

to one's dying day for the rest of one's life.

E

eager

eager beaver (*coll.*) a person who is always active or eager for work.

eagle

eagle eye sharp sight, watchfulness.

ear

easy on the ear EASY.

from ear to ear very broadly (*smiling from ear to ear*).

head and ears HEAD[1].

in one ear and out the other heard but making no lasting impression (*My advice to her had obviously gone in one ear and out the other*).

music to one's ears MUSIC.

out on one's ear (*coll.*) sent away ignominiously (*If you carry on like that, you'll find yourself out on your ear!*).

over head and ears HEAD[1].

someone's ears are burning someone is being talked about. [From a superstition dating back to Roman times. A tingling sensation in the right ear is supposed to indicate that the talk is favourable; in the left ear it has the opposite meaning.]

thick ear THICK.

to be all ears (*coll.*) to listen carefully and with great interest.

to believe one's ears BELIEVE.

to bend someone's ear BEND.

to bring (down) about someone's ears to be responsible for causing (trouble etc.) to someone.

to fall by the ears to quarrel.

to fall on deaf ears DEAF.

to gain the ear of GAIN.

to give (an) ear to listen (to).

to have/ hold a wolf by the ears WOLF.

to have/ keep one's ear to the ground to be well informed about trends, rumours, opinions etc. [From a tracking technique used by American Indians etc.]

to have someone's ear to be able to speak to and influence somebody.

to lend an ear LEND.

to make a pig's ear of PIG.

to meet the ear MEET.

to pin back one's ears PIN.

to play by ear to play without reading the printed music.

to play it by ear to react to a situation by responding instinctively to events as they occur, rather than by following a plan.

to prick up one's ears PRICK.

to set by the ears to incite or cause strife between.

to stop one's ears STOP.

to turn a deaf ear to DEAF.

up to one's ears (*coll.*) completely, so as to be overwhelmed (*up to her ears in debt*).

walls have ears WALL.

wet behind the ears WET.

with a flea in one's ear FLEA.

you can't make a silk purse out of a sow's ear SILK.

early

at one's earliest convenience as soon as possible.

at the earliest not before (*next week at the earliest*).

early bird (*coll.*) a person who gets up or arrives very early.

early days 1 early in the course of something, before it is clear how it will progress (*It's early days yet*). **2** (*Austral., New Zeal.*) during the settlement period in the 19th cent.

the early bird catches the worm those who are first to do something, such as starting work or taking advantage of an opportunity, are most likely to be successful.

earnest

in earnest 1 seriously, sincerely, not jokingly (*I say this in earnest*). **2** with determination (*get down to work in earnest*).

earth

all/ the four corners of the earth FOUR.

down to earth realistic, practical, sensible.

gone to earth in hiding. [The earth of a fox or badger is the hole where it lives.]

heaven on earth HEAVEN.

like nothing on earth NOTHING.

off/ from the face of the earth FACE.

on earth 1 (*after interrogatives, coll.*) used as an intensifier (*What on earth are you doing?*). **2** (*after superlatives, coll.*) in the world, of all (*the greatest show on earth*).

the salt of the earth SALT.

to come/ bring (back) down to earth to return/ cause to return to reality from daydreams or fantasy.

to/ from the ends of the earth END.

to move heaven and earth MOVE.

to pay the earth (*coll.*) to pay an excessive amount (*She must have paid the earth for that jacket*).

earthly

not an earthly (*coll.*) not a chance.

ease

at (one's) ease in a state free from anything likely to disturb, annoy or cause anxiety.

ill at ease ILL.

to ease off/ down/ away 1 (*Naut.*) to slacken (a rope etc.) gradually. **2** to become less oppressive (*The pain eased off*).

to ease oneself (*dated*) to urinate or defecate.

to set at ease 1 to relieve of anxiety, fear, bashfulness etc. **2** to make comfortable.

to stand at ease (*Mil.*) to stand with the legs apart and hands behind the back.

easy

easier said than done more difficult than it sounds.

easy ahead! move or steam at a moderate speed.

easy as pie/ winking/ falling off a log (*coll.*) very easy.

easy come, easy go what is obtained easily is just as easily spent or lost.

easy does it! move or go gently.

easy game/ meat/ prey (*coll.*) someone or something that is easily beaten or defeated.

easy mark (*dated, coll.*) a gullible person.

easy money (*coll.*) money acquired without much effort.

easy of access easy to get to or into.

easy on the eye/ ear agreeable to look at/ listen to.

Easy Street (*coll.*) a position of financial good fortune or security.

I'm easy (*coll.*) I have no particular preference or strong opinion.

of easy virtue (of a woman) promiscuous.

eat

eat, drink and be merry (for tomorrow we die) one should enjoy oneself while one can. [From the Bible, where parts of this phrase appear in at least four places, e.g. "Soul, thou hast much goods laid up for many years; take thine ease, eat, drink, and be merry" (Luke xii.19) and "Let us eat and drink; for tomorrow we shall die" (Isa. xxii.13).]

I'll eat my hat (*coll.*) used to express confidence that one's prediction will not prove mistaken (*If they're not divorced by this time next year, I'll eat my hat*).

the proof of the pudding is in the eating PROOF.

to eat away 1 to destroy. **2** to rust, to corrode.

to eat crow (*dated, coll.*) to (be made to) humiliate or abase oneself. [From an incident in the early 19th cent. when an American out hunting brought down a crow on British territory. A British officer took the man's gun and forced him to take a bite from the bird. By way of revenge, once his gun had been returned to him, the American made the officer eat the remainder of the crow.]

to eat dirt 1 to put up with insult and abuse without retaliation. **2** (*N Am.*) to make an embarrassing confession.

to eat humble pie 1 to apologize humbly. **2** to submit oneself to humiliation or insult. [Humble pie was made from the umbles (or entrails) of a deer and given to the menials at hunting feasts.]

to eat in to eat at home or where one is staying.

to eat into 1 to corrode. **2** to use time or resources, so reducing the amount available (*The running costs are eating into my savings*).

to eat like a horse (*coll.*) to eat a lot.

to eat one's heart out 1 to pine away. **2** to be extremely envious.

to eat one's words to retract what one has said.

to eat out to eat in a restaurant, café or hotel.

to eat out of house and home to cause

(someone) financial hardship or other problems by consuming all they have.

to eat out of someone's hand to be totally compliant or willing to obey a person (*She had the children eating out of her hand*).

to eat someone's salt (*dated*) to accept someone's hospitality.

to eat up 1 to eat completely, to finish. **2** to consume in (unnecessarily) large quantities. **3** to absorb.

what's eating you? (*coll.*) what's the matter?

ebb

at a low ebb LOW.

ebb and flow the continual improvement and deterioration of circumstances etc.

on the ebb 1 receding. **2** declining.

to ebb and flow 1 to rise and fall. **2** to increase and decrease; to improve and deteriorate.

eclipse

in eclipse 1 having been outshone, in decline. **2** (of a bird) having lost its distinctive plumage.

edge

on a knife-edge KNIFE-EDGE.

on edge irritable.

on the edge of very nearly (doing or being involved in).

razor's edge RAZOR.

to dull the edge of DULL.

to edge out to get rid of gradually.

to have the edge on/ over to have an advantage over (*He had the edge over his opponent*).

to set someone's teeth on edge TOOTH.

to take the edge off to weaken, to lessen the force of.

edit

to edit out to remove during editing.

eel

slippery as an eel SLIPPERY.

eff

effing and blinding swearing copiously.
[A euphemistic reference to taboo
words such as 'fuck' and 'bloody'.]

effect

for effect in order to produce a striking
impression.

in effect 1 in reality, substantially.
2 practically.

of no effect 1 without validity or force.
2 without result.

to bring/ carry into effect to accomplish.

to give effect to 1 to carry out. **2** to make
operative.

to no effect in vain, uselessly.

to take effect 1 to operate. **2** to produce
its effect (*when the anaesthetic has
taken effect*).

to that effect with that meaning or having
that result (*I've already sent her a
message to that effect*).

to the effect that such that.

with effect from taking effect from (a
specified date).

without effect invalid, without result.

effigy

to burn/ hang in effigy to burn/ hang an
image of, to show hatred, dislike or
contempt of.

egg

bad egg BAD.

chicken-and-egg CHICKEN.

curate's egg CURATE.

good egg! GOOD.

nest egg NEST.

sure as eggs is eggs SURE.

to have egg on one's face to look foolish,
to be mistaken. [Alluding either to a
messy eater or to a person who has
been pelted with raw eggs.]

to kill the goose that lays the golden eggs
KILL.

to put all one's eggs in one basket to risk
everything in a single venture.

to teach one's grandmother to suck eggs
TEACH.

**you can't make an omelette without
breaking eggs** OMELETTE.

eight

to have (had) one over the eight (*coll.*) to
be or become slightly drunk.

elbow

at one's elbow near at hand.

elbow grease (*coll.*) hard and continued
manual exercise.

elbow room ample room for action.

more power to your elbow! POWER.

not to know one's arse from one's elbow
ARSE.

out at (the) elbows 1 shabby in dress; in
needy circumstances. **2** (of a coat etc.)
worn through at the elbows, shabby.

to bend the elbow BEND.

to crook/ lift the elbow (*coll.*) to drink
alcohol.

to give someone/ get the elbow to dismiss
or reject someone/ be dismissed or
rejected.

to jog someone's elbow JOG.

to rub elbows with RUB.

up to the elbows deeply engaged in
business.

element

in one's element doing what one most
enjoys.

out of one's element in an unfamiliar
situation.

elephant

pink elephants PINK.

white elephant WHITE.

eleventh

at the eleventh hour at the last moment.
[An allusion to the parable of the
labourers in the Bible (Matt. xx.1–16).
Those who had worked all day
complained because they received the
same pay as those hired at the
eleventh hour.]

else

or else! (*coll.*) used as a threat of some unspecified punishment (*Give it back, or else!*).

embryo

in embryo 1 in the first or earliest stage. **2** in a rudimentary or undeveloped state.

eminence

†**to have the eminence of** to be better than.

employ

in the employ of employed by.

empty

on an empty stomach not having eaten recently.

enamoured

to be enamoured of/ with 1 to be in love with. **2** to be fond of (*I'm not enamoured with this job*).

end

all ends up completely.
at a loose end LOOSE.
at an end 1 finished, completed. **2** exhausted, used up.
at loose ends LOOSE.
at one's wits' end WIT¹.
at the end of one's tether at the limit of one's strength, endurance or patience. [Alluding to an animal tethered to a post, which can go no further than the length of its rope or chain.]
at the end of the day eventually and inevitably, when all is said and done.
at the sharp end SHARP END.
business end BUSINESS.
dirty/ rough end of the stick (*coll.*) the most unpleasant part of a task or deal.
end of story (*coll.*) that is all, there is no more.
end of the line/ road the point beyond which a person or thing can no longer go on or survive.

end on with the end pointing towards one.
end to end with the ends touching, lengthwise.
fag end FAG.
in the end 1 finally. **2** after all.
means to an end MEANS.
never to hear the end of HEAR.
no end (*coll.*) very much (*We had no end of trouble finding the place*).
odds and ends ODDS.
on end 1 upright, erect. **2** continuously (*for days on end*).
on one's beam-ends BEAM-ENDS.
sticky end STICKY.
the beginning of the end BEGINNING.
the end justifies the means it is acceptable to do something bad if the result is good.
the end of the world (*coll.*) a disaster (*It's not the end of the world if we miss the train*).
the thin end of the wedge THIN.
to be at/ on the receiving end RECEIVE.
to be thrown in at the deep end DEEP END.
to burn the candle at both ends BURN.
to come to a bad end to have an unpleasant or disgraceful future.
to come to an end to end, to be finished; to be exhausted.
to end it all to commit suicide.
to end up 1 to arrive at finally. **2** to become at last.
to/ from the ends of the earth to/ from the remotest parts of the earth (*I'd follow her to the ends of the earth*).
to go (in) off the deep end DEEP END.
to jump in at the deep end JUMP.
to keep one's end up (*coll.*) to continue performing effectively, esp. in a joint operation, in face of difficulties.
to make an end of to bring to a close, to finish.
to make (both) ends meet to keep expenditure within income. [Possibly referring to the ends of the financial year, or to the bottom line on both sides of an account.]

to make someone's hair stand on end HAIR.

to put an end to 1 to terminate, to stop.
2 to abolish.

to see the light at the end of the tunnel
LIGHT[1].

to that end for that purpose.

to the bitter end BITTER.

to the end of the chapter throughout, to
the end.

without end 1 everlasting. 2 very long.
3 inexhaustible.

world without end WORLD.

wrong end of the stick WRONG.

endorse

to endorse over to transfer one's rights in
(a bill etc.) to another person.

enemy

how goes the enemy? (*dated, coll.*) what
is the time? [From *The Dramatist*
(1789), a play by Frederic Reynolds.]

to be one's own worst enemy to act in a
way that is hostile to one's interests or
that contributes to one's problems.

Englishman

an Englishman's home is his castle people
may do as they like in their own
homes and have a right to privacy
there. [From the writings of Sir
Edward Coke (1552–1634): "For a
man's house is his castle."]

enjoy

to enjoy oneself (*coll.*) to experience
pleasure or happiness.

enough

enough is as good as a feast a sufficient
amount is all one needs.

enough is enough no more can be
tolerated.

enough to wake the dead (*coll.*) very loud
(*The noise you made coming in last
night was enough to wake the dead*).

to give someone enough rope to hang
themselves to allow someone enough

freedom of speech or action to commit
a blunder or cause their downfall.

to have had enough of 1 to have had
sufficient of. 2 to have had too much
of; to be tired of (*I've had quite enough
of her insolence*).

enter

to enter an appearance (*dated*) to show
oneself.

to enter into 1 to join. 2 to engage in
(conversation, dialogue etc.). 3 to
become party to (an agreement,
treaty etc.). 4 to form a part of. 5 to
sympathize with.

to enter on to begin, to set out upon.

to enter someone's head to occur as a
thought in someone's mind (*It never
entered her head that we might be
worried*).

to enter the lists to enter into a contest.
[Alluding to a piece of ground used for
a jousting tournament in former times.]

to enter up 1 to set down in a regular
series. 2 to complete a series of entries.

to enter upon 1 to begin, to set out upon.
2 to begin to treat of (a subject etc.).
3 to take legal possession of.

entirety

in its entirety completely, as a whole.

envy

green with envy GREEN.

equal

to be equal to to have the courage,
intelligence etc. for.

to equal out to become equal or balanced.

equality

on an equality with on equal terms with.

err

to err on the side of to favour (a specified
side, aspect etc.) in one's actions,
often at the expense of strict accuracy
(*I erred on the side of caution in my
estimate*).

errand
fool's errand FOOL.

error
trial and error TRIAL.

erst
†at erst at earliest, at once.

escape
narrow escape NARROW.

escrow
in escrow (of a document) executed and placed in the custody of a third party.

escutcheon
blot on the escutcheon BLOT.

essence
in essence fundamentally.
of the essence of the greatest importance (*Time is of the essence*).

esteem
to hold in esteem to regard with respect or admiration (*Her work is held in high esteem*).

eternal
eternal triangle a sexual or emotional relationship involving three people, usu. two of one sex and one of the other, often resulting in tension or conflict.
the Eternal City the city of Rome.

Eve
daughter of Eve DAUGHTER.

even¹
even chance an equal likelihood of success or failure.
even money 1 evens. 2 just as likely to be or happen as not.
even Stephens a situation in which all have an equal chance of winning (*As they entered the last stage of the contest, it was even Stephens*). [The name Stephen was once a slang term for 'money', but in this phrase it is probably no more than a rhyme for 'even'.]
odd or even ODD.
on an even keel 1 (*Naut.*) (of a ship) drawing the same water fore and aft. 2 (of a person) well-balanced, emotionally, mentally or financially. 3 (of a situation) stable or calm.
to be even with to be quits with.
to even out to make or become even or level.
to even up to balance, to make or become equal, to bring or come up to the same level.
to get even with to revenge oneself on.

even²
even as at the very same time that (*even as we speak*).
even now 1 at this very moment. 2 now and before.
even so 1 exactly; yes. 2 nevertheless. 3 in that case also.
even though in spite of the fact that.

event
at all events in any case, whatever happens.
happy event HAPPY.
in any event in any case, whatever happens.
in the event 1 as it turns out, or turned out. 2 if it should so turn out.
in the event of if (the specified thing) occurs (*in the event of an accident*).
in the event that if it turns out that.
wise after the event WISE¹.

ever
did you ever? (*coll.*) did you ever see or hear anything like this?
ever after continually after a certain time (*live happily ever after*).
ever and anon now and then, at one time and another.

ever since continually since a certain time (*She's been afraid of water ever since*).

ever so to any degree or extent conceivable (*It's ever so easy*).

ever such a (*coll. or dial.*) a very (*ever such a nice person*).

for ever and ever for all future time.

every

every last the total number of (*every last drop of water*).

every now and again/ then from time to time.

every one each one.

every other every alternate (day, week etc.) (*She visits her parents every other Sunday*).

every so often occasionally, intermittently (*Every so often we meet for a drink*).

every which way 1 (*N Am., coll.*) in all directions or ways. **2** (*N Am., coll.*) in a disorderly fashion.

everything

everything comes to him who waits patience will be rewarded.

to have everything (*coll.*) to have every advantage, wealth, attractiveness etc.

evidence

in evidence 1 received or offered as tending to establish a fact or allegation in a court of law (*used in evidence against you*). **2** (*coll.*) plainly visible, conspicuous.

evil

evil days a period of misfortune (*They had fallen on evil days*).

evil eye 1 a look or glance believed to have the power to bewitch, injure or kill (*to give someone the evil eye*). **2** the power to bewitch etc. in this way.

to put off the evil hour to postpone doing something unpleasant.

ewe

ewe lamb (*fig.*) a dearest possession.

[From the Bible: "the poor man had nothing, save one little ewe lamb" (II Sam. xii.3).]

exactly

not exactly 1 (*iron.*) not at all (*It's not exactly my idea of a relaxing holiday*). **2** not precisely.

examiner

to satisfy the examiners SATISFY.

example

for example as an illustration.

to make an example of to punish as a deterrent to others.

excel

to excel oneself to do better than one (or others) had thought possible.

exception

the exception that proves the rule something that shows a rule to be valid because the rule applies in most other cases. [From the legal principle "the exception proves the rule in cases not excepted".]

to take exception 1 to object, to find fault (*They took exception to the way we were dressed*). **2** to express disapproval.

with the exception of omitting, not including.

excess

in excess of more than.

to/ in excess more than is normal or proper (*drinking to excess*).

exchange

fair exchange is no robbery FAIR.

in exchange (for) as something exchanged (for), in return (for).

to exchange blows/ words to quarrel physically/ verbally, to have a fight/ an argument.

exclusion
to the exclusion of so as to exclude.

excursion
alarums and excursions ALARUM.

excuse[1]
to be excused (*euphem.*) to go to the lavatory.
to excuse oneself 1 to (try to) justify one's actions. 2 to ask permission to leave.

excuse[2]
excuse for (*coll.*) a bad example of, a botched attempt at (*What sort of an excuse for a meal do you call this?*).

exercise
object of the exercise OBJECT.

exert
to exert oneself to strive, to use effort.

exhibition
to make an exhibition of oneself to behave so as to appear foolish or contemptible.

expect
expect me when you see me (*coll.*) said when someone is unable or unwilling to specify a time of arrival or return.

expense
at the expense of 1 at the cost of. 2 to the discredit or detriment of (*at the expense of her health*).

explain
to explain away 1 to get rid of (difficulties) by explanation. 2 to modify or do away with (a charge etc.) by explanation.
to explain oneself 1 to make one's meaning clear. 2 to give an account of one's motives, intentions, conduct etc.

expose
to expose oneself 1 to display one's genitals in public so as to shock or embarrass others, usu. for sexual gratification. 2 to reveal one's faults, weaknesses etc.

express
to express oneself to declare one's opinions or feelings in words (well, strongly etc.).

extend
to extend a welcome (to) to welcome cordially.

extreme
in the extreme 1 in the highest degree. 2 extremely (*His manner was unpleasant in the extreme*).
to go to extremes to resort to the most severe or drastic measures.
to take something to extremes to do something in a way that exceeds normal limits.
to the other extreme to the opposite opinion, course of action etc. (*There's no need to go to the other extreme*).

eye
all my eye (and Betty Martin) nonsense, rubbish. [Possibly a corruption of the phrase *O mihi, beate Martine* (an invocation to St Martin), heard by British sailors abroad and introduced into the English language in garbled form, perhaps influenced by the name of an 18th-century actress.]
an eye for an eye (and a tooth for a tooth) strict retaliation. [From the Bible: "Ye have heard that it hath been said, An eye for an eye, and a tooth for a tooth" (Matt. v.38), referring to Exod. xxi.24 and Deut. xix.21.]
apple of someone's eye APPLE.
beauty is in the eye of the beholder BEAUTY.
before one's (very) eyes right in front of one, in plain view.
bird's-eye view BIRD'S-EYE.

eagle eye EAGLE.

easy on the eye EASY.

evil eye EVIL.

eyes front (*Mil.*) turn your head and eyes to the front.

eyes in the back of one's head an ability to see in all directions at once (*You need to have eyes in the back of your head with these kids!*).

eyes left (*Mil.*) turn your head and eyes to the left.

eyes right (*Mil.*) turn your head and eyes to the right.

glad eye GLAD.

green in one's eye GREEN.

half an eye HALF.

in a pig's eye PIG.

in one's mind's eye MIND.

in the eye(s) of 1 in the regard, estimation or judgement of. 2 from the point of view of (*in the eyes of the law*).

in the public eye PUBLIC.

in the twinkling of an eye TWINKLE.

in the wind's eye WIND[1].

mind your eye MIND.

more than meets the eye MEET.

mud in your eye! MUD.

my eye! (*sl.*) used to express astonishment or disbelief.

one in the eye ONE.

out of the corner of one's eye CORNER.

roving eye ROVING.

sheep's eyes SHEEP.

someone's eyes are bigger than their stomach/ belly said when someone takes more food than they can eat.

the naked eye NAKED.

the scales fall/ are removed from someone's eyes SCALE[1].

to be all eyes (*coll.*) to watch intently.

to believe one's eyes BELIEVE.

to cast an eye over CAST.

to catch someone's eye CATCH.

to close one's eyes CLOSE[2].

to close/ shut one's eyes to to refuse or pretend not to see.

to do someone in the eye to defraud someone.

to eye askance to look at with suspicion or distrust.

to eye up (*coll.*) to assess visually, esp. admiringly.

to feast one's eyes on FEAST.

to get one's eye in to gain skill or proficiency.

to give someone the glad eye GLAD.

to have an eye for 1 to pay due regard to. 2 to appreciate. 3 to be on the lookout for (*have an eye for a bargain*).

to have an eye to to have as one's objective.

to have eyes for to be interested in (*He only had eyes for his fiancée*).

to have one's eye on to watch; to have designs on.

to have the sun in one's eyes SUN.

to hit someone between the eyes/ in the eye HIT.

to keep an eye on to watch carefully (*I hope you're keeping an eye on the time*).

to keep an eye open/ out to keep a lookout (for).

to keep a/ one's weather eye open WEATHER.

to keep one's eye in to retain skill or proficiency.

to keep one's eyes open/ peeled/ skinned to watch carefully; to be careful.

to leap to the eye LEAP.

to lower one's eyes LOWER.

to make eyes at to regard amorously.

to meet someone's eye MEET.

to meet the eye MEET.

to open someone's eyes OPEN.

to pass one's eye over to skim over, to read quickly.

to pipe one's eye PIPE.

to pull the wool over someone's eyes WOOL.

to put someone's eye out to make someone jealous.

to raise one's eyes RAISE.

to see eye to eye to be in complete agreement (with) (*The Prime Minister and the Chancellor are rumoured not to see eye to eye on tax reform*).

to see with half an eye HALF.

to set/ lay/ clap eyes on to see (*I've never clapped eyes on him before*).

to take one's eyes off to look away from, to take one's attention off (*I daren't take my eyes off her for a second*).

to throw dust in the eyes of DUST.

to turn a blind eye to BLIND.

to view with a friendly eye VIEW.

to view with a jealous eye VIEW.

to wipe one's eyes WIPE.

to wipe the eye of WIPE.

under the eye of watched or supervised by.

up to the eyes deeply or completely immersed (in debt etc.).

with one eye on directing part of one's mind to (*We had to work with one eye on the clock*).

with one eye shut without needing to pay much attention (*I could do that with one eye shut*).

with one's eyes on stalks (*coll.*) staring in astonishment or anticipation.

with one's eyes open aware of all the facts.

with one's eyes shut 1 not aware of all the facts. 2 very easily, without having to pay much attention (*She could do a job like that with her eyes shut*).

eyeball

eyeball to eyeball (of discussions etc.) at close quarters, face to face.

up to the eyeballs (*coll.*) deeply or completely immersed (in work etc.).

eyebrow

to raise an eyebrow RAISE.

to raise one's eyebrows RAISE.

eyelash

by an eyelash by a small margin.

to flutter one's eyelashes at FLUTTER.

eye-tooth

to cut one's eye-teeth to become worldly wise.

to give one's eye-teeth (*coll.*) to be willing to exchange or sacrifice anything one has in order to have or do something (*I'd give my eye-teeth for a figure like that!*).

F

face

black in the face BLACK.

face as long as a fiddle a sad, dismal face (*sitting there with a face as long as a fiddle*).

face down(wards)/ up(wards) with the face or front pointing downwards/ upwards.

face to face (with) 1 in someone's or each other's actual presence (*We came face to face with the enemy*). **2** opposite; in confrontation. **3** clearly, without anything interposed.

face value 1 the nominal value shown on coins, banknotes etc. **2** the apparent value or meaning of anything (*I took his remark at face value*).

in full face FULL.

in (the) face of 1 in spite of. **2** when encountering.

in your face (*sl.*) offering a direct challenge, aggressively provocative.

left/ right face (*Mil.*) turn left/ right without moving from the same position.

let's face it (*coll.*) let us look at the matter honestly and realistically (*Let's face it, he's not exactly our best player*).

long face LONG.

loss of face LOSS.

not just a pretty face PRETTY.

off/ from the face of the earth completely, altogether (*My calculator has disappeared from the face of the earth*).

on the face of it to judge by appearances.

plain as the nose on your face PLAIN.

slap in the face SLAP.

someone's face falls someone shows disappointment (*Her face fell when she heard the news*).

someone's face is their fortune said of a person whose good looks are their best asset.

to be staring someone in the face STARE.

to cut off one's nose to spite one's face NOSE.

to face down 1 to confront sternly or defiantly. **2** to force to give way.

to face off 1 to drop the puck or ball to start or restart a game of ice hockey or lacrosse. **2** to have a confrontation.

to face out to carry off by boldness or effrontery (*I tried to face it out*).

to face (the) facts to confront or acknowledge the unpleasant truth.

to face the music to suffer the unpleasant consequences of something, esp. punishment or criticism. [Possibly of theatrical or military origin.]

to face up to to meet courageously.

to fly in the face of FLY².

to have egg on one's face EGG.

to have the face to be impudent, cool or composed enough (to) (*She had the face to tell me I was wrong*).

to laugh in someone's face LAUGH.

to laugh on the other side of one's face LAUGH.

to lose face LOSE.

to make/ pull a face 1 to distort the features. **2** to grimace.

to put a bold/ brave/ good face on 1 to make the best of, to pretend that one is not unduly upset by. **2** to adopt a confident air.

to put a new face on NEW.

to put one's face on (*coll.*) to put on make-up.

to save (one's) face SAVE.

to set one's face against to oppose, to withstand firmly.

to show one's face to appear (*if she ever shows her face in here again*).

to shut one's face SHUT.

to someone's face **1** openly. **2** in plain words (*They told me to my face that I was incompetent*).

to wipe the smile off someone's face WIPE.

until one is blue in the face BLUE.

was someone's face red! someone was very embarrassed.

fact

as a matter of fact MATTER.

before/ after the fact before/ after the actual committing of a crime (*an accessory after the fact*).

facts of life **1** the details of esp. human reproduction. **2** the (often unpleasant) realities of a situation.

in (point of) fact in reality, actually; independently of theory or argument.

to face (the) facts FACE.

fade

to do a fade (*sl.*) to go away, to leave.

to fade away **1** to fade. **2** (*coll.*) to grow very thin.

to fade in/ out to cause (sound or a picture) to appear/ disappear gradually.

fag

fag end **1** (*coll.*) a cigarette butt. **2** the unimportant or worthless remaining part of anything. **3** (*Naut.*) the fringed or untwisted end of a rope. **4** the loose end of a web of cloth, generally of coarser texture.

fagged out exhausted.

fail

without fail certainly, assuredly, in spite of all hindrances.

faint

not to have the faintest (idea) (*coll.*) not to know at all (*I haven't the faintest idea what she meant*).

fair

all's fair in love and war any tactic is legitimate in situations involving emotion or conflict.

by fair means or foul by any means whatsoever.

fair and square **1** honourable, straightforward, above board. **2a** fairly, honestly, without trickery or deceit. **2b** exactly on target.

fair cop (*coll.*) a justified arrest (*It's a fair cop!*).

fair dinkum **1** (*Austral., New Zeal., coll.*) fair, genuine. **2** (*Austral., New Zeal., coll.*) fair play.

fair dos (*coll.*) fair play, equal shares etc., fair treatment.

fair enough (*coll.*) (indicating at least partial assent to a proposition, terms etc.) all right, OK.

fair exchange is no robbery neither party loses when things of equal value are exchanged.

fair game a legitimate target for attack, criticism or ridicule. [The phrase originally referred to birds and animals that could be lawfully hunted.]

fair play reasonable behaviour; just or equal conditions for all.

fair's fair (*coll.*) used as a protest or reminder that everyone is entitled to fair or equal treatment.

fair to middling (*coll.*) not bad, about average.

fair-weather friend a friend who is present only in times of prosperity and cannot be relied on in times of need.

for fair (*N Am., sl.*) absolutely.

to be in a fair way to stand a good chance.

to give someone a fair show to let someone have a chance.

fairness

in all fairness 1 it is only right or just that. **2** being strictly honest.

faith

in faith in truth.
in good faith GOOD.
on the faith of 1 in reliance on. **2** on the warrant of.
to keep faith with to be loyal to.

faithfully

yours faithfully a conventional way of ending a formal or business letter.

fall

pride goes before a fall PRIDE.
to fall about (*coll.*) to laugh hysterically.
to fall among to come among accidentally (*He fell among thieves*).
to fall apart/ to pieces to become unstitched, unstuck etc., to break or separate into parts or fragments; to collapse.
to fall astern (*Naut.*) to drop behind.
to fall away 1 to extend or slope downwards. **2** to become few or thin. **3** to decay, to languish. **4** to desert, to revolt; to abandon one's principles.
to fall back to recede, to give way.
to fall back on to have recourse to.
to fall behind 1 to be passed by, to lag behind (*She began to fall behind in her schoolwork*). **2** to become in arrears (with).
to fall down 1 to be thrown down, to drop. **2** to collapse. **3** to prostrate oneself. **4** to fail, to be inadequate.
to fall down on to fail to carry out.
to fall for 1 (*coll.*) to be impressed by; to fall in love with. **2** to be fooled by.
to fall from to drop away from, to desert, to forsake.
to fall in 1 (*Mil.*) to take one's place in line. **2** to give way inwards. **3** to become due. **4** to become the property of a person by expiration of time. **5** to run out, to lapse.

to fall into to come into the range of; to be classed with.
to fall in with 1 to meet with accidentally. **2** to agree to, to concur in. **3** to coincide with.
to fall off 1 to decrease in quality, quantity or amount; to become depreciated (*Orders began to fall off*). **2** to withdraw, to recede. **3** to prove faithless; to revolt. **4** (of a ship) to fail to keep its head to the wind.
to fall on/ upon 1 (of the eyes, glance etc.) to alight on, to be directed towards. **2** to attack. **3** to meet or discover by chance.
to fall out 1 to happen, to turn out. **2** to quarrel. **3** (of the hair etc.) to become separate from the body. **4** (*Mil.*) to leave the ranks.
to fall over 1 to tumble or be knocked down. **2** to trip or stumble over.
to fall over oneself 1 (*coll.*) to be eager or overeager (to do something) (*They were falling over themselves to help*). **2** (*coll.*) to stumble clumsily.
to fall through to fail, to come to nothing (*Our plans fell through*).
to fall to to begin hastily or eagerly, to set to, e.g. to begin eating.
to fall under 1 to be subject to. **2** to come within the range of; to be classed with or reckoned with or under.
to fall within to be included in.
to ride for a fall RIDE.
to try a fall TRY.

false

false alarm a needless warning; a cause of unnecessary anxiety or excitement.
false pretences (*Law*) misrepresentations made with intent to deceive or defraud.
false start 1 a disallowed start to a race, usu. caused by a competitor moving away too early. **2** an unsuccessful beginning to any activity.

false colours

to sail under false colours SAIL.

under false colours falsely. [False colours are flags to which a ship has no right, raised to deceive an enemy.]

familiarity

familiarity breeds contempt 1 a long relationship can lead to disrespect. **2** one often fails to appreciate the things one knows best.

family

in a family way 1 in a domestic way. **2** without ceremony.

in the family way pregnant.

the bosom of one's family BOSOM.

to keep something in the family to ensure that something, e.g. a possession or piece of information, does not pass outside the family or a select group.

famous

famous last words (*coll.*) what has just been said is likely to be proved wrong (*I'll never make that mistake again – famous last words!*).

fan

to fan out to radiate outwards in a fan shape, to move off in divergent directions.

to fan the flames to exacerbate a difficult situation.

when the shit hits the fan SHIT.

fancy

fancy man 1 (*sl., derog.*) a woman's lover. **2** a prostitute's pimp, a ponce.

fancy that! used to express surprise or disbelief.

fancy woman (*sl., derog.*) a mistress.

footloose and fancy free FOOTLOOSE.

to fancy one's chances to be (unduly) confident of success.

to fancy oneself to have an excessively high opinion of oneself or one's abilities (*He fancies himself as a philosopher*).

to take a fancy to to develop a liking or an affection for, to desire.

to take someone's fancy to attract or appeal to someone.

to tickle someone's fancy TICKLE.

Fanny

(sweet) Fanny Adams (*sl.*) nothing at all. [From the name of a young girl murdered in 1867, whose body was cut up into small pieces. The name was subsequently applied, with macabre humour, to tinned meat issued to the Royal Navy. It is now used as a euphemism for 'fuck all'.]

fantastic

to trip the light fantastic TRIP.

far

a far cry 1 a long way off (from). **2** something very different (from) (*a far cry from the reforms promised in their manifesto*).

as/ so far as 1 to the distance of (a certain point). **2** to the extent that (*as far as I know*).

by far in a very great measure; very greatly, exceedingly.

far and near everywhere.

far and wide over a large number of places; everywhere (*We searched far and wide*).

far be it from me I would not even consider; I am very reluctant (to do something).

far from 1 anything but, not at all. **2** (*followed by pres.p.*) used to indicate that the speaker's actions or intentions are the opposite of those stated (*Far from being pleased with this year's financial results, we are extremely disappointed*).

far from it on the contrary.

how far to what extent, distance etc.

in so/ as far as in such measure as.

so far 1 up to a specified point (*I agree with you so far*). **2** up to now.

so far so good used to express satisfaction with how something has progressed or developed up to now.

farm

to farm out 1 to delegate, to contract out. **2** to put (esp. a child) into someone's care.

fart

to fart about (*sl.*) to behave foolishly, to waste time.

farthing

not a brass farthing BRASS FARTHING.
not to give a brass farthing BRASS FARTHING.

fashion

after/ in a fashion satisfactorily, but not very well.
after the fashion of in the same way as, like.
(all shipshape and) Bristol fashion BRISTOL.
all the fashion very popular or fashionable.
in fashion popular and favoured at a particular time.
like it's going out of fashion (*coll.*) without restraint (*spending money like it's going out of fashion*).
out of fashion unpopular and disapproved of at a particular time (*It went out of fashion soon after I bought it*).
parrot-fashion PARROT.
to set the fashion to set the example in a new style of clothes or behaviour.

fast

fast and furious 1 quickly, energetically. **2** vigorous and eventful, noisy or heated.
†fast beside/ by close, very near.
not so fast! wait a minute!, slow down!
to make fast to fasten securely, to tie.
to pull a fast one (*coll.*) to trick, to deceive, to use underhand methods.

[From the game of cricket, referring to a ball bowled fast.]

fasten

to fasten on 1 to lay hold on. **2** to become aware of and concentrate (one's attention) on (something). **3** to attach (blame, responsibility, a nickname etc.) to.

fast lane

in the fast lane (*coll.*) where the pace of life is particularly fast, exciting or risky (*life in the fast lane*).

fat

a fat lot of (*coll., iron.*) not much (*That's a fat lot of good!*).
fat cat (*coll., derog.*) a very wealthy or influential person.
fat chance (*coll., iron.*) very little chance.
the fat is in the fire (*coll.*) there's going to be trouble.
to live off/ on the fat of the land LIVE[1].

fate

fate worse than death a calamitous experience (*They saved us from a fate worse than death*).
sure as fate SURE.
to seal someone's fate SEAL.

father

how's your father HOW.
like father, like son said when a boy or man behaves like his father.
the child is father of the man CHILD.
the father and mother of a very extreme example of.
the wish is father to the thought WISH.
to father on to suggest that (someone) is responsible for (*They tried to father the problem on the previous government*).

fault

at fault 1 to blame, in error. **2** at a loss, puzzled, embarrassed.

to a fault excessively (*She's conscientious to a fault*).

to find fault with to complain of, to blame, to censure, esp. in a carping manner.

favour

do me a favour! an exclamation of incredulity.

in favour 1 approved. **2** approving (*All those in favour, raise your hand*).

in favour of 1 approving, on the side of. **2** to the advantage of. **3** to the account of. **4** in preference to.

in someone's favour to someone's advantage (*The bank made an error in our favour*).

out of favour disapproved.

to curry favour CURRY.

to find favour (in the eyes of) 1 to be considered acceptable (by). **2** to be graciously received and treated (by).

without fear or favour FEAR.

fear

for fear 1 in order that not; lest. **2** in dread (that or lest).

in fear and trembling in a state of great fear.

never fear there is no need to worry or be afraid.

no fear (*coll.*) not likely; certainly not.

to put the fear of God into to make very frightened, to terrify.

without fear or favour showing no partiality.

feast

enough is as good as a feast ENOUGH.

skeleton at the feast SKELETON.

to feast one's eyes on to look at with great delight.

feather

birds of a feather (flock together) BIRD.

feather in one's cap an honour, a distinction that one can be proud of. [From a former custom among some

peoples of adding a feather to their headgear each time they killed an enemy.]

fine feathers make fine birds FINE[1].

in fine/ high feather in high spirits, elated.

light as a feather LIGHT[2].

to be spitting feathers SPITTING.

to cut a feather 1 (*Naut.*) to leave a foamy ripple, as a ship moving rapidly. **2** (*fig.*) to move briskly. **3** to make oneself conspicuous. **4** to make a fine impression.

to feather one's nest 1 to accumulate wealth for oneself. **2** to make provision for oneself.

to make the feathers fly to create a scene, to start a row.

to ruffle someone's feathers RUFFLE.

to show the white feather WHITE.

to smooth someone's (ruffled) feathers SMOOTH.

you could have knocked me down with a feather KNOCK.

feed

at feed eating, grazing.

chicken feed CHICKEN.

fed up (*coll.*) unhappy or bored (with).

off one's feed without appetite.

on the feed 1 feeding, eating. **2** (of fish) taking or looking out for food.

to be fed up (to the back teeth) with to have had more than enough of, to be sick of.

to feed down 1 to supply (material) continuously. **2** to bring down (a tool) into continuous operation. **3** (of cattle etc.) to eat away by pasturing.

to feed the fishes to be drowned.

to feed up 1 to give plenty to eat, to fatten. **2** to satiate.

feel

not to feel oneself to feel unwell.

to feel after to try to find out by the sense of touch, to search for as by groping.

to feel blue to feel depressed.

to **feel cheap** to feel ashamed or embarrassed.

to **feel for 1** to search for as by groping (*I felt for the light switch*). **2** to have sympathy or compassion for (*I feel for his wife and children*).

to **feel free** not to hesitate (to do something) (*Feel free to make yourself a cup of tea*).

to **feel like** to wish to, to be in the mood for.

to **feel one's legs** to begin to support oneself on one's legs.

to **feel one's oats** (*coll.*) to feel vitality or be full of self-esteem.

to **feel one's way** to move ahead cautiously.

to **feel out** to try to discover the opinions of, esp. indirectly, to sound out.

to **feel sick** to feel like vomiting.

to **feel small** to feel humiliated or insignificant.

to **feel someone's collar** (*dated, sl.*) to arrest someone.

to **feel something in one's bones** to have a premonition or intuition about something (*I can feel it in my bones*). [An allusion to people suffering from arthritis or rheumatism who can predict the onset of bad weather from the pain in their bones.]

to **feel strange** to feel unwell.

to **feel the draught** (*coll.*) to be aware of, or affected by, adverse (economic) conditions.

to **feel the pinch** to be affected by a lack of money.

to **feel up** (*sl.*) to touch (someone) in such a way as to arouse oneself or the other person sexually.

to **feel up to** (*coll.*) to feel able or strong enough to (*Do you feel up to coming downstairs today?*).

to **feel with** to have sympathy for.

to **feel wretched 1** to feel ill. **2** to feel embarrassed or ashamed.

to **get the feel of** to become familiar with.

feeling

hard feelings HARD.

mixed feelings MIXED.

sinking feeling SINKING.

to **relieve one's feelings** RELIEVE.

fell¹

flesh and fell FLESH.

fell²

at one fell swoop in a single action, on a single occasion. [From Shakespeare's *Macbeth*: "What! all my pretty chickens and their dam, / At one fell swoop?", referring to the murder of Macduff's wife and children.]

fellow

hail-fellow-well-met HAIL.

felony

to **compound the felony** COMPOUND.

fence

over the fence (*Austral., coll.*) unreasonable, utterly indecent.

the grass is always greener on the other side of the fence GRASS.

to **mend fences** MEND.

to **rush one's fences** RUSH.

to **sit on the fence** SIT.

fend

to **fend for** to provide or get a living for (*We were left to fend for ourselves*).

to **fend off** to ward off.

fetch

to **fetch about/ a compass** to take a circuitous route or method.

to **fetch and carry** to go to and fro with things; to perform menial tasks.

†to **fetch off** to get the better of.

to **fetch out** to bring out, to cause to appear.

to **fetch to** to revive, as from a faint.

to **fetch up 1** (*coll.*) to end up. **2** to vomit. **3** to recall, to bring to mind. **4** (*Naut.*)

to stop suddenly. **5** (*dated*) to recover, to make up (lost time etc.). **6** †to overtake. **7** (*dated, coll.*) to bring up, raise or rear (children).

fettle

in fine/ good fettle in good condition or health.

fever

fever pitch a state of extreme excitement or activity.

few

a few a small number (of).
a good few (*coll.*) a considerable number (of).
few and far between rare, occurring very infrequently.
in few (*dated*) shortly, briefly.
no fewer than as many as (a surprisingly large number).
not a few a considerable number (*There will be not a few disappointed customers*).
of few words reserved, habitually saying little (*a woman of few words*).
some few SOME.
the few 1 the minority. **2** the elect.
to have a few (*coll.*) to consume several alcoholic drinks.

fiction

truth is stranger than fiction TRUTH.

fiddle

face as long as a fiddle FACE.
fit as a fiddle FIT.
on the fiddle (*coll.*) cheating, being dishonest, falsifying accounts etc. for one's own advantage.
to fiddle about/ around 1 to tinker, to fuss (with). **2** to interfere or tamper (with).
to fiddle while Rome burns to take no action to prevent the ruin or destruction of something important. [From a story about Emperor Nero, who is said to have played his lyre while Rome burned in AD 64.]

to play first fiddle FIRST.
to play second fiddle SECOND.

field

in the field 1 working away from the office, laboratory etc. **2** campaigning.
level playing field LEVEL.
to back the field BACK.
to bet/ lay against the field to bet on one or more horses, dogs etc. against all the others in a race.
to hold the field 1 to maintain one's ground against all comers. **2** to surpass all competitors.
to keep the field to continue a campaign.
to play the field to diversify one's interests or activities, esp. not to commit oneself to a steady boyfriend or girlfriend.
to take the field 1 to commence active military operations. **2** to begin a campaign. **3** to go on to the field of play.

field day

to have a field day to take gleeful advantage (*The press will have a field day when they hear about this*).

fifth

to take the fifth 1 (*N Am.*) to exercise the right to refuse to testify against oneself, guaranteed under the Fifth Amendment of the US Constitution. **2** (*N Am., coll.*) to avoid answering a question so as not to get oneself into trouble.

fig

in full fig FULL.
in good fig in good form or condition.
to fig out/ up to make (a horse) lively.

fight

to fight a losing battle to continue to struggle or resist although defeat or failure is inevitable (*fighting a losing battle against pollution*).

to **fight back 1** to resist. **2** to counter-attack. **3** to hold back (tears, an emotion) with an effort.

to **fight down** to hold back or suppress.

to **fight for 1** to campaign or strive on behalf of. **2** to try with determination to gain or achieve (*fighting for freedom*).

to **fight (it) out** to decide (a contest or wager) by fighting.

to **fight like cat and dog** to argue constantly or fiercely.

to **fight like Kilkenny cats** to fight so violently that both parties are destroyed. [From a game played by a group of soldiers in Kilkenny. Two cats were tied together by their tails and left to fight; when an officer approached, the soldiers released the cats by cutting off their tails and explained to the officer that the cats had eaten each other.]

to **fight off** to repel.

to **fight shy of** to avoid from a feeling of mistrust, dislike or fear.

to **fight tooth and nail** to fight with all one's power.

to **fight to the finish** to continue fighting until one of the parties is killed or completely defeated.

to **fight with the gloves off** to fight or contend in earnest; to show no mercy. [An allusion to boxing without gloves.]

to **make a fight of it** to offer resistance.

to **put up a fight/ show fight** not to give in without resistance.

fighting

fighting chance a chance of success if every effort is made.

fighting fit in peak condition.

fighting cock

to **live like fighting cocks** LIVE[1].

figure

ballpark figure BALLPARK.

figure of fun a person considered as being ridiculous.

that figures! (*sl.*) that is not surprising.

to **cut a figure** to look, appear or perform in a certain style (*He cuts a bold figure*).

to **figure on** (*coll.*) to plan to; to base one's plans or calculations on, to bargain on.

to **figure out 1** to ascertain by computation. **2** to understand (*I think I've figured out why she was upset*).

to **figure up** to add up, to reckon.

to **keep one's figure** to remain slim and attractive.

to **lose one's figure** LOSE.

to **put a figure on** (*coll.*) to state the exact number or amount of.

file[1]

in file drawn up or marching in a line or lines of people one behind another.

on file preserved and catalogued for reference.

rank and file RANK.

to **file away 1** to preserve or catalogue in a file. **2** to make a mental note of. **3** (*Mil.*) to go off in a military file.

to **file off** to go off in a military file.

†to **file with** to keep pace with.

file[2]

to **file away** to remove (roughness etc.) from a surface by means of a file.

to **gnaw a file** GNAW.

fill

to **fill an order** to execute a trade order.

to **fill in 1** to complete (anything that is unfinished, such as an outline or a form). **2** (*coll.*) to provide with necessary or up-to-date information (*She filled me in on everything that had happened in my absence*). **3** to occupy (time). **4** to act as a temporary substitute (for). **5** to fill (a hole) completely. **6** (*sl.*) to beat up.

to **fill out 1** to become bigger or fatter, to become distended. **2** to enlarge. **3** (*esp. N Am.*) to complete (a form etc.).

to **fill up 1** to fill or occupy completely. **2** to complete (a form etc.). **3** to fill the petrol tank of (a car etc.). **4** to become full. **5** to make up the deficiencies in, to supply what is wanting in. **6** to supply, to discharge; to fulfil, to satisfy. **7** to stop up by filling.

to **have one's fill of** to have rather too much of.

filter

to **filter out** to remove by filtering.

to **filter through 1** to pass through in diffused or diluted form. **2** to become known by degrees.

filthy

filthy lucre 1 gain obtained by dishonest methods. **2** (*facet.*) money. [From the Bible: "A bishop then must be … not greedy of filthy lucre" (I Tim. iii.2–3).]

find

all found (of a worker's wages) with food and lodging included free.

to **find against** (*Law*) to reach a verdict on (a person), judging them to be guilty or to have lost the case.

to **find for** (*Law*) to reach a verdict on (a person), judging them to be innocent or to have won the case.

to **find in** to provide with.

to **find oneself 1** to be or perceive oneself to be (in a certain situation). **2** to be or feel as regards health (*How do you find yourself today?*). **3** to provide oneself with the necessaries of life. **4** to realize one's own capabilities or vocation.

to **find out 1** to discover. **2** to get (information). **3** to unravel, to solve. **4** to detect, to discover the dishonesty of (*afraid of being found out*).

finder

finders keepers (*coll.*) whoever finds something has the right to keep it.

fine¹

fine and dandy quite satisfactory (*That's all very fine and dandy, but how are we going to pay for it?*).

fine feathers make fine birds anyone can look impressive in elegant or expensive clothes.

not to put too fine a point on it speaking frankly (*Not to put too fine a point on it, you're fired*).

to **cut/ run it fine** to reduce to the minimum; to take a risk by allowing little margin.

to **fine down 1** to clear or to become clear of grossness, opacity or impurities. **2** to reduce and improve by the removal of superfluous matter.

to **fine up** (*Austral., coll.*) (of the weather) to become fine.

to **get something down to a fine art** to learn to do something skilfully.

fine²

in fine 1 in conclusion, in short, finally. **2** to sum up.

to **fine down/ off** to pay a fine to secure a reduction of rent.

fine-tooth comb

to **go over with a fine-tooth comb** to examine minutely, to investigate very thoroughly. [Alluding to a comb with thin teeth set close together, used to find and remove fleas from an animal's coat or lice from a person's hair.]

finger

all fingers and thumbs clumsy or awkward (*I'm all fingers and thumbs today!*).

green fingers GREEN.

not to lift/ stir a finger to do nothing, to stand idly by (*He didn't lift a finger to help*).

someone's fingers itch someone is impatient (to do something).

to **burn one's fingers/ get one's fingers burnt** BURN.

to cross one's fingers CROSS.

to get/ pull one's finger out (*sl.*) to start making an effort.

to give someone the finger to make an obscene gesture to someone, as a sign of contempt, by raising the middle finger.

to have a finger in to be concerned in or mixed up with.

to have a finger in every pie to be involved in everything.

to have light/ sticky fingers to be given to stealing.

to have more ... in one's little finger than someone has in their whole body LITTLE FINGER.

to keep one's finger on the pulse to keep up to date with developments.

to keep one's fingers crossed to hope for good luck.

to lay/ put a finger on to touch, to interfere with in the slightest (*I never laid a finger on her!*).

to let slip through one's fingers SLIP¹.

to point the finger (at) POINT.

to put one's finger on to detect or point out precisely (the cause, meaning etc.).

to put the finger on (*sl.*) to identify or inform against.

to snap one's fingers (at) SNAP.

to stick to someone's fingers STICK².

to twist/ wind/ wrap around one's little finger LITTLE FINGER.

to work one's fingers to the bone WORK.

with one's fingers in the till stealing from one's employers (*She was caught with her fingers in the till*).

fingernail

to hang on by one's fingernails HANG.

fingertip

to have at one's fingertips to know thoroughly, to be well versed in.

to the fingertips completely.

finish

to fight to the finish FIGHT.

to finish off 1 to complete. 2 to consume or use up the remainder of. 3 to kill or destroy (someone or something already wounded or facing defeat or ruin).

to finish up 1 to consume or use up entirely. 2 to arrive, come to rest or end up.

to finish with to stop one's association with.

fink

to fink out (*chiefly N Am., sl.*) to go back on something; to let someone down.

fire

baptism of fire BAPTISM.

fire away! begin!

like a house on fire HOUSE.

no smoke without fire SMOKE.

on fire 1 burning, in flames. 2 excited, ardent, eager.

out of the frying pan into the fire FRYING PAN.

the fat is in the fire FAT.

to add fuel to the fire ADD.

to be firing on all cylinders (*coll.*) to be working properly or at full strength. [An allusion to the cylinders of an internal-combustion engine.]

to catch fire CATCH.

to draw fire to attract criticism to oneself, away from someone else.

to fire away to begin, to proceed.

to fire off 1 to discharge (a firearm). 2 to shoot (a round, a shell). 3 to utter in rapid succession (*He fired off a list of names*).

to fire out to expel forcibly, to chuck out.

to fire up 1 to start up (an engine etc.). 2 to fill with enthusiasm. 3 to kindle a fire. 4 to be inflamed with passion; to be irritated.

to go through fire and water to expose oneself to all dangers.

to hang fire HANG.

to have several irons in the fire IRON.

to heap coals of fire on someone's head
HEAP.

to miss fire MISS.

to open fire OPEN.

to play with fire to expose oneself to risk.

to pull the chestnuts out of the fire
CHESTNUT.

to set fire to to set on fire.

to set on fire 1 to kindle. **2** to excite, to
inflame.

to set the heather on fire HEATHER.

to set the world/ Thames on fire to do
something remarkable or striking.

under fire 1 exposed to the enemy's
firearms. **2** exposed to one's
opponent's questions or criticism.

firing line

to be in the firing line to be at the
forefront of any activity and exposed
to greatest risk.

first

at first 1 at the beginning. **2** originally.

at first sight immediately on seeing
someone or something, as a first
impression (*love at first sight*).

at (the) first blush at the first glance; at
first sight.

first and foremost most importantly,
before everything else.

first and last essentially; generally.

first come, first served people will be
attended to in the order in which they
arrive (rather than in any other order
of precedence).

first off (*coll.*) firstly, first of all.

first or last sooner or later.

first refusal the choice or option of
refusing something before it is offered
to others (*If we decide to sell, we'll
give you first refusal*).

first thing early, as the first action of the
day; before doing other things.

first things first things must be done in
order with the most important things
first.

first up (*coll.*) first of all.

from first to last 1 throughout. **2** altogether.

from the first from the outset.

in the first instance at the first stage; in
the first place.

in the first place as the first reason or
point.

not to know the first thing about to be
entirely ignorant of (*He doesn't know
the first thing about computers*).

of the first magnitude among the best,
worst, most important etc. of its kind
(*a disaster of the first magnitude*).

of the first water of the purest or finest
quality (*a genius of the first water*).
[From a method of grading diamonds.]

to make/ get to first base (*N Am., coll.*) to
complete the initial stage in a process.
[From the game of baseball.]

to make/ get to first base (with) (*N Am.,
coll.*) to have a sexual encounter
(with), to get off (with).

to play first fiddle to take a leading part.
[Alluding to the first violin section of
an orchestra, which usually plays a
leading role.]

first hand

at first hand as the original purchaser,
owner, hearer etc.

fish

a different/ another kettle of fish KETTLE.

a pretty/ fine kettle of fish KETTLE.

big fish in a little pond BIG.

fish out of water anyone out of their
element, in a strange or bewildering
situation.

loaves and fishes LOAF.

**neither fish, flesh nor fowl/ good red
herring** nondescript; neither one thing
nor the other.

other/ bigger fish to fry other more
important matters to attend to (*I have
other fish to fry*).

queer fish QUEER.

there are (plenty) more fish in the sea
there are (plenty) more people or
things to choose from; there will be
other opportunities.

to cry stinking fish CRY.

to drink like a fish DRINK.

to feed the fishes FEED.

to fish for compliments to lead people to pay compliments.

to fish in troubled waters to become involved in a difficult or unpleasant situation in order to gain some benefit for oneself.

to fish out 1 to find and draw out (*He fished out a photograph*). **2** to ascertain by cunning enquiry.

ye gods and little fishes! GOD.

fist

hand over fist HAND.

mailed fist MAILED.

to make a good/ poor fist (*coll.*) to make a good/ poor attempt (at).

to shake one's fist SHAKE.

fit¹

fit as a fiddle in good condition, ready for anything; very fit.

fit to be tied (*coll.*) very angry.

to fit a quart into a pint pot 1 (*usu. neg.*) to cram a large amount into a small space, esp. too small a space. **2** to attempt something impossible or barely possible.

to fit in 1 to find room or time for (*I can fit you in at four o'clock*). **2** to be esp. socially accommodating or suitable.

to fit like a glove to fit perfectly in size and shape.

to fit on to try on (a garment).

to fit out to equip, to furnish with things that are necessary or suitable.

to fit up 1 to furnish with the things suitable or necessary. **2** (*sl.*) to frame, to incriminate falsely.

to see fit to think advisable (*Pay them as much as you see fit*).

fit²

by/ in fits and starts intermittently.

in fits laughing uncontrollably (*The speaker had us in fits*).

to give someone a fit (*coll.*) to surprise or shock a person.

to have a fit (*coll.*) to be very angry or shocked.

five

bunch of fives BUNCH.

nine to five NINE.

to take five (*coll.*) to take a few minutes' break.

fix

of no fixed abode (*formal*) having no regular home or address, vagrant.

to fix on to determine on; to choose, to select (*Have you fixed on a name for the baby yet?*).

to fix up 1 (*coll.*) to arrange, to organize. **2** to accommodate. **3** to assemble or construct. **4** to provide.

fizzle

to fizzle out to end in a feeble or disappointing way.

flag

to dip the flag DIP.

to flag down to signal to (a vehicle) to stop.

to hoist one's flag HOIST.

to hoist the flag HOIST.

to keep the flag flying to continue to represent or stand up for e.g. a country or principles.

to put the flags out to celebrate a triumph, success etc.

to show the flag 1 to send an official representative or military unit to a place as a courtesy or a means of asserting a claim etc. **2** (*coll.*) to put in an appearance.

to show the white flag WHITE.

to strike/ lower the flag 1 to pull the flag down in token of surrender or submission. **2** (of an admiral) to relinquish the command.

flagpole

to run (something) up the flagpole to

sound out (an idea etc.), to test reactions to (something).

flake
to flake out (*coll.*) to collapse or fall asleep from exhaustion.

flame
old flame OLD.
to fan the flames FAN.
to flame out 1 (of a jet engine) to lose power because of the extinction of the flame. **2** (*esp. N Am.*) to fail, esp. in an obvious way.
to go up in flames to be destroyed, esp. by a fierce fire.
to shoot down in flames SHOOT.

flank
in flank at the side.

flare
to flare up 1 to blaze out. **2** to become angry suddenly. **3** (of war, illness etc.) break out suddenly and intensely.

flash
flash in the pan a moment of success or brilliance that does not last and is unlikely to be repeated. [From a flash produced by the hammer of a gun on a flint which then fails to explode the powder.]
in a flash suddenly, immediately.
quick as a flash QUICK.

flat
flat as a pancake very flat.
flat broke (*coll.*) having no money, skint.
flat out at full speed, with maximum effort; using all one's resources (*working flat out to meet a deadline*).
in a flat spin in a state of agitation. [In aviation, a flat spin is a spin in which the aircraft is almost horizontal.]
that's flat! (*coll.*) that is final or irrevocable (*You're not going, and that's flat!*).
to fall flat to be unsuccessful.

flavour
flavour of the month (*often facet.*) a person or thing much in favour at a particular time. [From marketing ploys and promotions used to introduce a new flavour of ice cream or increase sales of an old one.]

flea
with a flea in one's ear (*coll.*) with a sharp or contemptuous rebuke (*The headmaster sent him away with a flea in his ear*).

flesh
flesh and blood 1 the body. **2** human nature, esp. as alive, not imaginary, or as liable to infirmities. **3** one's children or near relatives.
flesh and fell 1 the entire body. **2** completely.
in the flesh in person, in bodily form.
more than flesh and blood can stand beyond the limits of human endurance.
neither fish, flesh nor fowl/ good red herring FISH.
pound of flesh POUND[1].
the way of all flesh WAY.
the world, the flesh and the devil WORLD.
to be made flesh to become incarnate. [From the Bible: "And the Word was made flesh, and dwelt among us" (John i.14), referring to Jesus Christ.]
to be one flesh to be closely united as in marriage.
to flesh out to elaborate, to give more substance or detail to (*a document fleshing out the proposals*).
to lose flesh LOSE.
to make someone's flesh creep to arouse (a physical sense of) horror in someone. [Popularized by the Fat Boy in Charles Dickens' *The Pickwick Papers* (1837): "I wants to make your flesh creep".]
to press the flesh PRESS.
to put on flesh to grow fatter.

flex

to flex one's muscles 1 to contract the muscles, esp. of the arm, in order to display them or as a preliminary to a trial of strength. **2** (*fig.*) to put on a show of power or strength.

flick

to flick through to read through quickly or inattentively; to turn over (pages etc.) quickly.

flicker

to flicker out to die away after an unsteady brightness.

flight[1]

in the first/ top flight taking a leading position; outstanding.
to wing one's flight WING.

flight[2]

to put to flight to cause to run away or disappear.
to take (to) flight to run away, to flee.

fling

to fling away to discard, to reject.
to fling down to cast or throw to the ground; to demolish, to ruin.
to fling off 1 to abandon, discard or disown. **2** to baffle in the chase.
to fling oneself into 1 to rush into. **2** to undertake (an activity) enthusiastically.
to fling oneself on to throw oneself on the mercy of.
to fling open to throw open suddenly or violently (*I flung open the window and screamed*).
to fling out 1 to be violent or unruly. **2** to make violent or insulting remarks. **3** to utter hastily or violently.
to fling to to shut violently (*He flung the door to*).
to fling up to abandon.
to have a fling at 1 to make a passing attempt at. **2** to gibe or scoff at.

to have one's fling 1 to give oneself up to unrestrained behaviour or enjoyment. **2** to have one's own way.

flip

to flip one's lid (*sl.*) to go berserk, to lose one's self-control.
to flip over to (cause to) turn over.
to flip through to read through quickly or carelessly.

flirt

to flirt with 1 to treat lightly; to risk carelessly. **2** to entertain thoughts of superficially, to toy with (*He flirted with the idea of setting up his own business*).

flit

moonlight flit MOONLIGHT.

flog

to flog a dead horse 1 to try to revive interest in something stale. **2** to pursue a hopeless task.
to flog to death (*coll.*) to talk about to the point of tedium (*I think we've flogged this subject to death*).

flood

before the Flood a very long time ago. [An allusion to the flood recorded in the Bible (Gen. vii).]
to flood out to drive from one's home etc. because of a flood.

floodgate

to open the floodgates OPEN.

floor

to cross the floor CROSS.
to get in on the ground floor GROUND.
to have the floor to be given the right to address a meeting, assembly etc.
to take the floor 1 to rise to speak, to take part in a debate. **2** to get up to dance.
to wipe/ mop the floor with someone (*coll.*) to defeat someone completely.

flotsam

flotsam and jetsam 1 wreckage or any property found floating or washed ashore. **2** odds and ends. **3** vagrants etc.

flourish

to cut a flourish to look flamboyant; to perform flamboyantly.

flow

ebb and flow EBB.

to go with the flow to do the same as others, not trying to do something different.

flower

in flower with the flowers appeared and opened.

fluence

to put the fluence on (*coll.*) to hypnotize.

flume

to go/ be up the flume (*N Am., sl.*) to come/ have come to grief.

flunk

to flunk out (*esp. N Am., coll.*) to be expelled for failure.

flush

to flush out to find and force to come out.

flutter

to flutter one's eyelashes at to flirt with.

to flutter the dovecotes to throw peaceful people into alarm; to scandalize conventional circles. [From Shakespeare's *Coriolanus*: "like an eagle in a dove-cote, I / Fluttered your Volscians in Corioli".]

fly¹

fly in the ointment a slight flaw or minor disadvantage that spoils the quality of something. [From the Bible: "Dead flies cause the ointment of the apothecary to send forth a stinking savour" (Eccles. x.1).]

fly on the wall an intimate, but unnoticed, observer of events.

like flies in vast numbers and offering no resistance (*They were dropping like flies from the disease*).

there are no flies on someone someone is no fool.

would not hurt/ harm a fly is very gentle.

fly²

fly-by-night 1 (an) unreliable or untrustworthy (person). **2** a runaway debtor. **3** a person who goes out at night to a place of entertainment.

to fly a kite 1 to try out an idea; to find out about a situation, public opinion etc. **2** (*sl.*) to raise money on an accommodation bill.

to fly at 1 to attack suddenly, to rush at with violence or fierceness. **2** to criticize severely. **3** (of a hawk) to soar at and attack.

to fly high 1 to be ambitious. **2** to succeed; to excel.

to fly in the face of 1 to defy openly. **2** to act in direct opposition to. [Originally referring to a bird or animal attacking a person.]

to fly off 1 to become suddenly detached. **2** †to revolt; to desert.

to fly off the handle (*coll.*) to become angry suddenly, to go into a rage. [Alluding to an axehead that flies off when the tool is swung violently.]

to fly open to open suddenly and violently (*The door flew open and a man ran out*).

to fly out 1 to burst into a passion. **2** to break out into licence or extravagance.

to fly the coop to escape.

to let fly 1 to shoot or throw out. **2** to direct a violent blow (at). **3** to use violent language. **4** (*Naut.*) to let go suddenly and entirely.

flying

flying start 1 the start of a race etc. in which the competitors are already travelling at speed as they pass the starting point. **2** a promising strong start giving initial advantage (*The meeting got off to a flying start*).

to send flying to knock over.

with flying colours brilliantly, successfully, with credit or distinction. [Alluding to the flag of a victorious army.]

foam

to foam at the mouth to be very angry. [From the frothy saliva around the mouth of an animal with rabies.]

fob

to fob off to put off with lies or excuses.

to fob off with to delude into accepting by a trick.

focus

in focus 1 adjusted so as to obtain a clear image. **2** clearly perceived or defined.

fodder

cannon fodder CANNON.

fog

in a fog confused, in a state of uncertainty.

foggy

not to have the foggiest (idea) (*coll.*) not to have the slightest notion.

fold

to return/ come back to the fold to rejoin a group, esp. a group of believers, after a period of absence. [Alluding to a sheep that returns to its pen.]

follow

as follows used as an introductory formula to a statement, list etc.

to follow in someone's footsteps to do the same as someone, esp. a relative, who has gone before (*She followed in her father's footsteps and became a butcher*).

to follow on 1 to continue without a break. **2** to continue from where somebody else left off. **3** in cricket, to bat again immediately after completing one's first innings because one is more than a certain number of runs behind.

to follow one's nose 1 to act according to one's instincts. **2** to go straight on (*Turn left at the crossroads, and follow your nose till you reach the church*).

to follow out to implement (an idea, instructions etc.).

to follow suit 1 to play a card of the suit led by someone else. **2** (*fig.*) to follow someone's example.

to follow the banner of to follow the cause of, to be an adherent of.

to follow the crowd to do the same as everyone else.

to follow the plough to be a ploughman or peasant.

to follow through 1 in golf, cricket etc., to continue the swing after hitting the ball. **2** to take further action consequent upon an initial act. **3** to follow to a conclusion.

to follow up 1 to pursue closely and steadily. **2** to pursue an advantage. **3** to make further efforts to the same end (*I followed up my visit with a phone call*). **4** to take appropriate action about. **5** (*Med.*) to re-examine a patient or check progress at intervals after treatment.

follower

camp follower CAMP[1].

fond

to be fond of to like very much, to love.

food

food for thought something that makes

one think, something worthy of
consideration.

food for worms a dead person, esp. after
burial.

fool

a fool and his money are soon parted
gullible people are easily persuaded
to waste their money on worthless
things.

fool's errand an absurd or fruitless errand
or quest, the pursuit of what cannot be
found.

fool's paradise a state of unreal or
deceptive joy or good fortune.

fools rush in where angels fear to tread
said when someone acts rashly
without forethought or tries to do
something that a wiser person would
not attempt. [From *An Essay on
Criticism* (1711) by Alexander Pope.]

more fool you (*coll.*) you are (or have
been) foolish (*more fool you for
lending him the money*).

nobody's fool NOBODY.

not to suffer fools gladly SUFFER.

to act/ play the fool to behave in a
foolish, playful way.

to fool around/ about 1 to behave
foolishly or irresponsibly. **2** to waste
time. **3** to trifle (with). **4** to engage in
sexual activity (with).

to fool with to meddle with in a careless
and risky manner (*Don't fool with
fireworks!*).

to make a fool of 1 to cause to appear
ridiculous. **2** to deceive, to disappoint.

foot

at someone's feet in someone's power
(*She had the world at her feet*).

at the feet of 1 humbly adoring or
supplicating. **2** submissive to. **3** as a
disciple or student of.

cold feet COLD.

feet of clay serious weakness in a person
who is admired. [From the Bible (Dan.
ii.31–34), referring to an image with a

head of gold, arms of silver, thighs of
brass and feet of iron and clay.]

foot in both camps a connection with
both of two mutually antagonistic
groups.

foot in the door 1 a first step towards a
desired end. **2** a favourable position
from which to advance. [Referring to
the act of putting one's foot in an open
doorway to stop someone from closing
the door.]

hand and foot HAND.

horse and foot HORSE.

my foot! used to express disbelief,
contradiction etc.

not to know B from a bull's foot B.

not to put a foot wrong to not make a
mistake.

off one's feet in such a state that one can
hardly stand (*be rushed off one's feet*).

on foot walking (*go somewhere on foot*).

on one's feet 1 standing up. **2** in good
health (*to get back on one's feet after
an illness*). **3** thriving, getting on well.

to catch someone on the wrong foot
CATCH.

to drag one's feet DRAG.

to fall/ land on one's feet to emerge safely
or successfully; to end up in an
advantageous situation. [Cats are
reputed always to land safely on their
feet after falling from a great height.]

to find one's feet to become accustomed
to, and able to function effectively in,
new circumstances.

to foot it 1 to go on foot. **2** to dance.

to foot the bill to pay the bill.

to foot up to (of items in an account) to
mount or total up to.

to get off on the wrong foot WRONG.

to get one's feet wet to begin to join in an
activity.

to have itchy feet ITCHY.

to have one foot in the grave to be very
old or near death.

to have one's/ both feet on the ground to
be realistic, sensible or practical.

to have the ball at one's feet BALL[1].

to have two left feet TWO.

to keep one's feet not to fall.

to keep on foot to maintain in a state of readiness (as a standing army).

to let the grass grow under one's feet GRASS.

to put one's best foot forward 1 to step out briskly. 2 to try to show oneself at one's best.

to put one's feet up (*coll.*) to rest.

to put one's foot down 1 to be firm, determined or repressive. 2 to go faster in a car etc.

to put one's foot in it to commit a blunder, esp. a gaffe.

to set foot on/ in to go on to, to enter (*the first person to set foot on the island*).

to set on foot 1 to put in motion. 2 to originate.

to shake the dust off one's feet SHAKE.

to sit at the feet of SIT.

to stand on one's own (two) feet to be independent, to manage without the help of others (*It's high time he learnt to stand on his own two feet*).

to sweep someone off their feet SWEEP.

to think on one's feet THINK.

to trample/ tread under foot 1 to destroy. 2 to treat with scorn.

to vote with one's feet VOTE.

to walk someone off their feet WALK.

under foot on the ground (*It was rather muddy under foot*).

under someone's feet in the way of someone.

footing

to keep one's footing not to fall.

to pay one's footing to pay a sum of money on doing anything for the first time, as on being admitted to a trade etc.

footloose

footloose and fancy free unbound by ties, esp. the ties of love or marriage.

footstep

to follow in someone's footsteps FOLLOW.

for

for all that nevertheless, in spite of all that.

oh for used to express a desire for something (*Oh for a drink!*).

to be for it (*coll.*) to be certainly heading for punishment or trouble.

forbidden

forbidden fruit anything desired but pronounced unlawful. [From the fruit of the tree of knowledge of good and evil, which Adam was commanded not to eat in the Bible (Gen. ii.17).]

force

brute force (and ignorance) BRUTE.

by force by compulsion.

by force of by means of (*by force of arms*).

force of circumstances circumstances beyond one's control.

force of habit a tendency to do or say something out of habit, rather than for any other reason.

in force 1 in operation. 2 valid, enforced. 3 in large numbers, in great strength (*They arrived in force*).

†of force of necessity.

show of force SHOW.

to be the driving force behind something DRIVING.

to come into force 1 to become valid. 2 to be enforced or carried out.

to force from 1 to elicit by force. 2 to wrest from.

to force one's way to push through obstacles by force.

to force out to drive out.

to force someone's hand to make someone take action against their will. [From card-playing.]

to force the bidding to make bids at an auction in order to increase the price quickly.

to force the issue to cause a decision to have to be taken immediately.

to force the pace to try to increase the speed or tempo of any activity.

to join forces JOIN.

fore

to come to the fore to become important or popular.

to the fore 1 to the front, prominent, conspicuous. **2** ready, available; forthcoming. **3** (*Sc.*) still surviving.

foregone

foregone conclusion 1 a conclusion determined beforehand or arrived at in advance of evidence or reasoning. **2** a result that might be foreseen.

forelock

to take time by the forelock TIME.

to touch/ tug one's forelock to raise one's hand to one's forehead as a sign of deference to a person of a higher social class.

forewarn

forewarned is forearmed a timely warning gives one the advantage of being prepared.

forget

forget it! an exclamation of dismissal.

to forget oneself 1 to lose one's self-control, to behave unbecomingly. **2** to act unselfishly. **3** to become unconscious.

forgive

to forgive and forget to pardon past wrongs and dismiss them from one's mind.

fork

to fork out/ up (*coll.*) to hand over or pay (money), esp. unwillingly (*I had to fork out £200 for a new set of tyres*).

to fork over 1 to turn over (soil) using a

fork. **2** (*coll.*) to hand over (money), esp. unwillingly.

forlorn

forlorn hope 1 a bold, desperate enterprise. **2** a faint hope. [From the Dutch phrase *verloren hoop*, meaning 'lost troop', referring to a body of soldiers selected for a dangerous mission.]

form

bad form BAD.

good form GOOD.

in any shape or form SHAPE.

matter of form MATTER.

off/ out of form playing or performing below one's usual standard.

on/ in form showing one's talent to advantage; playing, running or performing well.

forswear

to forswear oneself to perjure oneself.

fort

to hold the fort to cope temporarily, esp. in someone's absence. [Of military origin, popularized in the refrain of a song by Philip Paul Bliss (1838–76) "Hold the fort, for I am coming".]

fortune

someone's face is their fortune FACE.

to give a hostage to fortune HOSTAGE.

to make a/ one's fortune to gain great wealth (*They made a fortune buying and selling used cars*).

to tell someone's fortune TELL.

forty

forty winks a nap.

foul

foul play 1 unfair behaviour in a game or contest, a breach of the rules. **2** dishonest or treacherous conduct. **3** violence; murder.

to fall/ run foul of 1 to come or run against with force. **2** to come into collision, entanglement or conflict with. **3** to be contrary to, to go against (*to fall foul of the law*).

to foul one's (own) nest to harm or bring disgrace to oneself, one's family or one's own interests.

to foul up 1 to make dirty, to pollute. **2** to block; to entangle. **3** to become blocked or entangled. **4** (*coll.*) to blunder. **5** (*coll.*) to spoil or cause to break down by making mistakes etc.

four

all/ the four corners of the earth everywhere (*They came from all four corners of the earth*).

four-letter word any of a number of short English words referring to sex or excrement and considered vulgar or obscene.

on all fours crawling on the hands and feet or knees.

the four freedoms freedom of speech and religion and freedom from fear or want.

the four seas the seas surrounding Great Britain.

the four winds the four cardinal points.

freak

to freak out 1 (*coll.*) (to cause) to hallucinate. **2** (*coll.*) (to cause) to be in a highly emotional, excited or angry state. **3** to assume a strikingly unconventional lifestyle.

free

for free (*coll.*) gratis, for nothing.

free and easy 1 unconstrained, unceremonious, informal. **2** careless. **3** an unceremonious kind of social gathering or other entertainment.

free as a bird completely free.

free hand complete freedom to act as one wishes (*They gave me a free hand in the design of the exhibition*).

free of charge free, without charge.

to free up 1 (*coll.*) to make available (*free up some space on the shelves*). **2** (*coll.*) to cause to operate with fewer restrictions.

to make free to venture (to).

to make free with to treat without ceremony.

to set free to release.

freedom

the four freedoms FOUR.

freeze

to freeze on to (*sl.*) to seize or hold tightly.

to freeze out (*coll.*) to compel the retirement of from business, competition, society etc., by boycotting, contemptuous treatment or similar methods.

to freeze up to (cause to) be obstructed by the formation of ice (*The tank froze up while we were away*).

French

excuse/ pardon my French excuse my bad language.

French leave absence without permission. [From the discourteous act of leaving without saying goodbye to one's host, attributed to the French by the English and vice versa.]

fresh

fresh as a daisy 1 very fresh, not wilting. **2** not tired.

fresh out of (*coll.*) having recently (completely) run out of (*We're fresh out of milk*).

to get fresh to take undesired sexual liberties (with someone).

freshen

to freshen up 1 to refresh oneself, to have a wash or shower, change one's clothes etc. **2** to revive, to give a fresher, more attractive appearance to. **3** to replenish (a drink).

Freudian

Freudian slip an unintentional action, such as a slip of the tongue, held to betray an unconscious thought. [From the theories of the Austrian psycho-analyst Sigmund Freud (1856–1939).]

Friday

girl Friday GIRL.
man Friday MAN.

friend

a friend in need (is a friend indeed) a friend who helps one in times of trouble (is a true friend).
bosom friend BOSOM.
fair-weather friend FAIR.
friend at court a person who has influence to help another.
friends in high places people in important positions who can help one.
just good friends not having sexual relations.
my honourable friend HONOURABLE.
my learned friend LEARNED.
my noble friend NOBLE.
to be friends with to be friendly with.
to make friends to become friendly or reconciled (with).

frig

to frig about (*taboo, sl.*) to potter or mess about.

fright

to take fright to become frightened.

frighten

to frighten someone out of their wits to make someone very scared or terrified.

frightener

to put the frighteners on (*sl.*) to (attempt to) coerce or deter someone with threats (of violence).

fringe

lunatic fringe LUNATIC.

fritter

to fritter away to waste (esp. time or money).

fritz

on the fritz (*N Am., sl.*) not in working order.

frizzle

to frizzle up to burn or shrivel.

frog

frog in one's/ the throat (*coll.*) phlegm on the vocal chords impeding speech.

from

from out out from, forth from.

front

in front 1 in an advanced or the leading position. **2** facing or ahead of one.
in front of 1 before. **2** in advance of; ahead of. **3** in the presence of (*You shouldn't say such things in front of the children*).
out front in the audience or auditorium of a theatre.
to come to the front to take a prominent position.
to front up (*Austral.*) to turn up.
up front 1 at the front. **2** (of payments) in advance. **3** honest, straightforward.

fruit

forbidden fruit FORBIDDEN.
to bear fruit to have a successful outcome.

fruitcake

nutty as a fruitcake NUTTY.

fry¹

to fry up to heat or reheat in a frying pan.

fry²

to be small fry SMALL FRY.

frying pan

out of the frying pan into the fire out of one trouble into another that is worse.

fuck

fuck all (*taboo, sl.*) nothing at all.

not to give a fuck (*taboo, sl.*) not to care in the least.

to fuck about/ around 1 (*taboo, sl.*) to waste time, to mess around. **2** (*taboo, sl.*) to treat inconsiderately.

to fuck off (*taboo, sl.*) to go away.

to fuck up 1 (*taboo, sl.*) to botch; to damage. **2** (*taboo, sl.*) to make a mess of. **3** (*taboo, sl.*) to disturb emotionally.

fuel

to add fuel to the fire ADD.

full

at full blast 1 hard at work. **2** at maximum speed, volume etc.

at full length 1 lying stretched to the fullest extent. **2** of the standard length, not condensed or abridged.

at full pelt at full speed.

at full sea 1 at high tide. **2** at the acme or culmination.

at full stretch working etc. to full capacity, using all resources.

at full tilt at full speed or force.

at the full 1 at the height or the highest condition. **2** (of the moon) with the whole disc illuminated.

full and by (*Naut.*) close-hauled but with the sails filling.

full as a goog (*Austral., sl.*) very drunk. [A goog is an egg in Australian slang. The origin of this term is unknown.]

full marks 1 the highest score in a test, examination or other assessment. **2** great praise (*Full marks to Jenny for spotting the error*).

full of beans energetic and vigorous. [The phrase originally referred to a well-fed horse.]

full of oneself having an exaggerated view of one's own importance.

full of the joys of spring very happy, cheerful or merry.

full speed/ steam ahead used as an order to go or work as fast as possible.

in full completely, without abridgement, abatement or deduction (*paid in full*).

in full cry in hot pursuit. [Referring to the cry of hunting hounds.]

in full face with all the face visible towards the spectator.

in full fig (*coll.*) in full dress.

in full rig (*coll.*) smartly or formally dressed.

in full swing in full activity or operation.

in full view completely visible.

not the full quid (*Austral., sl.*) simple-minded.

on a full stomach after a large meal (*You shouldn't go swimming on a full stomach*).

the full monty (*coll.*) everything possible or necessary; the whole way. [The phrase is of uncertain origin: possible explanations include the full English breakfast eaten by Field Marshal Bernard Montgomery (nicknamed 'Monty'), a full three-piece suit from the men's outfitters Montague Burton, and the Spanish card game monte. The phrase was popularized by the comedian Ben Elton and others in the 1980s and 1990s and became the title of a 1997 comedy film about male strippers, in which it referred to full frontal nudity.]

(the) full whack the maximum rate, price etc.

to come full circle to come round to where one started.

to the full to the utmost extent.

fullness

in the fullness of time eventually (*She came to love him in the fullness of time*).

the fullness of the heart full, true feelings.

fun

figure of fun FIGURE.

for fun/ the fun of it simply for pleasure.

fun and games (*iron.*) frivolous activity; trouble (*We had fun and games getting the washing machine into the back of the car*).

in fun as a joke (*I only said it in fun*).

like fun 1 (*coll.*) energetically. **2** (*coll.*) thoroughly. **3** (*coll., iron.*) not at all.

to be great/ good fun to be very enjoyable or amusing.

to have fun to enjoy oneself.

to make fun of/ poke fun at 1 to hold up to ridicule, to mock (*They made fun of her accent*). **2** to banter.

what fun! how enjoyable.

fund

in funds (*coll.*) provided with cash, flush with money.

funeral

that's your funeral! (*coll.*) that's your problem; you must accept the consequences.

funk

in a (blue) funk 1 in a state of fear or panic. **2** (*N Am.*) in a state of despondency or depression.

funny

funny business 1 (*coll.*) dubious or suspicious goings-on; trickery. **2** jokes, drollery.

funny peculiar or funny ha-ha? addressed to someone who has used the word 'funny', to ascertain which meaning is intended. [From *The Housemaster* (1936), a play by Ian Hay.]

fur

the fur will fly there will be an argument. [Alluding to a fight between animals.]

to make the fur fly to create a scene, to start a row.

furniture

part of the furniture PART.

furrow

to plough a lonely furrow PLOUGH.

further

further to (*formal*) with reference to (an earlier letter etc.).

until further notice/ orders to continue until clearly changed.

furthest

at (the) furthest at the greatest distance; at most.

fury

like fury (*coll.*) with furious energy.

fuss

to make a fuss of to lavish attention on as a sign of affection (*He always makes a fuss of the children*).

to make/ kick up a fuss to cause a commotion, esp. by complaining.

future

in (the) future from now onwards (*Please be more careful in future*).

G

gab
the gift of the gab GIFT.

gad
by gad (*dated*) used as an oath or to
express surprise etc.

gaff
to blow the gaff BLOW¹.

gaiety
to add to/ increase the gaiety of nations to
cause general pleasure or amusement.

gain
to gain ground 1 to advance in any
undertaking. 2 to make progress.
to gain ground on to get nearer to
(someone or something pursued).
to gain on to get nearer to (an object of
pursuit) (*Hurry up, they're gaining on
us!*).
to gain over to win over to any side,
party or view.
to gain the ear of to secure favourable
consideration from.
to gain time to obtain delay for any
purpose.
what you gain on the swings you lose on
the roundabouts gains and losses,
advantages and disadvantages etc.
usually balance each other out.
[Alluding to the takings of fairground
operators.]

gait
to go one's (own) gait (*dated*) to go one's
own way.

gall
gall and wormwood all that is hateful,
exasperating and unwelcome. [From
the Bible: "Remembering mine
affliction and my misery, the
wormwood and the gall" (Lam. iii.19).]

gallery
to play to the gallery to court popular
applause. [The cheapest seats at a
theatre are in the gallery.]

gallop
at a gallop at the fastest speed.

gamble
to gamble away to squander or lose in
gambling (*He gambled away his
inheritance*).

game
fair game FAIR.
fun and games FUN.
game, set and match (*coll.*) a final and
convincing victory. [From the
announcement made at the end of a
tennis match.]
mug's game MUG¹.
off one's game playing or performing
below one's usual standard.
on one's game playing or performing
well.
the game is up 1 everything has failed.
2 the game (bird or animal) has started
up.
the name of the game NAME.
to be on the game (*coll.*) to be earning a
living as a prostitute.

to give the game away 1 to reveal a secret or strategy. **2** (*coll.*) to reject or abandon a competition etc.

to have the game in one's hands 1 to be sure of winning. **2** to have success in any contest, undertaking etc. at one's command.

to make (a) game of (*dated*) to turn into ridicule.

to play a shell game SHELL GAME.

to play/ beat someone at their own game to compete with/ do better than someone in their own sphere of activity.

to play the game 1 to abide by the rules. **2** to act in an honourable way.

two can play at that game TWO.

waiting game WAITING.

what's your/ their/ etc. game? what are you etc. up to?, what are your etc. intentions? (*What's his game?*).

gamut

to run the gamut of to go through the complete range of.

gander

what is sauce for the goose is sauce for the gander SAUCE.

gang

to gang up to join with others (in doing something).

to gang up on to join with others to make an attack on (someone).

gangway

to bring to the gangway (*Hist.*) to punish (a sailor) by tying up and flogging.

to sit below the gangway SIT.

gap

to stand in the gap to expose oneself for the protection of others.

to stop/ fill/ supply a gap to repair a defect or make up a deficiency.

gape

to gape at to open the mouth and gaze at with astonishment.

to gape for/ after to desire eagerly, to crave.

garbage

garbage in, garbage out (*Comput.*) if poor-quality or irrelevant data is entered or programmed, the results are worthless.

garden

common or garden COMMON.

everything in the garden is lovely everything appears to be well.

to lead up the garden path LEAD[1].

garter

to have someone's guts for garters GUT.

gasp

at the last gasp LAST[1].

to gasp out/ away to breathe out (one's life etc.) convulsively.

gate

like a bull at a gate BULL.

to give someone/ get the gate (*N Am., sl.*) to dismiss someone/ be dismissed.

gather

to gather head 1 to gain strength. **2** to ripen (as a boil etc.).

to gather (one's) breath to recover one's wind, to have respite.

to gather oneself together to concentrate all one's strength or faculties, as on an effort.

to gather speed to increase speed.

to gather way (of a vessel) to begin to move, to gain impetus, so as to answer to the helm.

gauge

to take the gauge of to estimate.

gauntlet

to run the gauntlet 1 to suffer the former military punishment of running between two lines of men armed with sticks or knotted ropes to strike the victim as he passed. **2** to be exposed to an ordeal, severe criticism etc. [In this phrase the word gauntlet comes from a Swedish word meaning 'passageway'.]

to throw down/ take up the gauntlet to make/ accept a challenge. [In this phrase the word gauntlet comes from the French word for 'glove'. A medieval knight would throw down his gauntlet, an armoured glove, as a challenge to one he wished to fight. By picking up the gauntlet his opponent accepted the challenge.]

gaze

†**at a gaze** gaping in wonder.

at gaze 1 (*Her.*) represented full-faced, as a deer. **2** as an intent spectator.

gear

in gear (of a machine or motor vehicle) connected up and ready for work.

out of gear 1 (of gearing or couplings) disconnected. **2** out of working order. **3** disturbed, upset.

to change gear CHANGE.

to gear down to decrease activity, facilities etc., usu. industrial, in response to a change in situation (*A fall in demand forced the company to gear down production*).

to gear up to increase activity, facilities etc., usu. industrial, in response to a change in situation.

gee

to take the gee (*Sc.*) to take offence.

general

as a general rule in most cases or in all ordinary cases.

caviar to the general CAVIAR.

in general 1 in the main, generally. **2** in most cases or in all ordinary cases, for the most part.

the general public people in general, as opposed to a specific group of people.

gentle

of gentle birth of honourable birth, belonging to the gentry, having good breeding.

George

by George! used to express surprise mixed with admiration.

germ

in germ existing in an undeveloped state.

get

get away/ along/ on! used to express mild disbelief.

to be getting on for to approach in time or age (*He must be getting on for eighty*).

to get about/ around 1 to be able to move or walk about (after an illness). **2** to become known, to be reported abroad. **3** to travel from place to place.

to get across 1 to communicate, to make understood (*trying to get the message across*). **2** to be communicated.

to get ahead 1 to prosper. **2** to move to a position in advance (of).

to get along 1 to proceed, to advance. **2** to succeed, to fare, to manage (well or badly). **3** (*coll.*) to go away. **4** (*coll.*) to have a friendly relationship (*They just don't get along*).

to get among 1 to become one of. **2** (*coll.*) to acquire, become involved with, esp. in a disruptive way.

to get at 1 to be able to reach. **2** to ascertain (*to get at the truth*). **3** (*sl.*) to criticize repeatedly, esp. in an annoying way. **4** to influence, corrupt, bribe (a jockey etc.). **5** to drug or illegally tamper with (a racehorse). **6** to imply, to hint at (*What are you getting at?*).

to get away 1 to escape. **2** to disengage oneself (from). **3** to quit.

to get away with 1 to make off with. **2** to escape discovery in connection with (something wrong or illegal), to escape blame or punishment for.

to get back 1 to receive back, to recover.
2 to return, to come back.

to get back at to retaliate against.

to get back to to contact again (*I'll get
back to you later*).

†to get before to arrive in front (of).

to get behind 1 to go back into the rear.
2 to lag. 3 to fall into arrears (*They got
behind with the rent*). 4 to penetrate,
to unravel.

to get by 1 (*coll.*) to have enough money
only for the things one needs, to
survive. 2 to elude. 3 to be good
enough.

to get down 1 to alight, to descend. 2 to
swallow. 3 (*coll.*) to make unhappy,
to depress (*Don't let it get you down*).
4 to write down.

to get down to 1 to concentrate upon.
2 to start work on.

to get forward to make progress, to
advance.

to get free/ loose to escape, to disengage
oneself.

to get his/ hers/ etc. 1 (*sl.*) to get his etc.
deserts. 2 (*sl.*) to be killed.

to get home 1 to arrive at one's home.
2 to arrive at the winning post.

to get in 1 to enter. 2 to collect and place
(crops etc.) under cover. 3 to make
room for. 4 to be elected. 5 to arrive
home (*I usually get in around six*).

to get into 1 to put on (clothes etc.).
2 (*coll.*) to become involved or
interested in (*I've been getting into
jazz recently*). 3 to possess, dominate
or take over (a person's mood,
personality etc.) (*What's got into you?*).

to get it 1 (*sl.*) to be in trouble, to be
punished. 2 (*coll.*) to understand (*I
don't get it*).

to get it together to become well
organized, to take control.

to get laid (*sl.*) to have sexual intercourse.

to get off 1 to dismount, to alight (from).
2 to escape, to be released (from). 3 to
be acquitted, to be let off (with or for)
(*We got off with a caution this time*).

4 to start. 5 to go to sleep. 6 to take off,
to remove. 7 to procure the acquittal
of. 8 to cause to go to sleep.

to get off on 1 (*coll.*) to be impressed by.
2 (*coll.*) to enjoy.

to get off with (*coll.*) to have a sexual
encounter with.

to get on 1 to put or pull on. 2 to move
on. 3 to advance. 4 to succeed or
prosper. 5 to grow late. 6 to grow old.
7 to have a friendly relationship (*She
doesn't get on with her brother-in-law*).
8 to do, fare or manage (with or
without). 9 to mount.

to get on to 1 to make contact with.
2 to become aware of, to discover.

to get out 1 to pull out, to extract. 2 to
escape from any place of confinement
or restraint. 3 to be divulged (*If this
gets out I'll be the laughing stock of
the school*). 4 to publish or say finally,
after difficulties. 5 to complete the
solution of (*None of my friends could
get the riddle out*).

to get out of 1 to avoid (doing something).
2 to obtain (something) from, with
some difficulty.

to get outside (of) (*sl.*) to eat or drink, to
ingest.

to get over 1 to surmount or overcome (a
difficulty etc.). 2 to recover from
(illness, surprise, disappointment etc.)
(*He never got over his wife's death*).
3 to make intelligible. 4 (*coll.*) to
persuade. 5 to finish (a task etc.) with
relief.

to get over with to finish (a task etc.) with
relief.

to get round 1 to coax by flattery or
deception (*You can't get round me
that easily!*). 2 to evade (a law or rule).

to get round/ around to to deal with in
due course (*One of these days I'll get
round to fixing that tap*).

to get there 1 (*coll.*) to succeed, esp. after
overcoming obstacles or difficulties
(*We're getting there!*). 2 (*coll.*) to
understand.

to get through 1 to reach a point beyond, to reach one's destination. **2** to succeed in doing, to complete, to finish (with). **3** to pass (an examination). **4** (of a bill) to be passed. **5** to use up (*She gets through two packets of cigarettes a day*). **6** to make a telephone connection.

to get through to 1 to make a telephone connection with. **2** (*coll.*) to make understand or pay attention.

to get to 1 to reach, to arrive at. **2** to begin (a task etc.). **3** (*coll.*) to annoy or irritate (*Don't let her get to you*). **4** (*coll.*) to affect emotionally.

to get together 1 to meet, to assemble. **2** to bring together, to amass.

to get up 1 to rise (as from a bed etc.). **2** to mount. **3** to dress up, to disguise. **4** (of the wind, waves etc.) to begin to rage or be violent. **5** to prepare, to get ready. **6** to learn, to work up. **7** to invent, to devise.

to get up to (*coll.*) to be doing, to be involved in, esp. wrongly.

to have got it bad (*sl.*) to be infatuated or obsessed with someone.

ghost

ghost of a chance the remotest possibility.

to give up the ghost to die, to expire. [From the Bible: "And Jesus cried with a loud voice, and gave up the ghost" (Mark xv.37). The phrase also occurs in the Old Testament and elsewhere in the New Testament.]

gift

God's gift GOD.

the gift of the gab (*coll.*) a talent for speaking, fluency.

to look a gift horse in the mouth to find fault with what cost one nothing. [From the practice of looking at a horse's teeth to ascertain its age before buying it.]

gill

green/ white about the gills pale in the face because of nausea, fear, exhaustion etc.

gilt

to take the gilt off the gingerbread to reveal the unattractive reality behind something which appears to be glamorous. [From the former practice of decorating gingerbread with gold leaf for sale at fairs etc.]

gingerbread

to take the gilt off the gingerbread GILT.

gird

to gird (up) one's loins 1 (*dated or facet.*) to get ready to do something. **2** (*dated or facet.*) to prepare oneself for (vigorous) action. [From the Bible: "Gird up now thy loins like a man" (Job xxxviii.3).]

girl

girl Friday a female secretary and general assistant in an office. [From Man Friday, the name of Robinson Crusoe's servant in Daniel Defoe's novel *Robinson Crusoe* (1719).]

give

don't give me that do not expect me to accept or believe that.

give me I prefer (*Give me Irish whiskey, any day!*).

given that granted that.

give or take (*coll.*) if you add or subtract (an amount or number) in making an estimate (*I weigh twelve stone, give or take a few pounds*).

to be given to to have a habit of, to be fond of (*He's given to exaggeration*).

to give and take 1 to be fair, to act fairly. **2** to exchange.

to give away 1 to make over as a gift, to transfer. **2** to hand over in marriage to a bridegroom during the wedding ceremony (*The bride is traditionally given away by her father*). **3** to let out or divulge inadvertently. **4** to give or concede to an opposing player or side by mistake. **5** (*Austral.*) to abandon, to lose interest in.

to give back to restore, to return (something to someone).

to give forth 1 to emit. **2** †to publish, to tell.

to give in 1 to yield. **2** to hand in.

to give it to (*coll.*) to scold, to punish severely or beat.

to give of to contribute (*He gave very freely of his time*).

to give off to emit (*It gives off an unpleasant smell*).

to give oneself (of a woman) to yield to sexual intercourse.

to give oneself up to surrender.

to give oneself up to to abandon or addict oneself to.

to give onto/ into to face, to lead into.

to give out 1 to emit. **2** to publish, to proclaim. **3** to distribute. **4** (*coll.*) to show, to profess. **5** to break down (*The engine gave out halfway up the hill*). **6** to run short. **7** (of an umpire in cricket) to indicate that (a batsman) is out.

to give over 1 to hand over, to transfer. **2** to abandon, to despair of. **3** (*in p.p.*) to devote or addict (*given over to gambling*). **4** to cease (from), to desist (*Give over!*). **5** to yield.

to give up 1 to surrender. **2** to resign (*give up one's job*). **3** to hand over. **4** to despair (*Sometimes I just feel like giving up*). **5** to stop doing (*give up smoking*).

what gives? (*coll.*) what is happening?

gizzard

to stick in someone's gizzard STICK².

glad

glad hand (*coll.*) a welcome, esp. a fulsome one.

glad rags 1 (*coll.*) one's best or smartest clothes. **2** (*coll.*) evening dress.

to give someone the glad eye (*coll.*) to ogle someone.

glamour

to cast a glamour over CAST.

glance

at a glance immediately, at a first look.

glass

glass ceiling a situation in an organization where promotion appears to be possible but is prevented by discrimination etc.

people who live in glass houses should not throw stones PEOPLE.

to raise one's glass to RAISE.

glassy

(just) the glassy (*Austral.*) just the job, the best.

glim

to douse the glim DOUSE.

glitter

all that glitters is not gold appearances can be deceptive.

glom

to glom on to 1 (*N Am.*) to take possession of. **2** (*N Am.*) to grab hold of.

glory

glory be! used to express surprise or annoyance. [A shortening of the exclamation 'Glory be to God!'.]

in (all) one's glory in all one's splendour, looking at one's best.

to glory in to be proud of.

to go to glory (*sl.*) to die, disintegrate, go wrong etc. (*That shot has gone to glory!*).

gloss

to gloss over to seek to avoid drawing

attention to by mentioning only briefly or misleadingly.

glove

hand in glove HAND.

the iron hand in the velvet glove IRON HAND.

to fight with the gloves off FIGHT.

to fit like a glove FIT.

to throw down/ take up the glove to make/ accept a challenge. [From the traditional way of challenging someone to a duel etc. and accepting such a challenge.]

with kid gloves KID GLOVE.

gloze

†**to gloze over** to explain away.

glutton

glutton for punishment a person eager to take on hard or unpleasant tasks.

gnat

to strain at a gnat and swallow a camel STRAIN.

gnaw

to gnaw a file to attempt obstinately a task that ends only in vexation.

gnome

gnomes of Zurich (*coll.*) international bankers thought to have great power and exercise a sinister and mysterious effect on world economics. [The phrase was used by Harold Wilson in a speech in Parliament in 1956: "all these financiers, all the little gnomes in Zurich and the other financial centres".]

go¹

from the word go WORD.

go ahead start, proceed without hesitation.

go on used to express mild disbelief.

go to hell/ blazes be off!

here goes! said by someone who is about to do something (*I don't know if it'll work, but here goes!*).

here we go again! said when the same unpleasant, predictable etc. thing seems to be about to happen again.

to go 1 remaining to be passed or dealt with (*only two more days to go*). **2** (*esp. N Am., coll.*) (of food) for taking away from the restaurant.

to go about 1 to set to work at, to tackle (*I'm not sure how to go about it*). **2** to go from place to place. **3** to take a circuitous course. **4** (*Naut.*) (of a vessel) to tack, to change course.

to go abroad 1 to go to a foreign country. **2** (*dated*) to go out of doors. **3** †to be disclosed.

to go against to be in opposition to (*It goes against her principles*).

to go ahead 1 to proceed in advance. **2** to make rapid progress. **3** to start.

to go aloft (*coll.*) to go to heaven, to die.

to go along with to agree with or to (a suggestion, plan etc.).

to go aside 1 to withdraw apart from others. **2** to go wrong.

to go astray to wander from the right path.

to go at 1 to attack. **2** to work at vigorously.

to go away to depart.

to go back on to fail to keep (one's word).

to go behind 1 to call in question. **2** to look beyond (the apparent facts etc.).

to go between to mediate between.

†**to go beyond** to cheat, to outdo.

to go by 1 to pass by or near to. **2** to pass by. **3** to pass unnoticed or disregarded. **4** to take as a criterion (*going by what it cost last time*).

to go down 1 to descend. **2** to fall, to become lower. **3** to set. **4** (of a ship) to founder. **5** to fall (before a conqueror). **6** to be beaten in a sports match (*We went down 3–0*). **7** to be set down in writing. **8** esp. in the UK, to leave university. **9** to be swallowed, to be palatable or acceptable. **10** to be received (*My joke about the president didn't go down very well*). **11** to fall ill (with) (*go down with chicken pox*).

to go downhill to deteriorate physically or morally.

to go easy to be careful, to slow down.

to go easy on 1 to use only a little of (*Go easy on the butter!*). **2** to treat (someone) gently or kindly.

to go far 1 to be successful (esp. in one's career). **2** (*esp. in neg.*) to be sufficient.

to go for 1 to go somewhere to obtain (something). **2** to attack. **3** to be true for, to include (*and that goes for her as well*). **4** to be attracted by. **5** to be sold for.

to go forth 1 to issue or depart from a place. **2** to be published or spread abroad.

to go forward to advance.

to go hard with (*dated, impers.*) to cause problems or difficulties for.

to go ill with (*dated, impers.*) to happen or fare badly with.

to go in 1 to enter. **2** (of the sun) to go behind clouds. **3** in cricket, to have an innings.

to go in and out to be perfectly at liberty.

to go in for 1 to be in favour of. **2** to follow as a pursuit or occupation (*I decided to go in for teaching*). **3** to enter or take part in (an examination or competition).

to go into 1 to enter. **2** to frequent. **3** to take part in. **4** to investigate or discuss.

†**to go in unto 1** to enter the presence of. **2** to have sexual intercourse with.

to go it 1 to carry on. **2** to keep a thing up. **3** to conduct oneself recklessly or outrageously.

to go it alone to carry on single-handedly.

to go off 1 to depart. **2** (of a gun, firework etc.) to be fired or explode. **3** to rot, perish or putrefy (*Most of the food had gone off*). **4** to fall away. **5** to become unconscious. **6** to die. **7** to cease to be perceptible. **8** to fare, to succeed (well or badly) (*The party went off well*).

to go on 1 to proceed, to continue, to persevere. **2** to grumble, to complain. **3** to talk at length (*going on about her daughter*). **4** (*coll.*) to behave (badly etc.). **5** to appear on the stage. **6** to happen. **7** in cricket, to begin a spell of bowling. **8** †to become chargeable to (the parish etc.). **9** to use as a basis (*We haven't got much to go on*).

to go on at someone to nag someone.

to go on to to advance, progress, move or travel to (a further level, position or place).

to go out 1 to depart, to leave (a room etc.). **2** to be extinguished (*The fire has gone out*). **3** to vacate office. **4** to leave home and enter employment. **5** to go into society. **6** to go on strike. **7** to lose consciousness. **8** to have a romantic or sexual relationship (with).

to go over 1 to cross, to pass over. **2** to change one's party or opinions. **3** to read, to examine. **4** to rehearse. **5** to retouch.

to go overboard 1 (*coll.*) to go to extremes of enthusiasm. **2** to go too far.

to go round 1 to pay a number of visits. **2** to encompass or be enough to encompass, to be enough for (the whole party etc.).

to go through 1 to pass through. **2** to undergo. **3** to suffer. **4** to examine. **5** (*coll.*) to overhaul, to ransack, to strip. **6** to discuss thoroughly (*She went through the report with us*). **7** to perform (a duty, ceremony etc.). **8** to be completed. **9** to use or consume.

to go through with to perform thoroughly, perh. despite reluctance, to complete (*I decided I couldn't go through with it*).

to go together 1 to harmonize, to be suitable to or match each other. **2** to have a romantic or sexual relationship.

to go too far to exceed reasonable limits.

to go to show to be evidence or proof (that).

to go under 1 to be known as (a title or a name). **2** to sink. **3** to be submerged or ruined (*The company's in danger of going under*). **4** to perish.

to go up 1 to climb, to pass upwards. **2** to rise, to increase (*The price has gone up*). **3** to be constructed (*Those houses went up about twenty years ago*). **4** to be destroyed, as by fire or explosion.

to go upon to act upon as a principle.

to go well with 1 to be approved by. **2** to complement, suit, match etc. **3** to happen or fare well with.

to go west 1 (*sl.*) to die. **2** (*sl.*) to be destroyed.

to go with 1 to accompany. **2** to follow the meaning of, to understand. **3** to be with (child). **4** to side or agree with. **5** to suit, to match (*The curtains don't go with the wallpaper*). **6** (*coll.*) to have a romantic or sexual relationship with.

to go without to be or manage without, to put up with the want of.

to have gone and (*coll.*) to have been foolish enough to have (*I've gone and locked myself out!*).

go²

all/ quite the go (*dated*) entirely in the fashion.

from the word go WORD.

it's all go (*coll.*) it's very busy.

it's no go (*coll.*) it's impossible, it's no use.

on the go 1 vigorously in motion. **2** on the move.

to have a go (*coll.*) to make an attempt.

to have a go at someone (*coll.*) to attack someone, physically or verbally.

to make a go of something to make something succeed (*a last-ditch attempt to make a go of their marriage*).

goal

to score an own goal SCORE.

goalpost

to move the goalposts MOVE.

goat

to act/ play the (giddy) goat to act in a foolish, playful way.

to get someone's goat to make someone angry (*Remarks like that really get my goat!*).

to separate the sheep from the goats SEPARATE¹.

go-by

to give the go-by to 1 to evade. **2** to cut, to slight. **3** to pass, to outstrip. **4** to dismiss as of no importance.

god

for God's sake used as a solemn adjuration or an expression of exasperation etc.

God almighty! used to express surprise or anger.

God forbid used to express the hope that a certain event etc. will not happen.

God help you/ her/ etc. 1 used to express sympathy, concern etc. **2** (*iron.*) used to imply that a person's situation is not to be envied.

God knows 1 a mild oath expressing apathy or annoyance. **2** God is my (etc.) witness that (*God knows I've tried*).

God rest his/ her soul may God grant the specified person's soul peace.

God's gift (*iron.*) a person of utmost importance (to) (*He thinks he's God's gift to women*).

God willing if circumstances permit.

in the lap/ on the knees of the gods outside human control, as yet undetermined. [Perhaps from the ancient practice of placing offerings on the knees of statues of seated gods in the hope that prayers will be answered. The phrase is found in Homer's *Iliad*.]

the mills of God grind slowly (but they grind exceedingly small) MILL.

there, but for the grace of God, go I GRACE.

tin god TIN.

to god it (*dated*) to behave as if one were godlike.

to play God to (seek to) control other people's destinies.

to put the fear of God into FEAR.

ye gods! used to express frustration, annoyance etc.

ye gods and little fishes! used to express surprise, protest etc.

going

going on (esp. of the time, one's age etc.) almost, nearly (*He must be going on 50*).

heavy going HEAVY.

to get going 1 to begin. 2 to make haste.

to get out/ go while the going's good to seize the chance of getting away or putting something into action.

gold

all that glitters is not gold GLITTER.

crock of gold CROCK.

gold mine 1 a place where gold is mined. 2 (*coll.*) a source of wealth or profit.

good as gold (esp. of children) very well behaved.

heart of gold HEART.

worth one's weight in gold WORTH.

gold dust

like gold dust very rare.

golden

golden boy/ girl a popular or successful person in a particular field.

golden calf (*fig.*) money as an aim in itself. [From the calf made by Aaron for the people of Israel to worship in the Bible (Exod. xxxii.1–4).]

golden handcuff (*coll.*) a payment or benefit given to an employee as an inducement to continue working for the same company.

golden handshake (*coll.*) a payment or benefit given to an employee on redundancy or retirement.

golden hello (*coll.*) a payment or benefit given to an employee on joining a company.

golden parachute (*coll.*) a clause in the contract of a company executive guaranteeing financial recompense in the event of redundancy following a merger, takeover etc.

golden rule 1 any important rule or principle. 2 the rule that one should treat others as one would like to be treated.

gone

gone a million (*Austral.*) completely beaten.

gone on (*sl.*) infatuated with.

good

as good as not less than, the same as, practically, virtually (*The building work is as good as finished*).

for good (and all) finally, definitely, completely.

good and completely, very (*good and ready; good and hot*).

good egg! (*dated, sl.*) excellent!

good form 1 good manners. 2 breeding.

good for/ on you! used to express approval, encouragement etc.

good heavens! used to express surprise, dismay, irritation etc.

good job (*coll.*) a satisfactory turn of affairs (*It's a good job you noticed*).

good riddance used to express relief at the loss, departure etc. of someone or something undesirable.

good Samaritan a person who helps another in need or adversity. [From a parable told by Jesus in the Bible (Luke x.30–37) about a man who had been attacked by thieves: a priest and a Levite ignored him and "passed by on the other side", but a Samaritan stopped to help him.]

good show! (that was) well done!

in good faith with honest intentions (*act in good faith*).

it's an ill wind that blows nobody any good ILL.

the good old days 1 better or happier former times. **2** the past viewed nostalgically.

the great and the good GREAT.

to be good for to be relied on to pay or bring in (a stated amount).

to come good 1 (*coll.*) esp. after a setback, to succeed or improve. **2** to recover one's health after illness etc.

to do someone a power of good POWER.

to do someone good to be beneficial to someone's health etc. (*A breath of fresh air will do you good*).

to do someone's heart good HEART.

to do someone the world of good WORLD.

to give as good as one gets to be a match for an opponent throughout a contest, argument etc.

to hold good 1 to remain valid (*I accept your objection, but my argument still holds good*). **2** to apply, to be relevant.

to hold it good to think it sensible (to do).

to make good 1 to perform, to fulfil, to become successful. **2** to supply a deficiency. **3** to replace or repair. **4** to compensate (for). **5** to confirm. **6** to prosper, to be successful.

to stand good to remain valid.

to take in good part not to take offence at (*I called her a fool, but she took it in good part*).

to the good extra, over and above, as a balance or profit (*We are £5 to the good*).

up to no good involved in crime or mischief.

goodbye

to kiss goodbye to KISS.

goodness

for goodness' sake used as a solemn adjuration or an expression of exasperation etc. [The word 'goodness' is used euphemistically in place of 'God' in a number of expressions.]

goodness gracious! used to express surprise etc.

goodness knows! used to express lack of knowledge etc.

goods

to deliver the goods DELIVER.

to sell someone a bill of goods SELL.

good turn

one good turn deserves another a favour should be repaid in kind.

goog

full as a goog FULL.

goose

all someone's geese are swans said of someone who habitually overestimates the merits of their family, their chances of success etc.

to cook someone's goose COOK.

to kill the goose that lays the golden eggs KILL.

what is sauce for the goose is sauce for the gander SAUCE.

wild-goose chase WILD.

would not say boo to a goose BOO.

gooseberry

to play gooseberry to act as an unwanted third party to a pair of lovers.

Gordian knot

to cut the Gordian knot to remove a difficulty by drastic measures. [From a knot in the harness of Gordius, king of Phrygia, which Alexander the Great is said to have cut with his sword on hearing the promise of the oracle that whoever could untie it should possess the empire of Asia.]

gorge

one's gorge rises at one is nauseated or disgusted by.

gown

town and gown TOWN.

grab

up for grabs 1 (*coll.*) on offer. 2 (*coll.*) for sale. 3 (*coll.*) ready for the taking.

grace

airs and graces AIR.

saving grace SAVING.

there, but for the grace of God, go I another person's misfortune etc. could easily have been mine. [From a comment made by John Bradford (?1510–55), on seeing some criminals being led to their execution: "But for the grace of God there goes John Bradford."]

to be in the good graces of to enjoy the favour of.

to fall from grace 1 to lose favour. 2 to fall into sin.

to grace with one's presence (*esp. iron.*) to condescend to attend (*Is your son going to grace us with his presence?*).

with a bad grace reluctantly.

with a good grace willingly.

gracious

gracious me! used to express surprise or protest.

grade

at grade (*N Am.*) at the same level (as of a place where two roads cross each other).

to grade up to improve (stock) by crossing with a better breed.

to make the grade to succeed.

grain

in grain downright, thorough, absolute, inveterate.

to go against the grain to be contrary to one's natural inclination, causing reluctance or aversion. [Alluding to the grain of wood: it is easier to cut wood along the grain than across it.]

grandeur

delusions of grandeur DELUSION.

grandmother

to teach one's grandmother to suck eggs TEACH.

grant

to take for granted 1 to assume as admitted basis of an argument. 2 to cease to show appreciation for another's help, work etc. due to familiarity.

grape

sour grapes SOUR.

grasp

to grasp at 1 to try to seize. 2 to be eager to accept.

to grasp the nettle to take decisive or bold action. [From the fact that nettles are more likely to sting if brushed lightly than if they are grasped firmly.]

within one's grasp able to be grasped, understood, obtained, achieved etc. by one.

grass

grass roots 1 the ordinary people. 2 the basic essentials, foundation, origin.

grass widow(er) a person whose husband or wife is away for a lengthy period. [The phrase originally referred to an unmarried woman who had conceived a child in an illicit sexual relationship, perhaps because such encounters often took place out of doors.]

green as grass GREEN.

snake in the grass SNAKE.

the grass is always greener on the other side of the fence the living or working conditions of others often seem better than one's own.

to go out to grass 1 to go out to pasture. 2 to go out from work, on a holiday, into retirement etc.

to let the grass grow under one's feet to waste time and so lose an opportunity.

to put/ send/ turn out to grass **1** to send out to pasture. **2** to send out from work, on a holiday, into retirement etc.

to send/ go to grass to knock/ be knocked down.

grasshopper

knee-high to a grasshopper KNEE-HIGH.

grave

from the cradle to the grave CRADLE.

on this side of the grave SIDE.

someone walking over one's grave WALK.

to dig one's own grave DIG.

to have one foot in the grave FOOT.

to turn in one's grave (of a dead person) to be (thought to be) shocked or distressed by some modern event (*an adaptation of the play that would make Shakespeare turn in his grave*).

gravy

gravy train (*sl.*) a job, course of action etc. requiring little effort in return for easy money, benefits etc.

grease¹

elbow grease ELBOW.

grease²

like greased lightning (*coll.*) very quickly.

great

great cry and little wool much ado about nothing.

great minds think alike said when two people find they share the same opinion, have the same idea etc.

no great shakes (*coll.*) of no great account. [Perhaps from the shaking of dice.]

the great and the good (*often iron.*) worthy and distinguished people.

the great mass the great majority, the bulk.

the great unpaid (*coll.*) unpaid magistrates etc.

the great unwashed (*coll.*) the mob, the rabble.

to be great at to be skilful at.

to go great guns (*coll.*) to make vigorous and successful progress. [Of naval origin, alluding to cannon fire.]

to go to great lengths to take great care, to go to a great deal of trouble (*They go to great lengths to ensure the safety of passengers*).

to make great strides to progress or develop rapidly.

Greek

at the Greek calends (*dated*) never. [The Greeks had no calends: the calends was the name of the first day of the month in the ancient Roman calendar.]

to be (all) Greek to to be incomprehensible to (*I read the small print on the contract, but it was all Greek to me*). [The phrase is used in Shakespeare's *Julius Caesar*, said by Casca of a speech in Greek by Cicero: "for mine own part, it was Greek to me", but is probably of earlier origin.]

when Greek meets Greek when one champion meets another, when equals encounter each other.

green

green as grass naive, inexperienced, immature.

green fingers skill at growing plants.

green in one's eye a sign that one is gullible.

green with envy very envious. [A greenish complexion was once thought to indicate jealousy.]

not as green as one is cabbage-looking not as naive, gullible or foolish as one looks.

the green-eyed monster jealousy. [From Shakespeare's *Othello*: "O! beware, my lord, of jealousy; / It is the green-ey'd monster which doth mock / The meat it feeds on."]

green light

to get the green light (*coll.*) to get permission to go ahead with a project.

grey

grey area an issue or situation that is not clear-cut.

grey matter 1 (*coll.*) intellect, intelligence. **2** the greyish tissue of the brain and spinal cord containing the nerve cells.

grief

to come to grief 1 to meet with disaster. **2** to fail. **3** to come to ruin.

grievance

to air a grievance AIR.

grim

like grim death tenaciously (*He clung on like grim death*).

the Grim Reaper REAPER.

grin

to grin and bear it to endure pain etc. with stoicism.

to grin like a Cheshire cat to grin broadly. [Usually associated with the Cheshire cat in Lewis Carroll's *Alice's Adventures in Wonderland* (1865), which faded away until all that was left was its grin. However, the phrase is of much earlier origin.]

grind

to grind to a halt to stop gradually, esp. because of a breakdown, failure etc. (*The traffic ground to a halt*).

grindstone

to keep one's nose to the grindstone NOSE.

grip

in the grip of dominated by, affected by, esp. in a negative way (*a country in the grip of fear*).

to come/ get to grips with to deal with or tackle (a problem etc.).

to get a grip on oneself to bring oneself under control, to discipline oneself.

to lose one's grip LOSE.

grist

grist to the mill something advantageous or profitable (*It's all grist to the mill*).

grit

to grit one's teeth to hide one's true feelings of fear, anger etc.

groan

to groan inwardly to feel disappointment etc. without expressing it.

groat

not worth a groat WORTH[1].

grog

to grog on (*Austral., coll.*) to take part in a session of heavy drinking.

gross

by the/ in gross 1 in bulk, wholesale. **2** in a general way, on the whole.

to gross up to convert (a net figure) to a gross figure (as net income to its pre-tax value).

ground

common ground COMMON.

down to the ground (*coll.*) thoroughly, in every respect (*It suits me down to the ground*).

ground rule (*often pl.*) a basic rule of a game, procedure etc.

happy hunting ground HAPPY.

on one's own ground in familiar and comfortable circumstances, on one's own subject or terms.

on the ground in practical conditions, at the place of operations as distinct from a place where related administrative decisions are made.

stamping ground STAMP.

thick on the ground THICK.

thin on the ground THIN.

to break ground BREAK.

to break new/ fresh ground BREAK.

to cut the ground from under someone/ someone's feet (*coll.*) to anticipate someone's arguments or actions etc.,

and thereby render them meaningless
or ineffective.

to fall on stony ground STONY.

to fall to the ground to come to nothing,
to fail.

to gain ground GAIN.

to gain ground on GAIN.

to get in on the ground floor to become
involved with a (potentially)
successful enterprise in its early
stages.

to get off the ground (*coll.*) to (cause
something to) make a start, esp. one
that is successful (*It'll never get off the
ground*).

to give ground to give way, to retire, to
yield.

to have/ keep one's ear to the ground EAR.

to have one's/ both feet on the ground
FOOT.

to hit the ground running HIT.

to hold one's ground not to yield or give
way.

to lose ground LOSE.

to run into the ground (*coll.*) to exhaust
or wear out with overwork or overuse
(*He ran his first car into the ground*).

to shift one's ground SHIFT.

to stand one's ground to remain resolute,
to stay in a fixed position.

to work into the ground WORK.

group

pressure group PRESSURE.

grouter

to come/ be in on the grouter 1 (*Austral.,
coll.*) to get an unfair advantage.
2 (*Austral., coll.*) in a game of two-up,
to bet on a change in the fall of the
coins.

grow

to grow downward to diminish.

to grow on one to increase in one's
estimation, to impress one more and
more (*I didn't like the colour at first,
but it grew on me*).

to grow on trees (*usu. with neg.*) to be
plentiful (*Money doesn't grow on trees*).

to grow out of 1 to issue from. 2 to
develop or result from. 3 to become
too big or mature for, to outgrow.

to grow together to become closely
united, to become incorporated in
each other.

to grow up 1 to arrive at manhood or
womanhood. 2 to advance to full
maturity. 3 to arise, to become
prevalent or common. 4 to begin to
behave sensibly (*Grow up!*).

grub

to grub along (*coll.*) to plod or drudge
along.

to grub up to dig up by the roots.

grudge

to owe someone a grudge OWE.

gruel

to give someone their gruel (*dated, coll.*)
to defeat, punish severely or kill
someone.

guard

off (one's) guard unprepared for attack,
surprise etc. (*She caught me off my
guard*).

old guard OLD.

on guard 1 on one's guard. 2 on duty as a
sentry etc.

on one's guard prepared for attack,
surprise etc. (*warning householders to
be on their guard against bogus
callers*).

to guard against to take precautionary
action to try to prevent (something
happening).

to mount guard MOUNT.

to raise one's guard RAISE.

to stand guard (of a sentry) to keep
watch.

guernsey

to get a guernsey 1 (*Austral.*) to be
selected for a football team.

2 (*Austral., coll.*) to win approval, to succeed. [From a type of sweater worn by Australian footballers.]

guess

anybody's guess ANYBODY.

I guess (*N Am., coll.*) I suppose so, I think it likely.

to keep someone guessing (*coll.*) to make another person remain in a state of uncertainty by withholding information.

your guess is as good as mine (*coll.*) I have no more idea than you.

guest

be my guest 1 please make use of the facilities available. **2** do whatever you wish.

gulp

to gulp back to keep back or suppress (esp. tears).

gum

to gum up the works (*coll.*) to interfere with, spoil or delay something.

gum tree

to be up a gum tree (*coll.*) to be cornered, in a fix or brought to bay.

gun

son of a gun SON.

sure as a gun SURE.

to blow great guns BLOW¹.

to give (something) the gun 1 (*coll.*) to increase the speed of (a car etc.). **2** to give (a task etc.) one's maximum effort.

to go great guns GREAT.

to gun for 1 (*coll.*) to seek to kill, harm or destroy (*They're gunning for me*). **2** to strive to obtain.

to jump/ beat the gun 1 to begin (a race) before the starting pistol has fired, to make a false start. **2** (*coll.*) to begin prematurely.

to spike someone's guns SPIKE.

to stick to one's guns STICK².

gunner

†**to kiss/ marry the gunner's daughter** (*Naut., sl.*) to be lashed to a gun and flogged.

gunpoint

at gunpoint under the threat of being shot (*robbed at gunpoint*).

gut

to bust a gut BUST.

to hate someone's guts HATE.

to have guts (*coll.*) to be courageous.

to have someone's guts for garters (*coll., facet.*) to punish someone severely (*If you break any of these glasses I'll have your guts for garters!*).

to slog/ work one's guts out (*coll.*) to work extremely hard.

gutser

to come a gutser 1 (*Austral., coll.*) to fall over. **2** to fail.

gyp

to give someone gyp to cause someone pain (*My shoulder's giving me gyp today*).

H

ha

ha ha! 1 used to express the sound of laughter. **2** used to express surprise, joy, suspicion or other sudden emotion.

habit

creature of habit CREATURE.

force of habit FORCE.

to be in the habit of to do (something) usually or regularly (*I'm not in the habit of falling asleep at my desk*).

to make a habit of to do (something) usually or regularly.

hackle

to make someone's hackles rise to make someone angry. [Alluding to the hairs or feathers on the neck of an animal or bird that stand erect when it is provoked or challenged.]

with its hackles up (of a dog, cock etc.) ready to fight.

hail

hail-fellow-well-met on easy, familiar terms.

within hailing distance/ hail close enough to be heard if one shouts.

hair

a hair's breadth 1 the breadth of a hair. **2** a very minute distance (*a hair's breadth away from discovery*).

by a hair by a very small margin (*win by a hair*).

hair of the dog (that bit one) (*coll.*) a small amount of what has proved harmful, esp. of alcohol during a hangover. [From the former practice of using hair from a dog as an antidote to its bite.]

keep your hair on! (*coll.*) don't lose your temper.

neither/ not hide nor hair of HIDE².

not to turn a hair not to show any sign of surprise or alarm.

to a hair to an extreme nicety, exactly.

to get in someone's hair to become a nuisance, to make someone irritated.

to harm a hair of someone's head HARM.

to let one's hair down 1 (*coll.*) to talk without restraint. **2** (*coll.*) to forget ceremony, to behave uninhibitedly (*Everyone lets their hair down at the Christmas party*).

to make someone's hair curl (*coll.*) to shock or scandalize someone greatly.

to make someone's hair stand on end to make someone very frightened or horrified.

to put hairs on someone's chest (*coll., facet.*) to make someone manly, strong, vigorous etc. (*Have a drink of this: it'll put hairs on your chest!*).

to split hairs SPLIT.

to stroke someone's hair the wrong way STROKE².

to tear one's hair TEAR¹.

halcyon

halcyon days a time of prosperity, peace and happiness. [The halcyon was a bird formerly supposed to have the power of calming the seas during its breeding season, a period of about two weeks in the winter solstice.]

half

... and a half (*coll.*) a particularly large or good example (*That was a meal and a half!*).

better half BETTER.

by halves badly, imperfectly (*She never does anything by halves*).

half a one half of a; roughly one half of a.

half a chance (*coll.*) the slightest opportunity (*She'd stay in bed all morning, given half a chance*).

half a loaf is better than no bread it is better to have something, however little, than nothing at all.

half an eye 1 some part of one's attention or perceptiveness (*I watched the proceedings with half an eye*). **2** a modicum of perceptiveness or intelligence (*Anyone with half an eye could tell he was unhappy*).

half past half an hour past (*half past three*).

half seas over (*sl.*) slightly drunk.

half the battle an immense advantage, an important part of what is needed for success (*If you can speak the language, that's half the battle*).

half the time (*coll.*) as often as not.

how the other half lives OTHER.

not half 1 (*iron.*) rather. **2** (*sl.*) not at all.

not to know the half of it to have only a vague notion of the truth.

other half OTHER.

six (of one) and half a dozen (of the other) SIX.

time and a half TIME.

to cry halves CRY.

to go halves to share equally (with another or in something).

too ... by half to an excessive degree (*too cocky by half*).

to see with half an eye to see easily.

half-cock

to go off at half-cock/ half-cocked to fail as a result of being too impetuous. [Alluding to a halfway position of the hammer of a gun in which it cannot be moved by the trigger to fire a shot.]

half-hour

on the half-hour at half past each hour, at 30 minutes past the hour.

half mast

at half mast (*coll., often facet.*) (of trousers etc.) around the knees, having slipped down. [From the position of a flag halfway down the mast denoting respect for a dead person.]

half-sword

at half-sword at close quarters.

halfway

halfway house 1 a compromise. **2** a place providing short-term accommodation for people leaving institutions such as prisons or mental hospitals to provide rehabilitation before going back into the community. **3** the midpoint in a progression. **4** an inn halfway between two towns etc.

halidom

†**by my halidom** used as an oath.

halt

to call a halt (to) to bring some activity to an end.

to grind to a halt GRIND.

ham

to ham up (*sl.*) to overact.

Hamlet

like Hamlet without the Prince of Denmark lacking the most important element. [Referring to Shakespeare's play *Hamlet (Prince of Denmark)*, in which most of the words and action centre on the title character.]

hammer

hammer and tongs 1 with great noise and

vigour (*going at it hammer and tongs*).
2 violently. [Alluding to a blacksmith's tools.]

to bring to/ come under the hammer to put up for/ be sold by auction. [From the small hammer (or gavel) used by an auctioneer to indicate that a sale has been made.]

to hammer down to fasten down by hammering.

to hammer home to stress greatly.

to hammer in 1 to drive in with a hammer. **2** to stress greatly.

to hammer out 1 to flatten with a hammer. **2** to produce (an agreement) after a lot of discussion and disagreement (*hammer out a deal*).
3 to play (a tune) heavy-handedly.

up to the hammer first-rate.

hand

a bird in the hand (is worth two in the bush) BIRD.

all hands on deck/ to the pumps everyone must help. [Of nautical origin.]

at all hands 1 by all parties. **2** from all quarters.

a tall man of his hands TALL.

†at any hand at any rate.

at first hand FIRST-HAND.

at hand 1 close by. **2** available. **3** about to happen.

at second hand SECOND-HAND.

at the hand(s) of 1 from or through (a person). **2** by the means or instrumentality of.

by hand 1 by a person, with the hands (as distinct from with instruments or machines). **2** by messenger or agent. **3** by artificial rearing (of children or the young of animals).

cap in hand CAP.

dab hand DAB.

for one's own hand (to play or act) for one's personal advantage.

free hand FREE .

from hand to hand from one person to another, bandied about.

(from) hand to mouth (*also attrib.*) having only just enough money or food (*living hand to mouth; a hand-to-mouth existence*).

glad hand GLAD.

hand and foot completely, attending to every need (*She waits on him hand and foot*).

handed to one on a plate/ platter (*coll.*) obtained without effort.

hand in glove on intimate terms (with), in close association (with).

hand in hand 1 holding hands (with each other). **2** in union, unitedly.

hand on heart honestly, sincerely.

hand over fist with rapid, unchecked progress (*making money hand over fist*).

hand over hand 1 by passing the hands alternately one above or before the other, as in climbing or hauling a rope. **2** with rapid, unchecked progress.

hands off! don't touch.

hands up! 1 raise hands, those who assent etc. **2** raise hands to assure surrender.

hand to hand 1 at close quarters. **2** in close fight.

heart and hand HEART.

heavy on hand HEAVY.

in hand 1 in a state of preparation or execution. **2** in possession. **3** under control (*We have the problem in hand*).

in the hands of in the possession or control of (*The National Health Service is safe in our hands*).

in the hollow of someone's hand HOLLOW.

in the palm of one's hand PALM².

light on hand LIGHT².

many hands make light work work is done more easily or quickly if everyone helps.

near at hand NEAR.

not to do a hand's turn (*coll.*) to do no work at all.

off one's hands 1 finished with. **2** no longer one's responsibility.

old hand OLD.

on every hand/ all hands everywhere, on all sides.

on hand 1 in present possession. 2 in stock.

on one's hands 1 (left) to one's responsibility. 2 (left) unsold.

on the one hand from this point of view.

on the other hand OTHER.

out of hand 1 done, ended, completed. 2 without further consideration; at once, directly, extempore (*They dismissed our allegations out of hand*). 3 out of control.

(ready) to hand 1 nearby. 2 available.

right-hand man RIGHT-HAND.

show of hands SHOW.

the devil finds work for idle hands DEVIL.

the iron hand in the velvet glove IRON HAND.

the left hand doesn't know what the right hand is doing LEFT[1].

to ask the hand of ASK.

†to bear in hand 1 to flatter with pretences. 2 to deceive. 3 to help.

to be putty in someone's hands PUTTY.

to bite the hand that feeds one BITE.

to change hands CHANGE.

to clasp hands CLASP.

to clasp one's hands CLASP.

to come to hand 1 to be received. 2 to arrive.

to eat out of someone's hand EAT.

to force someone's hand FORCE.

to gain/ get the upper hand UPPER HAND.

to get/ have/ keep one's hand in to get into/ be in/ keep oneself in practice.

to give a big hand to BIG.

to give one's hand to agree to marry.

to give the hand of to give permission to marry (a woman).

to hand down 1 to transmit, to give in succession. 2 to bequeath. 3 to pass on after use. 4 (*US*) to express authoritatively in court.

to hand in to deliver to an office etc.

to hand it to to give credit to, to acknowledge the superiority, victory etc. of (*You have to hand it to her*).

to hand off 1 to push off with the hand. 2 in American football, to pass the ball by hand.

to hand on to transmit, to give in succession.

to hand out 1 to distribute (*handing out leaflets*). 2 to allocate.

to hand over to deliver (to someone).

to hand round/ around to distribute.

to have a hand for to be skilful at.

to have a hand in 1 to have a share in. 2 to be mixed up with.

to have one's hands full to be fully occupied (*My parents had their hands full, raising a family of six and running their own business*).

to have one's hands tied to have no freedom of action.

to have only one pair of hands PAIR.

to have the game in one's hands GAME.

to hold hands to hold each other's hand.

to hold hands with to hold the other person's hand.

†to hold one's hand to refrain from action.

to hold someone's hand to make something easier for someone by helping and supporting them, showing them how to do something etc.

to join hand in hand JOIN.

to join hands JOIN.

to kiss hands KISS.

to know like the back of one's hand BACK.

to lay hands on 1 to touch. 2 to assault. 3 to seize. 4 to lay the hands on the head of (in ordination, confirmation etc.).

to lay one's hands on 1 to get, to acquire, to seize. 2 to find.

to lend/ give/ bear a hand to help, to give assistance (*I'll give you a hand with the washing up*).

to lie on one's hands LIE[2].

to overplay one's hand OVERPLAY.

to play into someone's hands to unknowingly give the advantage to one's opponent.

to put one's hand in one's pocket to spend or give money.

to put one's hand to the plough to begin a task or undertaking.

†to put/ stretch forth one's hand against 1 to use violence against. 2 to attack.

to raise/ lift a/ one's hand (to) to threaten, to strike a blow (at).

to rub one's hands RUB.

to set one's hand to 1 to begin (a task). 2 to sign (a document).

to shake hands/ someone by the hand SHAKE.

to sit on one's hands SIT.

to stay one's hand STAY.

to strengthen someone's hand STRENGTHEN.

to strike hands STRIKE.

to take a hand to take part in a game, esp. of cards.

to take a hand in 1 to take a share in. 2 to get mixed up with.

to take by the hand to take (someone) under one's protection, care or guidance.

to take in hand 1 to undertake, to attempt. 2 to deal with, to manage. 3 to discipline (*That child needs taking in hand*).

to take one's courage in both hands COURAGE.

to take one's life in one's hands LIFE.

to take the law into one's own hands LAW.

to throw one's hand in 1 to stop participating in a particular hand of a gambling card game. 2 to give up a job etc. as hopeless.

to tie someone's hands TIE.

to try one's hand TRY.

to turn one's hand to to undertake; to apply oneself to.

to wash one's hands WASH.

to wash one's hands of WASH.

to win hands down WIN.

to wring one's hands WRING.

†to wring someone's hand WRING.

under one's hand with one's proper signature.

whip hand WHIP.

with a heavy hand HEAVY.

with a high hand HIGH.

with clean hands CLEAN.

with one's bare hands BARE.

handcuff
golden handcuff GOLDEN.

handkerchief
to throw the handkerchief to 1 to call on (a player) to take a turn, esp. to pursue (in certain games). 2 to single out patronizingly.

handle
a handle to one's name (*sl.*) a title.

to fly off the handle FLY².

to get a handle on (*coll.*) to find a means of understanding etc.

to give a handle to to furnish an occasion or advantage that may be utilized.

handsaw
to know a hawk from a handsaw HAWK.

handshake
golden handshake GOLDEN.

handsome
handsome is as handsome does good actions are more important than a pleasant appearance.

to come down handsome (*sl.*) to pay a handsome price, compensation or reward.

hang
hang it/ I'll be hanged! used to express annoyance or surprise.

not to care/ give a hang (*coll.*) to be totally unconcerned.

one might as well be hung for a sheep as for a lamb if punishment is inevitable, one might as well gain maximum advantage from one's wrongdoing or folly. [Alluding to the former death penalty for sheep-stealing, which took no account of the age or size of the animal.]

thereby hangs a tale there are things that could be said by way of background, explanation etc. [From Shakespeare's *As You Like It*: "And so, from hour to hour, we ripe and ripe, / and then, from hour to hour, we rot and rot: / And thereby hangs a tale."]

to get the hang of 1 to understand the drift or connection of. **2** to get the knack of (*It seems hard at first, but you'll soon get the hang of it*).

to go hang (*coll.*) to be no longer of interest or concern.

to hang about/ around 1 to loiter, to loaf (*hanging around on street corners*). **2** to stay near, to frequent. **3** to wait. **4** to associate (with).

to hang back 1 to act reluctantly, to hesitate. **2** to stay behind.

to hang by a thread to be in a very precarious state.

to hang down to droop.

to hang fire 1 to hesitate. **2** (of a charge in a firearm) not to ignite immediately. **3** to be wanting in life or spirit.

to hang heavy (of time) to go slowly.

to hang in 1 (*esp. N Am., coll.*) to persist (*Hang in there!*). **2** (*esp. N Am., coll.*) to linger.

to hang in doubt to be in suspense.

to hang in the balance to be unresolved.

to hang loose (*N Am., coll.*) to behave in a relaxed and informal manner.

to hang on 1 to grasp or hold. **2** to persist. **3** to depend on. **4** (*coll.*) to wait (*Hang on a minute*). **5** to listen closely to.

to hang on by one's fingernails to make a desperate or determined effort to keep something or to remain in a particular position.

to hang one's head to bow one's head in shame, to be ashamed.

to hang on someone's lips to listen eagerly for every word spoken by someone.

to hang on to 1 to keep holding. **2** to retain.

to hang out 1 to suspend from a window etc. **2** (of a tongue) to protrude loosely. **3** (*sl.*) to live (in a particular place); to spend a lot of time (somewhere).

to hang over 1 to be hanging or immobile above. **2** to be oppressively present to. **3** to be overhanging. **4** to spend time.

to hang together 1 to be consistent, to make sense (*Their explanation doesn't hang together*). **2** to be closely united.

to hang up 1 to suspend. **2** to replace a telephone receiver and so end the call. **3** to put aside, to leave undecided. **4** to defer indefinitely. **5** (*sl.*) to cause neurosis or anxiety in.

to hang upon 1 to be dependent on. **2** to listen closely to (*He hangs upon her every word*). **3** to adhere closely to. **4** to be a weight or drag on. **5** to rest, to dwell upon.

to hang up one's boots to retire.

to hang up one's hat to make oneself at home (in another house).

to let it all hang out (*sl.*) to be completely relaxed, to abandon inhibition.

ha'p'orth

to spoil the ship for a ha'p'orth of tar SPOIL.

happen

as it happens actually, in fact.

it's all happening (*coll.*) there is a lot of activity.

happy

happy as a lark very happy or cheerful.

happy as a sandboy happily engrossed.

happy as Larry very pleased or happy. [Possibly from Larry Foley (1847–1917), a famous boxer.]

happy as the day is long very happy or contented.

happy event (*coll.*) the birth of a baby.

happy hunting ground (*coll.*) an area of activity offering easy rewards. [From the North American Indians' name for heaven or paradise.]

happy medium a compromise; a state of affairs avoiding extremes.

many happy returns (of the day) a birthday greeting.

hard

hard and fast strict; that must be strictly adhered to.

hard as nails 1 callous, unsympathetic. **2** physically tough.

hard by 1 close by. **2** close at hand.

hard case 1 a tough or violent person. **2** (*Austral., New Zeal.*) an amusing or eccentric person. **3** a difficult case. **4** a case of hardship.

hard cheese (*coll., iron.*) hard luck.

hard done by treated unfairly or badly.

hard feelings feelings of bitterness and resentment (*no hard feelings*).

hard hit seriously damaged or affected, esp. by monetary losses.

hard lines (*coll.*) hard luck.

hard luck 1 (*int.*) used to express commiseration. **2** misfortune, undeserved lack of success.

hard nut to crack 1 a problem that is difficult to solve. **2** something that is difficult to understand. **3** a person who is not easily convinced.

hard of hearing having defective hearing.

hard on 1 difficult for. **2** unkind to, unpleasant to. **3** critical of (*Don't be too hard on her*). **4** close behind.

hard put to unlikely to find it easy to (*You'd be hard put to tell the difference*).

hard put to it in difficulties.

hard row to hoe a difficult task.

hard stuff (*coll.*) the strongest alcoholic drink, spirits, esp. whisky.

hard up in need, esp. of money, very poor.

hard up for in need of, short of.

hard upon close behind.

to play hard to get (*coll.*) to act coyly, esp. as a come-on.

to put the hard word on (*Austral., New Zeal., sl.*) to ask or pressurize (someone) to do something.

harden

to harden off to make (a plant) more able to withstand cold conditions by increasing periods of exposure.

†**to harden the neck** to grow obstinate.

hardly

hardly any very few, very little.

hardly ever very seldom.

hare

mad as a March hare MAD.

to run with the hare and hunt with the hounds to keep in with both sides.

to start a hare START.

hark

hark forward/ away! cries to urge hounds.

to hark back to to return to (some point or matter from which a temporary digression has been made). [Originally a hunting term, meaning to call hounds back when they have passed the scent.]

harm

out of harm's way safe.

to come to harm to be injured or damaged.

to harm a hair of someone's head to harm someone in the slightest (*If he harms a hair of her head, I'll kill him!*).

harmless

to hold harmless (*Law*) to indemnify.

harmony

in harmony 1 producing musical chords or chord progressions. **2** in agreement.

harness

in harness at one's work.

to die in harness DIE[1].

harrow

under the harrow in distress or tribulation.

Harry

Tom, Dick and Harry TOM.

hash

to make a hash of (*coll.*) to make a mess of.

to settle someone's hash SETTLE.

haste

in haste speedily, precipitately.

marry in haste, repent at leisure MARRY.

more haste, less speed when you try to do something too quickly you make careless mistakes that slow you down.

to make haste 1 to be quick. 2 to be in a hurry.

hat

at the drop of a hat DROP.

brass hat BRASS.

hats off to used to express admiration for or approval of.

I'll eat my hat EAT.

old hat OLD.

out of a hat 1 (selected) at random. 2 as if by a clever trick or magic.

to hang up one's hat HANG.

to keep under one's hat (*coll.*) to keep secret.

to knock into a cocked hat KNOCK.

to pass/ send round the hat to ask for contributions of money, donations etc.

to raise the hat to RAISE.

to take off one's hat to (*coll.*) to express admiration for or approval of.

to talk through one's hat TALK.

to throw one's hat into the ring to enter a contest, election etc. [From a way of challenging (or accepting a challenge from) a prizefighter at a show etc.]

hatch¹

down the hatch! (*coll.*) drink up! (as a toast).

to batten down the hatches BATTEN.

under hatches 1 (*Naut.*) confined below; out of sight. 2 in a state of bondage or repression. 3 dead.

hatch²

hatches, matches and dispatches (*coll.*) newspaper announcements of births, marriages and deaths.

hatchet

hatchet job (*coll.*) a fiercely critical speech or piece of writing.

hatchet man 1 a person hired to carry out violent or illegal tasks. 2 a person appointed to sack people in an organization.

to bury the hatchet BURY.

to throw the hatchet to tell lies or fabulous stories. [From an old game in which hatchets were thrown at a target.]

hate

to hate someone's guts (*coll.*) to dislike someone intensely.

hatter

mad as a hatter MAD.

haul

to haul over the coals 1 to call to account. 2 to reprimand. [An allusion to a former method of punishment or torture.]

to haul up (*coll.*) to bring for trial in a court of law (*hauled up before the magistrate*).

have

†have after (*imper.*) follow, let us follow.

†have at (*imper.*) attack, encounter.

†have with you 1 I will go with you. 2 come on, agreed.

to be had to be taken in.

to have about one to be carrying, to have with one.

to have (got) to to be obliged to (*You have to admit it sounds unlikely*).

to have had it 1 (*coll.*) to have let one's opportunity or moment go by. 2 (*coll.*) to have done something that will have serious consequences for one. **3** (*coll.*) to have been killed or overcome. **4** (*coll.*) to be old, unfashionable or worn out (*I think these boots have had it*). **5** to be exhausted.

to have it 1 to have found the solution. **2** to win a vote etc.

to have it in for to want to harm.

to have it in one to be capable, to have the ability (*I knew you had it in you!*).

to have it off/ away (*taboo sl.*) to have sexual intercourse.

to have it out to settle a quarrel or dispute by fighting, debate etc.

to have it that to maintain or argue that.

to have on 1 to be wearing (something). **2** to have (something) planned. **3** to deceive (someone), to trick (someone) (*I thought she was having me on*).

to have out to have (a tooth etc.) removed or extracted.

to have something on someone 1 to have evidence that a person has done something wrong. **2** to have an advantage over another person.

to have up (*coll.*) to cause to be prosecuted in court.

to have what it takes (*coll.*) to show the necessary talent, qualities or stamina.

havoc

to cry havoc CRY.

to play havoc with 1 to damage. **2** to upset.

haw

to hum/ hem and haw 1 to hesitate in speaking. **2** to refrain from giving a decisive answer.

hawk

to know a hawk from a handsaw to be intelligent and discriminating. [From Shakespeare's *Hamlet*: "I am but mad north-north-west; when the wind is southerly, I know a hawk from a handsaw."]

to watch like a hawk WATCH.

hay

a roll in the hay ROLL.

to make hay to turn, toss and expose mown grass to the sun for drying.

to make hay of to throw into confusion.

to make hay while the sun shines to take advantage of every favourable opportunity.

haystack

to look for a needle in a haystack NEEDLE.

haywire

to go haywire to become chaotic or disordered, to go wrong (*All our plans went haywire*). [From the wire used to bind hay, which tangles easily and has a tendency to spring apart out of control when cut.]

head[1]

a head for an ability to understand or tolerate (*to have a head for heights*).

an old head on young shoulders OLD.

a price on someone's head PRICE.

a roof over one's head ROOF.

by a head by a narrow margin (*We won by a head*). [From horse racing.]

eyes in the back of one's head EYE[1].

from head to foot/ toe over the whole person.

head and ears 1 the whole person. **2** completely.

head and shoulders above much better than (*She stands head and shoulders above the other candidates for the job*).

head over heels 1 turning upside down. **2** completely (in love).

heads I win, tails you lose I cannot lose and you cannot win.

head start 1 an advantage given or taken at the beginning of a race etc. **2** an advantageous beginning to any enterprise.

heads will roll people will be severely punished. [An allusion to beheading as a form of capital punishment.]

in one's head 1 by thinking only, without physical aids. **2** in one's mind.

off one's head 1 out of one's mind. **2** wildly excited, demented.

off the top of one's head TOP[1].

one's head off very loudly or to excess (*laughing their heads off*).

on one's (own) head being one's own responsibility; at one's own risk (*On your own head be it!*).

out of one's head 1 off one's head. **2** out of one's own head. **3** delirious, intoxicated.

out of one's own head 1 by one's own invention. **2** of one's own accord.

over/ above someone's head 1 beyond someone's understanding. **2** appealing to a higher authority than someone (*I went over his head and complained to the manager*). **3** without regard for someone's higher status.

over head and ears deeply (immersed).

soft in the head SOFT.

standing on one's head very easily, without any difficulty (*I could do that standing on my head*).

to bang/ knock/ run one's head against a brick wall to have one's efforts come to nothing.

to bite someone's head off BITE.

to break a head BREAK.

to bury one's head in the sand BURY.

to come into someone's head to occur as a thought in someone's mind (*I just said the first thing that came into my head*).

to come to a head 1 to reach a crisis or culminating point. **2** (of an ulcer or boil) to suppurate. **3** to ripen.

to count heads COUNT.

to enter someone's head ENTER.

to gather head GATHER.

to get it into one's head to become convinced (that).

to get one's head down 1 (*sl.*) to start working seriously. **2** (*sl.*) to go to sleep.

to get one's head together to collect one's thoughts, to achieve a more balanced state of mind.

to give someone/ let someone have their head to give liberty or licence to someone. [When a horse is given its head, it is allowed to go as it pleases.]

to go off one's head (*coll.*) to become insane.

to go to one's head 1 (of alcoholic drink) to make one slightly drunk. **2** (of success etc.) to make one vain, arrogant etc.

to hang one's head HANG.

to harm a hair of someone's head HARM.

to have a head like a sieve (*coll.*) to be very forgetful.

to have eyes in the back of one's head EYE.

to have one's head screwed on the right way to be sensible or well-balanced.

to heap coals of fire on someone's head HEAP.

to hide one's head HIDE[1].

to hit the nail on the head HIT.

to hold a pistol to someone's head PISTOL.

to hold one's head high to behave proudly or arrogantly; to retain one's dignity.

to hold one's head up to be unashamed (*I'll never be able to hold my head up in the town again*).

to keep a civil tongue in one's head CIVIL.

to keep one's head to remain calm.

to keep one's head above water to avoid financial ruin.

to keep one's head down (*coll.*) to avoid being noticed when there are problems.

to knock one's head against KNOCK.

to knock on the head KNOCK.

to lay heads together to deliberate, to confer.

to lie on the head of LIE[2].

to lift up one's head LIFT.

to lose one's head LOSE.

to make head 1 to push forward. **2** to struggle (against) effectually.

to make head or tail of (*usu. neg.*) to have the slightest understanding of (*I couldn't make head or tail of their message*).

to need/ ought to have one's head
examined (*coll.*) to be very foolish or
slightly insane (*Anyone who buys a car
like that needs their head examined*).

to need (something) like a hole in the head
NEED.

to put ideas into someone's head IDEA.

to put one's head in a noose to put oneself
into a dangerous or exposed situation.
[An allusion to death by hanging.]

to put one's head on the block to lay
oneself open to blame, criticism,
failure, defeat etc. [An allusion to
capital punishment.]

to put our/ their/ etc. heads together to
consider (a problem) together (*Could
you put your heads together and come
up with a proposal for next Friday's
meeting?*).

to rear/ raise its (ugly) head to become
apparent, esp. in an ominous way
(*The question of finance reared its
ugly head*).

to scratch one's head SCRATCH.

to shake one's head SHAKE.

to snap someone's head off SNAP.

to take it into one's head 1 to fix on the
idea or belief (that), esp. with no
supporting evidence. 2 to resolve (to
do something).

to toss one's head TOSS.

to turn someone's head to cause someone
to be vain or infatuated.

to wet the baby's head WET.

two heads are better than one TWO.

with one's head in the clouds being
unrealistic; daydreaming.

head²

to head back 1 to intercept, to get ahead
of and turn back or aside. 2 to return
to one's starting point.

to head off 1 to intercept, to get ahead
and turn back or aside (*head them off
at the crossroads*). 2 to leave, to set off.
3 to forestall.

to head up to be in charge of (a team of
people etc.).

headline

to hit/ make the headlines to gain
notoriety, to get notice in the press.

headway

to make headway to advance, to make
progress.

healing

the healing art the art of medicine.

health

clean bill of health CLEAN.

to drink the health of DRINK.

heap

on the rubbish heap RUBBISH HEAP.

on the scrap heap SCRAP HEAP.

struck all of a heap STRIKE.

to heap coals of fire on someone's head to
return good for evil, causing remorse
or repentance. [From the Bible: "If
thine enemy be hungry, give him
bread to eat; and if he be thirsty, give
him water to drink: For thou shalt
heap coals of fire upon his head"
(Prov. xxv.21–22).]

hear

hear! hear! used to express agreement or
approval.

I've heard that one before! used to express
disbelief.

never to hear the end of (*coll.*) to be
repeatedly reminded of or told about
(*If she wins this competition, we'll
never hear the end of it!*).

one can hear a pin drop it is very quiet
(*A stunned silence followed her
announcement: you could have heard
a pin drop*).

to hear someone out to listen to what a
person has to say without interrupting.

to hear tell/ say to have been told (of
something).

will not hear of will not consider
allowing or agreeing.

hearing
hard of hearing HARD.

heart
absence makes the heart grow fonder
ABSENCE.

after one's own heart exactly as one
desires; as one feels or thinks oneself
(*You're a woman after my own heart*).
[From the Bible: "the Lord hath
sought him a man after his own heart"
(I Sam. xiii.14).]

at heart **1** in reality, truly, at bottom. **2** in
one's inmost feelings.

by heart by rote, by or from memory.

change of heart CHANGE.

close to/ near one's heart **1** very dear to
one. **2** that has a strong emotional
effect on one.

from (the bottom of) one's heart **1** with
absolute sincerity. **2** fervently.

hand on heart HAND.

have a heart! be more considerate; do not
be so harsh.

heart and hand with enthusiastic energy.

heart and soul with full commitment,
devotedly.

heart of gold a kind and generous nature.

heart of oak **1** a person of courage. **2** a
courageous nature.

heart of stone an unfeeling or unyielding
nature.

home is where the heart is HOME.

in good heart **1** in good spirits. **2** in good
condition, fertile.

in one's heart (of hearts) inwardly,
secretly (*I knew in my heart that we
would fail*).

one's heart bleeds for someone (*iron.*) one
feels great pity for someone (*I hear
they may have to sell their yacht: my
heart bleeds for them!*).

one's heart goes out to someone one feels
genuine sympathy for someone (*My
heart went out to the parents of the
victims*).

out of heart **1** in low spirits, depressed.
2 (of land) exhausted of fertility.

the fullness of the heart FULLNESS.

to break someone's heart BREAK.

to cross one's heart (and hope to die)
CROSS.

to do someone's heart good to make
someone happy.

to eat one's heart out EAT.

to find it in one's heart to to be able to
bring oneself to (do); to be willing to
(*Can you find it in your heart to
forgive him?*).

to give one's heart to to fall deeply in love
with.

to have at heart to be earnestly set upon,
to cherish (a design etc.).

to have one's heart in (*usu. neg.*) to be
fully committed or devoted to.

to have one's heart in one's boots to feel
discouraged or apprehensive.

to have one's heart in one's mouth to be
frightened or startled.

to have one's heart in the right place to
have a kind nature; to have good
intentions.

to have the heart to (*usu. neg.*) to be able
or have the courage to (do something
unkind or unpleasant) (*I didn't have
the heart to tell her she was too late*).

to learn/ get by heart to commit to
memory.

to lie at one's heart LIE².

to lose heart LOSE.

to lose one's heart to LOSE.

to make someone's heart bleed (*iron.*) to
distress someone.

to one's heart's content as much as one
likes.

to put one's heart into to become fully
committed or devoted to, to do
wholeheartedly.

to set one's heart on to want very much
(*I had set my heart on a white
wedding*).

to set someone's heart at rest to
tranquillize or console someone.

to shut one's heart to SHUT.

to speak to someone's heart SPEAK.

to take heart to pluck up courage.

to take to heart to be greatly affected by (*He took her criticism to heart*).

to warm the cockles of the heart WARM.

to wear one's heart on one's sleeve WEAR.

with a heavy heart HEAVY.

with all one's/ one's whole heart 1 very willingly. **2** completely, utterly.

heat

if you can't stand the heat, get out of the kitchen anyone who can't cope with the pressures of their job or position should leave it. [Originally said by US president Harry S. Truman (1884–1972).]

in the heat of the moment without thinking; without prior consideration (because of the pressure of events).

more heat than light more anger or vehemence than enlightenment.

on heat (of a female mammal) ready for mating.

to take the heat out of to make (a situation) less emotional or tense.

to turn the heat on (*coll.*) to put (a person) under pressure; to direct criticism at (a person).

heather

to set the heather on fire to create a disturbance.

to take to the heather to become an outlaw.

heave

to heave down to turn (a ship) on one side in order to clean it.

to heave in(to) sight to come into sight.

to heave out to throw out.

to heave the log to determine a ship's speed with a float and line. [From the piece of wood originally used for this purpose.]

to heave to 1 (*Naut.*) to bring a ship to a standstill. **2** (*Naut.*) to bring the head of (a ship) to the wind and so stop its motion.

heave-ho

to give someone/ get the heave-ho (*coll.*) to dismiss someone/ be dismissed from employment.

heaven

for heaven's sake used as a solemn adjuration or an expression of exasperation etc.

good heavens! GOOD.

heaven forbid may it never happen (that).

†heaven forfend may it never happen (that).

heaven knows used to reinforce the seriousness or sincerity of a statement.

heaven on earth a perfect or very pleasant place or situation.

heavens above! used to express surprise, dismay, irritation etc.

manna from heaven MANNA.

pennies from heaven PENNY.

seventh heaven SEVENTH.

the heavens opened (*coll.*) it poured with rain.

to high heaven HIGH.

to move heaven and earth MOVE.

heavy

heavy going difficult to get through, laborious. [From hunting or horse racing, referring to wet ground that slows down the pace.]

heavy on 1 using a lot of (*This car is heavy on fuel*). **2** unduly strict with or harsh to. **3** giving hard wear to.

heavy on hand (of a horse etc.) hard to manage.

to make heavy weather of to exaggerate the difficulty of.

with a heavy hand 1 oppressively. **2** unstintingly, without sparing.

with a heavy heart sadly.

hedge

to hedge one's bets to protect oneself against risk of loss by doing or securing something that will provide compensation.

to look as if one has been dragged through a hedge backwards DRAG.

heed

to take/ give/ pay heed to pay attention (to).

heel

Achilles heel ACHILLES.

at heel (of a dog) close beside or behind.

at the heels of close behind.

down at heel 1 having worn heels. 2 shabby, disreputably dressed.

head over heels HEAD[1].

on the heels of following closely after.

to come to heel (of a dog) to walk close beside or behind in a controlled manner.

to cool one's heels COOL.

to dig one's heels in DIG.

to drag one's heels DRAG.

to heel 1 (of a dog) close beside or behind. 2 (of a person) under control.

to kick one's heels KICK.

to kick up one's heels KICK.

to lay/ clap by the heels to arrest, to imprison.

to show a clean pair of heels CLEAN.

to take to one's heels to run away.

to turn on one's heel to turn round sharply (She turned on her heel and stalked out).

height

the height of the most extreme example of (the height of fashion).

hell

a hell of a (coll.) a very good, bad, remarkable etc. (thing of its kind) (He had a hell of a bruise on his shin).

all hell broke loose there was chaos or commotion. [The phrase was popularized in this form by John Milton in his poem Paradise Lost (1667): "Wherefore with thee / Came not all hell broke loose?".]

as hell (coll.) extremely (mad as hell).

come hell or high water (coll.) whatever may happen.

for the hell of it for amusement, just for fun.

hell for leather (coll.) very fast (They ran hell for leather down the street).

hell to pay very unpleasant consequences (There'll be hell to pay if we don't deliver on time). [Perhaps alluding to a pact with the devil.]

like a bat out of hell BAT[2].

like hell 1 (coll.) very hard, much etc. 2 (coll.) used to deny a statement made by another (Like hell you will!).

not to have a cat in hell's chance CAT.

not to have a hope in hell HOPE.

not to have a snowball's chance in hell SNOWBALL.

till hell freezes over (coll.) forever.

to beat/ scare/ etc. the hell out of to beat etc. severely.

to get/ catch hell to be severely scolded or punished.

to give someone hell 1 to scold someone severely. 2 to make life very difficult for someone.

to hell with used to express a complete lack of concern for (To hell with the rules!).

to play (merry) hell with 1 (coll.) to harm or damage. 2 (coll.) to scold.

to raise hell RAISE.

what the hell what does it matter.

what/ who / etc. the hell (coll.) used as an intensifier (Where the hell has it gone?).

hello

golden hello GOLDEN.

helm

at the helm steering, in control, at the head.

to put up/ down the helm (Naut.) to bring the rudder to leeward/ windward.

to take the helm to take control.

help

it cannot be helped 1 there is no remedy.
2 it cannot be prevented or avoided.

so help me (God) a strong oath or
asseveration.

to help a lame dog over a stile to help
someone in need or trouble.

to help along 1 to help (an infirm person
etc.) to walk. **2** to advance
(negotiations etc.).

to help down to help (a person) in
descending.

to help off 1 to help (a person) to remove
or take off (a garment etc.) (*I need
someone to help me off with this
wetsuit*). **2** to help (a person) to alight
from (a step etc.).

to help on 1 to forward, to advance. **2** to
help (a person) put on (a garment etc.)
(*The waiter helped me on with my
jacket*).

to help oneself to refrain from acting (*He
tried not to laugh, but couldn't help
himself*).

to help oneself to to take for oneself
without waiting for offer or permission
(*She helped herself to a glass of wine*).

to help out to help to complete or to get
out of a difficulty.

to help over to enable to surmount.

to help to to supply with, to furnish with.

to help up to help (a person) in rising or
getting up (a stair etc.).

helve

to put the axe on the helve AXE.

herd

to ride herd on RIDE.

here

here and now right now, the present.

here and there 1 in this place and that.
2 hither and thither.

here's how! I drink to your good health.

here's to let us drink a toast to (*Here's to
the success of the mission*).

here, there and everywhere all over the
place, everywhere.

here today and gone tomorrow temporary,
transient, short-lived.

here we are said on arrival after a
journey.

here you are said on giving something to
someone by hand.

neither here nor there unimportant,
irrelevant (*Where the money comes
from is neither here nor there*).

hero

hero's welcome a rapturous welcome, as
given to a successful warrior.

herring

red herring RED.

to draw a red herring across the track RED.

hesitate

he who hesitates is lost one should act
quickly and grasp opportunities, there
is no time for indecision or delay.

hew

to hew one's way to make a passage etc.
for oneself by hewing.

hewer

hewers of wood and drawers of water
labourers and other such menials.
[From the Bible: "Let them live; but let
them be hewers of wood and drawers
of water unto all the congregation"
(Josh. ix.21).]

hide¹

to hide one's head to keep or remain out
of sight, esp. from shame.

to hide one's light under a bushel to
conceal one's skills or talents. [From
the Bible: "Neither do men light a
candle, and put it under a bushel, but
on a candlestick" (Matt. v.15).]

hide²

neither/ not hide nor hair of nothing at all
of (someone) (*I haven't seen hide nor
hair of him for days*).

to tan someone's hide TAN.

hiding
on a hiding to nothing unable to succeed, no matter what happens.

hidlings
in hidlings (*Sc.*) on the quiet, secretly.

high
from on high from aloft, from heaven.

high and dry 1 left behind, stranded without resources. **2** (*Naut.*) out of the water, aground.

high and low 1 everywhere (*They searched high and low for the mouse*). **2** (of people) all sorts and conditions. **3** (*sl.*) †false dice loaded for throwing high or low.

high and mighty 1 (*coll.*) arrogant. **2** †of exalted rank.

high as a kite (*coll.*) completely intoxicated, esp. by drugs.

high old time (*coll.*) an enjoyable and exciting time.

high spot (*coll.*) a moment or event of particular importance or interest.

high time 1 (*coll.*) the latest possible time, almost too late (*It's high time you cleaned that car*). **2** (*coll.*) an enjoyable and exciting time.

high, wide and handsome (*coll.*) in an exuberant or flamboyant manner.

in high dudgeon angry or resentful.

in high spirits in a vivacious, cheerful or lively mood.

on high 1 aloft. **2** to or in heaven.

on one's high horse (*coll.*) behaving arrogantly or affecting superiority. [From the tall horses ridden by people of rank in medieval times.]

to get high 1 to reach a state of pleasure or euphoria. **2** to become pleasurably affected by drugs etc.

to high heaven very strongly or offensively (*That cheese stinks to high heaven*).

with a high hand in an arrogant or arbitrary manner.

high day
high days and holidays special occasions.

high jump
to be for the high jump (*coll.*) to be liable to receive some form of severe punishment etc.

hightail
to hightail it to run away. [Alluding to the raised tail of a fleeing animal.]

high water
come hell or high water HELL.

hill
old as the hills OLD.

over the hill 1 (*coll.*) beyond one's prime. **2** (*coll.*) beyond the crisis.

up hill and down dale 1 up and down hills. **2** facing many difficulties or engaged on a difficult journey. **3** strenuously and persistently.

hilt
up to the hilt to the fullest extent. [Alluding to a sword or dagger plunged into someone's body as far as it will go.]

hinge
off the hinges 1 in a state of mental or physical disorder. **2** out of working order.

hint
to drop a hint DROP.

to hint at to mention indirectly.

hip
†**on the hip** at a disadvantage.

to shoot from the hip SHOOT.

to smite hip and thigh SMITE.

hire
on/ for hire available for service or temporary use in exchange for a fee.

to hire oneself out to make oneself available for employment.

to hire out 1 to allow the temporary use of for an agreed payment. **2** to pay independent contractors for (work to be done).

his

his and/ 'n' hers (*esp. facet.*) (of paired objects) for husband and wife, or a man and a woman.

history

ancient history ANCIENT.

to go down in history to be remembered (*This will go down in history as the end of the era of communism*).

to make history 1 to do something momentous. **2** to influence the course of history.

hit

hit and miss/ hit or miss succeeding and failing in a haphazard way.

not to know what hit one to be suddenly taken by surprise.

to hit back to retaliate.

to hit below the belt to act unfairly in a contest. [From the sport of boxing, in which such a blow is against the rules.]

to hit home to bring about a desirable realization (*Your remarks seem to have hit home*).

to hit it off to get along well, to agree (*They really hit it off together*).

to hit off to represent or describe rapidly or cleverly.

to hit on 1 to light or chance on. **2** to discover by luck. **3** (*N Am., sl.*) to try to establish a romantic or sexual relationship with.

to hit out to strike out straight from the shoulder.

to hit out at to attack vigorously, either physically or verbally (*hitting out at the proposed reforms*).

to hit skins (*esp. N Am., sl.*) to have sexual intercourse.

to hit someone between the eyes/ in the eye to astonish or shock someone.

to hit someone when they are down to cause someone further suffering when they are already in an unfortunate situation. [From the sport of boxing, in which such a blow is against the rules.]

to hit the bottle (*sl.*) to drink a great deal of alcoholic drink.

to hit the deck (*coll.*) to fall down quickly or suddenly.

to hit the ground running (*esp. N Am., coll.*) to begin an activity, esp. a job, in a dynamic or enthusiastic way.

to hit the high spots 1 to visit the key places in an area. **2** to go to excess or extremes.

to hit the jackpot 1 (*coll.*) to win a large prize. **2** (*coll.*) to have a big success.

to hit the nail on the head 1 to hit upon the true facts of a case. **2** to do exactly the right thing.

to hit the road (*sl.*) to leave, to begin travelling.

to hit the roof/ ceiling (*coll.*) to lose one's temper.

to hit the sack/ hay (*coll.*) to go to bed or sleep.

to hit the skids (*coll.*) to deteriorate fast.

to hit the spot (*coll.*) to be just what is needed.

to hit the trail (*N Am., sl.*) to hit the road.

to hit up in cricket, to score (runs) freely or with vigour.

to hit upon to discover by luck.

to make/ score a hit (with) to be a sudden success (with), to become popular (with).

hitch

to get hitched (*sl.*) to get married.

to hitch one's wagon to a star to rely on powers higher than one's own. [From an essay by Ralph Waldo Emerson (1803–82).]

to hitch up to lift (esp. clothing) with a jerk.

hither

hither and thither/ yon 1 to this place and that. **2** here and there.

hive

to hive off 1 to assign (part of a firm's work) to a subsidiary company. **2** to transfer (assets) from one concern to another such as in privatization. **3** to separate from a larger group.
to hive up to hoard.

hob

to play/ raise hob (*N Am., coll.*) to cause mischief.

Hobson

Hobson's choice no alternative. [From Thomas Hobson (?1544–1631), keeper of a Cambridge livery stable, who insisted that every customer take the first horse inside the stable door or none at all.]

hock

in hock in pawn, debt or prison.

hoe

to hoe in (*Austral., New Zeal., sl.*) to eat heartily.
to hoe into (*Austral., New Zeal., sl.*) to attack vigorously.

hog

to go the whole hog WHOLE.
to live high off the hog LIVE[1].

hoist

hoist with/ by one's own petard caught in one's own trap. [From Shakespeare's *Hamlet*: "For 'tis the sport to have the engineer / Hoist with his own petard." A petard was an engine of war used to blow up barricades etc.]
to hoist one's flag to signify that one is taking command.
to hoist the flag to stake one's claim to discovered territory by displaying a flag.

hold

hold everything! stop doing anything!

hold hard! (*dated, coll.*) stop!
hold it! 1 (*coll.*) stop! **2** (*coll.*) wait!
no holds barred observing no rules. [From the sport of wrestling, in which certain ways of grasping one's opponent are sometimes forbidden.]
on hold 1 (of a telephone call or caller) waiting to be connected. **2** deferred until later.
to get hold of 1 to grasp. **2** to get in contact with (*We couldn't get hold of the child's parents*).
to hold aloof to avoid communication with others.
to hold back 1 to restrain, to prevent (something or someone) from progressing. **2** to retain in one's possession. **3** to keep oneself in check. **4** to stop oneself from expressing (an emotion).
to hold by to adhere to.
to hold down 1 to repress, to restrain, to control. **2** to keep at a low level. **3** (*coll.*) to be good enough at (one's job etc.) to retain it.
to hold forth 1 to stretch or put forward. **2** (*often derog.*) to speak in public or for a long time (*holding forth about her new car*). **3** to propose, to offer.
to hold from/ of to derive title from.
to hold in 1 to restrain. **2** to keep quiet, to keep silent.
to hold off 1 to keep (someone or something) at a distance. **2** to remain at a distance. **3** to delay. **4** to refrain from. **5** to keep away, not to happen.
to hold on 1 to continue without interruption, to persist. **2** (*coll.*) to stop. **3** to wait a moment. **4** not to end a telephone connection.
to hold on to 1 to keep holding, to clutch (*Hold on to the rope*). **2** to retain possession of (*Hold on to your shares until the market improves*).
to hold out 1 to hold forward, to stretch out. **2** to offer. **3** to bear, to endure, not to yield. **4** to persist, to last.
to hold out for to continue demanding in

spite of alternative offers (*They're holding out for a higher price*).

to hold out on (*coll.*) to refuse or delay in telling etc. something to (a person).

to hold over 1 to keep back or reserve, to defer. **2** (*Law*) to keep possession of after the expiration of one's term. **3** to threaten (someone) with.

to hold something against someone to be resentful towards another because of a past action etc., to regard something as discreditable to them (*I won't hold it against you if you say no*).

to hold to 1 to bind to (bail, one's statement etc.). **2** to adhere to.

to hold together 1 to (cause to) cohere. **2** to continue united.

to hold under to derive title from.

to hold up 1 to raise, to lift up. **2** to support, to encourage. **3** to sustain. **4** to show forth, to exhibit (to ridicule etc.). **5** to stop and rob by violence or threats. **6** to arrest the progress of, to obstruct. **7** (of the weather) to remain fine. **8** to continue at the same speed.

to hold with to approve of, to side with (*I don't hold with letting children watch programmes like that*).

to lay hold of to grasp or seize.

to leave hold of to stop holding, to let go.

to take hold 1 to take a grip (of). **2** to become established.

to take hold of to seize.

hole

ace in the hole ACE.

hole-and-corner secret, clandestine.

in holes (of materials etc.) worn so much that holes have formed.

like the Black Hole of Calcutta BLACK.

round peg in a square hole ROUND.

square peg in a round hole SQUARE.

to burn a hole in someone's pocket BURN.

to hole out 1 in golf, to play the ball into the hole. **2** (of a batsman in cricket) to be caught out.

to hole up (*N Am., coll.*) to go into hiding.

to make a hole in to take or consume a large part of.

to need (something) like a hole in the head NEED.

to pick holes/ a hole in PICK.

holiday

busman's holiday BUSMAN.

high days and holidays HIGH DAY.

on holiday/ one's holidays 1 having a break from work. **2** during one's holidays.

†to make a holiday to have a break from work.

to take a holiday to have a break from work.

hollow

in the hollow of someone's hand in a state of subservience to someone.

to beat hollow to excel or surpass in a great degree.

holy

holier-than-thou (*coll.*) convinced of one's moral superiority, sanctimonious. [From the Bible: "Stand by thyself, come not near to me; for I am holier than thou" (Isa. lxv.5).]

holy of holies 1 the innermost and most sacred apartment of the Jewish Tabernacle and the Temple, where the ark was kept. **2** an innermost shrine. **3** something regarded as most sacred.

holy terror 1 (*coll.*) a formidable person, a troublesome person or thing. **2** the use of organized intimidation.

to take holy orders to be ordained.

home

an Englishman's home is his castle ENGLISHMAN.

at home 1 in one's own house, area or country. **2** at ease, comfortable (*Make yourself at home*). **3** conversant (with). **4** accessible to visitors, esp. when entertaining.

broken home BROKEN.

close to home CLOSE[1].

home and dry safe after having
successfully come through an
experience.

home from home a place other than one's
own home where one can be at ease.

home is where the heart is one's home is
wherever the people one loves are.

home, James! (*facet.*) drive home at once!
[From the phrase 'Home, James, and
don't spare the horses!', originally
addressed to a private coachman in the
19th century, James being a typical
name of such servants.]

home truth an unwelcome truth
expressed in a pointed way.

near home concerning one deeply.

to eat out of house and home EAT.

homework

to do one's homework (*coll.*) to prepare
well.

honest

honest Injun (*coll.*) genuinely, really.
[Originally used by children. Injun is
an offensive name for a North
American Indian.]

honest to God/ goodness genuinely, really,
completely.

to make an honest woman of (*coll. or
facet.*) to marry (esp. a pregnant
woman).

to make/ earn/ turn an honest penny
(*coll.*) to earn money legitimately or
fairly.

honesty

honesty is the best policy it is wise to be
honest.

honey

land of milk and honey LAND.

milk and honey MILK.

honour

honour bright (*dated, sl.*) used by
schoolchildren to pledge honour.

honours are even there is evenness in the
contest.

in honour bound under a moral
obligation.

in honour of out of respect for; as a
celebration of.

on/ upon one's honour used to pledge
one's honour or reputation on the
accuracy or good faith of a statement.

to be the soul of honour SOUL.

to do the honours 1 to perform the duties
of a host or hostess to guests. **2** (*coll.*)
to perform a social task, courtesy etc.,
such as serving food, proposing a toast
etc.

honourable

my honourable friend used in the House
of Commons to refer to another
member of one's own party.

hoof

on the hoof 1 (of livestock) alive; not yet
slaughtered. **2** (*coll.*) while standing up
or moving around.

to hoof it 1 (*sl.*) to walk, to go on foot.
2 (*sl.*) to dance.

to pad the hoof PAD.

hook

by hook or by crook by any means
whatsoever.

hook, line and sinker completely.
[Alluding to the parts at the end of a
fishing rod.]

off the hook 1 (*coll.*) no longer in danger,
difficulty or trouble (*I decided to let
them off the hook*). **2** (of a telephone
receiver) not on its rest. **3** ready-made.

off the hooks (*sl.*) dead.

on one's own hook (*sl.*) on one's own
account.

to hook it 1 (*sl.*) to decamp. **2** (*sl.*) to run
away.

to sling one's hook SLING.

hoop

to go/ be put through the hoop to go/ be

put through an ordeal. [Alluding to the circus trick of jumping through a blazing hoop.]

hoot
not to care two hoots CARE.

hoover
to hoover up to clean with or suck up etc. as if with a vacuum cleaner.

hop
on the hop 1 (*coll.*) unawares; unprepared. **2** (*coll.*) active.
to catch someone on the hop CATCH.
to hop in/ out (*coll.*) to get into/ out of a vehicle (*Hop in, and I'll drive you home*).
to hop it (*coll.*) to go away.
to hop off 1 (*coll.*) to get down or off lightly. **2** (*coll.*) to go away.
to hop the twig/ stick 1 to go away quickly. **2** (*sl.*) to die.

hope
forlorn hope FORLORN.
hope springs eternal (in the human breast) hope is part of human nature. [From *An Essay on Man* (1733) by Alexander Pope.]
not a hope! (*coll.*) that will never happen.
not to have a hope in hell not to have any chance at all.
some hope! (*coll.*) that will never happen.
to hope against hope to cling to a slight chance.
to hope and pray/ trust to hope very much.
where/ while there's life there's hope LIFE.
white hope WHITE.

horizon
on the horizon 1 (of an event etc.) imminent; likely to appear or happen soon. **2** visible.

horn
on the horns of a dilemma 1 in a situation involving a choice between two equally undesirable alternatives. **2** in an awkward situation.
to horn in (*sl.*) to push in, to intrude (on) (*He tried to horn in on our conversation*).
to lock horns LOCK.
to pull/ draw in one's horns 1 to repress one's ardour. **2** to curtail one's expenses. **3** to draw back, to check oneself. [Alluding to a snail retreating into its shell.]
to take the bull by the horns BULL.

hornet
to stir up a hornets' nest STIR.

horse
dark horse DARK.
horse and foot cavalry and infantry.
horse of another/ a different colour a completely different person, thing or matter.
horse sense (*coll.*) common sense.
horses for courses the matching of tasks to talents, skills etc. [From horse racing.]
one-horse race ONE-HORSE.
on one's high horse HIGH.
stalking horse STALK².
the horse's mouth (of information etc.) the most reliable source (*straight from the horse's mouth*). [The phrase may have originally referred to a betting tip in horse racing.]
to back the wrong horse BACK.
to change/ swap horses in midstream to alter plans, views etc. in the middle of a project.
to drive a coach and horses through DRIVE.
to eat like a horse EAT.
to flog a dead horse FLOG.
to hold one's horses 1 (*coll.*) to stop. **2** (*coll.*) to hesitate; to refrain from acting.
to horse! mount your horses.
to lock the stable door after the horse has bolted LOCK.

to look a gift horse in the mouth GIFT.

to put the cart before the horse CART.

to take horse 1 to mount a horse for the purpose of riding. **2** to travel on horseback.

Trojan horse TROJAN.

willing horse WILLING.

you can take a horse to water (but you cannot make it drink) you can give someone the opportunity to do what you want (but you cannot force them to do it).

horseback

on horseback mounted on a horse.

host[1]

to reckon without one's host RECKON.

host[2]

a host in oneself a person of extraordinary skills, resources etc.

hostage

to give a hostage to fortune to put oneself at a disadvantage by risking the loss of someone or something valued highly. [From Francis Bacon's essay 'Of Marriage and Single Life' (1625): "He that hath wife and children hath given hostages to fortune; for they are impediments to great enterprises, either of virtue or mischief." Bacon was echoing the words of the Roman poet Lucan (AD 39–65): "I have a wife, I have sons: all of them hostages given to fate."]

hot

hot air (*coll.*) boastful, empty talk.

hot and bothered flustered.

hot potato a controversial issue, something difficult or dangerous to deal with.

hot stuff 1 (*coll.*) an impressive or excellent thing or person. **2** (*coll.*) a very attractive person. **3** (*coll.*) a spirited, vigorous or passionate person. **4** (*coll.*) pornographic or erotic literature, film etc.

hot under the collar 1 indignant, angry. **2** embarrassed.

in hot water in trouble, difficulty or disgrace.

more ... than someone has had hot dinners (*coll.*) used in claims of greater experience (*I've fixed more cars than you've had hot dinners*).

not so hot (*coll.*) mediocre.

to give it someone hot (*sl.*) to punish, censure or abuse someone severely.

to go hot and cold to feel alternately hot and cold (owing to fear etc.).

to go/ sell like hot cakes to be sold very quickly.

to have the hots for (*sl.*) to be sexually attracted to.

to hot up to become more intense, exciting etc.

to make it hot for someone to make a situation unpleasant for someone.

hotfoot

to hotfoot it (*sl.*) to run or go quickly.

hot seat

in the hot seat in an awkward, difficult or dangerous position. [From a slang name for the electric chair used to execute criminals in the US.]

hound

to ride to hounds RIDE.

to run with the hare and hunt with the hounds HARE.

hour

after hours after closing time.

at all hours at all times.

at the eleventh hour ELEVENTH.

from hour to hour as the hours pass; hourly.

hour of need a time when help is needed (*They helped us in our hour of need*).

on the half-hour HALF-HOUR.

on the hour at exactly one, two etc. o'clock (*Buses leave on the hour*).

small hours SMALL.

the witching hour WITCHING.

to keep good/ regular hours to be home at night early or punctually.

to put off the evil hour EVIL.

until all hours until very late at night (*I was up until all hours preparing food for the party*).

house

halfway house HALFWAY.

house of cards 1 a structure built of playing cards. 2 any scheme or enterprise of an insecure or precarious kind.

house of ill repute/ fame a brothel.

like a house on fire very quickly and successfully (*getting on like a house on fire*).

like the side of a house SIDE.

on the house (esp. of alcoholic drinks) given for no payment.

open house OPEN.

people who live in glass houses should not throw stones PEOPLE.

safe as houses SAFE.

to bring the house down to win tumultuous applause (*Her encore brought the house down*).

to eat out of house and home EAT.

to keep/ make a House to succeed in assembling a quorum or sufficient support in the House of Commons.

to keep (to) the house to be confined through illness.

to play house to play at being members of a family in their home.

to put/ set one's house in order to settle one's affairs.

to set up house to move into a separate dwelling.

household

household name/ word a familiar name/ word, a well-known person/ thing.

houseroom

not to give houseroom to not to own or accommodate under any circumstances (*It's a hideous vase: I wouldn't give it houseroom!*).

how

and how! (*sl.*) and how much more!

how about? 1 used to suggest a possible choice (*How about a swim?*). 2 what is the news about?

how are you? 1 what is your state of health, well-being etc.? 2 how do you do?

how many what number.

how much 1 what price (*How much is this carpet?*). 2 what amount.

†how now? what is the meaning of this, why is this so?

†how so? how can this be so?

how's that? 1 what is your opinion, explanation etc.? 2 used in cricket to ask for the batsman to be given out.

how's your father (*coll., facet.*) illicit goings-on, esp. of a sexual nature.

howl

to howl down to prevent (a speaker) from being heard by derisive shouting, laughter etc.

Hoyle

according to Hoyle exactly according to the rules. [Referring to Sir Edmund Hoyle (1672–1769), an English writer on card games.]

huddle

to go into a huddle to have a secretive discussion.

huff

in a huff annoyed, offended, in a mood (*He went off in a huff*).

hug

to hug oneself to congratulate oneself complacently.

hull

hull down (of a ship) so far off that only the superstructure is visible.

hum

to make things hum to stir people etc.
into productive activity.

humble pie

to eat humble pie EAT.

humour

out of humour in a bad mood,
displeased.

hump

over the hump past the difficult or
critical stage of something.
to get the hump (*coll.*) to become
annoyed or depressed.
to hump a shiralee (*Austral.*) to carry a
burden.
to hump one's bluey (*Austral.*) to tramp;
to carry one's bundle. [A bluey is a
bundle carried by a bushman.]
to live on one's hump LIVE[1].

hundred

a hundred and one (*coll.*) very many (*I've
got a hundred and one things to do*).
a/ one hundred per cent entirely, totally,
completely (*I'm not a hundred per
cent certain*).

hung up

hung up on neurotic about, obsessed by.

hunker

on one's hunkers squatting down.
to hunker down to apply oneself, to
knuckle down (to work etc.).

hunt

to hunt down 1 to track, pursue and
capture. 2 to destroy by persecution or
violence.
to hunt out to track out, to find by
searching.
to hunt up to search for.

hunting ground

happy hunting ground HAPPY.

hurry

in a hurry hurrying, in a rush.
not in a hurry not soon, not easily (*I
won't forget that name in a hurry*).
to hurry up/ along 1 to make haste.
2 to cause or cajole (someone) to
make haste.

hush

hush money a bribe paid to secure
silence (about a scandal etc.).
to hush up to keep concealed, to
suppress.

Hyde

Jekyll and Hyde JEKYLL.

I

I
to dot the i's and cross the t's DOT.

ice
on ice 1 in abeyance (*We put the project on ice*). 2 performed by ice-skaters.
on thin ice THIN.
to break the ice BREAK.
to cut no ice (*coll.*) to fail to make an impression, to be unimportant.
to skate on thin ice SKATE.

iceberg
tip of the iceberg TIP¹.

icing
icing on the cake an additional extra that is not necessary but is very pleasant or attractive.

idea
not one's idea of not what one considers to be (*It's not my idea of fun!*).
that's an idea that is something worth considering.
the very idea! that is ridiculous.
to get ideas 1 (*coll.*) to become overambitious. 2 (*coll.*) to develop the wrong expectations or impressions.
to have ideas to be ambitious.
to have no idea 1 to be unaware of what is going on. 2 (*coll.*) to be innocent or stupid.
to put ideas into someone's head to fill someone with overambitious and unrealistic thoughts, aspirations etc.
what's the big idea? BIG.

if
as if as it would be if.
ifs and ans things that might have been. [In this sense 'an' is an old or dialect word meaning 'if'.]
ifs and buts objections.
if so if that is the case.

ignorant
blissfully ignorant of quite unaware of.

ilk
of that ilk (*Sc.*) of the same name (used when the surname of a person is the same as the name of their estate).

ill
ill at ease uncomfortable, anxious.
it's an ill wind that blows nobody any good an unfavourable situation usually brings advantage to someone.
to be taken ill to fall sick.
to take ill/ in ill part to take offence at.

illusion
to be under the illusion to believe mistakenly (that).

image
spitting image SPITTING.

implication
by implication by indirect suggestion.

impose
to impose on/ upon 1 to act in a way that causes inconvenience to (someone).

2 to take advantage of (a person's good nature, kindness etc.). **3** to cheat, to deceive.

impress
to impress on/ upon to emphasize to (someone) (*He impressed on us the need for discretion*).

improve
to improve on/ upon to achieve something better than.

impunity
with impunity without having to suffer unpleasant consequences.

in
in absentia (*coll.*) in (his, her etc.) absence.
in at present at (*in at the start*).
in on **1** informed about (*in on the secret*). **2** participating in (*in on the deal*).
ins and outs the intricacies or details (of) (*the ins and outs of the tax system*).
in that **1** seeing that; since. **2** in so far as.
to be in for **1** to be about to experience (esp. something unpleasant) (*You're in for a disappointment*). **2** to be committed to or involved in. **3** to be entered for (a race etc.).
to be in with to be on good terms with.

inch
every inch **1** entirely, from head to foot (*He was every inch a gentleman*). **2** the whole area (*She knows every inch of the city*).
give someone an inch and they'll take a mile someone will take advantage of any concession one makes and ask for more.
inch by inch bit by bit; gradually; by very small degrees.
within an inch of very close to (*I came within an inch of losing my job*).

within an inch of one's life very close to death (*She thrashed him within an inch of his life*).

include
to include out (*coll. or facet.*) to exclude (*Include me out!*).

increase
on the increase increasing.

Indian
too many chiefs and not enough Indians CHIEF.

industry
captain of industry CAPTAIN.

influence
under the influence (*coll.*) drunk.

initiative
on one's own initiative without being prompted by others.
to have the initiative to have the advantage.
to take the initiative to take action before others.

Injun
honest Injun HONEST.

injury
to add insult to injury ADD.

injustice
to do someone an injustice to judge someone unfairly.

ink
to ink out to blot out with ink.

inner
inner man **1** the inner or spiritual part of a person. **2** (*facet.*) the stomach.

innings
to have a good innings (*coll.*) to have a long life. [From the game of cricket.]

inroad

to make inroads into 1 to encroach on.
  2 to start affecting, using or destroying
  (*The repair bill made inroads into my
  savings*).

inshore

inshore of closer to the shore than.

inside

inside of (*coll.*) within or in less than
  (*inside of an hour*).

inside out

to know inside out to have thorough
  knowledge of (*She knows her subject
  inside out*).
to turn inside out 1 to turn the inner side
  of (something) outwards. **2** (*coll.*) to
  cause chaos or a mess in.

insist

to insist on 1 to demand emphatically.
  2 to assert positively.

instance

at the instance of at the suggestion or
  desire of.
for instance for example.
in the first instance FIRST.
in the second instance SECOND.

insult

to add insult to injury ADD.

intent

to all intents and purposes practically,
  really, in reality.
to the intent that in order that.

interest

at interest (of money borrowed) on which
  interest is payable.
in the interest(s) of as a way of furthering
  or ensuring (*in the interests of
  hygiene*).
to declare an/ one's interest DECLARE.
to lose interest LOSE.

to take an interest in to show curiosity
  about or concern for.
with interest 1 with interest added.
  2 with added force etc. (*I paid her
  back with interest for the way she
  treated my brother*).

interval

at intervals 1 from time to time. **2** with
  spaces in between (*planted at intervals
  along the boundary*).

invention

necessity is the mother of invention
  NECESSITY.

iron

in irons in fetters.
Iron Curtain 1 (*Hist.*) the imperceptible
  barrier to communication between the
  former USSR with its satellites and the
  West. **2** (**iron curtain**) any similar
  barrier to communication.
to have several irons in the fire 1 to be
  engaged in several projects at the same
  time. **2** to have several expedients.
  [Alluding to the work of a blacksmith.]
to iron out 1 to correct (defects etc.).
  2 to find a solution to (problems etc.)
  (*We ironed out our differences*).
to pump iron PUMP.
to rule with a rod of iron RULE.
to strike while the iron is hot STRIKE.

iron hand

the iron hand in the velvet glove strict
  control which is at first concealed.

isolation

in isolation considered separately and
  not in relation to anything else.

issue

at issue 1 in dispute. **2** at variance.
to force the issue FORCE.
to join issue with JOIN.
to make an issue of to make a fuss about
  (something that one disagrees with).

to take issue with to argue against or disagree with.

it

that's it 1 that is what is wanted. **2** that is enough. **3** that is the difficulty or problem.

this is it 1 this is the moment when something that has been expected is about to actually happen. **2** this is the problem.

itch

to have an itching palm to be greedy for money. [From an old superstition that when someone's palm itches they are going to receive money.]

itchy

to have itchy feet 1 to want to travel. **2** to be restless.

itself

by itself alone; separately.

in itself independently of other things; in its essential qualities.

ivory

ivory tower a shelter from the realities of everyday life.

J

jack

all work and no play makes Jack a dull boy
WORK.

before one can say Jack Robinson quite
suddenly and unexpectedly or quickly.
[The name Jack Robinson was
probably chosen at random.]

every man jack MAN.

I'm all right, Jack RIGHT.

Jack is as good as his master all men are
equal, employees and employers are of
equal worth.

jack of all trades a person who can turn
their hand to any business, activity etc.

on one's jack/ Jack Jones (*sl.*) on one's
own. [From rhyming slang.]

to jack in (*sl.*) to abandon, to give up
(*She jacked in her job*).

to jack off (*taboo sl.*) to masturbate.

to jack up 1 to lift with a jack. **2** (*coll.*) to
increase (prices etc.). **3** (*sl.*) to inject
drugs.

jacket

to dust someone's jacket DUST.

jackpot

to hit the jackpot HIT.

jam¹

to be in a jam to be in a predicament.

jam²

jam on it (*coll.*) something extra, esp. in
addition to a benefit or advantage
already obtained (*They've just had a
huge pay rise, and now they want
jam on it*).

jam tomorrow better things promised but
usu. never forthcoming. [From Lewis
Carroll's *Through the Looking-Glass*
(1871): "The rule is, jam tomorrow and
jam yesterday – but never jam today."]

James

home, James! HOME.

Jane

plain Jane PLAIN.

jar

on the jar partly closed, ajar.

jaw

hold your jaw (*sl.*) shut up.

to set one's jaw to show determination or
resolution.

jazz

to jazz up 1 to quicken the tempo of
(a piece of music). **2** to make more
attractive, livelier, more colourful etc.

Jekyll

Jekyll and Hyde a person with a split
personality, one side evil, the other
good. [From Robert Louis Stevenson's
novel *The Strange Case of Dr Jekyll
and Mr Hyde* (1886), about a good
doctor who can transform himself into
a character that embodies all his evil
instincts.]

jerk

to jerk off (*taboo sl.*) to masturbate.

jest

in jest 1 as a jest or joke. **2** not seriously or in earnest.

jetsam

flotsam and jetsam FLOTSAM.

jib¹

the cut of someone's jib CUT.

jib²

to jib at 1 (of a person) to refuse to do (something). **2** to show aversion to (a person or thing).

jig

to jig about to fidget.

jiggered

I'm/ I'll be jiggered used to express surprise etc.

jingo

by jingo 1 used to express surprise etc. **2** used to emphasize a statement of intention etc.

Joan

Darby and Joan DARBY.

Job

Job's comforter a false friend who lacerates one's feelings whilst pretending to sympathize. [Alluding to the friends of Job in the Bible, who rebuked him in his grief: "miserable comforters are ye all" (Job xvi.2).]

job

good job GOOD.
hatchet job HATCHET.
jobs for the boys (*coll.*) jobs given to someone's supporters or favourites.
just the job (*coll.*) exactly what is wanted.
on the job 1 (*coll.*) at work, in activity. **2** (*coll., euphem.*) engaged in sexual activity.
out of a job unemployed.

put-up job PUT.
the devil's own job DEVIL.
to do the job for to ruin or kill.
to give up as a bad job to stop trying to do (something that seems impossible or bound to fail).
to job out to subcontract a piece of work.
to make a good/ clean job of (*coll.*) to do thoroughly or well.

jockey

to jockey for position 1 to try by skill to get an advantageous position. **2** to gain an unfair advantage.

jog

to jog on to get along (somehow or in some specified manner).
to jog someone's elbow to give someone a reminder.

John

John Barleycorn 1 barley personified as the grain from which malt liquor is made. **2** malt liquor.
John Bull 1 the English people personified. **2** an Englishman.

join

if you can't beat 'em, join 'em if you cannot make people change their ways, change yours instead.
join the club! I am (or we are) in the same unfortunate situation.
to join battle to commence a general combat.
to join forces to work together in a combined manner.
to join hand in hand to act in concert.
to join hands 1 to clasp hands (with). **2** to come to an understanding or combine (with).
to join in to take part.
to join issue with 1 to argue against or disagree with. **2** (*Law*) to submit an issue for discussion jointly with.
to join the colours to enlist.

to join the majority to die.
to join up **1** to enlist. **2** to connect.

joint
out of joint **1** dislocated. **2** out of order.
to put someone's nose out of joint NOSE.

joke
beyond a joke (*coll.*) no longer funny.
no joke (*coll.*) a serious, difficult or
  unpleasant matter (*It's no joke trying
  to raise a family on these wages*).
standing joke STANDING.

Jones
to keep up with the Joneses (*coll.*) to keep
  on the same social level as one's
  friends and neighbours. [From the title
  of a comic strip by Arthur R. Momand,
  based on personal experience, which
  began in the New York *Globe* in 1913
  and ran in various newspapers until
  1940.]

jot
not one jot or tittle not an iota, not the
  smallest amount. [From the Bible: "Till
  heaven and earth pass, one jot or one
  tittle shall in no wise pass from the
  law, till all be fulfilled" (Matt. v.18).]

Jove
by Jove! used to express surprise or
  approval.

jowl
cheek by jowl CHEEK.

joy
full of the joys of spring FULL.
pride and joy PRIDE.
to have no joy (*coll.*) to be unsuccessful
  in a task etc.
to wish someone joy of WISH.

judge
sober as a judge SOBER.

judgement
against one's better judgement contrary to
  one's preferred course of action.
to reserve judgement RESERVE.
to sit in judgement SIT.

jugular
to go for the jugular to attack someone
  where they are most vulnerable or
  most likely to be harmed. [Alluding to
  the jugular vein in the neck.]

juice
to juice up (*sl.*) to make more lively.
to stew in one's own juice STEW.

jump
one jump ahead one stage further than
  someone else (*trying to stay one jump
  ahead of the competition*).
on the jump (*coll.*) in a hurry.
take a running jump! RUNNING.
to be for the high jump HIGH JUMP.
to get/ have the jump on (*coll.*) to get or
  have an advantage over (a person).
to jump a claim to seize upon a mining
  claim by force or fraud.
to jump at to accept eagerly (*He jumped
  at the chance*).
to jump bail (*Law, coll.*) to fail to appear
  when required after release on bail.
to jump down someone's throat (*coll.*) to
  answer or interrupt someone violently.
to jump in at the deep end to start with
  the most difficult part, to start without
  much experience.
to jump on **1** to reprimand, abuse or
  assail violently. **2** to pounce on.
to jump out of one's skin (*coll.*) to be
  startled.
to jump ship (of a sailor etc.) to leave a
  ship without permission, to desert.
to jump the queue to get ahead of one's
  turn.
to jump to conclusions to make a
  premature judgement.
to jump to it (*coll.*) to act swiftly.

jungle
concrete jungle CONCRETE.
law of the jungle LAW.

jury
the jury is (still) out a decision has not yet
   been reached.
to poll a jury POLL.

just
just about 1 (*coll.*) nearly. 2 (*coll.*) more
   or less (*There's just about enough left*).
just now 1 a very short time ago, only a
   moment ago (*I saw her just now*). 2 at
   this instant.

just so 1 exactly. 2 that is right. 3 with
   great precision (*He likes everything to
   be done just so*).
to get one's just deserts to receive what
   one's behaviour merits.
to sleep the sleep of the just SLEEP.

justice
in justice to out of fairness to.
poetic justice POETIC.
to do justice to 1 to treat fairly. 2 to treat
   appreciatively.
to do oneself justice to acquit oneself
   worthily of one's ability.
with justice with good reason.

K

keel

on an even keel EVEN[1].

to keel over 1 to capsize, to turn over. **2** (*coll.*) to fall over.

keen

keen as mustard (*coll.*) very keen.

keen on enthusiastic about, interested in.

keep

for keeps permanently.

how are you keeping? how are you?

to keep at 1 to persist with. **2** to cause to persist with (*She kept us at it all afternoon*).

to keep away to prevent from approaching.

to keep away from not to approach, to avoid contact with.

to keep back 1 to restrain, to hold back. **2** to reserve, to withhold. **3** to keep secret. **4** to remain at a distance.

to keep down 1 to repress, to subdue. **2** to keep (expenses etc.) low. **3** to digest (food) without vomiting (*He managed to keep his breakfast down*).

to keep for 1 to reserve until (a future occasion). **2** to retain on behalf of.

to keep from 1 to abstain or refrain from. **2** not to tell (someone about something) (*Please keep this terrible news from your mother*). **3** to stop or prevent from. **4** to protect or preserve from.

to keep in 1 to repress, to restrain. **2** to confine, esp. after school hours (*The whole class was kept in as punishment*). **3** to maintain the combustion of (a fire). **4** to remain indoors.

to keep in with to remain on friendly terms with.

to keep off 1 to hinder from approach. **2** to avert. **3** to remain at a distance. **4** to abstain from. **5** to avoid mentioning or discussing.

to keep on 1 to continue to employ etc. **2** to continue (doing etc.), to persist. **3** to talk continuously, esp. in an annoying way; to nag.

to keep on at to nag at, to pester.

to keep oneself to oneself to avoid other people (*Our neighbours keep themselves to themselves*).

to keep out to hinder from entering or taking possession (of).

to keep someone going in to keep someone supplied with.

to keep to 1 to adhere strictly to. **2** not to stray from.

to keep together to (cause to) remain together or in harmony.

to keep to oneself 1 to avoid other people. **2** to tell no one else about.

to keep under to hold down, to repress.

to keep up 1 to maintain. **2** to keep in repair or good condition. **3** to prevent from falling or diminishing. **4** to carry on. **5** to cause to stay up at night (*We're not keeping you up, are we?*). **6** to bear up. **7** to go on at the same pace (with).

to keep up with 1 to stay informed about. **2** to maintain contact with.

keeper

am I my brother's keeper? BROTHER.

finders keepers FINDER.

keeping

in/ out of keeping in/ out of harmony (with) (*The extension is out of keeping with the rest of the house*).

ken

beyond one's ken beyond the limits of one's knowledge or experience.

in one's ken within the limits of one's knowledge.

kettle

a different/ another kettle of fish a matter to be considered separately. [A kettle of fish was originally a riverside picnic at which a freshly caught salmon was cooked and eaten.]

a pretty/ fine kettle of fish a mess, a muddle, a troublesome state of affairs.

the pot calling the kettle black POT.

to keep the kettle boiling (*coll.*) to maintain progress or activity, to keep the game alive.

key

in a minor key MINOR.

to have the key of the street to be homeless.

to key in to enter (data) into a computer using a keyboard.

to key up to brace up, to incite, to encourage.

under lock and key LOCK.

kibe

to gall/ tread on someone's kibes to irritate someone's feelings. [A kibe is a chilblain.]

kibosh

to put the kibosh on 1 to checkmate, to do for. **2** to put an end to.

kick

for kicks for pleasure.

kick in the teeth (*coll.*) a humiliating rejection, an unexpected personal attack.

to get a kick out of to get enjoyment from.

to kick about/ around 1 (*coll.*) to go from place to place aimlessly. **2** to be discarded and left lying about or forgotten. **3** to treat harshly. **4** to discuss informally, to raise but not consider seriously (*The idea was kicked around at the last meeting*).

to kick against the pricks to hurt oneself in unavailing struggle against something. [From the Bible: "I am Jesus whom thou persecutest: it is hard for thee to kick against the pricks" (Acts ix.5), said to Saul on the road to Damascus.]

to kick in 1 to break open (a door) by kicking. **2** to begin to function, to be activated. **3** (*N Am., Austral., sl.*) to pay one's share.

to kick off 1 to remove or discard by kicking. **2** in football, to give the ball the first kick, to start play. **3** to begin.

to kick oneself to be angry with oneself (*You'll kick yourself when I tell you the answer*).

to kick one's heels to stand idly waiting.

to kick out to eject or dismiss unceremoniously or with violence.

to kick over the traces to throw off any means of restraint or control. [In this phrase the word traces originally referred to the harness of a draught horse.]

to kick (some) ass (*N Am., sl.*) to behave forcefully or aggressively.

to kick the bucket (*sl.*) to die. [Perhaps from the Old French word *buquet*, denoting a beam from which slaughtered pigs were hung by their feet.]

to kick up one's heels to enjoy oneself with no inhibitions.

to **kick upstairs** (*coll.*) to promote, often to a less active or less powerful post.

kick-off
for a kick-off (*coll.*) for a start. [Alluding to the start of play in the game of football.]

kid[1]
kids' stuff 1 (*coll.*) something suitable for children. **2** (*coll.*) something childish or very easy.

kid[2]
no kidding (*sl.*) really, honestly.

kid glove
with kid gloves very carefully or tactfully (*People like that must be handled with kid gloves*).

Kilkenny
to fight like Kilkenny cats FIGHT.

kill
in at the kill present at the end or conclusion of something. [From hunting.]
kill or cure drastic in its effects.
to kill off 1 to get rid of by killing. **2** to destroy completely. **3** to remove (a fictional character) from a story by writing in their death.
to kill oneself 1 to commit suicide. **2** (*coll.*) to overexert oneself. **3** (*coll.*) to laugh uncontrollably.
to kill the fatted calf to have a lavish or extravagant celebration, esp. as a welcome. [From the prodigal son's reception in the Bible: "And bring hither the fatted calf, and kill it" (Luke xv.23).]
to kill the goose that lays the golden eggs to destroy the main source of one's profit or success, esp. through greed. [From Aesop's fable about a man whose goose laid golden eggs: the man killed the goose in the hope of finding

a store of golden eggs inside it and thus ended his supply of wealth.]
to kill time to pass time idly.
to kill two birds with one stone to achieve two things with a single action.
†**to kill up** to exterminate.
to kill with kindness to be too gentle or indulgent.

killing
to make a killing to make a large profit (*They made a killing on the stock market*). [The phrase was originally used of a large win at horse racing.]

kin
kith and kin KITH.
near of kin NEAR.
next of kin NEXT.

kind
after its kind according to its nature.
a kind of 1 a sort of. **2** roughly or approximately of the description or class expressed.
in kind 1 (of payment, wages etc.) in produce or commodities. **2** in the same way or manner (*She responded in kind*).
kind of (*coll.*) somewhat (*I was kind of sorry to see him go*).
nothing of the kind NOTHING.
of a kind 1 (*derog.*) a rudimentary or inadequate example of (*a writer of a kind*). **2** of the same type (*two of a kind*).
of one's kind of the type or class of person to which one belongs.
something of the kind SOMETHING.
to differ in kind DIFFER.
with kind regards with good wishes.

kindness
milk of human kindness MILK.
to kill with kindness KILL.

kindred
kindred spirit a person with the same interests and attitudes as one's own.

king

a cat may look at a king CAT.
king's ransom a large sum of money.
to king it (*coll.*) to behave as if one is
  superior to others.

kingdom

to come into/ to one's kingdom to reach
  one's desired status.

kingdom come

till kingdom come for ever. [From the
  Lord's Prayer in the Bible: "Thy
  kingdom come. Thy will be done in
  earth, as it is in heaven" (Matt. vi.10).]

kip

to kip down to lie down and go to sleep.

kirk

at kirk and market (*Sc., coll.*) on all
  occasions.

kiss

kiss and tell the practice of selling stories
  of one's sexual relationships to the
  press.
kiss of death something which will
  inevitably lead to failure. [An allusion
  to the kiss with which Judas betrayed
  Jesus in the Bible (Matt. xxvi.49).]
to blow a kiss BLOW[1].
to kiss away to wipe away by kissing.
to kiss goodbye to 1 to give a kiss to on
  parting. **2** (*coll.*) to accept the loss of.
to kiss hands to kiss one's sovereign's
  hands when one accepts office.
to kiss off 1 (*N Am., sl.*) to get rid of
  (someone) rudely. **2** (*N Am., sl.*) to die,
  to go away.
to kiss someone's arse (*taboo sl.*) to be
  obsequious towards someone.
to kiss the book to touch the Bible with
  the lips in taking an oath.
to kiss the dust 1 to be conquered, to
  yield. **2** to die, to be slain. [Alluding to
  a person falling face down when
  killed.]

to kiss the ground/ earth 1 to bow down,
  to prostrate oneself. **2** to be conquered.
to kiss the rod to submit tamely to
  punishment.

kit

the whole kit (and caboodle) WHOLE.

kitchen

all/ everything but the kitchen sink (*coll.*)
  an unnecessarily large number of
  things (*They take all but the kitchen
  sink with them when they go on
  holiday*).
**if you can't stand the heat, get out of the
  kitchen** HEAT.

kite

high as a kite HIGH.
to fly a kite FLY[2].

kith

kith and kin close friends and relations.

kitten

to have kittens (*coll.*) to be overexcited,
  very annoyed etc.
weak as a kitten WEAK.

knee

on bended knee(s) BEND.
the bee's knees BEE.
to bend the knee BEND.
to bring to one's knees to reduce to
  submission.
to give a knee to 1 to support on one's
  knee during a pause in a fight or
  contest. **2** to act as second to.

knee-high

knee-high to a grasshopper (*coll.*) young,
  small.

knickers

to get one's knickers in a twist (*coll.*) to be
  overanxious, upset etc. (*Don't get your
  knickers in a twist!*).

knife

before you can say knife (*coll.*) very soon, very quickly.

that one could cut with a knife 1 (*coll.*) (of an accent) thick, very marked. **2** (*coll.*) (of an atmosphere etc.) very tense, oppressive.

the knives are out (for someone) there are strong feelings of hostility or disloyalty (towards someone).

to get one's knife into someone to become vindictive towards someone.

to have one's knife in someone to be vindictive towards someone.

to the knife (of combat) mortal.

under the knife (*coll.*) undergoing a surgical operation.

knife-edge

on a knife-edge in a difficult situation where things could go either right or wrong (*His career was on a knife-edge*). [Alluding to a sharp edge used as the fulcrum for a balance.]

knifepoint

at knifepoint threatened by someone with a knife.

knight

knight in shining armour (*coll.*) a man who helps a woman in difficulty.

knit

to knit one's brows to frown.

to knit up 1 to repair by knitting. **2** to conclude, to wind up (a speech, argument etc.).

knob

with knobs on (*sl.*) even more so.

knock

knock it off! (*sl.*) stop it!

to knock about/ around 1 to strike with repeated blows. **2** to handle violently. **3** (*coll.*) to wander about, to lead an irregular life. **4** to keep company (with). **5** to be somewhere for no particular reason.

to knock against 1 to collide with. **2** to encounter casually.

to knock back 1 (*coll.*) to drink quickly, to eat up. **2** (*coll.*) to cost (a person) (*How much did that knock you back?*). **3** (*coll.*) to shock. **4** (*Austral., New Zeal., coll.*) to reject, to rebuff.

to knock cold 1 to knock unconscious. **2** to shock.

to knock down 1 to fell with a blow. **2** to demolish. **3** to prostrate (with astonishment etc.). **4** to sell (with a blow of the hammer) to a bidder at an auction. **5** (*coll.*) to lower in price, quality etc. **6** to dismantle (furniture etc.). **7** (*N Am., sl.*) to earn. **8** (*Austral., New Zeal.*) to spend (wages etc.) freely.

to knock into a cocked hat 1 to defeat utterly. **2** to amaze or confound. [Possibly alluding to a triangular formation in the game of ninepins.]

to knock into shape to make acceptable or workable, to put into a presentable form.

to knock into the middle of next week (*coll.*) to butt or strike (a person) very hard, to send flying.

to knock off 1 to strike off, with a blow. **2** to dispatch, to do or finish quickly. **3** to cease work (*In those days we knocked off at half past five*). **4** to leave off (work). **5** to deduct (from a price etc.). **6** (*sl.*) to steal. **7** (*sl.*) to kill. **8** (*taboo sl., offensive*) to have sex with.

to knock on in rugby, to play (the ball) with the hand or arm and in the direction of the opponents' goal line.

to knock oneself out (*coll.*) to exhaust oneself.

to knock one's head against to come into collision with (awkward facts etc.).

to knock on the head 1 to stun or kill with a blow on the head. **2** to frustrate, to spoil, to defeat (*I quickly knocked that idea on the head*).

to **knock (on) wood** (*N Am.*) to touch wood (for luck etc.).

to **knock out 1** to make unconscious by a blow to the head. **2** to force out with a blow. **3** to defeat (a boxer) by knocking down for a count of ten. **4** to eliminate from a contest by defeating (*We were knocked out in the first round*). **5** (*coll.*) to astonish or impress. **6** (*coll.*) to do or make quickly. **7** (*sl.*) to earn. **8** to empty tobacco from (a pipe) by tapping.

to **knock sideways** to knock off course, to destroy the composure of.

to **knock someone off their perch 1** to beat or destroy someone. **2** to lower the esteem in which someone is held.

to **knock spots off** to outdo easily. [Perhaps from a shooting contest in which the target is a playing card.]

to **knock the bottom out of 1** to refute (an argument). **2** to destroy the usefulness of.

to **knock the socks off 1** (*coll.*) to defeat resoundingly. **2** (*coll.*) to astonish.

to **knock the stuffing out of** to beat (an opponent) thoroughly.

to **knock together** to put hastily or roughly into shape.

to **knock under** (*coll.*) to acknowledge oneself beaten.

to **knock up 1** to strike or force upwards. **2** to arouse by knocking. **3** to fatigue, to wear out, to exhaust. **4** to put together or make up hastily. **5** to score (runs) quickly at cricket. **6** (*sl.*) to make (someone) pregnant. **7** to practise before starting to play a ball game.

you **could have knocked me down with a feather** I was very surprised.

knocker

on the knocker 1 (*coll.*) door-to-door. **2** (*coll.*) on credit. **3** (*Austral., New Zeal.*) promptly, at once.

up to the knocker 1 (*sl.*) in excellent condition. **2** (*sl.*) to the highest standard.

knocking

knocking shop (*sl.*) a brothel.

knot

at a rate of knots RATE.

get knotted! (*sl.*) an expression of anger, exasperation etc.

to **cut the Gordian knot** GORDIAN KNOT.

to **tie in knots** TIE.

to **tie the knot** TIE.

know

all one knows (how) 1 all one is able. **2** as much as one can.

before one knows where one is surprisingly quickly.

don't I know it! (*coll.*) used to express ironic agreement.

don't you know (*coll. or facet.*) used to express emphasis.

for all/ aught I know as far as I am aware (*He could be lying, for all I know*).

I knew it! I imagined that this would happen.

I know what I have an idea.

in the know 1 in the secret. **2** acquainted with what is going on.

not that I know of not as far as I am aware.

not to be in the know 1 to have no way of finding out. **2** not to be informed or told.

not to know where to put oneself (*coll.*) to be very embarrassed (*When he told them my nickname I didn't know where to put myself!*).

there is no knowing one can never tell.

to **have been known to** to have done in the past.

to **know best** to be the most informed person, in the best position for making decisions etc.

to **know better than to** to have enough intelligence, common sense or courtesy not to (*I know better than to interfere in such matters*).

to **know how** to know the way to accomplish something.

to know of 1 to be informed of, to have heard of. **2** †to ask, to inquire.

to know what's what 1 (*coll.*) to be experienced, to know the ways of the world. **2** to appreciate a good thing.

to know who's who (*coll.*) to be able to name or identify everybody.

what do you know (about that)? an expression of incredulity.

you know 1 (*coll.*) used as a meaningless filler in conversation. **2** used as a reminder that the person addressed is familiar with who or what is mentioned.

you know something/ what? (*coll.*) used to introduce information regarded as new.

you never know things are never certain.

knowledge

common knowledge COMMON.

not to my knowledge not as far as I know.

to come to someone's knowledge to become known by someone.

to the best of one's knowledge as far as one knows.

knuckle

knuckle sandwich (*sl.*) a punch.

near the knuckle verging on the indecent (*Some of his jokes were a bit near the knuckle*).

to go the knuckle (*Austral., sl.*) to get into a fight.

to knuckle down to get down to some hard work.

to knuckle under to bow to the pressure of authority.

to rap on/ over the knuckles RAP[1].

L

labour
labour of love work done without expectation of payment.

lace
to lace into to attack vigorously.

lack
for/ through lack of because of an absence or insufficiency of (*weary for lack of sleep*).
to be lacking 1 to be absent; to be in short supply. **2** to be deficient (in). **3** (*coll.*) (of a person) to be mentally deficient.
to lack for (*usu. neg.*) to be without, to lack (*Their children lacked for nothing*).

ladle
to ladle out to give or hand out freely; to distribute liberally.

lady
ladies'/ lady's man a man who enjoys the company of women or is particularly attentive to them or successful in attracting or seducing them.
Lady Bountiful a wealthy woman charitable in her neighbourhood. [From the name of a character in George Farquhar's play *The Beaux' Stratagem* (1707).]
Lady Muck (*sl., derog.*) a woman with social pretensions.

lam¹
to lam into to hit hard; to thrash.

lam²
on the lam escaping, on the run, esp. from the police.
to take it on the lam to make a quick escape, to flee.

lamb
ewe lamb EWE.
like a lamb without fuss or protest.
like a lamb to the slaughter defenceless, innocent, unresisting. [From the Bible: "he is brought as a lamb to the slaughter" (Isa. liii.7).]
mutton dressed as lamb MUTTON.
one might as well be hung for a sheep as for a lamb HANG.

lame
lame duck 1 a weak, ineffective or disabled person. **2** a defaulter on the Stock Exchange. **3** a company in financial difficulties, esp. one requiring government assistance.
4 (*N Am.*) an elected official (esp. the President) whose term of office is about to expire and whose successor has already been chosen.

lamp
to smell of the lamp SMELL.

land
cloud-cuckoo-land CLOUD.
how the land lies how matters stand, the state of play in a situation (*See how the land lies before you make a decision*).
land of milk and honey 1 the fertile land

promised by God to the Israelites.
2 any extremely fertile land. **3** a place or country offering wealth and ease. [From the Bible: "a land flowing with milk and honey" (Exod. iii.8).]

land of Nod 1 the land to which Cain was exiled after killing Abel. **2** the state of being asleep. [From the Bible: "And Cain went out from the presence of the Lord, and dwelt in the land of Nod, on the east of Eden" (Gen. iv.16). The idiomatic use of this phrase is a pun based on 'nod' in the sense of 'sleep'.]

land of the living (*facet.*) the state of being alive or being awake. [From the Bible: "for he was cut off out of the land of the living" (Isa. liii.8).]

lie of the land LIE².

never-never land NEVER-NEVER.

no man's land NO¹.

promised land PROMISE.

to land up to end up.

to land with to burden with (*I always get landed with the dirty jobs*).

to live off/ on the fat of the land LIVE¹.

to make (the) land to come in sight of land as one's ship approaches it from the sea.

landscape

blot on the landscape BLOT.

lane

in the fast lane FAST LANE.

it's a long lane that has no turning LONG.

memory lane MEMORY.

language

to speak the same language SPEAK.

lap¹

lap of luxury a state of wealth and ease (*living in the lap of luxury*).

to drop into someone's lap DROP.

lap²

the last lap LAST¹.

lap³

to lap up 1 to eat or drink, esp. eagerly or greedily. **2** to take great and often vain or self-indulgent delight in (*lapping up the publicity*). **3** to accept or believe uncritically.

large

at large 1 (esp. of a criminal) at liberty, free; roaming without constraint. **2** as a whole, in general. **3** diffusely, with ample detail. **4** freely, without restraint; without a particular target. **5** (of a political representative in the US) representing a whole area, not a subdivision of it.

large as life unmistakably present or real.

larger than life remarkably vivid or eye-catching.

lark

happy as a lark HAPPY.

to rise/ get up with the lark to rise very early in the morning.

Larry

happy as Larry HAPPY.

lash

to lash out 1 to make a strong, usu. sudden physical or verbal attack. **2** to be extravagant with money. **3** to be unruly.

last¹

at last after a long time or interval, esp. after a long period of waiting; after too long a time.

at long last LONG.

at the last gasp 1 at the last extremity. **2** at the point of death. [From the Apocrypha: "When he was at the last gasp" (II Macc. vii.9).]

last but not least no less important than those previously mentioned (*And last but not least, may I introduce my wife?*).

last resort 1 something to which one comes for aid or relief when all else has failed. **2** a final attempt.

last straw the thing that finally takes one past the limit of endurance or patience. [From the saying 'It is the last straw that breaks the camel's back.']

last word 1 a concluding statement. **2** a final decision. **3** the latest improvement, the most up-to-date model (*These seats are the last word in comfort*).

on its last legs (of a machine etc.) near the end of its useful life, nearly worn-out.

on one's last legs 1 in an extreme state of exhaustion. **2** near to death, ruin etc.

the last lap the beginning of the end, the closing stages.

to breathe one's last BREATHE.

to have the last laugh to be ultimately triumphant after a former setback.

to pay one's last respects to show respect for someone who has just died, by attending their funeral.

to the last 1 to the end. **2** till death.

last²

to last out 1 to endure to the end, to persevere, to survive. **2** to be enough to meet one's requirements till the end of (a period of time).

last³

to stick to one's last STICK².

latch

on the latch fastened by the latch only, not locked.

to latch on to 1 (*coll.*) to understand the meaning of. **2** to attach oneself to.

late

at the latest no later than (*I need it by next Thursday at the latest*).

better late than never said when someone or something is late.

late in the day 1 at an advanced stage in proceedings. **2** too late.

later on at some unspecified later or future time.

of late 1 a short time ago, lately, recently. **2** latterly, formerly.

the late 1 the recently deceased, resigned etc. (*the late president*). **2** the recent.

laugh

a laugh a minute 1 very funny or amusing. **2** (*iron.*) very unfunny.

don't make me laugh an expression of scornful disbelief.

he who laughs last laughs longest do not rejoice too soon.

to be laughing (*coll.*) to have no further problems; to be in an advantageous position (*If we can sell them for £10 each, we're laughing*).

to have the last laugh LAST¹.

to laugh at to mock, to deride, to ridicule.

to laugh away 1 to dismiss with a laugh (*He laughed away our suspicions*). **2** to pass (time) in a happy or merry way.

to laugh down to suppress or silence with derisive laughter.

to laugh in someone's face to show someone open contempt or ridicule.

to laugh like a drain to laugh in a loud and unrestrained way.

to laugh off to treat as of trifling importance.

to laugh on the other side of one's face 1 to feel vexation or disappointment after amusement or satisfaction. **2** to cry.

to laugh out of court to treat as not worth considering or listening to (*They laughed my suggestion out of court*).

to laugh over to talk about or recall to mind with amusement.

to laugh to scorn to treat with the utmost contempt.

to laugh up/ in one's sleeve to be inwardly amused while one's expression remains serious or demure.

laughing

laughing stock 1 an object of ridicule.
2 a butt.

no laughing matter something serious,
not a proper subject for levity.

laughter

laughter is the best medicine cheerfulness
banishes stress and anxiety.

to shriek with laughter SHRIEK.

launch

to launch into 1 to propel oneself into a
new activity, career etc. with vigour
and enthusiasm. **2** to embark on a long
speech, story or explanation.

to launch out 1 to enter on a new and
usu. more ambitious sphere of activity.
2 (*coll.*) to spend money freely.

laurel

to look to one's laurels to guard against
rivalry, to take care not to lose one's
pre-eminence. [Alluding to a laurel
wreath worn as a symbol of victory,
honour or distinction.]

to rest on one's laurels REST[1].

law

in/ at law according to the law.

law of the jungle a state of merciless
competitiveness.

Murphy's law MURPHY.

possession is nine-tenths of the law
POSSESSION.

Sod's law SOD[2].

the letter of the law LETTER.

the long arm of the law LONG.

to be a law unto oneself to act in
accordance with one's principles,
wishes etc. in defiance of customs,
rules etc. [From the Bible: "these,
having not the law, are a law unto
themselves" (Rom. ii.14).]

to go to law to take legal proceedings.

to have the law on 1 to take legal
proceedings against. **2** to report to the
police (*I'll have the law on you!*).

to lay down the law to talk or direct in a
dictatorial manner.

to take the law into one's own hands to try
to secure satisfaction or retaliation by
one's own methods or actions.

lawyer

barrack-room lawyer BARRACK.

lay

in lay (of hens) laying eggs.

to lay about one 1 to hit out on all sides;
to fight vigorously. **2** to issue criticism,
reprimands etc. indiscriminately.

†to lay apart to put away.

to lay aside 1 to put to one side. **2** to give
up, to abandon. **3** to store for future
use.

to lay away 1 to reserve for future use.
2 to reserve (a purchase) while
payments are being made.

to lay back to place or construct sloping
back from the vertical.

to lay before 1 to exhibit to. **2** to bring to
the notice of.

to lay by 1 to save. **2** to reserve for a
future occasion.

to lay down 1 to put down. **2** to resign, to
surrender. **3** to declare; to stipulate.
4 to formulate, to draw up. **5** to put
down the main structural parts of.
6 to record on paper. **7** to sacrifice
(*lay down one's life*). **8** to store (wine
etc.). **9** (*coll.*) to wager. **10** to pay. **11** to
convert (land) to pasture. **12** to record
(tracks of an album).

to lay fast to seize and keep fast, to
prevent from escaping.

†to lay for (*coll.*) to lie in wait for.

to lay in to acquire a store of.

to lay into (*coll.*) to assault physically or
verbally.

to lay it on 1 to speak or flatter
extravagantly. **2** to charge exorbitantly.
3 to strike or beat hard. **4** to criticize
severely.

to lay low 1 to fell or destroy. **2** to cause
to become weak or ill (*laid low by
pneumonia*).

to lay off 1 to suspend from employment. **2** to discharge (workers) permanently. **3** to stop (*Lay off teasing your sister!*). **4** to avoid.

to lay on 1 (*coll.*) to provide (facility, entertainment). **2** to install and supply (water, gas). **3** to impose, to inflict. **4** to deal (blows etc.). **5** to apply. **6** to prepare or arrange for printing.

to lay oneself out (*coll.*) to busy or exert oneself to do something.

to lay out 1 to arrange according to a plan (*I don't like the way the kitchen is laid out*). **2** to spread out. **3** to expound, to explain. **4** to expend. **5** to dress in grave-clothes and prepare for burial. **6** (*coll.*) to knock to the ground or render unconscious.

to lay over 1 to spread over, to overlay. **2** (*N Am.*) to stop over during a journey. **3** (*N Am.*) to postpone.

to lay to 1 (*Naut.*) to check the motion of a ship; to heave to. **2** (*Naut.*) to bring (a ship) into harbour. **3** to apply oneself vigorously.

to lay together 1 to place side by side. **2** to add together.

to lay under to subject to.

to lay up 1 to store, to save. **2** (of illness) to confine (someone) to their bed or room (*She ran the business while her father was laid up*). **3** to decommission (a ship) or take (a ship) out of service.

lead[1]

to lead a charmed life to be very lucky in avoiding harm, as if protected by occult powers.

to lead a dog's life 1 to lead a life of continual wretchedness. **2** to be continually bickering.

to lead astray to lead into error, misbehaviour, crime or sin.

to lead by the nose to cause to follow unthinkingly; to deceive. [Alluding to an animal led by means of a ring through its nose.]

to lead off 1 to make a start. **2** (*coll.*) to lose one's temper.

to lead on 1 to entice, to draw further towards some end. **2** to fool, to trick.

to lead someone a (merry) dance to cause someone trouble or delay.

to lead the way 1 to go first so as to point the way. **2** to take precedence.

to lead to the altar to marry (a woman).

to lead up the garden path (*coll.*) to mislead; to trick, to deceive.

to lead up to 1 to conduct conversation towards (some particular subject). **2** to conduct towards. **3** to pave the way for. **4** in cards, to play so as to induce an opponent to play (a certain card).

lead[2]

to go down like a lead balloon 1 to be utterly useless, to be a complete failure. **2** to be poorly received (*My joke about the president went down like a lead balloon*).

to put lead in someone's pencil (*coll., facet.*) to make someone more sexually potent (*Drink this: it'll put lead in your pencil!*).

to swing the lead SWING.

leading

leading light 1 an expert in a particular field. **2** an influential or prominent member of a movement, group etc.

leading question a question (esp. in cross-examination) that suggests a certain answer.

leading-strings

to be in leading-strings (*dated*) to be in a state of dependence on others. [Leading-strings were reins used to support or restrain a young child learning to walk.]

leaf

in leaf with its leaves out (*a shady spot when the trees are in leaf*).

to leaf through to turn the pages of (a book, magazine etc.) in a casual way.

to shake like a leaf SHAKE.

to take a leaf out of someone's book to follow someone's example, to imitate someone.

to turn over a new leaf NEW.

league

in league with having formed an alliance with, usu. for a dubious purpose.

not in the same league SAME.

leak

to leak out to become gradually known or public, esp. in an underhand manner.

to spring a leak SPRING.

lean

to lean on (*coll.*) to coerce or threaten (someone) (*I need the money: my creditors are leaning on me*).

leap

by leaps and bounds with astonishing speed (*improved by leaps and bounds*).

leap in the dark a hazardous step or action, one whose consequences cannot be foreseen. [From the last words of the English philosopher Thomas Hobbes (1588–1679): "I am about to take my last voyage, a great leap in the dark."]

look before you leap be cautious before acting.

to leap to the eye to be very prominent or noticeable.

learn

to learn of to find out, to ascertain, to be informed of.

to learn one's lesson to gain wisdom or learn prudence as a result of usu. bitter experience.

learned

my learned friend used in a court of law by one lawyer to refer to another lawyer.

lease

new lease of life NEW.

leash

straining at the leash STRAIN.

least

at least 1 at any rate, whatever else may be said on the subject. 2 if nothing else. 3 at the minimum (*It'll take at least four hours*).

at the least at the minimum.

in the least in the slightest degree, at all (*She wasn't in the least concerned*).

least said, soonest mended it is best to say little, or nothing at all, to avoid making matters worse.

not least particularly, especially.

to say the least not to put in stronger terms; without any exaggeration (*It's risky, to say the least*).

leather

hell for leather HELL.

leave[1]

to leave be to avoid disturbing or interfering with (*Leave me be!*).

to leave behind 1 to go away without. 2 to outstrip. 3 to leave as a record, mark, consequence etc.

to leave go 1 to release. 2 to relinquish hold of. 3 to cease to retain.

to leave it at that not to do or say any more.

to leave off 1 to stop, to cease (*Shall we carry on from where we left off?*). 2 to desist from (*Would you leave off talking, you're disturbing me*). 3 to cease to wear.

to leave out to omit.

to leave over to leave for future consideration etc.

to leave someone to themselves to refrain from disturbing, approaching or becoming involved with someone.

to leave well alone to refrain strictly from interfering with, approaching, becoming involved with etc.

leave²

by/ with your leave (*often iron.*) with your permission.

French leave FRENCH.

on leave 1 absent from duty by permission. **2** on holiday.

to take leave of one's senses to think or act contrary to reason.

to take leave to (*formal*) to venture to, to be so bold as to.

to take (one's) leave 1 to say goodbye. **2** to depart.

lecture

curtain lecture CURTAIN.

lee

under the lee of 1 on the sheltered side of. **2** protected from the wind by.

leech

like a leech persistently, tenaciously (*She stuck to me like leech all evening*).

leery

to be leery of to be wary of.

leeway

to make up leeway to recover lost ground or time. [Of nautical origin: leeway is the sideward drift of a vessel caused by the action of wind and water.]

left¹

left, right and centre everywhere, all over the place (*giving away money left, right and centre*).

the left hand doesn't know what the right hand is doing there is a lack of communication, esp. between parts of a large organization.

left²

to be left standing to prove much the weaker competitor, to be left at the starting post.

to be left with 1 to retain (an impression, feeling etc.) as a result of usu. lengthy exposure to something. **2** to have to deal with after an event.

to be well left to have ample provision made for one in a will etc.

to get left (*coll.*) to be abandoned or beaten.

to have left to have remaining.

leg

an arm and a leg ARM¹.

break a leg! BREAK.

leg before (*coll.*) leg before wicket.

leg before wicket a grounds for dismissal in cricket, stoppage by the batsman's leg of a ball when it would have hit the wicket.

not to have a leg to stand on to have no support or basis for one's position (e.g. in a controversy).

on its last legs LAST¹.

on one's (hind) legs 1 standing up, esp. in order to make a speech. **2** able to stand or walk about again after illness.

on one's last legs LAST¹.

sea legs SEA.

to feel one's legs FEEL.

to find one's legs to attain ease or mastery.

to get one's leg over (*sl.*) (of a man) to have sexual intercourse.

to give leg bail to run away.

to have no legs (of a golf ball etc.) not to have enough impetus to reach the point aimed at.

to have the legs of to be able to go further or faster than.

to leg it 1 (*coll.*) to run away. **2** (*coll.*) to run, hurry. **3** (*coll.*) to go on foot.

to pull someone's leg 1 to hoax or make a fool of someone. **2** to tease someone (*Ignore him: he's only pulling your leg!*).

to shake a leg SHAKE.

to show a leg 1 to get out of bed. **2** to make an appearance.

to stretch one's legs/ a leg STRETCH.

to talk the hind legs off a donkey TALK.

with one's tail between one's legs TAIL¹.

leisure

at leisure 1 not busy or occupied.
  2 without hurry. **3** deliberately.
at one's leisure when one has the time, at one's convenience.
marry in haste, repent at leisure MARRY.

lend

to lend an ear to listen (to).
to lend itself to to have the right qualities for, to be appropriate for using as (*The poem lends itself to being set to music*).
to lend oneself to to give support to.

length

at arm's length ARM[1].
at full length FULL.
at length 1 to the full extent, in full detail (*Although I explained the problem at length, they still didn't understand*). **2** at last (*At length a ship appeared on the horizon*).
to go to any length(s) 1 to stop at no obstacle. **2** to be restrained by no scruples.
to go to great lengths GREAT.
to measure one's length MEASURE.

leopard

a leopard cannot change its spots a person's basic nature or character never changes. [From the Bible: "Can the Ethiopian change his skin, or the leopard his spots?" (Jer. xiii.23).]

less

less and less gradually diminishing.
much/ still less used to introduce an alternative which is even less the case (*I've never met him, much less gone out with him*).
no less (than) 1 as much (as) (*She is demanding a salary of no less than £100,000*). **2** as important or special (as) (*He received a personal call from the prime minister, no less*). **3** no fewer (than).

lesson

object lesson OBJECT.
to learn one's lesson LEARN.
to teach someone a lesson TEACH.

let

let me see used to ask for time to consider or reflect.
to let available for renting.
to let be not to interfere with.
to let down 1 to allow to sink or fall.
  2 to fail or disappoint (someone) (*I felt I had let my family down*). **3** to make (a garment) longer by lowering the hem. **4** to deflate. **5** to untie (hair) and allow to hang loose.
to let down gently to avoid humiliating or causing too great distress or disappointment to.
to let fall 1 to drop. **2** to mention by accident, or as if by accident.
to let go 1 to release. **2** to relinquish hold of. **3** to cease to retain. **4** to dismiss from the mind. **5** to drop anchor.
to let in 1 to allow to enter. **2** to insert. **3** to inlay. **4** to cheat, to defraud.
to let in for to involve in (something unpleasant, difficult etc.) (*I didn't know what I was letting myself in for*).
to let in on to allow to be involved in or to profit from (*They offered to let me in on the deal*).
to let into 1 to allow to enter. **2** to allow to have knowledge of. **3** to set within another surface.
to let off 1 to refrain from punishing or to punish lightly (*They let us off with a warning*). **2** to excuse or dispense from. **3** to discharge, to fire off (an arrow, gun etc.); to detonate (a bomb, firework etc.). **4** to allow to alight or disembark. **5** to allow or cause (air, liquid etc.) to escape from. **6** to rent out (part of a building).
to let on 1 to divulge, to let out. **2** to pretend.

to let oneself go 1 to give way to any impulse. **2** to lose interest in maintaining one's appearance.

to let oneself in to use one's own key to enter a building.

to let out 1 to open the door for. **2** to allow to go out. **3** to free from restraint. **4** to divulge. **5** to utter, to give vent to (*He let out a scream*). **6** to enlarge or make less tight-fitting. **7** to lease or let on hire. **8** to allow (air, liquid etc.) to escape. **9** to disqualify, to rule out. **10** to exculpate.

to let someone have it (*coll.*) to punish, censure or abuse someone.

to let through 1 to allow to pass. **2** to overlook, to fail to correct, emend etc.

to let up to become less (severe), to abate (*The storm showed no sign of letting up*).

to let up on to treat less harshly; to stop harassing, pressing etc.

letter

bread-and-butter letter BREAD.

dead letter DEAD.

four-letter word FOUR.

red-letter day RED-LETTER.

the letter of the law literal or precise definition of the law.

to the letter exactly (*We followed the instructions to the letter*).

level

level pegging 1 equal. **2** (of contestants etc.) the state of being at the same level or at the same place in a race etc. [Alluding to pegs on a scoreboard.]

level playing field a situation in which no participant or contestant starts with an unfair advantage over the others.

on a level with on the same horizontal plane as.

on the level honest, genuine.

to do one's level best to do the best one can. [From the days of the gold rush, alluding to the act of washing and shaking sand or gravel in a flat dish to level the surface and reveal the gold.]

to find its (own) level 1 (of liquids) to reach the same height in a number of interconnecting vessels or chambers. **2** to reach a stable level, usu. with respect to something else.

to find one's level to settle in a position, office, rank etc. suitable for one's abilities, qualities or powers.

to level down to bring down to the level or standard of something or someone else.

to level off 1 to make flat. **2** to reach and stay in a state of equilibrium. **3** (of an aircraft) to return to horizontal flight after a dive.

to level out 1 to make or become level (*The land levels out towards the coast*). **2** to remove differences between. **3** (of an aircraft) to return to horizontal flight after a dive.

to level up to bring up to the level or standard of something or someone else.

to level with (*sl.*) to be honest with, to come clean with.

liberty

at liberty 1 free. **2** having the right (to do etc.) (*I am not at liberty to disclose that information*). **3** disengaged, not occupied.

to set at liberty to free from confinement or restraint.

to take liberties (with) 1 to be unduly familiar or presumptuous (with). **2** to transgress (rules or usages). **3** to falsify.

to take the liberty 1 to venture. **2** to do something without permission.

licence

poetic licence POETIC.

lick

a lick and a promise (*coll.*) something done very quickly, esp. a quick or superficial wash.

to lick into shape to bring into a satisfactory condition or shape (*My job is to lick the new recruits into shape*). [From the notion that young bears are born shapeless, and are licked into shape by their mother.]

to lick one's lips/ chops to anticipate or remember something with pleasure.

to lick one's wounds to withdraw after a defeat to recuperate physically or mentally.

to lick someone's boots/ shoes to be servile towards someone.

to lick the dust 1 to be beaten, to be killed. **2** †to act in a servile manner.

to lick up to consume, to devour.

licking

to take a licking to take a beating.

lid

to blow/ lift/ take the lid off (*coll.*) to reveal or uncover (esp. something clandestine or corrupt).

to flip one's lid FLIP.

to put the (tin) lid on it 1 (*coll.*) to be a final blow, misfortune etc. **2** (*coll.*) to curb or to put an end to something.

lie¹

to give the lie to 1 to show to be false; to disprove (*The results of the test gave the lie to her claims*). **2** to accuse of lying.

to lie in one's throat to lie outrageously.

to lie through/ in one's teeth to lie blatantly and unashamedly.

to live a lie LIVE¹.

white lie WHITE.

lie²

as far as in me lies to the best of my ability.

lie of the land 1 the topography of a place. **2** the nature of the situation as it stands and as it is likely to develop.

to let lie not to bring forward for discussion (because likely to cause controversy).

to lie about/ around to be left scattered randomly over an area.

to lie ahead to be in prospect or in store (*Who knows what lies ahead?*).

†to lie at one's heart to be a source of anxiety, care or desire.

to lie at the door of to be the fault or responsibility of.

to lie back to rest in a comfortable reclining position.

to lie behind to be the cause of or explanation for.

to lie by 1 to be put aside. **2** to remain unused. **3** to rest. **4** to be quiet. **5** to be or stay near.

to lie doggo (*coll.*) to wait silently and motionlessly.

to lie down 1 to take up a lying position. **2** to take a short rest. **3** to submit tamely. **4** †to sink into the grave.

to lie hard/ heavy on to oppress, to be a weight upon.

to lie in 1 to remain in bed later than normal. **2** †to be in bed to give birth to a child.

to lie in someone to be in someone's power or capacity.

to lie in state (of an important dead person) to lie in a coffin in some place where the public may come to visit as a token of respect.

to lie in the way to be an obstacle or impediment.

to lie in wait (for) 1 to wait in ambush or concealment (in order to waylay). **2** to be in store (for).

to lie low 1 to remain in hiding. **2** to conceal one's knowledge or intentions in order to outwit, forestall etc.

to lie off (*Naut.*) (of a ship) to stay at a distance from the shore or another ship.

to lie on one's hands 1 to remain unsold or undisposed of. **2** (of time) to go slowly.

to lie on the head of to be imputable or chargeable to.

to **lie on/ upon 1** to be incumbent upon. **2** to depend or be dependent upon.

to **lie over 1** to be deferred. **2** to remain unpaid.

to **lie perdu 1** (*Mil.*) to lie in ambush. **2** (*Mil.*) to be in a hazardous situation. **3** to be hidden or out of sight.

to **lie to** (*Naut.*) (of a ship) to be checked or stopped with its head to the wind.

to **lie under** to be subject to or oppressed by.

to **lie up 1** to rest, to stay in bed or in one's room to recuperate. **2** (of a ship) to go into dock.

to **lie with 1** to be the responsibility or duty of (*It lies with you to inform the next of kin*). **2** †to have sexual intercourse with. **3** †to lodge or sleep with.

to **take lying down** to accept (an insult, rebuff) without retaliation, resistance or complaint.

lief
†**had/ would as lief** would as willingly.

lieu
in lieu (of) instead (of), as a substitute (for) (*board and lodging in lieu of payment*).

life
facts of life FACT.

for dear/ one's life with extreme vigour, in order to escape death (*They rowed for dear life towards the shore*).

for the life of me even if my life depended upon it (used to indicate one's utter inability to do something) (*I can't for the life of me remember his name*).

large as life LARGE.

larger than life LARGE.

matter of life and death MATTER.

new lease of life NEW.

not on your life under no circumstances.

od's life OD.

slice of life SLICE.

that's life! said when something undesirable happens that cannot be avoided and must be accepted.

the life and soul the liveliest or most entertaining person, esp. at a party.

the life of Riley (*coll.*) an easy, carefree existence. [Perhaps from a popular song of the late 19th century.]

the light of one's life LIGHT[1].

there's life in the old dog yet used when an old person proves they are still active and able.

the time of one's life TIME.

to attempt the life of ATTEMPT.

to bring to life to give animation to, to enliven, to make interesting or exciting (*The exhibition brings history to life*).

to come to life 1 to emerge from unconsciousness, inactivity, torpor etc. **2** (of an inanimate object) to become animate. **3** (of a machine, engine etc.) to start operating.

to give one's life 1 to die in a self-sacrificial way. **2** to devote all one's time, energy and care.

to lead a charmed life LEAD[1].

to lead a dog's life LEAD[1].

to risk life and limb RISK.

to save one's life SAVE.

to save someone's life SAVE.

to see life to gain experience of the world.

to sell one's life dear(ly) SELL.

to take one's life in one's hands to risk death (*You take your life in your hands crossing this road*).

to the life 1 (of the way in which a likeness has been made) with great fidelity to the original. **2** (of a likeness) as if the original stood before one.

true to life TRUE.

upon my life a mild oath.

variety is the spice of life VARIETY.

walk of life WALK.

where/ while there's life there's hope do not despair if there is the remotest chance of improvement or success in an unpleasant or difficult situation.

within an inch of one's life INCH.

lift

to lift down to pick up and move to a lower position.

to lift off 1 (of a spacecraft or rocket) to take off vertically from a launching pad. **2** to remove or detach by raising slightly. **3** to be removable by lifting; to come away easily from a surface to which it adheres.

to lift one's head to hold one's head with pride.

to lift up one's voice (to begin) to sing out loud.

to thumb a lift THUMB.

light[1]

according to one's lights according to one's information or knowledge of a situation.

all sweetness and light SWEETNESS.

between the lights in the twilight.

bright lights BRIGHT.

in a bad/ poor light in such a way as to reflect discredit on.

in a good/ favourable light in such a way as to reflect credit on.

in the cold light of day COLD.

in the light of considering, allowing for.

leading light LEADING.

more heat than light HEAT.

strike a light! STRIKE.

the light of one's life (*usu. facet.*) a much loved person or thing (*Her grandson is the light of her life*).

to bring to light to discover, to detect, to disclose.

to cast light on CAST.

to come to light to become known.

to get the green light GREEN LIGHT.

to go/ be out like a light to fall asleep very quickly or lose consciousness suddenly.

to hide one's light under a bushel HIDE[1].

to light up 1 (*coll.*) to light a cigarette, pipe etc. **2** to illuminate. **3** to switch on (car) lights. **4** to become cheerful or animated suddenly (*Their faces lit up when they saw the cake*).

to see the light 1 to be born. **2** to realize the truth. **3** to be converted to a religion or to any other belief.

to see the light at the end of the tunnel to be approaching the end of a difficult task or unpleasant period at last.

to see the light of day to come into existence.

to see the red light RED LIGHT.

to shed/ throw light on to elucidate, to explain.

to stand in one's own light to frustrate one's own purposes or wishes.

to strike a light STRIKE.

light[2]

light as a feather very light in weight.

light on (*coll.*) short of, having insufficient.

light on hand (of a horse etc.) easy to manage.

to make light of 1 to treat as insignificant (*He made light of his disability*). **2** to treat as pardonable or excusable.

light[3]

to light into (*sl.*) to attack physically or verbally.

to light on/ upon to happen on, to find by chance.

to light out (*sl.*) to leave in a hurry.

to light up (*Naut.*) to slacken.

lightning

lightning never strikes in the same place twice the same misfortune is unlikely to happen again to the same person.

like greased lightning GREASE[2].

like[1]

and the like and other similar things, etcetera.

(as) like as not very probably.

just like that (*coll.*) effortlessly, without hesitation.

like so in this way, thus.

like that 1 of the kind referred to. **2** in

that way. **3** (*coll.*) effortlessly, without hesitation.

more like it nearer or more closely resembling what is desired.

nothing like 1 in no way similar to or comparable with. **2** far short of (what is required).

of like mind holding a similar or identical opinion.

something like 1 in some way or nearly resembling. **2** first-rate, highly satisfactory.

the likes of (*coll., usu. derog.*) people such as (*I wouldn't lend money to the likes of her*).

what is he/ she/ it/ etc. like? what are his etc. main characteristics?

like²

I like that! (*iron.*) a reaction to a piece of brazen effrontery.

like it or lump it put up with it as there is no alternative.

like it or not (*coll.*) whether one is pleased or not.

not to like the look of to find alarming or threatening (*I don't like the look of those clouds*).

likely

a likely story! (*iron.*) an exclamation of disbelief.

liking

to one's liking to one's taste (*The show was not to their liking*).

lily

to gild/ paint the lily to try to improve what is already perfect, to spoil beauty by overembellishing. [From Shakespeare's *King John*: "To gild refined gold, to paint the lily…Is wasteful and ridiculous excess."]

limb

out on a limb 1 in a precarious or exposed position. **2** isolated. [Alluding to a branch of a tree.]

to risk life and limb RISK.

to tear limb from limb TEAR¹.

limber

to limber up 1 to stretch and flex the muscles in preparation for physical exercise. **2** to make (something) flexible, to loosen up.

limit

off limits out of bounds, esp. to military personnel.

the sky is the limit SKY.

to be the limit to be unacceptable, intolerable or extremely annoying (*That's the limit!*).

within limits to a certain degree or extent.

without limit unrestrictedly; indefinitely.

limpet

like a limpet tenaciously (*clinging like a limpet to the ledge*).

line¹

above the line 1 in accounting, above a horizontal line on a profit and loss account dividing entries that establish a profit or loss from those that show how profit is distributed. **2** in marketing, relating to or denoting advertising through the media and by posters, for which a commission is paid to an agency. **3** in bridge, denoting bonus points entered above a horizontal line on the scoresheet that do not count towards game.

all along the line at every point, throughout.

below the line 1 in accounting, below a horizontal line on a profit and loss account dividing entries that establish a profit and loss from those that show how profit is distributed. **2** in marketing, relating to or denoting advertising by such means as free gifts or samples, mailshots etc. that are organized internally. **3** in bridge, denoting points that count towards game or rubber.

hard lines HARD.

hook, line and sinker HOOK.

in line for likely to receive; a candidate for (*in line for promotion*).

in line with 1 in accordance with (*not in line with council policy*). **2** in alignment with.

in the line of during or as part of the normal course of (esp. duty).

line of country one's special field of interest.

line of least resistance the easiest course of action.

on the line 1 available to be communicated with, esp. by telephone. **2** at risk (*Our jobs were on the line*).

out of line (of a person) acting in an inappropriate, improper or unruly manner.

out of line with 1 not in accordance with. **2** out of alignment with.

to be in the firing line FIRING LINE.

to come/ bring into line to conform/ cause to conform (with).

to draw the line at to refuse to go as far as (*She drew the line at posing in the nude*).

to drop someone a line DROP.

to fall into line 1 to form ranks, to take one's place in a row. **2** to do as others do, to conform.

to get a line on (*coll.*) to learn or discover useful information about.

to hold the line 1 not to give in. **2** not to end a telephone connection.

to lay it on the line to speak out frankly or uncompromisingly.

to lay/ put on the line to put at risk (*putting their lives on the line*).

to line up 1 to arrange in a line or lines. **2** to align. **3** to queue. **4** to secure or arrange for the appearance of (a speaker, celebrity). **5** to prepare. **6** to take a stand (for or against).

to read between the lines READ.

to shoot a line SHOOT.

to sign on the dotted line SIGN.

to step out of line STEP.

to toe the line TOE.

line²

to line one's pockets to abuse a position of trust in order to make money for oneself.

linen

to wash one's dirty linen in public WASH.

lining

every cloud has a silver lining CLOUD.

lion

the lion's mouth a dangerous place. [Alluding to the circus act of putting one's head in a lion's open mouth.]

the lion's share the largest part or the whole. [From Aesop's fable about a lion who went hunting with a group of animals: he claimed three-quarters of the kill for himself and defied the other animals to fight him for the remaining portion.]

to beard the lion in his den BEARD.

to throw to the lions to put (someone) in a dangerous or unpleasant situation in order to save or protect oneself. [From the ancient Roman practice of having people killed by lions as public entertainment.]

lip

one's lips are sealed one must keep a secret.

there's many a slip 'twixt cup and lip SLIP¹.

to bite one's lip BITE.

to button one's lip BUTTON.

to curl one's lip CURL.

to hang on someone's lips HANG.

to keep a stiff upper lip STIFF.

†**to make a lip** to pout the lips in sullenness or contempt.

to pass one's lips to be eaten, drunk or spoken (*Not a drop of alcohol has passed my lips since that day*).

to smack one's lips SMACK.

lip-service

to pay lip-service to express agreement without taking appropriate action (*They did no more than pay lip-service to government policy*).

liquidation

to go into liquidation (of a company) to have its affairs terminated and its assets apportioned among creditors.

liquor

in liquor (*dated*) drunk.

to liquor up 1 (*N Am.*) to take a lot of drink. **2** (*N Am.*) to cause to become drunk.

list¹

on the sick list SICK LIST.

list²

to enter the lists ENTER.

listen

to listen in 1 to be present at, but not contribute to, a conversation, discussion etc. **2** to eavesdrop; to intercept and listen to a telephone or radio communication. **3** to listen to a radio broadcast.

to listen out to wait in the hope or expectation of hearing.

to listen up (*N Am., coll.*) to pay attention.

little

a little to a small extent, slightly (*feeling a little better*).

a little bird told me (*coll.*) used to avoid revealing a source of information or gossip.

a little knowledge/ learning is a dangerous thing inadequate knowledge may lead to worse mistakes than complete ignorance. [From *An Essay on Criticism* (1711) by Alexander Pope: "A little learning is a dang'rous thing; / Drink deep, or taste not the Pierian spring."]

in little in miniature.

little by little by small degrees, (very) gradually.

little or nothing scarcely anything.

little things please little minds said disparagingly when someone is amused by trivia or childish pursuits.

no little considerable; a fair amount of (*It takes no little courage to do a job like that*).

not a little 1 very, greatly, extremely. **2** a great deal.

to make little of 1 to have a low opinion of. **2** to treat as of little importance. **3** to have little benefit from.

little finger

to have more ... in one's little finger than someone has in their whole body to be far superior to someone in the specified attribute.

to twist/ wind/ wrap around one's little finger to have (someone) in one's power, to be able to do as one likes with (someone).

live¹

as I live and breathe! used to express astonishment or resolution.

long live an expression of loyal good wishes to a particular person, institution etc. (*Long live the Queen!*).

to live a lie to lead a false life.

to live and breathe to be utterly devoted to or obsessed with (an activity, a pastime).

to live and learn to continue to learn new things, esp. by experience.

to live and let live to be tolerant of the deficiencies of others in return for indulgence of one's own.

to live by to order one's life in accordance with (a principle, creed).

to live by one's wits to live by cunning or ingenuity rather than regular employment.

to live down to efface the recollection of (former mistakes, scandal etc.) by one's conduct (*If my students find out about this, I'll never live it down!*).

to live high off the hog to have an affluent and luxurious lifestyle. [Alluding to the position of the choicest cuts of meat on a pig.]

to live in 1 (of an employee) to reside at one's place of work. **2** (of a student) to reside on the campus.

to live in sin (of a couple) to cohabit without being married.

to live it up (*coll.*) to enjoy oneself without restraint, to go on a spree.

to live like a lord to live affluently.

to live like fighting cocks to get the best of food and drink.

to live off 1 to be dependent on financially, for one's livelihood. **2** to feed oneself (exclusively) on.

to live off/ on the fat of the land to have the best of everything. [From the Bible: "I will give you the good of the land of Egypt, and ye shall eat the fat of the land" (Gen. xlv.18).]

to live on 1 to continue to exist, to endure, to survive. **2** to support oneself on (a specific amount of money). **3** to feed oneself (exclusively) on (*children who live on burgers and chips*).

to live on one's hump to be self-sufficient. [Alluding to the camel, which stores fat in its hump to sustain it during long periods without food or water.]

to live out 1 a to spend the whole or the remainder of (one's life, one's days). **b** to survive until the end of (*She won't live out the month*). **2** to express, manifest or fulfil in one's life and conduct (*live out one's principles*). **3** (of an employee) to reside away from one's place of work. **4** (of a student) not to reside on campus.

to live out of a suitcase to be restricted to and dependent on the things, usu. clothes, that one has with one in a suitcase (*I'd hate to be a commercial traveller, living out of a suitcase*).

to live through to experience and survive (an unpleasant experience).

to live to to live long enough to reach (a particular age).

to live together to cohabit.

to live to oneself to live in isolation.

to live to tell the tale to survive.

to live up to to be worthy of, to conform to (a prescribed standard) (*The car lived up to its reputation for poor handling*).

to live with 1 to cohabit with. **2** to accept or tolerate.

to live within/ beyond one's means to spend less/ more than one earns.

live²

live wire 1 a wire through which an electric current is flowing. **2** (*coll.*) an energetic person.

to go live (*Comput.*) (of a system) to become operational.

lively

look lively! hurry up, make haste.

livery

at livery kept at a stable for the owner at a fixed charge.

living

land of the living LAND.

to beat/ knock the living daylights out of to beat severely.

to scare/ frighten the living daylights out of to frighten greatly.

within living memory within the memory of people still alive (*the coldest winter within living memory*).

lo

lo and behold (*esp. facet.*) used to introduce a startling fact or revelation.

load

a load of (*coll.*) used for emphasis when dismissing something as merely or completely rubbish, nonsense etc.

a load off one's mind a great relief (from anxiety).

to get a load of (*sl.*) to listen to, to pay attention to; to look at (*Get a load of this!*).

to have a load on (*sl.*) to be drunk.

to load the dice against someone to prejudice someone's chances of success. [Loaded dice are weighted so that they fall with a required face up.]

loaded

loaded question a question with hidden implications designed to trap the answerer.

loaf

half a loaf is better than no bread HALF.

loaves and fishes personal gains, material benefits, as an inducement in religious profession or public service. [From the miracle performed by Jesus in the Bible (Matt. xiv.15–21), when 5000 people were fed with five loaves and two fishes.]

to use one's loaf USE[1].

loan

on loan 1 given or taken as a loan. **2** (of staff) temporarily transferred.

loath

nothing loath 1 quite willing. **2** willingly.

location

on location (of filming etc.) outside the studio.

lock

lock, stock and barrel the whole lot. [Alluding to the parts of a gun.]

to lock away 1 to hide or keep in a secure place. **2** to imprison. **3** to make unavailable or inaccessible. **4** to invest (money) so that it cannot be readily realized.

to lock horns to become engaged in an argument or combat. [Alluding to a fight between horned animals.]

to lock in to keep in, confine or imprison by locking doors etc.

to lock on (to) to track automatically by means of a radar beam or sensor.

to lock out 1 to prevent from entering by locking doors etc. **2** to prevent (workers) from working during an industrial dispute usu. by closing premises.

to lock the stable door after the horse has bolted to respond to an undesirable event by taking precautionary measures that would have prevented it.

to lock up 1 to fasten or secure with lock and key. **2** to close and lock all the doors and windows of (a building). **3** to hide or keep in a secure place. **4** to imprison. **5** to make unavailable or inaccessible. **6** to invest (money) so that it cannot be readily realized.

under lock and key securely locked up.

locker

Davy Jones's locker DAVY.

not a shot in one's locker SHOT.

lodging

board and lodging BOARD.

log

easy as falling off a log EASY.

to heave the log HEAVE.

to log in/ on 1 to begin to use a computer system. **2** to gain access to a computer system (by means of a code, password etc.).

to log out/ off to exit from or conclude the use of a computer system.

to log up to spend (a specified amount of time) working, flying etc. as recorded in a logbook or other record.

to sleep like a log SLEEP.

loggerhead

at loggerheads in conflict, locked in dispute.

logic

to chop logic CHOP².

loin

to gird up one's loins GIRD.

lone

lone wolf a person who prefers to be or to operate alone.

lonesome

on one's lonesome alone.

long

as long as 1 provided that, only if (*You can stay and watch as long as you don't make a noise*). **2** for the whole of the time that.

at long last after a very long delay or period of waiting.

before long soon, shortly.

by a long chalk by a great deal, by far (*He's not good enough to play for the first team – not by a long chalk*). [Alluding to a chalk line marking the score in a game.]

for a long while for a long time (*I haven't been to the cinema for a long while*).

in the long run 1 in the end, eventually. **2** over a long period of time.

it's a long lane that has no turning things are bound to change (for the better).

long as your arm (*coll.*) extremely long.

long face a gloomy or dejected expression.

long in the tooth elderly, old. [From the fact that the gums recede with age, making the teeth look longer, and the practice of inspecting a horse's teeth to ascertain its age.]

long on well supplied with, strong in.

long shot 1 a camera shot from a long distance. **2** a random guess, a remote possibility. **3** a bet at long odds.

long time no see used to greet someone one has not seen for a long time.

no/ not any longer formerly but not now.

(not) by a long shot/ sight (not) by any means (*not finished by a long sight*).

so long! (*coll.*) goodbye.

so long as provided that, on condition that (*so long as no one minds*).

the long and the short of it 1 the whole matter in a few words. **2** the eventual outcome.

the long arm of the law the wide-ranging and far-reaching power of the police or the courts.

to be long to take a long time (*I won't be long*).

to cut a long story short used to announce that one is omitting many details and coming directly to the point.

to draw the long bow to tell incredible stories. [Perhaps from the exaggerated tales told about the exploits of archers using longbows, such as their alleged ability to shoot an arrow over a distance of a mile.]

to go a long way 1 to make a substantial contribution (towards). **2** (of food, money etc.) to last for a long time, to provide material or the means to do many things. **3** to be successful.

look

dirty look DIRTY.

look here! used to attract attention, esp. in order to register a complaint or protest.

not much to look at unattractive, plain; unprepossessing.

not to like the look of LIKE¹.

to be looking at (*coll.*) to have at a rough estimate, to expect to pay, spend etc.

to look after 1 to take care of. **2** to attend to. **3** to follow (a departing person, thing) with one's eyes. **4** †to seek.

to look as if to seem or suggest from the available evidence that (*It looks as if she was telling the truth*).

to look askance at 1 to look at obliquely. **2** to view with mistrust, suspicion or disapproval.

to look back 1 to turn and look in the direction from which one has come. **2** to refer back (to). **3** to review or return (to a period, event, experience in the past) in one's mind. **4** (*usu. neg.*) to cease to make progress (*I never looked back after that*). **5** to pay another short visit.

to look down on 1 to despise. **2** to assume superiority over.

to look for 1 to seek. **2** to hope for. **3** to expect, to anticipate, to be on the watch for.

to look forward to to anticipate or hope for with pleasure.

to look in 1 to call, to pay a brief visit. **2** (*coll.*) to watch television.

to look into 1 to inspect carefully, to investigate (*The police are looking into the matter*). **2** to examine the inside of.

to look kindly on to be favourably disposed towards.

to look like 1 to resemble; to have the appearance of. **2** to seem to be going to. **3** to threaten or promise (e.g. rain). **4** to suggest the presence of.

to look on 1 to be a mere spectator. **2** to regard, to consider (as, with etc.).

to look oneself to look healthy; to have one's customary air and appearance.

to look out 1 to be on the watch, to be prepared (for). **2** to put one's head out of a window etc. **3** to search for or select and give to. **4** to have a view or outlook (over).

to look over 1 to inspect by making a tour of. **2** to read or examine cursorily. **3** †to overlook.

to look round/ around 1 to look behind one, or in another direction than in front. **2** to make a tour of and inspect. **3** to examine various options, possible purchases etc. before coming to a decision.

to look someone in the eye(s)/ face to look at someone steadily, unflinchingly and without shame (*I don't know how he could look me in the eye and say that!*).

to look through 1 to see or direct the eyes through. **2** to penetrate with one's sight

or insight. **3** to examine the contents of. **4** to ignore, or seem to ignore, the presence of (another person) (*I smiled and waved, but she looked straight through me*).

to look to 1 to direct one's eyes or thoughts towards. **2** to take heed for, to be careful about, to keep a watch over. **3** to rely upon (for).

to look up 1 to search for, esp. in a book. **2** to pay a visit to. **3** to improve, to become more prosperous (*Things are looking up at last*).

to look up and down to examine (a person) from head to foot attentively or with disdain or contempt.

to look upon to regard (as or with).

to look up to to admire and respect.

look-in

to get a look-in (*usu. neg.*) to have a chance, esp. of success or victory (*The other team didn't get a look-in*).

lookout

on the lookout on the watch.

to be someone's (own) lookout (*coll.*) to be someone's own business or responsibility (*If he wants to throw away the chance of a lifetime, that's his lookout!*).

loom

to loom large to be threateningly close or prominent (*The prospect of redundancy loomed large*).

to loom over to overhang, overshadow or stand tall beside, to seem to threaten.

loop

to loop the loop to travel round in a vertical loop in an aeroplane etc.

loose

at a loose end (*coll.*) with nothing in particular to do.

at loose ends (*N Am.*) at a loose end.

on the loose 1 no longer in captivity. **2** having a spree.

to cut loose 1 to escape or get away (from). **2** to begin to act without restraint.

to give loose to to give free vent to (one's tongue, feelings etc.).

to let loose 1 to free from restraint, to release. **2** to utter abruptly and violently. **3** to discharge, to fire off, to unleash abruptly.

to set loose to set at liberty.

loosen

to loosen someone's tongue to make someone talk more freely, often indiscreetly.

to loosen up 1 to limber up. **2** to relax, to become less shy or restrained.

lord

drunk as a lord DRUNK.

in the year of Our Lord YEAR.

Lord Muck (*sl., derog.*) a man with social pretensions.

someone's lord and master (*facet.*) someone's husband.

to live like a lord LIVE¹.

to lord it over to behave as if one is superior to (*After winning the championship, he began to lord it over his friends at the club*).

lorry

to fall off the back of a lorry BACK.

lose

to have lost sight of to have fallen out of touch with, no longer to know the whereabouts of.

to lose caste 1 to descend in the social scale. **2** to lose favour or consideration.

to lose count to be unable to keep count (*I've lost count of the number of times I've told her*).

to lose countenance to become embarrassed.

to lose courage to be overcome by fear.

to lose face 1 to be humiliated. **2** to suffer loss of personal prestige.

to lose flesh to lose plumpness, to become thin.

to lose ground 1 to be driven back, to give way. **2** to lose advantage or credit. **3** to decline, to fall off.

to lose heart to become discouraged.

to lose interest to stop being interested or interesting.

to lose no time to act immediately.

to lose one's balance 1 to tumble. **2** to be upset mentally.

to lose one's bearings to be uncertain of one's position.

to lose one's bottle (*sl.*) to lose confidence, to become afraid.

to lose one's cool (*coll.*) to become upset, flustered or angry.

to lose oneself 1 to lose one's way. **2** to become bewildered. **3** to become rapt or engrossed (in).

to lose one's figure to become rather fat.

to lose one's grip to lose control or mastery.

to lose one's head 1 to be carried away by excitement. **2** to lose one's presence of mind. **3** to be decapitated.

to lose one's heart to to fall deeply in love with.

to lose one's marbles (*coll.*) to go mad.

to lose one's nerve to lose confidence, to become afraid.

to lose one's rag (*sl.*) to become angry.

to lose one's shirt (*coll.*) to lose all one has.

to lose one's temper to become angry.

to lose one's/ the way to become lost, to take a false direction, to go astray.

to lose one's tongue to become silent.

to lose one's touch to cease to be skilful.

to lose out 1 (*coll.*) to make a loss, to be at a disadvantage. **2** to fail to obtain or take advantage of something.

to lose out to to be defeated by (a competitor or rival).

to lose sight of 1 to cease to see. **2** to overlook, to forget.

to lose sleep over to worry about (*It's a mystery, but I'm not going to lose any sleep over it*).

to lose the plot (*coll.*) to be no longer able to understand or handle events, developments etc., to become confused or unable to cope.

to lose the thread to stop following an argument, conversation, story etc.

to lose time 1 to delay or be delayed. **2** (of a watch) to go more slowly than required.

to lose touch 1 to cease regular communication (with). **2** to cease to be well-informed.

to lose track of to cease to be aware of (events, developments etc.).

to lose weight to become lighter or thinner.

loss

at a loss for less than the buying price; with costs, expenditure etc. exceeding income (*Because of the slump in the housing market, we were forced to sell at a loss*).

dead loss DEAD.

loss of face humiliation, loss of personal prestige.

profit and loss PROFIT.

to bear a loss 1 to sustain a loss without giving way. **2** to make good a loss.

to be at a loss to be embarrassed or puzzled.

to be at a loss for to be rendered helpless for lack of (*I was at a loss for words*).

to cut one's losses/ a loss to write off as lost, to abandon a speculation.

lost

get lost! go away.

lost cause 1 a futile endeavour. **2** a person whom one can no longer influence or help.

to be lost for words to be speechless with amazement, disbelief, admiration etc.

to be lost in 1 to be engrossed in. **2** to merge or be obscured in.

to be lost on to make no impression on, to be wasted on (*My sarcastic remarks were lost on him*).

to be lost to 1 (of a valuable thing or person) to be no longer available or accessible to (*Many of London's buildings were lost to us during the blitz*). **2** (of a person) to be impervious or unresponsive to.

to be lost without to be dependent on.

lot

a fat lot of FAT.

a lot (*coll.*) much (*I feel a lot better today*).

a whole lot WHOLE.

bad lot BAD.

that's your lot! (*coll.*) that is all you are getting.

the (whole) lot all, everything.

to cast lots CAST.

to cast/ throw in one's lot with to join with or make common cause with and share the fortunes of.

to draw lots to determine by drawing one name etc. from a number.

to fall to someone's lot to be someone's responsibility (to do something usu. unpleasant).

to think a lot of THINK.

loud

loud and clear very clearly (*I got the message loud and clear*).

out loud 1 aloud. **2** loudly.

louse

to louse up to spoil, to make a mess of.

lousy

lousy with swarming with, excessively supplied with.

love

all's fair in love and war FAIR.

calf love CALF.

cupboard love CUPBOARD.

for love for pleasure or out of benevolence, affection etc., not for payment (*I did it for love*).

for love or money (*usu. neg.*) by any

means, in any circumstances (*I wouldn't do that for love or money*).

for the love of for the sake of (esp. in adjuration) (*Slow down, for the love of God!*).

for the love of Mike used to express frustration, pleading etc.

I must love you and leave you (*coll.*) it's time for me to go.

in love feeling a strong desire and attachment (for another person, for each other).

labour of love LABOUR.

love all in tennis etc., nothing scored in a game on either side.

love in a cottage marriage for love without sufficient money to live in comfort or maintain one's social status.

love is blind people cannot see any faults in those they love.

love me, love my dog if you like a person you must learn to tolerate their faults and weaknesses or to accept their friends and relations.

out of love no longer in love.

puppy love PUPPY.

there's no love lost between them they feel great mutual dislike or hostility.

to fall in love to begin to feel love.

to give/ send one's love to give/ send an affectionate message (*Give my love to your sister*).

to make love to 1 to have sexual intercourse with. **2** †to woo, to pay court or attentions to.

to play for love to play without stakes.

low

at a low ebb weak, in a state of decline.

in low spirits dejected, depressed.

low profile (*also attrib.*) a reserved or inconspicuous attitude or manner to avoid attention or publicity (*to keep a low profile; a low-profile campaign*).

lower

to lower one's eyes to look down towards the ground.

to lower one's sights to settle for less, to become less ambitious.

to lower the tone to make a conversation, social gathering etc. less refined, prestigious or edifying.

luck

as luck would have it fortunately.

down on one's luck not having much luck.

for luck in the hope of gaining good fortune.

hard luck HARD.

just someone's luck someone's usual misfortune (*It was just my luck that the train was on time that day and I missed it*).

no such luck unfortunately not.

the luck of the devil/ Irish very good fortune.

the luck of the draw the way things happen by chance.

to luck into (*sl.*) to acquire or achieve by good fortune or chance.

to luck out (*N Am., sl.*) to be successful or fortunate, esp. by chance.

to push one's luck PUSH.

to take pot luck POT LUCK.

to try one's luck TRY.

with luck if everything goes well.

worse luck unfortunately.

lucky

lucky dog (*coll.*) a lucky fellow.

someone should be so lucky (*coll., iron., facet.*) someone is unlikely to be so fortunate (*A new car? I should be so lucky!*).

lucre

filthy lucre FILTHY.

lull

to lull into a false sense of security to make (someone) feel safer than they really are.

lump

in the lump 1 the whole taken together. **2** altogether, in gross.

lump in the throat a feeling of constriction in the throat caused by emotion.

to take one's lumps (*sl.*) to put up with hard knocks, assaults or defeats.

lunatic

lunatic fringe members of society or of a group regarded as holding extreme or fanatical views.

lunch

out to lunch (*coll.*) crazy.

to do lunch 1 to have lunch together, esp. for a business discussion. **2** to make or serve lunch.

lurch

to leave in the lurch to leave in difficulties. [The lurch is a losing position in cribbage and some other games.]

lute

rift in the lute RIFT.

luxury

lap of luxury LAP[1].

M

machine
cog in the machine COG.

mackerel
sprat to catch a mackerel SPRAT.

mad
like mad (*coll.*) violently, wildly,
  excitedly.
mad as a hatter quite mad. [Possibly from
  a substance formerly used in making
  hats, which caused a nervous
  disorder.]
mad as a March hare quite mad. [Perhaps
  from the wild behaviour of hares in
  the mating season.]

made
made for perfectly suited to.
made of money (*coll.*) very wealthy.
to have it made to be certain of success.
what someone is made of someone's true
  qualities, worth etc. (*This is your
  chance to show what you're made of*).

madness
method in one's madness METHOD.
midsummer madness MIDSUMMER.

magic
like magic very quickly, effectively etc.
  (*It works like magic*).

magnitude
of the first magnitude FIRST.

maid
old maid OLD.

mailed
mailed fist the application of physical
  force.

main
in the main for the most part.
main chance 1 the most important issue.
  2 an opportunity for personal gain
  (*with an eye to the main chance*).
  3 self-interest.
with might and main MIGHT.

mainbrace
to splice the mainbrace SPLICE.

majority
in the majority belonging to the party
  etc. that has the greatest number of
  members.
silent majority SILENT.
to join the majority JOIN.

make
on the make 1 (*coll.*) intent on personal
  profit, after the main chance. 2 (*coll.*)
  seeking sexual partners.
†to make after to pursue.
to make against to be unfavourable to, to
  tend to injure.
to make as if/ though to pretend (to), to
  feint (*I made as if to reach for my gun*).
to make at to attack.
to make away to hurry away.
to make away with 1 to get rid of, to kill.
  2 to waste, to squander.
to make do to cope or be satisfied (with)
  though the resources etc. are not
  completely adequate.

to **make for 1** to conduce to (*It makes for a more relaxed atmosphere*). **2** to corroborate. **3** to move towards (*We made for the exit*). **4** to attack.

to **make it 1** (*coll.*) to reach an objective. **2** (*coll.*) to succeed. **3** (*sl.*) to have sexual intercourse (with).

to **make it up 1** to be reconciled, to stop quarrelling. **2** to compensate for something missing.

to **make it up to** to compensate for an insult or injury to.

to **make like 1** (*esp. N Am.*) to pretend. **2** (*esp. N Am.*) to imitate.

to **make of 1** to understand as the meaning of (*What do you make of that?*). **2** to attach a specified degree of importance to. **3** to construct from.

to **make off 1** to hurry away. **2** to abscond.

to **make off with** to take away wrongfully (*The intruders made off with the family silver*).

to **make or break/ mar** to be crucial to the success or failure of.

to **make out 1** to identify or distinguish with the eyes or ears (*make out a ship on the horizon*). **2** to understand. **3** to prove, to establish. **4** to claim, to allege. **5** to draw up, to write out (*make out a cheque*). **6** (*coll.*) to be successful, to get on. **7** (*N Am., coll.*) **a** to engage in necking or petting. **b** to have sexual intercourse.

to **make over 1** to transfer. **2** to redesign, reshape etc., to give a new look to.

to **make up 1** to compose. **2** to compound. **3** to collect together. **4** to compile. **5** to fabricate, to concoct. **6** to complete, to supply (what is lacking). **7** to compensate (for). **8** to be reconciled, to stop quarrelling. **9** to settle, to adjust. **10** (of an actor) to dress up, to prepare the face to represent a character. **11** to prepare (a bed etc.) for use. **12** to repair. **13** to apply cosmetics to the face. **14** to apply cosmetics to the face of. **15** to arrange (type etc.) in columns or pages.

to **make up to** to make advances to.

to **make with 1** (*N Am., coll.*) to happen or proceed with. **2** (*N Am., coll.*) to show, to produce.

maker

one's **Maker** God.

to **meet one's Maker** MEET.

making

in the **making** gradually developing or being made.

to **be the making of** to play a crucial part in the successful development, outcome etc. of.

to **have the makings of** to have the potential to become (*She has the makings of a great musician*).

man

a **drowning man will clutch at a straw/ straws** DROWN.

as **one man** all together, in unison.

a **tall man of his hands** TALL.

dead men's shoes DEAD.

dirty old man DIRTY.

every man for himself everyone must take care of themselves (*When the boat began to sink it was every man for himself*).

every man has his price no one is above bribery.

every man jack every individual.

fancy man FANCY.

hatchet man HATCHET.

inner man INNER.

ladies'/ lady's man LADY.

man about town a fashionable man of leisure.

man alive! an expression of remonstration, often sarcastic.

man and boy from boyhood upwards (*He has worked on this farm man and boy*).

man Friday a personal servant, factotum. [From the name of Robinson Crusoe's servant in Daniel Defoe's novel *Robinson Crusoe* (1719).]

man in the moon the personage attributed to the semblance of a face on the surface of the moon as seen from earth.

man in the street an ordinary person.

man of (many) parts a versatile or accomplished person.

man of straw 1 a man of no substance. **2** a false argument or adversary put forward for the sake of being refuted.

man of the moment a man who is important, in the news etc. at a particular time.

man of the world an experienced, sophisticated and urbane man.

man on the street (*N. Am.*) man in the street.

man to man 1 as between individual people, one with or against the other (*They fought man to man*). **2** (*also attrib.*) with complete frankness (*a man-to-man talk*).

marked man MARKED.

may the best man win said at the beginning of a contest.

my (good) man used as a patronizing form of address to a man.

no man no one, no person, nobody.

no man's land NO[1].

odd man out ODD.

old man OLD.

one-man band/ show ONE-MAN.

one man's meat is another man's poison different people like different things.

right-hand man RIGHT-HAND.

the child is father of the man CHILD.

the man for the person needed or suitable for.

the next man NEXT.

time and tide wait for no man TIME.

to a man without exception (*slaughtered to a man*).

to be all things to all men THING.

to be man enough to be sufficiently manly.

to be one's own man to be of independent mind.

to be someone's man to be the person needed by someone (*If you can drive a fork-lift truck, you're our man*).

to play the man to be brave or courageous.

to separate/ sort out the men from the boys (*coll.*) to reveal those who are really tough or capable.

manger

dog in the manger DOG.

manna

manna from heaven anything very advantageous and unexpected. [From the food miraculously supplied to the Israelites in the wilderness, as recounted in the Bible (Exod. xvi.15).]

manner

all manner of all kinds of.

in a manner of speaking in a certain way, somewhat, so to speak.

to mend one's manners MEND.

to the manner born 1 (as if) accustomed to something from birth. **2** (*Shak.*) born to follow a certain practice or custom. [From Shakespeare's *Hamlet*: "But to my mind – though I am native here, / And to the manner born – it is a custom / More honour'd in the breach than the observance."]

many

a good many a large number.

a great many a very great number.

as many the same number of (*six ambulances and as many police cars*).

as many again the same number in addition (*ten there and as many again here*).

many a one many individuals.

too many 1 superfluous, not wanted, in the way. **2** (*coll.*) too clever, too able or skilful (for).

map

off the map 1 (*coll.*) of no account, not worth consideration, remote. **2** out of the way.

on the map important, well-known.

to map out to plan in detail, to lay out a plan of.

to put on the map to make (a place etc.) famous.

to wipe off the map WIPE.

marble

to lose one's marbles LOSE.

march

marching orders 1 (*Mil.*) instructions for service personnel to proceed to war. 2 (*coll.*) instructions by which a worker, lodger etc. is required to leave their job, lodging etc., a dismissal (*to get one's marching orders*).

on the march 1 advancing steadily. 2 making progress.

to march past to march in a review past a superior officer etc.

to steal a march on STEAL.

March hare

mad as a March hare MAD.

mare

shanks's mare SHANK.

marine

tell that to the marines TELL.

mark

below the mark not of the desired standard, unsatisfactory. [Alluding to the standard fixed by an assay office for gold and silver articles.]

dead on the mark DEAD.

easy mark EASY.

full marks FULL.

†(God) bless/ save the mark an exclamation of irony, deprecation or contempt. [Perhaps an allusion to the sign of the cross.]

mark my words used to add emphasis to a warning, prediction etc.

mark you (*coll.*) please note (*Mark you, this has never happened before*).

off the mark 1 making a start (*quick off the mark*). 2 wide of the mark.

of mark noteworthy.

on the mark accurate, straight.

on your marks an order from the starter in a race for runners to take their position on the starting line.

to make one's mark to do something that brings fame, recognition etc.

to mark down 1 to lower the price of. 2 to make a note of. 3 to decide to victimize. 4 to award a lower mark to.

to mark off to separate (one thing from another), to set boundaries.

to mark out 1 to set out (boundaries and levels) for a proposed building. 2 to set out (lines and marks) on material as a guide for cutting, drilling or other operations. 3 to set out plans for. 4 to destine (*marked out as a leader of men*).

to mark time 1 (*Mil.*) to move the feet alternately as in marching, without changing position. 2 to pause until further progress can be made. 3 to do something just to pass time.

to mark up 1 to raise the price of. 2 to write alterations or instructions on for keying etc.

to overshoot the mark OVERSHOOT.

to overstep the mark OVERSTEP.

to toe the mark TOE.

up to the mark up to standard, satisfactory. [Alluding to the standard fixed by an assay office for gold and silver articles.]

wide of/ beside the mark 1 not hitting the target. 2 not to the point, irrelevant.

marked

marked man 1 a person whose conduct is being scrutinized, esp. with suspicion or hostility. 2 a person apparently destined to succeed, because of recognition by superiors.

market

at kirk and market KIRK.

drug on the market DRUG.

the bottom has fallen out of the market BOTTOM.

to be in the market for to be ready to purchase or acquire (a particular item, commodity etc.).

to come into/ onto the market to be offered for sale.

to make a market to cause active dealing in a stock or shares.

to play the market to speculate on the stock market.

to price oneself out of the market PRICE.

to put on the market to offer for sale.

to raid the market RAID.

to rig the market RIG².

marriage

by marriage as a result of a marriage (*nephew by marriage*).

in marriage as a husband or wife (*given in marriage*; *taken in marriage*).

marrow

to the marrow right through, completely (*chilled to the marrow*). [Referring to the bone marrow.]

marry

marry in haste, repent at leisure a warning against marrying someone soon after meeting them.

to marry into 1 to gain (esp. money) by marrying. 2 to join (a family) by marrying.

to marry off to find a husband or wife for (a daughter or son).

to marry up to link or join (with).

martyr

a martyr to a continual sufferer from (*I'm a martyr to rheumatism*).

to make a martyr of oneself to feign or advertise suffering in order to gain sympathy.

mash

to be mashed on to be in love with.

mass

in the mass in the aggregate.

the great mass GREAT.

to be a mass of to be covered with, to have many.

mast

at half mast HALF MAST.

†before the mast 1 in the forecastle of a ship. 2 serving as a common sailor. [The common sailors' quarters were in the forecastle, in front of the foremast.]

to nail one's colours to the mast NAIL.

master

Jack is as good as his master JACK.

past master PAST.

someone's lord and master LORD.

to be one's own master to be free to do as one likes.

to make oneself (a) master to acquire a thorough knowledge (of) or competence (in).

mat

on the mat (*coll.*) being reprimanded.

match

game, set and match GAME.

hatches, matches and dispatches HATCH².

slanging match SLANGING.

to make a match to encourage and bring about a marriage.

to match matching, appropriate (*a shirt with tie to match*).

to match up to form a whole (with).

to match up to to be equal to or as good as.

to meet one's match MEET.

matchwood

to make matchwood of to smash to tiny pieces.

Matilda

to waltz/ walk Matilda (*Austral., coll.*) to carry a swag. [Matilda is a name given to a bushman's swag, or bag of belongings, carried from place to place.]

matter

a matter of approximately (*a matter of £500*).

as a matter of fact actually, in fact.

for that matter/ the matter of that 1 so far as that is concerned. **2** as an additional point.

grey matter GREY.

in the matter of as regards.

matter of course what may be expected in the natural course of events.

matter of form 1 an issue of etiquette or convention. **2** a purely routine matter.

matter of life and death something of vital importance.

matter of opinion a matter open to debate or question.

mind over matter MIND.

no laughing matter LAUGHING.

no matter 1 it does not matter. **2** regardless of (*no matter how hard I tried*).

what is the matter? what is wrong?

what matter? used to indicate that something is of no relevance, importance etc.

May

ne'er cast a clout till May is out CAST.

may

may/ might as well would be as sensible as not to (*I might as well go home*).

that is as may be that may or may not be the case (implying that there are further factors to consider).

McCoy

the real McCoy REAL.

me

me and mine me and my family.

meal

meal ticket 1 a ticket given in exchange for a meal, often at a subsidized price. **2** (*coll., often derog.*) a person upon whom one can depend for financial support.

to make a meal of 1 to exaggerate the importance, difficulty etc. of. **2** to eat as a meal.

mean¹

to mean business to be in earnest.

to mean it to be serious and not joking about something.

to mean to say to admit reluctantly (*Do you mean to say you have crashed my car!*).

to mean well to have good intentions.

mean²

no mean good, not to be underestimated (*no mean cricketer*).

means

by all (manner of) means certainly, undoubtedly.

by any means 1 in any way possible, somehow. **2** at all.

by fair means or foul FAIR.

by means of by the agency or instrumentality of.

by no (manner of) means certainly not, on no account whatever.

means to an end something done only to achieve a particular result.

the end justifies the means END.

to live within/ beyond one's means LIVE¹.

ways and means WAY.

measurable

within a measurable distance of almost at (a point of something undesirable etc.).

measure

beyond measure exceedingly, excessively.

for good measure as an additional amount, over and above that required.

in some/ a measure to some extent, to a certain degree.

to measure one's length to fall flat on one's face.

to measure swords **1** (of duellists) to see whether the swords are of the same length. **2** to try one's strength (with or against).

to measure up **1** to measure with a view to fitting something. **2** to take complete measurements. **3** to be good enough (*None of the candidates measured up*).

to measure up to to be adequate for.

to take measures to adopt means, to take steps (to).

to take someone's measure **1** to find out what kind of a person someone is. **2** to measure someone for clothes.

within measure in moderation.

without measure immoderately.

meat

†before/ after meat immediately before/ after a meal.

meat and drink something readily acceptable (to), a source of pleasure (to).

one man's meat is another man's poison MAN.

to sit at meat SIT.

medicine

a taste/ dose of one's own medicine unpleasant treatment in retaliation for the same.

laughter is the best medicine LAUGHTER.

to take one's medicine to accept stoically an unpleasant ordeal, duty, undertaking etc.

medium

happy medium HAPPY.

meet

more than meets the eye complexities or problems that are not apparent at first.

to meet halfway to compromise with.

to meet one's Maker to die.

to meet one's match to encounter someone who is equal to or better than one in combat, skill, argument etc.

to meet one's Waterloo to be finally or decisively defeated. [From the defeat of Napoleon at the Battle of Waterloo in Belgium in 1815.]

to meet someone's eye to exchange glances with someone, usu. in a knowing way.

to meet the eye/ ear to be seen/ heard.

to meet up to make contact (with), esp. by chance.

to meet with **1** to come across. **2** to have a meeting with. **3** to experience, to encounter, to engage, to receive (*to meet with problems*; *to meet with approval*).

to run to meet to anticipate (one's problems or troubles).

†well met welcome (a greeting).

Melba

to do a Melba **1** (*Austral.*) to come out of retirement. **2** (*Austral.*) to make several farewell appearances. [Referring to the operatic soprano Dame Nellie Melba (1861–1931).]

melt

to melt away to (make) disappear, esp. by liquefaction.

to melt down **1** to reduce (esp. metal articles) to a molten state by heat. **2** to become liquid or molten.

to melt in the mouth (of food) to be light and tasty.

melting pot

in the melting pot with an undecided future.

memory

from memory as far as one can remember without proper verification.

in memory of commemorating.

memory lane an imaginary route to nostalgic remembrance of the past (*a stroll down memory lane*).

to commit to memory COMMIT.

within living memory LIVING.

mend

on the mend improving, recuperating.

to make do and mend to manage with the things one has by repairing them or adapting them to one's current needs.

to mend fences to restore good relations (with someone), to make up differences.

to mend one's manners to improve one's behaviour.

to mend one's pace 1 to go faster. **2** to adjust one's pace to that of someone else.

to mend one's ways to reform, to improve one's behaviour, habits etc.

mention

don't mention it used to indicate that apologies or thanks are unnecessary.

mentioned in dispatches cited for bravery or valuable services.

not to mention to say nothing of (*There are four adults and ten children living in that house, not to mention their pets*).

to make mention to talk (of a subject).

to make no mention not to talk (of a subject).

mercy

at the mercy of wholly in the power of (*at the mercy of market forces*).

for mercy's sake used as a solemn adjuration or appeal.

small mercies SMALL.

tender mercies TENDER¹.

to cry mercy CRY.

to have mercy on/ upon to show mercy to.

mere

mere nothings trifling, unimportant things, events etc.

merit

on its merits on its intrinsic qualities, virtues etc. (*judge each case on its merits*).

to make a merit of to think or try to show

that (one's conduct, action etc.) deserves praise.

merry

to make merry to feast, to be jovial.

to make merry over to make a laughing matter of.

mesh

in mesh (of cogs) engaged.

mess

mess of pottage a material gain for which something of a higher value is sacrificed. [From the biblical story of Esau, who sold his birthright to his younger brother Jacob for a plate of lentil stew (Gen. xxv.29–34). The phrase 'mess of pottage' was used in a chapter heading for this story in an early edition of the Bible.]

to make a mess to make a bad job (of), to bungle.

to mess about/ around 1 to play or fool about. **2** to treat roughly. **3** to treat improperly or inconsiderately (*Our suppliers are messing us about*). **4** to potter about. **5** to flirt.

to mess up to ruin, to spoil (*The weather messed up her plans*).

to mess with to interfere with.

message

to get the message to understand what another person is trying to communicate.

method

method in one's madness careful thought underlying a seemingly careless action. [From Shakespeare's *Hamlet*: "Though this be madness, yet there is method in't."]

mettle

to put someone on their mettle to test someone's courage, determination etc.

mickey

to take the mickey/ mick (out of) (*coll.*) to tease, to make fun of someone or something (*Are you taking the mickey?*). [From the rhyming slang phrase 'to take the Mickey Bliss', used euphemistically for 'to take the piss'.]

mickle

many a mickle makes a muckle many small amounts accumulate to become a large amount.

Midas

Midas touch the facility for making money or achieving success. [Midas was a legendary king of Phrygia who had the power of turning everything he touched into gold.]

middle

in the middle of during, while.
in the middle of nowhere (*coll.*) in a remote location (*a village in the middle of nowhere*).
middle name 1 any name between a person's first given name and their family name. 2 (*coll.*) a person's most typical quality (*Punctuality is his middle name!*).
pig in the middle PIG.
to knock into the middle of next week KNOCK.

midnight

to burn the midnight oil BURN.

midst

in our/ your/ their midst among us, you etc. (*a traitor in our midst*).
in the midst of among, surrounded by or involved in (*in the midst of negotiations*).

midstream

to change/ swap horses in midstream HORSE.

midsummer

midsummer madness foolish behaviour, esp. associated with summer. [From Shakespeare's *Twelfth Night*: "Why, this is very midsummer madness."]

might

with all one's might using all one's strength, influence etc.
with might and main with all one's strength.

Mike

for the love of Mike LOVE.

milch

milch cow 1 a cow kept for milk. 2 a person from whom money is easily obtained.

mild

to draw it mild 1 (*coll.*) to state, describe or ask moderately, not to exaggerate or be exorbitant. 2 to draw beer from the cask of mild.

mile

a mile a minute (*coll.*) very rapidly (*talking a mile a minute*).
a miss is as good as a mile MISS.
give someone an inch and they'll take a mile INCH.
miles away lost in thought, daydreaming, preoccupied.
to run a mile to avoid someone or something undesirable by running away quickly.
to stick out a mile STICK².

milk

land of milk and honey LAND.
milk and honey prosperity, abundance.
milk and water (*also attrib.*) namby-pamby or mawkish talk, sentiment etc.
milk of human kindness the gentle nature considered natural to humanity. [From Shakespeare's *Macbeth*: "Yet do I fear thy nature; / It is too full o' the milk of

human kindness / To catch the nearest way."]

to cry over spilt milk CRY.

mill

grist to the mill GRIST.

run-of-the-mill RUN.

the mills of God grind slowly (but they grind exceedingly small) the punishment or reward one deserves may not come immediately but it will come eventually.

to go/ put through the mill to undergo/ subject to a harrowing, exhausting etc. experience.

million

gone a million GONE.

in a million extremely good or rare (*a chance in a million*).

to look/ feel (like) a million dollars to look or feel very attractive.

millpond

calm as/ like a millpond (of water) very smooth and still.

millstone

to be a millstone around someone's neck to be a great burden to someone.

to see far into a millstone to be remarkably acute.

mince

not to mince matters/ one's words to speak plainly.

mincemeat

to make mincemeat of to crush or destroy completely.

mind

all in the mind imaginary (*It's all in the mind*).

a load off one's mind LOAD.

at the back of one's mind BACK.

don't mind me (*usu. iron.*) do as you please, irrespective of my feelings, opinions etc.

do you mind? used to express irritation at a person's inconsiderate behaviour.

great minds think alike GREAT.

in one's mind's eye in one's imagination.

in one's right mind RIGHT.

in two minds TWO.

little things please little minds LITTLE.

mind out watch out (for), be careful.

mind over matter the power of the mind successfully exerted over the physical world.

mind you (*coll.*) used to qualify a previous statement (*I finished work early; mind you, I had done twice the usual amount*).

mind your back(s) used to indicate that one wants to get past.

mind your eye take care, look out.

never mind used to console someone.

never you mind used to rebut a prying question.

of like mind LIKE[1].

of unsound mind UNSOUND.

one-track mind ONE-TRACK.

out of one's mind mad, crazy.

out of sight, out of mind SIGHT.

peace of mind PEACE.

presence of mind PRESENCE.

the mind boggles used to express amazement or confusion at something that is hard to imagine or comprehend.

time out of mind TIME.

to bear in mind to remember, to take into account.

to blow someone's mind BLOW[1].

to bring/ call to mind to recall.

to change one's mind CHANGE.

to close one's mind CLOSE[2].

to come into someone's mind 1 to be remembered. **2** to form as an idea.

to come to mind to occur to one, to suggest itself.

to cross someone's mind CROSS.

to give someone a piece of one's mind PIECE.

to have a good/ half a mind to be inclined (to) (*I've a good mind to report him to the police*).

to **have in mind** to intend (*What exactly did you have in mind?*).

to **know one's own mind** to be decisive.

to **make up one's mind** to decide, to resolve (*I made up my mind to say nothing*).

to **mind one's own business 1** to attend to one's own affairs. **2** to refrain from meddling.

to **mind one's Ps and Qs** to be careful over details, esp. in behaviour. [Perhaps from a warning to printers' apprentices, or to children learning the alphabet, concerning the similarity between the lower-case letters p and q.]

to **mind the shop** to take charge temporarily.

to **one's mind** in one's opinion.

to **open one's mind** OPEN.

to **put in mind** to remind (of) (*It put me in mind of a game we used to play as children*).

to **put out of one's mind** to stop thinking about.

to **put/ set someone's mind at rest** to reassure someone.

to **read someone's mind** READ.

to **set one's mind on** to be determined to have or do.

to **shut one's mind to** SHUT.

to **slip someone's mind** SLIP[1].

to **speak one's mind** SPEAK.

to **spring to mind** SPRING.

to **take someone's mind off something** to stop someone thinking about something.

mine

gold mine GOLD.

mingle

to **mingle with** to go among (a group of people).

miniature

in miniature on a small scale.

minnow

Triton among the minnows TRITON.

minor

in a minor key conducted or passed quietly or uneventfully.

minority

in the minority in the state of being outnumbered.

mint

in mint condition/ state as perfect as when first produced. [Alluding to an unused coin.]

minute

a laugh a minute LAUGH.

a mile a minute MILE.

any minute now very soon, very shortly.

just/ wait a minute 1 (*coll.*) used to ask someone to wait for a short time. **2** (*coll.*) used as a prelude to a query or objection.

the minute (that) (*coll.*) as soon as (*We left the minute it stopped raining*).

there's one born every minute BORN.

up to the minute very modern.

mire

in the mire in difficulties.

mischief

to **do someone a mischief** to hurt or kill a person.

to **make/ get up to mischief** to cause trouble or ill-feeling.

misconduct

to **misconduct oneself** to misbehave.

misery

to **put someone/ something out of their/ its misery 1** to release an animal etc. from suffering, esp. by killing. **2** to release someone from the suspense of waiting (*They finally put us out of our misery and announced the results*).

miss

a miss is as good as a mile failure or escape, no matter how narrow the margin, is the point of importance.

not to miss a trick to be alert, esp. to any possible opportunity, advantage etc.

not to miss much to be alert and astute.

to be missing 1 to lack (something, esp. an integral part). **2** to be absent or lost.

to give a miss 1 not to take an opportunity to see, visit, enjoy etc. (something). **2** in billiards, to avoid hitting (the object ball) in order to leave one's own in a safe position.

to go missing to disappear or be lost.

to miss fire (of a gun, explosive etc.) to fail to go off.

to miss out 1 to omit. **2** to fail to receive or enjoy (*missing out on the joys of parenthood*).

to miss the boat/ bus (*coll.*) to miss an opportunity, to be too late.

mistake

by mistake accidentally, due to error.

make no mistake without doubt, certainly.

there is no mistaking one is certain to recognize (someone or something).

mitten

to give someone/ get the mitten (*sl.*) to reject or dismiss someone/ be rejected or dismissed (from office etc.).

mix

to be mixed up in to be involved in (esp. something dubious).

to be mixed up with to be involved with (esp. someone undesirable).

to mix and match to choose from a range of combinations, e.g. of fabrics, wallpaper etc.

to mix in to be sociable, to get on well with others.

to mix it to start a fight.

to mix it up (*N Am.*) to mix it.

to mix up 1 to mix thoroughly. **2** to confuse, to bewilder.

mixed

mixed bag/ bunch a diverse mixture of people or things, often in terms of quality.

mixed blessing something that has advantages and disadvantages.

mixed feelings a mixture of pleasure and sadness with regard to a single event etc. (*I had mixed feelings about the move*).

mixture

the mixture as before the same treatment repeated. [From a prescription for medicine.]

mock

to make (a) mock of to ridicule, to sneer at.

mocker

to put the mockers on 1 (*sl.*) to cause to fail. **2** (*sl.*) to make impossible.

moderation

in moderation not to excess, in a moderate manner or degree (*drink alcohol in moderation*).

molehill

to make a mountain out of a molehill MOUNTAIN.

moment

at a moment's notice with hardly any advance warning.

at the moment at the present, just now.

in a moment 1 in a short while (*I'll do it in a moment*). **2** instantly (*In a moment, she was gone*).

in the heat of the moment HEAT.

man of the moment MAN.

not for a moment never, emphatically not.

on the spur of the moment SPUR.

the moment of truth the crucial moment
when something is to be tested. [From
bullfighting, referring to the kill.]

this moment at once.

to have one's moments to be successful,
impressive, happy etc. on occasions.

money

a fool and his money are soon parted FOOL.

a (good) run for one's money RUN.

dirty money DIRTY.

easy money EASY.

even money EVEN[1].

for love or money LOVE.

for my money in my opinion.

hush money HUSH.

in the money having or having won a lot
of money.

made of money MADE.

money for jam/ old rope (coll.) money
made with little effort.

money talks wealth brings advantages.

money to burn more money than one
needs.

to coin money COIN.

to get one's money's worth to get good
value for one's expense or effort.

to make money to obtain an income, to
acquire wealth.

to put money into to invest in.

to put one's money where one's mouth is to
back up one's words or promises with
real action or financial commitment.

to see the colour of someone's money
COLOUR.

to spend money like water SPEND.

to throw good money after bad to waste
further money in a futile attempt to
rectify a bad situation that has already
cost money.

to throw money at to try to solve (a
problem) by spending money rather
than tackling the root cause.

you pays your money and you takes your
choice you are free to choose from a
range of equally likely, desirable etc.
options. [From a popular rhyme of the
19th century or earlier.]

monkey

cold enough to freeze the balls off a brass
monkey COLD.

monkey business 1 (coll.) devious or
underhand behaviour. 2 (coll.)
mischievous behaviour.

to get/ put someone's monkey up (coll.) to
make someone angry, to enrage
someone.

to have a monkey on one's back to be a
drug addict.

to make a monkey of to cause to seem
foolish.

monosyllable

in monosyllables in simple direct words.

monster

the green-eyed monster GREEN.

month

flavour of the month FLAVOUR.

month of Sundays an indefinitely long
period.

monty

the full monty FULL.

mood

in a mood experiencing a period of
sulkiness, gloom, withdrawal etc.
(The boss is in a mood this morning).

in the mood inclined (to or for), in a
positive state of mind (I'm not in the
mood).

moon

man in the moon MAN.

many moons ago a long time ago.

once in a blue moon BLUE MOON.

over the moon very pleased or happy.

to cry for the moon CRY.

moonlight

moonlight flit a removal of household
furniture after dark to escape paying
rent etc. (to do a moonlight flit).

mop[1]

to mop up 1 to wipe up with or as with a mop. 2 (*Mil.*) to clear (a place) of enemy troops etc. 3 (*sl.*) to seize, to appropriate, to get hold of. 4 to dispatch, to finish off.

mop[2]

mops and mows grimaces.

more

more and more with continual increase.

more of to a greater extent (*more of a director than an actor*).

more or less 1 about. 2 thereabouts. 3 to a greater or lesser extent.

more so to a greater extent or degree.

more than very (*I was more than grateful for their help*).

the more the merrier the pleasure will be greater, the more people are involved.

to be no more to be dead.

morning

in the morning tomorrow morning.

the morning after (the night before) a hangover.

Morpheus

in the arms of Morpheus ARM[1].

mortal

this mortal coil the bustle or troubles of earthly life. [From Shakespeare's *Hamlet*: "When we have shuffled off this mortal coil", part of the famous soliloquy in which Hamlet contemplates suicide.]

Moscow

gone to Moscow (*Austral., coll.*) pawned. [From a Yiddish corruption of the Hebrew word *mishken*, meaning 'to pawn'.]

moss

a rolling stone gathers no moss ROLLING.

most

at (the) most 1 as the greatest amount. 2 not more than.

for the most part in the main, usually.

to make the most of to use to the best advantage (*We made the most of the remaining time*).

mothball

in mothballs in long-term storage pending for possible future use.

to put into mothballs to defer execution of (a plan, project etc.).

mother

every mother's son all without exception.

like mother, like daughter said when a girl or woman behaves like her mother.

necessity is the mother of invention NECESSITY.

the mother and father of the greatest example of (*They had the mother and father of a row*).

to be mother (*coll.*) to pour out a drink, esp. tea (*Shall I be mother?*).

motion

in motion moving; not at rest.

to go through the motions to do something without enthusiasm or conviction (*I was just going through the motions*).

to put/ set in motion to set going or in operation.

to set the wheels in motion WHEEL.

motley

to wear motley WEAR.

mould

cast in the same mould CAST.

to break the mould BREAK.

mount

to mount guard to go on duty as a sentry etc.

mountain

to make a mountain out of a molehill to
make far more of an issue, task etc.
than is justified or reasonable.
to move mountains MOVE.

mouse

poor as a church mouse POOR.
quiet as a mouse QUIET.
to play cat and mouse with CAT.
when the cat's away the mice will play
CAT.

mouth

all mouth (and trousers) (*coll*.) full of talk
but slow to take action.
a plum in one's mouth PLUM.
born with a silver spoon in one's mouth
BORN.
by word of mouth WORD.
down in the mouth (*coll*.) unhappy.
(from) hand to mouth HAND.
the horse's mouth HORSE.
the lion's mouth LION.
to foam at the mouth FOAM.
to give mouth (of a dog) to bark or bay.
to have one's heart in one's mouth HEART.
to keep one's mouth shut (*coll*.) not to
speak, esp. not to reveal secrets.
to look a gift horse in the mouth GIFT.
to look as if butter wouldn't melt in one's
mouth BUTTER.
to make mouths/ a wry mouth to make
grimaces.
to make someone's mouth water 1 to
stimulate someone's appetite. 2 to
make someone very desirous.
to melt in the mouth MELT.
to put one's money where one's mouth is
MONEY.
to put words into someone's mouth WORD.
to shoot one's mouth off SHOOT.
to stop the mouth of STOP.
to take the bread out of someone's mouth
BREAD.
to take the words out of someone's mouth
WORD.

move

not to move a muscle to keep absolutely
still.
on the move 1 stirring. 2 moving from
place to place, travelling about.
to get a move on (*coll*.) to hurry.
to make a move 1 to go, to leave the table
etc. 2 to start. 3 to begin to go. 4 to
move a piece at chess etc.
to move away to go to live elsewhere,
esp. at some distance.
to move heaven and earth to make every
effort (to secure an object) (*I moved
heaven and earth to get you the job*).
to move in 1 to move into a new house
etc. 2 to take up a position of power,
influence, advantage etc. (*The police
moved in and took control*).
to move in with to start to share
accommodation with (an established
resident).
to move mountains to achieve what was
seemingly impossible by effort,
persistence etc.
to move on/ along to change one's
position, esp. to avoid crowding or to
accommodate others.
to move out 1 to go to live elsewhere. 2 to
leave a job, position etc.
to move over/ up to adjust one's position
to accommodate others.
to move the goalposts to change the
conditions, regulations, limits etc.
applying to a particular matter or
action.

mover

movers and shakers (*coll*.) people with
power and influence in politics,
business etc.

mow[1]

to mow down 1 to kill in great numbers.
2 to destroy indiscriminately.

mow[2]

mops and mows MOP[2].

Mr

Mr Right (*facet.*) the ideal marriage
partner for a woman.

much

a bit much (*coll.*) rather excessive,
unreasonable etc.

as much an equal quantity.

in as much as seeing that; since; in such
measure as.

much as even though (*much as I wanted
to stay*).

not much (*sl., sometimes iron.*) certainly
not, not likely.

not much in it little difference between
things being compared (*I thought this
one would be far more expensive, but
there's not much in it*).

not up to much (*coll.*) not very good, of
poor quality.

so much 1 a great deal, to a great extent
(*She's so much better!*). **2** a certain
(limited) amount (*I only have so much
patience*). **3** (*with neg.*) to a lesser
degree (*not so much a fashion as a
fad*).

so much as 1 (*with neg.*) even (*without so
much as a wave*). **2** however much, to
whatever extent.

so much for 1 I don't think much of
(*So much for their fabled speed*).
2 there is nothing more to be said
about (*So much for that*).

so much so to such a degree or extent
(that).

to make much of 1 (*usu. with neg.*) to
treat with fondness or favour. **2** to treat
as of great importance. **3** to derive
much benefit from.

too much more than enough.

too much for 1 superior to in a contest
etc., more than a match for. **2** beyond
what is acceptable to, endurable by etc.

muchness

much of a muchness practically the
same, very nearly alike. [From *The
Provok'd Husband* (1728), a play by
Sir John Vanbrugh.]

muck

common as muck COMMON.

Lady Muck LADY.

Lord Muck LORD.

to make a muck of to bungle, to make a
mess of.

to muck about/ around 1 to fool around,
to mess around. **2** to potter, to mess
about.

to muck in (*coll.*) to help others to do
something (*It won't take long if
everyone mucks in*).

to muck out to clean muck from (esp. a
stable).

to muck up 1 to make dirty or untidy.
2 to bungle, to make a mess of.

mucker

to come a mucker 1 to have a bad fall.
2 to come to grief.

to go a mucker 1 to plunge. **2** to be
extravagant.

muckle

many a mickle makes a muckle MICKLE.

muck sweat

in a muck sweat (*sl.*) sweating, esp. with
fear or confusion.

mud

clear as mud CLEAR.

mud in your eye! used as a drinking toast.

someone's name is mud NAME.

stick-in-the-mud STICK².

to drag through the mud DRAG.

to sling/ throw mud to make disgraceful
imputations.

muddle

to make a muddle of 1 to reduce to
disorder. **2** to bungle.

to muddle along to get along somehow.

to muddle on to keep going somehow.

to muddle through to attain a desired
result without any efficiency or
organization.

to muddle up to confuse (two or more
things).

muddy
to muddy the waters to confuse the issue.

mug¹
mug's game an unwise or unprofitable
activity.

mug²
to mug up to work hard (on) learning a
subject, esp. in a rapid, superficial way
(We'd better mug up on our French
before we go to Paris).

mule
stubborn as a mule STUBBORN.

multitude
to cover a multitude of sins COVER.

mum
mum's the word used to ask for silence or
discretion.

murder
murder will out a hidden matter will
certainly come to light.
to cry/ scream bloody murder (N Am., sl.)
to cry/ scream blue murder.
to cry/ scream blue murder (sl.) to make a
terrible din or commotion.
to get away with murder (coll.) to do
something criminal, outrageous etc.
without being punished.

Murphy
Murphy's law the maxim that if
something can go wrong, it will.

muscle
not to move a muscle MOVE.
to flex one's muscles FLEX.
to muscle in 1 to force one's way in. 2 to
interfere (She tried to muscle in on our
project).

music
music to one's ears something that one is
pleased to hear.
set to music (of a poem or other
composition) provided with music to
which it can be sung.
to face the music FACE.

must
I must say (coll.) used to add emphasis
(I must say I didn't expect such a
response).

mustard
keen as mustard KEEN.
to cut the mustard (N Am., sl.) to be up to
the required standard.

muster
to muster in (N Am.) to enrol (a recruit)
in the forces.
to muster out (N Am.) to discharge (a
soldier) from the army.
to pass muster 1 to be accepted as
satisfactory. 2 to pass inspection
without censure.

mute
to stand mute 1 to refuse or be unable to
speak. 2 (Law) to refuse to plead (usu.
from malice).

mutton
mutton dressed as lamb (coll., derog.) an
older woman dressed or made up to
look younger.

myself
I myself I, for my part.

mystery
to make a mystery of to treat something
with exaggerated secrecy.

N

N

to the nth (degree) 1 (*Math.*) to any power. **2** to the utmost.

nail

hard as nails HARD.

nail in the coffin of something likely to cause the death or end of (*another nail in the coffin of democracy*).

on the nail on the spot; at once (*paid cash on the nail*).

right as nails RIGHT.

to fight tooth and nail FIGHT.

to hit the nail on the head HIT.

to nail down 1 to extract a promise from. **2** to determine, to find out the identity or meaning of. **3** to fix with nails.

to nail one's colours to the mast to persist in one's support of something. [From the practice of nailing a ship's flag to the mast so that it could not be lowered as a sign of surrender.]

to nail up 1 to close or fasten up by nailing. **2** to fix at a height with nails.

naked

the naked ape modern man.

the naked eye the eye unassisted by any optical instrument.

name

a handle to one's name HANDLE.

by name called (*Mary Smith by name*).

by/ of the name of called (*a writer by the name of John Parker*).

give a dog a bad name DOG.

give it a name mention what you will have (to drink, as a present etc.).

in all but name virtually, practically.

in name only officially but not genuinely (*a marriage in name only*).

in one's own name by one's own authority.

in the name of 1 for the sake of (*destruction of the environment in the name of progress*). **2** by the authority of (*Stop, in the name of the law!*).

middle name MIDDLE.

name to conjure with a person of great influence.

no names, no pack drill (*coll.*) mention no names and no one gets into trouble. [Pack drill is a form of military punishment consisting of high-speed drill in full kit.]

someone's name is mud someone is in disgrace, unpopular etc.

the name of the game (*coll.*) the central or important thing; what something is all about (*Productivity is the name of the game*).

to call names to abuse verbally.

to clear someone's name CLEAR.

to have someone's name on it (of a bullet or bomb) to be destined to hit someone.

to have to one's name to own, to possess (*I didn't have a penny to my name*).

to know by name 1 to have heard mentioned. **2** to be able to provide the name of.

to make a name for oneself to become well known.

to name after to call by the same name as (*I am named after my grandmother; Pennsylvania is named after William Penn*).

to name for (*N Am.*) to name after.

to name names to mention people by name usu. in order to accuse or blame them.

to name the day to fix the date for one's wedding.

to put one's name down for 1 to apply for. **2** to promise to give.

to take someone's name in vain 1 to use someone's name, esp. God's, profanely or without due respect. **2** (*coll., facet.*) to mention someone's name. [From the Bible: "Thou shalt not take the name of the Lord thy God in vain" (Exod. xx.7), one of the Ten Commandments.]

what's in a name? the name is less important than the essence. [From Shakespeare's *Romeo and Juliet*: "What's in a name? that which we call a rose / By any other name would smell as sweet."]

you name it (*coll.*) whatever you want or think of (*There was smoked salmon, caviar, you name it*).

nap¹

to catch someone napping CATCH.

nap²

not to go nap on (*Austral., coll.*) not to like much.

to go nap 1 in the game of nap, to offer to take all five tricks. **2** to risk everything on one venture. **3** to win all the games or matches in a series.

nark

nark it! (*sl.*) stop it!

narrow

narrow escape a situation in which danger or trouble is only just avoided.

narrow squeak (*coll.*) a situation in which danger or trouble is only just avoided.

nasty

nasty piece of work (*coll.*) a nasty person.

something nasty in the woodshed something unpleasant or shocking, esp. from a person's past, kept hidden or secret. [From Stella Gibbons' novel *Cold Comfort Farm* (1932), referring to a traumatic childhood experience of the mad elderly matriarch of the story, Aunt Ada Doom, who "saw something nasty in the woodshed".]

nation

to add to/ increase the gaiety of nations GAIETY.

native

to go native to adopt the ways and customs of a place.

nature

against/ contrary to nature 1 unnatural. **2** miraculous; miraculously.

by nature innately.

call of nature CALL.

from nature in art, directly from the living model or natural landscape (*painted from nature*).

in a state of nature STATE.

in nature 1 in actual existence. **2** anywhere; at all. **3** in the sphere of possibility.

in the nature of rather like, more or less.

in the nature of things to be expected.

second nature SECOND.

to get back to nature to return to a simple way of life.

naught

to bring to naught to thwart, frustrate or defeat; to ruin.

to come to naught to be unsuccessful.

to set at naught to disregard.

near

near as dammit (*coll.*) very nearly.

near at hand close in distance or time.

nearest and dearest one's close relatives and friends.

near of kin closely related (by blood etc.).

near thing a situation in which danger or trouble is only just avoided.

†**near upon** close in time from.

to come near almost to (do something) (*I came near to losing my temper*).

to get near to approach within a small distance.

to go near to only just fail (to do something).

nearly

not nearly nowhere near, far from (*not nearly as good*).

necessity

necessity is the mother of invention said when one uses one's ingenuity to solve a problem, or when something is created to supply a need.

of necessity unavoidably, necessarily.

to make a virtue of necessity VIRTUE.

neck

brass neck BRASS.

by a neck by a very small margin (*We won by a neck*). [From horse racing, referring to the length of a horse's neck used to measure its lead.]

dead from the neck up DEAD.

neck and crop altogether, completely. [Alluding to the front and rear parts of an animal.]

neck and neck equal, very close (in a race or contest).

neck of the woods a particular part of the country (*in my neck of the woods*).

neck or nothing at all risks; desperately.

pain in the neck PAIN.

to be a millstone around someone's neck MILLSTONE.

to breathe down someone's neck BREATHE.

to get it in the neck 1 (*coll.*) to be reprimanded severely. **2** (*coll.*) to be hit hard.

to harden the neck HARDEN.

to risk one's neck RISK.

to stick one's neck out STICK².

up to one's neck deeply involved (in).

need

a friend in need (is a friend indeed) FRIEND.

at need at a time of need.

crying need CRYING.

†**had need** ought to, should.

hour of need HOUR.

in need poor or in distress.

in need of requiring, needing.

need not have did not need to (*I need not have worried*).

needs must (when the devil drives) said when one is forced to do something one would rather not do.

to have need of to require, to need.

to have need to to require to, to need to.

to need (something) like a hole in the head (*sl.*) not to need (something) at all, to regard (something) as an unwelcome addition to one's existing problems.

to serve someone's need(s) SERVE.

needle

on pins and needles PIN.

to get the needle (*sl.*) to become irritated or bad-tempered.

to look for a needle in a haystack to engage in a hopeless search.

needless

needless to say obviously, of course.

negative

in the negative indicating dissent or refusal.

neighbourhood

in the neighbourhood of approximately.

nelly

not on your nelly (*sl.*) certainly not.

nerve

bundle of nerves BUNDLE.

to get on someone's nerves (*coll.*) to irritate someone.

to have nerves of steel/ iron to be strong and courageous and not easily frightened.

to lose one's nerve LOSE.

to touch/ hit a nerve to upset someone by mentioning a sensitive subject.

war of nerves WAR.

nest

cuckoo in the nest CUCKOO.

nest egg 1 a sum of money laid by as savings for the future. 2 a real or artificial egg left in a nest to encourage hens to lay eggs there.

to feather one's nest FEATHER.

to foul one's (own) nest FOUL.

to stir up a hornets' nest STIR.

nettle

to grasp the nettle GRASP.

network

old boy network OLD.

never

never a one not a single person etc., none.

†never so to an unlimited extent; exceedingly.

well I never! (coll.) used to express surprise.

never-never

never-never land an imaginary place with conditions too ideal to exist in real life. [From the name of the land where the Lost Boys lived in J. M. Barrie's *Peter Pan* (1904).]

on the never-never on hire purchase.

new

a new broom sweeps clean people often make radical changes on taking up a new post, position etc.

new blood a person with fresh talent or a refreshing influence.

new broom a recently appointed person who is expected to make many changes.

new lease of life an anticipated spell of life or enjoyment (e.g. after recovery from illness or release from trouble).

that's a new one on me (coll.) I have never heard of.that before.

to put a new face on to alter the appearance of.

to turn over a new leaf 1 to change one's mode of life or conduct for the better. 2 to make a new start. [Alluding to a page of a book.]

Newcastle

to carry coals to Newcastle COAL.

news

no news is good news a lack of news about someone or something is a sign that nothing bad has happened.

to break the news BREAK.

next

next of kin the nearest blood relation.

next, please let the next person come.

next to almost; all but.

next to nothing scarcely anything.

next world life after death.

the next man anyone else (*I'm as tolerant as the next man, but this really is too much!*).

what next? can anything exceed or surpass this?

next door

next door to 1 in or at the house adjoining. 2 almost, near to.

nib

his nibs 1 (*coll., facet.*) an important or self-important person. 2 (*sl.*) a burlesque title.

nice

nice and pleasantly, satisfactorily (*nice and cool; nice and early*).

nicety

to a nicety exactly, with precision.

nick

in the nick of time only just in time (*I got there in the nick of time*).

nigger

nigger in the woodpile a person who or something which spoils something good. [Note that the use of the word 'nigger' is considered offensive.]

night

day and night DAY.

dead of night DEAD.

fly-by-night FLY².

night owl 1 an exclusively nocturnal owl. **2** (*coll.*) a person who habitually stays up late.

one-night stand ONE.

ships that pass in the night SHIP.

the other night OTHER.

to make a night of it to spend an evening or night in enjoyment or festivity.

to stay the night STAY.

nine

dressed (up) to the nines DRESS.

nine days' wonder an event, person or thing that is a novelty for the moment but is soon forgotten. [The phrase may allude to the duration of certain Roman Catholic festivals, called novenas, or to the period of time a young animal remains blind after birth.]

nine times out of ten usually, generally.

nine to five normal office working hours.

possession is nine-tenths of the law POSSESSION.

ninepin

to go down/ fall like ninepins to become ill or fail in large numbers (*The staff were going down like ninepins*).

nineteen

to talk nineteen to the dozen TALK.

nip

nip and tuck 1 (*coll.*) a surgical operation performed for cosmetic reasons. **2** (*N Am.*) neck and neck.

to nip in the bud to put a stop to at the outset.

nit

to keep nit (*Austral., sl.*) to keep a lookout.

nix

to keep nix to keep watch.

no¹

no man's land 1 (*Mil.*) the contested land between two opposing forces. **2** waste or unclaimed land.

no way (*coll.*) definitely not, under no circumstances.

... or no ... 1 in spite of, regardless of (*Deadline or no deadline, you must take a break*). **2** with or without (*I'm going to the show, ticket or no ticket!*).

there is no ...ing it is impossible to ... (*There is no getting out of this visit*).

no²

no can do (*coll.*) I cannot do that.

not to take no for an answer not to be deterred by refusal or rejection (*I said I couldn't go, but they wouldn't take no for an answer*).

the noes have it the voters against the motion are in the majority.

to say no to refuse or disagree (*I wouldn't say no to a cup of tea!*).

noble

my noble friend used in the House of Lords to refer to another member of one's own party.

nobody

it's an ill wind that blows nobody any good ILL.

like nobody's business (*coll.*) very energetically or intensively.

nobody's fool a sensible or wise person.

nod

a nod is as good as a wink (to a blind horse) only a slight hint is needed.

land of Nod LAND.

on the nod 1 (*coll.*) without question or argument. **2** (*coll.*) on credit.

to give/ get the nod (*esp. N Am.*) to give/
be given approval or permission.

to nod off (*coll.*) to fall asleep.

to nod through 1 to pass (a motion etc.)
without formal discussion, voting etc.
2 in Parliament, to allow to vote by
proxy.

nodding

nodding acquaintance a slight
acquaintance or knowledge (*I have
only a nodding acquaintance with
computer terminology*).

noise

to make a noise to become well known or
notorious.

to make a noise about to complain about.

nonce

for the nonce for the time being.

nonsense

stuff and nonsense! STUFF.

nook

every nook and cranny everywhere (*We
looked in every nook and cranny but
we couldn't find the missing keys*).

noose

to put one's head in a noose HEAD[1].

north

north and south along a line running to
and from north and south.

north of farther north than.

to the north in a northerly direction.

nose

by a nose by the smallest possible
margin. [From horse racing.]

no skin off someone's nose SKIN.

on the nose exactly, precisely.

plain as the nose on your face PLAIN.

to bloody someone's nose BLOODY.

to count noses COUNT.

to cut off one's nose to spite one's face to

harm oneself in the course of trying to
harm someone else.

to follow one's nose FOLLOW.

to get up someone's nose (*sl.*) to annoy
someone.

to hold one's nose to pinch one's nostrils
so as to not be able to smell, inhale
water etc.

to keep one's nose clean (*sl.*) to behave
well, to stay out of trouble.

to keep one's nose to the grindstone to
stick to one's work.

to lead by the nose LEAD[1].

to look down one's nose at 1 to despise.
2 to assume superiority over.

to pay through the nose to pay an
exorbitant price. [Perhaps from a tax
imposed by the Danes on the Irish in
the 9th century. Those who failed to
pay had their noses slit.]

to put someone's nose out of joint to
upset, disconcert or supplant someone
(*Her promotion put her husband's
nose out of joint*).

to rub noses RUB.

to rub someone's nose in it RUB.

to see no further than (the end of) one's
nose to be short-sighted or lacking in
insight.

to speak through one's nose SPEAK.

to stick/ poke one's nose into to meddle
officiously in.

to thrust one's nose in THRUST.

to thumb one's nose THUMB.

to turn up one's nose at to show contempt
for (*She turned up her nose at my
humble offering*).

under someone's nose in someone's actual
presence or sight.

with one's nose in the air in a haughty
manner.

not

not at all a polite way of acknowledging
thanks.

not in it 1 (*coll.*) not aware of (a secret).
2 (*coll.*) not participating in (an
advantage). 3 (*coll.*) not in the running.

not on 1 (*sl.*) not possible. **2** (*sl.*) not morally, socially etc. acceptable (*It's just not on!*).

not quite 1 almost. **2** definitely not.

not that it is not meant however that (*not that I mind*).

not very 1 to a minor extent. **2** far from being.

notch

to notch up to score, to achieve.

note

of note 1 important, distinguished. **2** worth noticing or mentioning (*Nothing of note happened that day*).

to compare notes COMPARE.

to hit/ strike the right note RIGHT.

to take note to pay attention.

nothing

for nothing 1 free, without paying. **2** to no purpose.

like nothing on earth very bad, unpleasant or unattractive.

little or nothing LITTLE.

mere nothings MERE.

neck or nothing NECK.

next to nothing NEXT.

no nothing (*coll.*) (at the end of a list of negatives) not at all (*I was left with no house, no money, no nothing*).

nothing doing 1 (*coll.*) there is no chance of success. **2** (*coll.*) nothing is happening. **3** (*coll.*) I refuse (to do something).

nothing (else) for it no alternative.

nothing else than/ but merely, only, no more than (this or that).

nothing less than 1 positively, downright, absolutely (*It's nothing less than blackmail!*). **2** (*dated*) anything rather than.

nothing like LIKE[1].

nothing loath LOATH.

nothing of the kind 1 something quite different. **2** not at all (as a rejoinder).

nothing to show for no visible result of (one's efforts etc.) (*four hours' work and nothing to show for it*).

nothing to you not your business.

nothing ventured, nothing gained nothing can be achieved without taking risks or making an effort.

on a hiding to nothing HIDING.

sweet nothings SWEET.

there is nothing in it 1 it is untrue. **2** there is very little difference between two alternatives.

there is nothing to it it is extremely easy.

think nothing of it THINK.

to be nothing to 1 not to concern. **2** not to be comparable with.

to be nothing to do with 1 to be no concern or business of (*It's nothing to do with you!*). **2** not to be connected with.

to come to nothing 1 to turn out a failure. **2** to result in no amount.

to count/ go for nothing to have no importance or influence (*Qualifications count for nothing in this job*).

to do nothing for not to suit or appeal to (*That dress does nothing for her*).

to have nothing on someone 1 to have no evidence that a person has done something wrong. **2** to have no advantage over another person.

to have nothing to do with 1 not to be connected or involved with. **2** to have no communication or relationship with (*She has had nothing to do with her brother since their parents' death*).

to make nothing of to fail to understand or deal with.

to say nothing of not to mention.

to stop/ stick at nothing not to be deterred, to be ready to do anything to achieve one's ends.

to think nothing of THINK.

to want for nothing WANT.

notice

at a moment's notice MOMENT.

at short notice SHORT.

to give notice to intimate the termination of an agreement, particularly a contract of employment.

to take no notice of to pay no attention to; to ignore.

to take notice 1 to observe. **2** to show alertness. **3** to pay attention.

to take notice of to pay attention to, to heed.

under notice served with a formal notice.

now

as of now from this time.

for now until later.

from now on from this time onwards.

now and then/ again from time to time; occasionally.

now, now used as mild rebuke or warning, or to express sympathy.

now or never at this moment or the chance is gone for ever (*It's now or never!*).

nowhere

in the middle of nowhere MIDDLE.

nowhere near not nearly.

to come from nowhere 1 to appear suddenly or unexpectedly. **2** to achieve sudden or unexpected success.

to come in/ be nowhere (*coll.*) to be badly defeated in a race or other contest.

to get nowhere to make or cause to make little or no progress (*Let's try a different approach: this is getting us nowhere!*).

nuddy

in the nuddy naked. [From a jocular mispronunciation of the word 'nude'.]

null

null and void having no legal force or validity.

number

a number of several.

any number of 1 any particular number of. **2** (*coll.*) a large quantity of (*There are any number of possible explanations*).

back number BACK.

by numbers performed in simple stages, esp. with each one numbered.

number one 1 the first or most important in a series. **2** (*coll.*) oneself (*to look after number one*). **3** (*coll.*) the most senior person in an organization. **4** (*coll.*) the product which is at the top of a sales chart, esp. a pop record. **5** most important (*He was England's number one batsman for ten years*).

number two a deputy.

opposite number OPPOSITE.

someone's number is up (*coll.*) someone is going to die.

there's safety in numbers SAFETY.

to have someone's number (*coll.*) to understand someone's intentions, motives or character.

without number too many to be counted.

nut

hard nut to crack HARD.

nuts and bolts (*coll.*) the basic essential facts.

off one's nut 1 (*sl.*) mad. **2** (*sl.*) drunk.

someone can't do something for nuts (*coll.*) someone is very bad at something (*He can't dance for nuts*).

to be nuts about/ on (*coll.*) to delight in; to be very fond of.

to do one's nut (*sl.*) to become very angry.

tough nut to crack TOUGH.

nutshell

in a nutshell expressed in a very concise statement.

nutty

nutty about/ on very fond of or enthusiastic about.

nutty as a fruitcake very eccentric or insane.

oak
heart of oak HEART.

oar
to lay on one's oars (*N Am.*) to rest/ lie on one's oars.
to put/ stick one's oar in 1 to intrude into a conversation. 2 to interfere, esp. with unasked-for advice.
to rest/ lie on one's oars 1 to cease rowing without shipping the oars. 2 to stop for rest, to cease working.
to toss oars TOSS.

oat
off one's oats (*coll.*) off one's food; without appetite. [Originally used of horses.]
to feel one's oats FEEL.
to get one's oats (*sl.*) to have regular sexual intercourse.
to sow one's (wild) oats SOW¹.

oath
on/ under oath 1 sworn to attesting the truth. 2 pledged or attested by oath. 3 having taken an oath.
to take/ swear an oath to swear formally to the truth of one's attestations.

obedience
in obedience to in accordance with.

object
no object not an obstacle or restriction (*money no object*).
object lesson 1 a practical illustration. 2 a lesson in which the actual object described or a representation of it is used for illustration.
object of the exercise the purpose of a particular action or activity.

obligation
of obligation obligatory.
under an obligation indebted for some benefit, favour or kindness.

oblige
much obliged used to express thanks.

oblivion
to fall into oblivion to be forgotten.

observation
under observation in a state of being watched carefully, undergoing scrutiny.

occasion
as the occasion arises when needful, when circumstances demand.
on occasion now and then.
to rise to the occasion RISE.
to take the occasion to to take the opportunity of.

o'clock
†what o'clock is it? what time is it?

od
†od's bodikins by God's dear body.
†od's life by God's life.

odd
odd man out 1 a person who is left when

a number pair off. **2** a person who is at variance with or excluded from, or who stands out as dissimilar to, a group etc.

odd or even a game of chance.

odds and ends miscellaneous remnants, scraps etc.

odds and sods (*coll.*) miscellaneous remnants, scraps etc.

odds

against all (the) odds despite obstacles that make success seem impossible (*They succeeded against all the odds*).

at odds at variance.

over the odds higher, more than is acceptable, necessary, usual etc. (*We paid over the odds for it*).

the odds are it is likely or probable (that) (*The odds are that he's forgotten*).

to lay/ give odds to offer a bet with favourable odds.

to make no odds to make no difference, not to matter.

to shout the odds SHOUT.

to take odds to accept a bet with favourable odds.

what's the odds? (*coll.*) what difference does it make?

odour

in good/ bad odour 1 in good/ bad repute. **2** in/ out of favour.

odour of sanctity 1 a reputation for holiness. **2** (*facet.*) the odour of an unwashed body. **3** sanctimoniousness. [The phrase originally referred to a pleasant smell allegedly given off by the corpse of a saintly person at the time of death or exhumation.]

of

of an evening/ morning/ etc. 1 (*coll.*) usually in the evening etc. **2** (*coll.*) at some point during most evenings etc.

of one's belonging or relating to one (*a friend of mine*).

off

off and on intermittently, now and again.

off chance

on the off chance in the slim hope (that), just in case.

offence

to give offence to cause umbrage, to affront, to insult.

to take offence to be offended, to feel a grievance.

offer

on offer presented for sale, consumption etc., esp. at a bargain price.

under offer provisionally sold prior to and subject to the signing of a contract.

offing

in the offing likely to occur soon. [The offing is the part of the sea beyond the halfway line between the coast and the horizon.]

often

as often as not in roughly half of the instances.

more often than not (quite) frequently.

oh

oh well used to express resignation.

oil

to burn the midnight oil BURN.

to oil the wheels to facilitate matters, to help things go smoothly.

to pour oil on troubled waters POUR.

to strike oil STRIKE.

oiled

on oiled wheels very smoothly.

oil painting

no oil painting physically unattractive.

ointment

fly in the ointment FLY[3].

old

an old head on young shoulders referring to someone who is wise beyond their years.

for old times'/sake's sake in memory of pleasant times in the past.

of old 1 in or from ancient times. **2** long ago, formerly.

of old standing long established.

old as the hills (*coll.*) very old, ancient.

old boy/ girl 1 (*coll.*) used as a friendly form of address to a man or boy/ woman or girl. **2** (*coll.*) an elderly man/ woman.

old boy network (*coll.*) a network of former pupils of public schools and universities, who can use their contacts for employment opportunities etc.

old chestnut (*coll.*) a stale joke or anecdote.

old flame (*coll.*) a former boyfriend or girlfriend.

old guard the old or conservative members of a party etc. [The term originally referred to the veteran regiments of Napoleon's Imperial Guard, who made the last charge at the Battle of Waterloo.]

old hand 1 a person who is skilled or practised at a trade or craft of any kind. **2** any of the early convicts in Australia etc.

old hat 1 (*coll.*) outdated, old-fashioned. **2** (*coll.*) familiar and dull.

old maid 1 (*derog.*) an unmarried woman of advanced years or unlikely ever to marry. **2** a card game in which an unpaired queen at the end of a hand scores against one. **3** a precise, prudish, fidgety person of either sex.

old man 1 (*coll.*) a male sexual partner, a husband. **2** (*coll.*) a father. **3** (*coll.*) used as a friendly form of address to a man. **4** (*coll.*) an employer.

old pals act (*coll.*) the principle that friends should help one another.

old wives' tale a legend, a foolish story.

old woman 1 (*coll.*) a wife or mother. **2** (*coll.*) a timid, fidgety or fussy man.

the oldest profession (*coll. or facet.*) prostitution.

the (same) old story a familiar sequence of events, the usual thing.

to come the old soldier 1 to claim to have more experience or knowledge. **2** to feign illness or incapacity for work.

to make old bones to live to a great age.

old school

of the old school belonging to past ways, traditions etc.

old school tie 1 a tie sporting a public school's colours worn by its former pupils. **2** a symbol of the mutual allegiance of a group of (esp. privileged or upper class) people.

olive

olive branch 1 a branch of the olive tree as an emblem of peace. **2** something which indicates a desire for peace (e.g. a goodwill gesture, an offer of reconciliation).

Oliver

a Roland for an Oliver ROLAND.

omega

alpha and omega ALPHA.

omelette

you can't make an omelette without breaking eggs it is impossible to achieve something without losing or damaging something else.

on

on and off intermittently, now and again (*It rained on and off all afternoon*).

on and on ceaselessly, continuously.

to be on about to talk about, esp. tediously (*I hadn't a clue what she was on about*).

to be on at (*coll.*) to nag or grumble at.

to be on to 1 to be aware of, to have discovered (something secret, someone's trick etc.). **2** to get in touch with.

once

all at once all together, simultaneously, suddenly.

at once 1 immediately, without delay (*We must leave at once*). **2** simultaneously.

for once for one time or occasion only.

just this once on this occasion only.

not once or twice many times, often.

once again another time.

once (and) for all 1 finally. **2** definitively.

once in a while/ way occasionally.

once more another time.

once or twice a few times.

once upon a time at some past date or period (usu. beginning a fairytale).

one

all in one combined.

all one of no importance (to).

at one in accord or agreement.

for one being one; even if the only one (*I for one think it's a good idea*).

one and all jointly and severally.

one and only 1 unique. **2** unequalled.

one by one one at a time, one after another.

one for the road (*coll.*) a last drink before leaving.

one in the eye a disappointment or rebuff (for) (*It'll be one in the eye for him if you get the job*).

one-night stand 1 a single performance at one venue. **2** (*coll.*) a sexual encounter or relationship lasting one evening or night. **3** a person engaging in such an encounter.

one or two a few.

one with in harmony or unity with, synonymous with, part of the same whole as.

one with another on the average, in general.

to be one for to be an enthusiast for.

to be one up on (*coll.*) to be in a position of advantage over.

to go one better (than) to outdo (another person).

to have one too many to become drunk.

one-horse

one-horse race a race or competition which one particular person is certain to win.

one-man

one-man band/ show 1 a sole musician playing a variety of instruments simultaneously. **2** a company, enterprise etc., consisting of, or run by, a single person.

one-track

one-track mind a mind preoccupied with one thing.

onion

to know one's onions (*coll.*) to be knowledgeable in one's subject or competent in one's job.

only

if only 1 if for no other reason than (*It's worth going, if only for the music*). **2** used to express a desire or wish (*If only I'd been there*).

not the only pebble on the beach able to be replaced easily.

only too ... 1 more than (*only too willing to help*). **2** to an excessive or regrettable degree (*only too true*).

open

open-and-shut needing little deliberation, easily solved, simple (*an open-and-shut case*).

open book someone or something easily understood.

open door 1 free admission or unrestricted access. **2** a policy of equal trading with all nations.

open house 1 hospitality proffered to all comers. **2** (*N Am.*) an open day.

open secret an apparently undivulged secret which is however generally known.

open sesame 1 a magic formula for opening a door. **2** a key to a mystery etc. **3** an easy means of entry to a profession etc. [From a magic formula used to gain entry to the treasure cave of the forty thieves, discovered by Ali Baba in one of the stories of the *Arabian Nights*.]

to be open with to speak frankly to.

to bring into the open to disclose (what was hitherto hidden or secret).

to lay oneself open to to expose oneself to (criticism, attack etc.).

to lay open 1 to cut so as to expose the interior of. **2** to expose, to reveal. **3** to explain.

to open fire to begin firing ammunition.

to open one's mind to give thought (to something previously unconsidered or rejected).

to open out 1 to unfold, to expand. **2** to develop. **3** to reveal, to disclose. **4** to become communicative. **5** (*Naut.*) to bring into full view. **6** to accelerate. **7** to begin firing.

to open someone's eyes to astonish or enlighten someone (*Visiting the site opened their eyes to the extent of the problem*).

to open the ball 1 to lead off in the first dance. **2** to commence operations.

to open the door to to allow the possibility of.

to open the floodgates to cause an uncontrolled outpouring or inrush, esp. of something undesirable, by removing all restraints or barriers.

to open the trenches to begin to dig or to form trenches or lines of approach.

to open up 1 to make accessible. **2** to reveal. **3** to discover, to explore, to colonize, to make ready for trade. **4** to accelerate. **5** to begin firing. **6** to talk openly.

under the open sky outside, out of doors.

with open arms enthusiastically (*welcomed with open arms*).

opener
for openers (*coll.*) to start with.

opinion
in one's opinion according to one's view or belief.

matter of opinion MATTER.

to be of the opinion that to believe or think that.

opportunity
opportunity knocks an opportunity occurs.

oppose
as opposed to in contrast with.

opposite
opposite number 1 a person in the corresponding position on another side. **2** a counterpart.

opt
to opt out 1 to choose not to be involved in something. **2** (of a school, hospital etc.) to choose no longer to be under the control or management of a local authority.

option
soft option SOFT.

to have no option but to to have to.

to keep/ leave one's options open to refrain from committing oneself.

oracle
to work the oracle WORK.

order
apple-pie order APPLE PIE.

by order according to direction by proper authority.

in bad order not working properly.

in good order working properly.

in/ of the order of approximately the size or quantity specified.

in order 1 properly or systematically arranged. **2** in due sequence. **3** ready and fit for use.

in order that so that.

in order to 1 to the end that. **2** so as to.

in short order SHORT.

marching orders MARCH.

not in order not working.

on order having been ordered but not yet arrived.

order of the day 1 business arranged beforehand, esp. the programme of business in a legislative assembly. **2** the prevailing state of things.

Order! Order! used to call for silence, esp. by the Speaker of the House of Commons.

out of order 1 disarranged. **2** untidy. **3** not consecutive. **4** not systematically arranged. **5** not fit for work or use. **6** (*coll.*) (of behaviour) not acceptable.

pecking order PECK.

tall order TALL.

to fill an order FILL.

to keep order to enforce or maintain order.

to order according to, or in compliance with, an order (*made to order*).

to order about 1 to send from one place to another. **2** to domineer over.

to order arms (*Mil.*) to bring rifles vertically against the right side with the butts resting on the ground.

to put/ set one's house in order HOUSE.

to set in order 1 to arrange, to adjust. **2** to reform.

to take holy orders HOLY.

to take orders 1 to accept commissions, commands etc. **2** to be ordained.

under starter's orders STARTER.

ordinary

in ordinary in actual and constant service.

in the ordinary way in normal circumstances.

out of the ordinary exceptional.

orient

to orient oneself to check one's position according to one's surroundings.

other

how the other half lives how people of a different social class live (*He spent a week on a council estate to see how the other half lives*).

in other words expressing the same thing in a different way.

none other than exactly, precisely (the person or thing specified).

of all others out of the many possible or likely.

on the other hand from that point of view.

other half one's spouse or partner.

pull the other one (*coll.*) used as an expression of disbelief (i.e. pull the other leg).

somehow/ somewhere or other in an unspecified way/ place.

someone/ something or other an unspecified person/ thing.

the other day/ night on a day/ night recently (*I saw Jack the other day*).

the other side of the coin the opposite point of view.

the other thing (*esp. facet.*) an unexpressed alternative.

the other way round in the opposite direction; in a reversed, inverted etc. position.

the other week during a week recently.

to look the other way to ignore or disregard someone or something.

to pass by on the other side to ignore someone in need of help. [From the Bible (Luke x.31–32), part of the parable of the good Samaritan.]

to turn the other cheek to accept a physical or verbal attack without retaliation. [From the Bible: "resist not evil: but whosoever shall smite thee on thy right cheek, turn to him the other also" (Matt. v.39).]

otherwise

and/ or otherwise the negation or opposite (of a specified thing) (*the truth or otherwise of what he said*).

out

at outs at variance, at odds.

from out out of.

ins and outs IN.

not out 1 (of a side or batsman in cricket) not having been caught, bowled etc. **2** having reached the end of a cricket innings or of play for the day without being dismissed.

out and about able to get up and go outside.

out and out 1 complete, thorough. **2** completely, unreservedly.

out for striving for.

out of it 1 not included, neglected (*I felt a bit out of it at the reception*). **2** at a loss. **3** in error, mistaken. **4** (*coll.*) unaware of one's surroundings due to drink, drugs etc.

out to aiming to, working to.

out with 1 away with. **2** not friendly with.

out with it say what you are thinking.

outgrow

to outgrow one's strength to become thin and weak through too rapid growth.

outline

in outline sketched or represented as an outline.

outrun

to outrun the constable (*dated*) to get into debt.

outset

at/ from the outset at or from the beginning.

outside

at the outside at the most (*It should take two weeks at the outside*).

outside and in outside and inside.

outside in having the outer side turned in, and vice versa.

outward

to outward seeming apparently.

oven

to have a bun in the oven BUN.

over

not over not very (*I'm not over keen on the colour*).

over-age AGE.

over all taken as a whole.

over and above 1 in addition to. **2** besides.

over and done with completely finished.

over and over 1 so as to turn completely round several times. **2** repeatedly.

to get it over with to do something unpleasant that has to be done.

overdo

to overdo it/ things to exhaust oneself, to do too much.

overleap

to overleap oneself to miss one's aim by leaping too far or too high.

overplay

to overplay one's hand 1 to overestimate one's capabilities. **2** to defeat one's object by going too far.

overreach

to overreach oneself 1 to strain oneself by reaching too far. **2** to defeat one's object by going too far.

overseas

from overseas from abroad.

overshoot

to overshoot oneself 1 to go too far, to overreach oneself. **2** to make assertions that cannot be substantiated.

to overshoot the mark to go beyond what
is intended.

overstep

to overstep the mark to violate
conventions of behaviour.

owe

to owe it to oneself to feel the need to do
something that is in one's own
interests.

to owe someone a grudge to hold a grudge
against a person.

owl

night owl NIGHT.

own¹

of one's own belonging to oneself.

on one's own without aid from other
people, independently.

to call one's own to regard as one's
possession, to own.

to come into one's own 1 to gain what
one is due. 2 to have one's talents or
potential acknowledged.

to get one's own back to be even with.

to hold one's own 1 to maintain one's
position. 2 to survive.

own²

to own up to confess (to).

own goal

to score an own goal SCORE.

oyster

the world is someone's oyster WORLD.

P

P
to mind one's Ps and Qs MIND.

pace
snail's pace SNAIL.

to force the pace FORCE.

to go the pace 1 to go very fast. 2 to lead a life of dissipation or recklessness.

to keep pace with to go or progress at equal rate with (*Wages are not keeping pace with inflation*).

to mend one's pace MEND.

to put someone through their paces to examine someone closely, to test someone. [The phrase originally referred to horses being tested for the quality of their training and performance in the four main gaits (walk, trot, canter and gallop).]

to set/ make the pace to fix the rate of going in a race or any other activity.

to stand/ stay the pace to keep up with other people.

pack
packed like sardines packed or crowded very closely together. [From the way sardines are packed in tins.]

packed out (*coll.*) full of people.

to pack a punch 1 (*coll.*) to be able to punch hard. 2 (*coll.*) to be forceful or effective. 3 (*coll.*) to be unexpectedly strong (*That cocktail certainly packs a punch!*).

to pack in 1 (*coll.*) to stop doing (something) (*Pack it in!*). 2 (*coll.*) to stop going out with (someone).

to pack off (*coll.*) to send or go away (*They packed him off to boarding school*).

to pack on all sail (*Naut.*) to put on the maximum amount of sail.

to pack one's bags to leave, esp. in anger.

to pack up 1 (*coll.*) to stop functioning; to break down. 2 (*coll.*) to stop doing something.

to send packing (*coll.*) to dismiss summarily.

pack drill
no names, no pack drill NAME.

pad
to pad the hoof (*sl.*) to tramp on foot.

paddle
to paddle one's own canoe to be independent.

paid
to put paid to (*coll.*) to end, to destroy.

pain
for one's pains (*usu. iron.*) as a reward for one's effort (*I delivered the goods to their door and got a parking ticket for my pains!*).

in pain feeling pain.

on/ under pain of subject to the penalty of (*on pain of death*).

pain in the neck (*coll.*) a nuisance.

to be at pains to to take trouble to, to be careful to.

to take pains to take trouble (to), to labour hard or be exceedingly careful (to).

paint

to paint out to efface by painting over.

to paint the town red to have a riotous time.

painting

no oil painting OIL PAINTING.

pair

in pairs in twos.

to have only one pair of hands to be unable to do several things at once (*I've only got one pair of hands, you know!*).

to pair off 1 to separate into couples. **2** to go off in pairs.

to show a clean pair of heels CLEAN.

pal

old pals act OLD.

to pal up with (*coll.*) to become friendly with.

pale¹

pale as death very pale.

pale²

beyond the pale unacceptable. [The word 'pale' here refers to a limit or boundary, esp. that around the part of Ireland ruled by the English in the late Middle Ages. Those who lived beyond it were considered uncivilized.]

in pale (*Her.*) arranged vertically.

palm¹

to bear the palm to have pre-eminence. [From the palm branch awarded to a victorious gladiator in ancient Rome.]

palm²

in the palm of one's hand under one's control; in one's power.

to cross someone's palm (with silver) CROSS.

to grease/ oil someone's palm (*coll.*) to bribe someone.

to have an itching palm ITCH.

to palm off to foist (on). [Alluding to conjurors who hide things in the palm of their hand.]

pan

flash in the pan FLASH.

out of the frying pan into the fire FRYING PAN.

to pan out 1 to have a specified result (*My plan panned out well*). **2** to yield gold.

pancake

flat as a pancake FLAT.

to toss a pancake TOSS.

panic button

to press the panic button PRESS.

pants

by the seat of one's pants SEAT.

to bore the pants off someone BORE.

to have ants in one's pants ANT.

to scare the pants off someone SCARE.

paper

not worth the paper it is written on WORTH.

on paper 1 written down. **2** theoretically, rather than in reality.

paper profits hypothetical profits shown on a company's prospectus etc.

paper tiger a person or thing that is apparently threatening or powerful, but is not so in reality.

someone could not punch their way out of a paper bag PUNCH.

to commit to paper COMMIT.

to paper over to disguise or cover up (a dispute, mistake etc.).

to paper over the cracks to disguise or conceal faults or problems. [Alluding to wallpaper covering a cracked wall.]

to put pen to paper PEN.

to send in one's papers to resign.

par

above par 1 at a price above the face value, at a premium. **2** of superior quality.

at par at face value.

below par 1 at a discount. **2** tired, slightly unwell.

on a par with of equal value, degree etc. to.

par for the course what is to be expected, usual. [From the sport of golf, par being the number of shots a good player is expected to take.]

up to par of the required standard.

parachute

golden parachute GOLDEN.

parade

on parade 1 taking part in a parade. **2** being paraded, on display.

paradise

fool's paradise FOOL.

parallel

in parallel (of electrical circuits) arranged across a common voltage supply.

parcel

part and parcel PART.

pardon

I beg your pardon/ pardon me excuse me, a polite apology for an action, contradiction or failure to hear or understand what is said.

to beg someone's pardon BEG.

parenthesis

in parenthesis as an aside, by the way.

parish

on the parish (*Hist.*) being financially supported by the parish.

park

to park oneself (*coll.*) to sit down.

parole

on parole (of a prisoner) released under certain conditions, esp. good behaviour.

parrot

parrot-fashion accurately but without understanding the meaning. [Alluding to the parrot's ability to imitate the human voice.]

sick as a parrot SICK.

part

for my part so far as I am concerned.

for the most part MOST.

in part(s) partly.

man of (many) parts MAN.

on the part of done by or proceeding from.

part and parcel an essential part or element.

part of the furniture a person who is almost always present and therefore often ignored.

the best/ better part of the largest/ larger part of, most of (*I waited for the best part of an hour*).

to look the part to appear to be exactly right for a role.

to part company to separate.

to part with to relinquish, to give up.

to play a part 1 to assist, to be involved. **2** to act deceitfully. **3** to act in a play or film.

to take in good part GOOD.

to take part to assist or participate (in).

to take the part of to back up, to support.

to top one's part TOP[1].

particular

in particular particularly.

parting

parting of the ways the point at which people must separate or follow different paths in life (*We have come to the parting of the ways*). [From the Bible: "For the king of Babylon stood at the parting of the way, at the head of the two ways" (Ezek. xxi.21).]

party

the party's over (*coll.*) something enjoyable, pleasant etc. is at an end.

pas

to have the pas of to take precedence over.

pass

to come to a pretty pass PRETTY.

to make a pass at (*coll.*) to attempt to seduce.

to pass around (*N Am.*) to pass round.

to pass away (*euphem.*) to die, to come to an end.

to pass by 1 to go past. **2** to omit, to disregard.

to pass for/ as to be mistaken for or accepted as (*She's 50, but she could pass for 35*).

to pass off 1 to disappear gradually. **2** to proceed in a specified manner (*to pass off without a hitch*). **3** to cause to be accepted (as something or someone else), to misrepresent (*He evaded capture by passing himself off as a parish priest*).

to pass out 1 to faint. **2** (*Mil.*) (of an officer cadet) to complete training at a military academy. **3** to hand out, to distribute.

to pass over 1 to go across. **2** to allow to go by without notice, to overlook (*She passed over his sarcastic remarks*). **3** to omit. **4** to die.

to pass round to hand round, to distribute.

to pass through to undergo, to experience.

to pass up (*coll.*) to renounce (*I couldn't pass up an opportunity like that*).

to sell the pass SELL.

passage

bird of passage BIRD.

to work one's passage WORK.

passing

in passing casually, without making direct reference (*He mentioned in passing that his wife had left him*).

past

not to put it past someone to do something not to be surprised if someone does something (*I wouldn't put it past him to lie about his age*).

past it (*coll.*) no longer young and vigorous.

past master 1 a thorough master (of a subject etc.). **2** a person who has been master of a Freemasons' lodge, a guild etc.

pasture

pastures new new places, areas of activity etc. (*It's time we moved on to pastures new*). [From John Milton's poem *Lycidas* (1637): "To-morrow to fresh woods, and pastures new."]

pat[1]

pat on the back a demonstration of approval.

to have off/ down pat to have learned or prepared thoroughly (*I had my speech off pat*).

to pat on the back to praise or congratulate.

to stand pat 1 (*esp. N Am.*) to stand by one's decision or beliefs. **2** in poker, to play with the hand one has been dealt, without drawing other cards.

pat[2]

on one's pat (*Austral., sl.*) on one's own, all alone. [From the rhyming slang phrase 'on one's Pat Malone'.]

patch

not a patch on (*coll.*) not nearly as good as.

to patch up 1 to mend. **2** to resolve (differences, a quarrel etc.), esp. temporarily.

path

primrose path PRIMROSE.

to beat a path to someone's door to visit someone in large numbers, esp. someone who has suddenly become famous, popular etc. [From a remark attributed to Ralph Waldo Emerson (1803–82): "If a man write a better book, preach a better sermon, or make a better mousetrap than his neighbour, though he build his house in the woods, the world will make a beaten path to his door."]

to cross the path of CROSS.

to lead up the garden path LEAD¹.

patience

out of patience with unable to stand or put up with.

to (be enough to) try the patience of a saint TRY.

to have no patience with 1 to be unable to stand or put up with. **2** to be irritated by.

Paul

to rob Peter to pay Paul ROB.

pause

to give someone pause to cause someone to hesitate and reconsider. [From Shakespeare's *Hamlet*: "For in that sleep of death what dreams may come / When we have shuffled off this mortal coil, / Must give us pause."]

pave

to pave the way for to prepare for, to make possible.

paw

cat's paw CAT.

pawn

at/ in pawn deposited as a pledge or security.

pay

in the pay of employed by.

to pay away 1 to let (a rope) run out by slackening it. **2** to hand out (money, a fund etc.) in wages etc.

to pay back 1 to repay. **2** to take revenge on. **3** to return (a favour etc.).

to pay dearly for 1 to pay with a lot of money or effort for. **2** to suffer as a result of (*You'll pay dearly for that!*).

to pay for 1 to make a payment for. **2** to suffer as a result of.

to pay in to deposit in a bank account.

to pay off 1 to make (an employee) redundant, with a final payment. **2** (*coll.*) to be profitable or rewarding (*Our efforts finally paid off.*). **3** to pay the full amount of, to pay in full and discharge (*now that we've paid off the mortgage*). **4** (*Naut.*) to turn to leeward.

to pay out 1 to spend or distribute (money), to disburse. **2** to punish. **3** to cause (a rope) to run out.

to pay up to pay someone what is owed or due to them.

payment

to stop payment STOP.

to suspend payment SUSPEND.

pea

alike as/ like (two) peas in a pod very similar, esp. in appearance.

peace

at peace 1 in a state of harmony or tranquillity. **2** (*euphem.*) dead.

peace and quiet tranquil silence, esp. after noise (*I escaped to the garden for a bit of peace and quiet*).

peace be with you a solemn formula of leave-taking.

peace of mind freedom from anxiety.

to hold one's peace to stay silent.

to keep the peace 1 to abstain from strife. **2** to prevent a conflict.

to make one's peace with to end one's quarrel with.

to make peace 1 to reconcile or be reconciled (with). **2** to bring about a treaty of peace.

peacock
proud as a peacock PROUD.

pearl
to cast pearls before swine CAST.

pebble
not the only pebble on the beach ONLY.

peck
pecking order the hierarchical order of
importance in any social group. [From
the natural hierarchy in a group of
domestic fowl or other birds.]
to peck at 1 to nibble at. 2 to nag. 3 to
bite at (something) with a beak.

pecker
to keep one's pecker up (*coll.*) to stay
cheerful.

pedestal
on a pedestal in a position of (excessive)
respect or devotion (*He put his wife on
a pedestal*).

peel
to peel off 1 to leave and move away from
(e.g. a column of marchers). 2 (*coll.*) to
undress.

peep
peeping Tom a person who is guilty of
prurient curiosity, a voyeur. [From the
name of a tailor who spied on Lady
Godiva as she rode naked through the
streets of Coventry in 1040 and was
struck blind as a consequence.]

peg
level pegging LEVEL.
off the peg ready-made.
peg to hang something on an appropriate
occasion for something, such as an
idea, to be aired or expressed.
round peg in a square hole ROUND.
square peg in a round hole SQUARE.
to peg away at to work at or struggle
with persistently.

to peg down 1 to restrict (to rules etc.).
2 to fasten down with pegs.
to peg out 1 (*sl.*) to die. 2 in cribbage, to
win by attaining the final hole in the
cribbage board. 3 in croquet, to go out
by hitting the final peg. 4 to mark out
the boundaries of. 5 (*sl.*) to fail, to be
ruined.
to take someone down a peg (or two) to
humiliate or deflate the ego of
someone. [Possibly alluding to a
musical instrument tuned by turning
pegs, or to pegs on a scoreboard.]

pelt
at full pelt FULL.

pen
to put pen to paper to write something,
esp. in a purposeful way.

penalty
the penalty of something unpleasant
resulting from (an action or
circumstance).
under/ on penalty of under the threat of.

penance
to do penance to do something
unpleasant to atone for sin.

pencil
to pencil in to agree or arrange something
provisionally.
to put lead in someone's pencil LEAD².

pendulum
swing of the pendulum SWING.

penny
a penny for your thoughts what are you
thinking about?
a pretty penny PRETTY.
in for a penny, in for a pound total
commitment is advisable.
like a bad penny repeatedly returning,
esp. when not wanted.
pennies from heaven an unexpected
bonus or advantage.

penny wise and pound foolish saving small sums at the risk of larger ones.

ten/ two a penny having little value because very common.

the penny drops (*coll.*) the truth is realized, something is made clear. [Alluding to a coin-operated machine.]

to make/ earn/ turn an honest penny HONEST.

to spend a penny SPEND.

without a penny to bless oneself with penniless, very poor. [Alluding to the cross on a silver penny.]

pension

to pension off 1 to cease to employ and to give a pension to. **2** to discard as useless, worn etc.

people

people who live in glass houses should not throw stones people susceptible to criticism through their own pursuits or opinions should not criticize others.

pep

to pep up 1 (*coll.*) to give energy, vigour etc. to. **2** (*coll.*) to cheer up.

percentage

to play the percentages (*coll.*) to play cautiously as regards odds in favour of success.

perch

to knock someone off their perch KNOCK.

perfection

to perfection completely, perfectly.

perfidious

perfidious Albion Britain or England as viewed by some of the French etc. [First used in 1793 in a poem by the Marquis de Ximenez, the phrase was popularized during the Napoleonic Wars (1799–1815).]

peril

at one's peril at risk of harm to oneself.

in peril of with great danger to.

perish

perish the thought used to express horror or disapproval.

perk

to perk up (*coll.*) (to cause) to be more cheerful or lively.

perpetuity

in/ for/ to perpetuity for ever.

person

in one's own person as oneself.

in person by oneself, not by deputy.

no respecter of persons RESPECTER.

perspective

in perspective 1 according to the laws of perspective. **2** in due proportion (*to keep things in perspective*).

out of perspective 1 not according to the laws of perspective. **2** not in due proportion (*to get things out of perspective*).

petard

hoist with/ by one's own petard HOIST.

Pete

for Pete's sake used as an expression of annoyance.

Peter

to rob Peter to pay Paul ROB.

peter

to peter out 1 to come to an end, to die out. **2** (of a lode or vein in mining) to thin or give out.

petto

in petto in secret, in reserve.

pew

to take a pew (*coll.*) to sit down.

phase

in phase happening together or in harmony.

out of phase not happening together or in harmony.

to phase in/ out to introduce/ discontinue gradually.

phrase

to coin a phrase COIN.

phut

to go phut (*coll.*) (of a plan) to falter, to be unsuccessful.

pick

to pick and choose to make a fastidious selection.

to pick at 1 to eat sparingly. **2** to criticize in a cavilling way.

to pick holes/ a hole in to find fault with.

to pick off 1 to gather or detach (fruit etc.) from a tree etc. **2** to shoot with careful aim one by one. **3** to eliminate (opposition) one by one. **4** in baseball, to put out by throwing the ball to a base.

to pick on 1 to single out for unpleasant treatment, to bully (*Stop picking on me!*). **2** to single out, to select.

to pick out 1 to select. **2** to distinguish (with the eye) from surroundings. **3** to play (a tune) by ear on the piano etc. **4** to relieve or variegate with or as if with distinctive colours. **5** to gather (the meaning of a passage etc.).

to pick over to examine carefully in order to reject unwanted items.

to pick someone's brains to consult someone with special expertise or experience.

to pick to pieces to analyse or criticize spitefully.

to pick up 1 to take up with the fingers, beak etc. **2** to raise (oneself) after a fall. **3** to raise (one's feet) off the ground. **4** to gather or acquire here and there or little by little (*I picked up some useful*

tips). **5** to collect and take away. **6** to accept and pay (a bill). **7** to arrest and detain (a suspect etc.). **8** to receive (an electronic signal etc.). **9** to make the acquaintance of, esp. with a view to establishing a sexual relationship. **10** to resume (*pick up where we left off*). **11** to regain or recover (health etc.). **12** to recover or improve (*until sales pick up*). **13** in golf, to pick up one's ball when conceding a hole.

to pick up the pieces to put things right after conflict or disruption.

to pick up the threads to resume an activity, way of life etc. after a break or period of absence.

to take one's pick to make a choice.

pickle

to have a rod in pickle ROD.

picnic

no picnic (*coll.*) a difficult or unpleasant experience.

picture

in the picture having all the relevant information (*You'd better put him in the picture*).

out of the picture not involved in a situation.

pretty as a picture PRETTY.

to get the picture to understand the situation.

pie

apple-pie bed APPLE PIE.

apple-pie order APPLE PIE.

pie in the sky an unrealistic aspiration. [From *The Preacher and the Slave* by Joe Hill (1879–1914): "You'll get pie in the sky when you die (That's a lie)".]

to eat humble pie EAT.

to have a finger in every pie FINGER.

piece

by the piece (of wages) according to the amount of work done.

conversation piece CONVERSATION.

in one piece 1 not broken. **2** not damaged
or hurt (*We were lucky to get out of
there in one piece*).

in pieces broken.

nasty piece of work NASTY.

of a piece of the same sort, uniform.

piece of cake something very easy.

piece of the action (*coll.*) active
involvement.

shot to pieces SHOT.

to break to pieces BREAK.

to cut to pieces to exterminate, to
massacre.

to give someone a piece of one's mind to
criticize or reprimand someone
sharply.

to go to pieces to collapse emotionally
(*After the death of his wife, he went to
pieces*).

to pick to pieces PICK.

to pick up the pieces PICK.

to piece on to fit on (to).

to piece out 1 to complete by adding one
or more pieces. **2** to eke out.

to piece up to patch up.

to pull to pieces 1 to tear (something) up.
2 to criticize, to abuse (*pulling each
other to pieces*).

to say one's piece to express one's
opinion.

to take to pieces 1 to separate (something)
into its various components. **2** to
criticize harshly (*She took my essay
to pieces*).

villain of the piece VILLAIN.

pig

in a pig's eye (*coll.*) certainly not.

in pig (of a sow) pregnant.

pig in a poke goods purchased without
being seen beforehand. [Referring to a
trick in which customers were sold a
bag that allegedly contained a piglet
but actually contained a cat. Many
foolish people did not look in the bag
before handing over their money.]

pig in the middle a person who is
unwillingly involved in a dispute
between two other parties. [From a
children's game in which one person
stands between two others and tries to
intercept a ball thrown by one to the
other.]

pigs might fly (if they had wings) (*iron.*)
used to express disbelief.

to bleed like a (stuck) pig BLEED.

to make a pig of oneself to eat too much.

to make a pig's ear of (*sl.*) to make a mess
of, to botch.

to pig it 1 to live in squalor. **2** to behave
in an unmannerly way.

to pig out (*esp. N Am., sl.*) to make a pig
of oneself.

to sweat like a pig SWEAT.

pigeon[1]

to put/ set the cat among the pigeons CAT.

pigeon[2]

not my pigeon (*coll.*) not my business,
not my concern. [Originally 'not my
pidgin', from the supposed Chinese
mispronunciation of the English word
'business' that gave rise to a name for
hybrid languages used in international
trade.]

pike[1]

to pike on (*esp. Austral., coll.*) to back
out of, to withdraw timidly from (a
plan, agreement etc.).

pike[2]

to come down the pike (*N Am.*) to come
to attention, to arrive. [Alluding to a
turnpike road.]

pikestaff

plain as a pikestaff PLAIN.

pile

to pile it on (*coll.*) to exaggerate.

to pile on the agony (*coll.*) to exaggerate
an account, to describe something in
the most sensational terms.

to pile up 1 to accumulate. 2 to be or cause (a vehicle) to be involved in a multiple collision.

pill

bitter pill BITTER.

to gild/ sugar/ sweeten the pill to make something unpleasant more acceptable.

pillar

from pillar to post 1 from one place to another. 2 from one difficult situation to another. [From the game of real tennis.]

pin

for two pins TWO.

one can hear a pin drop HEAR.

on one's pins in good condition.

on pins and needles in a state of nervousness.

to pin back one's ears to begin to listen attentively.

to pin down 1 to bind to a promise or obligation. 2 to force (someone) to make a decision. 3 to restrict the movements of. 4 to try to discover the identity or location of. 5 to hold down by force.

to pin one's hopes/ faith on to place full reliance on.

pinch

at/ in a pinch in an urgent case, if hard pressed (*We could manage with just one car at a pinch*).

to feel the pinch FEEL.

pink

in the pink in fine condition.

pink elephants (*coll.*) hallucinations induced by intoxication with alcohol.

tickled pink TICKLE.

pint pot

to fit a quart into a pint pot FIT[1].

pip[1]

to get the pip 1 (*sl.*) to be out of sorts or dejected. 2 (*sl.*) to become annoyed. [Alluding to a disease of poultry.]

to give someone the pip (*sl.*) to annoy or upset someone.

to have the pip (*sl.*) to be out of sorts or dejected.

pip[2]

to pip at the post to beat, outdo etc. at the last moment, e.g. in a race or contest (*pipped at the post by our closest rivals*).

to pip out to die.

pipe

pipe dream a fantastic notion, an unrealistic hope. [The phrase may have originally referred to the effects of smoking opium.]

put that in your pipe and smoke it (*coll.*) accept that unwelcome fact.

to pipe away to signal the departure of (a boat).

to pipe down 1 (*coll.*) to stop talking. 2 (*Naut.*) to dismiss from duty.

to pipe one's eye (*dated, sl.*) to weep.

to pipe up 1 to begin to sing, to sing the first notes of. 2 (*coll.*) to begin to speak.

pipeline

in the pipeline under preparation, soon to be supplied, produced etc.

piper

he who pays the piper calls the tune the person who finances a venture has the right to decide how it should be run.

piss

to piss about (*sl.*) to waste time in foolish behaviour.

to piss down (*sl.*) to rain heavily.

to piss in the wind (*sl.*) to do something futile or detrimental to oneself.

to piss off 1 (*sl.*) to go away. 2 (*sl.*) to annoy, to bore, to make discontented (*The way they treat their employees really pisses me off*).

to piss on (*sl.*) to treat with deep contempt, to humiliate.

to piss oneself 1 (*sl.*) to urinate in one's clothes. 2 (*sl.*) to laugh uncontrollably. 3 (*sl.*) to be frightened or nervous.

to take the piss (*sl.*) to tease, to make fun of someone or something (*Are you taking the piss?*).

pistol

to hold a pistol to someone's head to force someone to do something by threats.

pit

to dig a pit for DIG.

to pit one's wits against to engage in an intellectual struggle with.

pitch

fever pitch FEVER.

pitched battle 1 a fierce fight or argument. 2 (*Mil.*) a battle for which both sides have made deliberate preparations.

to pitch in 1 (*coll.*) to begin or set to vigorously. 2 (*coll.*) to participate or contribute.

to pitch into 1 (*coll.*) to assail with blows, abuse, etc. 2 (*coll.*) to attack vigorously.

to pitch on/ upon 1 to select, to decide upon. 2 to happen upon.

to pitch up in cricket, to bowl (the ball) to bounce near the batsman.

to queer someone's pitch QUEER.

pity

for pity's sake a solemn adjuration.

more's the pity unfortunately.

to take pity on to feel compassionate or act compassionately towards.

what a pity! how unfortunate!

place

all over the place in a mess, in chaos.

between a rock and a hard place ROCK[1].

friends in high places FRIEND.

in place 1 suitable, appropriate. 2 (*N Am.*) on the spot (*to run in place*).

in place of instead of.

in places at several points.

in the first place FIRST.

in the second place SECOND.

lightning never strikes in the same place twice LIGHTNING.

out of place 1 in the wrong position. 2 unsuitable, inappropriate.

place in the sun a favourable situation, scope for action etc.

pride of place PRIDE.

to be someone's place to be someone's duty or responsibility (*It's not my place to tell them what to do*).

to fall into place to become clear to the understanding.

to give place to 1 to make room for. 2 to give precedence to, to give way to. 3 to be succeeded by.

to go places (*coll.*) to be successful (*At last we're going places!*).

to have one's heart in the right place HEART.

to keep someone in their place to remind someone of their lowly status or rank.

to know one's place to be aware of one's lowly status or rank and behave accordingly.

to put oneself in another's place to imagine what one would do if one was in someone else's situation (*Put yourself in my place: how could I refuse?*).

to put someone in their place to humiliate someone who is arrogant, presumptuous etc.

to take one's place to go to one's rightful position.

to take place to happen, to occur.

to take the place of to be substituted for.

plague

†a plague on ...! used to express irritation.

to avoid like the plague AVOID.

plain

plain as a pikestaff perfectly clear or obvious. [The phrase originally referred to something that was simple or unornamented, like a staff worn smooth by constant use.]

plain as the nose on your face clearly to be seen.

plain Jane (*coll.*) an unattractive woman or girl.

plain sailing 1 sailing a straightforward course. **2** a simple course of action. [From 'plane sailing', a nautical term referring to a method of navigation originally based on the assumption that the earth was flat and subsequently used to simplify calculations over short distances.]

to be plain with to speak candidly to.

plan

to go according to plan to happen as intended or desired.

to plan on (*coll.*) to intend.

plank

thick as two short planks THICK.

to walk the plank WALK.

plant

to plant out to plant (young plants) outdoors.

plate

to clean one's plate CLEAN.

to have on one's plate to have waiting to be done, to be burdened with (*I've got rather a lot on my plate at the moment*).

play

all work and no play makes Jack a dull boy WORK.

at play engaged in playing.

child's play CHILD.

fair play FAIR.

foul play FOUL.

in play in fun, not seriously.

played out tired out, worn out, used up.

to bring into play to make operative.

to call into play to put into operation, to introduce as an influence or factor.

to come into play to become operative.

to make a play for (*coll.*) to try to get.

to make (great) play with to parade, to flourish ostentatiously.

to make play to act effectively.

to play about to act in a frivolous or irresponsible manner.

to play along (with) to seem to agree or cooperate (with).

to play around 1 to play about. **2** to have casual sexual relationships.

to play at 1 to engage in (a game). **2** to perform or execute in a frivolous or half-hearted way. **3** to pretend to be.

to play back to replay (something just recorded).

to play down to treat as unimportant (*They tried to play down their defeat in the by-election*).

to play fast and loose 1 to be fickle. **2** to act recklessly. [From the name of a trick formerly played with loops in a piece of string.]

to play foul to hit or deal with an opponent or competitor in a manner forbidden by the rules.

to play high 1 to play or gamble for heavy amounts. **2** to play a high card.

to play off 1 to oppose (one person) against another, esp. for one's own advantage (*Children often play off one parent against the other*). **2** to take part in an extra game to decide the final winner of a competition. **3** in golf, to tee off. **4** to pass (something) off as something else. **5** to show off.

to play on 1 to move about lightly or unsteadily on. **2** to continue to play. **3** to exploit (*playing on their fears*). **4** in cricket, to play the ball on to one's own wicket. **5** to perform upon.

to play oneself in to accustom oneself to the conditions in a game etc.

to play safe/ for safety to take no risks.

to play someone false to deceive or betray someone.

to play up 1 to cause trouble or suffering (to) (*My back's playing up this morning*). **2** to misbehave. **3** to malfunction. **4** to give prominence to. **5** to play more vigorously.

to play upon to exploit (something or somebody).

to play up to to humour, to flatter.

to play with 1 to treat with levity. **2** to amuse oneself with.

playing field

level playing field LEVEL.

plea

to cop a plea COP.

plead

to plead guilty (*Law*) to admit guilt or liability.

to plead not guilty (*Law*) to deny guilt or liability.

to plead with to entreat, to supplicate.

please

if you please 1 if it is agreeable to you, with your permission. **2** (*iron.*) expressing sarcasm or protest.

may it please you (*dated*) please.

please yourself do as you wish.

pleased

pleased as Punch highly delighted. [Alluding to the chief character in the popular puppet show of Punch and Judy.]

pleasure

to take pleasure in to get enjoyment from.

with pleasure gladly, willingly.

pledge

to take/ sign the pledge to vow to abstain from alcoholic drink.

plot

the plot thickens the situation or affair is becoming more complex, intriguing, exciting etc. [From the play *The Rehearsal* (1671) by George Villiers, Duke of Buckingham: "Ay, now the plot thickens very much upon us."]

to lose the plot LOSE.

plough

to follow the plough FOLLOW.

to plough a lonely furrow to be alone in one's work or beliefs; to have few friends, helpers or supporters.

to plough back 1 to plough (grass etc.) into the soil for enrichment. **2** to reinvest (profits).

to plough in to bury or cover with earth by ploughing.

to plough into to collide with violently (*The car ploughed into a crowd of spectators*).

to plough out to root out or remove by ploughing.

to plough the sands to labour in vain.

to plough through 1 to smash a way through. **2** to work or read through laboriously.

to plough under to bury in the soil by ploughing.

to plough up to break up by ploughing.

to put one's hand to the plough HAND.

plug

to plug away at to work doggedly and persistently at.

to plug in to establish an electrical connection (with).

to pull the plug on (*coll.*) to bring to an (abrupt) end (*They've pulled the plug on our project*).

plum

a plum in one's mouth a voice which is rich to the point of affectation.

plumb[1]

out of plumb not exactly vertical.

to plumb the depths (of) to experience
(something unpleasant) in the extreme,
to sink to the lowest level (of)
(*plumbing the depths of loneliness*).

plumb²

to plumb in to connect to a water main
and/or drainage system (*We plumbed
in the washing machine*).

plume

borrowed plumes BORROWED.

plump¹

to plump up to make (pillows or
cushions) rounded and soft by shaking.

plump²

to plump for to decide in favour of, to
choose.

plunge

to take the plunge (*coll.*) to commit
oneself after hesitating.

pocket

in pocket 1 having made a profit. 2 (of
money) available.
in someone's pocket 1 under someone's
influence or control. 2 intimate with
someone.
out of pocket having made a loss, having
less money than before.
to burn a hole in someone's pocket BURN.
to have in one's pocket to be assured of
winning (*She had the race in her
pocket as she entered the last lap*).
to line one's pockets LINE².
to put one's hand in one's pocket HAND.
to put one's pride in one's pocket PRIDE.

pod

alike as/ like (two) peas in a pod TWO.
in pod (*coll.*) pregnant.

poetic

poetic justice punishment or reward
ideally (often ironically) well-deserved.

poetic licence the latitude in grammar etc.
allowed to poets.

point

at all points 1 in every part or direction.
2 completely, perfectly.
at/ on the point on the verge (of).
†at point in readiness.
beside/ off the point irrelevant.
case in point CASE.
in point apposite, relevant.
not to put too fine a point on it FINE¹.
on the point of about to do.
point of no return 1 a critical point (at
which one must commit oneself
irrevocably to a course of action).
2 the point in a flight where shortage
of fuel makes it necessary to go on as
return is impossible.
point of view 1 the position from which a
thing is looked at. 2 a way of regarding
a matter.
point taken I understand.
sore point SORE.
to carry one's point to prevail in an
argument or dispute.
to come to a point 1 to taper. 2 to
culminate. 3 to reach a crisis.
to have a point to have an effective or
relevant argument.
to make a point 1 to score a point. 2 to
establish a point in argument.
to make a point of 1 to attach special
importance to. 2 to take special care to
(*I made a point of writing my address
on the back of the envelope*).
to make one's point to establish a point in
argument, to make one's opinion clear.
to point a/ the bone 1 (*Austral.*) in
Aboriginal magic, to will the death of
an enemy. 2 (*Austral.*) to put a jinx on
someone.
to point out to indicate, to draw attention
to.
to point the finger (at) 1 to accuse, to
blame. 2 to censure.
to point up to emphasize, to highlight.
to prove one's point PROVE.

to score points SCORE.

to score points off SCORE.

to stretch a point STRETCH.

to take someone's point to understand someone's argument.

to the point appropriate, apposite, pertinent (*brief and to the point*).

to win on points WIN.

up to a point partially, not completely (*I agree with him up to a point*).

poison

one man's meat is another man's poison MAN.

what's your poison? (*coll.*) what would you like to drink?

poke

pig in a poke PIG.

pole¹

up the pole 1 (*sl.*) crazy, mad. 2 mistaken, wrong.

pole²

poles apart 1 as far apart as possible. 2 having widely divergent views, attitudes etc.

policy

honesty is the best policy HONESTY.

polish

spit and polish SPIT.

to polish off 1 (*coll.*) to finish speedily. 2 to get rid of.

to polish up 1 to give a polish to. 2 to improve or refresh (one's knowledge of something) by study.

poll

to poll a jury (*N Am.*) to examine each juror as to their concurrence in a verdict.

ponce

to ponce about/ around 1 to act in an ostentatious or effeminate manner. 2 to fool about, to waste time.

pond

big fish in a little pond BIG.

pony

shanks's pony SHANK.

pool

to scoop the pool SCOOP.

poop

to poop out 1 to become exhausted. 2 to give up.

poor

poor as a church mouse very poor.

poor relation a person or thing looked down on, considered inferior, or shabbily treated in comparison to others (*the poor relation of the computer industry*).

pop¹

in pop (*sl.*) in pawn.

to go pop to make, or burst with, a popping sound.

to pop off 1 (*coll.*) to leave hastily. 2 to die.

to pop the question (*coll.*) to propose marriage.

to pop up to appear suddenly.

pop²

top of the pops TOP¹.

port

any port in a storm any resource, opportunity, solution etc., esp. in times of trouble or difficulty (*I wouldn't normally ask my in-laws for money, but any port in a storm*).

posh

to posh up to smarten up, to polish.

position

in a position to able to.

to jockey for position JOCKEY.

posse

in posse within possibility, possible.

possess

to be possessed of to own.

to possess oneself of to acquire, to obtain as one's own.

what possessed you? a rhetorical question expressing shock or disapproval of another's actions.

possession

in possession 1 in actual occupancy. **2** holding, possessing.

in possession of owning, possessing.

in the possession of owned or possessed by.

possession is nine-tenths of the law in disputes of ownership, the person who possesses the property in question is in the strongest position.

to give possession to put another in possession.

to take possession of 1 to become the possessor of. **2** to seize.

possum

to play possum to feign ignorance or unawareness, to dissemble. [An allusion to the opossum, which feigns death on the approach of danger.]

post¹

deaf as a post DEAF.

from pillar to post PILLAR.

to be left at the post to be left far behind at the beginning of a race, contest etc.; to be beaten by a wide margin.

to pip at the post PIP².

post²

to keep someone posted to keep someone supplied with up-to-date information.

to post up 1 to complete (a ledger) with entries of accounts from a day-book etc. **2** to supply with full information.

to ride post RIDE.

pot

a watched pot never boils WATCH.

in the melting pot MELTING POT.

the pot calling the kettle black adverse criticism from someone with the same faults.

to fit a quart into a pint pot FIT¹.

to go (all) to pot (*sl.*) to be ruined or done for, to degenerate. [Alluding to meat etc. that is fit only for stewing.]

to keep the pot boiling (*coll.*) to maintain progress or activity, to keep the game alive.

to pot on to transfer (a plant) to a larger pot.

to pot up to plant (a seedling) into a pot.

potato

couch potato COUCH.

hot potato HOT.

small potatoes SMALL.

to drop like a hot potato DROP.

pot luck

to take pot luck 1 to take whatever food may be available. **2** to take a chance, to take whatever luck may offer.

pottage

mess of pottage MESS.

pound¹

in for a penny, in for a pound PENNY.

penny wise and pound foolish PENNY.

pound of flesh the exact amount owing to one, esp. when recovering it involves one's debtor in considerable suffering or trouble. [From Shakespeare's play *The Merchant of Venice*, in which the moneylender Shylock demands a pound of flesh from the citizen Antonio for failing to repay a loan.]

pound²

to pound out to produce with or as if with heavy blows (esp. on a typewriter) (*pound out a tune on the piano*).

pour

to pour oil on troubled waters to exercise a soothing, calming or conciliatory influence. [Oil poured on rough water spreads over the surface in a thin layer and flattens the waves.]

to pour out vials of wrath 1 to take vengeance. **2** to give vent to one's anger or resentment. [From the Bible: "And I heard a great voice out of the temple saying to the seven angels, Go your ways, and pour out the vials of the wrath of God upon the earth" (Rev. xvi.1).]

to pour scorn on to express contempt or disdain for.

powder

to keep one's powder dry to take precautions and wait for an opportunity to act. [Referring to gunpowder.]

to take a powder (*N Am., coll.*) to run away, to leave quickly. [Possibly of French origin.]

power

in power in office.

in someone's power 1 within the limits of someone's capabilities or authority. **2** under someone's control, at someone's mercy.

more power to your elbow! (*coll.*) used to express one's approval of someone's efforts, urging someone to continue and even intensify them.

the power behind the throne a person with no official position in government who exercises a strong personal influence on a ruler.

the powers that be (*often facet.*) established authority. [From the Bible: "there is no power but of God: the powers that be are ordained of God" (Rom. xiii.1).]

to do someone a power of good to be very beneficial to someone.

to power up/ down to switch on/ off, to increase/ decrease the power supply to.

pox

†**a pox on ...!** used to express anger or dislike of a person or thing.

practice

in practice 1 in the sphere of action. **2** in reality rather than in theory. **3** in training, in condition for working, acting, playing etc. effectively (*to keep in practice*).

out of practice out of training.

practice makes perfect by doing something many times one may learn to do it without mistakes.

sharp practice SHARP.

to put something into practice to convert an idea or theory into reality, to do something previously only thought of.

practise

to practise what one preaches to do what one tells others to do, to set an example by following one's own advice.

praise

praise be! an exclamation expressing gratitude and pleasure.

to damn with faint praise DAMN.

to praise someone/ something to the skies to praise someone/ something lavishly or extravagantly.

to sing the praises of SING.

prawn

to come the raw prawn RAW.

prayer

not to have a prayer (*N Am., coll.*) to have not the slightest chance or hope.

on a wing and a prayer WING.

preach

to preach down 1 to denounce or disparage by preaching. **2** to preach against.

to preach to the converted to advocate an opinion etc. to people already in favour.

precedence

to take precedence to have a higher priority (over).

preference

in preference to rather than.

prejudice

without prejudice (*Law*) without impairing any pre-existing right, detracting from any subsequent claim, or admitting any liability.

preliminary

preliminary to 1 in advance of. 2 as a preparation for.

premise

on the premises actually in the building referred to.

premium

at a premium 1 above their nominal value, above par. 2 in great esteem or demand because scarce (*Time is at a premium*).

to put a premium on 1 to render more than usually valuable or advantageous. 2 to provide, or to be, an incentive to.

prepared

to be prepared 1 to be ready (for). 2 to be willing (to).

presence

in the presence of in front of, within sight of (a person).

presence of mind a calm, collected state of mind, esp. in danger or emergency.

to grace with one's presence GRACE.

to make one's presence felt to do something that causes people to be aware of one's presence.

present¹

at present at the present time, now (*There's little we can do about it at present*).

by these presents (*Law*) by this document.

for the present 1 for the time being. 2 just now. 3 so far as the time being is concerned.

present company excepted with the exception of the people here now (*The British have less fashion sense than some of their European neighbours – present company excepted, of course!*).

the present day modern times.

(there's) no time like the present TIME.

present²

to present arms to hold a rifle etc. in a perpendicular position in front of the body to salute a superior officer.

to present oneself to appear, to come forward.

present³

to make a present of to give as a gift.

preserve

to trespass on someone's preserves TRESPASS.

press

in (the)/ at press 1 being printed. 2 on the eve of publication.

to be pressed for to have very little of (esp. time).

to go to press to start printing, to begin to be printed.

to press on/ ahead/ forward 1 to continue (determinedly) on one's way. 2 to proceed, esp. in spite of difficulties or opposition.

to press the button 1 to start a machine etc. by pressing a button. 2 (*fig.*) to set a train of events in motion.

to press the flesh (*sl.*) (esp. of politicians) to shake hands.

to press the panic button to panic or cause others to panic.

to send to press to send for printing.

pressure

pressure group a group or small party exerting pressure on government etc. to promote a particular interest.

to bring pressure to bear on to try to force (someone to do something).

presume

to presume on/ upon 1 to rely on, to depend on. **2** to take unfair advantage of.

pretence

false pretences FALSE.

pretext

on/ under the pretext of putting forward as an excuse.

pretty

a pretty penny 1 considerable cost or expense. **2** a good round sum.

not just a pretty face (*coll.*) able or intelligent (*Of course I can fix it – I'm not just a pretty face, you know!*).

pretty as a picture very pretty.

sitting pretty SIT.

to come to a pretty pass to develop into an undesirable situation (*Things have come to a pretty pass when pupils start threatening their teachers*).

prevail

to prevail on/ upon to succeed in persuading, to induce (*They prevailed on him to vote against the proposal*).

prey

to be prey to to be subject to, to suffer from.

to prey on 1 to rob, to plunder. **2** to chase and seize as food. **3** to make a victim of, to subject to robbery, extortion etc. (*confidence tricksters who prey on the elderly*). **4** to have a depressing or obsessive effect on (*to prey on one's mind*).

price

a price on someone's head a reward offered for someone's killing or capture.

at any price no matter what the cost (*in pursuit of success at any price*).

at a price for a lot of money etc.

beyond/ above/ without price priceless, invaluable.

every man has his price MAN.

not at any price under no circumstances (*I wouldn't take such a risk at any price*).

to price oneself out of the market to lose trade by charging too high prices.

to set the price of to state the price of.

what price ...? 1 what are the chances of (something) happening? **2** (*iron.*) so much for (something) (*What price democracy?*).

prick

to kick against the pricks KICK.

to prick out/ off 1 to mark (a pattern) out with dots. **2** to plant (seedlings) more widely apart with a view to transplanting later to their permanent quarters.

to prick up one's ears 1 to begin to listen attentively. **2** (of dogs etc.) to raise the ears as if listening.

pride

pride and joy someone or something that one is very proud of (*The garden is his pride and joy*).

pride goes before a fall a display of pride is often followed by misfortune. [From the Bible: "Pride goeth before destruction, and an haughty spirit before a fall" (Prov. xvi.18).]

pride of place the highest, most prominent or most important position (*The trophy took pride of place on top of the bookcase*).

to pride oneself on to be proud of oneself for (*She prides herself on her patience*).

to put one's pride in one's pocket to
swallow one's pride.

to swallow/ pocket one's pride not to
stand on one's dignity, to humble
oneself.

to take (a) pride in 1 to be proud of. 2 to
be conscientious about the
maintenance of (*to take a pride in
one's appearance*).

primrose

primrose path the pursuit of ease and
pleasure, esp. as leading to perdition.
[From Shakespeare's *Hamlet*: "like a
puff'd and reckless libertine, / Himself
the primrose path of dalliance treads".]

prince

like Hamlet without the Prince of
Denmark HAMLET.

principle

in principle as far as the basic idea or
theory is concerned (*I agree in
principle*).

on principle because of the fundamental
(moral) issue involved; in order to
assert a principle (*We refused on
principle*).

print

in print 1 in a printed form. 2 (of a
printed book etc.) on sale.

out of print no longer obtainable from
the publisher.

small print SMALL.

to appear in print APPEAR.

to print out 1 to print. 2 to produce a
printout (of).

to rush into print RUSH.

prisoner

to take prisoner 1 to capture. 2 to arrest
and hold in custody.

private

in private 1 privately, confidentially. 2 in
private life.

pro

pro and con for and against; on both
sides.

pro and contra for and against.

pros and cons reasons or arguments for
and against (*weighing up the pros and
cons*).

probability

in all probability most likely.

probation

on probation 1 being tested for suitability
etc. 2 (*Law*) under the supervision of a
probation officer.

problem

no problem 1 it's all right. 2 it doesn't
matter.

that's your problem (*coll.*) you must deal
with that yourself, it is nothing to do
with me.

to have a problem/ problems 1 to have
difficulty (with) (*He has problems
with reading*). 2 to be in trouble.

process

in process of time as time goes on.

in the process during the carrying out
(of a specified operation).

in the process of 1 engaged in.
2 undergoing.

procinct

†in procinct 1 ready, prepared. 2 at hand,
close.

production

to make a production (out) of (*coll.*) to
make an unnecessary fuss about.

profession

the oldest profession OLD.

the three professions THREE.

profile

in profile as seen from the side.

low profile LOW.

profit

at a profit making a financial gain.

paper profits PAPER.

profit and loss 1 income and gains credited and expenditure and losses debited in an account so as to show the net loss or profit. **2** the arithmetical rule by which such gain or loss is calculated.

small profits and quick returns SMALL.

progress

in progress going on, developing, proceeding.

promise

a lick and a promise LICK.

promised land 1 any place of expected happiness or prosperity. **2** heaven. **3** the land of Canaan promised to Abraham and his descendants.

to promise ill to hold out unfavourable prospects.

to promise oneself to look forward to (something pleasant).

to promise well to hold out favourable prospects.

promotion

on promotion 1 awaiting, expecting or preparing oneself for promotion. **2** on one's best behaviour.

proof

above proof (of alcoholic liquor) of a stronger than standard strength.

proof positive convincing proof.

the proof of the pudding is in the eating the true worth of something cannot be fully assessed until it is tested or used.

prop

to prop up 1 to support in an upright position. **2** to keep (something or someone) going with financial etc. help.

to prop up the bar to frequent a particular public house (*propping up the bar at the Crown*).

prophet

prophet of doom a person who is continually predicting ruin and disaster.

proportion

in proportion 1 in due relation as to magnitude, number etc. **2** consistent with the real importance of the matter in hand (*Try to keep things in proportion*).

out of proportion 1 not in due relation as to magnitude, number etc. **2** not or no longer consistent with the real importance of the matter in hand (*You're getting things out of proportion*).

proposition

not a proposition not likely to succeed.

protest

under protest unwillingly; having expressed objections (*They left under protest*).

proud

proud as a peacock very proud.

to do someone proud 1 to entertain someone lavishly. **2** to give someone cause to be proud.

prove

not proven (*Sc. Law*) not proved (a verdict given when there is not sufficient evidence to convict).

to go to prove to be evidence or proof (that).

to prove oneself to do something which shows one's qualities, esp. courage.

to prove one's point to establish the truth of one's assertion.

prowl

on the prowl prowling in search of prey.

pry

to pry out to discover by prying.

psych

to psych out 1 to work out, to divine, to anticipate correctly (a person's motivation etc.). **2** to intimidate or defeat by psychological means. **3** (*coll.*) to have a psychological breakdown.

to psych up to prepare or stimulate psychologically as a preliminary to action (*He was really psyched up for the final*).

public

in public openly, publicly.

in the public eye famous.

the general public GENERAL.

to go public 1 to become a public company. **2** to make something publicly known.

pudding

the proof of the pudding is in the eating PROOF.

puff

in all one's puff (*coll.*) in all one's life.

to puff and blow to breathe hard or noisily.

puffed

puffed up 1 inflated. **2** swollen up with conceit or self-importance.

pull

to pull about to pull to and fro, to handle roughly.

to pull ahead to move ahead, or into the lead.

to pull apart 1 to pull asunder or into pieces. **2** to become separated. **3** to criticize severely.

to pull away to move (further) into the lead.

to pull back to (cause to) retreat; to withdraw.

to pull down 1 to demolish (*The school was pulled down years ago*). **2** to degrade, to humble. **3** to weaken, to cause (prices etc.) to be reduced. **4** (*sl.*) to earn (a specified amount of money).

to pull in 1 to retract, to make tighter. **2** (of a train) to enter a station. **3** (of a vehicle or driver) to stop (at), to pull over. **4** (*coll.*) to attract (audiences etc.) (*pulling in the crowds*). **5** (*sl.*) to arrest. **6** to earn.

to pull off 1 to remove by pulling. **2** to accomplish (something difficult or risky) (*Do you think you can pull it off?*).

to pull oneself together to regain one's composure or self-control.

to pull out 1 to remove by pulling. **2** to leave, to depart. **3** to withdraw. **4** to cease to participate. **5** to move out from the side of the road or from behind another vehicle (*She pulled out to overtake*). **6** (of an aircraft) to level off after a dive.

to pull over (of a vehicle or its driver) to draw in to the side of the road (and stop).

to pull round to (cause to) recover.

to pull through to (cause to) survive or recover.

to pull together to cooperate.

to pull up 1 to drag up forcibly. **2** to pluck out of the ground. **3** to cause to stop. **4** to come to a stop (*A taxi pulled up outside the house*). **5** to rebuke. **6** to gain on, to draw level (with).

pulse

to feel/ take someone's pulse 1 to gauge the rate or regularity of a person's pulse as a sign of health etc. **2** to sound someone's intentions, views etc.

to keep one's finger on the pulse FINGER.

pump

to pump iron to do weight-lifting exercises.

to pump up 1 to inflate (a tyre). **2** to inflate the tyres of (a cycle etc.).

Punch

pleased as Punch PLEASED.

punch

someone could not punch their way out of a paper bag someone is very weak.

to pack a punch PACK.

to pull one's punches (*usu. in neg.*) to strike or criticize with less than full force (*The reviewer didn't pull her punches*). [Alluding to a boxer who pulls back his fist at the moment of striking to lessen the force of the blow.]

punishment

glutton for punishment GLUTTON.

pup

in pup (of a bitch) pregnant.

to sell a pup to SELL.

puppy

puppy love temporary infatuation in adolescence.

pure

pure and simple nothing but, nothing other than (*It was a mistake, pure and simple*).

pure as the driven snow utterly pure or chaste.

purler

to come a purler to take a heavy fall.

purple

born in the purple BORN.

purpose

accidentally on purpose (*coll.*) deliberately, but with the appearance of an accident.

at cross purposes CROSS PURPOSE.

of set purpose intentionally, deliberately.

on purpose 1 intentionally, designedly, not by accident. **2** in order (that).

to all intents and purposes INTENT.

to no purpose with no useful result.

to serve a purpose SERVE.

to serve the purpose of SERVE.

to the purpose 1 with close relation to the matter in hand, relevantly. **2** usefully.

purse

you can't make a silk purse out of a sow's ear SILK.

purse strings

to hold the purse strings to control the expenditure (of a household etc.).

pursuit

in pursuit of pursuing.

push

at a push if really necessary.

if it comes to the push if really necessary.

pushing up (the) daisies dead (and buried).

to be pushed for (*coll.*) to be short of (time or money).

to give someone/ get the push (*sl.*) to dismiss someone/ be dismissed, esp. from a job.

to push about/ around 1 (*coll.*) to bully, to treat with contempt. **2** to move around roughly or aimlessly.

to push along (*coll.*) to go away.

to push for (*coll.*) to advocate vigorously, to make strenuous efforts to achieve (*pushing for a shorter working week*).

to push in (*coll.*) to force one's way in (esp. into a queue) ahead of others.

to push off 1 to push against the bank with an oar so as to move a boat off. **2** (*coll.*) to go away.

to push on 1 to press forward, to hasten. **2** to urge or drive on.

to push one's luck (*coll.*) to take risks, esp. by overplaying an existing advantage (*Don't push your luck!*).

to push the boat out (*coll.*) to celebrate expensively.

to push through to secure the acceptance of (a plan, proposal etc.) speedily or by compulsion.

when push comes to shove (*coll.*) when the time for action comes.

put

not to put it past someone to consider a person capable of (the activity under discussion) (*I wouldn't put it past her to tell the police*).

put it there! (*coll.*) shake my hand (said on holding out one's hand).

put-up job something secretly pre-arranged for purposes of deception.

to put about 1 to inconvenience. **2** (*Naut.*) to go about, to change the course of to the opposite tack. **3** (*coll.*) to make public, to spread abroad.

to put across 1 to communicate effectively. **2** to make acceptable.

to put away 1 to return to its proper place. **2** to lay by. **3** to shut up (in a prison, mental institution etc.). **4** (*coll.*) to consume (food or drink) (*He had put away six pints of lager*). **5** to put (an animal) to death because of old age etc. **6** to remove. **7** to divorce.

to put back 1 to retard, to check the forward motion of. **2** to postpone. **3** to move the hands of (a clock) back. **4** to replace. **5** (*Naut.*) to return (to land etc.).

to put behind one 1 to get on with one's life after. **2** to refuse to think about.

to put by 1 to put, set or lay aside for future use. **2** to evade. **3** to put off with evasion. **4** to desist from.

to put down 1 to suppress, to crush. **2** to snub, to degrade. **3** to confute, to silence. **4** to reduce, to diminish. **5** to write down, to enter. **6** to reckon, to attribute (*I put her behaviour down to jealousy*). **7** to put (a baby) to bed. **8** to kill (esp. an old or ill animal). **9** to pay (as a deposit). **10** (of an aircraft) to land. **11** (of a bus etc.) to stop to let (passengers) off. **12** to preserve, to store, to pickle.

to put forth 1 (*formal*) **a** to present to notice. **b** to publish, to put into circulation. **2** to extend. **3** to shoot out. **4** to exert. **5** (of a plant) to produce (buds, shoots etc.).

to put forward 1 to set forth, to advance, to propose. **2** to thrust (oneself) into prominence. **3** to move the hands of (a clock) onwards.

to put in 1 to introduce, to interject, to interpose. **2** to insert, to enter. **3** to install in office etc. **4 a** to present, to submit (an application, request etc.). **b** to submit a claim (for something). **5** to be a candidate (for). **6** to enter a harbour. **7** (*coll.*) to spend, to pass (time), to devote (effort) (*We had put in a lot of unpaid overtime*).

to put it across someone (*coll.*) to defeat someone by ingenuity.

to put it mildly with understatement (*His behaviour was unconventional, to put it mildly*).

to put it on 1 to pretend (to be ill etc.). **2** to exaggerate.

to put it to someone 1 to suggest to a person (that). **2** to challenge a person to deny (that).

to put off 1 to lay aside, to discard. **2 a** to postpone (an appointment). **b** to postpone an appointment with (a person). **3** to disappoint, to evade (a person). **4** to hinder, to distract the attention of. **5** to dissuade (from). **6** to cause aversion to (*It put me off Australian wine for years*). **7** to foist, to palm off (with).

to put on 1 to take on. **2** to clothe oneself with. **3 a** to assume (a disguise etc.). **b** to pretend to feel (an emotion). **4** to add, to apply. **5** to add on (weight etc.). **6** to bring into play, to exert. **7** to cause to operate (a light etc.). **8** to cause to be available. **9** to stage, to produce (a play etc.). **10** to appoint. **11** to move the hands of (a clock) forward. **12** to send (a bowler) on to the field in cricket.

to put one over on/ across (*coll.*) to deceive into believing or accepting something.

to put on to to make (a person) aware of; to put (a person) in touch with.

to put out 1 to eject. **2** to extinguish (a light). **3** to disconcert; to annoy. **4** to inconvenience (*I hope I'm not putting you out*). **5** to exert (strength). **6** to dislocate (a joint). **7** to publish, to broadcast. **8** to give out (work) to be done at different premises. **9** to render unconscious. **10** to invest, to place (at interest). **11** in cricket, to dismiss (a batsman or a side). **12** to blind (someone's eyes).

to put over 1 to communicate effectively. **2** (*N Am.*) to postpone. **3** (*N Am.*) to pass off.

to put through 1 to connect (someone) by telephone (to someone else). **2** to see to a conclusion, to accomplish. **3** to cause to undergo (esp. suffering).

to put together to assemble (things, parts) to form a finished whole.

to put to it 1 to distress. **2** to press hard.

to put under to render unconscious by the use of an anaesthetic.

to put up 1 to raise (a hand etc.). **2** to erect, to build. **3** to offer for sale. **4** to increase (a price etc.). **5** to show (a fight, resistance etc.). **6** to lodge and entertain (*Can you put us up for a couple of nights?*). **7** to take lodgings. **8** to display (a notice etc.). **9** to publish (banns etc.). **10** to provide (money, a prize). **11** to offer (oneself) as a candidate. **12** to present as a candidate. **13** to pack up. **14** to place in a safe place. **15** to lay aside. **16** to sheathe (a sword). **17** to cause (game birds) to come out of cover.

to put upon 1 to impose upon; to take undue advantage of. **2** to victimize.

to put up to 1 to incite to (*Who put you up to this?*). **2** to make conversant with.

to put up with to tolerate.

putt

to putt out to putt the ball into the hole and so complete a hole in a round of golf.

putty

to be putty in someone's hands to be easily manipulated by someone.

up to putty (*Austral., sl.*) no good, valueless, of bad quality.

puzzle

to puzzle out to work out by mental labour.

Pyrrhic

Pyrrhic victory a victory that is as costly as a defeat. [From Pyrrhus, king of Epirus, who won a victory over the Romans at Asculum in 279 BC but suffered heavy losses.]

Q

Q
to mind one's Ps and Qs MIND.

q.t.
on the q.t. (*coll.*) secretly, on the sly, on the quiet.

quadruplicate
in quadruplicate written out or copied four times.

quantity
unknown quantity UNKNOWN.

quart
to fit a quart into a pint pot FIT[1].

quarter
at close quarters CLOSE QUARTERS.
to come to close quarters CLOSE QUARTERS.

queen
to queen it to act in a superior or arrogant way (over).

Queen Anne
Queen Anne is dead stale news.

queer
queer fish (*coll.*) a strange person.
Queer Street (*coll.*) trouble, esp. financial difficulty.
to queer someone's pitch to spoil someone's chances. [Alluding to the pitch of a trader.]

quest
in quest of searching for.

question
beyond (all) question undoubtedly, unquestionably.
in question referred to, under discussion (*the money in question*).
leading question LEADING.
loaded question LOADED.
†out of question doubtless.
out of the question not worth discussing, impossible.
past/ without question undoubtedly.
sixty-four thousand dollar question SIXTY.
to beg the question BEG.
to call in/ into question to dispute.
to pop the question POP[1].
to put to the question to put to the vote, to divide the meeting or House upon.

queue
to jump the queue JUMP.

quick
quick as a flash very quickly.
quick on the draw 1 fast to draw and shoot a gun. 2 fast to act or respond.
quick on the trigger fast to react.
†quick with child pregnant, esp. when movement of the foetus is perceptible.
the quick and the dead the living and the dead.
to be cut to the quick to be deeply offended. [Alluding to a wound to the most sensitive part of the flesh.]

quid
not the full quid FULL.
quids in (*sl.*) in a profitable position.

quiet

at quiet at peace, peaceful.

on the quiet (*coll.*) secretly.

peace and quiet PEACE.

quiet as a mouse very quiet.

to keep quiet (about) to refrain from talking or disclosing information (about).

quintuplicate

in quintuplicate written out or copied five times.

quit

to be quits to be even or left on even terms, so that neither has the advantage.

to call it/ cry quits to declare things to be even, to agree not to go on with a contest, quarrel etc., to make it a draw.

†**to quit cost** to pay or balance the cost.

to quit scores to balance or make things even.

to quit the scene to die or leave.

quite

quite so I agree.

quiver

to have one's quiver full to have many children.

qui vive

on the qui vive on the lookout, alert, expectant. [From the words used by a French sentry as a challenge, meaning 'Which side do you support?' (literally 'Long live who?').]

quote

quote ... unquote an expression used to show the beginning and end of a quotation.

R

R
the three R's THREE.

rabbit
to breed like rabbits BREED.
to let the dog see the rabbit DOG.

race
one-horse race ONE-HORSE.
rat race RAT.

rack¹
on the rack 1 under torture. 2 under great
stress.
to rack one's brains to use great mental
effort. [Referring to the rack used as an
instrument of torture, to stretch the
victim's body.]
to rack up (*esp. N Am.*) to accumulate
(points or a score).

rack²
to go to rack and ruin to fall into a state
of complete ruin or neglect.

racket
to stand the racket 1 (*dated*) to stand the
expenses, to pay the score. 2 (*dated*)
to put up with the consequences.
3 (*dated*) to get through without
mishap.

rag¹
glad rags GLAD.
like a red rag to a bull RED RAG.
rags-to-riches denoting someone who
starts off poor and becomes rich, or a
story describing this progress.

rag²
to lose one's rag LOSE.

rage
all the rage an object of general desire,
quite the fashion.

ragged
to run someone ragged to exhaust
someone.

ragtag
ragtag and bobtail the riff-raff, the rabble.

raid
to raid the market to upset stock market
prices artificially for future gain.

rail
to go off the rails 1 to go mad. 2 to go
awry. [Alluding to a derailed train.]

rain
(come) rain or (come) shine whatever the
weather, whatever the circumstances.
it never rains but it pours misfortunes
always happen several at a time or in
quick succession.
right as rain RIGHT.
to be rained off to be cancelled or
postponed because of rain or bad
weather.
to be rained out (*N Am.*) to be rained
off.
to rain cats and dogs (*coll.*) to rain very
heavily. [Possibly from the dead
animals that would appear in the
gutters in former times when heavy

rain caused the drainage systems to overflow.]

rainbow
to chase rainbows CHASE.

rain check
to take a rain check to postpone accepting an invitation till a later date. [In N America, a rain check is a ticket for a sports event that allows readmission on another day if rain stops play.]

rainy
rainy day a time of misfortune or distress, esp. pecuniary need (*to save something for a rainy day*).

raise
to be raised to the bench (*Law*) to be made a judge.
to raise an eyebrow 1 to show surprise or disapproval by raising an eyebrow. 2 to cause surprise or disapproval (*Her behaviour raised a few eyebrows*).
to raise Cain (*sl.*) to make a disturbance, to make trouble. [Referring to Cain, brother and murderer of Abel in the Bible (Genesis iv).]
to raise hell (*coll.*) to make a lot of trouble.
to raise one's eyebrows to show surprise or disapproval by raising one's eyebrows.
to raise one's eyes 1 to look up from the ground. 2 to look upwards (to).
to raise one's glass to to drink a toast to.
to raise one's guard to become vigilant against danger.
to raise the devil (*coll.*) to make a disturbance or commotion.
to raise the hat to to greet, to salute.
to raise the roof 1 to lose one's temper. 2 (*coll.*) to make a lot of noise.
to raise the standard to rally supporters to the cause in preparation for war or some other campaign.
to raise the wind 1 (*sl.*) to make a disturbance or commotion. 2 (*sl.*) to get hold of cash.
†to raise up seed to have children.

rake
thin as a rake THIN.
to rake in (*coll.*) to accumulate (usu. money).
to rake off (*coll.*) to receive (a share of the profits from an illegal job).
to rake up/ over (*coll.*) to revive/ dwell on the memory of (a quarrel, the past etc.).

rally
to rally round to come to someone's aid morally or financially (*After her husband's death, the neighbours rallied round*).

ram
to ram home to force recognition or acceptance of.

rampage
on the rampage 1 violently excited. 2 on a drunken spree.

random
at random 1 without direction or definite purpose, haphazardly (*five numbers chosen at random*). 2 †at great speed.

range
to range oneself 1 to take sides (with). 2 to adopt a more settled course of life, to settle down (as by marrying).

rank
rank and file 1 common soldiers. 2 ordinary people (*rank-and-file opinion*). [From a body of soldiers standing side by side (in ranks) and one behind the other (in files).]
to break rank(s) BREAK.

to **close ranks** CLOSE².

to **keep rank** (of soldiers) to remain in
line.

to **pull rank** to take precedence by virtue
of higher rank, sometimes unfairly.

to **reduce to the ranks** REDUCE.

to **rise from the ranks** RISE.

to **take rank with** to be placed on a level
or be ranked with.

ransom

king's ransom KING.

to **hold to ransom 1** to keep in
confinement until a ransom is paid.
2 to put in a difficult or unpleasant
situation until certain demands are
met (*The strikers are holding the
country to ransom*).

rant

to **rant and rave** to express anger in a
loud uncontrolled manner.

rap¹

to **beat the rap** (*N Am., sl.*) to be acquitted
of a crime, to escape punishment.

to **rap on/ over the knuckles** to reprove, to
reprimand.

to **take the rap** (*coll.*) to take the blame
for another.

rap²

not worth a rap WORTH.

rare

rare bird a rarity, something very rarely
met with. [A translation of the Latin
phrase *rara avis*, which is also used
with this meaning in English.]

raring

raring to go eager to get started.

rat

like a drowned rat DROWN.

rat race the continual competitive
scramble of everyday life (*trying to get
out of the rat race*).

to **rat on** (*coll.*) to betray, to divulge
secret information, to inform against.

to **smell a rat** SMELL.

rate

at any rate 1 in any case. **2** even so.

at a rate of knots (*coll.*) very quickly.

at this/ that rate if this/ that is so, typical
or true.

to **rate up** to subject to a higher rate or
premium in order to cover increased
risks.

rather

had/ would rather would prefer to.

the rather by so much the more.

rattle

to **rattle one's dags** (*Austral., New Zeal.,
coll.*) to hurry up.

raw

in the raw 1 in its natural state. **2** naked.

raw deal (*coll.*) unfair treatment.

to **come the raw prawn** (*Austral., sl.*) to
try to deceive.

to **touch on the raw** TOUCH.

razoo

not a brass razoo BRASS.

razor

razor's edge 1 the edge of a razor. **2** a keen
edge. **3** a sharp crest or ridge, as of a
mountain. **4** a critical situation, a
crisis. **5** a sharp line of demarcation,
esp. between parties or opinions.

sharp as a razor SHARP.

razzle

on the razzle on a spree or binge, esp.
involving excessive drinking.

reach

out of reach unable to be reached or
gained.

within arm's reach ARM¹.

within reach able to be reached or gained.

read

to read between the lines to detect the hidden or unexpressed meaning of a letter, speech etc. [Perhaps from a method of deciphering a coded message by reading alternate lines.]

to read in to transfer (data) into a computer memory etc.

to read into to extract or assume (a meaning not explicit) from (something spoken or written).

to read off to take (a reading or information) from a recording instrument, e.g. a thermometer.

to read out 1 to read aloud (*She read out a list of names*). **2** to retrieve (data) from storage in a computer memory etc. **3** (*N Am.*) to expel from a political party or other organization. **4** †to read through or to the end.

to read someone a lecture/ lesson to scold or reprimand someone.

to read someone like a book to have full understanding of a person's motives etc. (*I know exactly what you're up to: I can read you like a book!*).

to read someone's mind to make an accurate guess as to what someone is thinking.

to read the riot act to give a severe warning that something must stop; to reprimand severely. [From the Riot Act of 1715, which enjoined riotous people to disperse within an hour of a proclamation to this effect being read by a magistrate.]

to read up to get information by reading (*I read up about the company before my interview*).

to take as read to assume, to accept without discussion. [From the literal use of this phrase at the beginning of a meeting, when time may be saved by not reading the minutes of the previous meeting.]

ready

at/ to the ready 1 prepared for action.
2 (of a firearm) held in the position preparatory to aiming and firing.

get ready, get set, go! used as a command to start a race.

ready, steady, go! used as a command to start a race.

to make ready 1 to prepare. **2** to prepare a forme before printing.

to ready up (*Austral., coll.*) to swindle.

real

for real 1 (*coll.*) in reality, genuine. **2** in earnest.

the real McCoy 1 the genuine article. **2** the best. [Possibly from a brand of whisky originally brewed in Scotland in the late 19th century. The phrase was subsequently associated with a US boxer of the 1890s.]

the real thing the genuine article and not a substitute.

reality

in reality in fact.

reap

to (sow the wind and) reap the whirlwind to suffer the consequences of a bad or foolish action. [From the Bible: "For they have sown the wind, and they shall reap the whirlwind" (Hos. viii.7), referring to the fate of Israel.]

reaper

the (Grim) Reaper death. [Death is often personified as a hooded figure carrying a scythe.]

rear

in the rear at the back.
to bring up the rear to come last.
to drop to the rear DROP.
to take in the rear (*Mil.*) to attack from behind.

reason

by reason of because, on account of, in consequence of.
it stands to reason it follows logically.

ours not to reason why it is not for us to question something. [From Tennyson's poem *The Charge of the Light Brigade* (1854): "Theirs not to make reply, / Theirs not to reason why, / Theirs but to do and die".]

to see/ listen to reason 1 to recognize and accept the logical force of an argument (*She tried to make her parents see reason*). 2 to be persuaded to act in a reasonable manner.

within/ in reason 1 in moderation. 2 according to good sense.

without rhyme or reason RHYME.

with reason with justifiable cause, for a good reason.

rebound

on the rebound 1 in the act of bouncing back. 2 as a reaction to a disappointment, esp. in love (*I married him on the rebound*).

receipt

in receipt of having received.

receive

to be at/ on the receiving end to be the recipient of something unpleasant.

reckon

to be reckoned with meriting consideration because formidable, influential etc. (*The company has become a force to be reckoned with in the industry*).

to reckon on 1 to rely upon. 2 to expect.

to reckon with to take into account.

to reckon without to fail to take into account.

to reckon without one's host to underestimate.

reckoning

day of reckoning DAY.

out of one's reckoning mistaken in one's judgement or expectation.

record

for the record for the sake of accuracy.

off the record in confidence, not said officially (*He told me off the record that he was planning to resign*).

on record 1 recorded, esp. with legal or official authentication. 2 publicly known.

to beat/ break the record to surpass all former achievements or events of the kind.

to go on record to state one's beliefs publicly.

to have a record to be a known, previously convicted criminal.

to put/ set the record straight to correct an error or false impression.

track record TRACK.

recourse

to have recourse to to turn or apply to for help.

without recourse an endorsement of a bill of exchange etc. protecting the endorser from liability for non-payment.

red

in the red overdrawn at the bank. [From the use of red ink on the debit side of an account.]

red as a beetroot very red in the face, as through embarrassment.

red herring 1 herring, dried and smoked. 2 anything which diverts attention from the real issue or line of enquiry.

red tape extreme adherence to official routine and formality. [From the red tape formerly used to tie up official documents.]

to draw a red herring across the track to distract attention by starting an irrelevant discussion. [From an attempt to mislead hunting hounds by dragging a strong-smelling smoked herring across the path of a hunted animal.]

to see red to become enraged.

red carpet

to put out the red carpet to give an impressive welcome. [From the strip of red carpet put out for a celebrity or important person to walk on.]

red cent

not to have a red cent (*N Am., coll.*) to have no money at all.

red-letter

red-letter day an auspicious or memorable day. [From the use of red ink to mark special or significant days on the calendar.]

red light

to see the red light to become aware of possible danger ahead.

red rag

like a red rag to a bull likely to excite rage. [From the red cape waved by bullfighters to make the bull charge, leading to the common misconception that bulls are enraged by the colour red.]

redress

to redress the balance to make things equal again.

reduce

in reduced circumstances poor, hard-up.

to reduce to silence to defeat with an unanswerable argument.

to reduce to the ranks (*Mil.*) to demote to the rank of private soldier.

reed

broken reed BROKEN.

reef

to take in a reef 1 (*Naut.*) to reduce the working area of a sail temporarily, as in bad weather. 2 to proceed with caution or in moderation.

reel

to reel in 1 to draw (a fish etc.) towards one by using a reel. 2 to wind (thread, a line etc.) on a reel.

to reel off 1 to unwind or pay out from a reel. 2 to tell or recite fluently and without a hitch (*He reeled off a list of numbers that he had memorized*).

to reel up 1 to wind up entirely on a reel. 2 to reel in.

refer

refer to drawer the words used by a bank to notify the payee of a cheque that payment of the cheque has been suspended.

reference

in/ with reference to with regard to, as regards, concerning.

without reference to irrespective of, regardless of.

reflect

to reflect on/ upon 1 to think about, to ponder. 2 to cast censure or blame upon (*The results reflect badly on the school*).

refusal

first refusal FIRST.

regard

as regards respecting, concerning.

in this regard on this point.

in/ with regard to 1 regarding. 2 in connection with.

with kind regards KIND.

regardless

regardless of in spite of.

region

in the region of 1 near. 2 approximately (*a sum in the region of £50,000*).

register
in **register** (of printed matter,
photographic and colour plates etc.)
exactly corresponding.

regular
regular as clockwork with unfailing
regularity.

rein
to give (free) rein to to leave unrestrained,
to allow to proceed without check.
to give the reins to 1 to leave unrestrained.
2 to allow (a horse) to go its own way.
to keep a tight rein on TIGHT.
to rein in to cause (a horse) to stop by
pulling on the reins.
to take the reins to assume guidance,
direction, office etc.

reinvent
to reinvent the wheel 1 to devise
something that already exists. **2** to
spend time unnecessarily on things
which have already been done,
covered etc.

rejoice
to rejoice in 1 to be glad because of.
2 (*often iron.*) to be fortunate to have
(*He rejoices in the name of Rufus T.
Firefly*).

relation
poor relation POOR.

relief
on relief (*esp. N Am.*) in receipt of
government financial assistance.

relieve
to relieve oneself/ nature (*euphem.*) to
defecate or urinate.
to relieve one's feelings (*euphem.*) to use
strong language when angry.

religion
to get religion (*coll.*) to be converted.

remand
to be on remand to be in custody
awaiting trial.

remember
something to remember someone by (*coll.*)
a physical or verbal attack (*If you do
that again, I'll give you something to
remember me by!*).
to remember oneself to recover or retain
one's good manners.

removed
once removed separated by one
generation younger or older (*first
cousin once removed*).
twice removed separated by two
generations younger or older.

rent
for rent available for use or tenancy on
payment of a rent.

repair
in bad/ out of repair in a dilapidated
condition, needing repair.
in (good) repair in sound working
condition, in good order.

repeat
to bear repeating to be worth repeating.
to repeat itself to recur in the same form
or order (*History repeats itself*).
to repeat oneself to say or do the same
thing over again.

report
to report back 1 to submit a report to the
person, company etc. for whom one is
acting. **2** to present oneself as having
returned.
to report sick to inform someone in
authority that one is ill and unable to
attend to one's work or duties.

reproach
above/ beyond reproach perfect,
blameless.

request
on/ by request if or when asked for (*Extra tickets are available on request*).

requisition
under/ in requisition in use, being applied.

reserve
in reserve reserved and ready for use in an emergency.

to reserve judgement to delay making a judgement about someone or something until more information is available.

with all (proper) reserve without endorsing.

without reserve 1 fully, without reservation. **2** (offered for sale) to the highest bidder without the condition of a reserve price.

residence
in residence 1 actually resident. **2** (of an artist, writer etc.) acting in a regular capacity for a limited period at a gallery, university etc.

to take up residence to make one's home or begin to live (in a particular place).

resist
unable to resist strongly inclined to, strongly attracted to.

resistance
line of least resistance LINE[1].

resort
last resort LAST[1].

resource
one's own resources one's own abilities.

respect
in respect of 1 with regard to, concerning. **2** †in comparison with.

in respect that because.

to pay one's last respects LAST[1].

to pay one's respects to send a message of esteem or compliment.

with (all due) respect a polite phrase used to precede the expression of a disagreement.

with/ in respect to with regard to, concerning.

respecter
no respecter of persons a person who pays no consideration to and is not biased by wealth and social standing. [From the Bible: "God is no respecter of persons" (Acts x.34).]

responsibility
on one's own responsibility without authorization.

rest[1]
at rest 1 reposing, not in motion, still. **2** not disturbed, agitated or troubled. **3** (*euphem.*) dead, in the grave.

give it a rest! (*coll.*) stop it!

to come to rest to stop, to cease moving.

to lay to rest 1 to bury. **2** to prevent from causing further trouble or dispute. **3** to calm, to assuage.

to put/ set someone's mind at rest MIND.

to rest one's case to conclude one's arguments. [Of legal origin.]

to rest on one's laurels to be satisfied with what one has achieved and not to strive for further success. [Alluding to a laurel wreath worn as a symbol of victory, honour, or distinction.]

to rest up (*N Am.*) to have a rest.

to set someone's heart at rest HEART.

rest[2]
and all the rest and all the others.

(as) for the rest as regards the remaining persons, matters or things, as regards anything else.

to rest assured to be secure in the knowledge (that).

to rest with to be left in the hands of.

restraint
in restraint of in order to restrain.

result
without result in vain.

retard
in retard delayed.

retire
to retire from the world to become
reclusive.
to retire into oneself to become
withdrawn or uncommunicative.

retreat
to beat a retreat to retire to avoid
confrontation (*We beat a hasty
retreat*). [Of military origin, referring
to the drum signal for a retreat.]

retrospect
in retrospect looking back on something
that has happened (*In retrospect, it
was not the best way to handle the
situation*).

return
by return (of post) by the next post back
to the sender.
in return 1 in reply or response, in
requital. 2 sent, given etc. back.
many happy returns (of the day) HAPPY.
point of no return POINT.
small profits and quick returns SMALL.
to return thanks 1 to offer thanks. 2 to
answer a toast.
to return the compliment 1 to pay a
compliment in return for one received.
2 to retaliate in kind.
to return to the charge to begin again.

reveal
to be revealed/ reveal oneself to come to
attention.

reverence
saving your reverence (*dated*) with all
respect to you.

†to do reverence to to treat with
reverence.

reverse
to reverse arms to hold a rifle with the
butt upwards.
to reverse the charges to make a
telephone call for which the recipient
pays.

revolve
to revolve around to have (something) as
an important central feature or focus
(*His life revolves around his family*).

rhyme
without rhyme or reason 1 unreasonable,
purposeless. 2 inconsiderately,
thoughtlessly.

rib
to stick to someone's ribs STICK².

rich
rich as Croesus very wealthy. [Croesus,
king of Lydia in the 6th century BC,
was a very wealthy man.]

riches
rags-to-riches RAG¹.

rid
to get/ be rid of to free oneself of or
become free of.

riddance
good riddance GOOD.

riddle
riddled with full of (*furniture riddled
with woodworm*).

ride
along for the ride accompanying others
out of interest, or to make up numbers,
but not taking part in the main activity
(*They said I could go along for the
ride*).
rough ride ROUGH.

to let something ride to let something continue without interference.

to ride again to return to a former activity.

to ride and tie (of two people having only one horse) to ride and walk alternately.

to ride down 1 to overtake by riding. **2** to trample on in riding.

to ride for a fall to act recklessly.

to ride hard (*Naut.*) to pitch violently when at anchor.

to ride herd on (*N Am.*) to guard, to watch over.

to ride high to be popular or successful.

to ride out 1 to come safely through (a storm etc.). **2** to endure successfully.

to ride post (*Hist.*) to ride with post-horses; to ride in haste.

to ride roughshod over to treat in a domineering and inconsiderate way. [A roughshod horse has roughened shoes to improve its grip on the road.]

to ride shotgun 1 (*esp. N Am.*) to travel as a guard, sitting beside the driver of a vehicle. **2** (*esp. N Am.*) to travel in the passenger seat of a vehicle. **3** (*esp. N Am.*) to act as a protector.

to ride the stang to be carried on a pole in derision, an old method of punishment.

to ride to death to overdo.

to ride to hounds to hunt.

to ride up (of a skirt etc.) to move up out of the normal position.

to take for a ride 1 (*coll.*) to play a trick on. **2** (*coll.*) to kidnap and murder.

rift

rift in the lute (*poet.*) a small fault or problem that will develop into something more significant, leading to ruin or failure. [From Tennyson's poem 'Merlin and Vivien', part of *The Idylls of the King* (1842–85): "It is the little rift within the lute, / That by and by will make the music mute".]

rig¹

in full rig FULL.

rig²

to rig the market to manipulate the market so as to raise or lower prices for underhand purposes.

to run the rig to indulge in practical joking.

right

a right one (*coll.*) a foolish person.

(as) of right legally or morally entitled.

bang to rights BANG.

by right(s) properly, with justice.

I'm all right, Jack used to express an attitude of self-interest or self-satisfaction and lack of concern for others.

in one's own right because of one's own efforts (*She became famous in her own right*).

in one's right mind sane, lucid.

in the right correct, in accordance with reason or justice.

in the right ballpark (*coll.*) approximately right, on the right lines.

Mr Right MR.

on the right track/ tack/ lines following the correct line of thought, inquiry, action etc.

right and left 1 in all directions. **2** on every side. **3** with both hands etc.

right as a trivet 1 (*coll.*) firm, stable. **2** (*coll.*) in first-rate health, circumstances, position etc.

right as nails (*coll.*) perfectly right.

right as rain (*coll.*) perfectly all right (*I was right as rain the following morning*).

right away/ off at once, immediately.

right ho/ oh! used to express agreement or compliance.

right, left and centre in or from all directions (*losing money right, left and centre*).

right on! (*sl.*) used to express support or approval.

right you are! (*coll.*) used to express agreement or compliance.

she'll be right (*Austral., coll.*) that is all right.

that's right used to express approval, agreement etc.

to give one's right arm (*coll.*) to be willing to exchange or sacrifice anything in order to have or do something (*I'd give my right arm for a figure like that*).

to hit/ strike the right note to speak or act in an appropriate or suitable manner.

too right (*coll.*) used to express agreement.

to put/ set right to correct, to rectify.

to put/ set to rights to put in order (*putting the world to rights*).

to see someone right SEE.

two wrongs don't make a right TWO.

within one's rights legally or morally entitled.

right angle

at right angles placed at or forming a right angle.

right-hand

right-hand man 1 one's best or most efficient assistant, aid or support. **2** a soldier placed on the right side.

right side

on the right side of 1 pleasing, in the favour of (*Try to keep on the right side of your boss*). **2** below (a specified age) (*while I'm still on the right side of 40*).

right side out with the correct side facing outwards.

Riley

the life of Riley LIFE.

ring¹

three-ring circus THREE.

to run rings round (*coll.*) to be much more successful or skilful than (*run rings round an opponent*).

to throw one's hat into the ring HAT.

ring²

to ring a bell 1 to revive a memory. **2** to look or sound familiar (*His name rings a bell*).

to ring back to make a return telephone call to.

to ring down the curtain 1 to lower the curtain in a theatre. **2** to bring something to an end (*ring down the curtain on a relationship*). [From the former practice of ringing a bell as a signal to lower the curtain in a theatre.]

to ring false to appear insincere. [Coins were formerly shown to be genuine or counterfeit by the sound they made when dropped or struck.]

to ring in 1 to report in by telephone. **2** (*Austral., New Zeal., sl.*) to substitute fraudulently.

to ring in one's ears/ heart to stay in one's memory (*with the cheers of the crowd still ringing in his ears*).

to ring off to end a telephone call; to hang up the receiver.

to ring round to telephone several people (*ringing round for insurance quotations*).

to ring the changes 1 to vary the ways of doing something. **2** (*dated*) to swindle by counterfeit money, or in changing a coin. [From bell-ringing, in which the phrase refers to the ringing of a set of bells repeatedly but in slightly varying order.]

to ring true to seem genuine.

to ring up to call on the telephone.

to ring up the curtain to raise the curtain in a theatre.

ringer

dead ringer DEAD.

to be a ringer for to look exactly like.

riot

to read the riot act READ.

to run riot 1 to act without control or restraint. **2** to grow luxuriantly.

rip

to let it rip (*coll.*) to allow something to proceed without restraint.

to let rip 1 (*coll.*) to speak, act or proceed without restraint. **2** (*coll.*) not to check the speed of.

to rip into to attack or criticize verbally.

to rip off 1 (*coll.*) to cheat (*ripping off unsuspecting tourists*). **2** (*coll.*) to steal (from).

rise

on the rise increasing.

rise and shine (*coll.*) get up out of bed. [From the Bible: "Arise, shine; for thy light is come, and the glory of the Lord is risen upon thee" is Is. lx.1).]

to get/ take a rise out of (*coll.*) to tease, to provoke.

to give rise to to cause.

to rise above 1 to be superior to. **2** to remain unaffected by (problems or adverse conditions).

to rise from the ranks 1 (of a soldier) to be promoted from the ranks, to receive a commission. **2** to achieve success by one's own efforts.

to rise in the world to advance to a higher social position.

to rise to the bait to allow oneself to be provoked, to react in the expected way.

to rise to the occasion to be equal to a demanding event or situation.

to rise with the sun to get up early.

risk

at one's (own) risk accepting responsibility.

at risk in danger, vulnerable (*Our jobs are at risk*).

at the risk of with the possibility of (unpleasant consequences).

to put at risk to expose to danger.

to risk life and limb to put oneself in great danger of physical injury.

to risk one's neck to do something very dangerous.

to run/ take a risk to risk danger.

to run the risk to take the chance (of danger) (*We ran the risk of losing their goodwill*).

river

to sell down the river SELL.

road

all roads lead to Rome there are many different ways of achieving the same objective. [From the days of the Roman Empire, when Rome was the centre of the civilized world.]

by road using transport on the roads.

in someone's road (*coll.*) obstructing someone.

in the road (*coll.*) in the way.

one for the road ONE.

on the road passing through, travelling, touring (often as a way of life).

on the road to on the way to, heading towards (*He is now on the road to recovery*).

royal road ROYAL.

rule of the road RULE.

to get in someone's road (*coll.*) to obstruct someone.

to get in the road to get in the way.

to get out of someone's road (*coll.*) to stop obstructing someone.

to get out of the road (*coll.*) to get out of the way.

to get the show on the road SHOW.

to hit the road HIT.

to take to the road to set out, to begin travelling.

roaring

roaring trade (*coll.*) thriving and profitable business (*We did a roaring trade selling cold drinks to the runners*).

rob

to rob Peter to pay Paul 1 to take away from one person in order to give to another. **2** to pay off one debt by incurring a new one. [The phrase is associated with an event of the mid-16th century, when revenue from the church of St Peter in Westminster was used for repairs to St Paul's cathedral, but it had been a common saying more than 150 years earlier.]

to rob someone blind (*coll.*) to obtain money from someone by deception, overcharging etc.

robbery

daylight/ highway robbery flagrant extortion or overpricing (*£2.50 for a cup of coffee – that's daylight robbery!*).

fair exchange is no robbery FAIR.

rock¹

between a rock and a hard place (*N Am.*) having to decide between two equally unpleasant courses of action.

on the rocks 1 (*coll.*) poor, hard up. **2** (*coll.*) (of a marriage) at an end, destroyed. **3** (of a drink) served with ice. [Alluding to a shipwreck.]

steady as a rock STEADY.

to get one's rocks off (*sl.*) to achieve esp. sexual gratification.

rock²

to rock the boat to disrupt existing conditions, to cause trouble (*I didn't want to rock the boat, so I said nothing*).

rocker

off one's rocker (*coll.*) crazy.

rod

spare the rod and spoil the child SPARE.

to have a rod in pickle to have a beating or scolding in store.

to kiss the rod KISS.

to make a rod for one's own back to do something that will cause one trouble later.

to rule with a rod of iron RULE.

Roland

a Roland for an Oliver 1 an effective retort. **2** a blow for a blow, a story capping another. [From the medieval heroes Roland and Oliver, knights at Charlemagne's court, who were evenly matched in exploits and combat.]

roll

a roll in the hay 1 (*coll.*) sexual intercourse. **2** (*coll.*) a period of sexual play.

on a roll (*sl.*) having a period of great success.

rolled into one combined together (*You have to be teacher, umpire and counsellor rolled into one*).

roll on! (of a day, date or event) hurry along, come quickly (*Roll on the holidays!*).

to roll along 1 to walk in a casual manner or with an undulating gait. **2** to have a casual or unambitious approach to life. **3** to move or push along by rolling.

to roll back (*N Am.*) to cause to decrease.

to roll in 1 to come in quantities or numbers (*when the money starts rolling in*). **2** (*coll.*) to arrive in a casual manner. **3** to wind in. **4** to push in by rolling.

to roll on 1 to knock over. **2** to repay (maturing stock) by an issue of new stock.

to roll up 1 (*coll.*) to assemble, to come up. **2** to make (a cigarette) by hand. **3** to wind into a cylinder. **4** (*Mil.*) to drive back (an enemy line) so that it is shortened or surrounded. **5** to wind up (a car window etc.).

to roll up one's sleeves to get ready for hard work, a fight etc.

to strike off the rolls STRIKE.

rolling

a rolling stone gathers no moss people who frequently move from place to place do not accumulate possessions, friends etc.

to be rolling in to have a lot of (*His parents are rolling in money*).

to be rolling (in it) (*coll.*) to be extremely wealthy.

Roman

when in Rome, do as the Romans do ROME.

Rome

all roads lead to Rome ROAD.

Rome was not built in a day accomplishments of any lasting worth require time and patience.

to fiddle while Rome burns FIDDLE.

when in Rome, do as the Romans do in a strange place or unfamiliar situation, one should follow the customs or example of those around one. [From the sayings of St Ambrose (c. 339–397), originally given as advice to St Augustine.]

romp

to romp home/ in (*coll.*) to win easily.

roof

a roof over one's head a place to live.

to go through the roof 1 (*coll.*) (of prices etc.) to increase suddenly and quickly. **2** to lose one's temper.

to raise the roof RAISE.

under one roof in the same building (*shopping and leisure facilities under one roof*).

under one's roof in one's home (*I don't want them sleeping together under my roof*).

room

barrack-room lawyer BARRACK.

elbow room ELBOW.

no room to swing a cat very little or not enough space. [Of several possible explanations of the origin of this phrase, the most popular is that it referred to the space needed to flog someone with a cat-o'-nine-tails (a whip with nine lashes used as an instrument of punishment).]

standing room STANDING.

to make room to move so as to leave space (for).

roost

to come home to roost to have undesirable consequences for the doer or initiator. [From the motto of Robert Southey's poem *The Curse of Kehama* (1810): "Curses are like young chickens, they always come home to roost."]

root

grass roots GRASS.

root and branch utterly, radically. [From the Bible: "the day that cometh shall burn them up, saith the Lord of hosts, that it shall leave them neither root nor branch" (Mal. iv.1).]

to pull up by the roots 1 to uproot. **2** to destroy.

to put down roots 1 to draw nourishment from the soil. **2** to become established.

to root out 1 to uproot. **2** to extirpate.

to strike at the root(s) of STRIKE.

to take/ strike root 1 to become planted and send out living roots or rootlets. **2** to become immovable or established (*The idea took root in her mind*).

rooted

rooted to the spot unable to move, as through fear, amazement etc.

rope

on the rope in mountaineering, roped together.

on the ropes 1 in boxing, forced against the ropes by one's opponent. **2** nearly defeated.

to give someone enough rope to hang themselves ENOUGH.

to know/ learn the ropes (*coll.*) to be/ become acquainted with the particular conditions of any affair or proceeding. [Alluding to the knowledge of a competent sailor.]

to rope in 1 to enlist or persuade (someone) to join a group or enter into an activity. **2** to capture or pull in (a steer, horse etc.) with a rope, to lasso.

to rope into to persuade (someone) to enter into (an activity).

to show someone the ropes (*coll.*) to acquaint someone with the particular conditions of any affair or proceeding.

rose

all roses/ roses all the way completely pleasant, unproblematic or easy.

bed of roses BED.

everything is coming up roses everything is turning out successfully.

to see through rose-coloured/ -tinted spectacles to take an overoptimistic or unrealistic view (of).

under the rose in secret, privately, confidentially, sub rosa. [The rose, an emblem of secrecy, was sometimes carved into the ceiling of a room where confidential discussions might take place.]

rotten

rotten apple (*coll.*) a member of a group who is immoral or corrupt.

rough

bit of rough BIT[1].

in the rough in general.

rough-and-ready hastily prepared, without finish or elaboration; provisional, makeshift.

rough-and-tumble 1 disorderly, irregular, haphazard. **2** an irregular fight, contest, scuffle etc. **3** in a disorderly, irregular or haphazard manner.

rough diamond a person with rough exterior or manners but a genuine or warm character.

rough ride a difficult experience (*Some of my customers had been giving me a rough ride*).

the rough edge/ side of one's tongue (*coll.*) a scolding, a rebuke.

to cut up rough (*sl.*) to become quarrelsome or savage.

to rough in to outline, to draw roughly.

to rough it to put up with hardships, to live without the ordinary conveniences.

to rough up 1 to ruffle (fur, hair or feathers) by rubbing in the wrong direction. **2** (*sl.*) to beat up, to injure during a beating.

to take the rough with the smooth to accept unpleasantness or difficulty as well as ease, happiness etc.

round

all round 1 all things considered; in most respects. **2** for everyone (present) (*drinks all round*).

in round numbers/ figures approximately, to the nearest hundred, thousand etc.

in the round 1 all things considered. **2** able to be viewed from every side.

round about 1 in or as if in a circle (round), all round. **2** approximately. **3** in an opposite direction. **4** circuitously, indirectly.

round and round several times round.

round peg in a square hole a person in an unsuitable job or function.

to go/ do the rounds (of news, a joke etc.) to be passed from person to person (*a virus that has been going the rounds in the office*).

to make/ do one's rounds to make a series of visits to different people or places.

to round down to lower (a number) to avoid fractions or reach a convenient figure.

to round off 1 to finish off, to complete, to perfect (*We rounded off the meal with a glass of port*). **2** to shape (angles etc.) to a round or less sharp form.

to round on to turn upon, to attack.

to round out 1 to finish off, to complete, to perfect. **2** to provide more information about. **3** to fill out, to become more plump.

to **round to** to turn the prow of a ship towards the wind, in order to heave to.

to **round up 1** to gather (horses, cattle etc.) together. **2** to raise (a number) to avoid fractions or reach a convenient figure (*Let's round it up to £50*).

roundabout

swings and roundabouts SWING.

what you gain on the swings you lose on the roundabouts GAIN.

rouse

to **rouse on** (*Austral.*) to scold, to tell off.

to **rouse oneself** to abandon inactivity.

roust

to **roust around** to rummage.

rout[1]

to **put to rout** to defeat utterly.

rout[2]

to **rout out** to hunt out.

roving

roving eye a promiscuous sexual interest.

row[1]

hard row to hoe HARD.

in a row 1 (placed) one beside the other. **2** (ordered) in succession.

row[2]

to **row down** to overtake by rowing, esp. in a bumping race.

to **row over** to win a rowing race very easily.

row[3]

to **make/ kick up a row** to make a loud, unpleasant noise.

royal

royal road an easy way or direct route (to a goal etc.). [The Greek mathematician Euclid (c. 300 BC) is said to have told Ptolemy I: "There is no royal road to geometry."]

rub

there's the rub that is the problem or difficulty. [From Shakespeare's *Hamlet*: "To sleep: perchance to dream: ay, there's the rub". A rub is an obstruction or hindrance, specifically an uneven patch on a bowling green.]

to **rub along/ on 1** (*coll.*) to manage, to just succeed, to cope despite difficulties. **2** (*coll.*) to keep on friendly terms.

to **rub down 1** to clean or dry by rubbing. **2** to make smooth.

to **rub elbows with** (*N Am.*) to rub shoulders with.

to **rub in** to force in by friction.

to **rub it in** to keep reminding someone of something embarrassing or unpleasant (*Don't rub it in!*).

to **rub noses** to rub one's nose against someone else's as an Eskimo (Inuit) greeting.

to **rub off** to remove by rubbing.

to **rub off on someone** to pass on to someone by example or close association (*My parents hoped my friend's good manners would rub off on me*).

to **rub one's hands** to express expectation, glee, satisfaction etc. by rubbing one's hands together.

to **rub out 1** to remove or erase. **2** (*N Am., sl.*) to kill.

to **rub salt into the wound** to make someone's sorrow or suffering worse. [Salt was formerly used as an antiseptic.]

to **rub shoulders with** to associate or mix with.

to **rub someone's nose in it** to refer to or remind someone of an error, indiscretion or misfortune. [Alluding to a method of house-training a pet by rubbing its nose in its excrement.]

to **rub up 1** to polish, to burnish. **2** to freshen (one's recollection of something). **3** to mix into a paste etc. by rubbing.

to rub (up) the wrong way to irritate. [An allusion to stroking an animal's fur in the wrong direction.]

rubbish heap

on the rubbish heap (*coll.*) discarded as ineffective or worthless.

Rubicon

to cross the Rubicon CROSS.

rude

to be rude to to speak impolitely to.

to have/ get a rude awakening to learn or discover something unpleasant very suddenly.

ruffle

to ruffle someone's feathers to make someone upset or angry.

rug

snug as a bug in a rug SNUG.

to pull the rug from under to put (someone) in a defenceless or discomposed state, to undermine (someone).

ruin

in ruins 1 in a state of ruin or decay. 2 completely spoiled.

to go to rack and ruin RACK².

rule

as a general rule GENERAL.

as a rule usually, generally (*We all eat together in the evening as a rule*).

by rule mechanically, automatically.

golden rule GOLDEN.

ground rule GROUND.

rule of the road a regulation governing the methods of passing each other for vehicles on the road, vessels on the water etc.

rule of thumb practical experience, as distinct from theory, as a guide in doing anything. [From the use of the thumb to make approximate measurements.]

the exception that proves the rule EXCEPTION.

to bend the rules BEND.

to be ruled by to be guided by.

to rule out to exclude, to eliminate (as a possibility).

to rule the roost/ roast to be the leader, to be dominant.

to rule with a rod of iron to exert strict discipline or control over (*She rules the workforce with a rod of iron*).

to run the rule over to check quickly for accuracy.

to work to rule WORK.

run

a (good) run for one's money 1 a strong challenge (*The other team gave us a good run for our money*). 2 pleasure derived from an activity. 3 return for one's money or effort. [From horse racing, referring to the excitement of watching a backed horse run, even if it does not win the race.]

at a/ the run running, in haste.

dry run DRY.

in the long run LONG.

on the run 1 in flight, fugitive. 2 rushing about.

run-of-the-mill undistinguished, ordinary, mediocre. [Probably alluding to the ungraded output of a mill.]

to have the run of to have free use of or access to (*She has the run of the house at the weekends*).

to run about 1 to rush from place to place. 2 (of children) to play freely, without restraint.

to run across 1 to encounter by chance, to discover by accident. 2 to make a quick visit (to). 3 to cross at a run.

to run after 1 to try to form a sexual or romantic relationship with. 2 to cultivate, to devote oneself to. 3 to chase.

to run against 1 to compete against (someone) for election. 2 †to happen on.

to run along (*coll.*) to leave, to go away (*Run along, and don't get into mischief!*).

to run amok to rush about in a wild, uncontrollable rage, attacking people indiscriminately.

to run around 1 to transport from place to place by car. **2** to deceive repeatedly. **3** (*coll.*) to have casual sexual relations (with).

to run at to rush at, to attack.

to run atilt to attack.

to run away 1 to flee, to abscond. **2** to elope. **3** (of a horse) to bolt.

to run away with 1 to carry off. **2** to win (an easy victory). **3** to accept (an idea) rashly. **4** to cost (a lot of money). **5** (of a horse) to bolt with. **6** to elope with. **7** (of enthusiasm, emotions etc.) to deprive of self-control and common sense (*I let my imagination run away with me*).

to run down 1 to stop through not being wound up, recharged etc. **2** to make enfeebled by overwork etc. **3** to pursue and overtake. **4** to search for and discover. **5** to disparage (*He's always running his students down*). **6** to collide with. **7** to reduce in size or amount.

to run dry 1 to stop flowing (*The river had run dry*). **2** (of a supply) to end.

to run for it to make an escape attempt, to run away.

to run high 1 (of the sea) to have a strong current with high tide. **2** (of emotions) to be strongly felt (*Feelings were running high*).

to run in 1 (*coll.*) to arrest, to take into custody. **2** to break in (a motor vehicle, machine etc.) by running or operating. **3** to insert (printed matter etc.). **4** to approach. **5** to incur (a debt). **6** to drive (cattle etc.) in. **7** to call, to drop in.

to run in the family/ blood to be hereditary.

to run into 1 to incur, to fall into. **2** to collide with. **3** to reach (a specified number, amount etc.). **4** to meet by chance (*I ran into my old headmaster at the library*). **5** to be continuous with.

to run low (on) to have a depleted supply (of).

to run off 1 to print. **2** to decide (a race or contest) after a series of heats. **3** to cause to pour or flow out. **4** to write fluently. **5** to digress.

to run off with 1 to elope with. **2** to steal, to remove.

to run on 1 to continue without a break. **2** to talk volubly or incessantly. **3** to elapse. **4** (of the mind) to be absorbed by.

to run out 1 to come to an end. **2** to leak. **3** in cricket, to dismiss (a batsman) by breaking the wicket when they are not in their ground. **4** (of a rope) to pass out. **5** to jut out. **6** to end a contest in a specified position. **7** to finish (a race). **8** to point (a gun). **9** to exhaust oneself by running.

to run out of to have no more supplies of (*The printer has run out of paper*).

to run out on (*coll.*) to abandon.

to run over 1 to review or examine cursorily. **2** to recapitulate. **3** to overflow. **4** to pass, ride or drive over. **5** to touch (piano keys) lightly in quick succession. **6** to go for a quick visit (to).

to run short to exhaust the stock in hand (of a commodity).

to run someone close/ hard to be a serious challenge to.

to run through 1 to go through or examine rapidly (*Can we just run through tomorrow's schedule?*). **2** to take, deal with, spend etc. one after another, to squander. **3** to pass through by running. **4** to pervade. **5** to transfix, to pierce with a weapon. **6** to strike out by drawing a line through.

to run to 1 to afford. **2** to extend to. **3** to have a tendency to. **4** to amount to. **5** to have the resources for. **6** to fall into (ruin).

to run to earth/ ground to track down, to
find after hard or prolonged searching.
[From hunting, referring to the hole
where a fox or badger lives.]

to run together to fuse, to blend, to mix.

to run up 1 to grow rapidly. 2 (of prices)
to increase quickly. 3 to accumulate
(a debt etc.). 4 to force up (prices etc.).
5 to amount (to). 6 to add up (a column
of figures). 7 to make a quick visit (to).
8 to build, make or sew in a hasty
manner (*I ran up a dress for the
party*). 9 to raise or hoist.

to run up against to encounter
(problems).

to run upon 1 to dwell on, to be absorbed
by. 2 to meet suddenly and
accidentally.

runner

to do a runner (*sl.*) to leave, esp. in order
to avoid paying for something.

running

in the running having a chance of
winning.

out of the running not having a chance of
winning.

running battle 1 a battle between
pursuers and pursued. 2 a continuous
or long-running argument.

running commentary an oral description,
usu. by broadcasting, of an event in
progress, e.g. a race.

take a running jump! 1 (*coll.*) under no
circumstances! 2 (*coll.*) go away!

to make/ take up the running to set the
pace.

rush

the bum's rush BUM.

to rush into print to write to a newspaper
or publish a book without adequate
justification.

to rush one's fences to act too hastily or
precipitously.

rustle

to rustle up 1 (*coll.*) to prepare or make
quickly, or without preparation or
prior notice (*He rustled up some
sandwiches*). 2 to gather up, to put
together.

rut

in a rut stuck in tedious routine.

S

sack

to give someone/ get the sack to dismiss someone/ be dismissed from employment. [From the bag in which workers carried the tools of their trade.]

sackcloth

in sackcloth and ashes penitent or contrite. [From the ancient practice, mentioned frequently in the Bible, of showing sorrow or repentance by wearing coarse sackcloth and sprinkling ashes over one's head.]

sacred

sacred cow (*coll.*) an institution, custom etc. regarded with reverence and as beyond criticism. [The cow is a sacred animal in some religions, such as Hinduism.]

sacrifice

to make the supreme sacrifice SUPREME.

saddle

boot and saddle BOOT[1].
in the saddle 1 mounted. **2** in control.
to saddle someone with something to burden someone with an unpleasant task or responsibility.

safe

better (to be) safe than sorry used when taking a precaution.
safe and sound secure and unharmed.
safe as houses completely safe.
to be on the safe side as a precaution (*We left early, to be on the safe side*).

safety

safety first used to advise caution.
there's safety in numbers it seems safer to do something risky if many people are doing it.

sail

to make sail 1 to set sail. **2** to extend an additional quantity of sail.
to pack on all sail PACK.
to sail close to the wind 1 (*Naut.*) to keep a vessel's head as near the direction from which the wind is blowing as possible while keeping the sails filled. **2** to take risks.
to sail into (*coll.*) to tackle or attack vigorously.
to sail under false colours to assume a false character. [False colours are flags to which a ship has no right, raised to deceive an enemy.]
to set sail to begin a voyage.
to shorten sail SHORTEN.
to strike sail STRIKE.
to take in sail 1 to furl the sails of a vessel. **2** to moderate one's ambitions.
to take the wind out of someone's sails WIND[1].
to trim one's sails TRIM.
under sail with sails spread.

sailing

plain sailing PLAIN.

saint

saints preserve us! used as an expression of exasperation.

to (be enough to) try the patience of a
     saint TRY.

sake

for Christ's sake CHRIST.
for conscience's sake CONSCIENCE.
for God's sake GOD.
for goodness' sake GOODNESS.
for heaven's sake HEAVEN.
for mercy's sake MERCY.
for old times'/ sake's sake OLD.
for Pete's sake PETE.
for pity's sake PITY.
for the sake of 1 because of, out of
     consideration for (*They stayed together
     for the sake of the children*). 2 in order
     to obtain or achieve (*It's not worth
     making a fuss for the sake of a few
     pounds*).

salad

salad days the time of youth and
     inexperience. [From Shakespeare's
     Antony and Cleopatra: "My salad
     days, / When I was green in
     judgement", the green colour of
     salad being associated with lack
     of experience.]

sale

on/ for sale offered for purchase.

Sally

Aunt Sally AUNT.

salt

above the salt among the more
     distinguished company. [From a
     position at the higher part of a dining
     table, above the salt cellar, where more
     important people were seated.]
below the salt among the less
     distinguished company. [From a
     position at the lower part of a dining
     table, below the salt cellar, where less
     important people were seated.]
in salt sprinkled with salt or steeped in
     brine for curing.

like a dose of salts DOSE.
not made of salt not put off by wet
     weather.
the salt of the earth a person or people of
     the utmost worth. [From the Bible: "Ye
     are the salt of the earth: but if the salt
     have lost his savour, wherewith shall
     it be salted?" (Matt. v.13).]
to eat someone's salt EAT.
to put salt on someone's tail to find or
     catch someone. [From children's
     attempts to put salt on a bird's tail in
     order to catch it.]
to rub salt into the wound RUB.
to salt an account/ the books (*sl.*) to show
     receipts as larger than they really are.
to salt something away (*sl.*) to save or
     hoard something, esp. money. [An
     allusion to the use of salt to preserve
     food.]
with a pinch/ grain of salt with doubt or
     reserve (*I took most of what she said
     with a pinch of salt*).
worth one's salt WORTH.

salute

to take the salute 1 (*Mil.*) (of an officer) to
     acknowledge a salute. 2 to receive
     ceremonial salutes.

Samaritan

good Samaritan GOOD.

same

all the same 1 nevertheless.
     2 notwithstanding what is said, done,
     altered etc.
at the same time nevertheless, yet.
in the same boat in the same (usu.
     undesirable) circumstances or
     position.
in the same breath done or said at the
     same time.
in the same canoe (*New Zeal.*) belonging
     to the same tribe.
just the same nevertheless, yet.
much the same with little change or
     difference.

not in the same league not in the same class, not on the same level of excellence etc.

not in the same street as not to be compared with, quite inferior to.

one and the same exactly the same, identical.

same here (*coll.*) me too, I agree.

the same as ever unchanged, no different.

the same to you! I wish you likewise.

the very same emphatically the same.

to be all the same to someone to be a matter of indifference to someone (*I'd rather go by train, if it's all the same to you*).

sanctity
odour of sanctity ODOUR.

sanctuary
to take sanctuary to hide in a place of refuge.

sand
the sands (of time) are running out the end is approaching, there is little time left. [An allusion to the sand in an hourglass.]

to build something on sand BUILD.

to bury one's head in the sand BURY.

to plough the sands PLOUGH.

sandboy
happy as a sandboy HAPPY.

sandwich
knuckle sandwich KNUCKLE.

sardine
packed like sardines PACK.

satiety
to satiety to an extent beyond what is desired.

satisfaction
to someone's satisfaction so that someone is satisfied.

satisfy
to satisfy oneself to be certain in one's own mind.

to satisfy the examiners to reach the standard required in an examination.

sauce
what is sauce for the goose is sauce for the gander what is appropriate for one person is also appropriate for another.

sausage
not a sausage (*coll.*) nothing at all.

save
saved by the bell rescued or reprieved at the last moment. [From the bell rung at the end of a round in boxing.]

saving grace a virtue or quality in a person or thing that compensates for other less admirable characteristics.

to save one's breath (to cool one's porridge) (*coll.*) to stop talking because no one is listening.

to save oneself the trouble/ bother to avoid wasted effort.

to save (one's) face to save oneself from disgrace or humiliation.

to save one's life under any circumstances at all (used to indicate one's utter inability to do something) (*He can't speak French to save his life*).

to save someone's bacon (*coll.*) to save someone from injury or loss.

to save someone's life 1 to prevent someone from dying. **2** (*coll.*) to help someone who is in serious difficulty.

to save (some)one's neck to (help someone to) escape injury, punishment etc.

to save (some)one's skin to (help someone to) escape injury or get off unscathed.

to save the day to find a solution that avoids difficulty or disaster.

to save the tide to get in and out of port etc. while the tide lasts.

say

how say you? (*Law*) how do you find?

I'll say (*coll.*) used to express agreement.

I say! an exclamation of mild surprise, protest etc. or calling for attention.

it is said it is generally reported or rumoured (*It is said that Henry VIII once slept in this bed*).

no sooner said than done used when something is done quickly, promptly or immediately.

not to say indeed one might say, perhaps even (*His dress sense is unusual, not to say eccentric!*).

say no more you have said enough to persuade, convince etc. me.

says you! (*sl.*) used to express incredulity.

say when (*coll.*) tell me when to stop pouring a drink etc.

that is to say 1 in other words. **2** or at least.

they say it is generally reported or rumoured.

to have one's say to express one's opinion.

to say for oneself to say by way of conversation etc.

to say much for (*often neg.*) to show the high quality of (*It doesn't say much for modern teaching standards*).

to say out to express fully.

what do/ would you say to? how about?

when all is said and done in the long run.

you can say that again! (*coll.*) used to express agreement.

you don't say (so)! (*coll.*) used to express amazement, disbelief etc.

you said it! (*coll.*) used to express agreement.

saying

as the saying goes used to introduce a proverb, cliché etc.

there is no saying it is impossible to know (*There is no saying how long it will take*).

to go without saying to be extremely obvious (*It goes without saying that we are all very pleased for her*).

scald

like a scalded cat moving very fast.

scale¹

the scales fall/ are removed from someone's eyes to reveal the truth to someone who has been deceived. [From the Bible: "And immediately there fell from his eyes as it had been scales: and he received sight forthwith, and arose, and was baptized" (Acts ix.18), referring to the conversion of Saul.]

scale²

to throw into the scale to add as a factor in a contest, debate etc.

to tip/ turn the scales 1 to cause one pan of a pair of scales to become lower than the other because of greater weight; to weigh in (at). **2** to make the significant difference.

scale³

in scale in proportion to the surroundings etc.

to play/ sing scales to play/ sing the notes of a scale as a musical exercise.

to scale in proportion to actual dimensions (*drawn to scale*).

to scale down to make smaller proportionately.

to scale up to make larger proportionately.

scarce

to make oneself scarce 1 (*coll.*) to keep out of the way. **2** (*coll.*) to be off, to decamp.

scare

to be scared shitless (*taboo sl.*) to be very scared.

to run scared to panic (*We had our rivals running scared*).

to scare the pants off someone (*coll.*) to scare someone greatly.

to scare up/ out 1 (*esp. N Am.*) to cause (game) to move out of cover. **2** (*coll.*) to find or produce quickly.

scarlet

scarlet woman 1 (*derog.*) a prostitute.
2 worldliness or sensuality. **3** pagan or
papal Rome. [From the Bible: "And
the woman was arrayed in purple
and scarlet colour,…having a golden
cup in her hand full of abominations
and filthiness of her fornication"
(Rev. xvii.4), a personification of
Babylon.]

scene

behind the scenes 1 at the back of the
stage. **2** (*also attrib.*) not generally
known, secretly (*a behind-the-scenes
investigation*).
to come on/ hit the scene to arrive, to
appear.
to make a scene to make a fuss.
to make the scene (*N Am.*) to come on/
hit the scene.
to quit the scene QUIT.
to set the scene 1 to describe the location
of events. **2** to give background
information.

scent

on the scent having a useful clue, lead
etc.
to scent out to discover by smelling or
searching.
to throw/ put someone off the scent to
mislead someone.

sceptre

to wield the sceptre WIELD.

schedule

according to schedule as planned (*if
everything goes according to
schedule*).
behind schedule late; not keeping up to
an arranged timetable.
on schedule on time.

school

at school attending lessons etc.
in school (*N Am.*) at school.
of the old school OLD SCHOOL.

old school tie OLD SCHOOL.
to go to school 1 to begin one's schooling.
2 to attend lessons.
to leave school to finish one's schooling.
to teach school TEACH.
to tell tales out of school TELL.

science

to blind someone with science BLIND.

scone

off one's scone 1 (*Austral., sl.*) angry.
2 (*Austral., sl.*) insane.

scoop

to scoop the pool 1 to win all the money
staked in a gambling game. **2** to come
away with everything, to be totally
successful.

score

on that score so far as that is concerned
(*You need have no worries on that
score*).
on the score of for the reason that;
because of.
to keep (the) score to record the score
during a game etc.
to know the score (*coll.*) to know the facts
of the situation.
to quit scores QUIT.
to run up a score to accumulate a debt.
to score an own goal (*coll.*) to do
something to one's disadvantage by
mistake. [In football etc., an own goal
is a goal scored by a player against
their own side by accident.]
to score off 1 (*coll.*) to get the better of.
2 (*coll.*) to triumph over in argument,
repartee etc.
to score out to cross out, to cancel.
to score points to outdo someone else; to
make a better impression.
to score points off to get the better of in
an argument.
to score under to underline.
to settle/ pay off a score to pay someone
out or have revenge for an offence of
old standing.

scorn

to laugh to scorn LAUGH.

to pour scorn on POUR.

†**to take scorn** to disdain, to scorn.

†**to think scorn of** to despise or disdain.

scran

bad scran to you! (*Ir.*) bad luck to you!

scrape

to scrape acquaintance with to contrive to make the acquaintance of, esp. for personal advantage.

to scrape along/ by (*coll.*) to keep going somehow (*scraping along on a meagre income*).

to scrape away to abrade, to reduce by scraping.

to scrape down 1 to scrape away. **2** to scrape from head to foot or top to bottom. **3** to silence or put down by scraping the feet.

to scrape (the bottom of) the barrel 1 to get the last remaining bit, to obtain the last scrap. **2** to be forced to use undesirable people or things because they are all that remain.

scrap heap

on the scrap heap no longer useful, esp. because of being unemployed (*He found himself on the scrap heap at the age of 50*).

scratch

to scratch along to keep going somehow.

to scratch one's head to be puzzled.

to scratch the surface 1 to gain a superficial understanding or provide a superficial analysis (*Your essay only scratches the surface*). **2** to investigate further (*Scratch the surface of that organization and you'll find some very shady goings-on*).

to start from scratch START.

up to scratch fulfilling the desired standard or requirements (*Her work was not up to scratch*). [From the sport of boxing, originally referring to a line scratched across the ring. A prize-fighter who could not reach this line without help after being knocked down was deemed to have lost.]

you scratch my back and I'll scratch yours if you do me a favour, I'll do you one in return.

screw

to have a screw at (*Austral., coll.*) to take a look at.

to have a screw loose (*coll.*) to be slightly crazy.

to put the screws on (*coll.*) to put pressure on. [An allusion to thumbscrews, former instruments of torture.]

to screw around (*taboo sl.*) to have sexual intercourse with many partners.

to screw up 1 to tighten up with or as with a screw. **2** to fasten with a screw or screws. **3** to shut (a person) in thus. **4** to twist. **5** (*sl.*) to bungle, mess up (*It screwed up my chances of getting the job*). **6** (*sl.*) to make confused or neurotic. **7** to summon (one's courage).

scrimp

to scrimp and save/ scrape to be thrifty and economical.

scrounge

on the scrounge (*coll.*) engaged in cadging things (*He only comes to see us when he's on the scrounge*).

scrub

to scrub round (*coll.*) to avoid or ignore (*We can scrub round these instructions*).

Scylla

between Scylla and Charybdis caught between alternative risks, escape from one of which entails danger from the other. [In Greek mythology, Scylla and Charybdis were sea monsters (identified elsewhere as a rock and a

whirlpool) on either side of the Strait
of Messina between Sicily and Italy.
Sailors trying to avoid one would be
caught by the other.]

sea

all at sea perplexed, uncertain, confused.
at full sea FULL.
at sea 1 on the open sea. **2** out of sight of
land. **3** perplexed, uncertain, confused.
between the devil and the deep blue sea
DEVIL.
beyond seas overseas, abroad.
by sea in a ship.
half seas over HALF.
on the sea 1 in a ship at sea. **2** situated on
the coast.
sea legs ability to walk on the deck of a
vessel at sea on a stormy day (*to get
one's sea legs*).
the four seas FOUR.
there are (plenty) more fish in the sea
FISH.
to go to/ follow the sea to be or become a
sailor.
to put (out) to sea to leave port or land.
to ship a sea SHIP.
worse things happen at sea THING.

seal

to seal someone's fate to guarantee that
someone will suffer in the future.
to set one's seal on/ to to authorize.
under seal in a document authenticated
by a seal.

seam

bursting at the seams BURST.
to fall apart at the seams to collapse or
fail completely (*Our plans fell apart at
the seams*).

search

in search of trying to find (*She went off
in search of an ashtray*).
search me! (*coll.*) how should I know?,
I have no idea.

season

compliments of the season COMPLIMENT.
in season 1 in vogue. **2** in condition for
shooting, hatching, use, eating etc.
3 (of a female mammal) ready for
mating, on heat. **4** at a fit or opportune
time.
in season and out of season at all times,
continuously or indiscriminately.
silly season SILLY.

seat

back-seat driver BACK SEAT.
be seated sit down.
by the seat of one's pants (*coll.*) by
intuition or instinct. [From aviation,
where the phrase originally referred to
flying without instruments or in poor
visibility.]
in the box seat BOX[1].
in the driver's seat DRIVER.
in the driving seat DRIVING.
in the hot seat HOT SEAT.
to take a back seat BACK SEAT.
to take a/ one's seat to sit down (*Please
take a seat*; *The audience took their
seats*).

second

in the second instance at the second
stage; in the second place.
in the second place as a second
consideration etc.
second childhood childlike behaviour
during old age.
second nature something that has
become effortless or instinctual
through constant practice.
second sight the power of seeing things at
a distance in space or time as if they
were present, clairvoyance.
second thoughts reconsideration of a
previous opinion or decision (*to have
second thoughts*; *on second thoughts*).
second to none unsurpassed (*His treacle
pudding is second to none*).
second wind a renewed burst of energy,
stamina etc. after a concentrated effort
(*to get one's second wind*).

to play second fiddle to take a subordinate part. [Alluding to the second violin section of an orchestra, which often has a subordinate role.]

second-hand
at second hand as one deriving or learning through another purchaser, owner, hearer etc.

secrecy
sworn to secrecy SWEAR.

secret
in (on) the secret among the people who know a secret.
in secret secretly, privately.
open secret OPEN.
to keep a secret not to reveal a secret.

secure
to secure arms (Mil.) to hold a rifle muzzle downwards with the lock under the armpit as a protection from rain.

security
on security of using as a guarantee.
to lull into a false sense of security LULL.

see
as far as I can see to the best of my understanding, judgement etc. (As far as I can see, there's nothing we can do about it).
as I see it in my opinion.
do you see? do you understand?
I'll be seeing you (coll.) goodbye.
I see I understand.
see here! used to get attention etc.
seeing is believing one cannot believe in the truth or existence of something until one has seen it.
see you (later) (coll.) goodbye for the present.
to be ill seen in not to be versed in.
to be well seen in to be versed in.
to see about 1 to give attention to. 2 to make preparations for etc.

to see after 1 to take care of. 2 to see about.
to see into to investigate.
to see off 1 to escort on departure. 2 (coll.) to get rid of.
to see out 1 to escort out of a house etc. 2 to outlive, outlast. 3 to last to the end of. 4 to finish.
to see over to inspect.
to see someone right (coll.) to make sure that someone is taken care of, rewarded etc. (If you cooperate with us, we'll see you right).
to see through 1 to penetrate, not to be deceived by. 2 to persist in (a task etc.) until it is finished. 3 to help through a difficulty, danger etc.
to see to to take care of, to attend to (The nurse will see to you in a moment).
to see to it that to take care that.
we shall see 1 we will see what happens. 2 used to ask for time to consider something.
we will see about that (coll.) we will try to prevent that.
you see 1 you understand. 2 you will understand when I have explained.

seed
to raise up seed RAISE.
to run/ go to seed 1 to cease flowering as seeds are produced. 2 to become shabby, degenerate or unhealthy. 3 to lose self-respect.
to sow the seed(s) of SOW¹.

seek
(far/ much) to seek 1 (seriously) lacking or insufficient. 2 a long way off being found yet.
to seek out 1 to search for. 2 to cultivate the friendship of.

seem
I can't seem to (coll.) I am unable to.
it seems it appears, it is reported (that).
it would seem it appears, it seems to one.

not to seem to (*coll.*) somehow not to (*He doesn't seem to cope well with pressure*).

seeming
to outward seeming OUTWARD.

see-saw
to go see-saw to vacillate.

seise
seised of (*Law*) in possession of.

seize
seized of 1 in legal possession of. **2** aware or informed of.

self
a shadow of one's former self SHADOW.
one's better self one's nobler impulses.
one's former/ old self oneself as one was before (*It's good to see her back to her old self again*).

sell
sold on enthusiastic about (*I'm not sold on the idea*).
to sell a dummy to feign a pass or move in rugby or football.
to sell a pup to (*sl.*) to trick into buying something worthless; to swindle.
to sell down the river (*coll.*) to let down, to betray. [From the former American practice of selling slaves to landowners further down the Mississippi, where working conditions were much harsher.]
to sell off 1 to sell the remainder of (goods). **2** to clear out (stock), esp. at reduced prices.
to sell oneself 1 to try to persuade someone of one's abilities. **2** to offer one's services for money etc.
to sell one's life dear(ly) to injure one's enemy before they kill one.
to sell one's soul to do anything, esp. something that would normally be against one's conscience or principles,
in order to get what one wants. [From stories, such as that of Faust, in which people sell their souls to the devil in return for wealth and other pleasures in life.]
to sell out 1 to sell off (one's stock etc.). **2** to sell completely. **3** to dispose of (one's shares in a company etc.). **4** to betray.
to sell short 1 to sell (stocks) for future delivery. **2** to cheat. **3** to disparage.
to sell someone a bill of goods to deceive someone.
to sell the pass to betray a cause.
to sell up 1 to sell the goods of (a debtor) to pay their debt. **2** to sell one's business, one's house and possessions etc. (*They sold up and moved to the country*).

sell-by date
past its/ one's sell-by date no longer effective or useful, past its/ one's prime (*Our relationship is past its sell-by date*). [From the date marked on the packaging of a perishable product.]

send
to send away/ off for to order (goods) by post.
to send down 1 to suspend from university. **2** to send to prison. **3** in cricket, to bowl (a ball or an over).
to send for 1 to require the attendance of a person or the bringing of a thing. **2** to summon. **3** to order.
to send forth/ out 1 to put forth. **2** to emit.
to send in 1 to cause to go in. **2** to submit (something, such as a competition entry).
to send off 1 to dispatch. **2** to give a friendly demonstration of good wishes to (a person who is departing). **3** in sport, to order (a player) off the field because of an infringement of the rules.
to send on 1 to forward (mail). **2** to send (luggage) in advance.

to send up 1 to parody. 2 to ridicule.
3 to cause to go up. 4 (*N Am.*) to send
to prison. 5 to pass to a higher
authority.

sensation

to cause/ create a sensation to cause
surprise and excitement.

sense

horse sense HORSE.
in a/ one sense from one point of view.
in one's senses sane.
out of one's senses insane.
sixth sense SIXTH.
to bring someone to their senses 1 to make
someone understand that they are
doing something wrong, silly etc. 2 to
make someone conscious after they
have been unconscious.
to come to one's senses 1 to recover
consciousness. 2 to become sensible.
to lull into a false sense of security LULL.
to make sense to be intelligible (*The
message doesn't make sense*).
to make sense of to understand.
to take leave of one's senses LEAVE².
under a sense of wrong feeling wronged.

sentence

under sentence having received sentence
or judgement.
under sentence of condemned to (*under
sentence of death*).

separate¹

to separate the sheep from the goats to
sort a group into inferior and superior
members. [From the Bible: "And
before him shall be gathered all
nations: and he shall separate them
one from another, as a shepherd
divideth his sheep from the goats"
(Matt. xxv.32).]
to separate the wheat from the chaff to
separate or distinguish good things
from bad or useless things.

separate²

under separate cover in another envelope
or parcel (*invoice to follow under
separate cover*).

sepulchre

whited sepulchre WHITE.

sequel

in the sequel as things developed
afterwards.

serene

all serene (*sl.*) all right.

series

in series 1 in ordered succession. 2 (of
circuits etc.) arranged in a series.

serve

it will serve it will be adequate.
to serve a purpose to be useful.
to serve at table to act as waiter or
waitress.
to serve one's time 1 to serve one's
sentence. 2 to go through an
apprenticeship. 3 to hold an office etc.
for the full period.
to serve out 1 to distribute (portions of
food) to those at table. 2 (*dated, coll.*)
to have one's revenge on.
to serve out one's time (*esp. N Am.*) to
serve one's time.
to serve someone right to be what
someone deserved (as a punishment or
misfortune) (*It serves you right!*).
to serve someone's need(s) to be adequate
for someone.
to serve someone's purpose/ turn to be
suitable or adequate for someone's
needs.
to serve the purpose of to be used as.
to serve the turn to be adequate.
to serve up to serve out (food).

service

at someone's service ready to help
someone.

in service 1 working as a servant.
2 available for use. **3** on active
service.

on (active) service engaged in actual duty
in the army, navy etc.

out of service not available for use
(*The cash dispenser was out of
service*).

to be of service to be available to help.

to pay lip-service LIP-SERVICE.

to see service 1 to have experience, esp.
as a soldier or sailor. **2** to be put to
long or hard use.

to take service with to become a servant
to.

sesame

open sesame OPEN.

session

in session assembled for business.

set¹

all set (*coll.*) ready to start.

dead set against utterly opposed to.

dead set on determined on.

to get set 1 to get ready. **2** (*esp. Austral.,
coll.*) to place a bet.

to set about 1 to begin. **2** to prepare or
take steps (to do etc.). **3** (*coll.*) to
attack.

to set against 1 to oppose. **2** to balance
(one thing) against another. **3** to make
(a person) unfriendly to or prejudiced
against.

to set apart to separate, to reserve (for
some special purpose).

to set aside 1 to reserve (*I had set aside
some money for the fare home*). **2** to
reject. **3** to annul, to quash.

to set back 1 to turn backwards. **2** to
hinder the progress of, to impede.
3 (*coll.*) to cost (someone) usu. a large
amount of money (*That new car must
have set you back a bit*).

to set by 1 (*esp. N Am.*) to reserve.
2 (*esp. N Am.*) to lay by, to save.

to set down 1 to put on the ground. **2** to

let (a passenger) alight from a vehicle.
3 to put in writing, to note. **4** to
attribute. **5** to explain (as). **6** to snub, to
rebuke.

to set forth 1 to start (on a journey etc.).
2 to show, to demonstrate, to make
known. **3** to recommend.

to set forward 1 to promote, to help. **2** to
begin going forward.

to set in 1 to begin in a steady manner.
2 to come into fashion. **3** (of the tide)
to move steadily shoreward. **4** (of the
weather) to become settled. **5** to insert
(esp. a sleeve).

to set much/ little by to value highly/
little.

to set off 1 to make more attractive or
brilliant by contrast (*The shrubs at the
back of the border set off the daffodils
to perfection*). **2** to act as a foil to.
3 to beautify, to adorn. **4** to place over,
against, as an equivalent. **5** to start
(laughing etc.). **6** to set out. **7** to
detonate.

to set oneself 1 to apply oneself, to
undertake. **2** to resolve.

to set oneself up as to pretend to be.

to set on/ upon 1 to incite, to urge (to
attack) (*I'll set the dogs on you!*).
2 to employ (on a task). **3** to make an
attack on.

to set out 1 to start (upon a journey etc.).
2 to intend. **3** to display, to state at
length. **4** to mark off. **5** to assign, to
allot. **6** to equip. **7** to adorn, to
embellish. **8** to plant out. **9** to lay (a
stone etc.) so as to project.

to set over to put in authority over or in
control of.

to set to 1 to apply oneself vigorously.
2 to begin to fight.

to set up 1 to erect, to display. **2** to raise,
to exalt. **3** to establish. **4** to start a
business (as). **5** to cause to develop,
to occasion. **6** to begin to utter.
7 (*coll.*) to arrange for (someone else)
to be blamed, to frame. **8** to compose
(type). **9** to put (copy etc.) in type.

10 to supply the needs of. **11** to prepare. **12** to restore the health of. **13** to put forward (a theory).

set²

game, set and match GAME.

to have a set on (*Austral.*) to intend mischief to.

to make a dead set at DEAD.

settle

to settle down **1** to become regular in one's mode of life (*It's high time you got married and settled down*). **2** to begin to apply oneself (to a task etc.). **3** to become quiet, calm or orderly.

to settle for to accept, to be content with (*I had to settle for a cheaper model*).

to settle in to make or become comfortably established.

to settle someone's hash (*coll.*) to defeat someone completely.

to settle up **1** to pay what is owing. **2** to arrange (a matter) finally.

to settle with **1** to pay money due to (a creditor). **2** to deal with. **3** to get one's revenge for.

seven

at sixes and sevens SIX.

seventh

seventh heaven **1** the highest of the seven heavens believed by cabbalists and Muslims to be the dwelling place of God. **2** a state of supreme happiness (*in seventh heaven*).

sew

to sew up **1** to mend, join etc. by sewing. **2** (*sl.*) to exhaust, to nonplus. **3** (*sl.*) to complete satisfactorily (*I thought we had the deal sewn up*).

sex

the fair(er)/ gentle(r) sex the female sex, women.

shack

to shack up (with) (*sl.*) to live (with), usu. having a sexual relationship.

shade

to put in the shade to be superior to; to outdo.

shadow

a shadow of one's former self much less strong, healthy, cheerful etc. than before.

to cast a shadow over CAST.

worn to a shadow WORN.

shaggy

shaggy-dog story a long, inconsequential story, funny but lacking a punchline.

shake

in two shakes (of a lamb's tail) TWO.

no great shakes GREAT.

to shake a leg (*often imper.*) to hurry up.

to shake down **1** to bring down (fruit etc.) by shaking. **2** to cause (grain etc.) to settle into a compact mass. **3** to become compact. **4** to settle down into a comfortable or harmonious state. **5** (*N Am., sl.*) to extort money from.

to shake hands/ someone by the hand to clasp each other's right hand in token of friendship etc.

to shake in one's shoes to be very frightened.

to shake like a leaf to tremble violently, esp. with fear.

to shake off **1** to get rid of by shaking, to cast off. **2** to get rid of (someone who is following one) (*We finally managed to shake off the police*).

to shake one's fist to wave a clenched fist as a gesture of anger.

to shake one's head to move the head from side to side in token of refusal, dissent, disapproval etc.

to shake out **1** to open out or empty by shaking. **2** (*coll.*) to reduce (staff) as part of a drastic reorganization.

to shake the dust off one's feet to leave angrily. [From the Bible: "And whosoever shall not receive you, nor hear your words, when ye depart out of that house or city, shake off the dust of your feet" (Matt. x.14).]

to shake up 1 to mix, disturb etc. by shaking. **2** (*coll.*) to reorganize drastically. **3** to reshape by shaking. **4** to rouse or shock.

shaker

movers and shakers MOVER.

shall

shall I? do you want me to?

shame

crying shame CRYING.

for shame! used to reprove someone who should be ashamed.

shame on you! you should be ashamed.

to cry shame on CRY.

to put to shame to humiliate by exhibiting better qualities.

what a shame! how unfortunate!

shank

shanks's mare (*esp. N Am.*) shanks's pony.

shanks's pony one's legs for walking as opposed to riding etc. (*I came home on shanks's pony*).

shape

in any shape or form of any kind; at all (*I can't stand modern music in any shape or form*).

in the shape of in the form of (*temptation in the shape of a large cream cake*).

to knock into shape KNOCK.

to lick into shape LICK.

to shape up 1 to develop a shape. **2** to develop satisfactorily.

to take shape to become recognizable as or develop into something definite.

share

share and share alike in equal shares.

the lion's share LION.

to go shares to divide equally with others.

to share out to divide into equal shares and distribute.

sharp

sharp as a razor 1 very sharp. **2** very keen-witted.

sharp practice (*coll.*) underhand or questionable dealings.

to look sharp to be quick, to make haste.

sharp end

at the sharp end taking the most important or difficult part in any enterprise.

shave

close shave CLOSE[1].

shear

to shear off to break off vertically.

sheathe

to sheathe the sword to make peace.

sheep

black sheep BLACK.

one might as well be hung for a sheep as for a lamb HANG.

sheep's eyes 1 a bashful or diffident look. **2** a wishful or amorous glance (*to make sheep's eyes at someone*).

to count sheep COUNT.

to separate the sheep from the goats SEPARATE[1].

wolf in sheep's clothing WOLF.

sheer

to sheer off to move off, to go away.

sheet[1]

in sheets 1 (of a book) not bound. **2** (of rain) very heavy.

white as a sheet WHITE.

sheet²

sheet anchor 1 a large anchor, usu. one of two carried outside the waist of a ship for use in emergencies. **2** a chief support, a last refuge.

three sheets in/ to the wind THREE.

to sheet home to secure a sail with the sheet.

shelf

on the shelf 1 put aside, discarded.
2 (of a woman) considered too old to marry.

shell

to come out of one's shell to stop being shy or reserved. [Alluding to any animal that retreats into its shell when frightened.]

to shell out (*coll.*) to pay up, to pay the required sum.

shell game

to play a shell game (*coll.*) to trick or deceive someone. [Alluding to a trick performed by sleight of hand with three inverted containers under one of which something is hidden.]

shift

to make shift to manage, to contrive (to do, to get on etc.).

to shift about 1 to turn right round. **2** to prevaricate. **3** to be shifted from side to side.

to shift for oneself to depend on one's own efforts.

to shift off to get rid of, to defer.

to shift one's ground 1 to change the basis or premises of one's reasoning. **2** to try a different plan.

shilling

to take the King's/ Queen's shilling (*dated*) to enlist during the reign of a king or queen. [An allusion to the former practice of giving recruits a shilling as token of a contract.]

shine

(come) rain or (come) shine RAIN.

to take a shine to to like at first sight.

to take the shine off 1 to surpass, to eclipse. **2** to spoil the brilliance etc. of.

ship

ships that pass in the night people who meet briefly by chance. [From Henry Wadsworth Longfellow's poem 'The Theologian's Tale' (1874), from *Tales of a Wayside Inn*: "Ships that pass in the night, and speak each other in passing".]

to jump ship JUMP.

to run a tight ship TIGHT.

to ship a sea to have a wave come over the side of a vessel.

to ship off 1 to send by ship. **2** (*coll.*) to send (a person) away.

to spoil the ship for a ha'p'orth of tar SPOIL.

to take ship to embark.

when one's ship comes in/ home when one becomes rich. [Alluding to a merchant ship returning from foreign lands with valuable cargo.]

shipboard

on shipboard on board ship.

shipping

to take shipping to embark on board ship.

shiralee

to hump a shiralee HUMP.

shirt

stuffed shirt STUFFED.

the shirt off one's back (*coll.*) one's last remaining possessions.

to keep one's shirt on (*coll.*) to keep calm.

to lose one's shirt LOSE.

to put one's shirt on (*coll.*) to bet all one has on.

shirtsleeve

in one's shirtsleeves with one's coat off.

shit

in the shit (*taboo sl.*) in trouble.

no shit! (*taboo sl., esp. N Am.*) no fooling.

not to give a shit (*taboo sl.*) not to care at all.

up shit creek (without a paddle) (*taboo sl.*) in a very awkward situation.

when the shit hits the fan (*taboo sl.*) when the expected trouble arrives.

shiver[1]

to send shivers up/ down someone's spine to make someone tremble with fear, excitement etc.

shiver[2]

shiver my timbers an oath supposedly used by pirates.

shoe

dead men's shoes DEAD.

if the shoe fits (*N Am.*) if the general remark applies to you.

to be in someone's shoes to be in another's place or plight (*I wouldn't like to be in your shoes when the boss finds out!*).

to die in one's shoes DIE[1].

to shake in one's shoes SHAKE.

to step into someone's shoes STEP.

where the shoe pinches where one's problem is.

shook

shook on (*Austral., coll.*) keen on.

shook up (*coll.*) disturbed emotionally or physically; upset.

shoot

to have shot one's bolt to be unable to take further action. [From the bolt or arrow used in a crossbow.]

to shoot ahead to get swiftly to the front in running, swimming etc.

to shoot a line (*sl.*) to boast, to exaggerate.

to shoot down 1 to destroy or kill by shooting. **2** to defeat the argument of.

to shoot down in flames 1 to criticize severely. **2** to defeat soundly.

to shoot from the hip (*coll.*) to speak plainly or carelessly.

to shoot home to hit the target or mark.

to shoot it out (*sl.*) to fight using guns in order to settle a dispute.

to shoot one's bolt to do all in one's power.

to shoot one's mouth off (*sl.*) to speak boastfully or ill-advisedly (*shooting his mouth off about his enormous salary*).

to shoot through (*Austral., sl.*) to depart; to escape.

to shoot up 1 to grow rapidly. **2** (*sl.*) to inject drugs. **3** to terrorize (an area) by shooting.

shop

all over the shop 1 (*coll.*) scattered around. **2** (*coll.*) in every place. **3** (*coll.*) wildly.

bull in a china shop BULL.

knocking shop KNOCKING.

to mind the shop MIND.

to set up shop to start a business.

to shop around to try several shops to find the best value.

to shut up shop SHUT.

to talk shop TALK.

shore

in shore on the water near to the shore.

on shore ashore.

short

at short notice with little advance warning.

for short as an abbreviation (*called Nick for short*).

in short briefly, in few words.

in short order (*N Am.*) straight away. [A short order is an order in a restaurant for food that can be prepared quickly.]

in short supply scarce.

in the short run/ term over a short period of time.

short and sweet (*esp. iron.*) brief and pleasant.

short commons a scanty allowance of food.

short for a shortened form of.

short of 1 deficient in; lacking. **2** less than (*Her request was nothing short of blackmail*). **3** distant from. **4** except.

short of breath out of breath, short-winded.

short on (*coll.*) deficient in; lacking.

short shrift summary treatment (*to give someone short shrift*). [The phrase originally referred to the few minutes allowed for the confession of a criminal about to be executed.]

the long and the short of it LONG.

to be caught/ taken short 1 (*coll.*) to feel a sudden need to urinate or defecate. **2** to be put at a disadvantage.

to bring/ pull/ cut up short to check or pause abruptly.

to come short to be deficient, to fail.

to cut short 1 to hinder by interruption. **2** to abridge.

to draw the short straw to be the one selected for a difficult or unpleasant task. [From a method of drawing lots.]

to fall short 1 to be deficient. **2** to drop before reaching the mark or target.

to fall short of to fail to attain.

to get/ have by the short and curlies (*coll.*) to get/ have (someone) in one's power. [An allusion to seizing someone by the pubic hair.]

to go short not to have enough (*Her family never went short*).

to make short work of to deal with quickly and expeditiously.

shorten

to shorten sail to reduce the amount of sail spread.

shot[1]

like a shot immediately, eagerly.

long shot LONG.

not a shot in one's locker (having) no money in one's pocket. [Alluding to a store of ammunition.]

Parthian/ parting shot a look, word etc. delivered as a parting blow. [From the arrows shot by the Parthians, inhabitants of an ancient Asian kingdom, as they fled.]

shot across the bows a warning.

shot in the arm 1 (*coll.*) a hypodermic injection. **2** (*coll.*) something which encourages or invigorates.

shot in the dark a random guess.

to call the shots to be in charge, to determine what is going to happen.

to get shot of (*coll.*) to get rid of.

to give it one's best shot (*coll.*) to try one's very best.

to make a bad shot to guess incorrectly.

shot[2]

shot to pieces completely ruined or destroyed.

shotgun

shotgun wedding/ marriage (*coll.*) a hurried wedding, esp. because the bride is pregnant. [Probably from the idea that the bride's parents will shoot the groom unless he marries their daughter.]

to ride shotgun RIDE.

shoulder

an old head on young shoulders OLD.

chip on one's shoulder CHIP.

head and shoulders HEAD[1].

shoulder to cry on a person who listens sympathetically to the troubles of another.

shoulder to shoulder 1 (standing in rank) with shoulders nearly touching. **2** with hearty cooperation, with mutual effort.

straight from the shoulder STRAIGHT.

to give someone the cold shoulder COLD.

to have broad shoulders BROAD.

to put/ set one's shoulder to the wheel
to set to work enthusiastically or in
earnest. [Originally referring to the
wheel of a cart or wagon stuck in the
mud or a rut.]

to rub shoulders with RUB.

to shoulder arms to hold a rifle with the
barrel against one's shoulder.

to shrug one's shoulders SHRUG.

shout

all over bar the shouting (*coll.*) virtually
decided. [Referring to the official
announcement of the winner and the
cheering that follows.]

to shout down to silence or render
inaudible by shouting.

to shout for to call for by shouting.

to shout from the rooftops/ housetops to
announce very publicly.

to shout the odds (*coll.*) to talk loudly,
stridently, vehemently etc.

shove

to shove off 1 to push off from the shore
etc. 2 (*sl.*) to go away.

when push comes to shove PUSH.

show

bad show BAD.

for show for the sake of appearance.

good show! GOOD.

on show being displayed.

show of force a demonstration of
willingness to use force.

show of hands the raising of hands in
voting.

to get the show on the road (*coll.*) to
make a start, to put something into
operation or effect. [Originally
referring to a touring theatre
company.]

to give someone a fair show FAIR.

to give the (whole) show away 1 to let
out the real nature of something
pretentious. 2 to reveal a secret.

to run the show (*coll.*) to manage, to have
control of something in one's own
hands.

to show around (*N Am.*) to show round.

†to show forth to display, to make
manifest.

to show in to lead in.

to show off 1 to set off, to show to
advantage. 2 (*coll.*) to make a display
of oneself, one's talents etc.

to show oneself 1 to appear in public.
2 to reveal oneself (to be).

to show one's hand/ cards to reveal one's
intentions. [The phrase originally
referred to the act of showing the cards
in one's hand.]

to show out to lead out.

to show round to guide round (*The
foreman showed us round the factory*).

to show through 1 to be visible through.
2 to be revealed inadvertently.

to show up 1 to expose. 2 to be clearly
visible. 3 to arrive or be present.
4 (*coll.*) to embarrass or humiliate
(*She showed him up in front of his
team-mates*).

to steal the show STEAL.

shred

to tear to shreds TEAR[1].

shriek

to shriek of to give a clear indication of,
to reveal blatantly.

to shriek out to utter in a shriek.

to shriek with laughter to laugh
uncontrollably.

shrift

short shrift SHORT.

shrink

to shrink into oneself to become
withdrawn.

to shrink on to put (a tyre etc.) on in a
heated condition so that it may
become firmly fixed in contracting.

shrinking

shrinking violet (*coll.*) a shy, hesitant
person.

shrug

to shrug off 1 to disregard, to ignore (*He
shrugged off their criticism*). 2 to throw
off, to get rid of.

to shrug one's shoulders to show a lack of
interest or concern.

shtook

in shtook (*sl.*) in trouble.

shtoom

to keep shtoom (*sl.*) to keep quiet.

shuck

to shuck off to strip off.

shuffle

to shuffle the cards to change policy etc.

shut

put up or shut up! either defend yourself
or remain silent.

to get/ be shut of (*sl.*) to get/ be rid of.

to shut down 1 to pull or push down (a
window-sash etc.). 2 (of a factory) to
stop working. 3 to stop (a factory etc.)
from operating.

to shut in 1 to confine. 2 to encircle.
3 to prevent escape from or access to.

to shut off 1 to stop the inflow or escape
of (gas etc.) by closing a tap etc. 2 to
separate.

to shut one's face (*esp. imper., sl.*) to be
quiet (*Shut your face!*).

to shut one's heart to to refuse to or
pretend not to feel sympathy for.

to shut one's mind to to refuse to or
pretend not to think about.

to shut out 1 to exclude, to bar. 2 to
prevent the possibility of. 3 to block
from the memory. 4 (*N Am.*) to prevent
from scoring.

to shut the door on to prevent the
possibility of.

to shut to 1 to close (a door). 2 (of a door)
to shut.

to shut up 1 to close all the doors,
windows etc. of (a house). 2 to close
and fasten up (a box etc.). 3 to put
away in a box etc. 4 to confine. 5 (*coll.*)
to stop, to make an end. 6 (*esp. imper.,
coll.*) (to cause someone) to become
silent or stop talking.

to shut up shop to give up doing
something.

shutter

to put up the shutters to cease business.

shy

to have a shy at 1 (*coll.*) to try to hit with
an object. 2 (*coll.*) to try. 3 (*coll.*) to jeer
at.

sick

sick and tired of bored and exhausted by,
fed up with (*I'm sick and tired of this
job*).

sick as a dog very sick, vomiting
profusely.

sick as a parrot (*coll., facet.*) extremely
upset or disappointed. [Perhaps an
allusion to parrot fever or psittacosis.]

sick to death thoroughly fed up (*I'm sick
to death of hearing about her
wonderful daughter*).

sick to one's stomach 1 (*esp. N Am.*)
affected with nausea, vomiting.
2 (*esp. N Am.*) disgusted, revolted.

to be sick to vomit.

to go sick to be absent from one's work or
duties through illness (real or claimed).

to look sick (*coll.*) to be outranked or
outshone, to be deficient in
comparison.

to make someone sick to disgust or
nauseate someone (*It makes me sick to
see taxpayers' money being wasted in
this way*).

to sick out (*N Am., W Ind.*) (of a
workforce) to report sick universally
and simultaneously.

to take sick (*esp. N Am.*) to become ill.

sick list
on the sick list laid up by illness.

side
bit on the side BIT[1].

born on the wrong side of the blanket
BORN.

by the side of 1 alongside, close to. **2** in
comparison with.

from all sides from every direction.

from side to side 1 all the way across.
2 one way then the other from a
central line or path (*swaying from
side to side*).

like the side of a house (*coll.*) very large
or fat.

on all sides in every direction,
everywhere.

on one side 1 away in one direction from
a central or principal position. **2** aside.

on the right side of RIGHT SIDE.

on the short/ long/ etc. side slightly too
short, long etc. (*He's a bit on the
young side for this job*).

on the side 1 in addition to the usual,
principal or known. **2** in addition to,
or apart from, the main aim, or one's
main occupation or income, applied
esp. to an underhand or illicit
arrangement.

on the side of the angels agreeing with
what seems morally correct. [From a
speech made in 1864 by Benjamin
Disraeli on the subject of Darwin's
theory of evolution: "Is man an ape or
an angel? Now I am on the side of the
angels."]

on the wrong side of WRONG.

on the wrong side of the tracks WRONG.

on this side of the grave during one's life.

right side out RIGHT SIDE.

side by side close together (for strength or
support etc.).

sunny side up SUNNY SIDE.

the other side of the coin OTHER.

this side of not going as far as, short of
(*Keep this side of plagiarism*).

to be on the safe side SAFE.

to change sides CHANGE.

to choose sides CHOOSE.

to err on the side of ERR.

to get on the wrong side of WRONG.

**to know which side one's bread is buttered
(on)** to know where one's best interests
lie.

to laugh on the other side of one's face
LAUGH.

to let the side down (*coll.*) (of an
individual) to bring discredit on a
team or group by failing to achieve
the same standard of performance or
behaviour as its other members.

to look on the bright side BRIGHT.

to pass by on the other side OTHER.

to split one's sides SPLIT.

to take sides to support one side in an
argument etc.

wrong side out WRONG.

sideline
on/ from the sidelines in/ from a position
that is at some distance from the main
action (*His injury kept him out of the
match, and he could only watch from
the sidelines*).

siege
to lay siege to 1 to besiege. **2** to
importune.

under siege 1 being besieged. **2** subjected
to constant attack or criticism.

sieve
to have a head like a sieve HEAD[1].

sight
a sight (*coll.*) a great deal (*She's got a
sight more common sense than you
have*).

at first sight FIRST.

in/ within sight 1 visible. **2** having a view
(of). **3** not far off.

on/ at sight 1 as soon as seen,
immediately (*Intruders will be shot
on sight*). **2** (of a bill, to be paid) on
presentation.

out of sight 1 not in a position to be seen, or to have a view or be in view (of). **2** having disappeared, e.g. into the distance. **3** forgotten, ignored. **4** (*dated, coll.*) excellent.

out of sight, out of mind it is easy to forget people or things that are no longer present or visible.

second sight SECOND.

sight for sore eyes/ for the gods (*coll.*) a person or thing one is pleased to see, a welcome visitor.

sight unseen without previous inspection (of the object to be bought etc.).

to catch sight of CATCH.

to get a sight of to glimpse, to manage to see.

to have in one's sights 1 to have as the object of one's desires or ambition (*She has the presidency in her sights*). **2** to be close enough to (a target) to have hopes of reaching or achieving (*The Liberals have overtaken the Tories in the latest polls and now have Labour in their sights*). [Alluding to the sighting device on a firearm etc., used in taking aim.]

to have lost sight of LOSE.

to heave in(to) sight HEAVE.

to know by sight to know well enough to recognize (but not to speak to).

to look a sight to look untidy or disreputable.

to lose sight of LOSE.

to lower one's sights LOWER.

to put out of sight to put away, to ignore.

to set one's sights on to have as one's goal, or the object of one's desires or ambition. [Alluding to the sighting device on a firearm etc., used in taking aim.]

sign

sign of the times anything that serves as an indication of sociological change or development.

to sign away to transfer or convey by signing a deed.

to sign for to acknowledge receipt of by signing.

to sign in to record arrival by signing.

to sign off 1 to stop work for the time. **2** to end a letter by signing. **3** to stop broadcasting, with a verbal announcement etc. **4** to discharge from employment. **5** formally to cease collecting unemployment benefit. **6** in bridge, to make a conventional bid indicating that one wishes to end the bidding. **7** to declare (a sick person) temporarily unfit for work (*The doctor signed me off for two weeks*).

to sign on 1 to commit (oneself or another) to an undertaking or employment. **2** to register as unemployed. **3** to begin broadcasting, with a verbal announcement etc.

to sign on the dotted line to finalize a formal and binding agreement, esp. by signing a document.

to sign out to record departure by signing.

to sign up 1 to commit (oneself or another) to an undertaking or employment. **2** to enlist, to enrol.

signal

to signal off/ on to signal for/ against a train proceeding.

silence

conspiracy of silence CONSPIRACY.

in silence without a word or sound.

silence is golden it is often advisable to keep quiet. [From the old proverb 'speech is silver, silence is golden'.]

to reduce to silence REDUCE.

silent

silent majority the large majority of a population who have moderate views but who do not bother to express them. [The current meaning of this phrase dates from its use in a speech by the US president Richard Nixon in 1969. It originally referred to the dead.]

silhouette

in silhouette as a dark shape or outline.

silk

to take silk to exchange a gown of ordinary fabric for one of silk, esp. to become a KC or QC.

you can't make a silk purse out of a sow's ear you cannot produce something good from inferior materials.

silly

silly season the late summer, when newspapers are traditionally full of trivial stories, for lack of anything serious to print.

silver

born with a silver spoon in one's mouth BORN.

silver lining

every cloud has a silver lining CLOUD.

simmer

to simmer down to become less agitated or excited, to calm down.

sin

as sin (*coll.*) to a degree, extremely, very (*ugly as sin*).

for one's sins (*facet.*) literally, as a judgement upon one, meaning little more than 'as it happens' (*I'm a journalist, for my sins!*).

like sin (*coll.*) intensely (*She hates him like sin*).

to cover a multitude of sins COVER.

to live in sin LIVE[1].

sincerely

yours sincerely a conventional way of ending a formal or business letter.

sing

to sing along (of an audience) to accompany a performer in singing popular songs.

to sing for one's supper to perform a task in order to receive a benefit.

to sing out to call out loudly, to shout.

to sing the praises of to commend warmly, to proclaim the virtues of.

to sing up to sing more loudly and enthusiastically.

singe

to singe one's wings to take a risk and come off badly. [Perhaps an allusion to moths drawn to a flame, or to the Greek legend of Icarus, who flew too close to the sun.]

single

to single out to pick out from among others (*singled out for special treatment*).

sink

all/ everything but the kitchen sink KITCHEN.

to sink in 1 to become absorbed, to penetrate. 2 to become understood (*The full horror of the situation finally sank in*).

to sink or swim to face the alternatives of failure or success (in a venture etc.) (*They said the job was a demanding one, and it was up to me to sink or swim*).

sinker

hook, line and sinker HOOK.

sinking

sinking feeling the uncomfortable feeling in the abdomen brought on by e.g. nervousness or hunger.

sit

sitting pretty in an advantageous position.

to make someone sit up to surprise someone, or attract their attention (*This will make them sit up and take notice!*).

†to sit at meat to sit at table.

to sit at the feet of to be taught by (a certain teacher, esp. a famous one).

to sit back to withdraw from active participation (*I intend to sit back and let the others do all the work*).

to sit below the gangway to sit as a more or less independent member of the House of Commons.

to sit by to observe without taking an active part.

to sit down 1 to place oneself on a seat, or in a sitting position, after standing. 2 to place in a sitting position, to cause to sit. 3 to begin a siege.

to sit down under to submit meekly to (an insult or insulting treatment).

to sit for 1 to take (an examination). 2 to represent (a constituency in parliament). 3 to pose for (a portrait).

to sit heavy on the stomach to be difficult to digest.

to sit in to occupy premises as a form of protest.

to sit in judgement to pass judgement on the actions of others, to be critical.

to sit in on to observe, be present at, or participate in (a discussion, meeting, lecture etc.) as a visitor.

to sit loosely on (of the duties of office) to be taken rather lightly by.

to sit on 1 to hold a meeting, discussion or investigation over. 2 (*coll.*) to repress severely, to snub. 3 (*coll.*) to suppress or prevent from circulating.

to sit on one's hands 1 not to act or intervene. 2 not to applaud.

to sit on the fence to remain neutral in respect to opposing policies.

to sit out 1 to sit out of doors. 2 to sit apart from (a dance, meeting etc.). 3 to stay till the end of (a concert etc., or an uncomfortable episode). 4 to stay longer than (other visitors).

to sit tight to hold firm and do nothing.

to sit under to attend the ministrations of (a member of the clergy).

to sit up 1 to rise from a recumbent position. 2 to sit with the body erect. 3 suddenly to pay attention, take notice or become alert (*to sit up and take notice*). 4 not to go to bed.

site

on site (available) at the workplace or place of activity.

sitting

sitting duck/ target an easy target, someone in a defenceless position.

situation

situations vacant a heading used to introduce lists of jobs offered.

situations wanted a heading used to introduce lists of jobs sought.

six

at sixes and sevens in disorder or confusion. [Probably from a game of dice.]

six (of one) and half a dozen (of the other) a dilemma presenting alternatives of equal acceptability, merit etc. [From Captain Marryat's novel *The Pirate* (1836): "I never knows the children. It's just six of one and half-a-dozen of the other."]

six of the best a severe beating, esp. with a cane.

to knock/ hit for six 1 to overcome completely, to defeat. 2 to astonish. 3 to stagger. [From the game of cricket, referring to a hit over the boundary that is worth six runs.]

sixpence

on a sixpence 1 within a small area (*turn on a sixpence*). 2 easily, quickly.

sixth

sixth sense the power of intuition, or extrasensory perception.

sixty

sixty-four thousand dollar question the crucial question. [From the final and most difficult question in a television quiz show of US origin, this sum of money being the prize for the correct answer.]

size

of a size all having the same size.

of some size fairly big.

the size of as large as.

the size of it the situation as it really is (*That's about the size of it*).

to cut someone down to size to cause someone to feel less important or be less conceited by exposing their limitations.

to size up 1 to form a rough estimate of the size of. **2** to judge the capacity of (a person).

to try for size TRY.

what size? how big?

skate

to get one's skates on (*coll.*) to hurry up.

to skate around to avoid talking about or confronting (an issue, subject etc.) directly.

to skate on thin ice to take up a risky stance when not altogether certain of one's ground.

to skate over to gloss over or hurry over (a topic that calls for direct confrontation).

skeleton

skeleton at the feast a person or thing that acts as a reminder of something less happy or pleasant, often spoiling the enjoyment of others. [From the ancient Egyptian custom of placing a skeleton in a prominent position at their banquets.]

skeleton in the cupboard/ closet an unpleasant or shameful secret from the past.

skeleton staff a staff reduced to the minimum number able to run a factory, office etc.

skerrick

not a skerrick left (*esp. Austral., New Zeal.*) nothing left at all.

sketch

to sketch in/ out to indicate roughly or in outline only.

skew

on the skew skewed, slanting, crooked.

skid

on the skids 1 (*coll.*) due to be abandoned or defeated. **2** (*coll.*) due to be launched.

to hit the skids HIT.

to put the skids under 1 (*coll.*) to speed the collapse or departure of. **2** (*coll.*) to hurry (someone) up.

skim

to skim the cream off to remove the best part from.

skin

beauty is only skin deep BEAUTY.

by/ with the skin of one's teeth very narrowly (*We avoided defeat by the skin of our teeth*). [From the Bible: "My bone cleaveth to my skin and to my flesh, and I am escaped with the skin of my teeth" (Job xix.20).]

no skin off someone's nose making no difference to someone, possibly even encouraging rather than perturbing to someone (*If she wants to make a fool of herself, it's no skin off my nose*).

soaked/ wet to the skin with all one's clothing thoroughly soaked.

to be (all) skin and bone to be extremely thin or emaciated.

to get under someone's skin to interest or annoy someone intensely.

to have a thick skin THICK.

to have a thin skin THIN.
to hit skins HIT.
to jump out of one's skin JUMP.
with a whole skin WHOLE.

skip
skip it! (*coll.*) forget it! never mind!

skite
on the skite (*Sc.*) on a drinking spree.

skittle
beer and skittles BEER.
to skittle out in cricket, to dismiss
    (batsmen) in quick succession.

skull
out of one's skull 1 (*sl.*) out of one's mind,
    crazy. 2 (*sl.*) helplessly drunk.

sky
out of a clear sky CLEAR.
pie in the sky PIE.
the sky is the limit there's virtually no
    limit (e.g. to a potential sum, or to the
    possibilities for achievement).
to praise someone/ something to the skies
    PRAISE.
under the open sky OPEN.

slack
to slack off 1 to shirk work. 2 to slacken
    off.
to slack up 1 to slow down (a train)
    before stopping. 2 to ease off.
to take up the slack 1 to gather up the
    loose portion of a rope. 2 to use
    surplus resources or time to good
    effect.

slacken
to slacken off 1 to loosen, to reduce the
    tension on (a rope etc.). 2 to lose speed
    or momentum.

slag
to slag off (*sl.*) to make disparaging
    remarks about.

slanging
slanging match a quarrel in which strong
    insults are exchanged.

slant
on a/ the slant sloping, aslant.

slap
slap and tickle (*facet.*) flirtatious romping,
    kissing and cuddling.
slap in the face a rebuff.
slap on the back an offer of
    congratulations.
slap on the wrist a reprimand.
to slap down to rebuff or rebuke curtly
    and unequivocally.
to slap on the back to congratulate.

slate
on the slate on credit, recorded as a debt.
    [Alluding to a piece of slate used as a
    writing-tablet.]
to have a slate loose (*coll.*) to be slightly
    mentally unbalanced. [Alluding to a
    piece of slate used as a roofing-tile.]
to wipe the slate clean WIPE.

slaughter
like a lamb to the slaughter LAMB.

sledgehammer
to take a sledgehammer to crack a
    walnut/ nut to use an excessive
    amount of force, effort etc. to tackle a
    simple problem.

sleep
in one's sleep while asleep (*She talks in
    her sleep*).
not to sleep a wink to have no sleep at
    all.
to get to sleep to manage to go to sleep.
to go to sleep to fall asleep.
to let sleeping dogs lie to leave well alone.
to lose sleep over LOSE.
to put to sleep 1 to anaesthetize.
    2 (*euphem.*) to kill (an animal)
    painlessly, usu. by injection.

to sleep around (*coll.*) to be sexually promiscuous.

to sleep in 1 to sleep on the premises. **2** to oversleep.

to sleep like a log to sleep very soundly.

to sleep like a top to be in a deep sleep.

to sleep off to get rid of or recover from (e.g. the effects of alcohol) by sleeping.

to sleep on it to postpone making a decision until the next day.

to sleep out 1 to sleep out of doors. **2** to have one's sleeping accommodation away from one's place of work.

to sleep over to spend the night where one is visiting.

to sleep rough to sleep out of doors, esp. on the street.

to sleep the sleep of the just (*usu. facet.*) to enjoy sound untroubled sleep.

to sleep with someone (*euphem.*) to have sexual intercourse with someone, esp. in bed (*Are they sleeping together?*).

sleeve

ace/ card up one's sleeve a plan or resource held secretly in reserve or in readiness; an undisclosed advantage. [Alluding to a way of cheating in a game of cards by concealing a high-scoring card about one's person.]

to have up one's sleeve to hold secretly in reserve or in readiness. [From the tricks of a conjuror or someone cheating at cards.]

to laugh up/ in one's sleeve LAUGH.

to roll up one's sleeves ROLL.

to wear one's heart on one's sleeve WEAR.

slice

slice of life an experience that brings home the grim realities of life.

slice of the cake one's fair share of the benefits.

slide

to let things slide to leave things undone,

or take no positive action over them, to allow things to deteriorate.

slight

not in the slightest not at all.

to put a slight upon to belittle or disparage.

sling

to sling off at (*Austral., New Zeal., sl.*) to jeer at or disparage.

to sling one's hook 1 (*sl.*) to decamp. **2** (*sl.*) to run away.

slip¹

Freudian slip FREUDIAN.

slip of the tongue/ pen a mistake in speaking/ writing.

there's many a slip 'twixt cup and lip nothing is certain to succeed, things may go wrong at any stage.

to give the slip to escape from, to evade.

to let slip 1 to allow to escape. **2** to lose, to miss. **3** to reveal inadvertently (*He let slip that he had been in prison*).

to let slip through one's fingers 1 to lose hold of. **2** to miss the chance of getting (*I'm not going to let a job like that slip through my fingers!*).

to slip away/ off to leave quickly or unobtrusively.

to slip someone's mind to be forgotten.

to slip the collar to free oneself.

to slip up to make a mistake.

slip²

a slip of a merely a slight, young (girl etc.).

slippery

slippery as an eel 1 very difficult to grasp or keep hold of. **2** very evasive or dishonest.

slippy

to look slippy (*coll.*) to hurry, to look sharp.

slop

to slop about to shamble or slouch.

to slop out (of prisoners) to clean out slops from a chamber pot.

to slop over (*esp. N Am.*) to be too effusive, to gush.

slope

to slope arms to position a rifle on the shoulder with the barrel pointing up and back.

to slope off (*coll.*) to leave, esp. furtively, to sneak away.

slouch

to be no slouch (*coll.*) to be quick and efficient (at doing something).

slow

slow and sure steady and methodical.

slow but sure finally achieving results.

slug

to slug it out 1 to fight it out. **2** to stick it out, to keep going to the end.

slum

to slum it (*coll.*) to make do with less comfortable or luxurious conditions than one is used to.

sly

on the sly slyly, in secret, on the quiet.

sly dog a cunning or secretive person.

smack

smack in the eye/ face (*coll.*) a snub or rebuff.

to have a smack at (*coll.*) to tackle, to have a go at.

to smack one's lips to part one's lips making a loud smacking noise as a sign of appetite, gleeful anticipation etc.

small

in a small way on a small or unambitious scale.

it's a small world used to express surprise at a coincidence (*The chap sitting next to me on the flight turned out to have been at school with my sister: it's a small world!*).

no small considerable, substantial, significant, rather a lot of (*no small feat*; *with no small dismay*).

small hours the time from midnight till 3 or 4 a.m., the early hours of the morning.

small mercies minor benefits or lucky breaks that one is reminded to be grateful for (*We must be thankful for small mercies*).

small potatoes (*sl.*) an insignificant person or unimportant matter.

small print 1 matter printed in a small typeface. **2** the unobtrusively printed reservations or restrictions in a policy or contract document.

small profits and quick returns the policy of selling cheap but on a large scale.

small talk light social conversation on superficial topics (*I'm no good at small talk!*).

small wonder 1 it is hardly surprising (that etc.). **2** naturally, of course.

to look small to be publicly humiliated, to appear insignificant (*make someone look small*).

small beer

to be small beer 1 to be unimportant, trivial or insignificant. **2** to lack power and influence. [Small beer is beer of a mild, light or weak quality. The phrase is used figuratively in Shakespeare's *Othello*: "To suckle fools and chronicle small beer."]

small fry

to be small fry to be insignificant or unimportant. [Small fry are small young fishes.]

smart

smart alec (*coll.*) someone who thinks they know everything.

to look smart to hurry up, to be quick.

smash

to go to smash (*coll.*) to suffer financial ruin.

smell

to smell a rat to be suspicious.

to smell of the lamp (of a speech, sermon etc.) to show signs of laborious preparation. [Alluding to work that continues long into the night, done by the light of an oil lamp.]

to smell out 1 to detect by instinct or prying. **2** to pollute (e.g. a room with smoke).

smile

to be all smiles to look very happy.

to come up smiling to end up in a favourable state, esp. after misfortune.

to smile on to show favour or approval to (*Fortune smiled on us that day*).

to wipe the smile off someone's face WIPE.

wreathed in smiles WREATHE.

smite

to smite hip and thigh to overthrow completely, to slaughter without mercy. [From the Bible: "And he smote them hip and thigh with a great slaughter" (Judg. xv.8), referring to Samson's revenge on the Philistines.]

smoke

no smoke without fire rumours are usually not without foundation.

to go/ end up in smoke 1 (of a scheme, a desire) to come to nothing. **2** to be destroyed by fire.

to smoke like a chimney (*coll.*) to smoke a lot of cigarettes.

to smoke out 1 to exterminate or drive out with smoke. **2** to discover, to force into the open.

smooth

in smooth water out of difficulty, having passed the worst.

to smooth over to gloss over (a difficulty).

to smooth someone's (ruffled) feathers to calm someone down.

snail

snail's pace a slow rate of progress.

snake

snake in the grass a treacherous or underhand person. [From Virgil's *Eclogues* (42–37 BC): "There is a snake hidden in the grass."]

snap

to snap off 1 to break off. **2** to bite off.

to snap one's fingers (at) to show contempt or defiance (of).

to snap out to say crossly.

to snap out of it to change one's mood abruptly (for the better).

to snap someone's head/ nose off to retort abruptly, irritably or rudely.

to snap up 1 to take quick advantage of (a bargain etc.), to purchase eagerly. **2** to grab quickly. **3** to interrupt (someone) while they are still speaking.

snappy

to make it snappy to hurry up.

snarl

to snarl up to (cause to) become tangled, disordered, inoperable, immobile etc.

snatch

by/ in snatches desultorily, in fits and starts.

sneak

to sneak away/ off to leave unobtrusively.

sneeze

not to be sneezed at not to be despised, worth consideration.

sniff

to sniff at 1 to investigate by sniffing. **2** to express contempt or disdain for.

to sniff out to discover (as if) by sniffing, to find through investigation.

snit

in a snit (*N Am., coll.*) sulking, in a rage.

snook

to cock a snook COCK[2].

snow

pure as the driven snow PURE.
to snow under (*usu. pass.*) to overwhelm (with work etc.) (*I'm snowed under with essays to mark*).

snowball

not to have a snowball's chance in hell to have no likelihood of success whatsoever.

snuff[1]

to snuff it (*sl.*) to die. [An allusion to snuffing out a candle.]
to snuff out 1 to put out, to extinguish (a candle etc.). 2 (*sl.*) to kill.

snuff[2]

up to snuff 1 knowing, sharp, not easily imposed upon. 2 in good condition, fulfilling the desired standard or requirements.

snug

snug as a bug in a rug (*coll.*) very cosy or comfortable.

so

and so forth/ on and the rest, and the like.
is that so? really?
or so or thereabouts, or about that.
so-and-so 1 an indefinite person or thing. 2 an unpleasant person or disliked thing.
so as to in order to (*I kept pinching myself so as to keep awake*).
so be it let it be thus (in affirmation, resignation etc.).
so-so indifferent, middling, mediocre.
so that in order that (*We moved into town so that we could be nearer my mother*).
so what? what about it?

soak

to soak in to become fully understood, appreciated, felt etc., to penetrate.
to soak oneself in to become thoroughly acquainted with or steeped in (a subject etc.).

soap

soft soap SOFT.

sob

sob story a hard-luck story intended to elicit pity.

sober

sober as a judge entirely sober.

sock[1]

put a sock in it (*sl.*) be quiet, shut up.
to blow the socks off BLOW[1].
to knock the socks off KNOCK.
to pull one's socks up to make a vigorous effort to do better.

sock[2]

to sock it to to address or attack with great vigour or force.

sod[1]

under the sod in one's grave.

sod[2]

odds and sods ODD.
sod all (*sl.*) nothing at all.
sod off (*sl.*) go away, get lost.
Sod's law the maxim that if something can go wrong it will.

Sodom

apple of Sodom APPLE.

soft

soft in the head feeble-minded, foolish.
soft option an option offering least difficulty.
soft soap 1 semi-liquid soap made with potash. 2 (*coll.*) flattery, blarney.

to **be soft on 1** to be lenient or
sympathetic towards. **2** to be
amorously inclined towards.
to **have a soft spot for** to be fond of (a
person).

soften

to **soften up 1** to make more sympathetic.
2 to break down the resistance of.
3 to reduce the effectiveness of the
defences of (a targeted position etc.)
e.g. by preliminary bombing.

solace

to **solace oneself with** to find comfort in.

soldier

to **come the old soldier** OLD.
to **soldier on** to persevere doggedly, esp.
in the face of difficulty (*soldier on
regardless*).

some

and then some (*sl.*) and a lot more.
some few not a great number.

something

or something used to indicate a further
unspecified possibility (*The train must
be late or something*).
quite something a remarkable person or
thing.
something of to some extent, in some
way (*She's something of an expert on
early music*).
something of the kind something
similar.
something tells me I think, I suspect
(*Something tells me you've done this
before!*).
to **have something on someone** HAVE.
to **say something** to make a short
speech.
to **say something for** to show the high
quality of.
to **see something of** to meet (someone)
occasionally.

somewhat

more than somewhat considerably (*I was
more than somewhat annoyed*).

somewhere

somewhere about approximately (*aged
somewhere about 45*).
to **get somewhere** to make headway, to
progress.

son

every mother's son MOTHER.
like father, like son FATHER.
son of a bitch (*derog.*) a man.
son of a gun a rascal. [Of nautical origin,
referring to the son of a sailor or a
child of uncertain paternity born on
board ship.]

song

for a song for a trifle, very cheaply (*I
bought it for a song; going for a song*).
[From Shakespeare's *All's Well That
Ends Well*: "I know a man that had
this trick of melancholy sold a goodly
manor for a song."]
to **be on song** to be in top form, to be
performing at one's best.
to **make a song and dance** to make a fuss
(about).
wine, women and song WINE.

soon

as/ so soon as 1 at the moment that
(*as soon as possible*). **2** immediately
after (*I'll ring as soon as I hear*).
3 not later than (*He went to bed as
soon as the clock struck eleven*).

sooner

no sooner ... than immediately (*No
sooner did she make the promise
than she withdrew it*).
sooner or later 1 sometime or other.
2 inevitably, eventually.
the sooner the better as quickly as
possible.

sooth

†in good sooth in truth.

sop

sop to Cerberus a propitiatory bribe.
[In classical mythology, Cerberus was
a three-headed dog that guarded the
entrance of Hades. The ancient Greeks
and Romans used to put a cake in the
hands of a dead person as a bribe for
safe passage into the underworld.]

sore

sore point a subject etc. which arouses
irritation, annoyance, retrospective
hurt feelings etc.

sorrow

more in sorrow than in anger showing
or feeling sadness rather than anger.
[From Shakespeare's *Hamlet*: "A
countenance more in sorrow than
in anger", referring to the ghost of
Hamlet's father.]
to drown one's sorrows DROWN.

sort

after a sort in a (usu. inadequate) way or
fashion.
in some sort after a sort, to a certain
extent.
it takes all sorts (to make a world) a
comment on the diversity of human
opinion, taste, behaviour etc., usu. said
of someone who differs from oneself.
of sorts/ a sort of an inferior or
inadequate kind (*a dancer of sorts*).
out of sorts 1 irritable, moody. 2 slightly
unwell.
sort of rather, to a degree, as it were (*sort
of unsettled*).
to sort out 1 to solve or resolve. 2 to clear
out; to tidy up. 3 to separate. 4 to
arrange. 5 (*coll.*) to beat, to punish.

soul

bless/ upon my soul! used to express
surprise etc.

God rest his/ her soul GOD.
heart and soul HEART.
not able to call one's soul one's own in
someone else's control, not
independent.
the life and soul LIFE.
to bare one's soul BARE.
to be the soul of honour to be incapable
of acting dishonourably.
to keep body and soul together BODY.
to sell one's soul SELL.

sound[1]

to sound off 1 to boast. 2 to speak loudly,
volubly, angrily etc. (*sounding off
about the government*).

sound[2]

sound as a bell perfectly sound, free from
any flaw.

sound[3]

to sound out 1 to test, to examine, to
endeavour to discover (intentions,
feelings etc.). 2 to test the reaction of
(someone) to a proposition etc.

soup

in the soup (*sl.*) in difficulties, in trouble.
to soup up to modify (the engine of a car
or motorcycle) in order to increase its
power.

sour

sour grapes peevish disdain for a desired
object that is out of one's reach. [From
Aesop's fable about a fox who tried to
get at a bunch of grapes: on finding
them to be out of his reach he claimed
not to want them because they were
sour.]
to go/ turn sour 1 to become sour. 2 to
lose attraction or become distasteful.

source

at source at the point of issue (*tax
deducted at source*).

south
north and south NORTH.
south of further south than.
to the south in a southerly direction.

sow¹
to sow one's (wild) oats to indulge in youthful (esp. sexual) excess.
to sow the seed(s) of to introduce, initiate or implant (a doubt, a suspicion etc.).

sow²
you can't make a silk purse out of a sow's ear SILK.

space
to space out to place at wider intervals.

spade¹
to call a spade a spade to be outspoken, to speak plainly.

spade²
black as the ace of spades BLACK.
in spades (*coll.*) to an extreme degree. [From card games in which spades rank higher than other suits.]

span
spick and span SPICK.

spanner
spanner in the works an impediment, a cause of confusion or difficulty (*to throw a spanner in the works*).

spare
not to spare oneself to do one's utmost, to give utterly dedicated service.
spare the rod and spoil the child children should be strictly disciplined, punishment is good for a child. [From the Bible: "He that spareth his rod hateth his son: but he that loveth him chasteneth him betimes" (Prov. xiii.24).]
spare tyre 1 a tyre carried in a vehicle as a replacement in case of a puncture.

2 (*coll.*) a bulge of fat around the midriff.
to go spare (*coll.*) to become excessively angry, agitated or distraught.
to spare extra, surplus, more than required (*plenty to spare*).
to spare someone's blushes to avoid embarrassing someone by praising them too much.

spark
bright spark BRIGHT.
to make sparks fly to start a violent quarrel, to cause a row.
to spark off 1 to kindle (a process, someone's interest etc.). **2** to galvanize into activity.

speak
broadly speaking speaking in a general way.
nothing/ none to speak of nothing important or significant, none worth mentioning.
roughly speaking approximately.
so to speak in a sense, as it were.
spoken for allocated, reserved, claimed.
to speak as one finds to base one's opinions on personal experience.
to speak by the card to speak with exactness.
to speak evil of to slander, to defame.
to speak for 1 to be spokesperson for. **2** to act as an advocate for, to represent, to witness to.
to speak for itself (of a circumstance, condition etc.) not to need further evidence or explanation, to have an obvious meaning.
to speak for oneself to be one's own advocate.
to speak ill to speak unfavourably (of or about) (*Do not speak ill of the dead*).
to speak of to mention.
to speak one's mind to speak freely and frankly.
to speak out 1 to speak loudly and articulately. **2** to express one's opinion frankly.

to speak the same language to have a similar background, outlook, habits of mind, tastes etc.

to speak through one's nose to have a nasal quality to one's voice.

to speak to 1 to address. **2** to speak in support or confirmation of (*She spoke to the general view*). **3** (*coll.*) to reprimand, to reprove (*I shall have to speak to him*).

to speak too soon to make a statement that takes something as yet uncertain for granted (*Don't speak too soon: we could still lose*).

to speak to someone's heart to comfort, encourage or cheer someone.

to speak up 1 to speak loudly. **2** to speak without constraint, to express one's opinion freely.

to speak volumes 1 (of a circumstance) to be of great or peculiar significance **2** to constitute abundant evidence (for) (*His good manners speak volumes for the excellence of his upbringing*).

to speak well 1 to make favourable mention (of). **2** to be abundant evidence (for).

speaking

in a manner of speaking MANNER.

on speaking terms 1 amicable towards one another (*They're hardly on speaking terms these days*). **2** slightly acquainted.

spec

on spec (*coll.*) on the off chance, in the hope of success, as a gamble.

specie

in specie 1 in coin. **2** in kind.

spectacle

to make a spectacle of oneself to do something that makes people stare or laugh at one.

spectacles

to see through rose-coloured/ -tinted spectacles ROSE.

speed

at speed while moving quickly.

more haste, less speed HASTE.

to gather speed GATHER.

to speed up 1 to progress faster. **2** to cause to progress faster, to expedite.

spell¹

to spell it out to explain things fully and simply, as distinct from hinting or alluding (*Do I have to spell it out for you?*).

to spell out 1 to utter or write letter by letter (*She spelt out her name*). **2** to make clear or easy to understand. **3** to puzzle out.

spell²

under a spell dominated by, or as if by, a spell.

spend

to spend a penny (*coll.*) to urinate. [From the former cost of using public conveniences.]

to spend money like water to spend money rashly and in large quantities.

spice

variety is the spice of life VARIETY.

spick

spick and span clean and smart, new and fresh. [From the phrase 'spick and span new', applied e.g. to a ship in which every part is new.]

spike

to spike someone's guns to foil someone's plans. [From the former military practice of making an enemy cannon useless by plugging the priming hole with a spike.]

spill

thrills and spills THRILL.

to spill over 1 to overflow. **2** (of excess population) to be forced to move or spread.

to spill someone's blood to be responsible for someone's death.

to spill the beans to divulge a secret.

spin

in a flat spin FLAT.

to spin a yarn to tell a story.

to spin off to throw off, or be thrown off, by centrifugal force while spinning.

to spin out 1 to compose or tell (a story etc.) at great length. **2** to prolong, to protract. **3** to spend (time) in tedious discussion etc. **4** (*N Am.*) (of e.g. a vehicle) to go out of control in a skid etc. **5** (of a bowler in cricket) to dismiss (a batsman) by spin bowling.

spine

to send shivers up/ down someone's spine SHIVER[1].

spirit

if the spirit moves one if one feels inclined.

in high spirits HIGH.

in low spirits LOW.

in spirit 1 inwardly, in one's heart. **2** as a supportive presence, though not in person (*They are with us today in spirit*).

kindred spirit KINDRED.

the spirit is willing (but the flesh is weak) said when one lacks the physical strength or will-power to fulfil one's good intentions. [From the Bible: "Watch and pray, that ye enter not into temptation: the spirit indeed is willing, but the flesh is weak" (Matt. xxvi.41).]

to spirit up to cheer or encourage.

spit

spit and polish 1 the activities of cleaning and polishing, esp. as a soldier's duties. **2** (*coll.*) (obsessive) cleanliness,

attention to details, as in the army. [From the practice of spitting on leather boots etc. then rubbing them to make them shine.]

to spit chips (*Austral., sl.*) to be furious.

to spit it out (*coll.*) to say what is concerning one, to confess (*Come on – spit it out!*).

to spit up (*N Am.*) (usu. of a baby) to vomit.

spite

in spite of notwithstanding, despite.

in spite of oneself though behaving contrary to one's inclinations (*She laughed in spite of herself*).

spitting

spitting image (*coll.*) an exact likeness; a person or thing that exactly resembles another.

to be spitting feathers to be very angry.

within spitting distance a very small distance (*He lives within spitting distance of the sea*).

splash

to make a splash (*sl.*) to make a sensation, display, etc.

to splash down (of a spacecraft) to land on water when returning to earth.

to splash out (*coll.*) to spend money extravagantly (*We splashed out on a bottle of champagne*).

spleen

to vent one's spleen on VENT.

splice

to splice the mainbrace 1 to serve an extra rum ration (on a ship). **2** to have a (celebratory) drink of strong liquor. [The mainbrace, which controlled the largest sail, was an important rope on square-rigged ship. A worn mainbrace was usually replaced rather than repaired by splicing, so the phrase implied that receiving an extra ration of rum was a rare occurrence.]

split

to split hairs to quibble about trifles.

to split one's sides to laugh uproariously.

to split one's vote/ the ticket (*N Am.*) to vote for candidates of more than one party.

to split the difference to compromise by taking the average of two amounts.

spoil

spoilt for choice faced with so many attractive possibilities that one cannot choose between them.

to spoil the ship for a ha'p'orth of tar to lose or ruin something valuable by refusing to spend a relatively small sum on a necessary item. [The phrase originally had 'sheep' in place of 'ship' and referred to the tar used to treat a wounded animal.]

spoke

to put a spoke in someone's wheel to thwart someone. [Referring to a pin used to lock the wheels of a cart going downhill.]

sponge

to throw up/ in the sponge 1 (of a boxer or their second) to toss the sponge into the air as a token of defeat. **2** (*coll.*) to acknowledge oneself beaten, to give up the contest.

spoon

born with a silver spoon in one's mouth BORN.

he that sups with the devil must have a long spoon SUP.

wooden spoon WOODEN.

sport

in sport in fun, as a joke.

to have good sport to have a successful time hunting, shooting etc.

to make sport of to jeer at, to ridicule.

sporting

sporting chance some chance of succeeding.

spot

a leopard cannot change its spots LEOPARD.

black spot BLACK.

blind spot BLIND.

high spot HIGH.

in a spot in an awkward situation.

in a tight spot TIGHT.

on the spot 1 at the scene of action. **2** in the position of having to act or respond quickly. **3** at once, without change of place, there and then. **4** alert, wide awake.

rooted to the spot ROOTED.

spot on (*coll.*) absolutely accurate.

to have a soft spot for SOFT.

to hit the high spots HIT.

to hit the spot HIT.

to knock spots off KNOCK.

to put someone on the spot to put someone in an awkward position, to force someone to think fast.

to run on the spot to make running movements with the legs without moving forwards, for exercise.

spout

up the spout 1 (*sl.*) ruined, failed. **2** (*sl.*) at the pawnbroker's, in pawn. **3** (*sl.*) pregnant. [Alluding to the device formerly used to transport pawned articles from the pawnbroker's shop to the storeroom.]

sprat

sprat to catch a mackerel a small gift or concession made in hope of a larger gain.

spread

to spread like wildfire to spread very quickly.

spree

on the spree indulging in a bout of extravagance or excess.

spring

full of the joys of spring FULL.

spring chicken 1 (*N Am.*) a tender young chicken, usu. from 2 to 10 months old. **2** (*usu. with neg., coll.*) a young, active, inexperienced person (*He's no spring chicken*).

to spring a leak to open or crack so as to admit or let out water (*The boat sprang a leak and began to sink*).

to spring to mind to come suddenly to mind.

spud

to spud in 1 to begin drilling an oil well. **2** (*coll.*) to start work.

spur

on the spur of the moment on impulse, impromptu.

to set/ put spurs to 1 to spur (a horse). **2** to whet, to put an edge on (one's resolution).

to win one's spurs WIN.

whip and spur WHIP.

square

all square with no party in debt to any other, even, quits.

back to square one back to where one started without having made any progress. [Perhaps from a game played on a board with numbered squares, or from a printed grid of a football field formerly used by radio commentators and listeners to describe and follow the progress of the game.]

on the square 1 at right angles. **2** fair, honest; fairly, honestly. **3** belonging to the Freemasons.

out of square not square, not at right angles.

square deal 1 a fair bargain. **2** a fair deal, fair treatment.

square peg in a round hole a person in an unsuitable job or function.

to get square with to pay or make terms with (a creditor).

to square away (*N Am., coll.*) to put in order, to tidy up.

to square off 1 to assume a posture of defence or attack. **2** (*Austral.*) to placate. **3** to mark off in squares.

to square the circle 1 to construct geometrically a square equal in area to a given circle. **2** to attempt the impossible.

to square up to settle an account.

to square up to 1 to face (someone) in a fighting attitude. **2** to face up to, to tackle positively (one's problems etc.).

squeak

narrow squeak NARROW.

squeeze

to put the squeeze on (*coll.*) to put pressure on (someone), to coerce.

squib

damp squib DAMP.

stab

stab in the back a treacherous act.

to have/ make a stab at (*coll.*) to attempt, to have a go at (doing something).

to stab in the back 1 to betray. **2** to injure the reputation of (esp. a colleague, friend etc.).

stable door

to lock the stable door after the horse has bolted LOCK.

stack

to blow one's stack BLOW[1].

to stack the cards 1 to interfere with a deck of playing cards secretly for the purpose of cheating. **2** to arrange matters to the disadvantage or advantage of someone (*The cards are stacked against us*).

to stack up (*N Am., coll.*) to measure up, to compare satisfactorily.

staff

skeleton staff SKELETON.

stage

to go on the stage to become a professional actor or actress.

to hold the stage to dominate proceedings, to take the leading role, e.g. in a discussion.

to set the stage to arrange things in preparation (for an event etc.).

stair

below stairs 1 in the basement. **2** in the servants' quarters or relating to their affairs. **3** relating to the workforce as opposed to management.

stake¹

to pull up stakes to move home, to move on. [Referring to the pegs used to hold down a tent.]

to stake one's claim to assert one's right to possess something, to register or establish one's claim (to something).

to stake out to place under surveillance.

stake²

at stake 1 likely to be lost or damaged, at risk, endangered (*Many lives are at stake*). **2** at issue.

stalk¹

with one's eyes on stalks EYE.

stalk²

stalking-horse 1 a horse or figure like a horse behind which a hunter hides when stalking game. **2** a mask or pretence concealing one's true purpose.

stall

to stall off to evade, to stave off.

stamp

stamping ground a habitual meeting place, a favourite resort.

to stamp on to suppress, to crush out of existence.

to stamp out 1 to extinguish (a fire) by stamping. **2** to suppress.

stand

as it stands 1 in its present state, without alteration. **2** in the present circumstances, as things are.

one-night stand ONE.

stand easy! (*Mil.*) (an order to) stand at ease.

stand on me (*sl.*) depend on me.

to be at a stand 1 to be perplexed. **2** to be in doubt as to further progress.

to make a stand to make a show of resistance, opposition etc.

to stand back 1 to retire to a position further from the front. **2** to withdraw mentally from close involvement, usu. in order to get an objective view.

to stand by 1 to be present as a bystander; to look on passively (*I can't stand idly by and watch animals being ill-treated*). **2** to uphold, to support firmly. **3** to abide by (one's decision etc.). **4** to stand near in readiness to act promptly as directed. **5** (*Naut.*) to post oneself ready to operate (the anchor etc.).

to stand down 1 to withdraw or resign from a body, competition etc. **2** to leave the witness box in a law court. **3** (*Mil.*) to come off duty. **4** (of a committee) to be dissolved.

to stand fast to stay firm, to be unmoved.

to stand for 1 to represent, to imply (*What does the S in RSI stand for?*). **2** (*usu. with neg.*) to tolerate, to endure. **3** to support the cause of.

to stand high to have a high reputation.

to stand in for 1 to deputize for, to act in place of. **2** to take the place of (an actor etc. whose special skills are temporarily not required).

to stand in with to have an understanding or community of interest with, to league oneself with.

to stand off 1 to move away; to keep at a distance. **2** to suspend (an employee).

to stand off and on (*Naut.*) to tack in and out along shore.

to stand on/ upon 1 to insist on. 2 (*Naut.*) to keep on the same course.

to stand or fall by to be totally dependent on or committed to.

to stand out 1 to be conspicuous, prominent or outstanding. 2 to persist in opposition or support, to hold out (for or against). 3 to endure without giving way.

to stand over 1 to supervise closely in an annoying or threatening way. 2 to be deferred, to be postponed.

to stand to 1 (*Mil.*) to stand ready for an attack, e.g. after dark or before dawn. 2 to abide by. 3 not to desert. 4 to be liable to (lose, gain etc. something) (*She stands to win £100,000*). 5 to fall to, to set to work.

to stand to it to maintain (that).

to stand up 1 to rise to one's feet. 2 to be or remain erect; to set erect. 3 (of an argument etc.) to be valid, to hold water. 4 (*coll.*) to fail to keep an appointment with.

to stand up for to support, to take the side of.

to stand up to to oppose with determination.

to stand well with to be on good terms with, to be in the favour of.

to take one's stand on to have as the basis of one's argument.

standard
to raise the standard RAISE.

standby
on standby 1 held in readiness for use or service in an emergency etc. 2 (of an airline passenger) awaiting an empty seat, not having booked in advance.

standing
of old standing OLD.

standing joke a subject of constant ridicule.

standing room room for standing, esp. after all seats are filled (*It was standing room only at the protest meeting*).

to be in good standing with to be on good or friendly terms with.

stang
to ride the stang RIDE.

star
my stars! (*coll.*) used as an expression of astonishment.

to bless one's stars BLESS.

to hitch one's wagon to a star HITCH.

to see stars (*coll.*) to have flashes or dots before one's eyes, as when dazed or stunned.

to thank one's lucky stars THANK.

stare
to be staring someone in the face 1 to be only too obvious. 2 to be imminent, to be inexorably awaiting someone.

to stare out/ down to outstare.

stark
stark staring mad completely crazy.

start
by/ in fits and starts FIT².

false start FALSE.

flying start FLYING.

for a start in the first place, as the first consideration of several.

head start HEAD¹.

to get the start of to obtain an advantage over.

to start a hare to raise a topic of conversation.

to start from scratch to start from the very beginning, with no advantage. [From athletics, originally referring to a starting line scratched on the ground. Competitors with a handicap would start ahead of this line.]

to start in 1 to begin. 2 (*N Am.*) to make a beginning (on).

to start off 1 to begin (*start off with introductions*). 2 to set out on a journey.

to start on (*coll.*) to pick a fight with, to nag, to bully.

to start out 1 to begin a journey. **2** to begin in a certain way (*He started out as a teacher but eventually became an archaeologist*). **3** to take the first steps in a particular activity (*We started out making the usual mistakes of first-time buyers*).

to start over (*N Am.*) to start again.

to start something (*coll.*) to cause trouble or complications, esp. inadvertently.

to start up 1 to come into notice or occur to the mind suddenly; to arise, to occur. **2** (of an engine, machine etc.) to start. **3** to rise suddenly. **4** to establish (a business etc.).

to start with 1 in the first place, as the first consideration (*You should never have bought it to start with*). **2** in the beginning (*There were eight of us to start with*).

starter

for starters (*coll.*) in the first place, to begin with, as the first consideration (*You've spelt my name wrong, for starters!*).

under starter's orders (of racehorses etc.) ready to race, awaiting the signal to go.

state

in a state of nature 1 in an uncultivated state. **2** completely naked. **3** in an unregenerate state.

in state with proper ceremony (*She was received in state*).

of state relating to government (*affairs of state*).

state-of-the-art using the most advanced technology available at the time.

to lie in state LIE[2].

station

action stations! ACTION.

status

status quo the existing state of affairs.

status symbol a possession regarded as indicative of a person's elevated social rank or wealth.

stave

to stave in to crush.

stay

to be here/ have come to stay to be a fixture, to have qualities of a permanent nature.

to stay in to remain at home, to remain indoors.

†**to stay one's hand** to refrain from action.

to stay over (*coll.*) to remain overnight.

to stay put to remain where put or placed; to remain on the spot.

to stay the course to last out to the end of some difficult or demanding activity.

to stay the night to remain somewhere, esp. to sleep, until the next day.

to stay up not to go to bed till after one's normal bedtime.

stead

in someone's/ something's stead instead of someone or something.

to stand someone in good stead to be of service to someone (*Her knowledge of Italian will stand her in good stead*).

steady

steady as a rock 1 very steady. **2** very reliable.

steady on! calm down! take it easy!

to go steady (*coll.*) to have a relatively long-term romantic or sexual relationship (with).

to steady down to become steady.

steal

to steal a march on 1 to get to an objective before, to start in advance of. **2** to gain an advantage over. [From the distance covered by troops in a day, which could be easily calculated by the enemy. However, if an army set off under cover of darkness, they would be ahead of their expected position.]

to steal someone's thunder 1 to spoil the effect someone had hoped to achieve with a particular idea by using the idea oneself first. **2** to attract publicity away from someone towards oneself. [From a remark attributed to the playwright John Dennis (1657–1734), who had invented a device to produce stage thunder for one of his plays and was dismayed to hear it used in someone else's production.]

to steal the show to attract the most attention, approval etc., esp. unexpectedly (*The dancing horse stole the show*).

stealth
by stealth furtively, surreptitiously.

steam
steamed up 1 (of windows etc.) clouded by steam. **2** (*coll.*) angry, indignant.

to get up steam 1 to build up steam pressure, esp. sufficient to run a steam engine. **2** to collect one's forces or energy. **3** to work oneself up into an excited state.

to let off steam to give vent to one's feelings.

to run out of steam to lose momentum or energy.

to steam in (*sl.*) to initiate or join a fight, to weigh in.

to steam up to (cause to) become covered with condensed steam.

under one's own steam by one's own efforts, without help.

steel
cold steel COLD.

steep
steeped in imbued with, having a thorough knowledge of or familiarity with.

steer
bum steer BUM.
to steer clear of to avoid.

stem
from stem to stern from one end of a ship to the other.
to stem from to spring from.

step
in someone's steps following the example of someone.

in step 1 in marching, dancing etc., in conformity or time with others. **2** (*coll.*) in agreement (with).

out of step 1 not in step. **2** (*coll.*) not in agreement or harmony (with others) (*The unions are out of step with the workers they represent*).

step by step gradually, with deliberation, taking one step at a time.

step in the right direction an action that makes an initial contribution to the desired end result.

step this way please come this way, please follow me.

to break step BREAK.

to change step CHANGE.

to keep step to stay in step.

to step down 1 to resign, to relinquish one's position etc. **2** to decrease the voltage etc. of.

to step in 1 to enter a house or room, esp. briefly. **2** to intervene (*I stepped in to resolve the dispute*). **3** to stand in as a substitute for someone.

to step into someone's shoes to take over a job, position, responsibility etc. from someone else.

to step into the breach to help out, esp. by replacing someone.

to step it (*poet.*) to dance.

to step on it (*coll.*) to hurry, to increase speed. [From the action of pressing a car's accelerator with the foot.]

to step on the gas/ juice 1 (*coll.*) to accelerate a motor vehicle. **2** (*coll.*) to hurry.

to step out 1 to leave a room, house etc. briefly. **2** to be socially active. **3** (*N Am., dial., coll.*) to date, to go out (with). **4** to take longer, faster strides.

to step out of line to depart from normal or acceptable behaviour.

to step up 1 to advance by one or more stages. **2** to increase the power, voltage etc. of. **3** to come forward.

to take steps to take action.

to turn one's steps towards to head for, to walk in the direction of.

to watch/ mind one's step to take care, to guard one's behaviour.

Stephen

even Stephens EVEN[1].

stern

from stem to stern STEM.

stew

to stew in one's own juice to suffer alone the consequences of one's folly.

stick[1]

a stick with which to beat someone knowledge of someone's weaknesses, mistakes etc. that can be used to coerce them or make them suffer.

carrot and stick CARROT.

cross as two sticks CROSS.

dirty/ rough end of the stick END.

in a cleft stick CLEFT STICK.

to cut one's stick 1 (*coll.*) to go away. **2** (*coll.*) to run, to escape.

to give someone stick to blame or criticize someone.

to up sticks UP.

wrong end of the stick WRONG.

stick[2]

stick 'em up! (*coll.*) raise hands to assure surrender.

stick-in-the-mud 1 dull, slow, unprogressive. **2** an unenterprising person (*Don't be such an old stick-in-the-mud*).

to be stuck 1 to be unable to progress further. **2** to be confined (somewhere) (*I don't want to be stuck in the house all day*).

to be stuck for to lack, to need (*I'm a bit stuck for cash*).

to be stuck on (*coll.*) to be very keen on, or infatuated with.

to be stuck with (*coll.*) to have no choice but to have, to be landed with (*I'm stuck with a husband who won't dance*).

to get stuck in 1 to start doing a task vigorously. **2** (*coll.*) to eat hungrily.

to get stuck into 1 to start doing vigorously. **2** (*coll.*) to eat (something) hungrily. **3** to attack (someone) physically or verbally.

to stick around (*coll.*) to remain in the vicinity.

to stick at/ to it to persevere.

to stick by 1 to stay close to. **2** to remain faithful to, to support.

to stick fast 1 to adhere strongly. **2** to be fixed or trapped immovably.

to stick in someone's craw to be hard to accept. [The craw is the first stomach of birds and insects.]

to stick in someone's gizzard (*coll.*) to be very disagreeable to someone.

to stick in someone's throat to be repugnant to someone, to be against someone's principles.

to stick it on 1 (*coll.*) to overcharge. **2** (*coll.*) to exaggerate.

to stick it out to put up with something as long as is demanded of one.

to stick one's chin out to be resolute, to show determination.

to stick one's neck out 1 (*coll.*) to invite trouble. **2** (*coll.*) to take a risk. [From the sport of boxing.]

to stick out 1 to (cause to) protrude. **2** to be conspicuous or obvious.

to stick out a mile to be only too obvious.

to stick out for to demand, to insist on (*They stuck out for a higher price*).

to stick out like a sore thumb to be highly conspicuous.

to stick together to remain loyal to one another.

to stick to one's guns to maintain an opinion in the face of opposition.

to stick to one's last to concern oneself with what one knows about and is skilled in (and not meddle with other matters). [From the proverb 'the cobbler should stick to his last', which is said to have originated in ancient Greece in the 4th century BC, when a shoemaker presumed to criticize the way the artist Apelles had painted someone's leg.]

to stick to someone's fingers (*coll.*) (of money) to be embezzled by someone.

to stick to someone's ribs (of food) to satisfy someone's hunger.

to stick up 1 to put up, to erect. **2** to stand up, to be prominent. **3** to paste or post up. **4** (*coll.*) to hold up; to rob at gunpoint. **5** (*sl.*) to puzzle, to nonplus. **6** (*Austral., sl.*) to hold up, to bail up.

to stick up for to take the part of, to defend.

to stick up to to stand up against, to resist.

sticky

on a sticky wicket (*coll.*) in an unfavourable situation.

sticky end (*coll.*) a disagreeable end or death (*to come to a sticky end*).

stiff

stiff as a board very stiff, esp. after strenuous exercise (*I cycled to London last week and I was stiff as a board the next day*).

stiff as a poker/ ramrod very stiff, rigid.

stiff with (*coll.*) packed with, full of (*stiff with holidaymakers*).

to keep a stiff upper lip to be self-reliant, inflexible or unflinching.

stile

to help a lame dog over a stile HELP.

still

still and all (*coll.*) nevertheless, in spite of that.

still small voice the voice of conscience or reason. [From the Bible: "And after the earthquake a fire; but the Lord was not in the fire: and after the fire a still small voice" (I Kgs. xix.12).]

still waters run deep a quiet or inscrutable exterior may conceal an active mind, strong feelings etc. [Alluding to the calm surface of deep water.]

stilt

on stilts 1 mounted on stilts. **2** stilted, bombastic. **3** stiltedly, bombastically.

sting

sting in the tail an unexpected or ironic twist to finish with. [Alluding to the scorpion and other creatures that sting with their tails.]

to take the sting out of something to make something less unpleasant or painful.

stink

like stink (*sl.*) intensely, very hard.

to raise/ create a stink 1 (*sl.*) to complain. **2** (*sl.*) to stir up trouble, esp. adverse publicity.

to stink out 1 to drive out by creating an offensive smell. **2** to cause (a room etc.) to stink.

stir

to stir in to mix (an ingredient) into a mixture by stirring.

to stir one's stumps (*coll.*) to become active, to get going.

to stir the blood to rouse one emotionally, to evoke strong feelings.

to stir up 1 to mix by stirring vigorously. **2** to incite (trouble, rebellion etc.). **3** to agitate, to excite, to arouse.

to stir up a hornets' nest to stir up trouble or excite the animosity of other people.

stitch

a stitch in time (saves nine) a timely repair or remedy (will prevent the development of more serious faults or problems).

in stitches helpless with laughter (*The comedian had us in stitches*).

to drop a stitch DROP.

to stitch up 1 to sew together or mend. **2** (*sl.*) to incriminate by informing on or concocting evidence against.

stock

in stock available to be sold immediately.

laughing stock LAUGHING.

lock, stock and barrel LOCK.

on the stocks in preparation or construction. [Alluding to a timber framework on which a ship or boat rests during building.]

out of stock not available for sale, not in stock.

stock-in-trade 1 goods, tools and other requisites of a trade etc. **2** resources, capabilities. **3** a person's range of skills or ploys.

to stock up to take in supplies, to lay in stock.

to take stock 1 to make an inventory of goods etc. on hand. **2** to survey one's position, prospects etc. **3** to examine, to form an estimate (of a person, etc.).

to take stock in to attach importance to.

stocking

in one's stocking(ed) feet/ soles without one's shoes, e.g. when having one's height measured.

stoke

to stoke up 1 to feed a fire or furnace with fuel. **2** to fill oneself with food.

stomach

butterflies in the stomach BUTTERFLY.

on a full stomach FULL.

on an empty stomach EMPTY.

sick to one's stomach SICK.

to have no stomach for to be strongly disinclined to.

to sit heavy on the stomach SIT.

to turn someone's stomach to make someone feel sick or disgusted.

stone

a rolling stone gathers no moss ROLLING.

a stone's throw a short distance.

heart of stone HEART.

people who live in glass houses should not throw stones PEOPLE.

stone-cold sober utterly sober.

stone the crows! (*sl.*) used to express amazement.

to cast the first stone CAST.

to get blood from a stone BLOOD.

to kill two birds with one stone KILL.

to leave no stone unturned to use all available means to effect an object.

to throw stones to go in for criticizing people.

stony

to fall on stony ground (of advice etc.) to be ignored. [From the parable of the sower and his seed in the Bible: "Some fell upon stony places, where they had not much earth" (Matt. xiii.5).]

stool

to fall between two stools TWO.

stop

to pull out all the stops 1 to make the utmost effort. **2** to play at maximum volume. [Referring to the knobs that control the sound of an organ.]

to put a stop to to cause to cease, esp. abruptly.

to stop by to break one's journey (at a particular place) for a visit.

to stop dead to stop suddenly.

to stop down in photography, to reduce the aperture of (a lens) by means of a diaphragm.

to stop off/ over to break one's journey (at a particular place).

to stop one's ears 1 to put one's fingers in one's ears so as not to hear. **2** to refuse to listen.

to stop out 1 to stay out (*stopping out till two or three o'clock in the morning*).

2 in printing etc., to cover (part of a surface) to prevent printing, etching etc.

to stop payment 1 to declare oneself insolvent. **2** to instruct a bank to withhold payment on a cheque etc.

to stop short 1 to come to a sudden stop. **2** to fail to reach the point aimed at.

to stop short of not to go as far as (*She stopped short of calling him a liar*).

to stop the mouth of to silence.

stopper

conversation stopper CONVERSATION.

to put a stopper on 1 to prevent the continuance of. **2** to keep (someone) quiet.

storage

cold storage COLD.

store

in store 1 in reserve. **2** ready for use. **3** on hand. **4** awaiting one in the future (*Who knows what lies in store for us?*).

to set/ put/ lay store by/ on to value highly.

storm

any port in a storm PORT.

calm before the storm CALM.

storm in a teacup a fuss about nothing.

to take by storm 1 to capture by means of a violent assault. **2** to captivate or overwhelm (an audience, (the people of) a city etc.).

to weather the storm WEATHER.

story

a likely story! LIKELY.

cock and bull story COCK[1].

end of story END.

shaggy-dog story SHAGGY.

sob story SOB.

success story SUCCESS.

tall story TALL.

the (same) old story OLD.

the story goes it is commonly said.

to cut a long story short LONG.

stow

stow it (*sl.*) drop it! stop joking etc.

to stow away 1 to put (something) where it will be tidily out of the way; to pack or fold away. **2** to be a stowaway on board a ship or aircraft.

straight

straight as a die 1 very straight. **2** completely honest.

straight as an arrow completely straight, directly.

straight away at once, without delay.

straight face a controlled expression, usu. concealing an inclination to laugh (*I don't know how you managed to keep a straight face*).

straight from the shoulder 1 (of a physical blow) squarely delivered. **2** (of criticism etc.) frank, direct.

straight off/ out (*coll.*) without needing time for checking or deliberation (*I couldn't tell you the date straight off*).

straight up 1 (*coll.*) honestly, truly. **2** (*N Am., coll.*) without dilution or admixture.

the straight and narrow the honest and virtuous way of life. [Perhaps from the Bible: "strait is the gate and narrow is the way, which leadeth unto life" (Matt. vii.14).]

to go straight to abandon criminal activities and become honest.

straighten

to straighten out to resolve, to unscramble.

to straighten up to stand erect after bending.

strain

at (full) strain stretched or exerted to the utmost.

straining at the leash anxious or
impatient to begin.

to strain at a gnat and swallow a camel to
be scrupulous about trifles and lax in
matters of great importance. [From the
Bible: "Ye blind guides, which strain
at a gnat, and swallow a camel" (Matt.
xxiii.24), part of Jesus's denunciation
of the Pharisees.]

to strain oneself 1 to do oneself an injury
through effort or straining. **2** (*often
with neg., facet.*) to try unduly hard
(*Don't strain yourself!*).

strange

strange to say oddly enough; it is strange
to report that.

straw

**a drowning man will clutch at a straw/
straws** DROWN.

†in the straw in labour, giving birth.

last straw LAST[1].

man of straw MAN.

the straw that broke the camel's back the
thing that finally takes one past the
limit of endurance or patience. [From
the saying 'it is the last straw that
breaks the camel's back'.]

to clutch/ catch/ grasp at straws to resort
to desperate or manifestly inadequate
remedies or measures.

to draw the short straw SHORT.

to make bricks without straw BRICK.

stream

on stream (of a factory etc.) in operation,
in production.

to go with the stream to do the same as
other people, to behave conventionally.

street

Easy Street EASY.

in civvy street CIVVY.

in the street outside the houses.

man in the street MAN.

man on the street MAN.

not in the same street as SAME.

on the streets 1 living by prostitution.
2 homeless, destitute.

Queer Street QUEER.

streets ahead of far better than.

streets apart completely different.

to have the key of the street KEY.

to walk the streets WALK.

up/ down one's street ideally suited to
one's talents, inclinations etc. (*This
project is right up my street*).

strength

from strength from a strong position, for
the purpose of negotiation etc.

from strength to strength with
continually increasing success (*to go
from strength to strength*). [From the
Bible: "They go from strength to
strength, every one of them in Zion
appeareth before God" (Psa. lxxxiv.7).]

give me strength! an exclamation of
exasperation.

in strength in considerable numbers.

on the strength on the register of staff etc.

on the strength of 1 in reliance on. **2** on
the faith of.

the strength of the essence, gist or main
thrust of (*That's about the strength of
it*).

to outgrow one's strength OUTGROW.

tower of strength TOWER.

strengthen

to strengthen someone's hand to empower
someone to take action.

stress

to lay stress on to emphasize, to accord
importance to.

stretch

at a stretch 1 at one go. **2** continuously
(*for two weeks at a stretch*).

at full stretch FULL.

to stretch a point to go beyond what
might be expected.

to stretch one's legs/ a leg to take exercise,
esp. after inactivity.

to **stretch out 1** to extend (e.g. a hand or foot). **2** to lie or recline at full length. **3** to eke (money etc.) out. **4** to prolong.

stricken

†**stricken in years** elderly, feeble with age.

stride

to **get into one's stride** to reach one's usual or best rate of working, level of skill etc. [From athletics.]

to **make great strides** GREAT.

to **take in one's stride 1** to jump (an obstacle) without adjusting one's gait. **2** to achieve (something) or override (something) without difficulty or effort.

strike

on **strike** participating in an industrial strike.

strike a light! used to express astonishment.

strike me pink! used to express astonishment.

struck all of a heap (*coll.*) staggered, flabbergasted.

struck on (*coll.*) enamoured of, infatuated with (*I'm not struck on the colour scheme*).

to **strike a balance 1** to make a compromise. **2** to reckon up the balance on a statement of credit and debt.

to **strike a blow for** to show support for.

to **strike a chord 1** to cause someone to recall something. **2** to elicit an emotional response, esp. sympathy.

to **strike a light** to strike a match.

to **strike an attitude** to assume an exaggerated or theatrical posture.

to **strike at the root(s) of** to destroy deliberately.

to **strike back 1** to return a blow, to retaliate. **2** (of a gas burner) to burn from an internal point before the gas mixes with air.

to **strike down 1** to knock down. **2** to make ill or cause to die, esp. suddenly. **3** to bring low.

to **strike dumb** to confound; to astonish; to render speechless by astonishment.

†to **strike hands 1** to make a bargain. **2** to become surety.

to **strike home 1** to hit the intended target. **2** to achieve the desired effect (*Your remark seems to have struck home*).

to **strike in 1** to break into a conversation. **2** (of a disease) to spread into the interior of the body from the skin or surface.

to **strike (it) lucky** to have a success.

to **strike it rich 1** to find a deposit of oil, minerals etc. **2** to make an unexpected large financial gain.

to **strike off 1** to remove, separate, dislodge etc. by a blow. **2** to erase, to delete, to strike out (e.g. someone, or their name, from a register). **3** to print (copies of a document).

to **strike off the rolls** to remove from the official list of qualified solicitors, to debar, to expel.

to **strike oil 1** to find oil by sinking a shaft. **2** to have a success.

to **strike out 1** to hit from the shoulder (e.g. in boxing). **2** to take vigorous action. **3** to delete, to expunge. **4** to set off (*We struck out northwards*). **5** to make vigorous strokes (in skating, swimming etc.). **6** to devise, to contrive (a plan etc.). **7** to produce (coins, medals etc.) by striking. **8** in baseball, to dismiss (a batter) or be dismissed after three strikes.

to **strike sail 1** to lower sails suddenly. **2** to give way, to submit.

to **strike through** to delete (a word etc.) by drawing a line through it.

to **strike up 1** to enter into, to start (a conversation etc.). **2** to begin to play or sing. **3** to drive up with a blow.

to **strike upon 1** to think of or hit upon (an idea, solution etc.). **2** (of light) to shine upon, to illuminate.

to strike while the iron is hot to take advantage of an opportunity while conditions are favourable. [Alluding to the work of a blacksmith.]

striking

within striking distance near enough to strike, reach or achieve.

string

more than one string to one's bow more resources, plans or opportunities than one.

no strings attached (*coll.*) with no conditions or restrictions.

on a string 1 totally dependent, e.g. emotionally. **2** held in suspense.

tied to someone's apron strings TIE.

to be in leading-strings LEADING-STRINGS.

to hold the purse strings PURSE STRINGS.

to pull strings to exert influence unobtrusively. [From puppetry.]

to string along 1 (*coll.*) to accompany (*You can string along with us, if you like*). **2** to agree with, to go along with. **3** (*coll.*) to fool, to deceive (*They had been stringing me along all the time*).

to string out to prolong, esp. unnecessarily.

to string together to join up in a series (*stringing together sentences with commas*).

to string up (*coll.*) to hang (by the neck).

strip[1]

to strip down to dismantle.

strip[2]

to tear a strip off TEAR[1].

to tear someone off a strip TEAR[1].

stroke[1]

at a stroke by a single action.

off one's stroke not at one's best.

on the stroke punctually.

on the stroke of exactly at the time when the clock starts striking (a particular time).

to put someone off their stroke to hinder someone's progress, esp. by interrupting or distracting them. [From the sport of rowing.]

stroke[2]

to stroke down to mollify, to appease.

to stroke someone/ someone's hair the wrong way to ruffle or annoy someone.

strong

going strong 1 continuing to flourish. **2** still in action.

strong suit 1 in card-playing, a suit in which one can take tricks. **2** something at which one excels; one's forte.

to come it strong (*coll.*) to exaggerate.

to come on strong to behave forcefully or aggressively.

stubborn

stubborn as a mule very stubborn or obstinate.

stud

at/ out to stud (of a stallion) available for breeding, for a fee.

study

in a brown study BROWN.

to make a study of to examine or investigate thoroughly.

stuff

hard stuff HARD.

hot stuff HOT.

kids' stuff KID[1].

stuff and nonsense! an expression of contemptuous disbelief.

that's the stuff! that is just what is needed.

to do one's stuff (*coll.*) to act as one is expected.

to know one's stuff (*coll.*) to be competent in one's chosen field, to know what one needs to know.

stuffed

get stuffed! (*offensive*) used to express anger, contempt etc. against another person.

stuffed shirt (*coll.*) a pompous person.

stuffing

to knock the stuffing out of KNOCK.

stump

on the stump going about making political speeches. [From the use of a tree-stump as a platform for making such a speech.]

to stir one's stumps STIR.

to stump up 1 to pay up. **2** to produce the money required.

up a stump (*N Am.*) in difficulties.

style

to cramp someone's style CRAMP.

subject

on the subject of concerning.

subject to conditional(ly) upon.

to change the subject CHANGE.

subscribe

to subscribe for to agree to purchase (a copy or copies of a book) before publication.

to subscribe oneself to sign one's name as.

to subscribe to 1 to arrange to take (a periodical) regularly. **2** to give support to (*I don't subscribe to that theory*).

succeed

nothing succeeds like success success engenders further success.

success

nothing succeeds like success SUCCEED.

success story a person who or something which is very successful despite unfavourable circumstances.

succession

in (quick) succession one (soon) after another.

in succession to as the successor to or of.

such

as such in the sense or capacity of what has been named or mentioned (*He has no qualifications as such*; *Wrongdoers will be treated as such*).

such-and-such 1 an unknown or unspecified person or thing. **2** not known or specified, some (*such-and-such a person*).

such a one 1 such a person or thing. **2** †some unspecified person or thing.

such as 1 for example. **2** of a kind that. **3** those who.

such as it is despite its inadequacies.

suck

†to give suck (to) to suckle.

to suck dry 1 to empty by sucking. **2** to use up the sympathy, tolerance etc. of.

to suck in 1 to absorb. **2** to engulf, to draw (in). **3** to involve unwillingly in a bad situation.

to suck up 1 (*coll.*) to act in an obsequious manner, to toady (*sucking up to the boss*). **2** to absorb.

sudden

(all) of a sudden suddenly; unexpectedly.

†on a sudden suddenly; unexpectedly.

sue

to sue out to petition for and obtain (a writ, pardon etc.).

suffer

not to suffer fools gladly to be intolerant of foolish people. [From the Bible: "For ye suffer fools gladly, seeing ye yourselves are wise" (II Cor. xi.19).]

sufferance
on sufferance merely tolerated.

suffice
suffice it to say I will say only this.

sugar
sugar daddy (*sl.*) a well-to-do, elderly
    man who spends money on a young
    woman.

suggest
to suggest itself to arise in the mind.

suit
in one's birthday suit BIRTHDAY.
strong suit STRONG.
to follow suit FOLLOW.
to suit oneself **1** to do what one wants,
    regardless of other people's feelings.
    2 to find something which pleases
    one.
to suit someone's book to be agreeable or
    favourable to someone. [Possibly
    referring to a bookmaker who will
    only accept certain bets.]
to suit the action to the word to carry
    out a promise or threat. [From
    Shakespeare's *Hamlet*: "suit the
    action to the word, the word to the
    action", part of Hamlet's advice to
    the visiting actors.]

suitcase
to live out of a suitcase LIVE[1].

sum
in sum briefly, in summary.
to sum up **1** to recapitulate. **2** to form a
    rapid opinion or estimate of. **3** to put
    in a few words.

summer
one swallow does not make a summer
    SWALLOW.

sun
against the sun anticlockwise.

in the sun exposed to the rays of the
    sun.
one's sun is set one's prosperous period
    is over.
on which the sun never sets worldwide.
place in the sun PLACE.
to catch the sun CATCH.
to have the sun in one's eyes **1** to be
    dazzled by the sun. **2** to be intoxicated.
to make hay while the sun shines HAY.
to rise with the sun RISE.
to see the sun to be alive.
under/ beneath the sun in the world, on
    earth (*I've tried every remedy under
    the sun*).
with the sun clockwise.

Sunday
month of Sundays MONTH.
Sunday best (*coll., often facet.*) one's best
    clothes.
week of Sundays WEEK.

sunder
in sunder apart, in two.

sunny side
sunny side up (*esp. N Am.*) (of an egg)
    fried on one side only.

sup
a bit and a sup BIT[2].
he that sups with the devil must have a
    long spoon a warning of the need for
    caution when dealing with evil or
    dishonest people.

supper
to sing for one's supper SING.

supply
in short supply SHORT.
on supply (of a teacher etc.) temporarily
    filling the position of another.

support
in support of in order to support.

suppose

I suppose so used to express agreement with a degree of uncertainty.

supreme

to make the supreme sacrifice 1 to die for a cause. **2** (*facet.*) to surrender one's virginity.

sure

for sure (*coll.*) surely, certainly.
sure as a gun 1 undoubtedly. **2** absolutely certain.
sure as death quite certain(ly).
sure as eggs is eggs (*coll.*) quite certainly. [This phrase may have originated in the form 'sure as *x* is *x*', a statement used in logic.]
sure as fate without doubt, undoubtedly.
sure enough 1 (*coll.*) in reality, not merely in expectation. **2** (*coll.*) with near certainty.
to be sure 1 not to fail (to) (*Be sure to phone as soon as you get there*). **2** without doubt, certainly, of course. **3** it must be admitted.
to make sure 1 to make certain, to ascertain. **2** to make secure.
to make sure of to establish the truth of.
well, I'm sure used to express surprise.

surety

†**of/ for a surety** certainly.
to stand surety to act as a surety.

surface

to come to the surface to appear after being hidden.
to scratch the surface SCRATCH.

surprise

to take by surprise to strike with astonishment, to take unawares.

surrender

to surrender to bail (*Law*) to appear in court in discharge of bail.

suspend

to suspend payment to be unable to meet one's financial engagements.

suspense

to keep in suspense to delay giving (someone) vital information.

suspicion

above suspicion too honest or good to be suspected.
under suspicion suspected.

suss

on suss (*sl.*) on suspicion (of having committed a crime).
to suss out (*sl.*) to investigate, to find out about.

swallow

one swallow does not make a summer used as a warning against jumping to conclusions from a single piece of evidence. [The swallow is a summer visitor to Britain.]

swan

all someone's geese are swans GOOSE.

swath

to cut a wide swath WIDE.

swear

sworn to secrecy having promised to keep something a secret.
to swear at (*coll.*) (of colours or patterns) to clash with.
to swear blind (*coll.*) to state solemnly or emphatically.
to swear by (*coll.*) to have or profess great confidence in (*He swears by these pills for his rheumatism*).
to swear by all that is sacred (*coll.*) to state emphatically or solemnly.
to swear in to induct into office with the administration of an oath.
to swear like a trooper to swear strongly or excessively.

to swear off (*coll.*) to renounce solemnly.

to swear out (*N Am.*) to secure the issue of (a warrant for arrest) by making a charge on oath.

to swear to to testify firmly to the truth of.

sweat

by the sweat of one's brow by working hard.

cold sweat COLD.

in a muck sweat MUCK SWEAT.

no sweat (*sl.*) no difficulty or problem; without trouble.

to sweat blood (*sl.*) to work or worry to an extreme degree (*I've sweated blood over this project*).

to sweat bullets (*N Am., sl.*) to sweat profusely.

to sweat like a pig to sweat profusely.

to sweat out 1 to remove or get rid of by sweating. **2** (*coll.*) to endure, to live through.

sweep

to make a clean sweep of CLEAN.

to sweep aside/ away to remove quickly and completely.

to sweep someone off their feet to enrapture someone, to make a complete and sudden conquest of someone.

to sweep the board to win everything. [From betting games in which all the stakes are placed on the table.]

to sweep the decks 1 (*Naut.*) to clear the decks of boarders by a raking fire. **2** to win all the stakes.

sweet

she's sweet (*Austral., sl.*) everything is all right.

sweet nothings words of endearment (*whispering sweet nothings in each other's ears*).

sweet tooth a fondness for sweet-tasting things (*My husband has a sweet tooth*).

to be sweet on to be in love with; to be very fond of.

sweetness

all sweetness and light an apparently amiable attitude. [From Jonathan Swift's *The Battle of the Books* (1704): "Instead of dirt and poison we have rather chosen to fill our hives with honey and wax; thus furnishing mankind with the two noblest of things, which are sweetness and light." The phrase was subsequently popularized by Matthew Arnold in *Culture and Anarchy* (1869): "The pursuit of perfection, then, is the pursuit of sweetness and light".]

swim

in the swim involved in the main current activity.

swine

to cast pearls before swine CAST.

swing

in full swing FULL.

swing of the pendulum the regular pattern of change in public opinion, political power etc.

swings and roundabouts a situation in which there are as many gains as losses.

to get into the swing (of things) to become accustomed to a particular routine, activity etc.

to go with a swing to be lively or successful.

to swing it to play music with swing.

to swing the lead to malinger. [Of nautical origin, referring to the use of a line weighted with lead to measure the depth of water. The line was swung around and cast into the sea ahead of the ship, a task that could be drawn out for some time by lazy sailors anxious to avoid more arduous duties.]

what you gain on the swings you lose on the roundabouts GAIN.

switch

to switch off (*coll.*) to stop listening or
   paying attention, to lose interest.
to switch on (*coll.*) to become alive or
   responsive (to).
to switch over to change, to change over.

swivet

in a swivet (*esp. N Am.*) panicking,
   flustered.

swoop

at one fell swoop FELL[2].

sword

at half-sword HALF-SWORD.
sword of Damocles a situation of
   impending disaster. [According to
   classical legend, Damocles was invited
   to a banquet by Dionysius of Syracuse,
   whom he had grossly flattered, but
   was forced to sit through the meal
   with a sword suspended over his
   head by a single hair, showing the
   dangerous nature of such exalted
   positions.]
to cross swords CROSS.
to draw one's sword against to attack.

to measure swords MEASURE.
to put to the sword to kill (esp. those
   captured or defeated in war).
to sheathe the sword SHEATHE.

syllable

in words of one syllable WORD.

symbol

status symbol STATUS.

sympathy

in sympathy with 1 showing sympathy
   for. **2** showing loyalty or support for.

sync

in sync well matched, working well
   together.
out of sync badly matched, not working
   well together.

system

all systems go said when everything is
   ready to start. [A phrase used at the
   launch of a spacecraft.]
to get something out of one's system
   (*coll.*) to rid oneself of a worry or a
   preoccupation.

T

T
to a T perfectly, to a nicety (*The working hours suit her to a T*).
to dot the i's and cross the t's DOT.

tab
to keep tabs on 1 (*coll.*) to keep a watch on. 2 (*coll.*) to keep a record or account of.

table
at table taking a meal.
on the table 1 put forward for debate, discussion or acceptance.
2 (*esp. N Am.*) set aside indefinitely.
to drink someone under the table DRINK.
to lay the table to set a table with cutlery, crockery etc. for a forthcoming meal.
to put/ lay one's cards on the table CARD.
to serve at table SERVE.
to turn the tables to reverse the conditions or relations (*She turned the tables on them by threatening to sue*). [From a former method of reversing the fortunes of players in a board game.]
to wait at table WAIT.
to wait on table WAIT.
under the table 1 illicit, secret. 2 (*coll.*) drunk.

tack
brass tacks BRASS.

tad
a tad slightly, a little (*This wine is a tad too sweet for me*).

tag
to tag along with to go along with (someone), to follow.

tail¹
heads I win, tails you lose HEAD¹.
like a dog with two tails DOG.
on someone's coat-tails COAT-TAIL.
on someone's tail very close behind someone.
piece/ bit of tail (*sl., offensive*) a woman, esp. when thought of in sexual terms.
sting in the tail STING.
the tail wags the dog the least important member or group in a society, organization etc. has control over the most important.
to make head or tail of HEAD¹.
to put salt on someone's tail SALT.
to tail away to dwindle.
to tail back (of traffic) to form a queue stretching back from an obstruction.
to tail off to come to an end, or almost to an end (*Public interest in the issue has tailed off*).
to turn tail 1 to run away. 2 to turn one's back.
with one's tail between one's legs beaten, in a state of defeat. [Alluding to a beaten or defeated dog.]
with one's tail up in good spirits.

tail²
in tail controlled by or under limited ownership (*estate in tail*).

take¹
it takes one to know one (*coll.*) the same

(usu. disparaging) remark is true of the person who made it.

on the take making money dishonestly.

take it from me believe me (*Take it from me: there's no easy way to get rich!*).

take that! used when delivering a blow etc.

to be taken with to be charmed by or very pleased with.

to take aback to greatly surprise or shock (*He was taken aback by her proposal*).

to take after 1 to resemble physically, mentally etc. (*She takes after her father*). **2** to follow, esp. in the same career etc.

to take against to form a dislike for.

to take amiss to be offended by.

to take apart 1 to separate. **2** (*coll.*) to criticize severely. **3** (*coll.*) esp. in sport, to outplay, outclass or defeat (*Aberdeen took Rangers apart*).

to take aside to disengage and talk privately to.

to take away 1 to subtract. **2** to remove. **3** to buy ready to eat, for consumption elsewhere.

to take away from to detract from.

to take back 1 to withdraw, to retract. **2** to stimulate memories, esp. nostalgically (*These photos take me back to when I was a lad*). **3** (*Print.*) to reset on the previous line. **4** to return or accept the return of (something bought) for a replacement or refund. **5** to accept back into a relationship that had earlier been ended.

to take down 1 to write down. **2** to lower (a garment) to one's knees or ankles, esp. temporarily (*She took down her jeans*). **3** to swallow, to gulp down. **4** to take apart, to pull to pieces. **5** to humiliate, to humble.

to take for to mistake for (*What do you take me for – a fool?*).

to take from 1 to deduct from. **2** to diminish, to lessen. **3** to quote from (*a passage taken from the Bible*).

to take in 1 to admit, to receive (*They have started taking in lodgers*). **2** to undertake (washing, typewriting etc.) at home for pay. **3** to include, to comprise. **4** to understand, to receive into the mind, to accept as true. **5** to deceive, to cheat. **6** to contract, to furl (sails).

to take it 1 to accept misfortune or punishment. **2** to understand by deduction (*I take it that you want to hand in your notice*).

to take it easy to take one's time, to relax.

to take it on/ upon oneself to decide (to do) without prompting or authority.

to take it or leave it 1 to accept something, including its problems, or not at all (*This is the only one I have: take it or leave it*). **2** to have a lukewarm reaction to something.

to take it out of 1 (*coll.*) to get revenge, compensation or satisfaction from. **2** (*coll.*) to exhaust the strength or freshness of.

to take it out on to vent one's anger or frustration on.

to take kindly to to react favourably to (*She doesn't take kindly to being told how to run her own business*).

to take off 1 to remove, to withdraw. **2** to begin flight. **3** to become popular (*Cybercafés are taking off in a big way now*). **4** to carry away. **5** to deduct (from). **6** to spend (an amount of time) away from work etc., esp. by choice. **7** to jump (from). **8** to leave suddenly or hastily. **9** (*coll.*) to mimic, to ridicule (*an impersonator who takes off MPs*). **10** (*dated*) to drink off, to swallow.

to take on 1 to engage for work etc. **2** to undertake to do (work etc.). **3** to accept a challenge from, to engage in a contest with. **4** to acquire, to adopt. **5** (*coll.*) to be violently affected, to be upset.

to take oneself off to go away, to leave.

to take out 1 to remove, to extract. 2 to
invite and accompany on an outing
etc. 3 to obtain for oneself, to procure.
4 (*Law*) to have (a summons,
injunction etc.) put in place. 5 (*N Am.*)
to buy ready to eat, for consumption
elsewhere. 6 (*sl.*) to murder, to put out
of action. 7 in bridge, to remove by
bidding differently or no trumps.

to take over 1 to assume the management,
ownership etc. of. 2 to assume control
of. 3 (*Print.*) to reset on the next line.

to take someone out of themselves to
distract someone from their problems
or shyness.

to take someone up on 1 to argue or
disagree with someone about. 2 to
accept someone's challenge or offer
of (*I'll take you up on that offer of a
lift*).

to take to 1 to resort to. 2 to form a habit
of. 3 to adapt to. 4 to form a liking for.

to take up 1 to lift (up). 2 to begin to
engage or take an interest in. 3 to
adopt as a protégé. 4 to agree to act
on. 5 to resume, to pursue. 6 (of an
object) to occupy or fill physically.
7 (of an activity) to occupy, to engage,
to engross. 8 to accept as an office.
9 to interrupt, esp. to criticize. 10 to
shorten, esp. by sewing in place.
11 to receive into a vehicle. 12 to
absorb. 13 to arrest, to take into
custody.

to take up with to begin to associate
with.

tale

old wives' tale OLD.
thereby hangs a tale HANG.
to live to tell the tale LIVE[1].
to tell a tale TELL.
to tell its own tale TELL.
to tell one's own tale TELL.
to tell tales TELL.
to tell tales out of school TELL.
to tell the tale TELL.

talk

big talk BIG.
now you're talking (*coll.*) at last you're
saying something I can agree with or
relate to.
small talk SMALL.
talk about used to express ironic or
disparaging emphasis (*Talk about
ignorant! He didn't know Cyprus was
an island!*).
talking of while on the subject of,
concerning (*Talking of Helen, where is
she working now?*).
talk of the town the thing that everyone
is discussing or is interested in.
tall talk TALL.
to know what one is talking about to be
an expert on a particular subject.
to talk about 1 to discuss. 2 to gossip
about.
to talk at 1 to address remarks to, often
indirectly or incessantly. 2 to talk, esp.
offensively, about (a person) in their
presence.
to talk away 1 to spend or use up (time)
in talking. 2 to speak or carry on
speaking.
to talk back 1 to reply. 2 to answer
impudently.
to talk big to boast.
to talk down 1 to silence by loud or
persistent talking. 2 to guide (a pilot or
aeroplane) in to land by giving verbal
instructions.
to talk down to to speak to in a
patronizing or condescending way.
to talk into to persuade to do by
argument (*They talked me into buying
their old car*).
to talk nineteen to the dozen to talk
incessantly.
to talk of 1 to discuss. 2 to mention.
3 (*coll.*) to suggest, esp. tentatively.
to talk out to kill (a motion) by
discussing it until the time of
adjournment.
to talk out of to dissuade from doing by
argument.

to talk **over 1** to discuss at length. **2** to
persuade or convince by talking.
to talk **round 1** to discuss without
coming to a decision. **2** to persuade.
to talk **shop** to talk about work, esp.
tediously or at an inappropriate time.
to talk **tall** to boast.
to talk **the hind legs off a donkey** to talk a
lot.
to talk **through 1** to explain the stages of
(a procedure). **2** to discuss thoroughly
and come to a resolution about.
to talk **through one's hat** to talk about
something one does not understand.
to talk **to 1** to speak to. **2** (*coll.*) to
remonstrate with, to reprove.
to talk **turkey** (*esp. N Am., coll.*) to come
to the point, to talk business.
to talk **up 1** to speak loudly or boldly.
2 to praise.
you **can/ can't talk** used to remind the
listener that what is being said also
applies to them.

tall

†a **tall man of his hands** a dexterous
worker.
tall **order** a difficult or demanding task,
an exacting or unreasonable demand.
tall **story** an exaggerated account.
tall **talk** (*coll.*) exaggeration.

tan

to **tan someone's hide** to beat someone
very severely, to thrash someone.

tandem

in **tandem 1** with one thing behind
another. **2** in partnership, together.

tangent

to **go/ fly off at a tangent** to diverge
suddenly from a course of thought or
action.

tank

to **tank up 1** to fill a vehicle with fuel.
2 to drink, or cause to drink, a large
quantity of alcohol.

tap

on **tap 1** (of a cask etc.) tapped so that
liquor can be drawn off. **2** (of liquor)
ready to be drawn off by tap. **3** (*coll.*)
freely available for use.
to **tap the claret** (*dated, sl.*) to strike the
nose and make it bleed.

tape

on **tape** recorded on magnetic tape.
red **tape** RED.
to **breast the tape** BREAST.
to **have taped** (*coll.*) to have a complete
understanding of (a person or thing).

tapis

on **the tapis** under consideration.

tar

tarred with the same brush with the same
bad characteristics. [Perhaps from the
former practice of brushing a sheep's
sores with tar. The same brush would
be used for the whole flock.]
to **spoil the ship for a ha'p'orth of tar**
SPOIL.
to **tar and feather** to smear with tar and
then cover with feathers as a form of
punishment.

target

on **target 1** on the right course. **2** on
schedule.

tart

to **tart up 1** to make more showy.
2 to dress cheaply, in a vulgar way.

Tartar

to **catch a Tartar** CATCH.

task

to **take to task** to reprove, to reprimand.

taste

acquired taste ACQUIRE.
in **bad/ poor taste** unacceptable, tactless,
lacking discernment (*a joke in poor
taste*).

to leave a bad/ bitter taste (in someone's
mouth) (of an unpleasant experience
etc.) to make someone upset, regretful
etc.

to one's taste to one's liking.

to taste in the amount preferred or
needed to give a pleasant taste (*Add
seasoning to taste*).

to taste blood to want to repeat something
enjoyable or successful. [Alluding to
an animal after its first kill.]

tat

tit for tat TIT.

tatter

in tatters 1 torn to pieces. 2 in a state of
ruin or irretrievable breakdown.

tea

for all the tea in China (*usu. neg.*) under
any circumstances (*I wouldn't go back
to teaching for all the tea in China!*).

one's cup of tea CUP.

teach

that will teach someone that will punish
someone for doing something or
discourage them from doing the same
thing again (*That'll teach you to
complain about my cooking!*).

to teach one's grandmother to suck eggs to
seek presumptuously to advise a more
experienced or knowledgeable person.

to teach school (*esp. N Am.*) to be a
schoolteacher.

to teach someone a lesson to show
someone, esp. by punishing them, that
something is unwise, wrong etc.

you can't teach an old dog new tricks
older people are slow or unwilling to
adjust to new ideas.

teacup

storm in a teacup STORM.

tear¹

that's torn it (*sl.*) that's spoiled things.

to be torn between to be unable to
choose, or have difficulty choosing,
between.

to tear apart 1 to devastate, disrupt or
divide. 2 to make a mess of (a place),
esp. when trying to find something.
3 to criticize severely.

to tear a strip off (*coll.*) to reprimand.

to tear into 1 to reprimand or criticize
forcefully. 2 to embark on
energetically.

to tear limb from limb to dismember
savagely.

to tear oneself away to leave reluctantly.

to tear one's hair 1 to be overcome with
grief. 2 to be very puzzled, frustrated
etc.

to tear someone off a strip (*coll.*) to scold
someone angrily.

to tear to shreds 1 to ruin or destroy
completely. 2 to ridicule or criticize
mercilessly. 3 to completely refute or
demolish (an argument).

tear²

crocodile tears CROCODILE.

in tears crying, weeping.

to bore to tears BORE.

without tears that is in a form that can be
easily mastered. [From *French Without
Tears*, the title of a play by Terence
Rattigan, first performed in 1936.]

tease

to tease out to disentangle.

tee¹

to tee off 1 to play from a tee. 2 (*coll.*) to
begin.

tee²

to a tee perfectly, to a nicety (*This
arrangement suited him to a tee*).

teeter

to teeter on the brink/ edge to be close to
taking a step or decision that could
prove disastrous.

teething

teething troubles 1 the problems or difficulties that arise at the beginning of a new venture etc. and which can usu. be put right quite easily. **2** the soreness and irritation caused when cutting the first teeth.

telegraph

bush telegraph BUSH.

telephone

on the telephone 1 connected to a telephone system. **2** using the telephone.

over the telephone by means of or using the telephone.

tell

all told all included.

as far as one can tell using whatever evidence, information etc. is known or available.

I told you so said by someone whose prediction, warning etc. is proved right.

tell me another (*coll.*) used to express disbelief.

tell that to the marines an expression of incredulity and derision. [From a remark made by Charles II when he heard a story about flying fish. His courtiers were sceptical, but an officer of the Maritime Regiment vouched for the existence of such creatures. The king said, "Henceforward ere ever we cast doubts upon a tale that lacks likelihood we will first tell it to the marines." The phrase was subsequently used to show the contempt of naval seamen for the land-based marines.]

that would be telling (*coll.*) used to express a disinclination to give out any more information, esp. because doing so would disclose a secret.

there's no telling it would be impossible to know or guess (*There's no telling how long it has been here*).

to tell apart to distinguish between.

to tell a tale to have clear significance.

to tell its own tale 1 to be self-evident. **2** to have clear significance.

to tell off 1 (*coll.*) to scold. **2** to count off. **3** to select or detach on some special duty.

to tell on to report (someone).

to tell one's own tale to speak for oneself.

to tell someone's fortune to make predictions about someone's future, e.g. by looking at the lines on their hand.

to tell someone where to get off (*coll.*) to reprimand someone sharply.

to tell tales 1 to report malicious stories to someone in authority. **2** to tell lies.

to tell tales out of school to give away secrets, to break confidences.

to tell the tale (*coll.*) to tell a piteous story.

to tell the time to read the time from a clock or watch.

to tell the truth to be frank.

you're telling me (*coll.*) I completely agree with what you are saying.

temper

out of temper irritable, in a bad temper.

to keep one's temper to remain calm and rational.

to lose one's temper LOSE.

to show temper to be irritable or moody.

temperature

to run a temperature to have an abnormally high body temperature.

to take someone's temperature to use a device such as a thermometer to measure a person's (or an animal's) body heat, esp. as a way of checking on their health.

tempt

to be tempted to to be inclined to (*I'm tempted to tell her*).

to tempt fate/ providence to take a great risk.

ten
ten to one very likely or probably.

tender¹
tender mercies (*iron.*) care or treatment which may ultimately be beneficial but which also involves a degree of discomfort, unpleasantness etc. (*They left me to the tender mercies of the police*). [From the Bible: "A righteous man regardeth the life of his beast: but the tender mercies of the wicked are cruel" (Prov. xii.10).]

tender²
to put out to tender to invite or seek tenders for (work, services etc.).

tense
to tense up to make or become tense.

tenterhook
on tenterhooks in a state of suspense and anxiety, usu. because of uncertainty or awaiting an outcome or result. [Tenterhooks were hooks used to stretch cloth over a frame.]

term
contradiction in terms CONTRADICTION.
in no uncertain terms UNCERTAIN.
in set terms expressed in a specific way.
in terms explicitly.
in terms of 1 as measured or indicated by. **2** in relation to, with reference to (*In terms of cost-effectiveness, this is the best method*).
on speaking terms SPEAKING.
on terms 1 friendly. **2** of equal status or standing.
to bring to terms to force or induce to accept conditions.
to come to terms 1 to conclude an agreement (with). **2** to yield, to give way.
to come to terms with 1 to find a way of coping and living with (some difficulty). **2** to make an agreement with.
to make terms to conclude an agreement.

termination
to bring to a termination to end with no possibility of resumption.
to put a termination to to end with no possibility of resumption.

terror
holy terror HOLY.

test
acid test ACID.
to put to the test to test.
to stand the test of time to prove to be of lasting value, interest etc.
to test out to put to a practical test.

tether
at the end of one's tether END.

thank
I'll thank you (*iron.*) used to express disapproval, reproach, polite annoyance etc. (*I'll thank you not to smoke in here*).
no thanks to despite having the handicap of.
thank goodness/ God/ heavens/ etc. 1 (*coll.*) used to express relief, pleasure etc. **2** used to express pious gratitude.
thanks to because of, owing to (*Thanks to your carelessness, we could lose this contract*).
thank you used as a formula expressing thanks, polite refusal etc.
to give thanks to say grace before a meal.
to return thanks RETURN.
to thank kindly to thank sincerely.
to thank one's lucky stars to be very thankful.

that
all that (*coll.*) very, particularly (*It wasn't all that bad*).

and (all) that (*coll.*) and all the other
things associated with what has just
been mentioned.

that is used to introduce a rewording, a
simpler version or an explanation of
what has just been said.

that's more like it used to acknowledge an
improvement, something preferable
etc.

that's that used to indicate that there is
nothing more to be said or done about
something.

that there (*sl.*) used to indicate
something emphatically (*That
there dress is the one I want*).

that will do used to indicate that no more
is wanted or needed.

thaw

to thaw out 1 to return to normal from a
frozen condition. **2** to become more
relaxed or more friendly.

then

by then by that time.

then and there on the spot, immediately.

then or thenabouts about that time.

thence

from thence thence.

thenceforth

from thenceforth thenceforth.

there

all there 1 (*coll.*) of normal intelligence.
2 (*coll.*) fully competent, knowing all
about it.

not all there 1 (*coll.*) of less than normal
intelligence. **2** (*coll.*) not fully
competent.

so there! used to express derision or
triumph.

there again on the other hand.

there and then at that place and
immediately.

there it is that is the situation.

there you are/ go 1 here is what you

wanted. **2** used to express confirmation
of a situation in a triumphant or
resigned way.

to have been there before to have
experienced the same thing previously
and to know all about it.

thick

a bit thick (*coll.*) unreasonable.

in the thick at the busiest part (of).

thick and fast very quickly, frequently, in
great numbers etc.

thick as thieves (*coll.*) very friendly.

thick as two short planks (*coll.*) not at all
intelligent, very stupid.

thick ear (*coll.*) a swollen ear as a result
of a blow (*If you do that again, I'll give
you a thick ear!*).

thick on the ground numerous, plentiful.

through thick and thin under any
conditions, undauntedly, resolutely.

to have a thick skin to be impervious to
insults or criticism.

to lay it on thick to speak or flatter
extravagantly.

thief

set a thief to catch a thief reformed
wrongdoers are good at catching
criminals because they are familiar
with their methods.

thick as thieves THICK.

thigh

to smite hip and thigh SMITE.

thin

on thin ice in a vulnerable or dangerous
situation.

the thin end of the wedge a relatively
unimportant first step, measure or
change that is likely to lead to
something more important, serious etc.

thin air invisibility, a state of apparent
non-existence (*to vanish into thin air;
to produce something out of thin air*).

thin as a rake very thin (*You don't need
to diet: you're thin as a rake!*).

thin on the ground not numerous, sparse.

thin on top balding.

thin time a period of hardship, misery etc.

to have a thin skin to be sensitive to slights or criticism.

to thin out to remove fruit, flowers etc. from (a tree or plant) or some of a crop of (seedlings etc.) to improve the rest.

thing

all/ other things being equal conditions being unchanged.

all things considered taking everything into account.

as things stand in the present circumstances, as things are.

first thing FIRST.

first things first FIRST.

for one thing as a single consideration.

in the nature of things NATURE.

it's a good thing it is fortunate (that) (*It's a good thing you noticed the window was open*).

(just) one of those things a happening that one cannot do anything about.

little things please little minds LITTLE.

near thing NEAR.

not a thing nothing at all.

not to know the first thing about FIRST.

of all things out of all the possibilities (usu. referring to the least suitable, desirable etc.) (*She was wearing a bikini, of all things!*).

one's thing (*coll.*) one's usual sphere of interest or competence.

quite the thing quite proper or fashionable.

the best thing since sliced bread a very welcome innovation.

the done thing DONE.

the other thing OTHER.

the real thing REAL.

to be all things to all men to please or satisfy everybody, esp. by adaptation to individual needs, interests, opinions etc. [From the Bible: "I am made all things to all men, that I might by all means save some" (I Cor. ix.22).]

to be on to a good thing to be in a situation that is to one's advantage.

to do one's own thing (*coll.*) to do what one likes or what one pleases.

to do things to to affect (someone) in a strange and remarkable way.

to have a thing about 1 to have an unaccountable prejudice or fear about (*He has a thing about spiders*). **2** to have a strong liking for or preoccupation with (*She has a thing about hygiene*).

to hear things HEAR.

to know a thing or two (*coll.*) to have considerable experience, to be worldly-wise.

to make a good thing of to make a profit out of.

to make a thing of 1 to make an issue of, to cause a fuss about. **2** to exaggerate the importance of.

to see/ hear things to see/ hear things that are not there (*I thought I was seeing things when the table began to move*).

worse things happen at sea used as consolation in a difficult or unpleasant situation.

think

I don't think (*coll.*) used to negate the preceding statement or express an opposite opinion (*Your parents will be delighted, I don't think!*).

that's what someone thinks someone is mistaken in their opinion, belief etc. (*That's what you think!*).

think nothing of it there is no need for apology or thanks.

to have another think coming (*coll.*) to be wrong about what one assumes will happen (*If she thinks I'm going to pay, she's got another think coming!*).

to think again 1 to reconsider a previous decision. **2** to change a previous plan or decision.

to think a lot of to think highly of.

to think aloud to speak about one's thoughts as they occur.

to think back to reflect on the past, a past event etc.

to think better of to change one's mind, to decide not to pursue (a course of action) (*I was going to hand in my notice, but I thought better of it*).

to think big to have high ambitions.

to think fit to decide (to do something).

to think for oneself to be independent-minded.

to think highly of to hold in high regard, to respect or admire.

to think less of to regard (someone) in lower esteem than previously.

to think little of to consider (something) to be of little significance or unremarkable.

to think much of to hold in high regard, to be impressed by (*I don't think much of his handwriting*).

to think nothing of to do (something others would find difficult, unpleasant etc.) easily and without hesitation (*He thinks nothing of running ten miles before breakfast*).

to think of 1 to have in mind, to conceive, to imagine. **2** to call to mind, to remember. **3** to have a particular opinion or feeling about, to esteem.

to think on to consider, to think about.

to think on one's feet to react to situations as they arise.

to think out 1 to devise. **2** to solve by long thought.

to think over to consider (a proposition etc.).

to think the world of to love or respect greatly.

to think through to think fully about a situation, decision etc. and its consequences.

to think twice 1 to give extra thought to, to hesitate. **2** to change a decision.

to think up to devise, to invent.

thinking

to put on one's thinking cap to think hard about a problem.

wishful thinking WISHFUL.

third

third degree intimidation or torture, esp. to extract information (*to give someone the third degree*).

third time lucky said after two failures, in the belief that the third attempt will be successful, or after a successful third attempt.

this

this and that/ this, that and the other (*coll.*) random and usu. unimportant activities, subjects of conversation etc.

this here (*sl.*) this particular (person, object etc.) (*What's this here lever for?*).

Thomas

doubting Thomas DOUBT.

thorn

on thorns restless, uneasy.

thorn in one's side/ flesh a constant source of trouble. [From the Bible: "there was given to me a thorn in the flesh, the messenger of Satan to buffet me, lest I should be exalted above measure" (II Cor. xii.7).]

thought

a penny for your thoughts PENNY.

a thought (*coll.*) a very small degree etc., a shade, somewhat.

food for thought FOOD.

in thought in the act of thinking, meditating.

perish the thought PERISH.

second thoughts SECOND.

the wish is father to the thought WISH.

to give thought to to consider.

to take thought to consider something carefully.

thrash

to thrash out to discuss thoroughly in order to find a solution.

thread

thread and thrum good and bad together, all alike.

to hang by a thread HANG.
to lose the thread LOSE.
to pick up the threads PICK.

three

the three professions divinity, law and medicine.

the three R's reading, writing and arithmetic, the basic subjects of education.

three-ring circus 1 (*N Am.*) a circus with three rings. 2 an extravagant event or display. 3 a scene of confusion and complexity.

three sheets in/ to the wind (*Naut., sl.*) drunk. [A sheet is a rope used to control or move the free end of a sail. A sailor or vessel with three sheets in the wind would be completely out of control.]

thresh

to thresh out to discuss thoroughly in order to find a solution.

thrill

thrills and spills the excitement of a situation in which sudden success alternates with sudden failure.

throat

frog in one's/ the throat FROG.
lump in the throat LUMP.
to be at one another's throats to be fighting or quarrelling violently.
to clear one's throat CLEAR.
to cut one another's throats to engage in a mutually ruinous competition.
to cut one's own throat to adopt a policy that will harm or ruin one.
to jump down someone's throat JUMP.
to lie in one's throat LIE¹.
to ram/ thrust something down someone's throat to force someone to accept or listen to an idea, argument etc., esp. by aggressive repetition.
to stick in someone's throat STICK².

throe

in the throes of struggling with (a task etc.).

throne

the power behind the throne POWER.
to ascend the throne ASCEND.

throttle

to throttle back/ down to reduce the speed of an engine by controlling the throttle.

through

all through all the time, throughout.
through and through 1 completely, in every way. 2 searchingly. 3 through again and again.
to be through (*coll.*) to have finished.

throw

a stone's throw STONE.
to be thrown away (on) to be wasted (on).
to be thrown back on to be forced to resort to or rely on.
to throw about/ around 1 to throw carelessly in various directions. 2 to spend (money) recklessly or ostentatiously.
to throw away 1 to cast from one, to discard. 2 to reject carelessly. 3 to spend recklessly, to squander. 4 to lose through carelessness or neglect. 5 to fail to take advantage of. 6 to say in a deliberately unemphatic way.
to throw back 1 to reflect (light etc.). 2 to revert (to ancestral traits).
to throw down 1 to overturn. 2 to lay (oneself) down prostrate.
to throw in 1 to interject, to interpolate. 2 to put in without extra charge, to add as a contribution or extra (*The radio comes with a pair of batteries thrown in*). 3 in soccer, to restart play by throwing the ball two-handed from the place at which it went out. 4 in cricket etc., to throw (the ball) from the

outfield. **5** in cards, to give the lead to (someone) to that player's detriment.

to **throw off 1** to cast off, to get rid of, to abandon, to discard. **2** to produce without effort. **3** to evade (pursuit). **4** to begin hunting.

to **throw oneself at** to make a determined and blatant attempt to attract (a potential sexual partner or spouse).

to **throw oneself into** to take up (an activity) with enthusiasm and energy.

to **throw oneself on/ upon** to commit oneself to the protection, favour etc. of.

to **throw open 1** to open suddenly and completely. **2** to make freely accessible. **3** to open (a discussion etc.) to the audience.

to **throw out 1** to cast out, to reject, to expel. **2** to discard, to throw away. **3** to emit. **4** to give utterance to, to suggest. **5** to cause (a building etc.) to stand out or project. **6** to confuse. **7** in cricket, baseball etc., to run (someone) out by throwing the ball directly at the stumps, base etc. **8** to discomfit so as to lose the thread of argument etc.

to **throw over** to abandon, to desert.

to **throw overboard** to abandon, to discard.

to **throw together 1** to put together hurriedly or carelessly (*I threw together a meal*). **2** to bring into casual contact (*They were thrown together on the training course*).

to **throw up 1** to raise, erect or lift quickly. **2** to abandon, to resign from. **3** (*coll.*) to vomit. **4** to draw attention to.

thrum

thread and thrum THREAD.

thrust

cut and thrust CUT.

to **thrust oneself in 1** to intrude. **2** to interfere.

to **thrust one's nose in** to interfere.

to **thrust through** to pierce.

thumb

all fingers and thumbs FINGER.

one's fingers all thumbs FINGER.

rule of thumb RULE.

thumbs up/ down an indication of success or approval/ failure or disapproval. [From gestures made by the spectators at a gladiator fight in ancient Rome, indicating whether the loser should live or die.]

to be all thumbs to be clumsy and fumbling with one's hands.

to stick out like a sore thumb STICK².

to thumb a lift to get a lift from a passing car by signalling with a raised thumb.

to thumb one's nose to make a gesture of derision with the thumb to the nose and the fingers spread, to cock a snook.

to twiddle one's thumbs TWIDDLE.

under someone's thumb completely under someone's power or influence.

thunder

blood and thunder BLOOD.

to steal someone's thunder STEAL.

thunderstorm

like a dying duck in a thunderstorm DYING.

tick¹

in two ticks TWO.

to tick off 1 to mark off (a series) by ticks. **2** (*coll.*) to reprimand, to tell off.

to tick over 1 (of an engine) to run slowly with gear disconnected. **2** to operate smoothly, at a low level of activity (*He kept the business ticking over in our absence*).

what makes someone tick (*coll.*) a person's main motivation or interest.

tick²

on tick bought on credit, hire purchase etc.

ticket

(just) the ticket (*coll.*) the right, desirable or appropriate thing.

meal ticket MEAL.

to have tickets on oneself (*Austral.*) to be conceited.

tickle

slap and tickle SLAP.

tickled pink/ to death (*coll.*) very amused, very pleased.

to tickle someone's fancy to attract or amuse someone.

tide

time and tide wait for no man TIME.

to save the tide SAVE.

to tide over (to help) to surmount difficulties in a small way or temporarily (*She borrowed £50 to tide her over*).

to turn the tide to reverse the course of events.

to work double tides WORK.

tie

fit to be tied FIT.

old school tie OLD SCHOOL.

tied to someone's apron strings unduly controlled by someone (esp. a mother or wife).

to tie down to restrict, to constrain.

to tie in 1 to agree or coordinate (with). **2** to be associated or linked (with).

to tie in knots (*coll.*) to baffle (a person) completely, to confuse.

to tie someone's hands (*usu. pass.*) to prevent someone from taking action (*My hands were tied: I couldn't prevent it*).

to tie the knot (*coll.*) to get married.

to tie up 1 to fasten securely to a post etc. **2** to restrict, to bind by restrictive conditions. **3** to be compatible or coordinated (with). **4** to keep occupied to the exclusion of other activities. **5** to truss up. **6** to invest. **7** to bring to a close.

with one hand/ arm tied behind one's back very easily, without any difficulty (*I could do that with one arm tied behind my back*).

tiger

paper tiger PAPER.

tight

in a tight spot in a dangerous or complicated situation.

to keep a tight rein on to control carefully (*We must keep a tight rein on our spending*).

to run a tight ship to manage a department, organization etc. with strict control.

tighten

to tighten one's belt to make economies, to reduce expenditure.

tile

on the tiles (*coll.*) enjoying oneself wildly, usu. drunkenly (*a night on the tiles*). [Alluding to cats on the rooftops.]

to have a tile loose to be eccentric or half-crazy.

till[1]

till now up to the present time.

till then up to that time.

till[2]

with one's fingers in the till FINGER.

tilt

at full tilt FULL.

to tilt at windmills to fight imaginary adversaries. [From the hero of Cervantes' novel *Don Quixote* (1605), who mistook a group of windmills for giants and attacked them with his lance.]

timber

shiver my timbers SHIVER[2].

time

against time in a great hurry, at utmost speed in order to achieve a goal by a specified time, to a deadline.

ahead of one's time having progressive or revolutionary ideas that it is thought would be more generally acceptable at a future time.

ahead of time earlier than anticipated.

all in good time later, when the time is right, eventually.

all the time 1 continuously. **2** throughout a given period of time. **3** at all times.

any time now very soon, very shortly.

a stitch in time (saves nine) STITCH.

at a time separately at any one time (referring to a specified group or number) (*two at a time*).

at one time 1 once, in the past (referring to an unspecified time). **2** simultaneously.

at the best of times when everything is ideal or favourable.

at the same time SAME.

at times at intervals, now and then.

before one's time prematurely.

behind the times old-fashioned, out of date.

behind time late.

big time BIG.

borrowed time BORROWED.

every time 1 on each occasion, with no exception. **2** (*coll.*) yes, certainly.

for the time being for the present.

from time to time at intervals; now and then.

half the time HALF.

high old time HIGH.

high time HIGH.

in good time 1 at the right moment. **2** early. **3** (*often iron.*) fortunately, happily.

in (less than) no time very quickly (*We'll be there in no time*).

in one's own good time at a pace and time decided by oneself.

in one's own time outside working hours.

in one's time 1 in one's prime, in one's

heyday. **2** in a previous period of one's life.

in process of time PROCESS.

in the course of time COURSE.

in the fullness of time FULLNESS.

in the nick of time NICK.

in time 1 not too late, early enough. **2** in the course of time, some time or other, eventually. **3** in accordance with the time, rhythm etc.

long time no see LONG.

many a time often, many times.

many's the time often.

nine times out of ten NINE.

not before time 1 at the appropriate moment. **2** later than the appropriate moment (*You're here, and not before time!*).

no time a very short space of time.

once upon a time ONCE.

on one's own time (*N Am.*) in one's own time.

on time punctually.

out of one's time having served one's apprenticeship.

out of time 1 unseasonable. **2** too late. **3** not keeping rhythm correctly.

sign of the times SIGN.

(there's) no time like the present used to encourage immediate action.

the time of one's life an experience of unequalled pleasure (*He had the time of his life at the party*).

thin time THIN.

third time lucky THIRD.

time after time repeatedly.

time and a half payment at one and a half times the normal rate, usu. for working overtime, weekends etc.

time and tide wait for no man used to encourage immediate action.

time and (time) again repeatedly.

time enough soon enough.

time flies time passes very quickly. [A translation of the Latin phrase *tempus fugit*, which is also used with this meaning in English.]

time immemorial time beyond legal

memory, a very long time ago (*The family has lived here since time immemorial*).

time is up 1 the allotted time is past. **2** the appointed moment has arrived.

time of day 1 the hour by the clock. **2** a greeting appropriate to this. **3** (*sl.*) the latest aspect of affairs.

time out of mind 1 a longer time than anyone can remember. **2** many times.

time was (*coll.*) there was once a time (*Time was when you could buy a loaf for a halfpenny*).

to beat time (*Mus.*) to regulate or measure the time by a motion of the hand or foot.

to bide one's time BIDE.

to buy time BUY.

to do time to serve a prison sentence.

to gain time GAIN.

to have a time of it to have difficulty or trouble in doing something.

to have a whale of a time WHALE.

to have no time for 1 to dislike. **2** to be unwilling or unable to spend time on (something).

to have the time 1 to be able to spend the required time. **2** to know what the time is.

to keep good/ bad time 1 to be habitually punctual/ unpunctual. **2** (of a clock etc.) to be reliable/ unreliable.

to keep time to move, sing etc. in time with something else, esp. music.

to kill time KILL.

to know the time of day to know what is going on, to be well informed.

to lose no time LOSE.

to lose time LOSE.

to make time 1 to make oneself available (for an activity). **2** (*N Am., sl.*) to make sexual advances (to a person).

to mark time MARK.

to pass the time of day to greet each other, to exchange casual remarks.

to play/ stall for time to protract something deliberately to allow other events to catch up.

to serve one's time SERVE.

to serve out one's time SERVE.

to stand the test of time TEST.

to take one's time to proceed steadily and without hurry.

to take time by the forelock to grasp an opportunity.

to tell the time TELL.

to waste no time WASTE.

what time (*poet.*) when.

tin

tin god 1 a person of local, undeserved importance. **2** a self-important person.

tinker

not to give a tinker's cuss not to care at all.

tip¹

on the tip of one's tongue about to be uttered, esp. if difficult to recall.

tip of the iceberg the small and most obvious part of a difficulty, problem etc. that is much larger. [Alluding to the small part of an iceberg that is seen above the surface of the water.]

tip²

to tip off 1 to give a warning hint (*They had been tipped off about the raid*). **2** in basketball, to start play by throwing the ball high between players of the two sides.

to tip one's hat/ cap to touch or raise one's hat etc. in greeting or acknowledgement.

to tip (someone) the wink (*coll.*) to give a hint, to inform furtively.

to tip the balance to make the significant difference (*Her computing experience tipped the balance in her favour*).

tiptoe

on tiptoe on the tip of the toes.

tit

tit for tat blow for blow, retaliation in kind.

tittle

not one jot or tittle JOT.

to

to and fro 1 forwards and backwards.
  2 repeatedly from one place to another
  and back again.

toast

on toast 1 (of food) served on a piece of
  toast. **2** (*coll.*) at one's mercy.
warm as toast WARM.

tod

on one's tod (*sl.*) on one's own. [From
  the rhyming slang phrase 'on one's
  Tod Sloan'. Tod Sloan was a famous
  jockey of the 19th century.]

today

today week/ fortnight on this day next
  week/ fortnight, a week/ two weeks
  today.

toe

from top to toe TOP[1].
on one's toes alert, ready to act (*to keep
  them on their toes*).
to toe in/ out to turn the toes in/ out, in
  walking etc.
to toe the line to conform, to bow to
  discipline. [Alluding to the correct
  position of competitors' feet just
  behind the starting line of a race.]
to toe the mark 1 (*Mil.*) to touch a chalk
  line with the toes so as to be in rank
  abreast with others. **2** to do one's duty,
  to perform one's obligations.
to tread on someone's toes TREAD.
to turn up one's toes (*sl.*) to die.

toffee

someone can't do something for toffee
  (*coll.*) someone is very bad at
  something (*He couldn't play for
  toffee*).

together

together with as well as, in addition to.

token

by the same/ this token similarly, in
  corroboration.
more by token as further proof.

toll

to take its toll to have a damaging effect
  in terms of loss, injury, deterioration
  etc. (*A long spell in prison had taken
  its toll on her health*).

Tom

peeping Tom PEEP.
Tom, Dick and Harry (*derog.*) average
  commonplace people, any taken at
  random (*Every Tom, Dick and Harry
  can become a shareholder*).

tomorrow

like there's no tomorrow (*coll.*) recklessly,
  extravagantly (*spending money like
  there's no tomorrow*).
tomorrow is another day 1 there will be
  better things or other opportunities in
  the future. **2** used to express a lack
  of concern about the future. [Made
  famous as the closing words of
  Margaret Mitchell's novel *Gone with
  the Wind* (1936), uttered by Vivien
  Leigh as Scarlett O'Hara in the film
  version.]
tomorrow morning/ afternoon/ evening
  during the morning/ afternoon/ evening
  of tomorrow.
tomorrow never comes used to
  discourage procrastination.
tomorrow week on the day a week later
  than tomorrow, a week tomorrow.

ton

like a ton of bricks (*coll.*) with great force
  (*If she catches you doing that, she'll be
  down on you like a ton of bricks*).
to weigh a ton WEIGH.

tone

to lower the tone LOWER.

to tone down 1 to subdue, to soften (the tint, tone, pitch, intensity etc. of). 2 to modify, to reduce, to soften (a statement, demands etc.). 3 to become softer, less emphatic etc.

to tone up 1 (of muscles etc.) to become firmer or more vigorous. 2 to heighten, to intensify.

tongs

hammer and tongs HAMMER.

tongue

on the tip of one's tongue TIP[1].

the cat has (got) someone's tongue CAT.

the rough edge/ side of one's tongue ROUGH.

to find one's tongue to express oneself after a period of remaining silent.

to give tongue 1 to speak one's mind. 2 to bark esp. (of a hound) when in contact with the quarry.

to hold one's tongue to keep quiet.

to keep a civil tongue in one's head CIVIL.

to loosen someone's tongue LOOSEN.

to lose one's tongue LOSE.

tongue-in-cheek 1 said with irony; mischievously and drily humorous (a tongue-in-cheek comment/ remark). 2 ironically, insincerely (talk/ speak tongue-in-cheek).

with one's tongue hanging out eagerly, with avid expectation.

with one's tongue in one's cheek ironically.

too

none too hardly, not very, rather less than (The weather was none too promising).

tool

a bad workman blames his tools WORKMAN.

to down tools DOWN.

tooth

armed to the teeth ARMED.

by/ with the skin of one's teeth SKIN.

in the teeth of 1 in spite of. 2 in direct opposition to. 3 in the face of (the wind).

kick in the teeth KICK.

long in the tooth LONG.

sweet tooth SWEET.

to cast something in someone's teeth CAST.

to cut one's eye-teeth EYE-TOOTH.

to cut one's teeth to have one's teeth come through the gums.

to cut one's teeth on to gain experience through, to learn one's trade or profession through (As an actor, he cut his teeth on lighter comic roles).

to draw the teeth of to render harmless.

to fight tooth and nail FIGHT.

to get one's teeth into to tackle (a task etc.) in a determined and satisfying manner.

to give one's eye-teeth EYE-TOOTH.

to go over with a fine-tooth comb FINE-TOOTH COMB.

to grit one's teeth GRIT.

to lie through/ in one's teeth LIE[1].

to one's teeth 1 to one's face. 2 in open opposition.

to set one's teeth 1 to clench the teeth. 2 to be obstinate or determined.

to set someone's teeth on edge 1 to cause a tingling or grating sensation in someone's teeth. 2 to cause a feeling of irritation or revulsion in someone.

to show one's teeth to adopt a threatening attitude. [From animal behaviour.]

to take the bit between one's teeth BIT[2].

top[1]

at the top of one's voice as loudly as possible (I shouted at the top of my voice).

at the top (of the tree/ ladder) being the most successful, esp. in a particular field of achievement.

from top to toe completely, from head to foot.

off the top of one's head without preparation, impromptu.

on top **1** in the lead. **2** in control.

on top of **1** added to. **2** in control of.

on top of the world **1** very happy indeed, exuberant. **2** at the height of fame, achievement etc.

out of the top drawer of the highest quality or social status.

over the top **1** on the attack. **2** to excess. **3** extreme, outrageous. [In World War I the phrase referred to soldiers climbing out of the trenches to attack the enemy.]

thin on top THIN.

to come to the top to achieve distinction.

top brass (*sl.*) the highest-ranking officials or officers.

top dog (*coll.*) the uppermost person, the boss.

top drawer **1** the uppermost drawer in a chest of drawers. **2** the highest social background or status.

top of the pops **1** (a record, singer etc.) currently (among) the most popular in terms of sales. **2** a person or thing which is currently enjoying great popularity.

to take it from the top (*coll.*) to start (again) from the beginning.

to the top of one's bent to one's utmost capacity.

to top off **1** to complete by putting the top or uppermost part to. **2** to finish, to complete.

to top oneself (*sl.*) to commit suicide.

to top one's part in the theatre, to play one's role to perfection.

to top out to put the last or highest girder etc. on (a building).

to top up to fill up (with petrol, oil etc.).

up top (*coll.*) in one's head or brain (*He hasn't got much up top*).

top²

to sleep like a top SLEEP.

torch

to carry a torch to suffer from unrequited love (for).

to put to the torch to burn down (as an act of war etc.).

toss

to argue the toss ARGUE.

to take a toss to be thrown by a horse.

to toss a pancake to turn a pancake over in the pan by flipping it in the air.

to toss oars to salute by raising oars to an upright position.

to toss off **1** to swallow at a draught. **2** to produce or do quickly or perfunctorily. **3** (*taboo sl.*) to masturbate.

to toss one's head to throw one's head back in anger, disgust, impatience etc.

to toss up to toss a coin in order to decide something.

to win the toss WIN.

tot

to tot up to to total, to amount to.

tote

to tote fair to act fairly.

tother

to tell tother from which to distinguish between two people or things.

touch

at a touch with very little manual effort (*The door opened at a touch*).

common touch COMMON.

in touch **1** in communication (with). **2** up to date, au fait with events etc. **3** aware, understanding of, conscious of, empathetic.

Midas touch MIDAS.

out of touch **1** not up to date or well-informed. **2** not in regular communication (with).

soft/ easy touch (*sl.*) someone easily influenced or imposed upon, esp. someone who is easily convinced to part with their money.

to get in/ into touch to communicate (with).

to keep in touch **1** to maintain regular

communication (with). **2** to be up to date or well-informed.

to lose one's touch LOSE.

to lose touch LOSE.

to put in/ into touch to cause or facilitate communication.

to touch at (of a ship) to come to land or call at (a port etc.).

to touch base to make esp. prearranged contact (with).

to touch bottom 1 to reach the bed of a river, bottom of a swimming pool etc. with one's feet. **2** to reach one's furthest point of decline.

to touch down 1 in rugby, American football etc., to touch the ground with the ball behind the opponents' goal. **2** (of an aircraft or spacecraft) to make contact with the ground after a flight.

to touch lucky to have a stroke of luck.

to touch off 1 to cause to begin, to trigger. **2** to set alight.

to touch on the raw to wound in a sensitive spot.

to touch on/ upon 1 to allude to. **2** to deal with or mention in a slight or hasty manner.

to touch the right chord to elicit an appropriate emotional response.

to touch up 1 to correct or improve (paintwork, make-up etc.) by slight touches, to retouch. **2** to fondle (someone) in a sexual way. **3** to strike (a horse etc.) gently with a whip.

to touch wood to touch something wooden as a supposed protection against bad luck. [From an ancient superstition about the protective power of certain trees, such as oak and ash.]

touch-and-go 1 highly uncertain, very risky or hazardous. **2** a state of uncertainty. [Perhaps of nautical origin, referring to a vessel that touches the bottom but does not go aground.]

would not touch with a bargepole would not come near or have anything to do

with on account of some highly undesirable feature. [Referring to the very long pole used to propel a barge.]

tough

to tough it (out) to withstand difficult circumstances, to persevere with something difficult.

tough as old boots very tough or resilient.

tough nut to crack a difficult problem to solve.

tour

on tour (of a sports team, theatre company, band etc.) visiting a series of different places to play or perform.

tow

in tow 1 being towed. **2** following. **3** under control or guidance.

on tow (of a vehicle) being towed.

to have in tow 1 to be towing (a boat etc.). **2** to be accompanied by, esp. as the person in charge (*They had several small children in tow*).

to have on tow to be towing (a vehicle etc.).

towel

to throw in the towel 1 (of a boxer or their second) to throw a towel into the ring as a sign of submission. **2** (*coll.*) to admit defeat.

tower

ivory tower IVORY.

to tower above/ over 1 to be much taller or higher than (*She towered over her classmates*). **2** to be much greater than in ability, quality etc.

tower of strength a person who gives strong, stable, reliable support, esp. in another's time of difficulty. [From Shakespeare's *Richard III*: "The king's name is a tower of strength."]

town

man about town MAN.

on the town (*coll.*) out to enjoy oneself amongst the amusements and entertainments of a city at night.

talk of the town TALK.

to go to town to let oneself go, to drop all reserve.

to paint the town red PAINT.

town and gown the townspeople and the university staff and students in a university town, as opposed to or contrasted with each other.

toy

to toy with 1 to trifle with. **2** to touch or move idly. **3** to touch and nibble rather than eating normally. **4** to consider in an idle or casual way (*I toyed with the idea of starting my own business*).

trace

in the traces in harness.

to kick over the traces KICK.

track

across the tracks in a poor, less socially prestigious area of town.

in one's tracks where one stands (*a noise that stopped me in my tracks*).

off the beaten track BEATEN.

off the track away from the subject in hand.

one-track mind ONE-TRACK.

on someone's track 1 in pursuit of a person. **2** having knowledge of someone's plans, conduct etc.

on the wrong side of the tracks WRONG.

to cover one's tracks COVER.

to draw a red herring across the track RED.

to keep track of to remain aware of (events, developments etc.).

to lose track of LOSE.

to make tracks to run away, to bolt, to leave.

to make tracks for 1 to head for. **2** to go in pursuit of.

to track down to discover by tracking.

to track with (*Austral.*) to associate with, to go out with.

track record the past achievements, performance, experience etc. of a person or thing. [From athletics.]

trade

jack of all trades JACK.

roaring trade ROARING.

stock-in-trade STOCK.

to be in trade (*usu. derog.*) to be in commerce, esp. to run a shop.

to trade in to give in part payment.

to trade off to exchange (one thing for another), esp. as a compromise.

to trade on to take advantage of (*trading on her generosity*).

trick of the trade TRICK.

trail

to blaze a trail BLAZE[2].

to hit the trail HIT.

to trail arms (*Mil.*) to carry a rifle etc. in a horizontal or oblique position in the right hand with the arm extended.

to trail one's coat/ coat-tails to invite attack. [From a former custom of trailing one's coat on the ground and fighting anyone who dared to tread on one's coat-tails.]

to trail oneself to move wearily or reluctantly.

train

gravy train GRAVY.

in someone's train following behind a person.

in the train of as a consequence or sequel of.

in train in progress, happening according to an organized schedule.

to train down to lose weight by training.

to train fine to bring or be brought to a fine pitch of efficiency by training.

to train it (*coll.*) to go by train.

training

in training 1 at present undergoing physical training. **2** physically fit because of this.

out of **training** not physically fit.

to go into **training** to begin physical
training, usu. for a particular event etc.

trample

to **trample** on 1 to tread heavily on. 2 to
tread on with contempt.

transit

in **transit** being conveyed.

transport

in **transports** extremely joyful.

tread

to **tread** down 1 to press down or crush
with the feet. 2 to trample on. 3 to
destroy.

to **tread** in to press in or into with the
feet.

to **tread** on 1 to trample on. 2 to set the
foot on. 3 to follow closely.

to **tread** on someone's corns to upset or
offend a person's feelings.

to **tread** on someone's toes to offend
someone, usu. by encroaching on their
area of activity.

to **tread** out 1 to press out (wine etc.)
with the feet. 2 to extinguish by
stamping on.

to **tread** the boards/ stage to be or become
an actor or actress.

to **tread** water 1 to remain upright and
afloat in water by making walking
motions with the legs. 2 to undergo a
period of relative inactivity.

treat

a **treat** (*coll.*) excellently, very well (*It
worked a treat!*).

Dutch **treat** DUTCH.

to stand **treat** (*coll.*) to pay for drinks etc.

to **treat** like dirt to behave disrespectfully
towards (*They treat their clients like
dirt*).

tree

not to see the wood for the **trees** WOOD.

out of one's **tree** (*sl.*) crazy, insane.

to bark up the wrong **tree** BARK.

to be up a gum **tree** GUM TREE.

to grow on **trees** GROW.

up a **tree** (*esp. N Am.*) in a fix, cornered.

tremble

all of a **tremble** 1 (*coll.*) trembling. 2 (*coll.*)
very agitated.

trench

to open the **trenches** OPEN.

trespass

to **trespass** on someone's preserves to
interfere in someone's business.

trial

on **trial** 1 undergoing a test. 2 being tried
in a law court.

trial and error a method of solving
problems by trying several solutions
and choosing the most successful.

triangle

eternal **triangle** ETERNAL.

trice

in a **trice** in a moment.

trick

dirty **trick** DIRTY.

how's **tricks**? (*coll.*) how are you?

not to miss a **trick** MISS.

the whole bag of **tricks** WHOLE.

to be up to one's **tricks** (*coll.*) to behave
badly.

to be up to someone's **tricks** to be aware of
the ruses or stratagems that someone is
likely to use.

to do the **trick** (*coll.*) to achieve the
required effect (*That should do the
trick*).

to know a **trick** worth two of that to know
of some expedient.

to **trick** out/ up to decorate, to dress up.

to turn a **trick** (*sl.*) (of a prostitute) to
have sexual relations with a client.

trick of the trade a process known only by members of a particular trade or occupation.

you can't teach an old dog new tricks TEACH.

trifle

to trifle with 1 to treat with levity, disrespect or lack of proper seriousness. **2** to dally with, to toy with. **3** to flirt with.

trigger

quick on the trigger QUICK.

trim

in trim (*esp. Naut.*) looking smart or neat.

out of trim not in good order.

to trim one's sails to restrain oneself or modify one's actions in accordance with the prevailing circumstances. [On a boat, trimming the sails involves adjusting the sails in order to use the wind to best advantage.]

trip

to trip the light fantastic (*facet.*) to dance. [From John Milton's poem *L'Allegro* (1632): "Come, and trip it as ye go / On the light fantastic toe".]

triplicate

in triplicate written out or copied three times.

Triton

Triton among the minnows a person greater than their fellows. [In Greek mythology, Triton was a sea-god.]

trivet

right as a trivet RIGHT.

Trojan

Trojan horse 1 the huge wooden horse in which the Greeks secretly entered Troy. **2** any subterfuge intended to undermine an organization etc. from within.

trolley

off one's trolley (*sl.*) crazy, insane.

trooper

to swear like a trooper SWEAR.

trot

on the trot (*coll.*) one after the other, successively (*for six weeks on the trot*).

to trot out 1 to cause (a horse) to trot to show its paces. **2** (*coll.*) to utter (esp. something familiar or trite).

troth

to pledge/ plight one's troth to pledge faith or fidelity, esp. to make a promise of marriage.

trouble

in trouble 1 liable to suffer punishment or misfortune. **2** (*coll.*) pregnant when not married.

teething troubles TEETHING.

to ask for trouble ASK.

to be no trouble not to cause any difficulty, inconvenience etc.

to get into trouble 1 to incur censure or punishment. **2** to become pregnant. **3** to make pregnant.

to go to the trouble of/ a lot of etc. trouble to to make great efforts (to do something) (*They went to a lot of trouble to get the costumes right*).

to look for trouble 1 (*coll.*) to try to cause trouble. **2** (*coll.*) to behave in a way that invites trouble.

to take (the) trouble to make great efforts (to do something).

to trouble someone for to ask someone to pass etc. (*Could I trouble you for the salt and pepper?*).

trowel

to lay it on with a trowel to flatter grossly.

truant

to play truant to stay away from school without leave.

truck

to have no truck with to have no dealings with.

truckload

by the truckload in large quantities or numbers.

true

in true correctly aligned.

not true (*coll.*) amazing, incredible (*They're so alike, it's just not true!*).

out of true not correctly aligned.

to come true to happen (*to make your dreams come true*).

to hold true 1 to remain valid. **2** to apply, to be relevant.

to show one's true colours 1 to reveal one's opinions, feelings or designs. **2** to throw off disguise.

true to life exactly how it is in life.

true to type/ form normal, what might be expected.

truly

yours truly a conventional way of ending a formal or business letter.

trump

†**to be put to one's trumps** to be reduced to one's last expedient.

to come/ turn up trumps (*coll.*) to be useful or helpful at an opportune moment.

to trump up to invent or fabricate (a charge etc.).

trump card 1 the card turned up to determine which suit is to be trumps. **2** any card of this suit. **3** (*coll.*) an infallible expedient.

trumpet

to blow one's own trumpet BLOW[1].

truss

to truss up 1 to make up into a bundle. **2** to bind or tie up. **3** to hang.

trust

in trust (*Law*) held for safekeeping or as a trustee.

on trust 1 on credit. **2** without questioning.

to take on trust to accept without questioning.

truth

home truth HOME.

in truth in reality, in fact, truly.

†**of a truth** in reality, in fact, truly.

the moment of truth MOMENT.

to tell the truth TELL.

truth is stranger than fiction things happen in real life that are stranger than anything invented by a writer.

truth to tell to be frank.

truth will out the truth cannot be hidden for ever.

try

a damned good try DAMNED.

to (be enough to) try the patience of a saint to be extremely annoying (*a task that would try the patience of a saint*).

to try a fall 1 to have a bout at wrestling. **2** to engage in a contest of any kind.

to try conclusions to engage in competition (with).

to try for 1 to aim at. **2** to attempt to secure. **3** to apply for.

to try for size to try out, to test for suitability etc.

to try it on 1 (*coll.*) to see how far one can go before provoking someone. **2** (*coll.*) to try to deceive, outwit or seduce someone.

to try on to put (clothes) on to see if they fit.

to try one's hand to try to do something new requiring skill (*I tried my hand at making a soufflé*).

to try one's luck to attempt something.

to try out to test.

tuck

nip and tuck NIP.

to tuck away 1 to eat heartily. 2 to place somewhere hidden or isolated.

to tuck in(to) (*coll.*) to eat heartily.

tucker
best bib and tucker BIB.

tumble
rough-and-tumble ROUGH.

to tumble home (*Naut.*) (of the sides of ships) to incline inwards from the line of greatest breadth.

to tumble in 1 to fit (a piece of timber) into another. 2 (*coll.*) to go to bed, to turn in.

tune
he who pays the piper calls the tune PIPER.

in tune 1 at the correct pitch. 2 correctly adjusted for pitch. 3 in harmony, sympathy or agreement (with).

out of tune 1 not at the correct pitch. 2 incorrectly adjusted for pitch. 3 not in harmony, sympathy or agreement (with).

the devil has (all) the best tunes DEVIL.

to call the tune to give orders, to say what is to be done.

to change one's tune CHANGE.

to dance to someone's tune DANCE.

to the tune of (*coll.*) to the sum or amount of (*demanding compensation to the tune of half a million pounds*).

to tune in 1 to adjust a radio circuit to obtain resonance at a required frequency. 2 to switch on a radio or TV set and start listening or watching.

to tune up 1 (of a group of musicians) to adjust (instruments) to a common pitch before playing. 2 to start to play or sing. 3 to improve the performance of (an engine) by tuning.

tuned in (to) (*coll.*) up to date (with); acquainted (with); knowledgeable (about).

tunnel
to see the light at the end of the tunnel LIGHT[1].

turf
to turf out (*coll.*) to throw out, to eject forcibly.

turkey
to talk turkey TALK.

turn
at every turn 1 constantly. 2 everywhere.

by turns 1 alternately. 2 at intervals.

done to a turn DONE.

in one's turn when one's turn, chance etc. comes.

in turn in order of succession, in rotation.

not to do a hand's turn HAND.

not to know which way/ where to turn to be unsure what to do, where to go etc.

one good turn deserves another GOOD TURN.

on the turn 1 (of the tide) just turning. 2 beginning to go sour. 3 on the point of changing.

out of turn 1 out of the proper order of succession. 2 at an inappropriate time.

take a turn for the better/ worse to improve/ deteriorate.

to serve the turn SERVE.

to take a turn for the better/ worse to improve/ deteriorate.

to take (it in) turns to alternate, to perform or participate in rotation or succession.

to turn about 1 to turn the face in another direction. 2 to turn round.

to turn adrift 1 to unmoor (a boat) and allow to float away. 2 to cast off, to abandon without support.

†to turn again to return.

to turn against 1 to (cause to) become hostile to (*She turned my family against me*). 2 to use against.

to turn around (*esp. N Am.*) to turn round.

to turn aside 1 to deviate. 2 to divert, to avert.

to turn away 1 to turn to face the other way. **2** to reject. **3** to send away, dismiss.

to turn back 1 to send back. **2** to begin to go back. **3** to fold back.

to turn down 1 to fold or double down. **2** to lower (a light, the volume on a radio etc.). **3** to lay (a card) face downwards. **4** to reject.

to turn in 1 to direct or incline inwards. **2** to fold or double in. **3** to send, put or drive in. **4** to hand over, to surrender. **5** to give, to execute (a performance etc.). **6** (*coll.*) to go to bed. **7** to achieve (a score). **8** to hand in. **9** (*coll.*) to abandon (a plan etc.).

to turn into to change or be changed into (*The caterpillar turns into a butterfly*).

to turn off 1 to deflect. **2** to deviate. **3** to dismiss. **4** to shut or switch off. **5** to achieve, to produce, to accomplish. **6** †to hang (a criminal). **7** (*coll.*) to cause to lose interest in, esp. sexually.

to turn on 1 to open a way to (gas etc.) by turning a tap. **2** to switch on. **3** to direct, to aim. **4** to hinge or depend upon. **5** to attack. **6** (*coll.*) to excite, to arouse the interest of, esp. sexually (*Whatever turns you on!*). **7** (*sl.*) to introduce to drugs. **8** (*sl.*) to take and get high on drugs.

to turn out 1 to drive out, to expel. **2** to point or to cause to point outwards. **3** to turn (pockets etc.) inside out. **4** to clean (a room) thoroughly. **5** to bring to view. **6** to produce, as the result of labour. **7** to prove to be (*The weather turned out fine*). **8** to switch off. **9** to dress, to groom, to look after the appearance of. **10** (*coll.*) to gather, to assemble. **11** (*coll.*) to go out. **12** (*coll.*) to get out of bed. **13** (*Mil.*) to call (a guard) from the guardroom. **14** to become.

to turn over 1 to change the position of, to invert, to reverse. **2** (of an engine) to (cause to) start or run at low revolutions. **3** to surrender, to hand over. **4** to transfer (to), to put under other control. **5** to cause to turn over, to upset. **6** to do business to the amount of (*turning over £10 million a year*). **7** to consider, to ponder. **8** (*sl.*) to rob.

to turn round 1 to face about. **2** to adopt a new view, attitude, policy etc. **3** to complete the processing of. **4** to complete the unloading and loading of (a ship, aircraft etc.). **5** to restore to profitability.

to turn to 1 to have recourse to. **2** to change or be changed to (*The water turns to steam*). **3** to direct towards. **4** to find (a page) in a book. **5** to set to work. **6** to seek the help of.

to turn up 1 to bring to the surface. **2** to unearth, to bring to light. **3** to place (a card etc.) with the face upwards. **4** to tilt up. **5** to find and refer to (a passage) in a book. **6** to point upwards. **7** to come to light. **8** to happen. **9** to make one's appearance. **10** (*coll.*) to cause to vomit. **11** to shorten (a garment etc.). **12** to increase (the brightness of a light, the volume of a radio etc.).

to turn upon 1 to hinge on. **2** to attack. **3** to direct or aim at.

turn and turn about alternately, successively.

turning

it's a long lane that has no turning LONG.

turn-up

turn-up for the book(s) (*coll.*) a sudden and unexpected (fortunate) occurrence. [From horse racing.]

turtle

to turn turtle to turn completely over, to capsize.

twain

in twain in two, asunder.

twiddle

to twiddle one's thumbs 1 to rotate one's thumbs around each other, as a gesture of nervousness or boredom. **2** to sit idle, to have nothing to do but wait.

twinkle

in a twinkle/ twinkling in an instant.
in the twinkling of an eye in an instant. [From the Bible: "we shall all be changed, In a moment, in the twinkling of an eye, at the last trump" (I Cor. xv.51–2).]

twist

round the twist (*coll.*) crazy (*This puzzle is driving me round the twist!*).
to get one's knickers in a twist KNICKERS.
to twist off to remove or break off by twisting.
to twist someone's arm to use force or psychological pressure to persuade someone.

two

for two pins given the slightest opportunity or reason (*For two pins I'd have driven off and left him there*).
in two 1 into two parts. **2** asunder (*split in two*).
in two minds unable to choose between alternatives, undecided (*I'm in two minds about selling the car*).
in two shakes (of a lamb's tail) very quickly.
in two ticks (*coll.*) in a very short time.
or two denoting several (*We've had a complaint or two about it*).

that makes two of us (*coll.*) the same thing applies to me.
there are no two ways about it it cannot be disputed.
to fall between two stools 1 to fail through being unable to choose between two alternatives. **2** to be neither one thing nor the other.
to have two left feet to be very clumsy, esp. in dancing.
to put two and two together (and make four) to draw inferences.
two bites at the cherry 1 a second chance (*You can't have two bites at the cherry*). **2** a bungling attempt.
two by/ and two in pairs.
two can play at that game (*coll.*) someone can be copied, to their disadvantage.
two heads are better than one a problem may be solved more quickly or easily by two people working together than by one alone.
two or three a few.
two's company, three's a crowd said when a third person would spoil the pleasure or enjoyment of two people doing something together.
two wrongs don't make a right one should not retaliate for one wrong with another.

twopenn'orth

to add/ put in one's twopenn'orth (*coll.*) to give one's views.

type

in type set in type.

tyre

spare tyre SPARE.

U

ugly
ugly duckling an unpromising person or thing that turns out surprisingly successful etc. [From a story by Hans Christian Andersen (1805–75) about a young bird that is rejected as the ugliest of a brood of ducklings but grows into a beautiful swan.]

unaccounted
unaccounted for not explained; not included in an account or list.

unawares
at unawares unexpectedly.

uncalled
uncalled for not necessary; gratuitous.

uncertain
in no uncertain terms forcefully and unambiguously.

uncle
bob's your uncle BOB².
Dutch uncle DUTCH.

unco
the unco guid (*esp. derog., Sc.*) people of narrow, excessively religious outlook.

understand
to give to understand to inform authoritatively; to lead to believe (*I was given to understand that the tickets were free*).

to understand each other 1 to know and be sympathetic to each other's feelings. **2** to have an agreement with each other.

understanding
on the understanding that provided that.

university
at university studying at a university.

unknown
unknown quantity a person, thing or number whose importance or value is unknown.
unknown to without the knowledge of (*Unknown to me she'd already gone*).

unsaid
to leave unsaid to refrain from stating (*Some things are better left unsaid*).

unsound
of unsound mind mentally unbalanced.

unstick
to come unstuck (*coll.*) (of a plan etc.) to go wrong or fail.

up
on the up and up 1 (*coll.*) becoming steadily more successful. **2** (*esp. N Am., coll.*) straight, honest.
something is up (*coll.*) something unusual or strange is happening.
to be all up with to be hopeless for.
to up sticks (*coll.*) to move house, to go and live elsewhere, to make off.

[Perhaps referring to the removal of furniture.]

to up the ante 1 to increase the (asking) price or cost. **2** to increase the risks, demands, etc. involved in something. [The ante is the opening stake in a game of poker.]

up against 1 confronting, having to deal with (*to find out what we're up against*). **2** close to. **3** touching.

up against it (*coll.*) facing stiff opposition or great difficulties.

up and about having got out of bed.

up-and-coming (*coll.*) (of a person) enterprising and promising.

up and doing active and busy.

up and down 1 alternately backwards and forwards. **2** alternately upwards and downwards. **3** in every direction. **4** (*coll.*) varying in moods or states of health.

up and running functioning (*once we get the computer system up and running*).

up for put forward for or being considered for (office).

up on knowledgeable about.

ups and downs 1 rises and falls, undulations. **2** vicissitudes, changes of fortune.

up to 1 until (*up to now*). **2** as far as (*up to my shoulder*). **3** as many or as much as (*up to five goes*). **4** incumbent upon (*It's not up to me to decide*). **5** capable of; equal to (a task etc.). **6** occupied with (*What are you up to?*).

up to anything (*coll.*) ready for any mischief, sport etc.

up with used to express support for something (*Up with the republic!*).

up yours (*sl., offensive*) used to express contempt, defiance etc.

what's up? 1 (*coll.*) what is going on? **2** (*coll.*) what is the matter?

upgrade

on the upgrade improving, advancing or progressing.

upper

on one's uppers (*coll.*) destitute. [Alluding to someone who has worn out the soles of their shoes.]

upper crust (*coll.*) the upper class.

upper hand

to gain/ get the upper hand to be victorious.

upset

to upset the apple-cart to disrupt plans or arrangements.

uptake

quick/ slow on the uptake quick/ slow to understand or learn.

upwards

upwards of more than.

use[1]

in use 1 being employed. **2** in customary practice.

to convert to one's own use CONVERT.

to have no use for 1 to dislike, to disapprove of. **2** to find no use for.

to make use of 1 to use, to employ. **2** to take advantage of.

use and wont common or customary practice.

use[2]

could use (*coll.*) would appreciate having (*I could use a drink!*).

to use one's discretion to make decisions based on one's own judgement.

to use one's loaf (*coll.*) to use one's brain or common sense. [From rhyming slang: loaf (of bread) = head.]

to use someone's name to quote a person as a reference etc.

to use up 1 to finish; to consume completely. **2** to find some use or purpose for (something left over). **3** to exhaust or wear out.

useful

to make oneself **useful** to be of service to someone.

usual

as per usual as usually happens.

usury

with usury (*poet.*) with interest.

utmost

to do one's **utmost** to do everything that one can.

V

vacuum
in a vacuum in isolation, without the normally attendant context, circumstances etc.

vain
in vain unsuccessfully, without result (*We tried in vain to find a replacement*).

value
face value FACE.

variance
at variance 1 conflicting, not in accord (with one another). 2 (of people) in disagreement or dispute.

variety
variety is the spice of life doing many different things makes life more interesting and enjoyable. [From William Cowper's poem *The Task* (1785): "Variety's the very spice of life, / That gives it all its flavour."]

veil
beyond the veil in the unknown state that follows death.
to take the veil 1 to assume the veil according to the custom of a woman when she becomes a nun. 2 to retire to a convent.

velvet
on velvet (*coll.*) in a position of comfort, luxury, wealth etc.

velvet glove
the iron hand in the velvet glove IRON HAND.

vengeance
with a vengeance to a greater degree than was anticipated or wished; forcibly, emphatically, undoubtedly, extremely.

vent
to give vent to 1 to give (often angry or violent) expression to, to express freely. 2 to allow to break out.
to vent one's spleen on to berate angrily or spitefully, often without just cause.

venture
at a venture at random; without planning, preparation, forethought etc.
to venture on/ upon to (dare to) enter upon or engage in etc.

verge
on the verge of on the brink of.
to verge on 1 to border on, to be next to. 2 to come near to, to nearly be (*eccentricity verging on madness*).

verity
†of a verity in truth, surely.

verse
chapter and verse CHAPTER.
to cap verses CAP.
to verse in to instruct in, to make conversant with or knowledgeable about (*She was well versed in computer terminology*).

very

very well/ good used to indicate assent or approval.

vial

to pour out vials of wrath POUR.

vicinity

in the vicinity nearby.

vicious

vicious circle 1 a situation in which progressing from cause to effect or from problem to solution merely brings one back to one's starting point and aggravates the original state of things. **2** circular reasoning, providing a proof or explanation for something which depends for its truth or validity on the truth or validity of the thing one is setting out to prove or explain.

victory

Pyrrhic victory PYRRHIC.

view

bird's-eye view BIRD'S-EYE.
in full view FULL.
in view 1 in sight. **2** in mind when forming an opinion. **3** as one's object or aim.
in view of considering, having regard to (*in view of his lack of experience*).
on view open to public inspection.
point of view POINT.
to take a dim/ poor view of (*coll.*) to regard pessimistically, to view with suspicion or disfavour (*I take a dim view of your refusal to cooperate*).
†to the view so as to be seen by everybody.
to view with a friendly eye to regard in a kind or friendly manner.
to view with a jealous eye to regard with jealousy.
with a view to 1 with the intention of. **2** in hopes or anticipation of.

villain

villain of the piece the principal wicked character.

vim

full of vim and vigour abounding in energy and vitality.

vine

clinging vine CLING.

violence

to do violence to 1 to do a physical injury to. **2** to violate. **3** to distort the meaning or intent of.

violet

shrinking violet SHRINKING.

viper

viper in one's bosom a close friend or associate who harms or betrays one. [From Aesop's fable about a peasant who took a dying snake into his home and nursed it back to health, only to receive a fatal bite from the recovered reptile.]

virtue

by/ in virtue of by or through the efficacy or authority of, on the strength of.
of easy virtue EASY.
to make a virtue of necessity to attempt to derive some benefit from consciously opting to undertake, or undertaking with a good grace, something that one is in any event compelled to do.

vogue

in vogue fashionable, currently popular or widespread.

voice

at the top of one's voice TOP[1].
in (good) voice in a condition to sing or speak well.
out of voice not in a condition to sing or speak well.
still small voice STILL.

to give voice to to utter, to express, to make known.

to lift up one's voice LIFT.

voice in the wilderness a person whose suggestions, advice, pleas etc. are unheeded or ignored. [From the Bible: "The voice of one crying in the wilderness" (Matt. iii.3), referring to John the Baptist.]

with one voice unanimously.

volition

of/ by one's own volition voluntarily.

volley

on the volley before the ball hits the ground.

volume

to speak volumes SPEAK.

vote

to put to a/ the vote to obtain a decision regarding (a proposal) by holding a vote.

to vote down to defeat or suppress by vote.

to vote in to elect.

to vote off to remove from (a committee etc.) by voting.

to vote out to dismiss from office by voting.

to vote with one's feet to indicate one's dissatisfaction by leaving or going elsewhere (*Customers will vote with their feet*).

vow

to take vows to enter a religious order and commit oneself to the vows of chastity, poverty and obedience.

W

wade

to **wade in/ into** (*coll.*) to tackle or attack vigorously.

to **wade through** to read (a book etc.) with difficulty or effort.

wager

to **hold a wager** to bet.

wagon

off the (water) wagon (*coll.*) no longer abstaining from alcohol.

on the (water) wagon (*coll.*) abstaining from alcohol.

to **hitch one's wagon to a star** HITCH.

wait

I can't wait I am impatient (for or to do something).

to **lie in wait (for)** LIE².

to **wait and see** to wait patiently for some future event.

to **wait at table** to act as a waiter in a hotel, restaurant etc.

to **wait on table** (*N Am.*) to wait at table.

to **wait on/ upon 1** to attend on as a waiter or servant. **2** to pay a visit to deferentially. **3** to await. **4** (of consequences etc.) to follow. **5** †to accompany, to escort. **6** †to watch.

to **wait up** to remain out of bed waiting (for).

wait for it! 1 do not begin too soon. **2** used to introduce an unexpected remark, a punchline etc.

wait on! be patient!, wait!

you wait! used to threaten or warn.

waiting

in waiting in attendance, esp. on the sovereign.

waiting game a holding back of action in the hope of more advantageous circumstances later (*to play a waiting game*).

wake¹

to **be a wake-up** (*Austral., coll.*) to be alert (to).

wake²

in the wake of following.

walk

cock-of-the-walk COCK¹.

in a walk easily, without effort.

someone walking over one's grave a momentary feeling of uneasiness, without apparent cause, that makes one tremble.

to **walk about** to stroll around.

to **walk all over 1** (*coll.*) to defeat easily or conclusively. **2** (*coll.*) to take advantage of.

to **walk away from 1** to go much faster than, esp. in a race. **2** to refuse to deal with (*to walk away from one's responsibilities*). **3** to survive without serious injury (*to walk away from an accident*).

to **walk away with** to win or gain easily.

to **walk in** to enter.

to **walk in on** to interrupt.

to **walk into 1** to enter or encounter unwittingly (*to walk into a trap*). **2** to gain easily (*to walk into a job*). **3** (*sl.*)

†to thrash. **4** †to abuse. **5** †to eat (something) heartily.

to walk it 1 to go on foot. **2** (*coll.*) to win or achieve something without effort.

to walk off 1 to depart abruptly. **2** to get rid of by walking (*to walk off one's depression*). **3** to get rid of the effects of (a meal etc.) by walking.

to walk off with 1 (*coll.*) to carry off, to steal. **2** to win or gain easily.

to walk one's chalks to be off, to depart without ceremony. [From the former practice of putting a chalk mark on the door of a house or room to be vacated.]

to walk out 1 to depart suddenly, esp. in anger. **2** to stop work as a protest.

to walk out on to abandon.

to walk out with (*dated*) to go courting with.

to walk over 1 (*coll.*) to walk all over. **2** to walk or go slowly over (a racecourse etc.) because one is the only competitor, or because one's opponents are weak.

to walk someone off their feet to make a person walk so far or so fast that they are exhausted.

to walk tall (*coll.*) to feel proud.

to walk the boards to be an actor.

to walk the chalk to follow a straight course as by walking along a chalk line. [Originally a test of sobriety.]

to walk the plank to be compelled to walk blindfold along a plank thrust over a ship's side (a pirates' mode of putting to death).

to walk the streets 1 to be a prostitute. **2** to wander round a town or city, esp. in search of work, accommodation etc.

to walk the wards/ hospitals to be a medical student in a hospital.

to walk up to to approach.

walk of life one's profession, occupation, sphere of action etc.

walk up! used to invite spectators to a circus etc.

walkabout

to go walkabout 1 (of Australian Aborigines) to go on a wandering journey through the bush. **2** (*coll.*) to go missing (*My car keys have gone walkabout*).

walkies

to go walkies 1 (*coll. or facet.*) to go for a walk. **2** (*coll. or facet.*) to disappear, to go missing.

walking

within walking distance close enough to walk to.

wall

fly on the wall FLY[1].

off the wall eccentric, unexpected.

the writing on the wall WRITING.

to bang/ knock/ run one's head against a brick wall HEAD[1].

to drive up the wall DRIVE.

to give the wall to to allow as a courtesy to walk or pass by on the side of a pavement etc. away from the gutter.

to go to the wall 1 (*coll.*) to be defeated in a contest. **2** (*coll.*) to be pushed aside. **3** (*coll.*) to fail (*Several other companies have gone to the wall*).

to have one's back to the wall BACK.

to see through a brick wall BRICK.

up the wall (*coll.*) in or into a state of distraction or exasperation (*to go up the wall*).

walls have ears beware of eavesdroppers.

wallaby

on the wallaby (track) (*Austral., sl.*) tramping about looking for work etc.

waltz

to waltz into (*coll.*) to rebuke severely.

to waltz off with 1 to take quickly or casually; to steal. **2** to win, esp. easily.

wand

to wave one's magic wand WAVE.

wane
on the wane waning, decreasing, declining.

wanion
†**with a wanion** with a curse (to you).

want
not to want to to be unwilling to.
not to want to know to prefer to ignore (*I tried to explain, but she didn't want to know*).
to want for nothing to have everything one needs.

wanting
to be found wanting to fail to meet the required or expected standard. [From the Bible: "Thou art weighed in the balances, and art found wanting" (Dan. v.27).]

war
all's fair in love and war FAIR.
at war engaged in hostilities (with).
in the wars (*coll.*) bruised or injured as from fighting or quarrelling.
†**to go to the wars** to serve as a soldier, esp. in a foreign country.
to go to war 1 to begin a war. **2** to begin active service in a war.
war of attrition a long-drawn-out conflict in which each side tries to wear down the other.
war of nerves a conflict involving the use of psychological tactics.

ward
to ward off 1 to parry, to turn aside, to keep off. **2** to avert.

warm
to warm the cockles of the heart to cause a deep feeling of warmth or contentment. [Perhaps from the Latin phrase *cochleae cordis*, referring to the ventricles of the heart.]
to warm up 1 to make or become warm.

2 to reheat (cooked food). **3** to prepare for a contest, performance etc., esp. by exercising or practising. **4** to make (an audience) more receptive to a show or act by a preliminary entertainment.
warm as toast pleasantly warm (*My feet were warm as toast in my new fur-lined boots*).

warpath
on the warpath 1 ready for or engaged in conflict. **2** (*coll.*) thoroughly roused or incensed.

warrant
death warrant DEATH.
I('ll) warrant I am sure.

wart
warts and all (*coll.*) without concealing any blemishes, shortcomings etc. [From instructions given by Oliver Cromwell (1599–1658) to his portrait painter: "Mr Lely, I desire you would use all your skill to paint my picture truly like me, and not flatter me at all; but remark all these roughnesses, pimples, warts, and everything as you see me".]

wash
to come out in the wash 1 to be removed in washing. **2** (*coll.*) to be resolved or revealed in the end (*It'll all come out in the wash*).
to wash away 1 to remove or be removed by or as by water. **2** to sweep or be swept away by or as by the action of moving liquid.
to wash down 1 to wash the whole of. **2** to accompany (food) with a drink.
to wash off to remove or be removed by washing.
to wash one's dirty linen in public to expose one's private scandals, quarrels etc. to public attention.
to wash one's hands (*euphem.*) to go to the lavatory.

to **wash one's hands of** to disclaim responsibility for. [From Pontius Pilate's symbolic washing of his hands in the Bible (Matt. xxvii.24) to disclaim responsibility for the crucifixion of Jesus Christ.]

to **wash out 1** to remove or be removed by washing. **2** to wash free of something unwanted. **3** to cause to be cancelled because of rain. **4** (*coll.*) to cancel, to annul. **5** to erode. **6** (of a flood etc.) to cause a breach in.

to **wash over** to happen around, without affecting (a person) (*His parents are always arguing, but it just washes over him*).

to **wash up 1** to wash dishes etc. **2** (*esp. N Am.*) to wash one's hands and face.

waste

to **go/ run to waste** to be wasted.

to **lay waste 1** to render desolate. **2** to devastate, to ruin.

to **waste no time** to act immediately.

to **waste one's breath** to talk to no avail.

to **waste words** to talk in vain or without effect.

waste not, want not if you do not waste things, you will have them when they are needed.

watch

a **watched pot never boils** impatience makes the awaited event seem slower to happen.

on the **watch** vigilant, on the lookout.

on **watch** on duty, esp. as a lookout.

to **keep watch** to be on guard, esp. at night while others are asleep.

to **set the watch** (*esp. Naut.*) to station lookouts etc.

to **watch like a hawk** to watch (someone or something) very closely.

to **watch out 1** to be on the lookout (for). **2** to take care (*Watch out!*).

to **watch over** to look after (someone), making sure no harm comes to them.

to **watch the clock** to look at the time frequently while working, esp. so as not to work any longer than necessary.

watch it/ yourself! (*coll.*) be careful! (*Watch yourself! The floor's covered in broken glass.*).

water

between wind and water WIND[1].

blood is thicker than water BLOOD.

by water in a boat or ship.

come hell or high water HELL.

fish out of water FISH.

hewers of wood and drawers of water HEWER.

in deep water DEEP.

in hot water HOT.

in smooth water SMOOTH.

like water off a duck's back (*coll.*) completely without effect. [Water runs straight off the oily feathers on a duck's back.]

milk and water MILK.

of the first water FIRST.

on the water in a boat or ship.

still waters run deep STILL.

to **back water** BACK.

to **cast one's bread upon the waters** CAST.

to **fish in troubled waters** FISH.

to **go through fire and water** FIRE.

to **hold water** to be sound or valid, to stand scrutiny.

to **keep one's head above water** HEAD[1].

to **make water 1** to urinate. **2** (*Naut.*) to leak.

to **muddy the waters** MUDDY.

to **pass water** to urinate.

to **pour oil on troubled waters** POUR.

to **pour/ throw cold water on** COLD.

to **spend money like water** SPEND.

to **take the waters** to take a cure at a watering spa.

to **take to (something) like a duck to water** DUCK[1].

to **tread water** TREAD.

to **water down 1** to dilute with water. **2** to make less forceful, offensive, harsh, vivid etc.

under water beneath the surface of the water.

water under the bridge past events, experiences etc. that are over and done with.

you can take a horse to water (but you cannot make it drink) HORSE.

Waterloo

to meet one's Waterloo MEET.

wave

to make waves 1 (*coll.*) to cause trouble. **2** (*coll.*) to make an impression.

to wave aside to dismiss with or as with a wave of the hand.

to wave down to wave as a signal to (a driver or vehicle) to stop.

to wave one's magic wand to achieve something or make something happen as if by magic.

way

across the way opposite, on the other side of the road etc.

all the way 1 the full distance. **2** completely.

by the way 1 in passing, parenthetically. **2** during the journey.

by way of 1 by the route of, via. **2** for the purpose of. **3** as a form of or substitute for, to serve as (*by way of introduction*).

†**come your way** come, come on.

in a bad way ill, seriously out of sorts.

in a big way BIG.

in a small way SMALL.

in a way 1 to some degree. **2** from one point of view.

in its way considered from an appropriate standpoint.

in no way by no means.

in the way in a position or of a nature to obstruct or hinder.

in the way of as a form or example of, by way of (*What do you have in the way of garden furniture?*).

not to know which way to turn (*coll.*) to be in a state of great confusion, anxiety etc.

no way NO[1].

one way and another altogether, on balance.

on one's way travelling, moving on.

on the way 1 in progress. **2** travelling or in transit. **3** (*coll.*) not yet born (*She's got four kids and another one on the way*).

on the way out 1 going out of fashion or favour. **2** dying.

out of one's way away from one's intended or desired route.

out of the way 1 unusual. **2** remote.

over the way across the street.

parting of the ways PARTING.

step this way STEP.

the other way round OTHER.

there are no two ways about it TWO.

the way of all flesh death. [From the biblical phrase 'to go the way of all the earth', used by Joshua (Josh. xxiii.14) and David (I Kgs. ii.2) in their dying days.]

the way the cookie crumbles the way things are or happen, an unalterable state of affairs (*I know it seems unfair, but that's the way the cookie crumbles*).

to be on one's way 1 to set off (*We must be on our way*). **2** to be travelling or in transit. **3** to be on course (to do, achieve or become something) (*She's on her way to becoming the first female president of the club*).

to break a way BREAK.

to clear the way CLEAR.

to come someone's way 1 to become available to someone. **2** to fall to someone's lot (*You must take whatever comes your way*).

to cut both ways BOTH.

to feel one's way FEEL.

to find a way to discover a means (of).

to find one's way 1 to succeed in reaching a place. **2** to come, esp. by chance.

to force one's way FORCE.

to gather way GATHER.

to get/ have one's (own) way to get what one wants.

to give way 1 to yield, to fail to resist. **2** to make concessions. **3** to make room for. **4** to be superseded. **5** to break down, to collapse (*The whole structure gave way*). **6** to abandon oneself (to). **7** to be depreciated in value. **8** to begin to row. **9** to row with increased energy.

to go down the wrong way WRONG.

to go one's own (sweet) way to follow one's own plan, to act independently.

to go one's way to depart.

to go out of one's way to take great trouble (to), to make a special effort (to).

to go someone's way 1 to travel in the same direction as someone. **2** (of events etc.) to be in someone's favour.

to have a way with to be good at using or handling something (*to have a way with words*).

to have it both ways BOTH.

to hew one's way HEW.

to hold on one's way to keep going steadily.

to lead the way LEAD¹.

to lie in the way LIE².

to look the other way OTHER.

to lose one's/ the way LOSE.

to make one's way 1 to proceed (*We made our way to the exit*). **2** to prosper, esp. by one's own exertions.

to make way 1 to make room, to open a passage. **2** to progress.

to mend one's ways MEND.

to pave the way for PAVE.

to pay its way to cover costs.

to pay one's way to keep out of debt or contribute to shared expenses.

to put someone in the way of to help someone to obtain (*I can put you in the way of a good deal*).

to rub (up) the wrong way RUB.

to see one's way clear to to feel able to.

to show the way to show what has to be done, which way to go etc. by leading.

to stand in someone's way to prevent someone from doing something (*If he wants to go back to university, I won't stand in his way*).

to take one's way 1 to set out. **2** to go in some direction.

under way 1 (of a ship etc.) in motion. **2** in progress.

way back (*coll.*) a long time ago.

ways and means 1 methods of doing or achieving something. **2** methods of raising money, esp. government revenue.

wrong way round WRONG.

wayside

to fall by the wayside to fail or drop out during the course of an undertaking. [From a parable told by Jesus in the Bible: "A sower went out to sow his seed: and as he sowed, some fell by the way side" (Luke viii.5).]

weak

weak as a kitten (of a person) very weak (*A bout of the flu had left him weak as a kitten*).

wean

to be weaned on to be familiar or grow up with from an early age.

wear

in wear being worn regularly.

the worse for wear 1 shabby, worn. **2** (*coll.*) tired, untidy etc.

to wear away 1 to efface or diminish by rubbing, use etc. **2** to be effaced or diminished by rubbing, use etc.

to wear blinkers (*coll.*) not to see or understand what is going on around one.

to wear down 1 to overcome gradually by persistent pressure. **2** to efface or diminish by rubbing, use etc.

to wear motley to play the fool. [Referring to the multicoloured costume of a jester.]

to wear off 1 to efface or diminish by rubbing, use etc. **2** to be effaced or diminished by rubbing, use etc. **3** to decline or pass away gradually (*when the effects of the drugs wear off*).

to wear one's heart on one's sleeve 1 to be excessively frank and unreserved. **2** to reveal one's inmost feelings and thoughts. [The phrase is used by Iago in Shakespeare's *Othello*: "I will wear my heart upon my sleeve / For daws to peck at", but it may be of earlier origin.]

to wear out 1 to use until no longer of use, to consume or render worthless by use. **2** to exhaust, to tire out. **3** to be used up, consumed or rendered worthless by rubbing, use etc.

to wear the trousers/ breeches to be in the dominant position, esp. in a marriage.

to wear thin 1 to become thin through use. **2** (of patience) to diminish. **3** (of excuses) to become less convincing or acceptable.

weather
fair-weather friend FAIR.

to keep a/ one's weather eye open 1 (*coll.*) to be on the alert. **2** (*coll.*) to have one's wits about one.

to make good/ bad weather (of a vessel) to behave well/ badly in a storm.

to make heavy weather of HEAVY.

to weather the storm to endure and come through a difficult period.

under the weather 1 poorly, unwell. **2** depressed, in low spirits. **3** drunk, intoxicated.

wind and weather WIND[1].

weave
to get weaving 1 (*sl.*) to begin. **2** (*sl.*) to hurry.

wedge
the thin end of the wedge THIN.

wedlock
born in/ out of wedlock BORN.

week
the other week OTHER.

to knock into the middle of next week KNOCK.

week of Sundays 1 (*coll.*) seven weeks. **2** (*coll.*) a long time.

weekend
dirty weekend DIRTY.

weigh
to weigh anchor to raise the anchor preparatory to sailing.

to weigh a ton to be heavy to lift, carry etc.

to weigh down 1 to cause to sink by weight, to force down. **2** to hold or keep down by weight. **3** to oppress.

to weigh in 1 (of a jockey, boxer etc.) to be weighed before a race, contest etc. **2** (*coll.*) to intervene (with) (*She weighed in with an argument about traffic congestion*).

to weigh into to attack.

to weigh one's words to choose one's words carefully.

to weigh out 1 to take (a particular weight of something) from a quantity. **2** to distribute or apportion in quantities measured by scales. **3** (of a jockey) to be weighed before a race. **4** (*sl.*) to pay (money) out.

to weigh up 1 (*coll.*) to assess, to judge. **2** (*coll.*) to consider carefully (*to weigh up the pros and cons*).

under weigh (*Naut.*) under way.

weight
to carry weight to be important or influential.

to lose weight LOSE.

to pull one's weight to take one's due share of work or responsibility.

to put on weight to become heavier or fatter.

to throw one's weight about/ around (*coll.*) to act in a domineering or aggressively self-assertive way.

worth one's weight in gold WORTH.

weird

to dree one's weird DREE.

weird and wonderful strange but impressive (*weird and wonderful plans for the new theatre*).

welcome

hero's welcome HERO.

to extend a welcome (to) EXTEND.

to make welcome to receive in a kind or hospitable way.

to outstay/ overstay one's welcome to stay too long.

you're welcome! used in response to thanks.

well

all's well that ends well said when a difficult situation reaches a satisfactory conclusion. [From the title of a play by Shakespeare.]

(all) well and good used to express calm or dispassionate acceptance.

as well 1 in addition. **2** equally, as much (as), not less than. **3** proper, right, not unadvisable (to) (*It's as well to switch it off first*).

(just) as well just as reasonably, with no worse results (*We might as well stay*).

not (too) well feeling rather unwell.

well and truly completely, utterly.

well away 1 making or having made rapid progress. **2** (*coll.*) drunk. **3** (*coll.*) fast asleep.

well in (*coll.*) on good terms (with).

well off 1 in good circumstances. **2** wealthy, prosperous.

well off for having plenty of (*We're not very well off for newsagents around here*).

well out of fortunate not to be involved with.

well up having ample knowledge or information (*I'm not very well up on medical terminology*).

well worth certainly worth (*well worth the trouble; well worth avoiding*).

welly

give it some welly (*coll.*) used to encourage someone to apply more force, make more effort etc.

wet

to wet one's whistle (*coll.*) to have a drink.

to wet the baby's head to have a celebratory drink after the birth of a child.

wet behind the ears immature, inexperienced. [Alluding to a young animal licked behind the ears by its mother.]

wet blanket (*coll.*) a person who dampens enthusiasm, zeal etc.

wet through thoroughly soaked.

whack

out of whack (*N Am., Austral., sl.*) out of order.

(the) full whack FULL.

to have a whack at (*sl.*) to try, to attempt.

whale

to have a whale of a time to have a very enjoyable or exciting time.

whammy

double whammy DOUBLE.

what

to give someone what for (*coll.*) to give someone a severe reprimand or punishment.

what about what do you think, feel, know etc. about; what is the position concerning (*What about Jonathan?*).

what ever what at all (*What ever is she talking about?*).

what for for what reason, purpose etc.

what for no? (*Sc.*) why not?

what have you (*coll.*) anything else of the kind (*picking up bits of broken glass and what have you*).

what ho! (*dated*) used in greeting or accosting.

what if 1 what would happen if (*What if it rains?*). **2** what does it matter if (*What if I am being selfish?*).

what is more moreover.

what not (*coll.*) anything else of the kind (*coins, keys and what not*).

what of what is the news about.

what of it? why does that matter?

what's what (*coll.*) the real or important thing or situation.

what with (*coll.*) because of (*We're a bit short-staffed today, what with the flu epidemic and the rail strike*).

whatever

or whatever (*coll.*) or some similar or suitable thing (*Use a knife, a screwdriver or whatever*).

wheat

to separate the wheat from the chaff SEPARATE¹.

wheel

at the wheel 1 driving a motor vehicle. **2** steering a vessel. **3** directing, in control, in charge.

on oiled wheels OILED.

to break on the wheel BREAK.

to oil the wheels OIL.

to put a spoke in someone's wheel SPOKE.

to put/ set one's shoulder to the wheel SHOULDER.

to reinvent the wheel REINVENT.

to set the wheels in motion to cause or enable something to begin.

to wheel and deal to operate shrewdly and often ruthlessly in business, politics etc. [An allusion to the gambling games of roulette and cards.]

wheels within wheels 1 intricate machinery. **2** (*coll.*) concealed reasons or interdependent circumstances. [From the Bible: "and their appearance and their work was as it were a wheel in the middle of a wheel" (Ezek. i.16).]

whenever

or whenever (*coll.*) or at any similar or suitable time.

wherever

or wherever (*coll.*) or in any similar or suitable place.

whet

to whet someone's appetite to make someone hungry for or desirous of more.

whether

whether or no 1 in any case. **2** which (of two opposite cases).

which

which is which used when people or things are difficult to tell apart (*I can never remember which is which*).

while

a good while a long time (*a good while later*).

all the while all the time, during the whole time.

for a long while LONG.

for a while for some time.

in a while soon.

the while 1 during. **2** at the time.

to be worth (someone's) while WORTH.

to while away to pass (time etc.) pleasantly or in a leisurely manner.

whip

(fair) crack of the whip CRACK.

to crack the whip CRACK.

to whip in to bring (hunting hounds) together.

to whip on to urge forward or into action.

to whip round to have an informal or impromptu collection of money.

to whip the cat (*Austral., coll.*) to waste time regretting something that cannot be undone.

to whip up 1 to excite, arouse or stimulate. **2** to produce hurriedly. **3** to summon (*to whip up attendance*).

†**whip and spur** with the greatest haste.

whip hand 1 the hand holding the whip. **2** the advantage or control (*to have the whip hand*).

whipping

whipping boy 1 a scapegoat. **2** (*Hist.*) a boy educated with a young prince and taking his punishments for him.

whirl

to give something a whirl (*coll.*) to try or attempt something.

whirlwind

to (sow the wind and) reap the whirlwind REAP.

whisker

to have whiskers (*coll.*) to be very old.

whisper

it is whispered that it is rumoured that.

whistle

clean as a whistle CLEAN.

to blow the whistle on BLOW[1].

to wet one's whistle WET.

to whistle down the wind 1 to let go. **2** to set (a hawk) loose.

to whistle for to seek or ask for in vain, to stand little or no chance of getting.

to whistle for a wind to whistle in a calm, the superstitious practice of old sailors.

to whistle in the dark to hide one's fear with a show of nonchalance or boldness.

whit

every whit wholly.

no whit not at all, not in the least.

white

to show the white feather to show signs of cowardice or timidity. [From the belief that a white feather in the tail of a fighting cock was a sign of bad breeding or cowardice.]

to show the white flag to surrender. [From the use of a white flag to indicate that the enemy has a peaceful communication to make.]

white as a sheet extremely pale in the face.

whited sepulchre a hypocrite. [From the Bible: "Woe unto you, scribes and Pharisees, hypocrites! for ye are like unto whited sepulchres, which indeed appear beautiful outward, but are within full of dead men's bones" (Matt. xxiii.27).]

white elephant a useless and expensive possession. [The kings of Siam used to present a white elephant – a rare animal held in high regard – to those who had lost their favour, knowing that the cost of its keep would ruin them.]

white hope a member of a group, team, organization etc. who is expected to achieve much or bring glory. [From the sport of boxing, where the phrase originally referred to a white fighter thought capable of beating a black champion.]

white lie a pardonable fiction or misstatement.

who

who goes there? used as a challenge by a sentry etc.

whole

as a whole considered as an organic unity.

a whole lot (*coll.*) very much.

on the whole 1 all things considered. **2** in most cases.

the whole bag of tricks 1 everything. **2** all means or expedients.

the whole boiling (lot) (*sl.*) all, everything.

the whole (kit and) caboodle (*coll.*) all, everything.

the whole of everybody in (*The whole of the village heard the explosion*).

the whole shooting match/ shoot (*coll.*) the whole amount, everything.

to go the whole hog (*coll.*) to do a job completely, making no compromise or reservations. [Probably referring to a pig bought or eaten in its entirety. An alternative explanation is based on the fact that the word 'hog' was once a slang term for 'shilling'.]

with a whole skin unharmed or unwounded.

whoop

to whoop it up 1 (*coll.*) to engage in riotous enjoyment. **2** (*coll., N Am.*) to stir up enthusiasm etc.

whoopee

to make whoopee 1 (*coll.*) to whoop it up. **2** (*coll.*) to make love.

why

whys and wherefores all the reasons, details etc.

why so? for what reason? on what grounds?

wick

to dip one's wick DIP.

to get on someone's wick (*coll.*) to annoy or irritate someone.

wicket

at the wicket in cricket, batting.

leg before wicket LEG.

on a good wicket (*coll.*) in a favourable situation.

on a sticky wicket STICKY.

to take a wicket in cricket, to get a batsman out.

wide

the wide world all the world.

to cut a wide swath (*N Am.*) to make a bold or stylish impression.

to give a wide berth to 1 to keep away from. **2** to steer clear of. [Of nautical origin, a berth being the space needed for a ship or boat to manoeuvre.]

to the wide completely, absolutely.

widow

grass widow(er) GRASS.

wield

to wield the sceptre to rule with supreme command.

wife

all the world and his wife WORLD.

old wives' tale OLD.

†to have/ take to wife to marry.

wiggle

to get a wiggle on (*sl.*) to hurry up.

wild

beyond one's wildest dreams much more or better than one could imagine or hope for (*She found herself rich beyond her wildest dreams*).

in the wild in its natural state.

(out) in the wilds (*coll.*) a long way from human habitation (*to live out in the wilds*).

to run wild 1 to grow or become unrestrained or uncontrolled. **2** to grow unchecked. **3** to behave in an uncontrolled way.

wild and woolly unrefined, uncultivated.

wild-goose chase a foolish or hopeless enterprise. [Perhaps from a medieval game in which players on horseback had to follow an erratic course imitating that of wild geese in flight.]

wilderness

in the wilderness out of office, not wielding power.

voice in the wilderness VOICE.

wildfire
to spread like wildfire SPREAD.

wild oat
to sow one's wild oats SOW[1].

will[1]
will do (*coll.*) used to express willingness to comply.

will[2]
at will 1 at one's pleasure or discretion. 2 (*Law*) (of a tenant) that can be evicted without notice.

to have one's will to get what one desires.

to work one's will on/ upon WORK.

where there's a will there's a way anything can be achieved with determination.

with a will heartily, zealously.

with the best will in the world no matter how good one's intentions are, however determined one is.

willing
to show willing to indicate a readiness to help, comply etc.

willing horse a person who is always keen to work hard or help others.

wimp
to wimp out (*sl.*) to withdraw from something through fear, to chicken out.

win
to win by a canvas in boat racing, to win by a small margin. [Referring to the covered part at the ends of a racing boat.]

to win hands down to win without an effort, easily. [From horse racing: jockeys can relax their hold on the reins when they are winning easily.]

to win one's spurs 1 to achieve distinction, to make oneself famous. 2 (*Hist.*) to gain knighthood. [From the former practice of awarding a pair of gilt spurs to a newly dubbed knight.]

to win on points in boxing, to win by scoring more points, not by a knockout.

to win over to persuade, to secure the support, favour or assent of.

to win the toss to have something decided in one's favour by correctly predicting on which side a tossed coin will land (*Surrey won the toss and chose to bat*).

to win through/ out to be successful, to prevail.

you can't win (*coll.*) it is impossible to succeed.

you can't win them all (*coll.*) used to express resignation or consolation on failure, defeat etc.

wind[1]
between wind and water in a vulnerable place or position.

capful of wind CAPFUL.

how the wind blows the position or state of affairs.

in the wind showing signs of occurring.

in the wind's eye towards the precise point from which the wind blows, directly against the wind.

it's an ill wind that blows nobody any good ILL.

like the wind very swiftly (*She ran like the wind*).

on/ off the wind (*Naut.*) near/ away from the direction from which the wind is blowing.

second wind SECOND.

the four winds FOUR.

three sheets in/ to the wind THREE.

to break wind BREAK.

to get the wind up (*coll.*) to get nervous, to become frightened.

to get wind of 1 (*coll.*) to hear about. 2 (*coll.*) to smell out.

to piss in the wind PISS.

to put the wind up (*coll.*) to frighten.

to raise the wind RAISE.

to sail close to the wind SAIL.

to take the wind out of someone's sails
1 (*Naut.*) to sail to the windward of
someone. 2 to frustrate someone's
plans, to disconcert someone.

to take wind to become known.

to the (four) winds 1 in all directions
(*scattered to the four winds*). 2 into a
state of abandonment (*to cast caution
to the winds*).

to throw caution to the winds CAUTION.

to whistle down the wind WHISTLE.

to whistle for a wind WHISTLE.

which way the wind blows the position or
state of affairs.

wind and weather the effects of wind,
rain etc.

wind[2]

to wind down 1 to lower by winding.
2 to reduce gradually. 3 to relax. 4 to
unwind. 5 gradually to reduce the
amount of work in (something), before
it stops completely.

to wind off 1 to unwind. 2 to stop talking.

to wind up 1 to coil up. 2 to coil or
tighten up the spring of (a watch etc.).
3 (*coll.*) to put into a state of tension or
readiness for activity. 4 (*coll.*) to
irritate, to annoy. 5 (*sl.*) to tease (*Ignore
him: he's just winding you up*). 6 to
bring to a conclusion, to conclude.
7 to come to a conclusion. 8 to arrange
the final settlement of the affairs of (a
business etc.). 9 to go into liquidation.
10 (*coll.*) to end up in a certain state or
situation (*They wound up in hospital*).

windmill

to throw one's cap over the windmill CAP.

to tilt at windmills TILT.

window

out of the window (*coll.*) discarded,
dispensed with, no longer taken into
account.

windward

to get to the windward of 1 to get to the
side of (someone or something)
towards which the wind blows.
2 to get the advantage over.

wine

to wine and dine to entertain with food
and alcohol.

wine, women and song the
entertainments and indulgences
traditionally enjoyed by men
(*He squandered his inheritance on
wine, women and song*). [From a
rhyme attributed to Martin Luther
(1483–1546): "Who loves not wine,
woman and song / Remains a fool his
whole life long."]

wing

in the wings waiting in readiness. [An
allusion to the sides of a theatre stage,
where actors wait for their cue.]

on a wing and a prayer with no more
than a slight chance of success.

on the wing 1 flying. 2 in motion.

to clip the wings of CLIP.

to give/ lend wings to to make faster, to
speed up.

to singe one's wings SINGE.

to spread/ stretch one's wings to develop
or make full use of one's powers,
abilities etc.

to take under one's wing to take under
one's protection.

to take wing 1 to begin flying, to fly
away. 2 to disappear.

to wing one's flight to fly.

wink

a nod is as good as a wink (to a blind
horse) NOD.

forty winks FORTY.

in a wink very quickly.

like winking 1 very rapidly. 2 with great
vigour.

not to sleep a wink SLEEP.

to tip (someone) the wink TIP[2].

to wink at 1 to pretend not to see.
2 to connive at.

winkle

to winkle out 1 (*coll.*) to extract with difficulty. **2** (*coll.*) to elicit (information etc.) with difficulty. **3** to extract (sharpshooters and small bodies of enemy troops) from hiding-places. [Alluding to the difficulty of removing a winkle from its shell.]

wipe

to wipe away 1 to remove by wiping. **2** to get rid of.

to wipe down to clean (a surface) by wiping.

to wipe off 1 to clear away. **2** to cancel.

to wipe off the map to remove or destroy completely.

to wipe one's eyes to stop weeping.

to wipe out 1 to clean out by wiping. **2** to efface, to obliterate. **3** to destroy, to annihilate. **4** (*sl.*) to murder.

to wipe the eye of 1 to show up the foolishness of. **2** to shoot what someone has missed.

to wipe the slate clean to start afresh, to erase past crimes, errors etc. [Alluding to a piece of slate used as a writing tablet.]

to wipe the smile off someone's face to make someone less smug, contented, proud etc.

to wipe up 1 to remove (a liquid etc.) by wiping. **2** to dry (dishes etc.).

wire

by wire by telegraph or telegram.

live wire LIVE[2].

to cross wires/ get one's wires crossed CROSS.

to pull the wires 1 to manipulate puppets. **2** (*esp. N Am.*) to control politics etc. by clandestine means. **3** to exert influence unobtrusively, to pull strings.

to wire in (*dated, coll.*) to apply oneself vigorously.

wisdom

in one's wisdom (*iron.*) thinking that this is a wise thing to do (*Her father, in his wisdom, let her borrow the car*).

wise[1]

none the wiser having no more knowledge or understanding than before.

to put someone wise to inform someone.

to wise up 1 (*esp. N Am., coll.*) to be or become aware or informed. **2** (*esp. N Am., coll.*) to make aware, to inform.

wise after the event able to judge or understand something with hindsight.

wise to aware of, alert to.

without anyone being the wiser without anyone knowing, without detection.

wise[2]

in no wise not at all.

wish

the wish is father to the thought we believe what we wish to be true. [From Shakespeare's *Henry IV* Part 2: "Thy wish was father, Harry, to that thought."]

to wish someone joy of (*iron.*) to be gladly rid of (what that person has).

to wish something on someone to foist something on someone (*I wouldn't wish a job like that on anyone!*).

wishful

wishful thinking belief based on desires rather than facts.

wit[1]

at one's wits' end at a complete loss as to what further steps to take, in a state of despair or desperation.

out of one's wits mad.

to frighten someone out of their wits FRIGHTEN.

to have/ keep one's wits about one to be alert.

to live by one's wits LIVE[1].

to pit one's wits against PIT.

to set one's wits to to argue with.

wit[2]

to wit namely.

witching

the witching hour midnight, the time when witches are supposed to become active.

with

to be with someone 1 to support someone. 2 to agree with someone. 3 (*coll.*) to understand someone, to follow what someone is saying (*I'm not with you*).

with it 1 (*coll.*) up to date, fashionable. 2 (*coll.*) alert to what is being done or said. 3 besides, in addition.

with that thereupon.

withers

to wring someone's withers WRING.

witness

to bear witness 1 to give testimony. 2 to be a sign of (*Their response bears witness to their lack of concern*).

to call to witness to summon, appeal to or ask for confirmation or testimony.

woe

woe betide may misfortune befall; used to warn of unpleasant consequences (*Woe betide anyone who touches my new computer!*).

woe is me! (*facet.*) used to express great distress.

†woe worth the day! cursed be the day.

wolf

lone wolf LONE.

to cry wolf CRY.

to have/ hold a wolf by the ears to be in a precarious or desperate situation.

to keep the wolf from the door to keep off starvation.

to throw to the wolves to send to certain destruction, to sacrifice or abandon without scruple or remorse.

wolf in sheep's clothing a person who disguises malicious intentions behind a pretence of innocence. [From Aesop's fable about a wolf who disguises itself in a fleece to get into the sheepfold. The image is also found in the Bible: "Beware of false prophets, which come to you in sheep's clothing, but inwardly they are ravening wolves" (Matt. vii.15).]

woman

fancy woman FANCY.

old woman OLD.

scarlet woman SCARLET.

to be one's own woman (of a woman) to be of independent mind.

to make an honest woman of HONEST.

to play the woman 1 to weep. 2 to give vent to emotion, esp. fear.

wine, women and song WINE.

wonder

I shouldn't wonder (*coll.*) I think it probable or likely.

I wonder I doubt it.

nine days' wonder NINE.

no wonder it is not surprising (that) (*I didn't realize it was her car: no wonder she was annoyed!*).

small wonder SMALL.

to work/ do wonders to achieve remarkable or miraculous results.

wonders will never cease! used to express great surprise.

wood

dead wood DEAD.

from the wood from the cask.

hewers of wood and drawers of water HEWER.

neck of the woods NECK.

not to see the wood for the trees to be prevented by excessive details from getting an overall view.

out of the wood out of danger or difficulty.

out of the woods (*esp. N Am.*) out of the wood.

to knock (on) wood KNOCK.

to touch wood TOUCH.

wooden

wooden spoon 1 a spoon made of wood, used in cooking. **2** a booby prize, esp. in sports competitions. [From a booby prize awarded to the student who came last in the mathematics examination at Cambridge University.]

woodpile

nigger in the woodpile NIGGER.

woodshed

something nasty in the woodshed NASTY.

woodwork

to crawl/ come out of the woodwork (of something unpleasant or undesirable) to appear, to come to light, to become known.

wool

dyed-in-the-wool DYE.

great cry and little wool GREAT.

to pull the wool over someone's eyes to deceive someone. [Perhaps from the former practice of pulling someone's wig over their eyes, blinding them temporarily, in order to rob or play a trick on them.]

wrapped (up) in cotton wool WRAPPED.

word

actions speak louder than words ACTION.

as good as one's word 1 fulfilling one's promises. **2** trustworthy. **3** not to be deterred.

at a word as soon as asked, at once.

a word (is enough) to the wise there is no need to be more explicit.

by word of mouth by actual speaking, orally.

dirty word DIRTY.

famous last words FAMOUS.

four-letter word FOUR.

from the word go (*coll.*) from the very beginning (*This car has been nothing but trouble from the word go*).

in a/ one word 1 briefly, in short. **2** to sum up.

in other words OTHER.

in so many words explicitly, precisely, bluntly.

in word and deed not in speech only.

in words of one syllable expressed clearly or plainly.

last word LAST[1].

mark my words MARK.

mum's the word MUM.

not the word for it an inadequate description (*Unattractive is not the word for it – it's an eyesore!*).

not to breathe a word BREATHE.

of few words FEW.

of one's word able to be relied upon to do what one says one will do (*a man of his word*).

on my word (of honour) used to make a promise or give a solemn assurance.

to bandy words BANDY.

to be lost for words LOST.

to break one's word BREAK.

to eat one's words EAT.

to exchange words EXCHANGE.

to get a word in edgeways (*often neg.*) to succeed in interrupting a talkative person or breaking into a conversation between such people.

to give one's word to promise, to give one's assurance.

to have a word with to have a brief conversation with.

to have no words for to be unable to express, describe etc.

to have words with to have a dispute with, to reproach.

to keep one's word to keep one's promise, to fulfil an undertaking.

too ... for words extremely ... , too ... to describe (*This is too ridiculous for words*).

to put in a good word for to recommend or praise (someone).

to put into words to express in speech or writing.

to put the hard word on HARD.

to put words into someone's mouth to represent, often incorrectly, what one assumes another person means.

to say the word 1 to say that you agree. **2** to give the order etc.

to send word to send information.

to suit the action to the word SUIT.

to take someone at their word to assume that someone means what they say.

to take someone's word for it to believe someone without proof or further investigation.

to take the words out of someone's mouth to say what another person was about to say (*You took the words right out of my mouth!*).

to waste words WASTE.

to weigh one's words WEIGH.

(upon) my word! used to express surprise, indignation etc.

word for word in exactly the same words, verbatim.

words fail me! used to express disbelief, exasperation, astonishment etc.

work

all work and no play makes Jack a dull boy people who spend all their time working and have no outside interests are not good company (used as a reason for taking a break from work).

at work 1 doing work, in action or operation. **2** at one's place of employment.

dirty work DIRTY.

donkey work DONKEY.

in work in paid employment.

many hands make light work HAND.

nasty piece of work NASTY.

out of work not in paid employment, unemployed.

spanner in the works SPANNER.

the devil finds work for idle hands DEVIL.

to get the works (*coll.*) to get the full or appropriate treatment.

to give someone the works (*coll.*) to give someone a violent beating.

to gum up the works GUM.

to have one's work cut out to have a hard task.

to make short work of SHORT.

to set to work 1 to begin on a task. **2** to cause to begin working.

to work double tides to work twice as hard or twice as long as usual.

to work in 1 to introduce or combine by manipulation. **2** to find space or time for.

to work into the ground to exhaust or wear out with overwork.

to work it (*coll.*) to arrange things, to bring it about (*She worked it so that he couldn't refuse*).

to work like a dog/ horse/ Trojan to work very hard.

to work off 1 to get rid of, esp. by effort, activity etc. **2** to pay off (a debt etc.) by working. **3** to produce. **4** (*coll.*) to palm off.

to work on to continue to work.

to work one's fingers to the bone to do hard esp. physical work, without thanks or reward.

to work one's passage 1 to work as a sailor etc., receiving a free passage in lieu of wages. **2** to work one's way without help from influence etc.

†to work one's will on/ upon to make do or perform as one wants.

to work out 1 to compute, to solve, to find out, to understand. **2** to accomplish, to effect. **3** to devise, to formulate (*to work out a plan of action*). **4** to have a result (*It didn't work out as well as we'd hoped*). **5** to undertake a series of exercises to get fit. **6** to exhaust. **7** to expiate. **8** to be successful. **9** to add up to (a certain amount).

to work over 1 to examine carefully.
2 (*coll.*) to beat severely, to mug.

to work the oracle 1 to secure by craft a desired answer from the mouthpiece of an oracle. **2** to obtain some object by secret influence. **3** to gain one's point by stratagem.

to work to rule to follow working rules so strictly that productivity is reduced, esp. as a form of industrial action.

to work up 1 to elaborate, to bring gradually into shape or efficiency. **2** to excite gradually, to stir up, to rouse. **3** to advance or increase gradually (*working up to a dramatic climax*). **4** to mingle together. **5** to study (a subject) perseveringly.

workman

a bad workman blames his tools said when a careless or incompetent person blames their equipment, materials etc. for a bad piece of work or for something they have done wrong.

world

all the world everybody.

all the world and his wife a large mixed group of people.

(all) the world over everywhere.

dead to the world DEAD.

for all the world exactly, precisely (*It sounded for all the world like an explosion*).

for the world on any account (*I wouldn't hurt you for the world*).

in a world of one's own daydreaming; not aware of what is going on around one.

in the world at all, possibly (*How in the world did that happen?*).

it's a small world SMALL.

man of the world MAN.

next world NEXT.

on top of the world TOP[1].

out of this world 1 (*coll.*) remarkable, striking. **2** (*coll.*) excellent.

the best of both worlds the benefits of two different or incompatible things, ways of life, sets of ideas etc. (*to get the best of both worlds*).

the end of the world END.

the wide world WIDE.

the world is someone's oyster a person has every opportunity for success, prosperity etc. (*Graduates leave university thinking the world is their oyster*). [From Shakespeare's *The Merry Wives of Windsor*: "Why, then the world's my oyster, / Which I with sword will open."]

the world, the flesh and the devil all forms of temptation. [From *The Litany* in the Book of Common Prayer (1662): "from all the deceits of the world, the flesh, and the devil, Good Lord, deliver us."]

the world to come life after death, the hereafter.

this world existence, this mortal life.

to bring into the world 1 to give birth to. **2** to deliver (a baby).

to carry the world before one to have complete success.

to come into the world to be born.

to do someone the world of good to be very beneficial to someone.

to retire from the world RETIRE.

to rise in the world RISE.

to see the world to travel far and wide.

to think the world of THINK.

with the best will in the world WILL[2].

worlds apart very different.

world without end to all eternity, everlastingly. [Used several times in the Book of Common Prayer and the Bible.]

worm

can of worms CAN.

(even) a worm will turn the most humble or submissive person will retaliate under extreme provocation.

food for worms FOOD.

the early bird catches the worm EARLY.

wormwood

gall and wormwood GALL.

worn

worn to a shadow thoroughly exhausted.

worried

worried sick extremely worried.

worry

not to worry (*coll*.) there's no need to worry.

to worry along/ through to get along somehow in spite of trouble and difficulty.

to worry out to solve (a problem) by perseverance.

worse

for the worse tending towards deterioration (*a change for the worse*).

none the worse not damaged, harmed or adversely affected.

or worse or some even worse eventuality.

the worse for damaged or harmed by.

worse off in a poorer condition or financial situation.

worst

at (the) worst 1 in the worst circumstances. **2** in the least favourable view.

do your worst used to express defiance.

if the worst comes to the worst if the worst of all possible things happens.

to come off worst to be defeated.

to get the worst of it to be defeated.

worth

for all one is worth (*coll*.) with all one's strength, energy etc. (*They leapt into the boat and paddled for all they were worth*).

for what it's worth used to express doubt about the truth or value of something.

not worth a bean/ button/ fig worthless.

not worth a groat worthless.

not worth a rap worthless. [A rap was originally a counterfeit Irish coin passing for a halfpenny.]

not worth the paper it is written on worthless.

(the game is) not worth the candle (something is) not worth the trouble, expense etc. [Alluding to the cost of a candle used for illumination, originally during a gambling game.]

to be worth (someone's) while to be worth the time, labour or expense involved.

to get one's money's worth MONEY.

worth it worthwhile.

worth one's salt worth keeping, worth one's wages. [From the former practice of paying workers or soldiers with salt, an essential commodity for good health, or with money to buy salt, from which the word 'salary' is derived.]

worth one's weight in gold extremely useful, valuable etc.

wound

to lick one's wounds LICK.

to rub salt into the wound RUB.

wrap

to take the wraps off to reveal or disclose.

to wrap round (*sl*.) to crash (a car etc.) into (*He wrapped his bike round a tree*).

to wrap up 1 to fold paper etc. round (*to wrap up a present*). **2** to dress warmly. **3** to bring to a conclusion. **4** (*usu. in p.p.*) to absorb, to engross (*wrapped up in her work*). **5** (*usu. imper., sl.*) to be quiet.

under wraps secret, in secrecy.

wrapped

wrapped (up) in cotton wool pampered, protected from hard reality.

wrath

to pour out vials of wrath POUR.

wreathe

wreathed in smiles smiling a lot.

wriggle

to wriggle out of (*coll.*) to evade, avoid or shirk.

wring

to wring one's hands to press one's hands together convulsively, as in great distress.

to wring someone's hand to clasp or squeeze someone's hand with great force or emotion.

to wring someone's withers to appeal passionately to someone's pity.

wringer

to put someone through the wringer to cause someone to undergo a difficult or stressful experience.

wrist

slap on the wrist SLAP.

writ

someone's writ runs someone has the specified authority.

write

nothing/ not much to write home about (*coll.*) not very impressive, great etc.

to write down 1 to put in writing, to record. **2** to depreciate, to criticize unfavourably in writing. **3** to write in such a way as to appeal to low standards of taste, intelligence etc. **4** in accounting, to reduce the book value of.

to write in 1 to send a letter, request, query, suggestion etc. to a magazine, radio station etc. **2** (*N Am.*) to add (a name) to a ballot paper when voting.

to write off 1 to write and send a letter etc. **2** to cancel (a debt etc.) from a written record. **3** to consider (a loss etc.) as irrecoverable. **4** to damage (a car) beyond repair. **5** to discard as useless, insignificant etc. **6** to compose rapidly and easily.

to write oneself out to exhaust one's powers of literary production.

to write out 1 to write the whole of. **2** to write in finished form. **3** to remove (a character, episode etc.) from a drama series, book etc.

to write up 1 to praise in writing. **2** to bring (a diary, account book etc.) up to date. **3** to give full details of in writing.

writ large 1 set down or recorded in large letters. **2** magnified, emphasized, very obvious, on a large scale.

writing

in writing in written form.

the writing on the wall a sign of approaching disaster or the end of something (*The writing is on the wall for our hopes of a peaceful settlement*). [An allusion to the writing that appeared on the wall of King Belshazzar's palace in the Bible (Dan. v.5–28), warning of the end of his kingdom.]

wrong

in the wrong 1 guilty, responsible. **2** in error.

in the wrong box mistaken, out of place.

on the wrong side of more than, esp. in age (*on the wrong side of forty*).

on the wrong side of the tracks in a poor, less socially prestigious area of town (*to live on the wrong side of the tracks*). [Alluding to a railway line separating rich and poor districts of a town.]

on the wrong track/ tack/ lines following the incorrect line of thought, inquiry, action etc.

to do wrong to commit a crime, sin etc.

to do wrong to to mistreat.

to get in wrong with (*coll.*) to fall into disfavour with.

to get off on the wrong foot to make a bad start, esp. in personal relations with someone.

to get on the wrong side of to fall into disfavour with.

to get wrong 1 to misunderstand (*Don't get me wrong, I'm not criticizing you*). 2 to fail to give or obtain the correct answer to.

to go down the wrong way (of food or drink) to pass into the windpipe instead of the gullet.

to go wrong 1 to fail morally, to fall into sin. 2 to fail to operate correctly. 3 to fall into error. 4 to take the wrong road, path etc.

two wrongs don't make a right TWO.

under a sense of wrong SENSE.

wrong end of the stick the contrary to what is meant (*I seem to have got hold of the wrong end of the stick*).

wrong side out inside out.

wrong way round back to front, in reverse of the proper sequence.

Y

yard
by the yard **1** in great quantities. **2** at great length.

yarn
to spin a yarn SPIN.

yea
to yea and nay to be indecisive, to shilly-shally.

yeah
oh yeah? used to express incredulity.

year
a year and a day (*Law*) a period sometimes specified in law to ensure the completion of a full calendar year.
donkey's years DONKEY.
from year to year as the years pass; yearly.
in the year of Our Lord in a specified year AD (*in the year of Our Lord 1665*).
of the year outstanding in a particular year (*sports personality of the year*).
stricken in years STRICKEN.
the year dot as long ago as can be remembered.
year by year as the years go by.
year in, year out constantly over a very long period, without cessation.

yes
to say yes to agree.
yes, and a verbal prelude to stronger words (*The thief was caught – yes, and still with the money*).
yes and no a response indicating that what has been said is partly true but also partly untrue.

yesterday
yesterday morning/ afternoon/ evening during the morning/ afternoon/ evening of yesterday.

yet
as yet up to this or that time, so far.
just yet (*with neg.*) in the immediate future.
nor yet and also not (*He had not finished the exam nor yet started the last question*).
not yet not up to the present time.

yore
of yore (*poet.*) formerly, of old time, long ago (*days of yore*).

you
you and yours you and your family, property etc.

young
with young pregnant.
young blood a new accession of vigour or enterprise.

yourself
how's yourself? (*coll.*) how are you? (esp. following a similar question).

Z

Z
from A to Z A.

zero
to zero in on **1** to focus attention on, to fix on. **2** to aim for. **3** to converge on, to home in on.

zip
to zip along to move swiftly.
to zip through to finish quickly.
to zip up to fasten by means of a zip.

zonk
to zonk out (*sl.*) to overcome with sleep, alcohol, drugs etc.

zoom
to zoom in/ out with a zoom lens, to go from long shot to close-up/ from close-up to long shot, when taking a photograph, a film shot etc.

Zurich
gnomes of Zurich GNOME.